Short Wave

International

Frequency Handbook

—— Spa Publishing Ltd ——
22, Main Road, Hockley, Essex. SS5 4QS

ISBN 1 873076 05 3

Printed in Great Britain by
Whitstable Litho Ltd, Whitstable, Kent

CONTENTS

INTRODUCTION

A warm welcome to this new edition of "Short Wave International Frequency Handbook", the second under this title. Many thousands of our previous editions have been sold around the world and we are grateful for the helpful comments and suggestions received from readers. These help us to maintain the accuracy and reliability for which this book is renowned.

While our main sources of information are derived from UK based monitoring stations our verification procedures are not limited to the UK. Reference materials from many other countries are consulted as part of the thorough review which takes place between each edition. Nevertheless, monitoring is maintained on a daily basis in order to continually update our computer database.

This new edition incorporates many changes; the result of many hours of "hands-on" monitoring and checking. To all those who supply material, we offer our thanks. Regular contributors and readers of this guide know that there is a continuous process of change throughout the short wave section of the radio spectrum. It is our aim to find these changes and, through fast and comprehensive compilation techniques, present the results in each new edition.

The use of "in house" typesetting has again helped us to maintain the superb value of this directory of frequencies. No other publication comes anywhere near offering the same value for money. To this end, we have written computer software that allows us to directly transfer data from our database to our typesetting equipment in a matter of minutes. The large A4 format has been retained as many readers seem to prefer this. The larger page area also permits personal logging notes to be made.

As always, we have been faced with the problem of deciding what to leave out and what to include. The main criteria for each decision has been whether information is of sufficient detail to warrant inclusion and whether it has been corroborated by other monitors. Vague reports are excluded as are those that appear suspect and could be the result of wrong interpretation of the signal heard or perhaps the listener's receiver suffering image response problems.

We have again included some unidentified stations (designated "UNID") where, despite the absence of information, it is likely that such transmissions may be heard regularly. This edition includes only those stations which have been monitored since the publication of the last edition. We are grateful to those readers who have written in with the results of their detective work which has resulted in identification of some previous "UNIDS". Please keep up the flow of information.

All times shown are taken from log entries, although often it is possible to indicate additional scheduled transmission times Of course Utility stations may transmit any time of the day although many press, marine and weather stations tend to maintain set time schedules.

It is always fascinating to look at other publications which list similar information to that contained within this edition. Some have entries which are not included within these pages. The reason is quite simple. A lot of entries in these publications are "dead" and should have been removed years ago. When we update our database, we not only add hundreds - we remove hundreds. The less scrupulous publishers simply keep adding new ones without bothering to prune out entries which are no longer valid.

In this new edition, you will find more call sign changes for countries of the former USSR. These have been made quite recently as a result of further re-allocations by the International Telecommunications Union (ITU). Stations noted with changes include Archangel, St. Petersburg, Kiev, Odessa and Mariupol. We have again closely monitored frequencies for marine traffic and for your interest, have included a considerable number of ship names and call signs in the CW and RTTY sub-bands. A lot of the former USSR vessels are not included in official (and expensive) ITU publications. We have again featured broadcast stations in the listings and this is a significant improvement over other frequency guides of a similar kind. The listings are not exhaustive, as we have listed only those stations which have been monitored in Europe. The times can only be regarded as a guide and do not indicate transmission schedules, which change throughout the seasons of the year. There is also a separate section listing monitored broadcasting stations with frequencies and monitored details. All can be regularly heard in Europe. The more avid broadcast listener would do well to invest in the latest edition of the "World Radio and TV Handbook" which can be purchased from most amateur radio dealers and large book shops. While that publication provides very comprehensive details of frequencies and schedules of broadcast transmissions, it does not cover the utility stations contained in this guide.

Not only does this latest edition include many new stations (both broadcast and utility), all existing entries have been reviewed in the light of continuous monitoring information. The overriding aim is to provide accuracy on which the reader can rely. You may see some entries which note that the frequency varies. This results from monitoring by the same receiving station using the same equipment, but noting slight variations of the transmitted frequency.

The layout has been designed so that the listener may have a good idea where to listen for the particular stations of interest to him or her. Each section has a heading giving the internationally agreed types of services permitted to operate under a particular band of frequencies. As the marine service makes extensive use of duplex arrangements under which the coast station transmits on a different frequency to that of the ship, the frequency "pairings" have been clearly shown in our listings.

Finally, we hope that this frequency guide proves its worth to you and that you find the content both useful and informative. We also hope that it will make you want to purchase some of our other guides that are regularly advertised in the radio magazines and stocked by most good amateur radio stockists. In case of difficulty copies may be purchased direct from the distributors, Waters and Stanton Electronics, Spa House, 22, Main Road, Hockley, Essex, SS5 4QS.

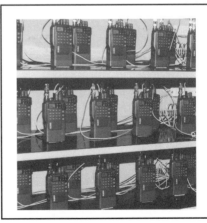

NEW TO SHORT WAVE LISTENING?

If you are new to short-wave listening and you have just purchased your first receiver, then understandably you may be somewhat puzzled by the apparent complexity of the hobby. Perhaps you are not sure of some controls on your radio and their functions. Maybe you do not know what to expect or where to listen, or you might just be totally confused by other aspects or perhaps the many strange noises that you come across as you tune your radio. Well take heart, you are in good company. There are many enthusiasts who have experienced the same bewilderment when they first came into the hobby.

Rather surprisingly there is very little literature published on the subject to help. Most books either cover the basics in just a few paragraphs or make the assumption that you are an experienced listener and plunge straight into the more technical aspects. Clearly the growing interest in the hobby demands better coverage of the basics, particularly as for many, short-wave listening is the prelude to a much greater interest in radio generally. Who knows, it might even culminate in you obtaining a full amateur radio licence or perhaps one of the new novice licences. This enables the owner to share in some of the fun and transmit signals on the short-wave bands from the comfort of his or her home. A worthy ambition, as there can be little doubt that the pleasure and satisfaction of talking with fellow enthusiasts across the world has no parallels with any other hobby. But turning our attention back to basics, how can you learn a little more about the skill and art of listening? Make no mistake listening is an art and knowing where and when to listen is something that only comes with experience.

To the newcomer, one of the initial puzzles are the strange noises that can be heard all over the band, perhaps with an apparent lack of interesting, or at least signals that appear to carry any useful information. Looking at the listings within these pages you may just wonder why many of these interesting signals, cannot be heard at the first attempt. The most likely reason is that you are not listening at the correct times. Although broadcast stations transmit for longer periods of time and to specific schedules, non broadcast stations (often called utility stations) are there to fulfil a function and will only transmit when it is necessary to do so. In other words, if such stations have no traffic, then clearly they won't be heard. You need patience, experience and skill. Also, radio conditions are continually changing and reception of some more distant stations will only be possible at certain times of the day or night. Now this may sound to be stating the obvious, but it is quite common to make the mistake of assuming that if you listen on a given frequency you will immediately hear the listed station. Not so! Be patient and you will be rewarded.

If you thought that the quality of reception on the short-wave bands would be similar to that experienced when listening to local broadcasts on the domestic radio, then you are in for a big disappointment. Radio signals are rarely totally without some kind of background noise, often caused by interference from the many stations fighting for a space in this crowded part of the radio spectrum. Other noises will be caused by electrical interference from domestic appliances, power cables, television receivers and the like. Also, particularly in the summer months, static caused by electrical charges in the air can be a problem. All these different sources of noise therefore come together and cause a general melee of noise and interference that affects the fidelity of reception. But don't let this put you off. There is absolutely nothing that you can do about it, and rather surprisingly you will soon get used to it and learn to ignore these extraneous noises in favour of the signals that you are trying to copy. If this paints a rather black picture of reception, then take comfort from the fact that there will often be times when conditions are good, signals are strong, and interference very low. The main point to bear in mind is that reception can be noisy and reception very variable. Don't expect hi-fi reception, even from broadcast stations. The system can at best only give you the same quality as that obtained from stations on the medium wave band. But the thrill of hearing signals from the remote corners of the world will more than offset this minor limitation.

Do take time to read the instructions that come with your receiver. Some documentation is better than others, but it is essential to understand the function of the controls. Many modern designs now have quite complex memory systems for storage of popular frequencies. This may be very useful, but can also cause confusion. So if things seem to go wrong take time to consider whether you are doing anything wrong before you go back to the dealer from whom you purchased the receiver. The standard of reliability is now very high, particularly from equipment produced by the major manufacturers. Rarely does new equipment arrive faulty so check the instructions carefully before assuming the worst.

The tuning in of signals requires a little practice and should always be carried out slowly and carefully. This applies particularly when trying to receive Single Sideband (SSB) signals. Some receivers are easier than others to operate in this respect. Practice on strong signals, tuning carefully, and if you have a choice of USB and LSB, try switching from one to the other. Most commercial voice services use USB, but amateur signals below 10MHz and a few commercial transmissions use LSB. It's a knack that comes quickly after a few hours of practice.

Simple changes to your station can often make significant improvements. Try using an external aerial, rather than a whip or short piece of wire. The importance of a good aerial should not be underestimated. We are dealing with weak signals from transmitters running hundreds of times less power than the national broadcast stations, and a good aerial is a prerequisite for good reception. Use a wire at least 50ft long, outside if possible. The wire does not have to be in a straight line but the longer it is the better. Height is far less important than may be imagined. Certainly it does affect reception but in the early stages just worry about getting out a decent length of wire. Later, as you get further into the hobby you will want to study the performance of specially designed aerials and learn more about the various factors that can improve reception, particularly over longer distances. You will learn how raising the aerial height can improve long distance reception while reducing the strength of local signals. Aerials can be directional or omni directional. There are hundreds of designs and most of them can be home constructed at very low cost. Actually there are very few commercial aerials made for listening. This is partly because most specialised aerials have their best performance over particular areas of the short wave band and the more popular "long wire" hardly needs to be specially packaged. A length of wire is a length of wire! And no, it doesn't matter one little bit how thick or thin it is and whether or not it is covered in PVC. Frequent questions often asked by the newcomer, but not always accurately answered!

Clearly, there will be many listeners who are working on a budget and may have purchased a low cost receiver, or perhaps a second hand receiver. In fact the latter choice can be an excellent way of reducing the initial outlay. There have been so many new models produced over the past few years that there can be some major savings made by investigating the used market. The more fortunate may be lucky enough to be able to afford one of the top current models. But in the early stages results are more dependent on knowledge and understanding the vagaries of the short-wave spectrum rather than the price paid for the receiver. Obviously there are a few really cheap ones that cannot be regarded as having any serious potential. If you are purchasing from new, then it is likely that you will have to pay something over £100 for anything that will be capable of providing lasting interest, and receiving transmissions other than the stronger broadcast ones. If there is a common weakness of receivers at the cheaper end of the market, it is their poor SSB reception (or lack of it) and inability to provide good reception on external aerials particularly at night when the bands can be very crowded with strong signals. It may seem ironic, but one of the problems at this time of day is the strength of the signals on the short wave band. Sometimes signals are so strong they overload the receiver causing apparent interference. These strong interfering signals are sometimes well removed from the ones that you are trying to receive, yet their sheer strength is such as to cause problems within the receiver. Many receivers are fitted with attenuators or RF gain controls. Switching in the attenuator or reducing the RF gain control level can often cause a marked improvement. If you happen to be listening between 5MHz and 10MHz at night, try it and see. If you do not have either of these controls fitted you may find a significant improvement by reverting to the whip aerial usually found on cheaper receivers, and only using the external aerial for reception during the day when all signals are somewhat weaker. Never be frightened of experimenting. After all this is part of the fun. Never make assumptions; everything is worth trying in order to improve reception. Over the years amateurs have contributed much to the art of radio communications. Often it is simple curiosity that has been the spark that has ultimately resulted in discoveries of new aerials and communications techniques.

One of the most important aspects of short-wave listening is that of log keeping. If you keep an efficient log you will add enormously to your listening pleasure. So often one hears a station that sounds interesting but it ceases transmission before it can be identified. When this happens, log the date, day, time, frequency and any other relevant information. In this way you can go back on some future occasion to check if the station has a regular schedule.

Finally, do try and do some further reading on the more technical aspects of receivers, aerials and propagation. The better understanding you have of the various aspects, the more skilful you will become. But like any other hobby it will take time. You cannot become an expert overnight. Also, try to learn the best times to listen by observing and logging signals. Pay particular attention to the times of the day that signals from some parts of the world are normally heard. Also, consider world time differences. This may mean late night listening or early morning monitoring. And if you happen to have trouble in sleeping, try switching on your receiver at some unearthly hour such as three o'clock in the morning. The world doesn't stop when you go to sleep and you might just hear something interesting!

<u>Yaesu FRG-100 HF Receiver</u>

RADIO CONDITIONS 1994 - 1995

We are now well past the sunspot maximum in the present 11 year cycle. Opinions differ about how conditions are changing as we descend the slope. It will not be until the beginning of the new millennium that we experience really good conditions again. But don't become too disheartened, many of us have been through several of these doldrums periods and with the improvement in equipment things are a lot better than they would have been twenty years ago.

The general trend will be for conditions to worsen, particularly in the summer months. At times the bands above 20MHz will be very quiet, although winter can provide a bit of an uplift in conditions. It's worth checking around 25 - 30 MHz in the summer months for sporadic-E propagation. This can bring a dead band back into life without warning. Often it's short lived and very specific geographically, but is very interesting nevertheless. Sporadic-E is normally noticeable on the higher frequencies and can extend well into the lower VHF regions.

Those new readers who have never experienced a sunspot maximum before will have to wait until the year 2000/2001. Those dead areas above 25MHz suddenly spring into life and stations from around the world not normally heard, appear, often with tremendous strength. World wide propagation is not confined to the range below 30MHz. The band of frequencies up to, and often above 50MHz, will at times support propagation over thousands of miles. Amateur radio operators who frequent the 10 metre band will know that even modest power levels of only a few watts can produce good contacts across the Atlantic and beyond. It is sometimes possible to hear the many American services that operate in the area between 30MHz and 40MHz. There are many radio beacons that operate in the amateur

radio band between 28MHz and 30MHz on a 24-hourly basis and these provide a good indication of radio conditions.

The outlook over the next few years is, therefore, not very good but this has to be viewed in context. Newcomers will have nothing to compare the present propagation with and old timers will have been through it all before. The use of a modern, sensitive receiver together with a good aerial will still provide plenty of opportunities for long distance reception.

Nostalgia

Perhaps a measure of nostalgia should be felt when listening to marine traffic and possibly the aeronautical bands. It is almost certain that when the next sunspot maximum occurs at the turn of the century most of this traffic will be carried via satellites. There will always be a certain amount of communications by these services on the short waves for there will need to be a backup system to use if the satellites should fail. Satellites will always be vulnerable to accidental or intentional damage. For all the vagaries of short wave propagation, one thing is sure, those reflective layers around the earth will always be there to support cheap, effective and fairly reliable long range communications.

As we descend the current sun spot cycle there is likely to be a much greater level of activity and a noticeable improvement in radio conditions on the lower frequency bands. There are some listeners who specialise in listening on the lower frequencies and there is certainly a measure of satisfaction from hearing long distance signals "the hard way." The best times to listen are after the hours of darkness and often this means late at night or in the early hours of the morning. Signals may often be weak and subject to interference from more local stations. This becomes less of a problem as the night progresses.

Sunspot Watching

The eleven-year sunspot cycle has been well documented and recorded over the years but despite this there is still remarkably little known about exactly how it can have such a dramatic affect on radio propagation. Nevertheless sunspot activity does give a very good indication of what we can expect in the way of radio conditions on the short waves. High sunspot counts mean good conditions. Sudden sunspot flares can mean high levels of disturbance to radio propagation and it is sometimes possible to even monitor the solar noise which manifests itself in the form of an increase in receiver background noise.

Sunspots can be viewed by indirect observation achieved by projecting an image of the sun onto a suitable surface. This is a worthwhile study project that costs virtually nothing other than the time taken to make and record drawings of the sunspots on a regular basis. On no account should any attempt be made at direct observations of the sun unless a suitable light absorbing filter is used. Observations of the sunspots provide an interesting exercise, particularly when trying to correlate the visual observations with radio conditions. Although the cycle of events takes eleven years to complete there is also a less predictable, but noticeable, monthly cycle associated with hf conditions and sunspots.

Sunspot activity can normally be associated with a sudden, and often dramatic, change in radio propagation. Certainly there will be scientists around the world carrying out observations and in many respects the amateur is on an equal footing with his professional counterpart. Much research remains to be done into how and why sunspot activity can have such remarkable affects on the reflection and absorption of short-wave signals by the ionised layers above the Earth's surface. Only careful and systematic observations are likely to provide clues to the many, as yet, unsolved questions.

One final thought on the subject of sunspots concerns whether the eleven-year cycle is simply part of a much larger cycle measured in hundreds of years rather than tens of years. Observations so far carried out suggest that there is a certain amount of circumstantial evidence to support such a theory. Unfortunately none of us will live long enough to prove this one way or the other, but by keeping careful records and studying past sunspot cycles it is possible that we will gradually obtain a better idea of whether such a theory can be supported. Meanwhile, make the most of the current period, radio may never be quite like it again as many services currently using the short-wave bands will be operating in the GHz range by the year 2000, the time of the next sunspot maximum!

RECEIVERS

A question often asked by newcomers to the hobby is "what receiver would you recommend?" It is a question to which there is no one answer applicable to all circumstances. Enthusiasts place different demands on receivers and have different priorities. One that is right for one person may be entirely wrong for the next. And it would be equally incorrect to suppose that the most expensive receiver has everything that one could wish for. Indeed, some professional receivers that sell for several thousand pounds, look positively bereft of features when compared with those offered on the hobby market. Probably the most accurate answer to the question although no more informative, is that the receiver best suited to your needs is the one that does everything you require of it at minimum cost.

As with many hobbies, "the most expensive" is not necessarily "the best," particularly for the newcomer. For example, a receiver may have many accessories and controls that are of no useful purpose to the purchaser, but have no SSB or CW facility. If such a receiver were to be used for broadcast listening only, then this omission would be of no consequence. On the other hand, if the receiver was intended to be used for the

The latest SW-100E miniature receiver from SONY. It provides full shortwave reception AM and SSB

reception of the kind of stations listed in this book, it would prove wholly unsuitable. It is all a question of "horses for courses." Therefore, whilst no one receiver will suit everybody's needs, there are certain basic criteria that should be met by any receiver that is going to used for serious short-wave listening.

Firstly the receiver must cover the range 1.6-30MHz, or 170 to 10 metres for those of you who may be returning to the hobby from the old days when frequencies were often referred to in metres. Do make sure that the receiver has no gaps in its range. Some of the lower priced models have gaps in their range which can be most frustrating to the purchaser when he finds that his receiver misses out the very range that carries the traffic he or she wishes to listen to.

The next point of consideration must be that the receiver is suitable for the type of stations you wish to receive. Now this may seem obvious, but it is quite surprising how many people actually purchase "blind" or base their choice on ill founded advice. Transmissions on the short-wave band make extensive use of Single Sideband (SSB) and receivers must be fitted with a Beat Frequency Oscillator (BFO) or product detector. Sounds complicated? Well the easiest method of knowing whether your receiver has the necessary facility is to look for a switch or selector button that is labelled either "SSB" or "LSB & USB." If there is no such facility indicated, then don't purchase it. Don't be tempted by the £30 receiver that promises world-wide reception if you intend to take your hobby seriously. The salesman may impress you by telling you that it can receive stations from all over the world. What he really means is that it receives Radio Moscow and

Voice of America; stations that are so strong, even an old "crystal set" could probably receive them!

All modern receivers possess digital displays, and whilst this is not a feature that directly affects performance, it is something that is very useful for two reasons. The first is the fairly obvious one that it provides a very accurate frequency display and enables the user to read out the precise frequency and log it for the future. The second, and much less obvious reason is that by definition a digital receiver will normally have very good frequency stability. Any respectable receiver should be capable of remaining tuned to the selected frequency and the digital read-out should remain perfectly stable. If it does not, and the read-out shows a tendency to change, then the receiver is unstable and should be avoided. Fortunately this is becoming a thing of the past and all current receivers from reputable manufacturers have no such deficiencies. This defect is only likely to be found in really cheap receivers and some second-hand models that are some years old.

There are some basic features which any serious receiver should have and we list these below together with a brief description of their functions.

RF gain control.

This permits the level of the signal fed from the aerial to the early stages of the receiver to be adjusted. Its function is quite different from an audio gain control. The main purpose of the RF gain control is to prevent the early rf stages of the receiver from being overloaded by strong signals. This can occur when the receiver is used in close proximity to a transmitting station. It is more likely to occur at night time when very strong signals can arrive at the aerial terminals. Overloading of this kind manifests itself in various ways and can produce a general "clutter" on and around the frequency to which you are tuned. Technical terms such as cross modulation and

intermodulation are frequently used to describe these problems. Detailed accounts of these receiver shortcomings are described in most good text books on receiver design. Of course even the best receivers will eventually be affected by strong signals but they will tolerate much higher strengths of signal before the onset of any problems. The main point to bear in mind is that if you find at night there is a considerable increase in background noise and adjusting the rf gain control improves it, then your receiver is suffering from strong signal overload. Make full use of the rf gain control, it is there for a purpose and sensible use can result in dramatic improvements in reception on crowded bands.

Attenuator.

Some receivers have an attenuator fitted instead of an rf gain control. Its function is very similar to that of the rf gain control described above. However, it does cope with serious cases of overloading somewhat better than the traditional rf gain control. Some receivers have both controls fitted. If you have a fairly cheap receiver and there is neither an rf gain control or attenuator fitted then there is an opportunity for you to make an improvement by undertaking a bit of home construction. Get a copy of an attenuator circuit and build it into a box that you can fit between the aerial and the aerial socket. The chances are that you will find a dramatic improvement in receiver performance, particularly at night.

Slow Motion Tuning.

Because you will be tuning in stations that are very close together, it is essential that the receiver is equipped with a main tuning control that is not too coarse in its rate of tuning. You should have enough slow motion movement to permit the smooth selection of stations, particularly on SSB. Some receivers are now equipped with dual rates of tuning, this is particularly useful for rapid tuning through the bands using the fastest rate, whilst having the means of selecting a slower rate for fine tuning and moving between adjacent stations. Also check for backlash. This is the tendency for the tuning control to move slightly, after removing your hand from the control. Only older receivers normally suffer from this effect.

External Aerial Socket.

If you want to be sure of receiving long distance signals you will need to employ some form of external aerial. If your receiver has a built-in whip aerial its performance will be limited to receiving only the strongest signals. Most good portables and all base station receivers have provisions for connecting to an external aerial system. If your receiver has no such provision then it is not likely to be suitable for serious listening.

Noise Blanker

The description gives a clue to its function. However, it is probably one of the most misunderstood controls on a receiver. On many occasions its use will appear to have no noticeable effect on background noise. Perhaps the name is misleading, perhaps it should be called a "pulse noise blanker." Noise blankers are best at coping with simple pulsed forms of noise such as may occur from a vehicle ignition system. Such noises are composed of noise pulses with short gaps in between. This occurs many times a second but the noise blanker is able to "blank off" the receiver for the duration of each pulse and thus dramatically reduce the offending noise. If you are near a busy road or likely to use your receiver in a moving vehicle you will find this device very useful.

Unfortunately noise blankers are of very little use in combating many other forms of noise and interference. They certainly won't help with interference from other stations and will have no effect on the dreaded TV time base noise that radiates from domestic TV receivers. This manifests itself in the form of noise every 10KHz or so along the receiver dial.

There is one device that we have tried and that seems to work pretty well to reduce locally generated electrical noises (including time base

interference). This is the "QRM eliminator" made by SEM in the Isle of Man. Interested readers who wish to pursue the use of this device can contact Mark Francis during office hours on 01702 203353.

AGC Slow & Fast:

All modern receivers have an automatic gain control circuit that electrically detects the level of the received signal and adjusts the internal gain of the receiver. This prevents overloading of the mixer and early stages of the receiver and also ensures that widely differing strengths of signal all produce the same level of audio to the speaker or headphones. Without agc it would be somewhat uncomfortable to have widely differing audio levels coming through the speaker or headphones.

Some receivers have different speeds of agc action normally referred to as "fast" and "slow." Slow agc will quickly reduce the gain of the receiver upon reception of a strong signal and hold the reduced gain for a significant time even after the signal has either ceased or reduced in level. This is particularly suitable for phone reception and avoids the "pumping" action associated with "fast" agc. The fast action is normally more suited to CW reception. It may also be possible to switch the agc completely off on some receivers. Under certain conditions this may be desirable and when used in conjunction with an rf gain control can sometimes achieve the best strong signal handling characteristics.

Modes: AM/SSB/CW/FM

Modern receivers cater for all the popular modes of transmission and the selection is made from a front panel control. If you wish to listen to broadcast stations you will need to select the "AM" position on the switch. This is the same mode used by broadcast stations on our medium and long wave bands. In fact it was the very first mode of transmission ever used for transmitting speech and music. Although superseded on our VHF bands by FM, AM is the only viable mode for entertainment broadcasts on the short wavebands because of its relatively narrow bandwidth.

If you wish to listen to marine, aircraft or amateur radio transmissions, your receiver must have the ability to resolve SSB (Single Sideband) signals. Normally you will have the option of switching between upper and lower sideband. (USB/LSB). USB is used for almost all commercial transmissions, whilst amateurs use LSB on bands below 10MHz and USB on bands above 10MHz.

Any receiver capable of receiving SSB can also receive CW signals and most other data signals such as fax and rtty. There is very little FM activity, in the main it is the preserve of Citizen Band operation on the 27MHz band and amateurs in the 29MHz band.

A few manufacturers also make available vhf converters for use with their radios. In these cases the receivers will have provision for the reception of FM. There are also some independent manufacturers of vhf converters. If you intend to use a converter it is essential to ensure your receiver is capable of FM reception. This mode is widely used on the vhf bands.

Squelch

This control cuts out the background noise from the receiver when no signal is present. It is particularly useful for FM reception in the vhf bands but has far less application on the short wave bands. The problem on the short wave bands is the high level of random noise and interference. This is enough to "break" the squelch even though the wanted signal may not be present. If, however, you are monitoring a channel that carries a very strong signal it may be possible to make use of the squelch control with careful adjustment.

Memories.

Many modern receivers are equipped with memories. These permit the storage of chosen frequencies and allow instant selection. Often the memories are used in conjunction with a scanning feature. If the receiver is fitted with a squelch control the it will be possible to scan the memories continually until a signal is present. Dependent on the design, the receiver will either lock onto this signal or halt temporarily. We have already mentioned the limitations of squelch on the short wave bands and this limitation applies when using a scanning receiver or scanning mode. Unless the squelch control is turned well up, the random noise is likely to open the squelch and halt the scanning. In other words, the receiver will treat random noise as a signal and halt on the frequency or memory channel.

POPULAR RECEIVERS

It is not the purpose of this book to cover in detail the various models available. Over the past ten years or so there have been a large number of receivers manufactured for the short wave bands. Some have become almost classic designs, selling widely. Others have come and gone almost unnoticed. There have also been many cheap imports from countries other than Japan. The list of receivers briefly described below is by no means exhaustive but probably includes most of the top sellers over the last few years. Many are no longer current but are nevertheless still freely advertised on the second-hand market. We have given an indication of prices and all these are based on the 1993 market. At the present time exchange rates are pushing prices up and this will also affect the second-hand market. Prices should be viewed with this fact in mind.

KENWOOD (TRIO) R1000

Very popular about ten years ago, this was the first of a successful line of receivers from Kenwood. Most models sold in the UK bore the legend of "Trio" but they came from the same factory. Although production has long since ceased, it still represents excellent value for money and features digital read-out. There are no memory or scanning provisions but it is regarded

as a worthwhile model to consider if you are looking at the second-hand market. Based on 1993 prices, expect to pay around £180 - £225.

KENWOOD (TRIO) R600

Really this is the little brother of the R1000 mentioned above. It also has been discontinued for some while but it has the same basic specification. One criticism of it has been the fairly fast tuning rate on the main dial. This is probably a personal moan and the intending purchaser would do well to check this point for himself. In all other respects it offers good value for money and if you can find one in good condition it is likely to give you an excellent return on your investment. Current prices are in the range £170 - £200.

KENWOOD R2000

Introduced several years ago production ceased towards the end of 1992. It was a radical update of the R1000/R600 series. It was one of the first receivers to offer memory channels as standard. It also offers scanning and is fitted with a squelch control. The optional VHF converter that plugs into the back (model VC-10) immediately transforms the receiver into a VHF monitor covering the range 118-174MHz). The basic receiver range is 150kHz - 30MHz and other features include noise blanker, three switched filters, step attenuator, 24 hour clock etc. The current used price is £300 - £350.

KENWOOD R5000.

Kenwood's only current production receiver, it has been popular for several years even though it is in the upper price bracket. The more experienced listener will appreciate its high technical specification and performance features. Its main competitors are the ICOM R71 and the NRD-535. The coverage of the R-5000 is 100kHz - 30MHz and with the addition of the optional

VC-20 VHF converter the coverage extends to include 108 - 174MHz. This receiver includes luxuries such as 10Hz vfo steps, 100 memories, selectable filters, dual mode noise blanker, numeric keypad frequency entry, optional computer interface, notch filter, IF shift and much more. The current listed price is £999.

YAESU FRG7

This is arguably one of the most successful receivers ever produced. Certainly getting on in years now and becoming somewhat scarce it still offers the newcomer on a budget, a good buy. It does not have digital read-out and uses the same filter for SSB and AM. Bandspread is adequate and stability is quite good. You will need to check its condition carefully as some specimens can be as old as 15 years. Nevertheless, one in good condition, carefully looked after is worth considering. Expect to pay between £80 and £135.

YAESU FRG-7700

This receiver was a radical improvement over the FRG-7 and really bears little resemblance to it. It has all the necessary features to make it a good choice for the serious listener and although not fitted as standard there was an optional memory bank available. Yaesu also produced a range of VHF converters for use with this receiver and these covered a combined range of 50MHz to 170MHz. Neither receivers or accessories are now available from new but the receiver is still regularly advertised in the second-hand columns of the magazines. Current prices are in the £300 region.

YAESU FRG-8800

This is a discontinued model from Yaesu, although it had now been in production for several years. Very much based on the FRG-7700 above it included memory bank as standard and is also capable of scanning. The VHF converter option was a module that slid directly into the back of the receiver. The basic range is 150kHz - 30MHz and with the optional converter the range covers 118MHz - 174MHz. Separate filters are used for SSB, AM and FM reception.

Other features include timer, clock, tone control, attenuator and wide/narrow AM filter. The selling price was £860.

YAESU FRG-100

Recently released this is Yaesu's new model and although it was announced as a budget class receiver with a high performance, the recent exchange rate changes have rather made the "budget" part of the description somewhat redundant! It uses a high first IF which should help to overcome any image problems and the frequency range is 50KHz to 30MHz. It features 50 memories, SSB/CW and AM reception with switched filters, FM as an option, squelch control, clock, timer, scanning etc. all built into a compact size of 238 x 93 x 243mm. Provisions are also made for installing narrow filters for CW work, either 500Hz or 250Hz. The current price is £559.

ICOM R70/R71.

These are basically the same receiver, the only significant difference being that the R71 has provisions for remote control using an optional infrared control unit. The R71 also offers the provision of direct frequency entry using a front panel keypad. The R70 is no longer in production. In the higher end of the price bracket these receivers offer excellent performance. They are particularly sensitive and are fitted with a switchable pre-amplifier. Very accurate dial read-

out to 100Hz, 10Hz tuning steps, and excellent strong signal handling capabilities are all features that make both models attractive. The listed price of the R71 is £875 and the used price of the R70 is £300 - £350.

ICOM R-72E

Now in its second year of production, the R-72 offers an excellent specification in the mid price bracket. The basic coverage is 30kHz to 30MHz and offers reception of USB, LSB, CW and AM with FM as an option. Great emphasis has been put on the front end performance and ICOM claim a dynamic range of 100dB. In layman's terms this means the receiver is able to operate on crowded bands with very strong signals without showing any distress in the form of increased background noise. This is a common fault with earlier receivers from all manufacturers. To preserve the sensitivity a switched pre-amplifier is included together with an attenuator, direct keypad entry, noise blanker, 99 memories, clock etc. At a price of £690 it provides good value for money.

ICOM R-9000

At a list price of just over £4,000 you are not likely to see this on many dealer's shelves. But our coverage would not be complete without making a brief mention of this fine receiver. It covers the staggering range of 30kHz to 2GHz without gaps and has so many features that it would be impossible to do it justice within the space available. Features include 5" CRT display, 1000 memories, spectrum scope capability, TV video signal capability, SSB, CW, FSK, AM and FM modes, IF shift, notch filter, noise

blanker to name just a few. A number of these receivers are known to have been sold to the professional market at which level they offer good value for money. Whether or not the average enthusiast can justify the cost really depends on one's devotion to the hobby and financial capability. However, it's still nice to dream!

SONY ICF-7600D

A truly portable little receiver that could almost fit into the larger pocket. It has stood the test of time and still sells as well as the updated SW-7600.. The weight and size is kept down by supplying the power supply in a separate module. The ICF-7600D covers the complete short wave band plus broadcast FM. It features digital display and provides reception of AM, SSB, CW and FM (76MHz - 108MHz). Also offered are ten memory channels, scanning, clock, timers, fine tuning for SSB and an RF attenuator. It uses a common filter for SSB and AM reception but this is a minor disadvantage in a receiver of this size and price. Current cost is typically £170.

SONY ICF-2001D

This is an advanced version of the ICF-7600D and much bigger, although still portable. Its specification enables it to be used as a base station receiver on an external aerial. Features

not included in the ICF-7600D are RF gain control, larger memory bank, continuous tuning down to 50Hz steps, 100Hz frequency resolution, synchronous detection for AM, switchable LSB/USB, separate filters for SSB and AM, and an improved front end amplifier. All UK models also have airband AM reception from 108MHz to 136MHz plus FM broadcast. Price is approximately £300

SONY ICF-SW55

Launched in 1992 this receiver has many similarities to both the ICF-7600D and the ICF-2001D. It covers all modes, provides full coverage of the short wave bands and also offers FM stereo reception through headphones. Its performance on its internal whip aerial is particularly good and can be thoroughly recommended for desk top operation. The memory bank offers the means of not only storing frequency, but also storing the name of the station. The memories can then be paged through rather like a computer menu. We checked one out and were very impressed. You also get a nice hard plastic carry case, universal power supply and wire aerial.

SONY ICF-SW55E

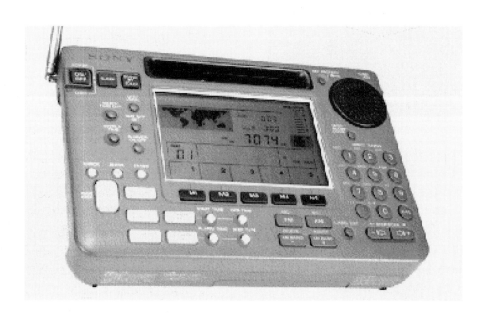

AERIALS

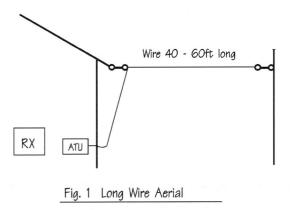

Fig. 1 Long Wire Aerial

Figure 1 gives a typical layout of a long wire aerial used by many listeners. Many operators do not use the aerial tuner shown, but there is no doubt that this is a very desirable accessory. This form of aerial does have a drawback in that it cane be prone to picking up electrical interference, particularly where it enters the premises. This form of aerial also tends to be more susceptible to picking up interference radiated from TV receivers. This interference manifests itself in the form of a rough note every 10kHz or so along the receiver dial. It is usually more of a problem on the lower frequencies rather than the higher ones. In order to overcome these problems some

No matter how good your receiver, its performance depends very much upon the aerial you use. The handbook with the receiver may give you some initial advice. Most modern receivers will give quite useful results from even a mediocre aerial and a random length of wire in the region of 50ft or so will often provide good DX reception. But for the best performance a more ambitious aerial system should be considered. There are a number of books regularly advertised in specialist radio magazines covering the subject, and these will give you an in depth understanding of the many different types of aerials that can be used together with dimensions and construction details.

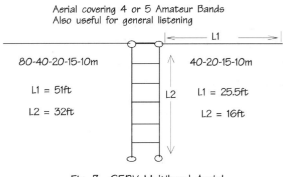

Fig. 3 G5RV Multiband Aerial

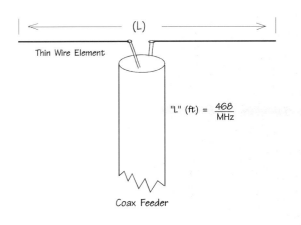

$$\text{"L" (ft)} = \frac{468}{\text{MHz}}$$

Fig, 2 Dipole Aerial

form of shielded feed between the aerial system and the receiver is recommended where the aerial approaches its entrance into the premises in the form of coaxial cable. Although it would be perfectly possible to connect the random length of wire shown in figure 1 to a short length of coaxial cable, the resultant poor match of impedance between the "low" of the cable and the "high" of the wire would cause a significant reduction in performance. However one does have to balance this against the reduction in electrical and TV interference that results.

An alternative to the wire is the dipole aerial which is a traditional aerial used by many, and is designed to be fed with coaxial cable. Unfortunately such an aerial is "frequency conscious", but it does provide excellent performance on its design frequency. A typical design is shown in figure 2 together with the formula for calculating dimensions for any frequency. The aerial will perform away from its design frequency but performance will fall off considerably. For practical purposes you can regard the aerial as usable over a bandwidth of approximately 10% of its frequency before any noticeable fall off in reception takes place. For amateur radio enthusiasts the G5RV antenna is worth considering, either in its full size version or half size version. See figure 3.

Finally, we should not ignore those who have very small gardens and cannot erect much or anything in the way of an outside aerial. For those in such a position it is recommended they try an active aerial. The two commercially available ones are the Sony AN-1 vertical and the Datong AD370 horizontal. Both only measure a few feet in length and can be erected indoors or outside. In essence they are a short antenna that is connected directly to an amplifier that has the dual role of providing gain and matching. The amplifier forms an integral part of the aerial system and is housed in a waterproof casing. From this amplifier runs a coaxial cable that conveys the signal back to the receiver and also provides the low voltage power feed back to the amplifier up at the aerial. The Sony unit uses batteries for power in the base module whilst the Datong uses a mains unit. Active aerials are capable of excellent results when no alternative is possible and can be thoroughly recommended.

The Lowe HF-150 Combo Station

RECEIVER AERIAL TUNERS

Global AT-2000 ATU with "Q" switch

What can an aerial tuner do for you? With the latest receiver designs using modern high gain solid state devices it is easy to wonder whether an aerial tuner can really effect much improvement. But in some respects this very technology is its own worst enemy. Unquestionably, the modern short-wave receiver is now an extremely sensitive machine and just poking a screwdriver into the aerial terminal will produce some signals. But when it comes to digging out the weaker signals, the shortcomings in many modern receivers start to show themselves.

An aerial comprising a random length of wire type presents a continually changing impedance to the receiver as we tune through the radio spectrum. At one frequency it may measure just a few hundred Ohms whilst at another this impedance can rise to several thousand Ohms. The length of the wire and the frequency at which it is being used determines the exact resistance. Odd multiples of quarter wavelengths present low impedances whilst even multiples present high impedances. Now the transfer of signal energy from aerial to receiver will only be at its maximum when the receiver input impedance matches that of the aerial. Almost all receivers are designed to have a 50 Ohm aerial impedance, but end fed wires are anything but that! As a consequence there is a loss of signal transfer which may not be too important for strong signals but can be very important for weak signal reception. However, the problems don't end

here. Most modern receivers have poor front end selectivity, in other words the early stages of the receiver will amplify signals over a wide frequency range equally well, both the signal you are tuned to and signals either side up to several MHz away. This can result in "cross modulation", a term used to describe the way in which strong signals well removed from the receive frequency, "modulate" and cause interference to the wanted signal.

An aerial tuner can help with both of the problems outlined above. Firstly it has the ability to transform the impedance of the aerial to 50 Ohms, and secondly, it can provide some of the missing front end selectivity and so "clean up" reception.

An item of equipment that does just that is the AT2000, a purpose designed receiver ATU that covers the range 150kHz to 30 MHz. It will handle most forms of aerials including long wires, coaxial fed dipoles and even tuned feeder. No power is required as the unit is entirely passive. Just connect the unit in between the aerial and the receiver and hear the difference! A novel feature found on this tuner is the "Q" switch. This enables you to adjust the front-end selectivity to match reception conditions. The AT-2000 is stocked by most good amateur radio dealers and Maplin Electronics.

STATIONS LISTED IN THIS BOOK

Whilst all stations listed are reported to have been active and heard in Europe, the transmissions are by nature, intermittent. In fact many may only transmit for very short periods during the day. Other stations appear on several different frequencies. Such entries indicate that the station uses several different channels. This does not imply that they transmit simultaneously on all frequencies, but rather that they will select the frequency most suitable for the time of day and year, together with distance involved. The main exceptions are the broadcast stations where it is quite common to find that they transmit the same programme on several different frequencies.

The listener should also be aware that some non-channelised stations vary their frequency to some degree, usually to avoid interference. Sometimes the short-wave band can appear a very disorganised place! For this reason it may sometimes be found that a listed station is slightly removed from its normal frequency. But maritime, aeronautical and news transmissions are not likely to vary. On the other hand, some broadcast stations have been heard to move, usually those from some of the less well developed countries, but not always.

It must not be assumed that because a transmission is heard on a particular frequency it is the same station as listed. Quite apart from the fact that the station may be operating away from its listed frequency, there are many stations that have not been identified. This is where you, the listener, can add to this list and build up your own personal log. Nothing can replace experience and as you become more skilled at listening you will find hunting out new stations becomes easier.

Our listings contain only those stations recorded as being active or that have been reliably monitored. We have also tried to include only those stations which there is a fair chance of hearing in Europe. For example there is not the slightest point in listing low power Pacific stations on 3MHz and 4MHz. The average enthusiast would not have the necessary aerials to be able to pick up such signals. Likewise the higher frequency listings have tended to favour the longer distance stations which are more likely to be heard at this end of the band.

Although international band plans have been agreed there are plenty of examples of stations throughout the world operating on frequency bands other than those allocated. This makes compiling an accurate list all the more difficult. It is further complicated by stations that tend to shift frequency from time to time, often at complete random. There are many frequencies that are shared, some on a planned basis and others on a non-voluntary basis.

Many services have a number of different frequencies allocated to them throughout the HF bands. This is necessary because radio signals tend to travel over varying distances at different times of the day and night, and also at different times of the year. In order to provide a reliable service, stations need to select the frequency that is most likely to provide reliable communications for the chosen period of operation. To a large extent the best frequency band to use can be predicted in advance. But sometimes even the best forecasts are wrong and stations have to move one band up or one band down to effect communication. But as a general rule, when night falls, stations move lower in frequency and as day breaks they move higher. In winter this shift from higher to lower frequencies becomes more dramatic at dusk, whereas in the summer months the shift may not be necessary until well after dark.

There is one more predictable variation that affects radio propagation; that is the eleven year sunspot cycle. As we have explained earlier in this book, this causes radio propagation to im-

prove, particularly on the higher frequency bands, as we approach the peak of the cycle. The next sunspot maximum is predicted to be some time during the turn of the century.

The new Grundig SSB and AM YB-400 receiver is a handy size and covers the complete medium wave, short wave

RTTY Explained

Here's a modern data controller from MFJ. The MFJ-1278 will permit you to copy RTTY and many other data modes including CW, AMTOR and PACTOR. You'll also need a computer and a modern short wave receiver.

Radio teletype or RTTY is a mode of radio transmission that is used widely for the transmission of messages. A keyboard is used to send characters either in plain language or code, by radio. The information is first received via a normal communications receiver and the output (usually audio) is passed to a terminal unit that decodes it for printing on paper or to display on a screen. The latter method is often favoured by amateurs but printing is used by professional networks in order to preserve hard copy. Almost any receiver capable of receiving Morse code will also receive RTTY, although frequency stability is critical for some of the more sophisticated RTTY modes such as VFT (Voice Frequency Transmission). Suitable terminals for decoding the signals and displaying them on either a monitor screen or on a domestic TV are available from most amateur radio dealers. With a simple arrangement, most amateur and many commercial transmissions can be copied. Several different types of RTTY transmissions are listed in this edition of the frequency handbook, ranging from standard 50 Baud press and meteorological stations (which simple decoders can read) to advanced ARQ systems for which the more expensive decoders (such as the POCOM, WAVECOM or UNIVERSAL models) are required. It is also possible to obtain software (such as HOKA) to run programmes for decoding by PCs. The basic RTTY type as transmitted by press and meteo stations, is one which uses the so-called "Baudot" code - originally devised for land-line teletype. The code alphabet is known as ITA2. Standard speeds of 50, 75 and 100 Baud will be encountered on

press/meteo stations and on many other services listed in this book. Amateur RTTY of this type uses 45 Baud speed. Marine, some Embassy and other services use an error-correcting system known as SITOR (or CCIR 476-3). The normal speed is 100 Baud. Amateurs also use a derivative of this system, known as AMTOR. SITOR/AMTOR has two modes. In essence, Mode A is an error correcting system that requires the receiving station to repeatedly acknowledge correct receipt of data by transmitting back an acknowledgement signal. This requires rapid switching at both ends of the link. The cycle takes place approximately twice each second, each character sent comprising a unique combination of bits - but with a common number of odd/even bits. This helps in recognition with any corruption of the signal (by interference, for example) causing the receiving station to send an automatic repeat request (ARQ). The system is very efficient over paths that are prone to weak signals or to interference. The Swedish system of SITOR (known as SWED-ARQ) uses good signal conditions to lengthen the "block" of characters transmitted at each "over". When conditions are not so good, the Swedish system reverts to a block length compatible with normal SITOR Mode A. Despite the drawbacks of SITOR, it is extensively used for Marine RTTY traffic and by some Embassy services. Contact is made by use of Selective Calling (SELCAL) and a list (not exhaustive) of some Selcal codes is given at the end of this book. There are many occasions, particularly in the marine service, where information of a general nature is transmitted to many stations rather than one particular receiver. Clearly

Mode A is not suitable for general transmissions of this type and to cater for these, whilst still retaining the error-correction facilities, Mode B is used. In this mode, each character is effectively sent twice. If the receiving station detects an error in the odd/even bit combination on the first pass, it picks the same character up again on the second pass. If the second is still an incorrect combination, the receiver will print a dash for the missing character. This system is a considerable improvement over the basic ITA2 Baudot RTTY and, in general, it works well. One application of SITOR Mode B is for the NAVTEX system for navigational information on 518kHz. When monitoring RTTY it is important to appreciate that many transmissions will not be able to be decoded; or the decoder may output what appears to be "gibberish". There can be several reasons for this. For example, there are many transmissions from stations which use the Cyrillic alphabet rather than the Latin alphabet. There are press transmissions using the Arabic keyboard but, with practice, it is possible to recognise the output from these stations as displayed or printed by a Latin-alphabet decoder. Some military signals are sent at non-standard speeds and use non-Baudot codes. The signal sounds like RTTY, but the decoder will not display. Even the more expensive decoders do not capture all these military signals. What these expensive decoders do have is the ability to copy the more advanced TDM (Time Division Multiplex) and other refinements of RTTY, many using what is known as the "Moore" code as opposed to the older Baudot code. It is beyond the scope of this publication to give detailed technical explanations of these systems, many examples of which appear in our handbook. Different equipment manufacturers use slightly different descriptions for the various systems. We use the descriptions applicable to the WAVECOM decoder. The systems encountered in this edition include ARQ/E (usually 96, 72 or 86Bd), ARQ/E3 (usually 100 or 48Bd), ARQ/M2 (usually 96 or 200Bd), ARQ/M4 (usually 192Bd), FEC-A (usually 96 or 144Bd), SI-ARQ (usually 96Bd), SI-FEC (usually 96Bd), DUP-ARQ (usually 125 Bd), SWED-ARQ (100Bd) and POL-ARQ(100Bd). Whilst there are other RTTY systems such as AUTOSPEC, they are quite rare. 100Bd ARQ/N is also encountered on rare occasions. For some ARQ systems, we give the repetition cycle of the system. Thus an entry which reads "72ARQ/E/4" would mean ARQ/E system at a speed of 72 Baud with a four-repetition cycle. The "shift" between the high and low tones transmitted to represent mark and space in Baudot RTTY will normally be 425Hz, with some services using 325Hz or 850Hz. Where the shift is known to be a narrower one, we show this before the Baud speed - i.e. 85/75 would be a 75 Baud speed transmission using a shift of 85Hz. CIS maritime stations normally use 170Hz. The phasing of the shift can either be "normal" or "reverse", depending on whether the mark signal is the high or the low one. Although some decoders do not have to be set for this phasing or polarity, simple ones may have to be set for correct polarity. We therefore give this information after the Baud speed. The letter "c" denotes known Cyrillic. Thus an entry of 170/50nc would indicate a 50 Baud transmission using 170Hz shift of normal polarity and using the Cyrillic alphabet. CIS and Baltic states are still using 50Bd Baudot although there is an increasing use of SITOR by these countries. The Cyrillic alphabet can be

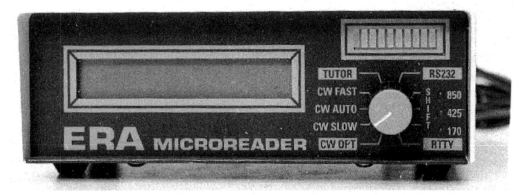

The ERA Microreader is an excellent way of starting off in RTTY. Its built-in screen means you don't need a computer for display.

displayed by some decoders (although not normally able to be printed). When monitoring Cyrillic, several decoders rely on the use of "Unshift On Space" (USOS) to force the decoder to display letters because the shift signal used for Cyrillic will change the display to figures and other upper case symbols. With USOS, the display will come back to letters after a space has been received. There are snags. There can be a problem when a word begins with the Cyrillic character for "ch". This will be printed as "4" and the rest of the word may well remain in upper case and appear unintelligible. It is possible to construct a transliteration table of the third-shift Cyrillic keyboard in order to "translate" into an English equivalent and there are some characters worth mentioning in that context. As well as the "4" meaning the "ch" sound, the letter "Q"

should be translated as the sound "ya" and an "X" should be ignored. Take the word which you receive as "OKTQBRXSKAQ". This is translated as "OKTYABRSKAYA". A little practice and you will master the system.....ASCII(American Standard Code for Information Interchange) may sometimes be encountered on Amateur bands and there are signals originating in Germany which use adapted ASCII. One such transmission can be found on 140.3kHz, using 300Bd speed. Also included in this edition are some frequencies where "packet" radio transmissions have been monitored on amateur, US military amateur transmissions and on the sector of 6MHz used by illegal "CB type" stations. These examples should help you to find where the "packet" transmissions can be sampled. The speed is usually 300Bd on HF.

FACSIMILE

These transmissions are employed for sending information of a graphical nature. They can in fact transmit any form of information but are used extensively for the transmission of weather maps and, to a lesser degree, press photographs. The main UK centres for weather map transmissions are Bracknell (Met Office) and Northwood (Royal Navy). A number of different frequencies are used and are shown in this book. Two main frequencies for Bracknell are 3289.5kHz and 4782.0kHz. Royal Navy transmissions can be found on 4307.0kHz and 6446.0kHz. Transmission times are slow and a chart might take 15 to 20 minutes to complete. The system relies on the action of a device which scans the document to be transmitted, a line at a time. Radio signals representing black and white shades are then

detected by the receiver and made to operate the FAX receiving equipment to reproduce the original document. Initially, the cost of FAX equipment was prohibitive, but the enthusiast can now obtain efficient FAX decoders at modest cost. Our monitoring is done with the British-made ICS FAX decoder, which is now available with 50Bd RTTY and "NAVTEX" receiving facilities. The decoder is connected to the audio output of a communications receiver (usually in LSB mode) and will give an output to a parallel interface to an Epson FX-80 compatible printer. Interested readers should consult the advertising pages of such magazines as Practical Wireless and Short Wave Magazine. Both magazines appear monthly and are available from most newsagents.

The Marine Services

The marine service is a very well organised system that makes great use of the HF bands and is divided into channels. The operator selects a channel on the HF band in much the same way as would be done on the VHF bands. The actual channel separation varies and depends on the mode of transmission. Narrow bandwidth signals such as RTTY and CW need only small amounts of space measured in hundreds of Hertz and can thus be grouped closely together. SSB voice signals require a much greater bandwidth and therefore have a larger channel separation, typically 3kHz. Telex and SSB channels are assigned numbers, often used by the operators in preference to the actual frequency. A new HF allocation plan was introduced from July 1991 and this edition includes results of our monitoring the implementation of the new sub-bands. There are isolated examples where the new allocation plan has not been implemented (e.g. Luanda Coast Radio is still using 22330.5 for CW although it is now allocated as a Telex frequency for use by ships). You will find that most coastal traffic operates R/T calls between 1.6MHz and 4MHz. The main voice calling frequency is 2182kHz, which is monitored continually by Coast Stations as part of the International Calling and Distress system. A new system of UK channel pairings, designed to relieve the pressure on 2182kHz and to even out R/T calls between groups of stations, was introduced by British Telecom. This was later overtaken by a complete re-allocation plan for MF R/T in the European area. Full details of pairings are given against the channel frequencies for these stations. However, 2182 remains in use for calling by most vessels. Coast stations regularly transmit traffic lists and special warnings. These are broadcast at set times of the day and night. We have listed times against some of these stations. All times are given in UTC. Traffic lists comprise call signs or names of ships for which the station holds traffic, very often telephone links for passengers or crew. Some Coast stations have several channels and will normally nominate a working channel for contact, thus leaving open a "calling" channel. Coastal traffic can also be heard using CW in the sector round 500kHz. Unlike other books, we include details of coast and ship working frequencies for this LF band. Ships outside coastal waters will generally use the higher frequency bands from 4MHz upwards. These frequencies support long distance communication much better than the lower ones. The actual frequency band used will be determined by the distances involved and the general propagation conditions prevailing. In the UK, the centre for long distance communication is Portishead Radio in the West of England. They have numerous frequencies, all of which you will find within these listings.

Navtex

Following experimental transmission using SITOR Mode B to promulgate navigation, weather and search & rescue messages, the use of the NAVTEX system is now well established and it will, in some circumstances, eventually become compulsory for ships to be fitted with equipment capable of receiving these broadcasts. Once the equipment is installed and switched on, it is not necessary for a radio operator to be on duty for the messages to be received. Each transmission (on 518kHz) is coded to show the transmitting station and the category of message. A four-character group at the start of the message will identify the station and the category, plus 2 further serial numbers. If these two numbers are "00", the message is urgent and will by-pass the selective element of the dedicated receiving equipment so that this urgent traffic is always printed.

Stations in Europe have the following identifiers:

Brest Le Conquet	**F**
Cullercoats	**G**
Haernoesand	**H**
Niton	**S**
Ostend	**T**
Portpatrick	**O**
Reykjavik	**R**
Rogoland	**L**
Scheveningen	**P**
Stockholm	**J**
Tallinn	**U**

Categories are:

A	**Navigation warnings**
B	**Gale warnings**
C	**Ice warnings**
D	**Search and Rescue**
E	**Weather forecasts**
Z	**Used to indicate no messages on hand at the scheduled transmission time.**

Aeronautical Communications

It comes as quite a surprise to many to learn just how much air traffic is dependent upon short-wave radio communications whilst crossing the world's oceans. In many cases, the only position information that controllers have of aircraft crossing the Atlantic is by means of their hourly updates. The main interest for UK listeners will be North Atlantic traffic. The busiest band at present is between 5.450MHz and 5.730MHz. All communication is by USB voice transmission. Once an aircraft is out of range of the VHF service, contact will be established with the Oceanic Area Control Centre on one of the HF frequencies, normally in the 5MHz band. The UK OACC is known as "Shanwick," a combination of Shannon and Prestwick. Unlike airways over land, airways across the Atlantic are not fixed but are revised twice daily. Listeners to the HF transmissions by aircraft will hear them providing co-ordinates of both their current and later estimated position. From this information it is a relatively simple task for the listener to plot the aircraft's course using an atlas. One feature of aviation HF communications worthy of mention is "SELCAL," an abbreviation for "selective calling." This is a special identity code in the form of a short tone combination that is superimposed on the signal at the start of trans-

missions. Each aircraft has a unique "SELCAL" code. The system enables the crew to switch their HF radio receiver to the stand-by mode whereby it can automatically be activated and the crew alerted that there is traffic for them by means of the ground station radiating the appropriate "SELCAL" signal. This avoids the inevitable fatigue and possible confusion that would arise if one of the crew members had to monitor the radio continuously. Other frequencies of interest to the HF listener on the aviation bands are those allocated for air-sea rescue. 5.680MHz is the main daytime channel and during a search becomes very busy indeed. There are two control centres in the UK. One located in the south is at Plymouth and the other in the north at Edinburgh. You will hear direct transmissions from both helicopters and control aircraft such as Nimrods. At nightfall some traffic switches to 3.022MHz. If you want to make a quick check on the overall weather scene then check RAF VOLMET on 4.722MHz or 11.200MHz. These are continuous voice transmissions on USB 24 hour as per day. There are also a number of other world VOLMET services you will find listed in the main body of this publication. For the main European civil airports check Shannon VOLMET on 5.505MHz USB. Not all VOLMET services are continuous.

Unusual Transmissions

No one can doubt that the short-wave spectrum has for many years provided an ideal medium for spy communications and the like. The years between 1935 and 1970 probably saw the greatest use of such transmissions with the war years providing great leaps forward in sophistication. Miniature short-wave transmitters behind enemy lines are not just James Bond fantasies, they actually exist. With the rapid growth in recent years in the number of satellites in space, it would be logical to think that the use of the short-wave spectrum no longer has any useful role to play in communications requiring secrecy. However, one cannot ignore the absolute simplicity of a short-wave transmitter sending CW. It is highly portable and requires little in the way of technical knowledge to operate. With the use of coded signals it still provides a very effective means of communications. Sophisticated high stability receivers with very narrow bandwidths enable even low power transmitters to provide reliable communications. Perhaps this brief background goes some way to explaining some of the strange transmissions to be heard on the bands. Take for example the single letter beacons often abbreviated "SLB." They appear to carry no useful information and yet are dotted around the spectrum running continuously. Do they provide propagation indications or do they serve a more sinister purpose? They have existed for well over 20 years and yet nobody seems to know the reason for their existence. Even more strange is the fact that their exact location is still not known. Attempts to direction find them have only provided vague ideas as to their location and yet somebody somewhere must maintain them. But who and where? Some listeners claim to have detected minor variations in the keying speeds and frequency and have concluded that this in itself may be some form of code. Others have observed that some of the transmissions are keyed in unison suggesting some form of central control. The most likely reason that they exist is as some form of beacon used for navigation or propagation and that they somehow fit into a much more complex communications network that so far has yet to be satisfactorily explained. The mystery remains! Another form of strange transmission that has been around for years is the phonetic alphabet station. These transmissions normally take the form of a female voice that repeats a series of phonetic letters followed by a number. The frequency used varies but the type of transmission is easily recognisable. No logical explanation has really been made as to their purpose or indeed their country of origin. Some have suggested Israel as a location whilst others have suggested that the signals emanate from an Eastern Bloc country. The transmissions are usually fairly strong in Europe and they are sent in plain language. Clearly they are intended to be received on a fairly modest receiving system. This would suggest the intended recipient is probably using a portable receiver and that the information is some form of key to a code or general situation indicator. It is unlikely that the transmissions themselves carry anything intelligible, as the code could easily be broken. There is also another group of stations sending numbers. The numbers are read out in groups. Again their origin is uncertain but some transmissions almost certainly originate from the other side of the Atlantic, possibly Cuba. Again they are strong and as they are in plain language the intention must be for them to be received by individuals on a pretty simple domestic receiving set-up. If this were not the case then it would be logical for the transmissions to be sent by CW or RTTY. It would be a fairly logical assumption to suppose that the transmissions are intended for use by agents. Again the meaning behind the transmissions remains an enigma and we as amateurs can have little hope of solving the mystery. They do, however, provide a fascinating talking point amongst enthusiasts! Finally may we wish you lots of fun and enjoyment in your listening. If you think that you may have something to contribute to any future edition then write care of the publishers. We would be glad to hear from you.

The Windom Antenna
Rebirth of a 1920's Design
Mike Lee G3VYF

D.M.U

132' Total Length

> The above dimensions are for the 80m version. Total length for a 40m version is 66ft.

Radiating Coaxaial Cable Section

L.I.

In the September 1929 edition of QST, the journal of the American Radio Relay League, Loren Windom W8GZ/ W8ZG published an article sub-titled, "Practical Design Data For The Single Wire Fed Hertz Antenna." The term "Hertz Antenna" was used at that time to describe a half-wave antenna, normally horizontally polarised. Vertical antennas, normally quarter waves fed against a radial ground system, were referred to as "Marconi Aerials." It's worth remembering that in these early days, coax cable that we now all take for granted, had not been introduced. All feed systems employed some form of open wire method, usually comprising single or twin wires.

The Hertz antenna was either fed at the end (high-impedance) via 600 Ohm twin open wire feeder, or at the centre (low impedance). However, Windom described an alternative method of feeding the antenna using a single wire feeder, tapped approximately one third from the end (medium impedance).

The construction employed 14 swg copper wire. It is worth quoting from the 1991 edition of the "ARRL Antenna Book" chapter 24, page26: "The characteristic impedance of the single wire line ranges from 500 to 600 Ohms for 12 to 14 swg

conductors at lengths of 10 to 30 ft." So what Windom and his colleagues from the Bell Telephone Laboratories had discovered was a simple and effective way of matching a half-wave antenna by choosing a point along its length which had the same impedance as the feeder, ie. 600 Ohms. It was claimed that this single wire feeder actually radiated very little energy when configured in this way.

It is evident that by modern standards, some energy would be radiated from the feeder, later developments of the Windom have sought to usefully turn this effect to some advantage.

Two technical developments have enabled the Windom antenna to be reborn in its present guise: one is the use of ferrite materials, the other is coaxial cable.

Taking ferrite material first, this has enabled the design and construction of wide-band transformers to be employed in a modern day version of the Windom, "The Carolina Windom." This design, produced in the USA by "Radio Works," has received wide acclaim from many users and a number of DX-peditions. In fact one station was recently heard on twenty metres to describe it as "the best wire antenna I've ever used." The Carolina Windom uses two ferrite transformers to achieve its results. One is termed a "Dedicated Matching Unit" (DMU) and the other is decribed as a "Line Isolator" (LI).

The DMU is a 6:1 balance - to unbalance transformer (Balun). Its function is to transform the impedance at the one-third point along the antenna from its medium impedance to 50 Ohms, the characteristic impedance of standard coax cable. A length of coax cable is then dropped vertically to the line isolator whose job is to prevent any radiation from taking place beyond this point. The coax cable being unbalanced and being connected at a point of imbalance along the antenna, exhibits what are known as "common mode" currents on its outer braid. In other words it is not decoupled completely from the horizontal section of the antenna and some energy is radiated from the feeder in the vertical plane. The "Line Isolator" is a 1:1 current balun which forces equal currents to flow in the coax feeder between itself and the transmitter, thus decoupling the feeder, rendering it "flat" and killing any further unwanted radiation that would otherwise take place.

The length of coax feeder between the DMU and the LI is not only part of the feed system, but also an effective vertical

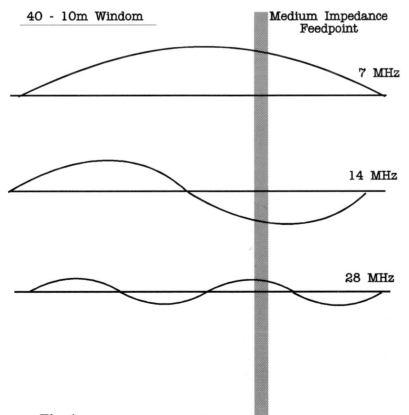

40 - 10m Windom

Medium Impedance Feedpoint

7 MHz

14 MHz

28 MHz

Fig. 1

radiator. It exhibits what is known as "controlled feeder radiation." Its length is chosen to maximise vertical radiation on a given band. The full size Carolina Windom has a 20ft section which is optimised for 20 metres and the half size version produces optimum vertical radiation on 10 metres.

An excellent introduction to the phenomenum of controlled feeder radiation is given by B, Sykes, G2HCG, in the May 1990 edition of "RADCOM." Although mention is made of the Windom antenna, it must be said the design of the baluns employed was somewhat rudimentary. The article nonetheless points out the many advantages of combining horizontal and vertical radiation into a single antenna design and highlights how feeder radiation can be turned to good use if correctly configured. G2HCG writes " This application of CFR has been used by the author when operating from Southern France, back to the UK on 7MHz, and has proved very effective indeed. Two days of deliberate operation without CFR and without announcing the fact, resulted in many comments on reduced signal strength."

A further advantage of the Windom antenna lies in its ability to function effectively at frequencies higher than its fundamental. It is in fact a useful multiband antenna as was observed from the outset when Windom himself noted, "at W8ZG a 7,00kc antenna has been working very effectively on 28,000kc."

A glance at the following diagrams will show that on even harmoinics, the medium impedance point at which the antenna is fed, shifts only slightly as the frequency of operation is raised harmonically. Refer to Fig. 1.

The actual feedpoint impedance is lowest at the fundamental 7MHz (200 Ohms), and highest at 28MHz (>300 Ohms) when operated at heights of 30 to 40ft.

We show the data derived from a test Carolina Windom erected as an inverted Vee with apex at 40ft and ends at 20ft. An MFJ-259 Antenna Analyser was used in the tests and the feedline was 45ft of UR67. Refer Fig. 2.

The broadband characteristics of the Wndom were noted by John Belrose, VE2CV and Peter Boulone, VE3KLO (QST, August 1990 "The Off-Centre Fed Dipole Revisited." They stressed the need to feed the Windom antenna via a current balun, noting that voltage baluns, as found in most ATU's are unsuitable for this application. (This does not mean that such ATU's cannot be used to tune out any residual reactance of the systems).

In conclusion, the Off-Centre Fed Dipole, or Windom antenna has made a big come-back. It will tune all bands via an ATU. Its medium impedance and broadband characteristics make it quite a "tame" antenna to use. The employment of a line isolator in keeping rf away from the shack and rig, further assures trouble-free operation and good immunity to rf interference.

Finally my thanks to Bridget DiCosimo, Technical Department Secretary of the ARRL who kindly supplied photo copies of the QST articles referred to in the text and to Peter Waters, G3OJV, who encouraged me to commit the above observations to print.

Finally, at our station in Hockley we have been using Carolina Windoms for somewhile now to demonstrate equipment and occasionally do some serious operation with. The results have been most encouraging and certainly seem to outperform the traditional G5RV on the higher frequencies.

Additional Notes:

These figures were obtained with the antenna in an inverted "V" configuration at approx. 40ft. Because the feeder between antenna and LI radiates it is important to keep it away from any metal support mast. This can easily be achieved if the antenna is supported at its natural centre, rather than the 1/3rd feedpoint.

It was found that the length needed to be increased by 70cm on the long leg and 35cm on the short leg to obtain best VSWR for UK operation. This is because the standard 40m version is cut for the US phone band, 7.2MHz - 7.3MHz.

The antenna has also been found to work on 6 metres. where a 2:1 VSWR is achieved. Using the Windom, contact was made with JY2SIX on SSB and CW.

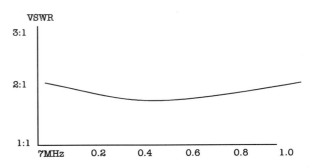

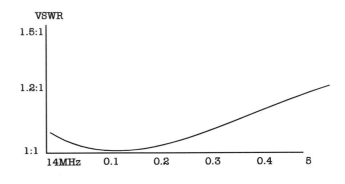

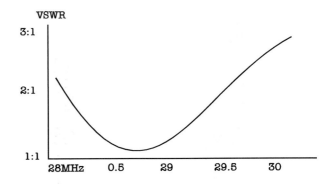

Fig. 2

cushcraft
CORPORATION

DX Verticals

"High Quality Engineering - Outperforms Conventional Verticals"

R-7
7MHz - 30MHz

* 1.8 Kw DX Design
* Low Angle Radiation
* Auto Switching
* Built To Last

R-5
14MHz - 30MHz

Don't Take Our Word For It!

*"It's an excellent solution for somebody who's looking for a low-profile homestation antenna that works well on 40 through 10 meters. . . ideal for portable operation because it easily breaks down into a small package, and you don't have to worry about a radial system or finding trees for supports." ***

QST, August 1992

*"The instructions are very detailed and clear. . .the antenna goes together in about 30 minutes. . . running 100 Watts and using the R7 I managed to work DXCC (actually 117 countries). . .hardware is of very outstanding material, and the antenna is best described as rugged." ***

CQ, August 1992

Frequency	R7 7 Bands 7 - 30MHz
....	R5 5 Bands 14 - 30MHz
Power	1.8kW
Radiation	16 degree angle
Height	R 7 6.9m
....	R5 5.2m
Mast Size	1.5 - 1.75"
Wind Load ...	R7 2.25m
....	R5 1.4m
Weight	R7 5.6kg
....	R5 4kg
Radials	49"

The R5 and R7 are the result of decades of experience in antenna design. They have proven themselves on Artic DX-peditions, tropical island contest stations, ocean vessels etc. Their great success though has been in amateur radio home stations throughout the world where they provide exceptional performance. What's more, as UK main distributors we can always promise you genuine factory spares.

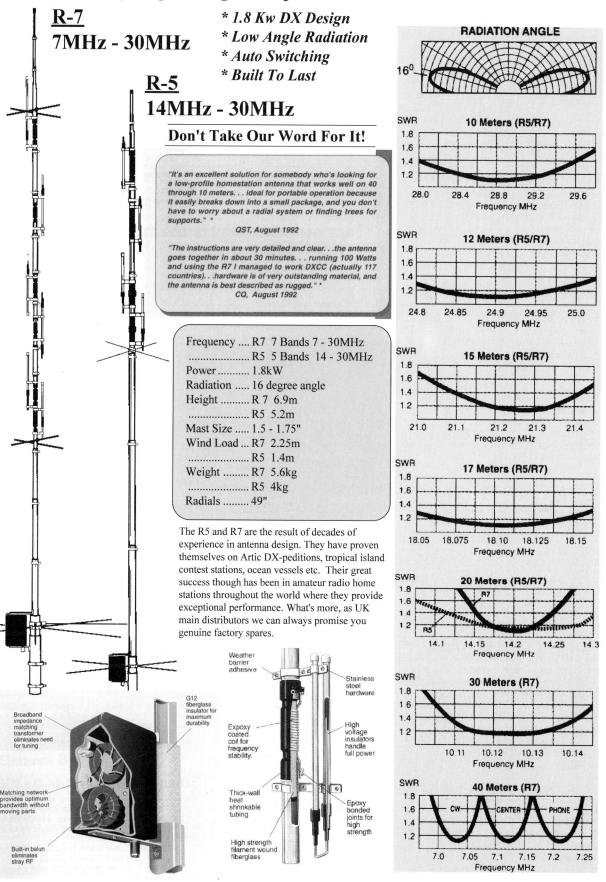

Country List of Radio Callsign Prefixes

The following is a list of internationally agreed callsign prefixes used by both commercial and amateur radio stations around the world. These prefixes are very useful when you have no idea of where the station is located. The prefixes are used by both commercial and amateur radio stations.

AAA-ALZ	USA	HZA-HZZ	SAUDI ARABIA
AMA-AOZ	SPAIN	H2	CYPRUS
APA-ASZ	PAKISTAN	H3	PANAMA
ATA-AWZ	INDIA	H4	SOLOMON ISLANDS
AXA-AXZ	AUSTRALIA	H6+H7	NICARAGUA
AYA-AZZ	ARGENTINA	H8+H9	PANAMA
A2	BOTSWANA	IAA-IZZ	ITALY
A3	TONGA	JAA-JSZ	JAPAN
A4	OMAN	JTA-JVZ	MONGOLIA
A5	BHUTAN	JWA-JXZ	NORWAY
A6	UNITED ARAB EMIRATES	JYA-JZZ	JORDAN
A7	QATAR	JZA-JZZ	INDONESIA
A8	LIBERIA	J2	DJIBOUTI
A9	BAHRAIN	J3	GRENADA
BAA-BZZ	CHINA	J4	GREECE
CAA-CEZ	CHILE	J5	GUINEA-BISSAU
CFA-CKZ	CANADA	J6	ST LUCIA
CLA-CMZ	CUBA	J7	DOMINICA
CNA-CNZ	MOROCCO	J8	ST VINCENT & GRENADINES
COA-COZ	CUBA	KAA-KZZ	USA
CPA-CPZ	BOLIVIA	LAA-LNZ	NORWAY
CQA-CUZ	PORTUGAL	LOA-LWZ	ARGENTINA
CVA-CXZ	URUGUAY	LXA-LXZ	LUXEMBOURG
CYA-CZZ	CANADA	LYA-LYZ	LITHUANIA
C2	NAURU	LZA-LZZ	BULGARIA
C3	ANDORRA	L2-L9	ARGENTINA
C4	CYPRUS	MAA-MZZ	UK
C5	GAMBIA	NAA-NZZ	USA
C6	BAHAMAS	OAA-OCZ	PERU
C7	WORLD MET ORGANISATION	ODA-ODZ	LEBANON
C8+C9	MOZAMBIQUE	OEA-OEZ	AUSTRIA
DAA-DRZ	GERMANY	OFA-OJZ	FINLAND
DSA-DTZ	S KOREA	OKA-OLZ	CZECH REPUBLIC
DUA-DZZ	PHILIPPINES	OMA-OMZ	SLOVAK REPUBLIC
D2+D3	ANGOLA	ONA-OTZ	BELGIUM
D4	CAPE VERDE	OUA-OZZ	DENMARK
D5	LIBERIA	PAA-PIZ	NETHERLANDS
D6	COMOROS	PJA-PJZ	NETHERLANDS ANTILLES
D7+D8+D9	S KOREA	PKA-POZ	INDONESIA
EAA-EHZ	SPAIN	PPA-PYZ	BRAZIL
EIA-EJZ	EIRE	PZA-PZZ	SURINAME
EKA-EKZ	ARMENIA	P2	PAPUA NEW GUINEA
ELA-ELZ	LIBERIA	P3	CYPRUS
EMA-EOZ	UKRAINE	P4	ARUBA
EPA-EQZ	IRAN	P5-P9 N	KOREA
ERA-ERZ	MOLDOVA	RAA-RZZ	RUSSIAN FEDERATION
ESA-ESZ	ESTONIA	SAA-SMZ	SWEDEN
ETA-ETZ	ETHIOPIA	SNA-SRZ	POLAND
EUA-EWZ	BELARUS	SSA-SSM	EGYPT
EXA-EXZ	RUSSIAN FEDERATION	SSN-STZ	SUDAN
EYA-EYZ	TAJIKISTAN	SUA-SUZ	EGYPT
EZA-EZZ	TURKMENISTAN	SVA-SZZ	GREECE
E2	THAILAND	S2+S3	BANGLADESH
E3	ERITREA	S5	SLOVENIA
FAA-FZZ	FRANCE	S6	SINGAPORE
GAA-GZZ	UK	S7	SEYCHELLES
HAA-HAZ	HUNGARY	S9 SAO	TOME & PRINCIPE
HBA-HBZ	SWITZERLAND	TAA-TCZ	TURKEY
HCA-HDZ	ECUADOR	TDA-TDZ	GUATEMALA
HEA-HEZ	SWITZERLAND	TEA-TEZ	COSTA RICA
HFA-HFZ	POLAND	TFA-TFZ	ICELAND
HGA-HGZ	HUNGARY	TGA-TGZ	GUATEMALA
HHA-HHZ	HAITI	THA-THZ	FRANCE
HIA-HIZ	DOMINICAN REPUBLIC	TIA-TIZ	COSTA RICA
HJA-HKZ	COLOMBIA	TJA-TJZ	CAMEROON
HLA-HLZ	S KOREA	TKA-TKZ	FRANCE
HMA-HMZ	N KOREA	TLA-TLZ	CENTRAL AFRICAN REPUBLIC
HNA-HNZ	IRAQ	TMA-TMZ	FRANCE
HOA-HPZ	PANAMA	TNA-TNZ	CONGO
HQA-HRZ	THAILAND	TOA-TQZ	FRANCE
HTA-HTZ	NICARAGUA	TRA-TRZ	GABON
HUA-HUZ	EL SALVADOR	TSA-TSZ	TUNISIA
HVA-HVZ	VATICAN STATE	TTA-TTZ	CHAD
HWA-HYZ	FRANCE	TUA-TUZ	IVORY COAST

TVA-TXZ	FRANCE	3Z	POLAND
TYA-TYZ	BENIN	4A-4C	MEXICO
TZA-TZZ	MALI	4D-4I	PHILIPPINES
T2	TUVALU	4J-4K	AZERBAIJAN
T3	KIRIBATI	4L	GEORGIA
T4	CUBA	4M	VENEZUELA
T5	SOMALIA	4N-4O	YUGOSLAVIA
T6	AFGHANISTAN	4P-4S	SRI LANKA
T7	SAN MARINO	4T	PERU
T9	BOSNIA & HERZEGOVINA	4U	UNITED NATIONS ORGANISATION
UAA-UIZ	RUSSIAN FEDERATION	4V	HAITI
UJA-UMZ	UZBEKISTAN	4X	ISRAEL
ULA-USZ	RUSSIAN FEDERATION	4Y	INTERNATIONAL CIVIL AVIATION
URA-UZZ	UKRAINE		ORGANISATION
VAA-VGZ	CANADA	4Z	ISRAEL
VHA-VNZ	AUSTRALIA	5A	LIBYA
VOA-VOZ	CANADA	5B	CYPRUS
VPA-VSZ	UK & DEPENDENCIES	5C-5G	MOROCCO
VTA-VWZ	INDIA	5H+5I	TANZANIA
VXA-VYZ	CANADA	5J+5K	COLOMBIA
VZA-VZZ	AUSTRALIA	5L+5M	LIBERIA
V2	ANTIGUA & BARBUDA	5N+5O	NIGERIA
V3	BELIZE	5P+5Q	DENMARK
V4	ST KITTS & NEVIS	5R+5S	MADAGASCAR
V6	MICRONESIA	5T	MAURITANIA
V7	MARSHALL ISLANDS	5U	NIGER
V8	BRUNEI	5V	TOGO
WAA-WZZ	USA	5W	WESTERN SAMOA
XAA-XIZ	MEXICO	5X	UGANDA
XJA-XOZ	CANADA	5Y+5Z	KENYA
XPA-XPZ	HILE	6A+6B	EGYPT
XSA-XSZ	CHINA & TAIWAN	6C	SYRIA
XTA-XTZ	BOURKINA FASO	6D-6J	MEXICO
XUA-XUZ	CAMBODIA	6K-6N	S KOREA
XVA-XVZ	VIETNAM	6O	SOMALIA
XWA-XWZ	LAOS	6P-6S	PAKISTAN
XXA-XXZ	PORTUGAL	6T-6U	SUDAN
XYA-XZZ	MYANMAR (BURMA)	6V+6W	SENEGAL
YAA-YAZ	AFGHANISTAN	6X	MADAGASCAR
YBA-YHZ	INDONESIA	6Y	JAMAICA
YIA-YIZ	IRAQ	6Z	LIBERIA
YJA-YJZ	VANUATU	7A-7I	INDONESIA
YKA-YKZ	SYRIA	7J-7N	JAPAN
YLA-YLZ	LATVIA	7O	YEMEN
YMA-YMZ	TURKEY	7P	LESOTHO
YNA-YNZ	NICARAGUA	7Q	MALAWI
YOA-YRZ	ROMANIA	7R	ALGERIA
YSA-YSZ	EL SALVADOR	7S	SWEDEN
YTA-YUZ	YUGOSLAVIA	7T-7Y	ALGERIA
YVA-YYZ	VENEZUELA	7Z	SAUDI ARABIA
YZA-YZZ	YUGOSLAVIA	8A-8I	INDONESIA
Y2-Y9	GERMANY	8J-8N	JAPAN
ZAA-ZAZ	ALBANIA	8O	BOTSWANA
ZBA-ZJZ	UK & DEPENDENCIES	8P	BARBADOS
ZKA-ZMZ	N ZEALAND	8Q	MALDIVES
ZNA-ZOZ	UK & DEPENDENCIES	8R	GUYANA
ZPA-ZPZ	PARAGUAY	8S	SWEDEN
ZQA-ZQZ	UK & DEPENDENCIES	8T-8Y	INDIA
ZRA-ZUZ	S AFRICA	8Z	SAUDI ARABIA
ZVA-ZZZ	BRAZIL	9A	CROATIA
Z2	ZIMBABWE	9B-9D	IRAN
Z3	MACEDONIA (former Yugoslav Republic)	9E+9F	ETHIOPIA
	UK & DEPENDENCIES	9G	GHANA
3A	MONACO	9H	MALTA
3B	MAURITIUS	9I+9J	ZAMBIA
3C	EQUATORIAL GUINEA	9K	KUWAIT
3DA-3DM	SWAZILAND	9L	SIERRA LEONE
3DN-3DZ	FIJI	9M	MALAYSIA
3E+3F	PANAMA	9N	NEPAL
3G	CHILE	9O-9T	ZAIRE
3H-3U	CHINA & TAIWAN	9U	BURUNDI
3V	TUNISIA	9V	SINGAPORE
3W	VIETNAM	9W	MALAYSIA
3X	GUINEA	9X	RWANDA
3Y	NORWAY	9Y+9Z	TRINIDAD & TOBAGO

kHz.	Station	Call	Mode / Heard/Times GMT
409.90	Spa Publications		

410-495
MARITIME MOBILE

kHz.	Station	Call	Mode / Heard/Times GMT
435.50	Karlskrona, Sweden	SAA	CW 1833 tfc list 0805 2140 wx (Eng) 0931 2131
436.00	Chatham, USA	WCC	CW tfc list 2253
436.00	Marseille, France	FFM	CW 0422 nav wngs (Fr) 1953 2057 2126 2212
436.50	Lisbon, Portugal	CUL	CW 2154 2240 tfc list 2031 2231 (listens 454kHz)
438.00	Cabo la Nao, Spain	EAV	CW 0011 2159 tfc list 0803 1603 2203 nav wng 2052 2128
438.00	Lyngby, Denmark	OXZ	CW 1705 tfc list 2051 2251 wx 2323
438.00	Reykjavik, Iceland	TFA	CW nav wng 2250
439.00	Ostend, Belgium	OST	CW 0842 1719 1954 tfc list 0802 1002 1602 1802 2202 wx 0820 1720
439.50	Kaliningrad, Russia	UIW2	CW 2138
440.50	Rome, Italy	IAR	CW 2109
441.00	Casablanca, Morocco	CNP	CW 2239 tfc list 2135
441.00	Cullercoats, UK	GCC	SEL-FEC (Marine paging system)
441.00	Istanbul, Turkey	TAH	CW nav wngs 2136
441.00	Niton, UK	GNI	SEL-FEC (Marine paging system)
442.00	Portpatrick, UK	GPK	CW 0832
442.50	Boulogne, France	FFB	CW 0720 0824 1927 wx 0625 2225 nav wng 1932 tfc list 2204
443.00	Malta	9HD	CW nav wngs (Eng) 2225 2240 2252
443.50	Brest-le-Conquet, France	FFU	CW 0622 0731 0806 tfc list 1501
444.00	Boulogne, France	FFB	CW tfc list 0703
444.00	Oran, Algeria	7TO	CW tfc list 0735
444.00	Stockholm, Sweden	SDJ	CW
444.50	Scheveningen, Holland	PCH	CW 0649 2234 tfc list even hrs + 50 (listens 454.0 & 484.5kHz)
445.00	French Naval, Cherbourg	FUC	CW "FDDO de FUC testing RYRY SGSG" 1900 2137 (NOT RTTY)
445.00	Ruegen, Germany	DHS	CW 0755 2155 wx (Eng) 2010 tfc list 2231
445.00	Tarifa, Spain	EAC	CW 2157 2203 2334 tfc list 0804 2203 nav wngs 2033
446.50	Las Palmas, Canaries	EAL	CW nav wng 2018 tfc list 2140
447.00	Gdynia, Poland	SPH	CW tfc list 0005 wx (Eng) 1905
447.00	Genoa, Italy	ICB	CW 2128 2142 tfc list 2220
447.00	Niton, UK	GNI	CW 0628 0833 2007 tfc list 0420 1556
447.00	Tanger, Morocco	CNW	CW tfc list 0825 2225 2325
447.00	Tunis, Tunisia	3VX	CW (with C6KI7) 0724
447.50	Rogaland, Norway	LGQ	CW 0821 2150 2217 nav wng 0718 wx 1435 tfc list 0800 1600 2200
448.00	Land's End, UK	GLD	CW 0811 1706 tfc list 0802 1555 nav wng 2003
448.00	Mariupol, Ukraine	UTW	CW
448.00	Stockholm, Sweden	SDJ	CW wx (Eng) 2105 2115
448.50	Ostend, Belgium	OST	CW reserve frequency
448.50	Tjome, Norway	LGT	CW 2310 wx 1418
449.00	Blaavand, Denmark	OXB	CW 0653 0720 1052 2253 tfc list 0651 0851 1851 2251
449.00	Cabo Penas, Spain	EAS	CW nav wng 0820 2020 wx (Span) 1818 tfc list 0803 1603 2203
449.50	Klaipeda Harbour, Lithuania	LYL	CW
450.00	Tallinn, Estonia	ESA	CW tfc list 1932 wx 2044
452.50	Murmansk, Russia	UMN	CW
454.00	Ships working		CW P3GP2 (to GLD) 2226
464.00	Sydney, Canada	VCO	CW wx & nav wngs 2230
468.00	Ships working		CW "Domodedov" (EMAJ) 0821 "Cervantes" (EADO) 2035
472.00	Finisterre, Spain	EAF	CW 1952 wx 1824 tfc list 0802 2202 nav wng (Eng) 2049 2054
478.00	St John's, Canada	VON	CW nav wngs 2308
479.00	Ships working		CW (clg freq to OST) "Handy Jack" (DUWL) 0832
480.00	Ships working		CW "Plopeni" (YQEA) 1957 "Kapitan Izmailov" (UVQE) 2327
482.00	Ships working		CW
483.50	Ships working		CW (to FFU) 0831
484.00	Haifa, Israel	4XO	CW 2155 tfc list 2230
484.00	Tarifa, Spain	EAC	CW (listens after tfc list on 485.0) tfc list 2200
484.50	Ships working		CW "Sithea" (LADO4) 0805
485.00	Ships working		CW ECAK 2156 "Cemenmar Cuatro" (EGXH) 2333
487.00	Ships working		CW 0732 2214
487.50	Ships working		CW GCLC 0658
488.00	Ships working		CW (to GLD)
489.00	Ancona, Italy	IPA	CW nav wng (Ital) 2132 (Eng) 2134 2154
494.90	Spa Publications		

495-505
MOBILE (DISTRESS & CALLING)

kHz.	Station	Call	Mode / Heard/Times GMT
500.00	International Calling & Distress		CW

kHz.	Station	Call	Mode / Heard/Times GMT
504.90	Spa Publications		

505-526.5
MARITIME MOBILE/AERONAUTICAL NAVIGATION

kHz.	Station	Call	Mode / Heard/Times GMT
510.50	Cullercoats, UK	GCC	CW tfc list 0830
510.50	Odessa, Ukraine	UTT	CW wx (Eng) 1600
511.00	Gdynia, Poland	SPH	CW tfc list 2005
511.50	Ancona, Italy	IPA	CW 2133 2140
511.50	Norddeich, Germany	DAN	CW 0731 0814 1642 2142 2316
511.50	Orlandet, Norway	LGD	CW (with LYDA) 2025 wx wng 2248 nav wng 2348
512.00	Ships working		CW "Adelaide" (H2PP) 1645 "Polar Crystal" (3EHS7) 2135
512.50	Klaipeda Harbour, Lithuania	LYL	CW
512.50	Torshavn, Faroes	OXJ	CW gale wng 0754 2135 2220 2250
512.50	Trieste, Italy	IQX	CW 2239
514.00	Helsinki, Finland	OHC	CW wx (in Eng for Gulf of Bothnia) 0839
514.50	Bari, Italy	IPB	CW 2141 2237
514.50	Swedish Military	HIA	170/50r 5 let grps 2229
515.00	Valentia, Eire	EJK	CW 2039 (to UJTQ) 2139 gale wng 2221 2251
515.50	Cullercoats, UK	GCC	CW 2148
515.50	Stettin, Poland	SPE	CW 2220 2231 tfc list 0615 2210 nav wngs (Eng) 2151
516.50	Lyngby, Denmark	OXZ	CW 1928 2209 tfc list 2050 gale wng 2252 wx 2331
517.00	Wick, UK	GKR	CW wx 0840 2032 nav wng 2052
518.00	Brest-le-Conquet, France	FFU	SITOR Mode B "NAVTEX" b/casts 0118 & 4 hrly (Station F)
518.00	Cullercoats, UK	GCC	SITOR Mode B "NAVTEX" b/casts 0048 & 4 hrly (Station G)
518.00	Dutch Coastguard	PBK	SITOR Mode B "NAVTEX" b/casts 0348 & 4 hrly (Station P)
518.00	Monsanto, Portugal	CTV	SITOR Mode B "NAVTEX" b/casts 0250 & 4 hrly (Station R)
518.00	Niton, UK	GNI	SITOR Mode B "NAVTEX" b/casts 0018 & 4 hrly (Station S)
518.00	Ostend, Belgium	OST	SITOR Mode B "NAVTEX" b/casts 0248 & 4 hrly (Station T)
518.00	Portpatrick, UK	GPK	SITOR Mode B "NAVTEX" b/casts 0130 & 4 hrly (Station O)
518.00	Rogaland, Norway	LGQ	SITOR Mode B "NAVTEX" b/casts 0148 & 4 hrly (Station L)
518.00	Stockholm, Sweden	SDJ	SITOR Mode B "NAVTEX" b/casts 0330 & 4 hrly (Station J)
518.00	Tallinn, Estonia	ESA	SITOR Mode B "NAVTEX" b/casts 0030 & 4 hrly (Station U)
519.00	Rome, Italy	IAR	CW 2001 tfc list 2325 wx 1900
519.00	Stockholm, Sweden	SDJ	CW 2113 2203 2339 wx 2105
520.50	Brest-le-Conquet, France	FFU	CW 1830 1950 2252 wx (Fr) 0830 nav wng 0822
521.50	Goeteborg, Sweden	SAG	CW 0712 nav wng (Eng) 1301 tfc list 0700 1900 2100
522.50	Tingstaede, Sweden	SAE	CW wx 2050
523.00	Klaipeda, Lithuania	LYK	CW 2102 (with LYAH) 2258
524.00	Genoa, Italy	ICB	CW nav wng (Eng) 2150
524.00	Riga, Latvia	UKB	CW
525.00	Kerkyra, Greece	SVK	CW wx (Eng) 2108
525.00	Norddeich, Germany	DAN	CW tfc list 0530 1530 1930 2130 nav wng (Eng) 2107 wx (Eng) 2002
1606.40	Spa Publications		

1606.5-1625.0
FIXED/LAND & MARITIME MOBILE

kHz.	Station	Call	Mode / Heard/Times GMT
1609.50	Rogaland, Norway	LGB	SITOR (dup. 2144.5) 0735 1604 1857 1933 2154
1611.50	Rogaland, Norway	LGB	SITOR (dup. 2146.5) 1709 1943 2157 2241
1612.50	Wick, UK	GKR1	SITOR (dup. 2147.5) 0650 2144 2226
1613.00	Lyngby, Denmark	OXZ	SITOR (dup. 2148.0) 1922 2155 2243
1615.00	Cullercoats, UK	GCC1	SITOR (dup. 2150.0) 1714 1848 2156 2214 tfc list 1900 2300
1619.50	Scheveningen, Holland	PCH85	SITOR (dup. 2154.5) 1900 1918 2155 2311
1634.90	Spa Publications		

1635-1810
FIXED/LAND & MARITIME MOBILE

kHz.	Station	Call	Mode / Heard/Times GMT
1635.00	Coast stations ch 241 (dup. 2060.0kHz)		USB
1635.00	Brest-le-Conquet, France	FFU	USB 0007 0647 0734 1933 2315 wx & tfc list 0614 2204
1637.00	UNID (pirate)		AM Dutch/Eng 1925 2146 2228 (freq varies)
1638.00	Coast stations ch 242 (dup. 2063.0kHz)		USB
1638.00	Helsinki, Finland	OHG	USB 2127 tfc list 2153
1641.00	Coast stations ch 243 (dup. 2066.0kHz)		USB
1641.00	Niton, UK	GNI	USB 0726 tfc list 2235 wx 0740 nav wngs 2236
1641.00	Torshavn, Faroes	OXJ	USB wx 1820
1642.00	UK cordless telephones base tx		FM (paired 47.45625 MHz)
1644.00	Coast stations ch 244 (dup. 2069.0kHz)		USB
1644.00	Malin Head, Eire	EJM	USB

kHz.	Station	Call	Mode / Heard/Times GMT
1647.00	Coast stations ch 245 (dup. 2072.0kHz)		USB
1650.00	Coast stations ch 246 (dup. 2075.0kHz)		USB
1650.00	Stockholm, Sweden	SDJ	USB
1650.00	Stonehaven, UK	GND	USB (UK ch "JULIET") 0143 1907 2152 2330
1653.00	Coast stations ch 247 (dup. 2078.0kHz)		USB
1653.00	Barcelona, Spain		USB nav wngs 2337
1653.00	Bergen, Norway	LGN	USB nav wng 1807 tfc list 2135
1656.00	Coast stations ch 248 (dup. 2081.0kHz)		USB
1656.00	Chipiona, Spain		USB 1840 1938 2137 tfc list 2337 (also listens 2045kHz)
1659.00	Coast stations ch 249 (dup. 2084.0kHz)		USB
1659.00	Bodo, Norway	LGP	USB 2255
1659.00	Jersey, Channel Islands		USB wx 0745 1845 2245
1659.00	Wick, UK	GNK	USB (UK ch "DELTA") 1837 1914 2315
1662.00	Coast stations ch 250 (dup. 2087.0kHz)		USB
1662.00	UK cordless telephones base tx		FM (paired 47.46875 MHz)
1662.50	Guernsey, Channel Isles		USB (Lifeboat & SAR work only)
1665.00	Coast stations ch 251 (dup. 2090.0kHz)		USB
1665.00	Ostend, Belgium	OST	USB 2044 (with MIMC5) 1626
1665.00	Tjome, Norway	LGT	USB 2214
1668.00	Coast stations ch 252 (dup. 2093.0kHz)		USB
1671.00	Coast stations ch 253 (dup. 2096.0kHz)		USB
1671.00	Brest-le Conquet, France	FFU	USB 0739 wx (Fr) 0733 1808 nav wng (Eng) 1937 tfc list 2153
1671.00	Farsund, Norway	LGZ	USB 2112 2247 2328
1674.00	Coast stations ch 254 (dup. 2099.0kHz)		USB
1674.00	Scheveningen, Holland	PCG	USB (Dutch ch "DELTA") 1921 wx 2140
1674.00	Stockholm, Sweden	SDJ	USB wx (Eng) & nav wngs 2133 2143
1674.00	Vardo, Norway	LGV	USB 2317
1677.00	Coast stations ch 255 (dup. 2102.0kHz)		USB
1677.00	Cabo Penas, Spain	EAS	USB (with 3EJL4) 1657
1677.00	Mariehamn, Finland	OFH	USB nav wngs (Eng) 2035
1677.00	Malin Head, Eire	EJM	USB 1852 1910 nav wng 1641
1677.00	Tarifa, Spain	EAC	USB tfc list 2150
1680.00	Coast stations ch 256 (dup. 2105.0kHz)		USB
1680.00	Athens, Greece	SVN	USB 2140
1680.00	Floroe, Norway	LGL	USB 1540 1715 2213 2223 nav wng 2134
1682.00	UK cordless telephones base tx		FM (paired 47.48125 MHz)
1683.00	Coast stations ch 257 (dup. 2108.0kHz)		USB
1683.00	Ostend, Belgium	OSU	USB 2245
1686.00	Coast stations ch 258 (dup. 2111.0kHz)		USB
1686.00	St Nazaire, France	FFO	USB 1856 nav wng 2107
1689.00	Coast stations ch 259 (dup. 2114.0kHz)		USB
1692.00	Coast stations ch 260 (dup. 2117.0kHz)		USB
1692.00	Boulogne, France	FFB	USB 0739 1841 1921 wx & nav wngs (Fr) 0733 1833 2133
1692.00	Gdynia, Poland	SPC	USB tfc list 2035
1692.00	Rogaland, Norway	LGQ	USB 2122 2133 tfc list 0333 & 4 hrly
1695.00	Coast stations ch 261 (dup. 2120.0kHz)		USB
1698.00	Coast stations ch 262 (dup. 2123.0kHz)		USB
1698.00	La Coruna, Spain		USB 1916 2141 2201 2334 tfc list odd hours + 33
1701.00	Coast stations ch 263 (dup. 2126.0kHz)		USB
1702.00	UK cordless telephones base tx		FM (paired 47.49375 MHz)
1704.00	Coast stations ch 264 (dup. 2129.0kHz)		USB
1704.00	Lyngby, Denmark	OXZ	USB 2140 nav wngs 2141 gale wng 2307
1704.00	Tarifa, Spain	EAC	USB 2042 2229 nav wng 2033
1707.00	Coast stations ch 265 (dup. 2132.0kHz)		USB
1707.00	Machichaco, Spain		USB 1700 nav wngs (Eng & Span) 2034
1707.00	North Foreland, UK	GNF	USB 2119 wx 1935 tfc list & nav wngs 2135 2334
1710.00	Coast stations ch 266 (dup. 2135.0kHz)		USB
1710.00	Bordeaux, France	FFC	USB
1710.00	Brest-Le Conquet	FFU	USB wx & nav wngs (Fr) 2204
1710.00	Goeteborg, Sweden	SAG	USB 2230 tfc list 1834 2233 wx (Eng) 2235 nav wng 2135
1710.00	Portpatrick, UK	GPK	USB (UK ch "YANKEE") 1808 1910
1713.00	Coast stations ch 267 (dup. 2138.0kHz)		USB
1713.00	Scheveningen, Holland	PCG	USB (Dutch ch "FOXTROT") wx 0340 0640 0940 1540 2140 nav wng 2333
1713.00	UK Coast Control		USB "GR" radio check 2138
1716.00	Coast stations ch 268 (dup. 2060.0kHz)		USB
1716.00	Scheveningen, Holland	PCG	USB (Dutch ch "BRAVO") 1859
1719.00	Coast stations ch 269 (dup. 2063.0kHz)		USB
1719.00	Floroe, Norway	LGL	USB
1719.00	Helsinki, Finland	OHG	USB 2131
1722.00	Coast stations ch 270 (dup. 2066.0kHz)		USB
1722.00	Ruegen, Germany	DHS	USB (dup. 2550.0) tfc list 1820 2120 2220 2320 nav wng 2333
1722.00	St Nazaire, France	FFO	USB wx & nav wng (Fr) 1835
1722.00	Stonehaven, UK	GND	USB (Autolink ch) 2117
1722.00	UK cordless telephones base tx		FM (paired 47.50625 MHz)
1725.00	Coast stations ch 271 (dup. 2069.0kHz)		USB
1725.00	Rogaland, Norway	LGQ	USB 1927 2143 nav wng 0735 2233 tfc list 2333

kHz.	Station	Call	Mode / Heard/Times GMT
1728.00	Coast stations ch 272 (dup. 2072.0kHz)		USB
1728.00	Ostend, Belgium	OSU	USB 1814
1728.00	Vardo, Norway	LGV	USB 2134 2148 2225
1731.00	Coast stations ch 273 (dup. 2075.0kHz)		USB
1731.00	Cabo de la Nao, Spain	EAV	USB nav wngs 2034
1731.00	Cullercoats, UK	GCC	USB (UK ch "NOVEMBER") (dup. 2527.0) with GBKP 1815
1734.00	Coast stations ch 274 (dup. 2078.0kHz)		USB
1734.00	Blaavand, Denmark	OXB	USB 1746 1829 2142 gale wng 2156 2205 2305 tfc list 2308
1737.00	Coast stations ch 275 (dup. 2081.0kHz)		USB
1737.00	Orlandet, Norway	LFO	USB
1740.00	Coast stations ch 276 (dup. 2084.0kHz)		USB
1742.00	UK cordless telephones base tx		FM (paired 47.51875 MHz)
1743.00	Coast stations ch 277 (dup. 2087.0kHz)		USB
1746.00	Coast stations ch 278 (dup. 2090.0kHz)		USB
1746.00	Valentia, Eire	EJK	USB
1749.00	Coast stations ch 279 (dup. 2093.0kHz)		USB
1752.00	Coast stations ch 280 (dup. 2096.0kHz)		USB
1752.00	Las Palmas, Canaries	EAL	USB 2157 2218
1752.00	Norddeich, Germany	DAN	USB
1752.00	Valentia, Eire	EJK	USB (listens 2045.0kHz) 2200 2308 nav wng 2232 wx 2037
1755.00	Coast stations ch 281 (dup. 2099.0kHz)		USB
1755.00	Wick, UK	GKR	USB (UK ch "GOLF") 1949
1758.00	Coast stations ch 282 (dup. 2102.0kHz)		USB
1758.00	Torshavn, Faroes	OXJ	USB 2238
1761.00	Coast stations ch 283 (dup. 2105.0kHz)		USB
1762.00	UK cordless telephones base tx		FM (paired 47.53125 MHz)
1764.00	Coast stations ch 284 (dup. 2108.0kHz)		USB
1764.00	Finisterre, Spain	EAF	USB 2121 tfc list 1535
1764.00	Guernsey, Channel Isles		USB (listens 2049 & 2056 kHz)
1764.00	Wick, UK	GKR	USB wx 1903 nav wng 0635 2234 tfc list 2235
1767.00	Coast stations ch 285 (dup. 2111.0kHz)		USB
1767.00	Blaavand, Denmark	OXB	USB 1914 1923
1767.00	Cabo Gata, Spain		USB 2236
1768.40	Tunis, Tunisia	3VT	USB (with "Habib") 2307
1770.00	Coast stations ch 286 (dup. 2114.0kHz)		USB
1770.00	Boulogne, France	FFB	USB 0740 1704 1922 2156 wx 1904 tfc list 2105
1770.00	Wick, UK	GNK	USB wx 1903
1773.00	Coast stations ch 287 (dup. 2117.0kHz)		USB
1776.00	Coast stations ch 288 (dup. 2120.0kHz)		USB
1779.00	Coast stations ch 289 (dup. 2123.0kHz)		USB
1779.00	Stockholm, Sweden	SDJ	USB wx & nav wngs 2138
1780.00	UK Coast Control		USB 2146 2312
1782.00	Coast stations ch 290 (dup. 2126.0kHz)		USB
1782.00	Orlandet, Norway	LFO	USB
1782.00	UK cordless telephones base tx		FM (paired 47.54375 MHz)
1785.00	Coast stations ch 291 (dup. 2129.0kHz)		USB
1785.00	Farsund, Norway	LGZ	USB 1750 1844 2155 2242 nav wng (Eng & Nor) 1852 2147
1788.00	Coast stations ch 292 (dup. 2132.0kHz)		USB
1788.00	Kiel, Germany	DAO	USB
1791.00	Coast stations ch 293 (dup. 2135.0kHz)		USB
1791.00	Ruegen, Germany	DHS	USB
1794.00	Coast stations ch 294 (dup. 2138.0kHz)		USB
1794.00	Stettin, Poland	SPO	USB 1928 2048 2158 2200 2249 tfc list 2238
1797.00	Coast stations ch 295 (dup. 2060.0kHz)		USB
1797.00	Stockholm, Sweden	SDJ	USB (with "Tavria") 2203 wx & nav wngs (Eng) 2139
1797.00	Wick, UK	GKR	USB (UK ch "FOXTROT") 0658 2038
1809.90	Spa Publications		

1810-2000
FIXED/MARITIME MOBILE/AMATEUR

kHz.	Station	Call	Mode / Heard/Times GMT
1818.00	Gdynia, Poland	SPC	USB
1856.00	Stonehaven, UK	GND	USB (UK ch "INDIA" dup. 2555.0) 1538 1845 2122 2206 2244
1862.00	Bordeaux, France	FFC	USB wx 0733
1866.00	Hebrides, UK	GHD	USB tfc list & nav wngs 0203 0603 1003 1403 1803 2203
1866.00	Hebrides, UK	GHD	USB (UK ch "ZULU" dup. 2534.0) 1834 1936 2256
1869.00	Humber, UK	GKZ	USB 2135 wx 0733 1933 tfc list & nav wng 0534
1876.00	Brest-le-Conquet, France	FFU	USB 0741 tfc list, wx & nav wng 2155
1876.00	Reykjavik, Iceland	TFA	USB wx (Eng) 2333
1877.00	Swedish Military	HIA	170/50r p/lang wx forecasts 1536 5 let grps 2201
1883.00	Kiel, Germany	DAO	USB (dup. 2566.0)
1883.00	Portpatrick, UK	GPK	USB wx 0303 0703 0903 1503 1903 2103 tfc/wngs 0203 & 4 hrly
1888.00	Civitavecchia, Italy	IPD	USB 1943 wx 1935 gale wng 2225

kHz.	Station	Call	Mode / Heard/Times GMT
1890.00	Scheveningen, Holland	PCG	USB (dup. 2051.0/2054.0/2057.0) 1540 wx 2140 gale wng 1725
1905.00	Goeteborg, Sweden	SAG	SITOR 1846 1930 2050 2156 2243
1906.00	Marseille, France	FFM	USB 1736 2154 nav wngs 1634 2149 tfc list 2140
1911.00	Norddeich, Germany	DAN	USB (dup. 2541.0)
1918.00	Kiel, Germany	DAO	USB (dup. 3161.0)
1922.00	Trapani, Italy	IQM	USB
1923.70	Wick, UK	GKR2	SITOR (dup. 2149.5) 1910 2051 2124 2200 2243
1925.00	Humber, UK	GKZ	USB (UK ch "QUEBEC" dup. 2105.0) 2012 2052 2310
1946.00	Stonehaven, UK	GND	USB (UK ch "KILO" dup. 2566.0) 0650 2035 2127
1953.00	Ships working		USB (UK ch "OSCAR" dup. 2828.0) 1950
1964.00	Ships working		USB (to Rogaland dup. 2878.0) 2148 2220
1971.50	Ships working		SITOR (to OST) 0746
1992.00	Ships working		USB (to Brest dup. 1635.0) 2115 "Lusevy" (FHUE to Brest) 2214
1995.00	Ships working		USB (to PCG dup. 2600.0) 1946
1999.00	Ships working		USB (UK ch "LIMA" dup. 2607.0) 1956
1999.90	Spa Publications		

2000-2170
FIXED/LAND & MARITIME MOBILE

kHz.	Station	Call	Mode / Heard/Times GMT
2000.20	Ships working		SITOR (to GNI1 dup. 3517.0) "Rosa Dan" (OWQN2) 2150
2002.00	Ships working		USB (UK ch "ROMEO" dup. 2684.0) 1817 2221
2006.00	Ships working		USB (UK ch "ALPHA" dup. 2751.0) 1652 1841 2210 2241
2009.00	Ships working		USB (UK ch "UNIFORM" dup. 2628.0) "HMS Invincible" (GUCL) 2222
2013.00	Ships working		USB (UK ch "CHARLIE" dup. 2604.0) 1931
2016.00	Ships working		USB (UK ch "TANGO" dup. 2698.0) 2054
2017.50	Grengel Met, Germnay		100r 2117
2023.00	Ships working		USB (to DAN dup. 2614.0) 1828 "Jessica S" (DCQZ) 2151
2040.00	Ships working		USB "Kavo Maleas" (9HYM3) (to IQX) 2215
2045.00	Ships working		USB (Dutch ch dup. 1890.0) 1848
2045.00	Ships working		USB (to EJK) 2201 ERQB (to PCG) 2256
2048.00	Ships working		USB 1923 "Otto" (P3SL2) 7TGW (to FFU) 2009
2049.00	Ships working		USB "Peppy" (SV9021) 1808 SZME (to PCG) 2243
2051.00	Ships working		USB (Dutch ch dup. 1890.0)
2052.00	Ships working		USB "Mary Wonsild" (ICWC to 9HD) 1932
2054.00	Ships working		USB (Dutch ch dup. 1890.0)
2056.00	Ships working		USB (Eng) 2200 (to FFU) 2152
2057.00	Ships working		USB (Dutch ch dup. 1890.0)
2060.00	Ships wkg ch 241 (dup. 1635.0kHz)		USB
2060.00	Ships wkg ch 268 (dup. 1716.0kHz)		USB (to PCG) 1859
2060.00	Ships wkg ch 295 (dup. 1797.0kHz)		USB (UK ch "FOXTROT") 2119 "Maersk Ranger" (GBKR) 0659
2063.00	Ships wkg ch 242 (dup. 1638.0kHz)		USB
2063.00	Ships wkg ch 269 (dup. 1719.0kHz)		USB
2066.00	Ships wkg ch 243 (dup. 1641.0kHz)		USB
2066.00	Ships wkg ch 270 (dup. 1722.0kHz)		USB (Stonehaven Autolink ch)
2069.00	Ships wkg ch 244 (dup. 1644.0kHz)		USB Fr 1911 2143
2069.00	Ships wkg ch 271 (dup. 1725.0kHz)		USB GSIR 2144
2072.00	Ships wkg ch 245 (dup. 1647.0kHz)		USB
2072.00	Ships wkg ch 272 (dup. 1728.0kHz)		USB (to LGV) 2150 2226
2075.00	Ships wkg ch 246 (dup. 1650.0kHz)		USB (UK ch "JULIET") 1818 2153
2075.00	Ships wkg ch 273 (dup. 1731.0kHz)		USB
2078.00	Ships wkg ch 247 (dup. 1653.0kHz)		USB
2078.00	Ships wkg ch 274 (dup. 1734.0kHz)		USB (to OXB) 1924 2158 2214 2306
2081.00	Ships wkg ch 248 (dup. 1656.0kHz)		USB
2081.00	Ships wkg ch 275 (dup. 1737.0kHz)		USB
2084.00	Ships wkg ch 249 (dup. 1659.0kHz)		USB (UK ch "DELTA") "Grampian Haven" (GCLG) 1838
2084.00	Ships wkg ch 276 (dup. 1740.0kHz)		USB
2087.00	Ships wkg ch 250 (dup. 1662.0kHz)		USB
2087.00	Ships wkg ch 277 (dup. 1743.0kHz)		USB
2090.00	Ships wkg ch 251 (dup. 1665.0kHz)		USB (to OST) 2045
2090.00	Ships wkg ch 278 (dup. 1746.0kHz)		USB
2093.00	Ships wkg ch 252 (dup. 1668.0kHz)		USB
2093.00	Ships wkg ch 279 (dup. 1749.0kHz)		USB
2093.00	Ship working		USB "Oualidia" (CNCT) to Boulogne on 1770kHz 2156
2096.00	Ships wkg ch 253 (dup. 1671.0kHz)		USB (to LGZ) 2120
2096.00	Ships wkg ch 280 (dup. 1752.0kHz)		USB
2099.00	Ships wkg ch 254 (dup. 1674.0kHz)		USB (to LGV) 2319
2099.00	Ships wkg ch 281 (dup. 1755.0kHz)		USB (UK ch "GOLF") 1948
2100.00	Ships working		170/50nc (to LYK) 2126
2102.00	Ships wkg ch 255 (dup. 1677.0kHz)		USB (to EJM) 1855 1911 (to OFH) 2034
2102.00	Ships wkg ch 282 (dup. 1758.0kHz)		USB (to OXP) 2157
2105.00	Ships wkg ch 256 (dup. 1680.0kHz)		USB (to LGL) 1539 2130 2212
2105.00	Ships wkg ch 283 (dup. 1761.0kHz)		USB

kHz.	Station	Call	Mode / Heard/Times GMT
2105.00	Ships working		USB (UK ch "QUEBEC" dup. 1925.0) 1809 MMNK8 2010
2108.00	Ships wkg ch 257 (dup. 1683.0kHz)		USB
2108.00	Ships wkg ch 284 (dup. 1764.0kHz)		USB (to EAF) 1625 2123 2145
2108.00	Ships working		USB (UK ch "HOTEL" dup. 2625.0) 2052
2111.00	Ships wkg ch 258 (dup. 1686.0kHz)		USB (to FFO) 1859
2111.00	Ships wkg ch 285 (dup. 1767.0kHz)		USB (to OXB) 1913
2111.00	Ships working		USB (UK ch "WHISKEY" dup. 2782.0) 2129 2249 EVPI 2215
2114.00	Ships wkg ch 259 (dup. 1689.0kHz)		USB
2114.00	Ships wkg ch 286 (dup. 1770.0kHz)		USB
2117.00	Ships wkg ch 260 (dup. 1692.0kHz)		USB (to LGQ) 2123
2117.00	Ships wkg ch 287 (dup. 1773.0kHz)		USB
2120.00	Ships wkg ch 261 (dup. 1695.0kHz)		USB
2120.00	Ships wkg ch 288 (dup. 1776.0kHz)		USB
2120.00	Ships working		USB (UK ch "X-RAY" dup. 3610.0)
2122.00	Ships working		USB (to La Coruna dup. 1748.0) 2129
2123.00	Ships wkg ch 262 (dup. 1698.0kHz)		USB 1915 2158 2240
2123.00	Ships wkg ch 289 (dup. 1779.0kHz)		USB 2320
2123.00	Ships working		USB (UK ch "PAPA" dup. 3750.0) 2052
2126.00	Ships wkg ch 263 (dup. 1701.0kHz)		USB
2126.00	Ships wkg ch 290 (dup. 1782.0kHz)		USB
2129.00	Ships wkg ch 264 (dup. 1704.0kHz)		USB (to EAC) 2044
2129.00	Ships wkg ch 291 (dup. 1785.0kHz)		USB (to LGZ) 1927 2157
2132.00	Ships wkg ch 265 (dup. 1707.0kHz)		USB (to Machichaco) 1701 (to GNF) 1917 2120
2132.00	Ships wkg ch 292 (dup. 1788.0kHz)		USB Portuguese 2247
2135.00	Ships wkg ch 266 (dup. 1710.0kHz)		USB (UK ch "YANKEE") 1809
2135.00	Ships wkg ch 293 (dup. 1791.0kHz)		USB
2138.00	Ships wkg ch 267 (dup. 1713.0kHz)		USB (to PCG) 1955 (to PCG on 1716.0) 1847
2138.00	Ships wkg ch 294 (dup. 1794.0kHz)		USB (to Stettin) 2055 2159 2250
2144.50	Ships working (paired 1609.5kHz)		SITOR "Maersk Jutlander" (OWEA6) 1925
2146.50	Ships working (paired 2696.7kHz)		SITOR 1917
2146.50	Ships working (paired 1611.5kHz)		SITOR "Norske Barde" (LCZO3) 2045
2147.00	Ships working (paired 3607.8kHz)		SITOR
2147.50	Ships working (paired 1612.5kHz)		SITOR "Resolution" (GBZX) 1928
2148.00	Ships working (paired 1613.0kHz)		SITOR 2315 "Pernille W" (OWBN6) 2126
2149.50	Ships working (paired 1923.7kHz)		SITOR 1838 Rig "Dundee Explorer" 0615
2150.00	Ships working (paired 1615.0kHz)		SITOR 1820 "Seaboard Invincible" (GOMV) 2322
2154.50	Ships working (paired 1619.5kHz)		SITOR 2240
2169.90	Spa Publications		

2170-2194
MARITIME MOBILE

kHz.	Station	Call	Mode / Heard/Times GMT
2170.50	Coastal calling		USB 1927
2182.00	INTERNATIONAL DISTRESS/CALLING		USB (Malin Head Radio Mayday relay 1930)
2187.50	Maritime safety channel		SITOR
2189.50	Ships working		SITOR Mode B Fr 2056
2191.00	Ships calling		USB (alt when 2182 in use for distress) 0745 1924 2120
2193.90	Spa Publications		

2194-2300
FIXED/MARITIME & AERONAUTICAL MOBILE

kHz.	Station	Call	Mode / Heard/Times GMT
2201.00	Intership working		USB Ger 2245
2210.00	Aasiaat, Greenland	OYR	USB 2000
2211.00	Intership working		USB (Irish) 2131 2137
2216.00	Ships working		USB (to SDJ dup. 1650.0) 2141 2207
2222.00	Ships working		SITOR 0746 1822 2124 2318
2226.00	Aberdeen Coastguard, Scotland		USB gale wng 2250
2226.00	Falmouth Coastguard, UK		USB wx forecast 2152
2226.00	Intership working		USB Eng "Grampian Falcon" (GCJK)/"Grampian Otter" (GDJX) 2141
2241.00	Intership working		USB ("Shetland Service" with another) 2118
2246.00	Intership working		USB "Seaboard Invincible" (GOMV) 1655 Oil Rig nav wng 2136
2246.50	French Military, Metz	FDC	CW 1830 2000 2215 2253
2249.00	Ships working		USB (to LGN) 2240
2254.00	Intership working		USB 2252
2266.00	Intership working		USB "Ocean Valiant" 2213
2268.50	French Military, Metz	FDC	CW 2158 2240
2270.00	Numbers Station		USB phonetics (female voice) 2244
2272.00	Intership working		USB Spanish 2154
2274.50	Italian Naval	IGJ	USB 2255
2277.00	Ships working		USB (UK ch "BRAVO" dup. 2840.6) 1758 1816 2251
2286.00	Intership working		USB Ital 2246

kHz.	Station	Call	Mode / Heard/Times GMT
2287.00	Caribbean Air traffic CAR A		USB
2295.90	UNID		96ARQ/E/8 Idle 2058 2148
2296.00	Intership working		USB Ital 2147 2153
2298.50	Intership working		USB Ger 2204
2299.90	Spa Publications		

2300-2495
FIXED AERONAUTICAL & MARITIME MOBILE

INTERNATIONAL BROADCASTING (SHARED)

kHz.	Station	Call	Mode / Heard/Times GMT
2301.00	Intership working		USB Eng 2129 2001 2225 Scottish 1950
2306.00	Intership working		USB Eng "Moray Firth 1" 1927 "Grampian Pride" (GDDK) 2228
2311.00	Intership working		USB (Irish) 2227
2326.00	Intership working		USB Ger 1842 1933 2219
2330.00	Intership working		USB Span 2200
2336.00	Intership working		USB (Scandinavian lang) 2249
2342.20	Grengel Met, Germany	DHJ51	FAX wx maps 1911 2002 2207 2253
2346.00	Intership working		USB Eng 2158 2207 2228
2351.00	Intership working		USB Ger 1857 1918
2357.50	Danish Naval	OUA	CW (also keyed with OVK) 1832 2208 2254 2308
2361.00	Intership working		USB Ger 0425 1859 2126
2364.00	Intership working		USB Greek 2159 2205
2366.00	Intership working		USB Dutch 0845 1940 Eng 2047
2374.00	British Naval	GYA	FAX wx maps 0847 1933 1950
2391.00	Intership working		USB Dutch 1833 1945 2158 2242
2396.00	Intership working		USB Ger 2224
2400.00	Intership working		USB Scottish 2132 2321
2411.00	Ship working		USB Ital ship dictating telegram 2201
2418.50	Intership working		USB Ger 1946 2220
2423.50	Goeteborg, Sweden	SAG	SITOR (dup. 3267.5) 1834 1947 2003 2128 2241
2429.00	RAF Pitreavie, Scotland	MKL	CW air wx forecasts (Tafs) 1902 2209 2309
2442.00	Pennsuco, USA	WOM	USB (dup. 2406.0)
2449.00	Ship working		USB (to CUL) 2212
2450.00	Intership working		USB Fr 1905
2450.00	New York (Ocean Gate), USA	WOO	USB (dup. 2366.0)
2458.00	Ships working		USB ICBI (to Livorno dup. 2591.0) 2207
2460.00	Intership working		USB Italian 2252
2460.00	Riga, Latvia	UDH	SITOR 2004 2140 2312 Mode B (to UEET) 1950 tfc list 1942
2461.50	Irish Naval	OA	SITOR 2317
2464.00	Ships working		CW LYDS (to LYK) 2006
2465.00	Ships working		USB "Benwalid" (TCJV) (to CUL) 2250
2474.00	Dutch Naval	PBC	75r 0748 1853 2155 2311
2484.00	Ostend, Belgium	OSU	USB (dup. 3178.0) 0748 0849 1753 1831 1942 2048
2485.00	ABC Katherine, Australia		AM Eng 2037
2490.00	Pennsuco, USA	WOM	USB (dup. 2031.5)
2491.00	Ships working		USB (to DAN dup. 2799.0) 0725 0846 2131 2154 SWQU (to CUL) 2219
2496.30	Ships working		SITOR (to GKZ dup. 3607.3) 2050 2259
2499.90	Spa Publications		

2500-2505
STANDARD FREQUENCY/TIME SIGNALS

kHz.	Station	Call	Mode / Heard/Times GMT
2503.50	UNID		SITOR Ger 2325 (ship position rpt, North Sea) 2006
2504.00	UNID		CW 5 fig grps 2157
2504.90	Spa Publications		

2505-2850
FIXED/LAND & SEA & AERONAUTICAL MOBILE

kHz.	Station	Call	Mode / Heard/Times GMT
2515.00	Ships working		SITOR (dup. 2780.7) 1907
2520.00	Ships working		USB (to PCG paired ch "ALPHA" 2824kHz) 2202 2243
2524.00	Ships working		USB (UK ch "ECHO" dup. 2705.0) 1751 "Grampian City" 2145
2525.00	Ships working		170/50nc "Klaipeda" (LYAH) (to LYK) 2300
2527.00	Ships working		USB (UK ch "NOVEMBER" dup. 1731.0) 0800 1753 2205
2529.50	Ships working		SITOR (SPB 2829.5kHz) 1815
2534.00	Ships working		USB (UK ch "ZULU" dup. 1866.0) 1837 1915 2300
2535.00	Ships working		SITOR 2152 (to UDH) "Ojars Vacietis" (UHNL) 1847
2538.00	Ships working		SITOR "Mindaugas" (LYOB) 1938
2538.00	St John's, Newfoundland	VON	USB 0309

kHz.	Station	Call	Mode / Heard/Times GMT
2543.50	Ships working		SITOR (to SPS dup. 2643.5) "Frycz Modrewski" (SPZC) 2225
2554.00	US Military		USB 2320
2555.00	Ships working		USB (UK ch "INDIA" dup. 1856.0) 2143 GYEC 2040
2557.50	Murmansk, Russia	UDK2	170/50nc
2558.00	New York (Ocean Gate), USA	WOO	USB (dup. 2166.0)
2562.00	Ships working		USB (UK ch "SIERRA" dup. 2810.0) 1958 "Pelikhan" (J8DJ9) 2207
2566.00	Pennsuco, USA	WOM	USB (dup. 2390.0)
2566.00	Ships working		USB (UK ch "KILO" dup. 1946.0) "Maersk Promoter" (OXBG5) 2117
2572.00	Mobile, USA	WLO	USB
2574.00	Ships working		SITOR (to GNK2 dup. 3542.7) 2202
2576.00	Ships working		SITOR (to GND1 dup. 3615.7) 2134
2577.00	Ships working		SITOR (to GNK1 dup. 2832.7) 1953 2251
2579.00	Bari, Italy	IPB	USB 2304
2586.00	Ronne, Denmark	OYE	USB 2305 tfc list odd hrs + 05
2590.00	Athens, Greece	SVN	USB 2246 tfc list even hours + 05
2591.00	Livorno, Italy	IPL	USB (dup. 2458.0) 2001 2209 wx wng (Eng) 1946 2248 nav wng (Eng) 2300
2593.00	Blaavand, Denmark	OXB	USB 1823 1923 2223
2598.00	Canadian CG	VON	USB wx 2210
2600.00	Scheveningen, Holland	PCG	USB (Dutch ch "CHARLIE" dup. 1995.0) 1818 1921 1946 2003
2604.00	Wick, UK	GNK	USB (UK ch "CHARLIE" dup. 2013.0) 1842 2118
2607.00	French Naval, Toulon	FUO	CW 2009 2127 2301 2314
2607.00	Stonehaven, UK	GND	USB (UK ch "LIMA" dup. 1999.0) 1955
2614.00	Norddeich, Germany	DAN	USB (dup. 2023.0) 0848 wx 0810 2010 2205 tfc list 1948 2245
2615.00	Dubrovnik, Croatia	9AD	USB 2206 tfc list odd hours + 20
2618.50	Bracknell Met, UK	GFA	FAX wx maps 1834 1917 2230 2321 (1800-0600)
2624.00	Trieste, Italy	IQX	USB (dup. 2040.0) 2206
2625.00	Malta	9HD	USB (dup. 2052.0) 1926
2625.00	St Petersburg, Russia	UGC	SITOR 1916 2017 2136 2207 Mode B tfc list 2020
2625.00	Wick, UK	GKR	USB (UK ch "HOTEL" dup. 2108.0) 2051
2626.00	Swedish Military	HIA	170/50r 2259 2305
2628.00	Niton, UK	GNI	USB (UK ch "UNIFORM" dup. 2009.0) 2221
2628.00	Numbers Station		USB phonetics (female voice) 2245
2632.00	Naples, Italy	IQH	USB 1926
2635.00	Orlandet, Norway	LFO	USB (dup. 3200.0) 1542 nav wng 1937 2135 tfc list 2335
2639.00	Witowo, Poland	SPS	USB (dup. 2090.0)
2642.00	Genoa, Italy	ICB	USB 1931
2642.00	Farsund, Norway	LGZ	USB (dup. 3146.0) 1837
2643.50	Witowo, Poland	SPS	SITOR (dup. 2543.5) 1922 1952 2042 2135 2231 2316
2645.00	Turkish Naval	TBO	CW 1953 2210 2315
2646.00	Orlandet, Norway	LFO	USB (dup. 3165.0) 2014 2157 Eng 2148 2207
2649.00	Floroe, Norway	LGL	USB (dup. 3217.0) 1544 2218 2255
2652.00	Italian Naval	IGJ41	CW 2203 2303
2653.00	Rogaland, Norway	LGQ	USB 1742 1906 2136
2656.00	Ancona, Italy	IPA	USB (dup. 3305kHz) 2158 wx 1935
2656.00	Rogaland, Norway	LGQ	USB (paired 2139.0) 2231
2663.00	Crotone, Italy	IPC	USB (dup. 2023.0) 1950 2143 wx (in Italian) 2003
2665.00	Ruegen, Germany	DHS	USB tfc list 1920
2667.00	Bergen, Norway	LGN	USB (dup. 3277.0) 2204
2670.00	Bergen, Norway	LGN	USB (dup. 3203.0) 1917
2670.00	Land's End, UK	GLD	USB wx 0303 0733 0903 1503 1933 2103 tfc/wngs 0233 & 4 hrly
2676.00	Farsund, Norway	LGZ	USB (dup. 3214.0)
2680.00	Cagliari, Italy	IDC	USB (with ICSB) 1916 nav wng 2003
2680.00	Israeli Naval	4XZ	CW 2254 2304
2684.00	Humber, UK	GKZ	USB (UK ch "ROMEO" dup. 2002.0) 1537 1637 2301 2335
2687.00	Norwegian Military	JWT	USB radio checks 2303
2691.00	Brest-le Conquet, France	FFU	USB 1935 2038 wx (Fr) 2155 tfc list even hours + 03
2691.00	Grengel Met, Germany		100n 2011
2691.00	Stonehaven, UK	GND	USB wx 0303 0703 0903 1503 1903 2103 tfc/wngs 0233 & 4 hrly
2694.00	Lisbon, Portugal	CUL	USB 2005 2157 2205 2258 tfc list even hours + 05
2696.70	Land's End, UK	GLD3	SITOR (dup. 2146.5) 0751 1954 2139 2239 Mode B tfc list 2102 2302
2698.00	Stonehaven, UK	GND	USB (UK ch "TANGO" dup. 2016.0) 1926
2698.00	Venice, Italy	ICZ	USB nav wng 2138
2700.00	Nicosia, Cyprus	5BA	USB 0016 1940
2702.00	UK Coast Control		USB 1820 2212 2310 (notice of Rig move) 1958
2705.00	Wick, UK	GKR	USB (UK ch "ECHO" dup. 2524.0) 0659 0852 1750 1918 2143
2712.00	Numbers Station		AM Slav 2307
2716.00	Goeteborg, Sweden	SAG	SITOR 0635 1751 1919 2012 2138
2719.00	Cullercoats, UK	GCC	USB wx 0303 0703 0903 1503 1903 tfc/wngs 0233 & 4 hrly
2719.00	Porto Torres, Sardinia	IZN	USB 2130 2252 nav wng 1835 gale wng 2208 2220
2719.00	Witowo, Poland	SPS	USB 1917 1928
2720.00	Samara Met, Russia	RDE73	FAX wx maps 2246

kHz.	Station	Call	Mode / Heard/Times GMT
2722.00	Genoa, Italy	ICB	USB (with IBQE) 1929
2725.00	Italian Naval	IDQ	CW 0427 2210 nav wng 2153 wx analysis 1931 wx 2114
2726.00	Brest-le Conquet, France	FFU	USB 2204
2726.00	Gdynia, Poland	SPC	USB 1936 tfc list 0035 (& each 4 hours) wx (Eng) 1936
2727.00	Norddeich, Germany	DAN	SITOR (dup. 2538.0) 0637 1854 2013 2148 Mode B tfc list 2201
2730.00	Limnos, Greece	SVL	USB 2000 2218 wx (Eng) 2141
2733.00	Stockholm, Sweden	SDJ	USB 2141 tfc list & wx (in Eng) 2150
2740.00	St Nazaire, France	FFO	USB 0621 nav wng 0819 wx 0805 1836
2749.00	Halifax, Canada	VCS	USB wx 2223
2751.00	Wick, UK	GNK	USB (UK ch "ALPHA" dup. 2006.0) 1650 1757 1955
2752.50	Spanish Police		SITOR p/lang 2133
2761.00	Ostend, Belgium	OSU	USB 1722 1834 2133 tfc list each hour + 20 wx 2235 nav wng 2208
2768.00	Tingstaede, Sweden	SAE	USB wx (Eng) 2207
2775.00	Bordeaux, France	FFC	USB wx (Fr) 0745
2775.00	Kiel, Germany	DAO	USB (dup. 2569.0) wx 0754 tfc list each hour + 25
2780.70	Stonehaven, UK	GND4	SITOR (dup. 2515.0) 0632 1753 2014 2211
2781.00	Lisbon, Portugal	CUL	USB 2121 2152 2221
2782.00	Land's End, UK	GLD	USB (UK ch "WHISKEY" dup. 2111.0) 0702 1540 2147 2200 2250
2789.00	Karlskrona, Sweden	SAA	USB wx (Eng) & tfc list 2154
2795.00	Tallinn, Estonia	ESA	SITOR (dup. 3180.0) 1836 2017 2116 2316
2799.00	Cabo de la Nao, Spain	EAV	USB
2799.00	Iraklion, Crete	SVH	USB 2136 nav wngs (in Eng) 2349
2799.00	Norddeich, Germany	DAM	USB (dup. 2491.0) 0847 1844 1921 2130 wx (Eng) 2149
2800.00	Israeli Naval	4XZ	CW 1844 1956 2145 2203 2247 2306
2806.00	Finisterre, Spain	EAF	USB (dup. 3283.0)
2806.00	Italian Naval	IGJ41	CW 1919 2015 2146 2214 2223
2810.00	Helsinki, Finland	OHG	USB 1938 wx 0703 1133 1933 tfc list 2153
2810.00	Humber, UK	GKZ	USB (UK ch "SIERRA" dup. 2562.0) 0815 1624 2208
2815.00	Italian Naval	IDR8	CW 1837 2157 2243 2314
2815.00	Moscow Met, Russia	RVO76	FAX wx maps 1957
2815.50	Ostend, Belgium	OST	SITOR 0638 1543 1836 2016 2154 2259
2820.00	Las Palmas, Canaries	EAL	USB (listens 3290.0) 2326
2822.00	Grengel Met	DHN	100r 0640 1920 2017 2221
2824.00	Scheveningen, Holland	PCG	USB (Dutch ch "ALPHA" dup. 2520.0) 2248 2313 wx (Eng) 2145
2828.00	Cullercoats, UK	GCC	USB (UK ch "OSCAR" dup. 1953.0) 0840 1821 2135
2829.50	Stettin, Poland	SPB	SITOR (dup. 2529.5) 1746 1827 2149 2315 Mode B tfc list 2155
2831.00	Stettin, Poland	SPO	USB (dup. 2090.0) tfc list 0640 1838 2238
2832.70	Wick, UK	GNK1	SITOR (dup. 2577.0) 0802 1545 1756 1954 2018 2208
2837.70	Oil Rig (North Sea)		SITOR 0641
2840.60	Wick, UK	GNK	USB (UK ch "BRAVO" dup. 2277.0) 1757 1822 2229
2843.00	Madeira	CUB	USB 2315
2845.00	Dutch Naval	PBB	75r 0752 1015 1759 1838 1943 2317
2848.00	Norddeich, Germany	DAN	USB (dup. 3161.0) 1650 1958
2849.90	Spa Publications		

2850-3025
AERONAUTICAL MOBILE (MAINLY CIVIL) 3KHz channels

kHz.	Station	Call	Mode / Heard/Times GMT
2850.00	Capetown, RSA	ZSC60	SITOR 2150 2200 2238
2851.00	N Central Asia Air traffic NCA 2		USB
2854.00	S Atlantic Air traffic SAT 2		USB
2854.00	Canaries ATC	GCCC	USB
2869.00	Cent East Pacific Air traffic CEP 1/2		USB
2869.00	CIS VOLMET channel	UWWW	USB 2148 2203 2308
2872.00	N Atlantic Air traffic NAT C		USB
2872.00	Gander ATC, Canada	CZQX	USB 0622 (with ASCOT 5773) 2320
2872.00	Reykjavik ATC, Iceland	BIRD	USB 0739
2872.00	Shanwick ATC, UK/Eire	EGGX	USB 0617 0733 2019
2878.00	Africa Air traffic AFI 4		USB
2878.00	Rogaland, Norway	LGQ	USB (dup. 1964.0) 1940 2152 2201 2216
2886.00	Intership working		USB Eng 2020 2226 2237 2319
2887.00	Caribbean Air traffic		USB
2892.20	British Naval	GYA/MTO	75r 0644 0849 1546 2301
2892.50	French Military, Orleans	FDY	CW 2209
2899.00	N Atlantic Air traffic NAT B		USB
2899.00	Gander ATC, Canada	CZQX	USB 0619 0741 2319
2899.00	Reykjavik ATC, Iceland	BIRD	USB
2899.00	Santa Maria ATC, Azores	LPAZ	USB
2899.00	Shanwick ATC, UK/Eire	EGGX	USB 0433 0607 0750 2137 2249 2327
2912.00	Intership working		USB Dutch 2203 2227
2920.00	Intership working		USB Scottish 2229
2929.00	Intership working		USB Eng 0754

kHz.	Station	Call	Mode / Heard/Times GMT
2932.00	North Pacific Air traffic NP		USB
2941.00	CIS VOLMET channel		USB 1909 2151 2205 2239 2323
2944.00	Middle East Air traffic MID 3		USB
2944.00	S America Air traffic SAM		USB
2962.00	N Atlantic Air traffic		USB
2962.00	Gander ATC, Canada	CZQX	USB
2962.00	Reykjavik ATC, Iceland	BIRD	USB
2962.00	Santa Maria ATC, Azores	LPAZ	USB 0613
2962.00	Shanwick ATC, UK/Eire	EGGX	USB 0620
2971.00	N Atlantic Air traffic NAT D		USB
2971.00	Bodo ATC, Norway	ENBO	USB
2971.00	Cambridge Bay ATC, Canada	CYCB	USB
2971.00	Churchill ATC, Canada	CYYQ	USB
2971.00	Reykjavik ATC, Iceland	BIRD	USB
2971.00	Shanwick ATC, UK/Eire	EGGX	USB 0538 2301
2978.50	Intership working		USB N Irish 2302
2992.00	Middle East Air traffic MID 1		USB
2992.00	Bahrain ATC	OBBB	USB
2998.00	Cent West Pacific Air traffic CWP 1/2		USB
3000.00	Intership working		USB Eng 1016 1725 Scand 2207
3004.00	N Cent Asia Air traffic NCA 3		USB
3008.00	Intership working		USB Ger 0145 1922 2205 Dutch 2308
3010.00	Berne (in-flight R/T service)		USB 2246 2306
3010.00	Intership working		USB Scottish 0629 2245
3011.50	Intership working		USB Scottish 2202
3016.00	E Asia Air traffic EA 1		USB
3016.00	N Atlantic Air traffic NAT A		USB
3016.00	Gander ATC, Canada	CZQX	USB 0551 0621 0813
3016.00	New York ATC, USA	KZNY	USB 0611
3016.00	Santa Maria ATC, Azores	LPAZ	USB 0428 0733
3016.00	Shanwick ATC, UK/Eire	EGGX	USB 0812 0820 2020 2209 2242
3019.00	N Cent Asia Air traffic NCA 3		USB
3023.00	Calling, Distress & Safety		USB Slav 0735
3023.00	Edinburgh MRCC		USB (with "Rescue 122") 1800
3023.00	Plymouth MRCC		USB (with "Rescue 172") 0640 ("Rescue 52") 2212
3023.00	Shanwick MRCC		USB 1945
3024.90	Spa Publications		

3025-3155
AERONAUTICAL MOBILE (MAINLY MILITARY) 3KHz channels

kHz.	Station	Call	Mode / Heard/Times GMT
3029.50	Ship working		SITOR "Helgoland" (DLVC) 2159
3030.00	Intership working		USB Eng 0629 Span 2145
3034.50	UNID		SITOR Fr p/lang 2254
3038.00	Swedish Military	HIA	170/50n 5 let grps 2146 tfc list 2201
3050.00	Intership working		USB Eng 0624 2150 2243
3051.00	Edinburgh MRCC, Scotland		USB 2022
3060.00	Irish Naval	OA	USB radio check with "20" 1837
3070.00	Intership working		USB Scottish 1846
3074.00	Intership working		USB Eng 1726
3104.50	Intership working		USB Scottish 2142
3108.00	Intership working		USB Ger 0836 1924
3134.00	Swedish Military	HIA	50r 5 let grps 2216
3146.00	Ships working		USB (to LGZ 2642.0) 1838
3150.00	Numbers Station		AM phonetics (female voice) 2302 2321
3154.90	Spa Publications		

3155-3200
FIXED/LAND & MARITIME MOBILE

kHz.	Station	Call	Mode / Heard/Times GMT
3161.00	Ships working		USB (to DAN 2848.0) 0625 SZQZ 1653
3172.50	Rome Met, Italy	IMB	50n 1841 2203 2303 2322
3178.00	Ships working		USB (to OST dup. 2484.0) 0755 1754 1829 1944
3182.00	Italian Naval	IDR	USB 2228 msg (in Eng) to "Q8P" 2306
3186.00	US Embassy frequency (rptd Athens)	KWS78	CW 2311
3190.00	Mariupol, Ukraine	USU	CW 2003 2256 2304 tfc list 1901 2001 2201
3191.00	Ships working		USB (to PCG ch "ECHO" dup. 3673.0)
3195.00	Single Letter Beacon	R	CW 1825 2231 2254 2323
3196.00	Prague Met, Czech Republic		50r 1832 2204 2228
3197.00	Intership working		USB Ger 0637 1842 2013
3199.90	Spa Publications		

kHz.	Station	Call	Mode / Heard/Times GMT

3200-3230
FIXED/LAND & MARITIME & AERONAUTICAL MOBILE

BROADCASTING

kHz.	Station	Call	Mode / Heard/Times GMT
3201.60	UNID		SITOR Selcal PKMV 2219
3203.00	Intership working		USB Scottish 0850 2143
3210.00	Klaipeda, Lithuania	LYK	CW (listens 2464.0) 2004 2104 2306
3210.00	Klaipeda, Lithuania	LYK	170/50nc (to LYCH) 2024
3210.00	Ships working		USB GUXN (to Rogaland dup. 2656.0) 2255
3215.00	St Petersburg, Russia	UGC	SITOR 1803 2048 2209 2253
3217.00	Ships working		USB (to LGL) 1545
3220.00	UNID		75r RYs & encrypted 0739
3222.00	R Kara, Togo		AM Fr 2204
3229.90	Spa Publications		

3230-3400
FIXED/LAND & MARITIME MOBILE

BROADCASTING

kHz.	Station	Call	Mode / Heard/Times GMT
3231.50	Grengel Met, Germany	DHJ	100n 1548 1833 1925 2206 2234
3232.00	Intership working		USB Scottish 2255
3233.50	CIS Naval	RMP	CW (with UJDO) 1951
3235.00	Minsk Met, Belarus	RSR71	FAX wx maps 1845 2138 2227 2236
3242.50	Boston, USA	NMF	FAX (0300-1055)
3245.00	Ships working		USB 2211
3249.00	Ships working		USB (UK ch "MIKE" dup. 3617.0)
3250.00	Murmansk, Russia	UDK2	CW
3252.00	Ships working		USB (dup. 3666.0) (Autolink ch to Stonehaven)
3255.00	BBC		AM Eng 2141 2148
3262.00	Numbers Station		USB Ger (female voice) 2144
3267.50	Ships working		SITOR (to SAG) 2159 "Baltic Trader" (SZYA) 2205
3270.00	R Namibia		AM Eng 2225
3273.00	German Govt net		96ARQ/E/8 1834 2313
3279.00	Grengel Met, Germany	DHJ	100n 2028 2208 2222
3280.00	Prague Telecom	OLX	CW 2356
3282.00	Intership working		USB Ger 1828 2226
3290.00	Kiev Met, Ukraine		50r 1835 1926 2149 2204
3291.00	Single Letter Beacon	P	CW 1843
3297.00	Portuguese Naval	RPFNF	75r p/lang 1824
3305.00	Ship working		USB "Ankara" (to IPA) 2156
3306.50	French Military	FDE2	CW 1836
3310.00	Tallinn, Estonia	ESA	CW 2047
3316.00	SLBS Freetown, Sierra Leone		AM Eng 2205 2212 2236
3320.00	French Military, Orleans	FDY	50r "Voyez le Brick..." 2016 2358
3320.00	R Orion, S Africa		AM 2208 classical music 2227
3326.00	R Nigeria		AM Eng 2109 2230 2246
3330.00	Moscow Met, Russia	RWZ72	50r 1837 1957 2145 2223
3330.00	Ottawa Time Station	CHU	CW/USB Eng & Fr 0756 2326
3333.00	Intership working		USB Scottish 1551 2154
3335.00	Ships working		USB (dup. 3775.0) (Autolink ch to Wick)
3338.00	Ships working		USB (dup. 3528.0) (Autolink ch to Wick)
3340.00	UNID		USB wx fcsts (French) for UK coastal areas 1845
3356.00	R Botswana		AM Eng 1812 2154
3357.00	US Naval	NAM	FAX wx maps
3360.00	Kiev Met, Ukraine		FAX wx maps 1838 2153 2256 2316
3360.50	Intership working		USB Ger 2052 2111
3366.00	GBC Radio, Ghana		AM Eng 0032 2146 2155 2214 2243
3377.00	Ankara Met, Turkey	YMA5	FAX wx maps 1929 2000 2215
3384.00	R Moscow feeder		USB Slav 1927 2040 2231
3390.00	Glasgow Naval	MGJ	75r test 1813 2001 2211
3399.90	Spa Publications		

3400-3500
AERONAUTICAL MOBILE (MAINLY CIVIL) 3khZ CHANNELS

kHz.	Station	Call	Mode / Heard/Times GMT
3407.00	CIS VOLMET channel		USB 1839 2212
3413.00	Cent E Pacific Air traffic CEP 1/2		USB
3413.00	Shannon VOLMET, Eire	EINN	USB 0015 0614 0636 0805 2008 2220 2325
3417.00	Numbers Station		AM phonetics (female voice) 2002 2229 "ART" 1833 2200 2213
3419.00	Africa Air traffic AFI 1		USB

kHz.	Station	Call	Mode / Heard/Times GMT
3451.50	Irish Naval	OA	SITOR 1832 2004 2258 2359 wx fcsts 0744
3452.00	Africa Air traffic AFI 1		USB
3452.00	Dakar ATC, Senegal	GOOO	USB
3452.00	S Atlantic Air traffic SAT 1		USB
3452.00	Canaries ATC	GCCC	USB 0528
3455.00	Caribbean Air traffic CAR B		USB
3455.00	New York ATC, USA	KZNY	USB
3467.00	Africa Air traffic AFI 3		USB
3467.00	Addis Ababa ATC, Ethiopia	HAAA	USB 2235
3467.00	Benghazi ATC, Libya	HLLB	USB
3467.00	Cairo ATC, Egypt	HECA	USB 2236
3467.00	Middle East Air traffic MID 2		USB
3467.00	Bombay ATC, India	VABF	USB (with Air India 356) 2156
3467.00	Delhi ATC, India	VIDF	USB 1848
3467.00	Kabul ATC, Afghanistan	OAKX	USB 2151
3467.00	Karachi ATC, Pakistan	OPKR	USB 2151 2230 2244
3467.00	Lahore ATC, Pakistan	OPLR	USB 2234 2243
3467.00	S Pacific Air traffic SP		USB
3470.00	S E Asia Air traffic SEA 1/3		USB
3470.00	Dhaka ATC, Bangladesh	VGFR	USB 1815
3470.00	Perth ATC, Australia	APGF	USB (with Cathay 107) 1821
3475.00	UNID		LSB CB style (Eng) 2144
3476.00	N Atlantic Air traffic NAT E		USB
3476.00	Gander ATC, Canada	CZQX	USB (with "Reach 6078") 0650
3476.00	New York ATC, USA	KZNY	USB
3476.00	Santa Maria ATC, Azores	LPAZ	USB 2325
3476.00	Shanwick ATC, Eire/UK	EGGX	USB 0626 (with American 92) 0432
3476.00	Indian Ocean traffic INO 1		USB
3479.00	Europe Air traffic EUR A		USB
3479.00	S America Air traffic SAM		USB
3485.00	E & S E Asia Air traffic EA 2 SEA 1		USB
3485.00	Gander VOLMET, Canada	CZQX	USB 0753 2054 2155 2258 2327
3485.00	New York VOLMET, USA	KZNY	USB 0001 0616 0738 2215 2232 2331
3490.00	UNID		LSB CB style (France) 2113
3491.00	E Asia Air Traffic		USB
3491.00	Calcutta ATC, India	VECF	USB 2137
3494.00	New York (in-flight R/T service)		USB
3494.00	Stockholm (in-flight R/T service)		USB 1630 2011 2255
3499.90	Spa Publications		

3500-3800
AMATEUR RADIO (SHARED)

FIXED/MARITIME MOBILE

kHz.	Station	Call	Mode / Heard/Times GMT
3517.00	Niton, UK	GNI1	SITOR (dup. 2000.2) 0630 1136 2217 2326 wx wng 2210
3519.00	Intership working		USB Eng 0755 2148
3528.00	Wick, UK	GNK	USB (dup. 3338.0) (Autolink ch)
3540.00	St Petersburg, Russia	UGC	CW 1928 2155 2220 2232
3541.50	Brent Oilfield traffic		68Bd AUTOSPEC msg 0813 2219
3542.70	Wick, UK	GNK2	SITOR (dup. 2574.0) 1629 1844 2227 2327
3550.00	Intership working		USB (Scand) 2115
3571.50	French Military, Orleans	FDY	50r "Voyez le Brick.." 2221
3581.50	French Military, Orleans	FDY	50r "Voyez le Brick.." 2239
3603.00	Amateur packet radio		300Bd packet net GB7BSX/GB7ERA 0633
3607.30	Humber, UK	GKZ1	SITOR (dup. 2496.3) 0819 1631 2152 2241 Mode B 1100
3607.80	Hebrides, UK	GHD2	SITOR (dup. 2147.0) 0739 1928 2116 2228
3610.00	Land's End, UK	GLD	USB (UK ch "X-RAY" dup. 2120.0) 2050
3615.70	Stonehaven, UK	GND1	SITOR (dup. 2576.0) 0802 0954 1633 2240 wx 1945 Mode B 0700
3617.00	Stonehaven, UK	GND	USB (UK ch "MIKE" dup. 3249.0) 0806
3618.00	French Military	RFFZ	72ARQ/E/4 Controle de Voie 1842
3628.00	Orlandet, Norway	LFO	USB (dup. 2463.0)
3631.00	Bergen, Norway	LGN	USB (dup. 2449.0) 2238
3639.00	Porto Torres, Sardinia	IZN	USB gale wng (Ital & Eng) 2236
3640.00	Numbers Station		USB Eng (female voice) 2018
3645.00	Floroe, Norway	LGL	USB (dup. 2576.0)
3652.00	British Naval	GYA	FAX wx maps 0620 0955
3652.50	Farsund, Norway	LGZ	USB (dup. 2442.0)
3652.50	Greek Naval	SXA	CW 2117 2156 2243
3655.00	Archangel Met, Russia	RVZ73	50n 1556
3666.00	Stonehaven, UK	GND	USB (dup. 3252.0) (Autolink ch)
3678.00	Greek Naval	SXH	CW 2118 2257
3712.90	Greek Naval	SXA33	CW 1930 2240

kHz.	Station	Call	Mode / Heard/Times GMT
3722.00	Brest-le-Conquet, France	FFU	USB 0618
3730.00	Klaipeda Harbour, Lithuania	LYL	CW (listens 4207.0kHz) 2203
3737.00	Kaliningrad, Russia	UIW	CW (to "Frio Brazil" P3YI3) 2210 nav wngs 2127
3740.00	Varna, Bulgaria	LZW	USB (dup. 4115.7)
3745.00	Tbilisi Met, Georgia	RIS70	FAX wx maps 1931 2227
3745.50	French Military, Orleans	FDY	50r "Voyez le Brick.." 2227
3750.00	Cullercoats, UK	GCC	USB (UK ch "PAPA" dup. 2123.0) 0738 0845 0901
3764.30	Dutch Naval	PBB	75r 0755 1557 1826 2230
3775.00	Wick, UK	GKR	USB (dup. 3335.0) (Autolink ch)
3778.00	UNID		AM Slav anns & music 2217
3781.50	French Military, Orleans	FDY	50r "Voyez le Brick.." 2258
3782.00	Portuguese Naval, Lisbon	CTP	CW 1847 2120 2020 2230
3787.00	French Military	FDE	CW 2231
3790.00	French Military	FDE	CW 1840
3795.00	Boulogne, France	FFB	USB (dup. 3314.0) 1827 2021 nav wngs (Fr & Eng) 0535 2137
3795.00	Marseille, France	FFM	USB nav wngs (Fr) 1913 2135 gale wng (Fr) 1910
3799.90	Spa Publications		

3800-4000
FIXED/AERONAUTICAL & LAND MOBILE

AMATEUR RADIO USA (SHARED)

BROADCAST

kHz.	Station	Call	Mode / Heard/Times GMT
3810.00	Minsk Met, Belarus	RST75	FAX wx maps 1848 2203 2243
3840.00	Numbers Station		AM phonetics (female voice) 2239
3855.00	Hamburg (Quickborn) Met, Germany	DDH3	FAX wx maps 0758
3874.50	French Military, Orleans	FDY	50r "Voyez le Brick.." 2300
3875.00	Moscow Met, Russia	RCI72	FAX wx maps 1916 2157
3881.00	French Military	FAV22	CW 1559 "QLH 3881/6825kHz" 0858
3900.00	Intership working		USB Scand 0636 2122
3905.00	All India Radio		AM Eng 1600
3910.00	Reflections Europe		AM Eng 2159 2229
3915.00	BBC		AM Eng 1601 2233
3930.00	Intership working		USB Eng 0822 0852
3939.30	Intership working		USB Eng 0800
3944.50	Scottish Free Radio (pirate)		AM Eng 2200
3945.00	UNID		AM Eng (religious) 2056
3955.00	BBC		AM Eng 0621 0713 1755 2246 (0300-0730 1700-2315)
3960.00	R Svoboda		AM Slav 1933 2243
3965.00	R France International		AM Fr 0034 0638 0813 1934 2210 2313 (0001-0900 1700-2400)
3970.00	R Svoboda		AM Romanian 2158
3980.00	VOA		AM Eng 0435 0623 0637 1831 1917 Slav 2314
3985.00	R China International		AM Eng 2124 2200 Ital 2232
3985.00	R Swiss International		AM Eng 0613 Fr 0640 0813 1842 Ger 2024
3995.00	Deutsche Welle		AM Ger 2012 2208 2247 2316
3999.90	Spa Publications		

4000-4063
FIXED MARITIME MOBILE

kHz.	Station	Call	Mode / Heard/Times GMT
4000.00	R Bafoussam, Cameroon		AM Fr 2011
4002.00	Bucharest Met, Romania	YRR6	50r 1851 2205 2235
4010.50	UNID		USB Irish fisherman (to home on illegal net) 2025
4014.00	Pretoria, RSA	ZRO	FAX wx maps
4015.00	USMARS	AGA7RM	300Bd packet net AE1FGT 0757 AFA7DW 1853 AE1KFD 2232
4036.50	UN marine monitoring (Adriatic)		USB "I9P"/"V2Y" 2207
4055.00	UNID		AM Chinese ?? 2202 2256
4061.50	French Police	FVA80	CW 0623
4062.90	Spa Publications		

4063-4438
MARITIME MOBILE

kHz.	Station	Call	Mode / Heard/Times GMT
4065.00	Ships wkg ch 1 dup. 4357.0kHz		USB 0700 0811 2115
4068.00	Ships wkg ch 2 dup. 4360.0kHz		USB 1347
4071.00	Ships wkg ch 3 dup. 4363.0kHz		USB
4071.70	Egyptian Embassy traffic		SITOR 1951
4074.00	Ships wkg ch 4 dup. 4366.0kHz		USB 1943

kHz.	Station	Call	Mode / Heard/Times GMT
4077.00	Ships wkg ch 5 dup. 4369.0kHz		USB 1855 1958 (to PCG) 2332
4080.00	Ships wkg ch 6 dup. 4372.0kHz		USB 0628 2112
4083.00	Ships wkg ch 7 dup. 4375.0kHz		USB 0648 2203
4083.00	Spanish Naval		USB simplex R/T 1952
4086.00	Ships wkg ch 8 dup. 4378.0kHz		USB 1844 1921
4088.00	Intership working		USB Eng 2033
4089.00	Ships wkg ch 9 dup. 4381.0kHz		USB 0619 0726 2248
4090.00	UN traffic		SITOR UNHCR convoy details for Sarajevo 2237
4092.00	Ships wkg ch 10 dup. 4384.0kHz		USB 1224 1856 "HMS Liverpool" (GZIS) 2110
4095.00	Ships wkg ch 11 dup. 4387.0kHz		USB 0755 (to OST) 1819
4098.00	Ships wkg ch 12 dup. 4390.0kHz		USB 0632
4100.00	Intership working		USB Eng 1547
4101.00	Ships wkg ch 13 dup. 4393.0kHz		USB 1940 2236
4104.00	Ships wkg ch 14 dup. 4396.0kHz		USB 0748
4107.00	Ships wkg ch 15 dup. 4399.0kHz		USB 0730 2234
4110.00	Ships wkg ch 16 dup. 4402.0kHz		USB 0048 0802 1839 2219
4113.00	Ships wkg ch 17 dup. 4405.0kHz		USB 1832 2135 2320
4116.00	Ships wkg ch 18 dup. 4408.0kHz		USB (to OXZ) 0804
4119.00	Ships wkg ch 19 dup. 4411.0kHz		USB 0957 1908 2147
4122.00	Ships wkg ch 20 dup. 4414.0kHz		USB 0630 1517 1645 2217
4125.00	Ships wkg ch 21 dup. 4417.0kHz		USB (common calling & distress/safety ch) 0656 0756
4128.00	Ships wkg ch 22 dup. 4420.0kHz		USB 0649 2148 (to ESA) 2242
4131.00	Ships wkg ch 23 dup. 4423.0kHz		USB 1756 2129
4134.00	Ships wkg ch 24 dup. 4426.0kHz		USB 0814
4137.00	Ships wkg ch 25 dup. 4429.0kHz		USB
4140.00	Ships wkg ch 26 dup. 4432.0kHz		USB 0638 2249 (to LGN) 1919
4141.00	Intership working		USB Spanish 0637 Scottish 2220
4143.00	Ships wkg ch 27 dup. 4435.0kHz		USB 1832 2141
4146.00	Ships/Coast stations simplex		USB 0620 1718 1902 2206 2315
4149.00	Ships/Coast stations simplex		USB 0624
4165.00	Numbers Station		AM "SYN2" (fem voice) 2231
4172.50	Ships wkg ch 1 dup. 4210.5kHz		SITOR "Cavendish" (VPGT) 1912 Selcal KYVS (Tallinn) 1827
4173.00	Ships wkg ch 2 dup. 4211.0kHz		SITOR "CTE Lucia" (HJWL) 2243
4173.50	Ships wkg ch 3 dup. 4211.5kHz		SITOR "Arild Viking" (LAIM) 1841 "Marian Buczek" (SQFQ) 2037
4174.00	Ships wkg ch 4 dup. 4212.0kHz		SITOR "Nikolay Vilkov" 1820 "Pomorye" (UZFE) 2237
4174.50	Ships wkg ch 5 dup. 4212.5kHz		SITOR ELOZ6 2230 "Zim Pusan" (SXZC) 2245
4175.00	Ships wkg ch 6 dup. 4213.0kHz		SITOR "Green Arctic" (LAIM4) 0808
4175.50	Ships wkg ch 7 dup. 4213.5kHz		SITOR "Zanis Griva" (YLCV) 0623 "Asari" (YLCR) 0810
4176.00	Ships wkg ch 8 dup. 4214.0kHz		SITOR "Alandia Wave (C6CN6) 1812 "Cast Polarbear" (C6JK9) 1851
4176.50	Ships wkg ch 9 dup. 4214.5kHz		SITOR "Heinrich Essberger" (DGHE) 0810 Selcal QSPV (Goteborg) 1843
4177.00	Ships wkg ch 10 dup. 4215.0kHz		170/50rc "Mariyampole" (LYAF) 1918 "Kapitonas Gudin" (LYBN) 2137
4177.50	Ship stations		RTTY Marine safety channel (Scand) 2035
4178.00	Ships wkg ch 12 dup. 4215.5kHz		SITOR "Pernille Kosan" (OUMH3) 0749 "Janne Terkol" (OYHX2) 0819
4178.50	Ships wkg ch 13 dup. 4216.0kHz		SITOR Selcal QFMP (Norddeich) 1740
4179.00	Ships wkg ch 14 dup. 4216.5kHz		SITOR "Framnaes" (SDBT 0805 & 170/50nc "Kapitonas Panfilov" (LYCH) 1820
4179.50	Ships wkg ch 15 dup. 4217.0kHz		SITOR "Rubene" (UFVK) 0755 "Smit-Lloyd 123" (PHSC) 2248
4180.00	Ships wkg ch 16 dup. 4217.5kHz		170/50nc "Pakruoyis" (LYDF) 1828
4180.00	Ship working		CW "Novolvovsk" (URFV) 0627
4180.50	Ships wkg ch 17 dup. 4218.0kHz		SITOR Selcal VFMV (Ostend) 1801
4181.00	Ships wkg ch 18 dup. 4218.5kHz		SITOR 1604 2255
4181.50	Ships wkg ch 19 dup. 4219.0kHz		RTTY
4182.00	Ships calling ch 1		CW "Birshtonas" (LYCR) 1835
4182.50	Ships calling ch 2		CW "Kompozitor Rakhmaninov" (UPIO) 2252 "Berezovka" (UUVT) 2255
4183.00	Ships calling ch 5		CW "Arctic Crystal" (3EKS7) 0917
4183.50	Ships calling ch 6		CW SVIT (to SVB) 1842 IBLU (to IQX) 2215
4184.00	Ships calling ch 3		CW "Kas" (TCCO) 2157 "Tadmor" (HQEN9) 2237 "Amazonia" (SWCR) 2248
4184.50	Ships calling ch 4		CW "Egnazia" (IBMD) 1922 TCXR (to TAH) 2133
4185.00	Ships calling ch 7		CW "Sealand Value" (WPKB) 1835
4185.50	Ships calling ch 8		CW "Proliv Vilkitskovo" (EMMD) 1908
4186.00	Ships calling ch 9		CW YLBH (to UDH) 2250
4186.50	Ships calling ch 10		CW "Nikolay Tulpin" (UEWA) 2318
4187.00	Ships working		CW P3YT3 1812 "Vishva Mamta" (ATGV) 1918
4187.50	Ships working		CW "Valle Azzurra" (IBLU) 2210
4188.00	Ships working		CW "Buona Speranza" (IBSN) 1832
4188.50	Ships working		CW 1928
4189.00	Ships working		CW "Slobozia" (YQCN) 1852 "Cesme 1" (TCBN) 2152
4189.50	Ships working		CW 1901
4190.00	Ships working		CW "Youcheng" (3EDO7) 2148
4190.50	Ships working		CW "Bazias 2" (YQOQ) 1920
4191.00	Ships working		CW "Zuetina" (5ALZ) 1924 "Penelope" (ELDU7) 2309

kHz.	Station	Call	Mode / Heard/Times GMT
4191.50	Ships working		CW 2008
4192.00	Ships working		CW "Zuetina" 1804 "Ob" (USNN) 2140
4193.00	Ships working		CW "Egizia" (ICYR) 0720
4193.50	Ships working		CW "Sekibeech" (3EZI2) 1735
4194.00	Ships working		CW "Viseu" (YQDH) 2000 "Portoria" (IBFM) 2131
4194.00	UNID	W9TL	CW (clg RMP) 1805 (clg RCV4) 2204
4194.50	Ships working		CW "Everdina" (C6BF8) 1908
4195.00	Ships working		CW "Istrian Express" (YJYA7) 0725
4195.50	Ships working		CW 3EYL3 2258
4196.00	Ships working		CW "Volga 4001" (UMFA) 2005 "Polluks" (UJPT) 2230
4197.00	Ships working		CW "Adige" (9HZV3) 2151 "Pyotr Alekseyev" (ULBJ) 2312
4198.00	CIS Naval	RMVQ	CW (clg RMP) 2219 & RMBE (clg RMP) 2155
4198.00	Ships working		CW "Ladoga 1" (EMXM) 2136
4198.50	Ships working		CW UKJO 2259
4199.00	Ships working		CW EMML 1940
4199.50	Ships working		CW "Sormovskiy 1002" 2020
4200.00	Ships working		CW "Shane" (9HAJ3) 0734 "Damiao De Gois" (CSBL) 2233
4201.00	Ships working		CW "Chusovoy" (P3RD3) 1839 "Hua De" (BPKQ) 2245
4202.00	Ships working		CW "Birshtonas" (LYCR) (to GKB) 1839
4202.00	Ships working		170/50nc "Novosibirsk" (UFJK) 1920
4202.50	Ships working (non paired)		170/50nc "Baltiyskaya Slava" (USYQ) 1906
4203.00	Ships working (non paired)		SITOR 0826 & 170/50nc "Novoaltaysk" (UOUW) 2250
4203.50	Ships working (non paired)		170/50nc 0810 "Abava" (YLAD) 1641
4204.00	Ships working (non paired)		SITOR 0758 2029 2154
4204.50	Ships working (non paired)		170/50nc "Nikolay Kremlyanskiy" (UYUE) 2213 "Berezovka" (UUVT) 2306
4205.00	Ships working (non paired)		SITOR 0831 1939 & 170/50nc "MA 0805" 2023
4205.50	Ships working (non paired)		RTTY
4206.00	Ships working (non paired)		SITOR "Sergey Kirov" (URMH) 2251
4206.50	Ships working (non paired)		RTTY
4207.00	Ships working (non paired)		170/50nc "MB 0365" 0805
4207.50	Maritime safety channel		SITOR
4208.00	Ships digital selective calling		SITOR "Auseklis" (YLAG) with Selcal KYVM (Riga) 2220
4208.50	Ships digital selective calling		SITOR 1822
4209.00	Ships digital selective calling		RTTY
4209.50	Coast stations		RTTY "NAVTEX" ch
4210.00	Maritime safety channel		RTTY
4210.00	Coast stations ch 1 dup. 4172.5kHz		RTTY
4210.50	Bahrain	A9M	SITOR 2235 2239 2310
4210.50	Rome, Italy	IAR	SITOR 1704 1909 2150 2237
4210.50	Singapore	9VG74	SITOR 2258
4210.50	Tallinn, Estonia	ESA	SITOR 0007 0736 1554 1925 2141 2305 Mode B 1722
4211.00	Coast stations ch 2 dup. 4173.0kHz		RTTY
4211.00	Lyngby, Denmark	OXZ	SITOR
4211.00	Novorossiysk, Russia	UFN	SITOR 2344
4211.00	Portishead, UK	GKE2	SITOR 1706 2251 2324 Mode B wx 0930 2130
4211.50	Coast stations ch 3 dup. 4173.5kHz		RTTY
4211.50	Gdynia, Poland	SPA21	SITOR 2042 2300 2325 tfc list 1653
4211.50	Mariupol, Ukraine	USU	SITOR 1846 2156 2205 2300
4211.50	Rogaland, Norway	LGB	SITOR 0656 0759 1724 1935 2226
4212.00	Coast stations ch 4 dup. 4174.0kHz		RTTY
4212.00	Portsmouth, USA	NMN	SITOR
4212.00	Scheveningen, Holland	PCH25	SITOR
4212.00	Tallinn, Estonia	ESA	SITOR 2156 2248 2307 0008
4212.50	Coast stations ch 5 dup. 4174.5kHz		RTTY
4212.50	New York (Ocean Gate), USA	WOO	SITOR
4212.50	St Lys, France	FFT21	SITOR 2235 Mode B nav info 1900 tfc list 1913 2300 wx 0805
4212.50	Stettin, Poland	SPC21	SITOR
4213.00	Coast stations ch 6 dup. 4175.0kHz		RTTY
4213.00	Athens, Greece	SVS2	SITOR
4213.00	Berne, Switzerland	HEC14	SITOR 2208
4213.00	Mobile, USA	WLO	SITOR
4213.00	Perth, Australia	VIP31	SITOR
4213.00	Rogaland, Norway	LGB	SITOR 0737 1706 1838 1926 2132 2222
4213.50	Coast stations ch 7 dup. 4175.5kHz		RTTY
4213.50	Gdynia, Poland	SPA22	SITOR
4213.50	Halifax, Canada	VCS	SITOR
4213.50	Norddeich, Germany	DCL	SITOR 0737 1458 1936 2143 2233 Mode B tfc list 2202
4213.50	Novorossiysk, Russia	UFN	SITOR 1634 1656 2145 2245
4213.50	Portishead, UK	GKL2	SITOR
4214.00	Coast stations ch 8 dup. 4176.0kHz		RTTY
4214.00	Capetown, RSA	ZSC61	SITOR 2207
4214.00	Portishead, UK	GKP2	SITOR 1457
4214.00	Italian Naval	IDR2	CW 1847 1911 2155 2256
4214.50	Coast stations ch 9 dup. 4176.5kHz		RTTY
4214.50	Goeteborg, Sweden	SAG	SITOR 0655 1707
4215.00	Coast stations ch 10 dup. 4177.0kHz		RTTY

kHz.	Station	Call	Mode / Heard/Times GMT
4215.00	Genoa, Italy	ICB	SITOR 0818
4215.00	Helsinki, Finland	OFJ	SITOR 2140
4215.00	Mobile, USA	WLO	SITOR 0927
4215.00	Sydney, Australia	VIS70	SITOR
4215.50	Coast stations ch 12 dup. 4178.0kHz		RTTY
4215.50	Berne, Switzerland	HEC24	SITOR 2122 2223 2302 Mode B tfc list 2030
4215.50	Lyngby, Denmark	OXZ	SITOR 0009 0716 0929 2037 2158 2253
4215.50	Perth, Australia	VIP41	SITOR tfc list 2335
4216.00	Coast stations ch 13 dup. 4178.5kHz		RTTY
4216.00	Athens, Greece	SVU2	SITOR
4216.00	Doha, Qatar	A7D	SITOR 1912 1937 2258
4216.00	Portishead, UK	GKY2	SITOR
4216.50	Coast stations ch 14 dup. 4179.0kHz		RTTY
4216.50	Chatham, USA	WCC	SITOR 2224
4216.50	Goeteborg, Sweden	SAG	SITOR 1914 2213
4216.50	Portishead, UK	GKQ2	SITOR
4216.50	Sydney, Australia	VIS61	SITOR
4217.00	Coast stations ch 15 dup. 4179.5kHz		RTTY
4217.00	Mobile, USA	WLO	SITOR
4217.00	Scheveningen, Holland	PCH26	SITOR 0141 0654 0930 1459 Mode B tfc list 0715 0915
4217.00	Stettin, Poland	SPB22	SITOR
4217.50	Coast stations ch 16 dup. 4180.0kHz		RTTY
4217.50	Dixon, USA	KMI	SITOR
4218.00	Coast stations ch 17 dup. 4180.5kHz		RTTY
4218.00	General Pacheco, Argentina	LPD	SITOR 2255 2307
4218.00	Ostend, Belgium	OST28	SITOR 0006 1000 1600 1829 1922 2205
4218.50	Coast stations ch 18 dup. 4181.0kHz		RTTY
4218.50	Riga, Latvia	UDH	SITOR 1725 1851 1928 2142 2227 2313
4219.00	Coast stations ch 19 dup. 4181.5kHz		RTTY
4219.00	General Pacheco, Argentina	LPD	SITOR
4219.00	UNID	PPQ	SITOR 2232
4219.50	Coast stations digital selective calling		RTTY
4220.00	Coast stations digital selective calling		RTTY
4220.00	PBS China		AM 0035 2326
4220.50	Coast stations digital selective calling		RTTY
4221.00	Gibraltar Naval	GYU	75n 1915 2003 2236 2314
4223.00	Athens, Greece	SVD2	CW 1835 2259 2327
4223.00	St Petersburg, Russia	UCW4	CW 1506
4224.30	Istanbul, Turkey	TCR	CW 2256 tfc list 2301
4227.00	Italian Naval	IGJ42	CW 0638 1659 1938 2038 2152 2216
4227.90	Greek Naval	SXA	CW 0036 1848 2045 2127 2213 2237 2304
4229.00	Klaipeda, Lithuania	LYK	CW nav wngs 1832 tfc list 2201 2302
4231.00	Doha, Qatar	A7D	CW 2033 2128 2217 2309 tfc list each even hour
4231.50	Gelendzhik, Russia	UVA	CW tfc list 1600 1702
4232.00	French Military, Martinique	FUF	CW 0037 0555 0809 0827
4232.50	Hong Kong	VPS8	CW 1850 1854
4235.00	Genoa, Italy	ICB	CW 0820 1917 2147 2219 2330
4236.00	Riga, Latvia	UDH	CW 1654 1809 1852 1939 2039 2158 2209 2325 tfc list 1700
4238.00	Haifa, Israel	4XO	CW 1727 1840 2129 2216 2315 tfc list even hours + 25
4238.00	Indian Naval	VTP	CW 2147
4239.00	Malaysian Naval	9MB2	CW 1928
4239.40	Athens, Greece	SVB2	CW 2041 2230 2310
4240.00	UNID	RPLT	CW 2302
4241.00	Israeli Naval	4XZ	CW 1842 2119 2220 2304
4241.50	Rogaland, Norway	LGW	CW 0656 0828 1502 1856 2149 2303 tfc list 0930
4242.00	Intership working		USB Scottish 0717
4244.00	Norddeich, Germany	DAL	CW 2300
4244.00	Rio de Janeiro, Brazil	PPR	CW 0639 2133 2221 2345
4245.00	Novorossiysk, Russia	UFN	CW 1715 1929 2212 2304 tfc list 1800 1900 2200
4245.00	Novorossiysk, Russia	UFN	170/50nc 1839 1859
4245.00	Sydney, Australia	VIS53	CW 1752 1941
4246.00	RSA Naval	ZRH	CW 0058 2120 2157
4248.00	RSA Naval	ZRQ	CW 0055 1753 1942 2218
4250.00	Scheveningen, Holland	PCH20	CW 0737 1525 1710 2042 2149 2222 2325 tfc list 1850
4251.00	Juncao, Brazil	PPJ	CW 0556 0740 2131 2150 2236 2348
4253.00	Archangel, Russia	UCE	SITOR 2240
4253.00	Istanbul, Turkey	TAH	CW 1716 2046 2138 2219 2240 tfc list 2305
4253.50	Dammam, Saudi Arabia	HZG	CW 1804 1854 2043 2151 2307
4255.00	Serapeum, Egypt	SUZ	CW nav wngs (in English) 1850
4256.00	Portishead, UK	GKD2	CW reserve frequency
4257.50	Mobile, USA	WLO2	CW 0038 0826 0942 2350
4258.40	British Naval	MTO	75r 0802 0916 1940 2149
4260.00	Murmansk, Russia	UDK2	CW (to "4LS") 2049 tfc list 2305
4260.00	Turkish Naval	TBA2	CW 2226 (freq varies to 4261.0)
4261.00	Spanish Naval	EBA	CW nav wngs 2020
4264.00	UNID	UPQ67	CW (clg UOD31) 1815

kHz.	Station	Call	Mode / Heard/Times GMT
4265.00	Belem, Brazil	PPL	CW 0059 2152 tfc list 0030 0430 0830 1230 1630 2030 wx 2205
4265.00	Norddeich, Germany	DAM	CW 1916 2204 2224 2326 tfc list 2139
4265.00	Mariupol, Ukraine	USU	CW 2051 wx 1703
4267.90	Portishead, UK	GKG2	CW (working frequency to ships) 0917 1711
4268.00	General Pacheco, Argentina	LPD68	CW 2156 2226 2352
4268.00	Indian Naval	VTG	CW 2023
4268.60	Goeteborg, Sweden	SAG	SITOR 0932 1220 1501 1941 2158
4270.00	Numbers Station		AM phonetics (female voice) 2309
4271.00	Halifax Met, Canada	CFH	FAX wx maps 0803 2218 2306
4271.00	Halifax Met, Canada	CFH	75r 0644
4271.00	Helsinki, Finland	OFJ4	CW 0626 2228 tfc list even hours + 05 wx/nav wngs 0825
4272.00	Gdynia, Poland	SPH22	CW
4273.00	French Military, Toulon	FUO	CW 2153
4274.00	Intership working		USB (2 UK vessels arranged after call on 2182) 2215
4274.00	Portishead, UK	GKB2	CW 0815 1537 1755 1943 2229 2301
4275.00	Karlskrona, Sweden	SAA	CW 2024 2237 2322
4275.00	Panama	HPP	CW 0040 0646 0834 2248 2353
4275.00	Turkish Naval	TBA5	CW 2055 2210 2241 2330
4277.00	Kaliningrad, Russia	UIW	CW 2249 (to "Baltiyskaya Slava") 1843
4277.00	Kaliningrad, Russia	UIW	170/50nc 2215
4280.00	Dutch Naval	PBC	75r 0814 1001 1749 1857
4281.00	Italian Naval	IDQ2	CW 1807 1937 2147 2207 (freq varies)
4282.00	Bourgas, Bulgaria	LZL2	CW 1910
4282.00	Mauritius	3BM2	CW 2310
4283.00	RSA Naval	ZSJ2	CW 1905 2045 2121 2150 2229 2316
4283.00	Tianjin, China	XSV	CW 2227
4284.00	Bahrain	A9M	CW 2100 2155 (to YQRK) 2148
4285.00	Halifax, Canada	VCS	CW 0648 0817 2314 wx 0130 0930 1530 2030 tfc list 0713
4285.00	Tallinn, Estonia	ESA	CW (listens 4185.5) 2203 2301
4286.00	Australian Naval	VHP	CW 0813 1855 1936 1944
4286.00	Portishead, UK	GKA2	CW wx 0930 1130 2130 tfc list 0000 1000 1400 1500 2100
4286.00	Sydney, Australia	VIX	CW 1741
4288.00	Boufarik, Algeria	7TF2	CW (with 7TAO) 2148
4290.00	Shanghai, China	XSG	CW 2057
4290.50	Ostend, Belgium	OST22	CW
4292.00	Rome, Italy	IAR24	CW 0650 2308 wx (Eng) 0805 1919 2046 (Ital) 1932 tfc list 1600
4294.00	Greek Naval	SXA34	CW 1920 2149 (also msrd 4296.0 & 4295.0)
4294.00	Slidell, USA	WNU	CW 0041 0805
4295.00	French Naval, Paris	HWN	CW 0738 2046 2145 2231 2302
4295.00	French Naval, Paris	HWN	75r RYs & SGs 0719
4296.00	Trieste, Italy	IQX	CW 0921 1746 1933 2054 2208 2308
4298.00	Olinda, Brazil	PPO	CW 0053 2124 2201 2232 2354
4298.00	Ostend, Belgium	OST2	CW
4302.00	Bahrain	A9M	CW 1756 1945 2047 2155 2231
4302.00	Single Letter Beacon	C	CW 2158 2216 2301
4303.00	Lyngby, Denmark	OXZ2	CW 0939 1504 1716 2143 2316 tfc list 1925 2126 2224
4307.00	British Naval	GYA	FAX wx maps 0621 0837 1006 1221 1732
4307.00	Murmansk, Russia	UMV	CW 1815
4308.00	Seoul, S Korea	HLG	CW tfc list 2215
4308.50	Norddeich, Germany	DAN	CW 1551 2212 2230 2316 2355
4308.50	Ras Tannurah, Saudi Arabia	HZY	CW 2356 tfc list 2000
4310.00	Slidell, USA	WNU41	CW 2310 2356
4313.00	Singapore	9VG33	CW 2218
4314.00	Varna, Bulgaria	LZW2	CW 1946 2210 2318 tfc list 1903 2108 2302
4314.50	Portishead, UK	GKH2	CW working frequency to ships 0719
4315.00	St Petersburg, Russia	UGC	CW (listens for wx 4201.0) 1935 wx 1600 tfc list 1833 1933
4315.00	St Petersburg, Russia	UGC	170/50rc 2218
4316.00	Portishead, UK	GKM2	CW reserve frequency
4317.00	Capetown. RSA	ZSC33	CW 2105 2214 2230
4317.50	Portishead, UK	GKI2	CW reserve frequency
4319.00	Gdynia, Poland	SPH23	CW
4320.00	Rome, Italy	IAR4	CW 0922 1802 1848 1926 2125 2202 2309 wx 0050
4323.00	Perth, Australia	VIP7	CW 2123 2244
4323.50	Constanza, Romania	YQI2	CW
4324.20	Single Letter Beacon	R	CW 0043 1936 2203
4325.70	Single Letter Beacon	R	CW 1608 2125 2231 2340
4326.50	Portishead, UK	GKJ2	CW reserve frequency
4328.00	St Lys, France	FFL2	CW 2312 wx 0814 1843 2211 tfc list 0835 1435 2235
4330.00	Archangel, Russia	UCE	CW 0726 1922 2229 tfc list 1810 2103
4331.00	Chatham, USA	WCC	CW 2314
4331.00	Israeli Naval	4XZ	CW 1757 2126 2242 wx (analysis) 1850 2205
4334.00	French Naval, Reunion	FUX	CW 2151 2250
4335.00	Riga, Latvia	UDH	CW 2112 tfc list 2033
4335.00	Riga, Latvia	UDH	170/50nc 2043 currency exchange rates 1945
4336.00	Portishead, UK	GKK2	CW reserve frequency

kHz.	Station	Call	Mode / Heard/Times GMT
4336.00	Prague Met, Czech Republic		50r 1717 1808
4337.00	Gdynia, Poland	SPH21	CW
4340.00	Guangzhou, China	XSQ	CW 2315
4343.00	Athens, Greece	SVA2	CW 1853 1947 2228 nav wng 1843 2306 tfc list 2200 wx 2118
4343.00	Mobile, USA	WLO	CW wx 0726
4343.00	Mobile, USA	WLO	SITOR Mode B wx 2344
4345.00	French Military, Toulon	FUO	CW 0658 0805 0827 1921
4346.00	Cerrito, Uruguay	CWA	CW 2205 2231
4346.00	Rijeka, Croatia	9AR	CW 1814 2135 2158 2228 tfc list 2007
4349.00	Valparaiso, Chile	CBV	CW 0729
4349.90	Norddeich, Germany	DAF	CW
4357.00	Coast stations ch 1 dup. 4065.0kHz		USB
4357.00	Goeteborg, Sweden	SAG	USB
4357.00	Istanbul, Turkey	TAN	USB (on request)
4357.00	Lyngby, Denmark	OXZ	USB 1825
4357.00	Norddeich, Germany	DAP	USB
4357.00	Riga, Latvia	UQK	USB 0714 0724
4359.00	UNID		50n 5 fig grps (time group is UTC + 1hr) 0944
4360.00	Coast stations ch 2 dup. 4068.0kHz		USB
4360.00	Gdynia, Poland	SPC23	USB
4360.00	Murmansk, Russia	UMV	USB 0813
4360.00	Portishead, UK	GKT22	USB (CW ID for GNI Niton heard on this channel)
4360.00	Numbers Station		AM "CIO2" 2251 "SYN2" Eng (female voice) 2335
4363.00	Coast stations ch 3 dup. 4071.0kHz		USB
4363.00	Pennsuco, USA	WOM	USB 2321 tfc list 2300 wx 2305
4363.00	Istanbul, Turkey	TAN	USB (on request)
4363.00	Monaco	3AC4	USB wx (Fr & Eng) 0803
4363.00	Rogaland, Norway	LGN	USB 2138 2258
4365.00	Tashkent Met	RPJ78	FAX wx maps 0024 1610 2129 2241
4366.00	Coast stations ch 4 dup. 4074.0kHz		USB
4366.00	Perth, Australia	VIP	USB
4366.00	St Lys, France	FFL	USB 0736 0923 1750 1815 2014 2210 2335 tfc list 0705
4366.00	Stettin, Poland	SPO21	USB 2226
4366.00	Townsville, Australia	VIT	USB
4369.00	Coast stations ch 5 dup. 4077.0kHz		USB
4369.00	Capetown, RSA	ZSC25	USB
4369.00	Klaipeda, Lithuania	LYK	USB 1857
4369.00	Mobile, USA	WLO	USB
4369.00	Scheveningen, Holland	PCG21	USB 2015 2333 tfc list 0706 1505 1706 2306
4369.00	Singapore	9VG60	USB
4369.00	St Lys, France	FFL	USB
4369.00	Sydney, Australia	VIS	USB
4372.00	Coast stations ch 6 dup. 4080.0kHz		USB
4372.00	Gdynia, Poland	SPC22	USB 2018
4372.00	Portishead, UK	GKT26	USB
4375.00	Coast stations ch 7 dup. 4083.0kHz		USB
4375.00	Rogaland, Norway	LGN	USB 0659 1816 1858 1922 2151
4375.00	Scheveningen, Holland	PCG24	USB
4378.00	Coast stations ch 8 dup. 4086.0kHz		USB
4378.00	Berne, Switzerland	HEB14	USB 2024 2239 tfc list 2115
4378.00	Genoa, Italy	ICB	USB
4378.00	Ostend, Belgium	OSU24	USB 1728
4378.00	Rijeka, Croatia	9AR	USB 1849 1856 2244
4378.00	Stettin, Poland	SPO22	USB 2019
4381.00	Coast stations ch 9 dup. 4089.0kHz		USB
4381.00	Genoa, Italy	ICB	USB 1858
4381.00	Rogaland, Norway	LGN	USB 0641 0759 1918 2016 2049 2356
4384.00	Coast stations ch 10 dup. 4092.0kHz		USB
4384.00	Haifa, Israel	4XO	USB 1857
4384.00	New York (Ocean Gate), USA	WOO	USB 2326 (with rig "Miss Milly") 0007
4384.00	Portishead, UK	GKT20	USB 1223 1729 (to "HMS Birmingham" GQEN) 2130 (to "QE2") 2205
4384.00	Scheveningen, Holland	PCG23	USB
4386.00	US Embassy traffic (rptd London)	KRH50	CW 2208 2223
4387.00	Coast stations ch 11 dup. 4095.0kHz		USB
4387.00	General Pacheco, Argentina	LPL	USB
4387.00	Istanbul, Turkey	TAN	USB (on request)
4387.00	Madrid, Spain	EHY	USB 0050
4387.00	New York (Ocean Gate), USA	WOO	USB 0801 2233 tfc list 0000 & 2 hrly wx 2201
4387.00	Ostend, Belgium	OSU21	USB 1534
4390.00	Coast stations ch 12 dup. 4098.0kHz		USB
4390.00	Kaliningrad, Russia	UIW	USB 0003 0831 1859 1928
4390.00	Norddeich, Germany	DAK	USB
4390.00	Pennsuco, USA	WOM	USB 0143 0739 2324
4390.00	Rome, Italy	IAR	USB
4390.00	Townsville, Australia	VIT	USB (on request)
4393.00	Coast stations ch 13 dup. 4101.0kHz		USB

kHz.	Station	Call	Mode / Heard/Times GMT
4393.00	Athens, Greece	SVN21	USB
4393.00	Helsinki, Finland	OJG2	USB 1632 1837 1910 tfc list 0855 1255 1855
4393.00	Lisbon, Portugal	CUL	USB 2151 tfc list 1900
4393.00	Luanda, Angola	D3E	USB
4393.00	Norddeich, Germany	DAH	USB
4395.00	Numbers Station		AM Ger (female voice) 0707 1506
4396.00	Coast stations ch 14 dup. 4104.0kHz		USB
4396.00	St Petersburg, Russia	UGC	USB
4396.00	Mobile, USA	WLO	USB
4396.00	Norddeich, Germany	DAJ	USB 0005 1735 2047
4399.00	Coast stations ch 15 dup. 4107.0kHz		USB
4399.00	Athens, Greece	SVN22	USB 1939 2253 2328
4399.00	Brisbane, Australia	VIB	USB
4399.00	Lyngby, Denmark	OXZ	USB
4402.00	Coast stations ch 16 dup. 4110.0kHz		USB
4402.00	St Lys, France	FFL	USB 2008
4405.00	Coast stations ch 17 dup. 4113.0kHz		USB
4405.00	Bar, Montenegro	YUW	USB 1857 2236
4405.00	Pennsuco, USA	WOM	USB 2238 2303
4405.00	Helsinki, Finland	OHG	USB 1848 2134
4405.00	Istanbul, Turkey	TAN	USB 2228
4405.00	Sydney, Australia	VIS	USB
4405.00	UK Coast Control		USB 0645
4408.00	Coast stations ch 18 dup. 4116.0kHz		USB
4408.00	Halifax, Canada	VCS	USB wx 0812 2207 ice wng 2338 tfc list 2135
4408.00	Lyngby, Denmark	OXZ	USB 0736 2234 2244 tfc list odd hours + 05 (1905-0705)
4411.00	Coast stations ch 19 dup. 4119.0kHz		USB
4411.00	Mobile, USA	WLO	USB
4411.00	Scheveningen, Holland	PCG22	USB
4411.00	St Lys, France	FFL	USB
4414.00	Coast stations ch 20 dup. 4122.0kHz		USB
4414.00	Goeteborg, Sweden	SAG	USB tfc list 1800
4414.00	Istanbul, Turkey	TAN	USB 2311
4417.00	Coast stations ch 21 dup. 4125.0kHz		USB common calling ch
4417.00	Capetown, RSA	ZSC53	USB
4417.00	Luanda, Angola	D3E	USB
4417.00	Ostend, Belgium	OSU26	USB
4417.00	Rome, Italy	IAR	USB 2200
4417.00	Scheveningen, Holland	PCG20	USB
4420.00	Coast stations ch 22 dup. 4128.0kHz		USB
4420.00	Berne, Switzerland	HEB34	USB
4420.00	Klaipeda Harbour, Lithuania	LYL	USB
4420.00	New York (Ocean Gate), USA	WOO	USB 0637
4420.00	Ostend, Belgium	OSU22	USB 2009
4420.00	Tallinn, Estonia	ESA	USB 1556 2240
4420.00	UK Coast Control		USB "GA" 0624 "GM" 1800 (to "Ship 22") 1552
4423.00	Coast stations ch 23 dup. 4131.0kHz		USB
4423.00	Gdynia, Poland	SPC21	USB
4423.00	Norddeich, Germany	DAI	USB
4423.00	Pennsuco, USA	WOM	USB 0020 2238 2300 2355
4423.00	Rome, Italy	IAR	USB
4426.00	Coast stations ch 24 dup. 4134.0kHz		USB
4426.00	Athens, Greece	SVN24	USB 2129
4426.00	Berne, Switzerland	HEB24	USB (with UPZX) 2025
4426.00	Goeteborg, Sweden	SAG	USB
4426.00	Lyngby, Denmark	OXZ	USB
4426.00	Perth, Australia	VIP	USB
4426.00	Sydney, Australia	VIS	USB wx 0333
4429.00	Coast stations ch 25 dup. 4137.0kHz		USB wx
4429.00	Athens, Greece	SVN25	USB
4429.00	Lyngby, Denmark	OXZ	USB
4429.00	Ostend, Belgium	OSU23	USB 0813
4432.00	Coast stations ch 26 dup. 4140.0kHz		USB
4432.00	Portishead, UK	GKV26	USB 2131
4432.00	Rogaland, Norway	LGN21	USB 1831 2134 2236
4435.00	Coast stations ch 27 dup. 4143.0kHz		USB
4437.90	Spa Publications		

4438-4650
FIXED/LAND & MARITIME & AERONAUTICAL MOBILE

kHz.	Station	Call	Mode / Heard/Times GMT
4442.50	Kiev Met, Ukraine		50r 0010 1904 1930 2154 2218
4443.00	UNID		96ARQ/E/8 Idle 0819 1720
4445.00	French Military	FAL21	USB (to FAL20) 0734
4445.00	Khabarovsk Met, Russia		50n 2135

kHz.	Station	Call	Mode / Heard/Times GMT
4450.00	Intership working		USB Scand 0708
4460.00	Numbers Station		AM Eng (female voice) 2203
4460.00	PBS China		AM Chinese 2225
4461.00	Numbers Station		USB phonetics (female voice) 2222
4463.00	Numbers Station		USB Eng (female voice) 1910 2133 2242 2316
4465.00	R Svoboda feeder		USB Slav (poss Romanian) 1931
4485.00	R Petropavlovsk		AM Slav 1611 1738 1943 2321
4489.00	Bracknell Met, UK	GFL26	50r 0721 0934 1342 1721 1810 2050 2132 2329
4500.00	PBS China		AM Chinese 2202 2318 English lessons 2245 (freq varies)
4525.00	Kiev Met, Ukraine		FAX wx maps 1905 2146 2246
4534.00	Swedish Military	HIA	50r nav wng 1621
4538.00	Numbers Station		AM Eng (female voice) 1906
4538.00	UNID		100ARQ/E3/8 Idle 0840 1624 1753
4542.50	French Military, Orleans	FDY	50r "Voyez le Brick.." 0944
4543.00	Numbers Station		AM Ger (female voice) 2241
4543.00	UNID	MHTO	CW (clg "S74R") 0742
4547.00	Italian Naval	IDR	USB radio check with "3MZ" 2228
4548.00	Swedish Military	HIA	170/50r 5 let grps 1723 2129
4550.00	Moscow Met, Russia	RWW79	FAX wx maps 1955 2234 (also noted on 4560.0)
4560.00	Numbers Station		AM phonetic letters (female voice) 1911 2149 2245
4570.00	Jeddah Met	HZN	100n 0012 1900 1919 2247 2307
4570.10	Grengel Met, Germany	DHJ51	FAX wx maps 0839 1225 1605
4575.00	Samara Met, Russia		FAX wx maps 1625
4583.00	British Military		USB road convoy route directions (S England) 1608
4583.00	Hamburg (Quickborn) Met, Germany	DDK	50r 0935 1739 1811 1859 2051 2127
4594.00	Numbers Station		AM Ger (female voice) 1945
4595.50	French Military	FDE	CW 0738 1830 2148
4601.50	Irish Naval	OA	SITOR 1626 (with "12") 0936 ("57" & "46") & Selcal XSFC 0741
4604.00	Single Letter Beacon	P	CW 1507
4610.00	Bracknell Met, UK	GFA	FAX wx maps 1344 1801 1907
4615.00	R Baghdad		AM Arab 2000 2312 (under jamming and varies frequency)
4623.00	US Naval, Spain	AOK	FAX wx maps 2247
4632.50	INTERPOL	FSB	SITOR 0013 1921 2126 2224
4633.00	British Military		USB "40B" radio check call 2301
4645.00	Tallinn VOLMET, Estonia		USB Eng 0646 0724 1628 1958
4649.90	Spa Publications		

4650-4700
AERONAUTICAL MOBILE (MAINLY CIVIL) 3KHz channels

kHz.	Station	Call	Mode / Heard/Times GMT
4654.00	Berne (in-flight R/T service)		USB (link call to Angola) 2250
4663.00	CIS VOLMET channel		USB (in Eng) 2211 2243
4665.00	Numbers Station		AM "VLB2" (female voice) 1946 2248
4666.00	Cent W Pacific Air traffic CWP 1/2		USB
4669.00	Middle East Air traffic MID 1/3		USB
4669.00	S America Air traffic SAM		USB
4675.00	N Atlantic Air traffic NAT D		USB
4675.00	Bodo ATC, Norway	ENBO	USB
4675.00	Gander ATC, Canada	CZQX	USB 0907 2123 2315
4675.00	Reykjavik ATC, Iceland	BIRD	USB 1619 1742
4675.00	Shanwick ATC, UK/Eire	EGXX	USB 1144 1335 1609 1741
4687.00	UNID		USB "UE" (clg Frankfurt, in English) 0626
4690.00	Intership working		USB Scottish 0710
4699.90	Spa Publications		

4700-4750
AERONAUTICAL MOBILE (MAINLY MILITARY) 3KHz channels

kHz.	Station	Call	Mode / Heard/Times GMT
4707.00	RAF Buchan, Scotland		USB interception position msg to "E6F" 1727
4707.00	RAF Neatishead, UK		USB (with "9IB") 1226 (with "R7F") 2218
4710.00	UNID		LSB CB style (Ital) 2232
4711.00	UN marine monitoring (Adriatic)		USB "5JB"/"8KM" 2232 "9UW" 2328
4712.00	CIS Air traffic		USB 1629 1852 2213
4722.00	RAF VOLMET, UK	MVU	USB 0001 0700 0938 1657 1813 2055 2248 2330
4725.00	USAF Incirlik, Turkey		USB 0047 2243
4725.00	USAF McClellan AFB		USB
4730.00	RAF Akrotiri, Cyprus		USB "CYPRUS FLIGHT WATCH" (LCRO) test 2211 wx 2016
4731.00	RAF Pitreavie, Scotland	MKL	CW wx 0703 1003 1601 1705 2002 2207 2303
4735.00	PBS China		AM Chinese 1614 2340
4740.00	Numbers Station		AM "32264" Eng (female voice) 2131
4740.00	R Dushanbe		AM Slav 1610 1947 2329
4742.00	RAF Ascension Island		USB "TURTLE" (2000-0800)
4742.00	RAF Falkland Isles		USB "VIPER"

kHz.	Station	Call	Mode / Heard/Times GMT
4742.00	RAF Gibraltar		USB
4742.00	RAF, UK		USB "ARCHITECT" 0002 0725 0856 0939 1615 1729 2213
4747.00	Intership working		USB Scottish 0701
4749.90	Spa Publications		

4650-4995
FIXED/AERONAUTICAL & LAND MOBILE
BROADCASTING
AERONAUTICAL (4750-4850)

kHz.	Station	Call	Mode / Heard/Times GMT
4750.00	PBS China		AM 2305
4757.00	USAF weather service		FAX wx maps 0030 0724
4758.00	US Military		USB "76" (clg "DSN26") 2316
4760.00	PBS China		AM 2248 2308 2359
4760.00	ELWA, Liberia		AM Eng 2201
4763.00	UN marine monitoring (Adriatic)		USB "U8P"/"3JZ"/"6ZE" 1006 "W6K"/"6WJ" 1604 "XAJ2" 1612
4765.00	R Brazzaville		AM Fr 1904 1920 2152 2208
4770.00	R Nigeria		AM Eng 2004 2132 2154 2212 2250 (0530-2300)
4777.50	Rome Met, Italy	IMB51	FAX wx maps 1903 2010 2341
4780.00	Numbers Station		AM "KPA2" (female voice) 2229
4782.00	Bracknell Met, UK	GFE21	FAX wx maps 0702 1509 1730 1814 2119
4783.00	RTM Bamako, Mali		AM Fr 2234 2310
4785.50	Grengel Met, Germany	DHJ51	100n 0843 1007 1613 1835
4788.00	Dakar Met, Senegal	6VU	50n 1913 2214 2233
4790.50	Dakar Met, Senegal	6VU23	FAX wx maps
4790.50	R Kashmir		AM Asian lang 1755
4795.00	R Cameroon		AM Fr 2148 2204 2220
4795.00	R Moscow		AM Eng 2135 2249 2301 2310 Slav 1640
4800.00	PBS China		AM Chinese 0015 2311 2342
4800.00	R Lesotho		AM 2213
4805.00	R Nac Amazonas, Brazil		AM Portuguese 0003 2223 2326
4807.00	Portishead (in-flight R/T service)		USB (with "Kestrel 128") 2123
4808.00	UNID		72ARQ/E/4 0701
4810.00	R Yerevan		AM Slav 1836 1921 2009 2251
4813.00	Sofia Met, Bulgaria	LZA	50n 1802 1835 1905 2057
4815.00	RTV Burkina Faso		AM Fr 2201
4815.00	UNID		AM Slav 2300
4820.00	R Moscow		AM Slav 1837 1903 2327
4820.50	British Military training net		USB "V10" 1632
4821.00	Numbers Station		AM Ger (female voice) 2206 2246
4825.00	R Ukraine International		AM Eng 2229 2252 Slav 0650 2214 Ger 0001
4830.00	R Botswana		AM Eng 2116 2318
4830.00	R Tachira, Venezuela		AM Span 2236 2306
4832.00	Numbers Station		AM Ger (female voice) 2227
4835.00	RTM Bamako, Mali		AM Fr 1929 2006 2250
4837.50	INTERPOL	FSB	SITOR 0940 1642 2112 2217
4845.00	R Nouakchott, Mauretania		AM Fr 1924 Arab 2032 2215 2245 2312
4850.00	R Tashkent		AM Slav 1839 1905 2139 2234
4850.00	R Yaounde, Cameroon		AM Fr 2202 2234
4857.00	UNID		CW 5 let grps (not Eng morse) 2111
4860.00	R Moscow		AM Eng 2133 2253 2314 Ger 2007 Slav 1906
4861.00	NATO exercise		USB British & German "1SH"/"G6M"/9QY" radio checks & msgs 0704 0819
4865.00	R Cinaruco, Colombia		AM Span 0534 0704 2327
4865.00	PBS China		AM Chinese 0017 2203 2342
4870.00	R Cotonou, Benin		AM Fr 1923 2226
4873.00	US Naval, Turkey	YMB	USB radio check with USN Naples 0003
4880.00	Numbers Station		AM "VLX2" (female voice) 2134 2214 "ULX" 2330
4885.00	R Belem, Brazil		AM Port 2141 2216
4885.00	R Kenya		AM Swahili 1840
4885.00	UNID		72ARQ/E/4 Idle 1936
4890.00	RTV Senegal		AM Fr 2227
4893.00	British Military		USB radio check "V31" 1733
4895.00	R Manaus, Brazil		AM Portuguese 0004 2256
4896.00	French Military		USB 0901
4900.00	Czech Embassy traffic		100n Slav p/lang 0845
4904.50	R Chad		AM Fr 1841 1912 2222
4910.00	R Zambia		AM Eng 1834
4910.00	US Embassy frequency (rptd Athens)	KWS78	CW 1907 2000 2119 2223
4915.00	R Accra, Ghana		AM Eng 0741 0818 1925 2008 2207 2230 2259
4915.00	UNID		AM Span 0814
4923.00	British Military	GXQ	50n(VFT) QBF & RYIs 1345 2327 (LSB 4926.0)
4925.50	French Military, Metz	FDC	CW 0703 1708 1913 2106 2235
4925.80	R Nacional, Equatorial Guinea		AM Span 2328
4930.00	R Moscow		AM Slav 1842 1950 2217

kHz.	Station	Call	Mode / Heard/Times GMT
4930.50	UN marine monitoring (Adriatic)		USB "4YR"/"K8S" 2210
4930.50	Warsaw, Poland	SPW	SITOR (dup. 4207.0) 2052 2156
4932.00	Warsaw, Poland	SPW	USB 2142 2239
4935.00	R Kenya		AM Eng 1819 1926
4940.00	R Moscow		AM Eng 2330 Slav 1745 1843
4940.50	British Military		USB "Q3" radio check 0707
4945.00	UNID		100ARQ/E3/8 Idle 1634
4955.00	British Military training net		CW 0903
4955.00	R Belem		AM Portuguese 2258
4957.50	R Baku		AM Slav 1844 1927 2012
4971.60	German Govt net		72ARQ/E/4 0947 1930
4972.50	German Govt net		96ARQ/E/8 1637
4975.00	PBS China		AM Chinese 2213
4975.00	R Moscow		AM Eng 1617
4976.00	R Kampala		AM Eng 2025
4980.00	R Ecos del Torbes, Venezuela		AM Span 0005 2227 2259 2320
4985.00	R Brazil Central		AM Portuguese 0006 2204
4990.00	R Nigeria		AM Eng 1931 2112 2231 2300
4993.50	Irish Naval	OA	SITOR (to "12" and "37") 0903
4996.00	Moscow Time Signal station	RWM	CW 1639 1747 1845 2013 2140 2240
4999.90	Spa Publications		

5000-5005
STANDARD FREQUENCY/TIME SIGNALS

kHz.	Station	Call	Mode / Heard/Times GMT
5000.00	Buenos Aires Time Station, Argentina	LOL	CW 2300
5000.00	Caracas Time Station, Venezuela	YVTO	USB 2120 2250
5000.00	Xian Time Station, China	BPM	CW 2300
5000.00	Fort Collins Time Station, USA	WWV	CW/USB 0706
5000.00	Rome Time Station, Italy	IAM	CW ID 0736
5000.00	Tashkent Time Station, Uzbekistan	RCH	CW 2132
5003.70	R Nacional, Equatorial Guinea		AM Span 2137 2146
5004.90	Spa Publications		

5005-5060
FIXED

BROADCASTING

kHz.	Station	Call	Mode / Heard/Times GMT
5008.50	French Military	FDE	CW 0724
5010.00	French Military	FDC	CW 0834
5010.00	R Cameroon		AM Fr 2148
5010.00	SBC Radio One, Singapore		AM Eng 1450
5015.00	Numbers Station		AM Ger (female voice) 1907 2242 "EL" 1932
5015.00	R Asgabat, Turkmenistan		AM Slav 2250
5020.00	Moscow Met, Russia	RWW74	50r 1434 1646 1712 1814 1847 1920 2053 2234 (freq varies)
5020.00	R Niamey, Niger		AM Fr 2237
5021.00	PBS China		AM 2240 2315
5024.00	German Police		96ARQ/E/8 1647
5025.00	RAF Akrotiri, Cyprus	MKD	50r (VFT) QBF & RYIs 1840 (LSB ch 5028.0)
5025.00	R Benin		AM Fr 2150
5026.00	R Kampala, Uganda		AM African lang 2038
5030.00	R Continente, Venezuela		AM Span 2141
5033.00	French Military		CW 1559
5034.90	R Bangui		AM Fr 0836 1815 2151
5035.00	R Almaty, Kazakhstan		AM Eng 1935 Slav 1618 1834
5040.00	R Ala, Russia		AM Slav 1538 1841 2055 2230
5045.00	R Cultura do Para, Brazil		AM Port 2251
5047.00	R Lome, Togo		AM Fr 0002 1750 1915 2152 2213 2308
5049.10	UNID	CSP	SITOR Mode B msgs in Portuguese from "COMGERPSP" 1649 1840
5050.00	R Tanzania		AM Eng 1810
5052.00	SBC Radio One, Singapore		AM 1619 2247
5055.00	Amman Press (PETRA)	JYF	50n Eng 1714 Arab 1654
5055.00	R Guyane, Fr Guiana		AM Fr 0536 2154 2205
5058.50	UNID		50r "de DV47/1AG1/1AG2/1AG5" & RYs 0628
5059.90	Spa Publications		

5060-5250
FIXED/LAND & MARITIME MOBILE

kHz.	Station	Call	Mode / Heard/Times GMT
5064.00	Georgetown Naval, Malaysia	9MB	CW 1836 1937 2155 2216 2248
5070.00	Czech Embassy traffic		100n p/lang 0847 0906 1538
5075.00	R Bogota, Colombia		AM Span 0632 0647 0833 2236 2258 2309
5083.00	Grengel Met, Germany		100n 0848 1540 1819
5091.00	Numbers Station		AM "JSR"/"JSR2" phonetics (fem voice) 1730 1807 1837 1930 2238
5100.00	Canberra Met, Australia	AXM32	FAX wx maps 1718 1854
5111.00	Single Letter Beacon	P	CW 0633
5112.00	Belgrade Press (TANJUG)	4OC3	75r Slav 0830 1716 1849
5117.00	RAF Akrotiri, Cyprus	MKD	50r (VFT) QBF & RYls 1923 2249 (LSB ch 5120.0)
5123.00	UNPROFOR, Bosnia		USB (British units) 1920
5125.00	Numbers Station		USB Ger 2254
5125.00	R Svoboda feeder		LSB Slav 2243
5140.00	Moscow Met, Russia	RWW73	50r 1436 1539 1718 1839 2013
5145.00	R China International		AM Slav 1518
5145.00	UNID		100ARQ/E3/8 Idle 0849 1850
5150.00	Moscow Met, Russia	RVO73	FAX wx maps 0834 1600 1808 1855 1927 2252
5151.50	UN traffic		SITOR (in Eng) 1852
5156.00	UNID		75n 5 let grps (long msg) 1909
5171.70	UNID		192ARQ/E3/8 Idle 1519
5174.00	CIS Naval	RMMV	CW 1918 2156
5178.00	British Military		USB test on ch 39 requesting mode for tx on channel 75 2200
5180.00	US Military		USB "KC" & "KD" radio checks 2231
5190.00	China Met		50n 1627 1851 1924
5202.00	UNID		USB simplex R/T ("TROIKA" & one other) 2251
5203.00	UNID		100ARQ/E3/8 Idle
5205.00	Numbers Station		AM Eng (female voice) 0634
5208.00	INTERPOL	FSB	SITOR 1855 2253 Selcal IPEP 0649 IPUX 2058
5210.00	Novosibirsk Met, Russia	ROF75	FAX wx maps 1837 1929
5210.00	UNID		100ARQ/E3/8 Idle 1719 1820 1902
5211.00	French Military		USB simplex R/T 0908
5212.00	Intership working		USB Scottish 1853
5220.00	Cairo Press (MENA)	SUA	75r Arab 1822 1842 1919 1930
5223.00	UNID		72ARQ/E/4 Idle 1618
5233.50	USAF weather service		75n 0651 1628 1809
5237.00	USAF weather service		FAX wx maps 0750 0949 1753 2240
5240.00	Belgrade Press (TANJUG)	4OC2	50r Eng 1643 1823 1901 2059 2150 2252 2302
5240.00	PBS China		AM 2242
5245.00	British Military cadet training net	MRQ55	USB with MRO44/MRC16/MRC01 1110
5249.90	Spa Publications		

5250-5450
FIXED/MARITIME & LAND MOBILE

kHz.	Station	Call	Mode / Heard/Times GMT
5260.00	R Almaty, Kazakhstan		AM Eng 1938 Slav 1619 1844 1931
5263.00	INTERPOL, Zurich	HEP	CW 1824 1855
5266.80	UNID		192ARQ/E3/8 Idle 0832 1521 1821
5269.00	Grengel Met, Germany	DHJ	100r 0635 0652 0835 1000 1308 1541 1631
5271.00	INTERPOL, Zurich	HEP	CW 2303
5272.00	UNID	2E2P	CW (clg "HZ3M") 1523
5275.00	Cairo Press (MENA)		75r Eng 1839 1857 Fr 1734 1825 1922
5275.00	WYFR, Taiwan		AM Chinese 1524
5280.00	Irkutsk Met, Russia	RKR76	FAX wx maps 1632 1858 1932
5282.00	Stockholm (in-flight R/T service)		USB with Condor "UE" 2314
5285.00	Tashkent Met, Uzbekistan	RBX71	FAX wx maps 0836 1644 1903 2245
5290.00	R Krasnoyarsk, Russia		AM Slav 0838 2101 2241 2303
5290.00	UNID		100ARQ/E3/8 Idle 1310 2152
5292.00	UNID		75n 5 let grps (long msg) 1856
5299.50	British Naval	MTO	75r ch test tape 1722
5301.00	Numbers Station		AM Slav (female voice) 1904 2102
5301.00	UNID		CW 5 fig grps 1810
5302.00	Prague, Czech Republic	OLX	CW 1658 1859 (& 5301.0 at 1756)
5305.80	Single Letter Beacon	S	CW 1723 1858 2153 2246
5306.00	Single Letter Beacon	C	CW 1840 1905 1932
5310.00	UN marine monitoring (Adriatic)		USB "MB"/"R5I" 2248 "6UD" 2251 "K4K" 2253 "J8G" 2301
5312.00	Serbian Embassy traffic	DFZG	75n Eng press reviews (TANJUG) 1528
5315.00	Numbers Station		AM Ger (female voice) 1900
5321.50	Spanish Police		SITOR p/lang 1758 1846
5325.00	Moscow Met, Russia	RND77	FAX wx maps 1659 1724 1933 2255 2304
5331.50	Intership working		USB Scottish 1311
5335.00	Tbilisi Met, Georgia	RDM78	50n 1529 1824 1847 2154 2247
5341.30	UNID		50n Spanish (possibly police or military) 1833 1902
5342.00	French Military, Orleans	FDY	CW 0910 1626 1700 1829
5342.00	French Military, Orleans	FDY	50r "Voyez le Brick.." 2200

kHz.	Station	Call	Mode / Heard/Times GMT
5345.00	Archangel Met, Russia	RSW71	50n 1439 1530 1825 2103 & msrd 5344.0
5347.00	Archangel Met, Russia	RSW71	FAX wx maps 2247
5355.00	Moscow Met, Russia	RND77	FAX wx maps 1621 1841 1934
5356.00	Intership working		USB Scottish 0751
5365.00	French Military		CW p/lang 0754 0839
5376.50	Ostend, Belgium	OST23	SITOR Mode B tfc list 1907 2105 (each hr + 05 mins)
5381.50	Spanish Police		SITOR 1629 1902 (msg from RETWLG) 1028 Selcal TWLA 1759
5385.00	US Military		USB exercise net 2307
5397.00	French Military	FDE	CW p/lang 1314
5397.50	French Military	RFFP	200ARQ/M2/4 ch B airnav msgs 1844 1928 5 let grps 1701
5400.00	Bucharest Met, Romania	YOG37	50r 1532 1725
5406.00	RAF London	MKK	50r (VFT) QBF & RYls 1935 (LSB 5409.0)
5421.00	UNID	T2XO	CW (clg IPLA) 1851
5422.50	UNID		CW(FSK) 5 fig grps 1441 2248
5426.00	US Embassy frequency (rptd London)	KRH50	CW 0642 0837 1030 1533 1622 1826 2201 2308
5430.00	Tashkent Met, Uzbekistan	RVM45	50n 1842 2158
5430.00	UNID		USB Slav R/T 2309
5437.00	Numbers Station		AM Eng (female voice) 1937 2106 2244 "ART2" 1702 2202
5440.00	Numbers Station		USB Ger (female voice) 2128
5440.00	PBS China		AM Chinese 0134 1630
5449.90	Spa Publications		

5450-5480
FIXED/AERONAUTICAL & LAND MOBILE

kHz.	Station	Call	Mode / Heard/Times GMT
5456.70	UNID		192ARQ/E3/8 Idle 1031 1914
5462.00	RAF Buchan, Scotland		USB with "8BV" & "5ID" 2311
5465.00	Intership working		USB Scottish 1840
5472.00	Beacon, Sveio, Norway	LN2A	CW propagation tests 0913 1929
5472.00	UK Coastguard		USB "COSMOS 4" 0756
5474.00	Santa Maria Air, Azores	CSY	50r ID & RYs 2259
5476.40	UNID		96ARQ/E/8 Idle 1032 1638 1842
5479.90	Spa Publications		

5480-5680
AERONAUTICAL MOBILE (MAINLY CIVIL) 3KHz channels

kHz.	Station	Call	Mode / Heard/Times GMT
5485.00	UNID		LSB CB style (Eng) 1933
5493.00	Africa Air traffic AFI 4		USB
5499.00	Brazzaville VOLMET	FCCC	USB Fr 2129 2249
5500.00	UNID		USB Portuguese simplex R/T (probably fishing vessels) 1843
5505.00	Shannon VOLMET, Eire	EINN	USB 0621 0838 1032 1340 1623 1939 2107 2310
5510.00	UNID		AM Fr 1639
5520.00	Caribbean Air traffic CAR B		USB
5520.00	New York ATC, USA	KZNY	USB 0622 0641 2235
5526.00	S America Air traffic SAM		USB
5526.00	Belem ATC, Brazil	SBBL	USB
5526.00	Manaus ATC, Brazil	SBMU	USB 0643 (with American 905) 0623
5526.00	Paramaribo ATC, Surinam	MEPM	USB 0735
5526.00	Piarco ATC, Trinidad	MKPP	USB 0729
5526.00	Porto Velho ATC, Brazil	SBPH	USB 0731 (with American 900) 0621
5526.90	Beijing Met, China	BAF6	FAX wx maps 2144 2218 2311
5532.00	KLM Company frequency		USB 0733 (with KLM 616) 0624
5532.00	Prague Company frequency		USB 0728 1640 2130 2227 2247
5535.00	British Airways Company frequency		USB 0645 0810
5535.00	Lima (in-flight R/T service)		USB 0746
5538.00	Gulf Air company frequency		USB 2120 2154 "Falcon Bahrain" 2306
5539.00	Intership working		USB (Irish fishing boats) 0633 1641
5541.00	Stockholm (in-flight R/T service)		USB 0729 1940 2121 2234 2314
5544.00	Saudi Airline Company frequency		USB 1804
5547.00	Central E Pacific Air traffic CEP 1/2		USB
5547.00	San Francisco ATC, USA	KSFO	USB
5550.00	Caribbean Air traffic CAR A		USB
5550.00	New York ATC, USA	KZNY	USB 0707 0732 0833 2220
5555.00	Intership working		USB Scand 0731 Scottish 2123
5562.00	Miami, USA	KJY74	USB (Hurricane hunters) 0700
5565.00	S Atlantic Air traffic SAT 2		USB
5565.00	Sal ATC, Cape Verde	GVSC	USB wx (in Portuguese) 0736
5567.00	Intership working		USB Scottish 0824
5568.00	LIAT air company frequency		USB 2250
5568.00	UNID		USB Russian air tfc 1833
5572.00	Intership working		USB Scottish 0810

kHz.	Station	Call	Mode / Heard/Times GMT
5574.00	Central E Pacific Air traffic CEP 1/2		USB
5598.00	N Atlantic Air traffic NAT A		USB
5598.00	Canaries ATC	GCCC	USB
5598.00	Gander ATC, Canada	CZQX	USB 0537 0644 0657 0740 0838 2127 2235
5598.00	New York ATC, USA	KZNY	USB 0608 0633 0701 0745 2317 2333
5598.00	Santa Maria ATC, Azores	LPAZ	USB 0643 0655 0724 2141 2250
5598.00	Shanwick ATC, UK/Eire	EGGX	USB 0645 0714 1033 2237 "HMS Newcastle" with radio check 0604
5601.00	Bombay ATC, India	VABB	USB 1845 2155 2318
5601.00	Karachi ATC, Pakistan	OPKR	USB 2215
5604.00	St John's (in-flight R/T service)		USB "Rainbow Radio" 0634
5610.00	Portishead (in-flight R/T service)	GKX	USB 0540 0656 (with VRCAR) 1548 (with Shamrock 4953) 2202
5616.00	N Atlantic Air traffic NAT B		USB
5616.00	Gander ATC, Canada	CZQX	USB 0627 0712 2147 2231 2310
5616.00	Reykjavik ATC, Iceland	BIRD	USB 0834 1341 2229
5616.00	Shanwick ATC, UK/Eire	EGGX	USB 0628 0701 1035 1142 1229 1408 1705 2121
5628.00	N Pacific Air traffic NP		USB
5628.00	Honolulu ATC	PHZH	USB 0745
5629.00	Numbers Station		AM Eng (female voice) "SYN6" 1830 "CIO2" 2148 "SYN2" 2232
5634.00	Indian Ocean Air traffic INO 1		USB
5634.00	Mauritius ATC	FIMM	USB 1729
5643.00	S Pacific Air traffic SP		USB
5643.00	Auckland ATC, N Zealand	NZZA	USB 1907
5643.00	Honolulu ATC, Hawaii	PHZH	USB
5643.00	Sydney ATC, Australia	ASSY	USB
5645.00	Dutch maritime pilotage service		USB (helicopter/ship frequency)
5646.00	N Central Asia Air traffic NCA 1		USB
5649.00	N Atlantic Air traffic NAT C		USB
5649.00	Gander ATC, Canada	CZQX	USB 0151 0628 0636 0709 0842 2212 2231
5649.00	Reykjavik ATC, Iceland	BIRD	USB 0651 0834
5649.00	Shanwick ATC, UK/Eire	EGGX	USB 0628 0715 0839 1341 1727 1853 2219
5649.00	E & S E Asia Air traffic EA 2 SEA 1		USB
5652.00	Africa Air traffic AFI 2		USB
5652.00	Algiers ATC	DAAA	USB 2103
5652.00	Niamey ATC, Niger	DRRR	USB 2334
5655.00	E & S E Asia Air traffic EA 2 SEA 1		USB
5655.00	Hong Kong ATC	VHHK	USB 1936
5658.00	Africa & M East Air traffic AFI 3 MID 2		USB
5658.00	Addis Ababa ATC, Ethiopia	HAAA	USB 2153 2246 2318
5658.00	Asmara, Ethiopia	HAAS	USB 2203
5658.00	Bombay ATC, India	VABF	USB 1733 1841 2127 2207 2303
5658.00	Cairo ATC, Egypt	HECA	USB 2334 (clg Khartoum) 2216
5658.00	Delhi ATC, India	VIDF	USB 1854 2218
5658.00	Kabul ATC, Afghanistan	OAKX	USB 2149 2223
5658.00	Karachi ATC, Pakistan	OPKR	USB 1622 1845 1928 2124 2233
5658.00	Khartoum ATC, Sudan	HSSS	USB 2155 2231 2250
5658.00	Lahore ATC, Pakistan	OPLR	USB 1745
5658.00	Mogadishu ATC, Somalia	HCMM	USB 1808
5658.00	Nairobi ATC, Kenya	HKNA	USB 2304
5658.00	Tehran ATC, Iran	OIIX	USB 2221
5658.00	Tripoli ATC, Libya	HLLL	USB 2040 2251 2308
5660.00	Intership working		USB Eng (West Indian accents) 0648
5661.00	Europe Air traffic EUR A		USB
5661.00	Malta (in-flight R/T service)		USB 0152 1853 2145
5664.00	N Central Asia Air traffic NCA 3		USB
5667.00	M East Air traffic		USB
5670.00	China Air traffic		USB 2254 2320
5679.90	Spa Publications		

5680-5730
AERONAUTICAL MOBILE (MAINLY MILITARY) 3KHz channels

kHz.	Station	Call	Mode / Heard/Times GMT
5680.00	INTERNATIONAL CALLING & DISTRESS		USB
5680.00	Aberdeen Coastguard, Scotland		USB
5680.00	Edinburgh RCC, Scotland		USB 1715 2110
5680.00	Flensburg Rescue, Germany		USB (with DRFJ) 0923
5680.00	Plymouth RCC, UK		USB (with "Rescue 172") 0637 (with "Rescue 194") 0915
5680.00	RAF Uxbridge		USB (with Plymouth Rescue) 0826
5680.00	Stockholm Rescue, Sweden		USB 0859 0957 (with "Rescue 240") 0841
5682.00	French Air Force		USB 2119
5685.00	Italian Air Force		USB 2208
5687.00	German Air Force		USB 0730 0735 0806
5690.00	Canadian Military		USB wx 2220 2316
5691.00	German Air Force		USB 2150
5695.00	Edinburgh MRCC, Scotland		USB (with "SRG137") 1000

kHz.	Station	Call	Mode / Heard/Times GMT
5695.20	Spanish Police		SITOR 0657
5696.00	Jamaican Coastguard	6YX	USB
5696.00	Boston CG, USA	NMF	USB "COMSTA BOSTON" 2238 (with "Rescue 6018") 2218
5696.00	Culdrose Naval Air Station, UK		USB with "I1I"/"J73"/"Navy821" 0957
5696.00	Kodiak CG, Alaska	NOJ	USB
5696.00	Miami CG, USA	NOM	USB "COMSTA MIAMI" 0800 2224 (with "Rescue 1406" 2328)
5696.00	Mobile CG, USA	NOQ	USB
5696.00	Chesapeake CG, USA	NMN	USB "COMSTA PORTSMOUTH" (with "Rescue 6019") 0647 ("1711") 2311
5696.00	San Juan CG, Costa Rica		USB 2312
5696.00	Chesapeake CG, USA		USB "CAMSLANT CHESAPEAKE" (working "1710") 2330
5696.00	UNID		USB Fr wx forecasts "Meteo de Corse" 0758
5708.00	Danish Naval	OVG	CW 1858
5711.00	French Air Force		USB 1810 flight plan 0705
5713.00	RAF, UK		USB "ARCHITECT" 0629 0703 0831 1402
5715.00	CIS VOLMET channel		USB 2236
5715.00	Numbers Station		AM "ZLW1" (female voice) 2306
5718.00	Canadian Military		USB with "Rescue 306" 0651
5723.00	French Air Force		USB 0708 0845
5725.00	French Air Force		USB 0837
5729.90	Spa Publications		

5730-5950
FIXED/LAND & MARITIME MOBILE

kHz.	Station	Call	Mode / Heard/Times GMT
5730.00	French Military, Metz	FDC	CW 0627 1859 2109 2214
5731.00	Bucharest Met	YRR	50n 1717
5732.00	Numbers Station		AM Ger (female voice) 1908 2313
5738.00	UNID		CW 5 fig grps 0748
5740.00	Jeddah Met, Saudi Arabia	HZN	50n 1639 1941
5740.00	Irkutsk Met, Russia	RKR78	50n 1836 1918 2007 2156
5743.00	Intership working		USB Scottish 1034
5746.00	Numbers Station		USB Eng (female voice) 1832 2205
5748.00	French Military	FDE13	CW ID 1817
5748.00	Numbers Station		AM Ger (female voice) 2309
5752.50	UN traffic		SITOR msg in Eng to Sarajevo 1637
5754.00	UNID		72ARQ/E/4 1911
5755.00	UNID		USB Slav R/T (simplex) 1833
5757.00	Swiss Embassy traffic	HBD	SITOR p/lang Ger 0707 5 let grps 0730 1640
5760.00	Danish Naval	OVG5	CW 0630 1342 1638 1729 1912 2317
5760.00	Danish Naval	OVG	75r p/lang news bulletin 0727
5761.20	Italian Police		50r msg from Rome to Milan 0647
5763.00	UNID		75n 5 let grps 1849
5765.00	Novosibirsk Met, Russia	RYO79	FAX wx maps 1642 1718 1834 1943 2110
5767.50	Swiss Embassy traffic	HBD	SITOR Selcal KPVP 1553
5773.10	Swiss Embassy traffic	HBD	SITOR 5 let grps 1651
5775.00	UNID		75n 5 let grps 1610
5779.00	French Police	FVA80	CW 1643
5781.50	Spanish Police	RETW	SITOR (to EHL) 0840 "JECOR TARRAGONA" 0800
5788.00	UNID		100ARQ/E3/8 Idle 0803
5790.00	Polish Embassy traffic		100POL-ARQ 5 fig grps 1628
5792.00	UNID		USB Slav R/T 1619
5792.50	UNID		100ARQ/E3/8 Idle 1036 1730 1851
5795.00	French Military, Orleans	FDY	50r "Voyez le Brick.." 0846 1613
5800.00	UNID		100ARQ/E3/8 Idle 1343
5804.50	French Military, Metz	FDC	CW 1629 1645 1900
5805.50	French Military	FAM20	USB radio checks & exercise with FAM10, FAM17 & FAM18 0710
5807.00	Auckland Met, N Zealand	ZKLF	CW p/lang wx forecast 0841 analysis 1813
5807.00	Auckland Met, N Zealand	ZKLF	FAX wx maps 0719 0733 1648 1837
5810.00	WWCR, USA		AM Eng 0738 0808
5810.00	French Military	FDE2	CW 1913
5810.00	UNID		75r "TOT 29/1000Z" (date/time group) 1000
5820.00	Numbers Station		AM phonetics (female voice) 1815 1907
5825.00	WEWN, USA		AM Ger 2313 2320
5825.00	UNID		AM Dutch (religious) 0529 Slav (religious) 0739
5826.00	UNID		75n 5 let grps (long msg) 1945
5834.00	UNID	U2K	USB radio check (English, heavy African accent) 2300
5845.00	UNID		AM Eng (US religious) 0840 Ger 1816
5850.00	Monitor Radio International		AM Eng 0136 0700 0740
5851.70	UNID		SITOR Selcal PKMV 0825
5860.50	French Military, Metz	FDC	CW 2301
5861.50	UNID		SITOR Spanish p/lang 1854
5862.50	UNID		72ARQ/E/8 Idle 1318 1616
5864.50	US Naval, Spain	AOK	FAX wx maps 0841 1719 1949

kHz.	Station	Call	Mode / Heard/Times GMT
5867.00	Baghdad Press (INA)	YIL	50r Arab 1720 1902
5868.00	French Military	FDE2	CW 1648 1845 2152
5870.00	Key West CG, USA	NAR	CW 0648 0750 0851 2255 2321
5870.00	UNID		AM Ger 0843
5875.00	BBC		AM Eng 1855 Slav 1651 1817 1903 2100
5880.00	R Australia		AM Eng 1917
5881.00	CIS Naval	RMP	CW (clg "RIQ86") 1103
5885.00	R Vatican		AM Eng 1950 Ital 2105 2202 2239 (freq varies to 5882.0kHz)
5887.50	Rome Met, Italy	IMB2	50n 1649 1733 1846 1948 2322
5890.00	R Australia		AM Eng 1707 1857
5890.00	Tashkent Met, Uzbekistan	RBV78	FAX wx maps 1857
5895.00	R Croatia		AM Slav 2236
5900.00	Kol Israel		AM Hebrew 1858
5905.00	R Moscow		AM Eng 1554 2237
5910.00	Numbers Station		AM Ger (female voice) 2202
5910.00	R Vlaanderen International		AM Eng 0650 1806 1818 Dutch 0742 0843 Ger 1734
5911.50	Spanish Police	RETXX	SITOR p/lang 0630 Selcal TWNC 1651
5912.00	British Military	GXQ	50r (VFT) QBF & RYIs 0846 (LSB ch 5915.0)
5915.00	R Almaty, Kazakhstan		AM Eng 2303
5915.00	R Slovakia International		AM Eng 1836 1859
5920.00	R Croatia		AM Slav 0855 2238
5920.00	R Moscow		AM Eng 2259 Ital 2140
5930.00	R Prague		AM Eng 1723 Fr 1953 Slav 1633 Span 1905 2301 2322
5935.00	R Riga		AM Eng 1820 1827
5935.00	WWCR, USA		AM Eng 0848
5940.00	R Moscow		AM Fr 2257
5945.00	R Austria International		AM Eng 1951 2137 Ger 1807 1848 2102 2203
5949.90	Spa Publications		

5950-6200
INTERNATIONAL BROADCASTING

kHz.	Station	Mode / Heard/Times GMT
5950.00	R Moscow	AM Eng 2155 2239
5950.00	Voice of Free China	AM Chinese 2300 2324
5955.00	R Svoboda	AM Slav 2157 2208
5955.00	R Netherland	AM Eng 0859 1319 1525 1558 Dutch 0743 0803 1653
5955.00	R Romania International	AM Eng 1945
5960.00	R Canada International	AM Eng 2218
5960.00	R Sarejevo	AM Slav 2325
5960.00	R Prague	AM Eng 2103 Slav 1920
5960.00	R Ukraine International	AM Eng 2241
5965.00	BBC	AM Eng 0138
5970.00	R Svoboda	AM Slav 1909 2200
5975.00	BBC	AM Eng 1634 2158 2241 2305
5975.00	R Japan	AM Eng 0728
5975.00	R Moscow	AM Eng 2201
5980.00	Radioropa Info	AM Ger 0717 1037 1122 1322 2210 2225
5985.00	R Moscow	AM Eng 2323
5985.00	R Svoboda	AM Slav 1346 1910
5985.00	R Ukraine International	AM Eng 2242
5990.00	RTV Italiana	AM Eng 2205 Ital 1631 Ger 1821
5995.00	Polish Radio Warsaw	AM Eng 1829 1849
5995.00	R Australia	AM Eng 0900
5995.00	R Canada International	AM Eng 2109 2150 2222 Slav 1635 Fr 1952 2104
5995.00	VOA	AM Eng 0612 0646
6000.00	R Moscow	AM Eng 1632 Span 2326
6000.00	R Sweden	AM Slav 1503
6005.00	RIAS, Berlin	AM Ger 0823 1347 1620 1735 1920 2204
6005.00	RTV Italiana	AM Ital 2245
6010.00	Deutsche Welle	AM Slav 1600
6010.00	R Moscow	AM Eng 2139 Ger 1943
6020.00	R Netherland	AM Dutch 0900 2110 2205
6020.00	R Ukraine International	AM Eng 2238
6030.00	BBC	AM Arab (Eng lang lesson) 1924
6030.00	SDR, Germany	AM Ger 0725 0806 1049 1404
6035.00	VOA	AM Eng 0636 2249
6040.00	Deutsche Welle	AM Span 2327
6040.00	R France International	AM Fr 2210
6040.00	VOA	AM Eng 0641 1654 1731 1809 1923 2000 2127 Span 2307
6045.00	R Moscow	AM Slav 1658
6050.00	R Japan	AM Eng 0702 0744 0807 2306 2330
6055.00	R Moscow	AM Eng 2240
6055.00	R Prague	AM Eng 0615 1039 1601 2103 2114 2208 Ger 0955 Fr 1635
6055.00	R Ukraine International	AM Eng 2217
6060.00	R Denmark	AM Danish 2331

kHz.	Station	Call	Mode / Heard/Times GMT
6060.00	RTV Italiana		AM Ital 0805
6060.00	R Japan		AM Eng 2309
6060.00	VOA		AM Eng 0637 Slav 0616 1700 1833
6065.00	R Sweden		AM Eng 1732 1840 2115 Ger 1830 Swed 0825
6070.00	R Svoboda		AM Slav 1810
6070.00	VOA		AM Eng 2224 2243
6075.00	Deutsche Welle		AM Ger 0703 1050 1123 1348 1623 2226 2325
6080.00	R Australia		AM Eng 1652 1811 1820
6085.00	Bayerische Rundfunk		AM Ger 1904 2116
6090.00	RTL		AM Fr 0721 0800 0858 1602
6090.00	R Ukraine International		AM Eng 2104 2142 (2100-2200 0000-0100) Ger 2310
6100.00	Deutsche Welle		AM Ger 2213 2327
6100.00	R Yugoslavia		AM Eng 1948 Fr 1700 2131 2147
6105.00	R Romania International		AM Eng 1946
6105.00	R Svoboda		AM Slav 0752 1349
6110.00	BBC		AM Eng 0644
6110.00	R Budapest		AM Eng 1906 2210 2250
6115.00	Deutsche Welle		AM Ger 1124 1405 1624 1811 2311
6120.00	R Finland		AM Eng 0646 0745 1834 1957 2142 Ger 1930 Russ 2000
6125.00	BBC		AM Eng 1249 1601 1705 Ger 1654 1812 1910
6125.00	REE Spain		AM Eng 2132 Span 0007 2333
6130.00	Deutsche Welle		AM Slav 1407
6130.00	R Moscow		AM Eng 2144 Ger 1745
6130.00	R Portugal International		AM Port 2200
6135.00	Polish Radio Warsaw		AM Eng 1350 Ger 1603 1816
6140.00	Deutsche Welle		AM Ger 0809 0900 1052 Span 1702
6140.00	VOA		AM Eng 0618 1638 Slav 2000
6145.00	R Moscow		AM Fr 1657 Ger 1713
6155.00	R Austria International		AM Eng 0850 1250 1440 1832 Ger 1002 1125 1819 Span 1351
6160.00	BBC		AM Eng 2314
6165.00	R Netherland		AM Eng 2338
6165.00	R Swiss International		AM Eng 1004 Ger 0723 1703 Fr 0950 Ital 1638
6175.00	R France International		AM Eng 1555 1645 Fr 1041 1126 1700 2001
6180.00	BBC		AM Eng 1704 1749 1835 1921
6180.00	VOA		AM Eng 1640
6183.10	R Nacional Amazonas		AM Port 2215 2302
6190.00	R Bremen		AM Ger 0951 1923
6195.00	BBC		AM Eng 0639 1721 1820 2002 2201 2251 2329
6199.90	Spa Publications		

6200-6525
MARITIME MOBILE

kHz.	Station	Call	Mode / Heard/Times GMT
6200.00	Ships wkg ch 1 dup. 6501.0kHz		USB (to DAJ) 2148
6203.00	Ships wkg ch 2 dup. 6504.0kHz		USB
6205.00	HCJB, Ecuador		AM Eng 0643 0738 0801 0825 1738
6206.00	Ships wkg ch 3 dup. 6507.0kHz		USB 1944 2231
6209.00	Ships wkg ch 4 dup. 6510.0kHz		USB
6210.00	R Bulgaria		AM Slav 1414 1803 Ital 2331
6212.00	Ships wkg ch 5 dup. 6513.0kHz		USB 0849
6215.00	Ships wkg ch 6 dup. 6516.0kHz		USB 0708 0825 1005
6218.00	Ships wkg ch 7 dup. 6519.0kHz		USB
6219.50	UNID (pirate)		AM Eng 1751
6220.00	European Christian Radio		AM Eng ID & Romanian 1700
6221.00	Ships wkg ch 8 dup. 6522.0kHz		USB 0637 0703 0809 1822
6221.50	UNID (pirate)		AM Eng 0850 1053 1352 1641
6224.00	Auckland, New Zealand	ZLD	USB wx 0734
6224.00	Ship/Coast working (simplex)		USB 0645 0902 2256
6226.10	R DLR-106 (Pirate)		AM Eng 1008 2201
6227.00	Ship/Coast working (simplex)		USB 1839
6229.00	UNID (pirate)		AM Eng 0811 0856 1127
6230.00	R Cairo		AM Arab 1627
6230.00	TWR		AM Ger 0830 Ital 1009
6230.00	Ship/Coast working (simplex)		USB 0646 2233 2301
6235.00	R Bulgaria		AM Eng 1845 1857 Fr 1807 Ger 1709
6238.80	R Merlin International (Pirate)		AM Eng 1011
6242.00	British Military		USB "3DW" "F9M" "6YT1" "9M1" radio checks 0816
6245.00	R Vatican		AM Eng 0637 Ital 1642 Fr 1013 1710 Ger 1924
6250.10	UNID (pirate)		AM Eng (probably Eire) 1129
6250.30	R Nacional, Equatorial Guinea		AM Span 2117 2200
6253.30	Italian Naval	Z2T	USB radio check call to IGJ 2156
6260.00	PBS China		AM Chinese 2258
6263.00	Ships wkg ch 1 dup. 6314.5kHz		SITOR "Eos" (LAOJ4) 0937 "Sea Victory" (ELXR) 1849
6263.50	Ships wkg ch 2 dup. 6315.0kHz		SITOR "Morven" (MBFQ6) 0755 "Mercury Cape" (ELHB5) 1907
6264.00	Ships wkg ch 3 dup. 6315.5kHz		170/50nc "Merkine" (LYCT) (to LYK) 0933

kHz.	Station	Call	Mode / Heard/Times GMT
6264.50	Ships wkg ch 4 dup. 6316.0kHz		SITOR "Auskelis" (YLAJ) 0807 "Mehanikis Fjodorovs" (YLBJ) 2156
6265.00	Ships wkg ch 5 dup. 6316.5kHz		SITOR "Hassir Mel" (7TCL) 0710 "Kapitonas Izmyakov" (LYBY) 0735
6265.50	Ships wkg ch 6 dup. 6317.0kHz		SITOR "Pioner Kazakhstana" (UJDG) 1857 "Indira Gandhi" (EODT) 2215
6266.00	Ships wkg ch 7 dup. 6317.5kHz		170/50nc "Birshtonas" (LYCR) 0813
6266.50	Ships wkg ch 8 dup. 6318.0kHz		SITOR Selcal QPPV (Rogaland) 2155
6267.00	Ships wkg ch 9 dup. 6318.5kHz		SITOR "Medallion" (OYEK2) 0820 "Arktis Bay" (OYMP2) 1832
6267.50	Ships wkg ch 10 dup. 6319.0kHz		SITOR "Sheldon Lykes" (KRJP) 0032
6268.00	Maritime Safety channel		RTTY Distress & Safety ch Mode B Fr Fisheries info 0845
6268.00	UNID (pirate)		AM Eng (Irish accent) 1056
6268.50	Ships wkg ch 12 dup. 6319.5kHz		SITOR "Cast Polarbear" (C6JX9) 0833 "Baltic Eagle" (GBBZ) 1009
6269.00	Ships wkg ch 13 dup. 6320.0kHz		SITOR "Baco-Liner 3" (DCMZ) 0638 5VNR (to DCL) 0956
6269.50	Ships wkg ch 14 dup. 6320.5kHz		SITOR "Vento di Grecale" (IVFC) 0645 "Presidente Ibanez" (3EIX2) 0830
6270.00	Ships wkg ch 15 dup. 6321.0kHz		SITOR 2216
6270.00	Numbers Station		AM "ULX2" (female voice) 2031
6270.50	Ships wkg ch 16 dup. 6321.5kHz		SITOR Selcal XYFV (Athens) 1920 2115
6271.00	Ships wkg ch 17 dup. 6322.0kHz		SITOR "Golconda 1" (3EIG2) 1807
6271.50	Ships wkg ch 18 dup. 6322.5kHz		SITOR 1024
6272.00	Ships wkg ch 19 dup. 6323.0kHz		SITOR "United Tiger" 0737 "Safe Holmia" 0818 "Amazon" 1800
6272.50	Ships wkg ch 20 dup. 6323.5kHz		SITOR "Houtmansgracht" (PEUD) 0840
6273.00	Ships wkg ch 21 dup. 6324.0kHz		SITOR Selcal KQQV (Portishead) 0848
6273.50	Ships wkg ch 22 dup. 6324.5kHz		SITOR Selcal KYVV (St Petersburg) 1926
6274.00	Ships wkg ch 23 dup. 6325.0kHz		SITOR Selcal KYVY (Murmansk) 1943
6274.50	Ships wkg ch 24 dup. 6325.5kHz		SITOR "Anatoliy Vasilyev" (UQJW) 1840 Selcal KYVV (St Petersburg) 2210
6275.00	Ships wkg ch 25 dup. 6326.0kHz		170/50nc "Kapitonas Izmiakov" (LYBY) 1557
6275.50	Ships wkg ch 26 dup. 6326.5kHz		SITOR "Romny" (UJYV) 2159
6276.00	Ships calling		CW HQKK7 (to YQI) 1919 8MOY (to ARL4) 2327
6276.50	Ships calling		CW (to JOS) 2147
6277.00	Ships calling		CW P3QO2 (to FFL3) 1922
6277.50	Ships calling		CW "Vissarion Belinskiy" (UTPK 1545 UROH (to USO5) 1915
6278.00	Ships calling		CW "Cielo D'Europa" (ELMC4) 0122 UHEL (to RIW) 2302
6278.50	Ships calling		CW "Klintsy" (UTRZ) 2245
6279.00	Ships calling		CW
6279.50	Ships calling		CW UYGT (to UGC) 1826
6280.00	King of Hope, Lebanon		AM Eng 0125 1853 2151
6280.00	Prague, Czech Republic	OLX	CW 0659 0756 0857
6280.00	Ships calling		CW "Oltshan" (LYHN) 0820
6280.50	Ships calling		CW
6281.00	Ships wkg ch 27 dup. 6327.0kHz		170/50nc "Kapitonas Stulpinas" (LYCN) 0735
6281.50	Ships wkg ch 28 dup. 6327.5kHz		SITOR "Slavyanka" (UGSH) 2052 Selcal KYVX (Moscow) 1925
6282.00	Ships wkg ch 29 dup. 6328.0kHz		RTTY
6282.50	Ships wkg ch 30 dup. 6328.5kHz		RTTY
6283.00	Ships wkg ch 31 dup. 6329.0kHz		SITOR "Rauf Bey" (TCGS) 1953 "Samsun 1" (TCSL) 2207
6283.50	Ships wkg ch 32 dup. 6329.5kHz		RTTY
6284.00	Ships wkg ch 33 dup. 6330.0kHz		SITOR 1740 1903
6284.50	Ships wkg ch 34 dup. 6330.5kHz		170/50nc "Plunge" (LYCP) 0804
6285.00	Ships working		CW "Candelaria" (J8GD2) 1912
6285.50	Ships working		CW 1541
6286.00	Ships working		CW 1929
6286.50	Ships working		CW "Ladoga 105" (UPAY) 1708 "Baltijskiy 107" (UKJO) 1817
6287.00	Ships working		CW "Amur 2521" (UTWK) 1531 "Risnov" 1912
6288.00	Ships working		CW 1859
6288.00	Italian Naval	IGJ43	CW 0633 0818 1913 2018 2252 (& msrd 6289.0)
6288.50	Ships working		CW 1844
6289.00	Ships working		CW "AB 0012" 2230
6290.00	Ships working		CW 2140 P3VO2 (to EAD) 2320
6290.50	Ships working		CW 0757 2249
6291.00	Ships working		CW "Kapitan Vasiliy Kulik" (UQZW) 2135 "Parallel" (UBOK) 2216
6292.00	Ships working		CW YQCK 2150 (to URD) 0820
6292.50	Ships working		CW 2120 UEBQ 1524
6293.00	Ships working		CW "Volgoneft 129" (UFDW) 0701 "Sevastopol" (P3ZV3) 1815
6294.00	Ships working		CW "Taganrog" (YLCM) 0758
6295.00	UNID (pirate)		AM Eng 1014 1130 1047
6295.00	Ships working		CW 1815 2250 2311 UZPF (to UUI) 2137
6295.50	Ships working		CW 2322
6296.00	Ships working		CW "Georghieni" (YQEC) 1817
6299.50	Ships working		CW 1931
6300.00	Intership working		USB Eng 1011
6300.00	Ships working		CW URAZ (to USO5) 1829
6300.00	Ships working		170/50nc "Meganom" (EOXG) 1532
6300.00	WYFR, USA		AM Chinese (Taiwan relay) 2228

kHz.	Station	Call	Mode / Heard/Times GMT
6300.50	Ships working (non paired)		170/50nc "Pertominsk" (UWFN) 2233
6300.50	UNID	I9MN	CW (clg LTOM) 1414
6301.00	Ships working		CW UKFU/UVLD/UVXB with wx to UCE 1810
6301.00	Ships working (non paired)		SITOR 1654
6301.50	Ships working (non paired)		SITOR 1815 2053
6302.00	Ships working (non paired)		SITOR "Cvijeta Zuzoric" (9ANB) 0643 "Vargas" 1240
6302.50	Ships working (non paired)		170/50nc "Labrador" (UHUS) 1933 "Roman Karmen" 1938
6303.00	Ships working (non paired)		170/50nc 1852
6303.50	Ships working (non paired)		170/50nc "Suzdal" (UVEQ) 1828
6304.00	Ships working (non paired)		170/50nc "Yakov Smirnitskiy" (to Archangel) 1740
6304.50	Ships working (non paired)		170/50nc 2019
6305.00	Ships working (non paired)		170/50nc "Maksim Starostin" (UDYN) 1911
6305.40	Voz del Cid		AM Span 0547 0640 0707 0800
6305.50	Ships working (non paired)		170/50nc 2238
6306.00	Ships working (non paired)		170/50nc "Utena" (LYDE) 0811 "Neringa" (LYMO) 1828
6306.50	Ships working (non paired)		SITOR Selcal KYVF (Archangel) 2209
6307.00	Ships working (non paired)		170/50nc 0812 UYHH 0738
6307.50	Ships working (non paired)		170/50nc "Plutonas" (LYAC) 2231
6308.00	Ships working (non paired)		170/50nc 2149
6308.50	Ships working (non paired)		RTTY
6309.00	Ships working (non paired)		170/50nc 0745
6309.50	Ships working (non paired)		RTTY
6310.00	CIS Naval	MCSX	CW (clg RMP) 1558
6310.00	Ships working (non paired)		170/50nc (to Izmail) 1732
6310.50	Ships working (non paired)		RTTY
6311.00	Ships working (non paired)		170/50nc "Moldavia" (UJLY) 0709
6311.50	Ships working (non paired)		170/50nc "Kapitan Bugrimov" (LYNZ) 2313
6312.00	Italian Naval	IDR3	CW 0750 1819
6312.00	Maritime Safety channel		RTTY
6312.50	Ships digital selective calling		RTTY
6313.00	Ships digital selective calling		RTTY
6313.50	Ships digital selective calling		RTTY
6314.50	Coast stations ch 1 dup. 6263.0kHz		RTTY
6314.50	Goeteborg, Sweden	SAG	SITOR 0819 1440 1536 1741 1817 1921 2301
6315.00	Coast stations ch 2 dup. 6263.5kHz		RTTY
6315.00	Portishead, UK	GKE3	SITOR 0126 1132 1355 1858 1928 Mode B tfc list 0900 wx 0930
6315.50	Coast stations ch 3 dup. 6264.0kHz		RTTY
6315.50	Gdynia, Poland	SPA31	SITOR 1941 2138 2322
6315.50	Mariupol, Ukraine	USU	SITOR 1833 2130 2259
6316.00	Coast stations ch 4 dup. 6264.5kHz		RTTY
6316.00	Argentine Radio	LSD836	SITOR 2227
6316.00	Chesapeake CG, USA	NMN	SITOR 0627 2319
6316.00	Riga, Latvia	UDH	SITOR 1803
6316.50	Coast stations ch 5 dup. 6265.0kHz		RTTY
6316.50	Scheveningen, Holland	PCH35	SITOR 0746 1048 1350 1628 1946
6317.00	Coast stations ch 6 dup. 6265.5kHz		RTTY
6317.00	Archangel, Russia	UCE	SITOR 1741 2020
6317.00	Mobile, USA	WLO	SITOR 0607 0846 0929 0955
6317.00	Odessa, Ukraine	UUI	SITOR 1911 2152 2253 2312
6317.00	Perth, Australia	VIP32	SITOR
6317.50	Coast stations ch 7 dup. 6266.0kHz		RTTY
6317.50	Halifax, Canada	VCS	SITOR 1900
6318.00	Coast stations ch 8 dup. 6266.5kHz		RTTY
6318.00	Rogaland, Norway	LGU2	SITOR 0737 1321 1430 1742 1845 2021
6318.00	Italian Naval	IDR3	CW 0930 1818 1914 2301
6318.50	Coast stations ch 9 dup. 6267.0kHz		RTTY
6318.50	Lyngby, Denmark	OXZ	SITOR 0820 1251 1716 1923 Mode B tfc list odd hours + 30
6318.50	Vancouver, Canada	VAI	SITOR
6319.00	Coast stations ch 10 dup. 6267.5kHz		RTTY
6319.00	Mobile, USA	WLO	SITOR 0714
6319.50	Coast stations ch 12 dup. 6268.5kHz		RTTY
6319.50	Boston CG, USA	NMF	SITOR 0735
6319.50	Perth, Australia	VIP42	SITOR
6319.50	Portishead, UK	GKP3	SITOR 0956 1012 1253 1629 1841 2211
6320.00	Coast stations ch 13 dup. 6269.0kHz		RTTY
6320.00	Norddeich, Germany	DCL	SITOR 2124 2153
6320.50	Coast stations ch 14 dup. 6269.5kHz		RTTY
6320.50	St Lys, France	FFT31	SITOR 1322 1830 1943 2222 Mode B wx 0706 tfc list 0900 1900
6321.00	Coast stations ch 15 dup. 6270.0kHz		RTTY
6321.00	Lyngby, Denmark	OXZ	SITOR
6321.00	Mobile, USA	WLO	SITOR 0931 2303
6321.50	Coast stations ch 16 dup. 6270.5kHz		RTTY
6321.50	Athens, Greece	SVU3	SITOR 1630 1902 2156 tfc list 2025
6321.50	Portishead, UK	GKL3	SITOR
6322.00	Coast stations ch 17 dup. 6271.0kHz		RTTY

kHz.	Station	Call	Mode / Heard/Times GMT
6322.00	Ostend, Belgium	OST	SITOR 0646 0821 1340 1820
6322.50	Coast stations ch 18 dup. 6271.5kHz		RTTY
6323.00	Coast stations ch 19 dup. 6272.0kHz		RTTY
6323.00	Goeteborg, Sweden	SAG	SITOR 1442 1630 1834
6323.00	Mobile, USA	WLO	SITOR 2323
6323.50	Coast stations ch 20 dup. 6272.5kHz		RTTY
6323.50	Scheveningen, Holland	PCH36	SITOR 1351 1608 2131 2242 Mode B tfc list 0915
6323.50	Singapore	9VG	SITOR 2144 wx 0030 1230
6324.00	Coast stations ch 21 dup. 6273.0kHz		RTTY
6324.00	Chatham, USA	WCC	SITOR 0740 2028 2130 2221 2305
6324.00	Italian Naval	IDR3	CW 2300
6324.00	Portishead, UK	GKQ3	SITOR
6324.50	Coast stations ch 22 dup. 6273.5kHz		RTTY
6325.00	Coast stations ch 23 dup. 6274.0kHz		RTTY
6325.00	Riga, Latvia	UDH	SITOR 2143 2254 2313
6325.00	Murmansk, Russia	UMV	SITOR 1944
6325.50	Coast stations ch 24 dup. 6274.5kHz		RTTY
6325.50	Mobile, USA	WLO	SITOR 0742 0957 2220 2235
6325.50	St Petersburg, Russia	UGC	SITOR 0748 1352 1540 1819 2141 (with UABC) 2034
6326.00	Coast stations ch 25 dup. 6275.0kHz		RTTY
6326.50	Coast stations ch 26 dup. 6275.5kHz		RTTY
6326.50	Dixon, USA	KMI	SITOR
6326.50	Mariupol, Ukraine	USU	SITOR 1456 1753 2306 (to "Akademik Artsimovich" UYWN) 1904
6327.00	Coast stations ch 27 dup. 6281.0kHz		RTTY
6327.00	General Pacheco, Argentina	LPD	SITOR
6327.50	Coast stations ch 28 dup. 6281.5kHz		RTTY
6327.50	Pennsuco, USA	WOM	SITOR
6327.50	Moscow, Russia	UAT	SITOR 1538 1835 1930 2036 2157
6328.00	Coast stations ch 29 dup. 6282.0kHz		RTTY
6328.00	General Pacheco, Argentina	LPD	SITOR
6328.00	New York (Ocean Gate), USA	WOO	SITOR Mode B 0638 2306 tfc list 0715
6328.00	Riga, Latvia	UDH	SITOR 2126 2228
6328.50	Coast stations ch 30 dup. 6282.5kHz		RTTY
6329.00	Coast stations ch 31 dup. 6283.0kHz		RTTY
6329.00	Istanbul, Turkey	TAH	SITOR 2000
6329.50	Coast stations ch 32 dup. 6283.5kHz		RTTY
6330.00	Coast stations ch 33 dup. 6284.0kHz		RTTY
6330.00	CIS Naval	RMP	CW ID 1547
6330.00	Varna, Bulgaria	LZW	SITOR 0743 1947 2230 2255
6330.50	Coast stations ch 34 dup. 6284.5kHz		RTTY
6331.00	Coast stations digital selective calling		RTTY
6331.50	Coast stations digital selective calling		RTTY
6332.00	Coast stations digital selective calling		RTTY
6335.50	Frobisher Bay (Iqualit), Canada	VFF	CW wx 2120
6336.10	British Naval	MTO	75r 0822 1325 1744 1826 1952
6337.00	Valparaiso, Chile	CBV	CW 0010 2256 2328
6338.50	RSA Naval	ZRQ	CW 1917
6339.70	New Zealand Naval	ZLO	CW 0609 1459 1733
6340.50	Singapore	9VG9	CW 1638 1754 1836 2205 2239
6341.50	Odessa, Ukraine	UUI	CW tfc list 0802 wx 2114 (Eng) 1500
6341.50	Riga, Latvia	UDH	CW 1954
6341.50	Riga, Latvia	UDH	170/50nc 1119 1946 (to "Skulptors Tomskis") 1632 tfc list 1418
6344.00	Athens, Greece	SVB3	CW 0127 1950 2133 2257 2304
6344.00	Mobile, USA	WLO2	CW 0630 0752 0825 0903 0934
6344.00	Mobile, USA	WLO	SITOR Mode B wx 0645 0744 news 0846
6348.00	French Naval, Paris	HWN	CW 0823 1022 1327 1718 1954 2038 2231
6348.00	French Naval, Paris	HWN	75r RYs & SGs 0647 2042
6353.00	Odessa, Ukraine	UUI	CW tfc list 1905
6353.00	Odessa, Ukraine	UUI	170/50rc 1917 2308
6354.00	St Petersburg, Russia	UGC	CW 1906 wx 1600
6354.00	St Petersburg, Russia	UGC	170/50nc 1847 2318 wx forecast 1706
6355.00	Mariupol, Ukraine	USU	CW tfc list 1825 1925
6355.00	Mariupol, Ukraine	USU	170/50nc 1716 1827
6357.00	Karlskrona, Sweden	SAA	CW (listens 6292.5) 0128 0832 1354 1741 2224 tfc list 2302
6358.50	Dutch Naval	PBC	75r 1013 1858
6363.50	Norddeich, Germany	DAF	CW
6364.50	Dammam, Saudi Arabia	HZG	CW 0650 2039
6368.50	Riga, Latvia	UDH	CW 0632 0702 2126 2226
6369.00	Luanda, Angola	D3E41	CW 2206 2232 2251
6370.00	St Petersburg, Russia	UGC	SITOR 1837 1932 2008 2300
6371.00	Gibraltar Naval	GYU	75n 0746 1814 1920 2137
6371.50	Archangel, Russia	RKLM	CW 1438 1606 1930 tfc list 0901 1801 2101
6374.90	Turkish Naval	TBO	CW 0754 1416 2148 2235
6375.00	Brazilian Naval	PWN33	CW 2311 (clg PWDO) 2253
6376.00	Chatham, USA	WCC	CW 0651 0743 0904 1847 2130 2207 tfc list 0856 2055 2251
6379.00	Israeli Naval	4XZ	CW 0129 1756 1956 2259 wx analysis 1607 1807 2318

kHz.	Station	Call	Mode / Heard/Times GMT
6380.00	Kholmsk, Russia	UQB	CW 1815 1907 2212 tfc list 1902
6380.00	St Petersburg, Russia	UCW4	CW 1015 1508 1607
6381.00	Ship working		SITOR "Inzhener Nechiporenko" (out of normal sub band) 1727
6382.00	Turkish Naval	TBA6	CW 2040 (& msrd 6383.0)
6382.20	Madrid, Spain	EAD2	CW 0824 1951 2044 2140 2240 tfc list 0802 2002
6383.00	Dakar, Senegal	6VA4	CW wx (Fr) 2200
6383.00	San Francisco CG, USA	NMC	CW 0610 0635
6383.00	Sebastopol, Ukraine	URL	CW 0652 1834 2208 2241
6383.00	Sebastopol, Ukraine	URL	170/50rc 2006
6385.00	French Military, Toulon	FUO	CW 0651
6385.00	Rio de Janeiro, Brazil	PPR	CW 0015 0650 2220 2257
6385.00	UNID	AQK	CW 1736
6386.00	Greek Naval	SXA	CW 0647 0707 1518 ¡558
6386.50	Buenaventura, Colombia	HKC	CW 0738 0803
6386.50	Izmail, Ukraine	USO5	CW 1519 1532 1614 1719 1829 tfc list 0736 1536
6386.50	Izmail, Ukraine	USO5	170/50nc 0639 1639
6386.50	RSA Naval	ZSJ3	CW 1814 1932 2041 2135 2225 2326
6388.00	Spanish Naval	EBA	CW 1952 nav wng 0925 1004 1657 1734 2003
6389.00	Portuguese Naval	CTP	CW 0756 2210 2253
6389.70	Slidell, USA	WNU42	CW 0648 0708 0848 2330
6390.00	Pakistan Naval	AQP4	CW 1720 1922 2255 2320 (freq varies)
6390.30	Italian Naval	IDQ3	CW 0652 1014 1356 1808 2147
6392.00	Prague Met, Czech Republic		50r 1721 1912
6393.50	Australian Naval	VHI	CW 1507 1758 1944 2042 2132 2225
6393.50	Murmansk, Russia	UDK2	CW (to 4LS) 0850 1024 1257 1559 1946 2201 tfc list 1935
6393.50	Murmansk, Russia	UDK2	170/50rc 0755 1910
6395.00	Turkish Naval	TBA3	CW 1439 1615 1809 2149 2301 nav wng (Eng) 2019 (freq varies)
6393.50	Pakistan Naval	AQP	CW 2138
6400.00	Murmansk, Russia	UMV	CW 1913 tfc list 2002 2102 2202
6400.00	R Pyongyang		AM Asian lang 2215
6400.00	Pirate Radio (UNID)		AM Eng 1240 1757
6404.00	General Pacheco, Argentina	LPD	CW
6405.00	Tallinn, Estonia	ESA	CW 0919 1840 1932 tfc list 1832
6407.50	Perth, Australia	VIP	CW 1803 1820 1935 2047 2133 2237
6408.00	RSA Naval	ZRQ	75r msg to "P9CV" & p/lang msg to "COMNAVOP" 1843
6408.50	Spanish Naval	EBA	CW wx (Span) 0930 1742 nav wng 1736
6410.00	Batumi, Georgia	UHK	CW 2211 tfc list 2106
6411.00	Ostend, Belgium	OST3	CW 1758 1849 2227 tfc list 1811
6412.00	Singapore	9VG55	CW 2141 2210 2332
6415.00	Boufarik, Algeria	7TF4	CW 0654 1936 2135 2208 2256 tfc list 0130
6416.00	Greek Naval	SXA	CW 1641
6416.00	Mobile, USA	WLO	CW wx 2325 tfc list 0800
6416.00	Mobile, USA	WLO	SITOR Mode B tfc list 0857
6418.00	Indian Naval	VTP5	CW 1813 2144 2205
6418.00	Rome, Italy	IAR26	CW 0629 2200 2208 2250
6418.50	Hamburg Press	DGF41	SITOR Mode B Ger news 1954 2009
6420.00	Baku, Azerbaijan	UON	CW 1920 1950 2123 tfc list 1800
6421.50	St Lys, France	FFL3	CW 1617 1938 2043 2125 wx 0758 1605 tfc list 1843
6421.50	Dutch Naval	PBB	75r 0905 1440 1850
6425.00	St Petersburg, Russia	UGC	CW 0900 1258 1328 1401 1618 1726 1955 2004 2153 2213
6427.00	Klaipeda, Lithuania	LYK	CW 1915 tfc list 1001 1701 1801 2301
6428.50	Australian Naval	VHP	CW 0710 1610 1640 1803 1937 2012 2150
6428.50	Sydney, Australia	VIS	CW wx 2049 (uses VIS call for wx)
6428.50	Sydney, Australia	VIX	CW 0736 0946 1739
6434.50	British Naval	GYA	100n RYs & encrypted msgs 0932
6435.00	Brazilian Naval	PWZ33	CW 2230 (also rptd using 75Bd RTTY)
6435.50	Norddeich, Germany	DAN	CW 0011
6439.00	Klaipeda, Lithuania	LYK	170/50nc nav warnings 0751 blind tfc 1903
6439.50	Murmansk, Russia	UDK2	CW 1942 wx (in Russian) 1734
6439.50	Murmansk, Russia	UDK2	170/50rc 2104
6444.50	Athens, Greece	SVD3	CW 0131 1841 1925 2111 2229 2245
6446.00	British Naval	GYA	FAX wx maps 0748 1343 1424 1708 2105
6446.50	Mobile, USA	WLO2	CW 0645
6446.70	Lyngby, Denmark	OXZ3	CW 2335 tfc list 1815
6447.00	Odessa, Ukraine	UUI	CW 1935
6450.00	UNID		CW Slav wx fcast (Baltic area) 1443 nav wngs 0935
6451.00	Seoul, S Korea	HLG	CW 1907 tfc list 2030
6454.00	Shanghai, China	XSG	CW 0853 tfc list 2230
6455.00	Murmansk, Russia	UDK2	CW (to 4LS) 2209 2240
6456.00	CIS Naval	RCV	CW ID 2108
6456.00	Vancouver Military, Canada	CKN	CW (to C13E) 0821 0914
6456.50	Norddeich, Germany	DAL	CW 0012
6459.00	Stettin, Poland	SPE31	CW 2241
6459.50	Gelendzhik, Russia	UVA	CW tfc list 1501 1601
6460.00	Goeteborg, Sweden	SAG	SITOR 0800 1330 1444 1735 2046 2109
6462.00	French Military, Tahiti	FUM	CW 0651 0800 0854

kHz.	Station	Call	Mode / Heard/Times GMT
6463.00	Barranquilla, Colombia	HKB	CW 2217 2323
6464.00	Sydney, Australia	VIS3	CW 1915 tfc list (for Sydney & Perth) 1925
6465.00	Kaliningrad, Russia	UIW	CW 1642 2112 2206 2215 tfc list 2200 nav wngs 2101
6465.00	Kaliningrad, Russia	UIW	170/50nc 2251
6465.50	Murmansk, Russia	ROD7	CW 0801 0900 1905 tfc list 1000 1800
6466.00	Intership working		USB Scottish 1028
6467.00	Choshi, Japan	JCS	CW 0855 1017 1851 tfc list 0800
6467.00	Indian Naval	VTG5	CW 1908 2152 2229 wx (Eng) 1833 1910 2033 (& msrd 6468.0)
6467.50	Rogaland, Norway	LGW	CW 2218 tfc list 0132
6470.00	Archangel, Russia	UCE	CW 0820 1239 1454 1627 1941 2124 2246 tfc list 2100
6470.00	Greek Naval	SXA	CW 2226
6470.40	Haifa, Israel	4XO	CW 1758 2015 2213 2231
6471.00	Greek Naval	SXA24	CW 0712 1619 2047 2113 2257 2337 (freq varies)
6473.50	Constanza, Romania	YQI3	CW 1800 1817 tfc list 1703 1803 2107 2302
6474.00	Intership working		USB Scottish 0738
6475.00	Klaipeda, Lithuania	LYK	CW 0811
6475.00	Klaipeda, Lithuania	LYK	170/50nc 1848
6475.00	Moscow, Russia	UAT	CW (wkg UOUW on 8373.5) 2137
6475.00	UN traffic		SITOR Selcals HCBB/HCYL & msg to Zagreb 1731
6475.50	Norddeich, Germany	DAM	CW 1926 2147
6477.50	Mariupol, Ukraine	USU	CW tfc list 0802
6478.70	Athens, Greece	SVA3	CW 1928 2145 2237 tfc list 2215 news 1847
6480.00	R Korea		AM Eng 2219 Slav 2016 Asian lang 1819
6481.00	St Petersburg, Russia	UGC	170/50nc tfc to several ships 0712 nav wngs 1630
6483.00	Dutch Naval	PBB	75r 0805 0853 1331 1421 1733
6484.50	Tuckerton, USA	WSC8	CW 2154 2208 2248 tfc list 0818
6485.00	Choshi, Japan	JCU	CW 0856
6485.00	Tallinn, Estonia	ESA	CW 1801 tfc list 1104 1832 1932
6485.00	Numbers Station		USB Eng (female voice) 2229
6490.00	Moscow, Russia	UJE	CW 1820 2146
6491.50	Curacao, Neth Antilles	PJC	CW tfc list 0700
6491.50	Halifax, Canada	VCS	CW 1859 2147 2211 2249 wx 2042 tfc list 2301
6491.50	Nagasaki, Japan	JOS	CW 1917 2150
6493.00	Vancouver, Canada	VAI	CW 0857
6493.50	Klaipeda Harbour, Lithuania	LYL	CW 1956 2017 2148 2209 2236
6493.50	Klaipeda Harbour, Lithuania	LYL	170/50nc 2057 2217
6495.00	Murmansk, Russia	UMV	CW 1850 2112 2210
6495.00	Murmansk, Russia	UMV	170/50nc 2325 (wx info in Eng for Barents Sea) 1709
6496.40	Halifax Met, Canada	CFH	FAX 0804 0906 2129 2209
6496.40	Halifax Met, Canada	CFH	75r 2250
6498.10	Ostend, Belgium	OST3	CW 1802 1822 1903 2230 tfc list 2216
6501.00	Coast stations ch 1 dup. 6200.0kHz		USB
6501.00	Inuvik, Canada	VFA	USB
6501.00	Norddeich, Germany	DAJ	USB tfc list 2146
6501.00	Chesapeake CG, USA	NMN	USB 0639 0942 wx 2208
6502.00	Turkish Naval	TBB6	CW 1712 2251
6504.00	Coast stations ch 2 dup. 6203.0kHz		USB
6504.00	Ostend, Belgium	OSU31	USB
6504.00	Rome, Italy	IAR	USB 1944
6504.00	Singapore	9VG62	USB
6507.00	Numbers Station		AM Ger (fem voice) 2117
6507.00	Coast stations ch 3 dup. 6206.0kHz		USB
6507.00	Athens, Greece	SVN32	USB 2213
6507.00	Darwin, Australia	VID	USB
6507.00	General Pacheco, Argentina	LPL	USB 2133 2232
6507.00	Haifa, Israel	4XO	USB 1945
6507.00	Lyngby, Denmark	OXZ	USB
6507.00	Melbourne, Australia	VIM	USB
6507.00	Murmansk, Russia	UDK2	USB
6507.00	Perth, Australia	VIP	USB wx
6507.00	Rogaland, Norway	LGN30	USB wx (Eng) 2305
6507.00	Sydney, Australia	VIS	USB wx
6507.00	Townsville, Australia	VIT	USB
6509.50	UK Coast Control		USB 1737 1853 wx inference msg 0826
6510.00	Coast stations ch 4 dup. 6209.0kHz		USB
6510.00	Haifa, Israel	4XO	USB
6510.00	Istanbul, Turkey	TAN	USB
6510.00	Stettin, Poland	SPO31	USB 2143 test tx 2239 tfc list 2235
6513.00	Coast stations ch 5 dup. 6212.0kHz		USB
6513.00	Frobisher Bay (Iqaluit), Canada	VFF	USB
6513.00	Halifax, Canada	VCS	USB wx 0805 2206
6513.00	Lyngby, Denmark	OXZ	USB
6513.00	Chesapeake CG, USA	NMN	USB
6513.00	St Lys, France	FFL	USB 0754 0815 1332 1613 2018
6513.00	Vancouver, Canada	VAI	USB
6515.00	UNID		LSB CB style (Italy) 1848

kHz.	Station	Call	Mode / Heard/Times GMT
6516.00	Coast stations ch 6 dup. 6215.0kHz		USB common calling ch
6516.00	Ostend, Belgium	OSU35	USB
6516.00	Rio de Janeiro, Brazil	PPR	USB
6519.00	Coast stations ch 7 dup. 6218.0kHz		USB
6519.00	St Lys, France	FFL	USB 0630
6519.00	Sydney, Australia	VIS	USB 0732
6522.00	Coast stations ch 8 dup. 6221.0kHz		USB
6524.90	Spa Publications		

6525-6685
AERONAUTICAL MOBILE (MAINLY CIVIL) 3KHz channels

kHz.	Station	Call	Mode / Heard/Times GMT
6530.00	UNID		LSB CB style (Italy) 2233 USB (Ital) 0814
6532.00	Central W Pacific Air traffic CWP 1/2		USB
6532.00	Israeli Naval	4XZ	CW 1614
6535.00	UNID		LSB CB style (Italy) 0633 2144
6535.00	Africa Air traffic AFI 1		USB
6535.00	Dakar ATC, Senegal	GOOO	USB 0649 2215 2229 2242
6535.00	S Atlantic Air traffic SAT 1		USB
6538.00	UNID		LSB CB style (Fr) 0825 1029 1035
6540.00	R Pyongyang		AM Asian lang 1824 1936 2019
6543.00	Intership working		USB Scottish 0734
6549.50	R Beirut		AM Arab 1713 1813 1941 2118 (freq varies to 6550)
6552.00	Intership working		USB (Scottish) 1738
6553.00	UNID		AM Ger (probably a Pirate) 0834
6555.50	Intership working		USB (Irish fishing boats) 2116
6555.60	UNID		LSB CB style (Slav) 0801
6556.00	S E Asia Air traffic SEA 1/3		USB
6556.00	Bombay ATC, India	VABF	USB 2220 2238
6556.00	Calcutta ATC, India	VECF	USB 1739 1826 2135 2224 2327
6556.00	Colombo ATC, Sri Lanka	VCCC	USB 1621 1714 2020 2222
6556.00	Dhaka ATC, Bangladesh	VGFR	USB 1825 1850 2048 2347
6556.00	Jakarta ATC, Indonesia	NIIZ	USB 1809
6556.00	Karachi ATC, Pakistan	OPKR	USB 1907 2032
6556.00	Kuala Lumpur ATC, Malaysia	WMFC	USB 1623
6556.00	Madras ATC, India	VPMF	USB 1659 1849 2021 2214 2314 (Singapore 242) 1633
6556.00	Male ATC, Maldives	VRMM	USB 1802 2257
6556.00	Perth ATC, Australia	APGF	USB 1549 1847
6556.00	Yangon ATC, Myanmar	VBRR	USB 1851
6560.00	R Baghdad		AM 1622 1740 1946
6561.00	UNID		LSB CB style (Italy) 2145
6562.00	Cent W Pacific Air traffic CWP 1/2		USB
6571.00	E Asia Air traffic EA 1		USB
6576.00	R Pyongyang		AM Eng 2046 Span 1814 Ger 1931 1942 Fr 1615 2119
6577.00	Caribbean Air traffic CAR A		USB
6577.00	Havana ATC, Cuba	MUHA	USB 0845
6577.00	New York ATC, USA	KZNY	USB 0046 0706 0754 0815 2243 2248 2256 2340
6577.00	Piarco ATC, Trinidad	MKPP	USB
6580.00	UNID		LSB CB style (Ital) 2153 2252
6583.00	Numbers Station		AM Slav (female voice) 1359
6585.00	UNID		LSB CB style (Fr) 1008 1422
6586.00	Caribbean Air traffic CAR B		USB
6586.00	New York ATC, USA	KZNY	USB 2208 2247 2340
6586.00	Accra ATC, Ghana		USB 2146 2218 2316
6588.00	UNID		LSB CB style (Fr) 0752 (Dutch) 1334
6592.00	N Central Asia air traffic		USB
6592.00	Moscow ATC, Russia		USB 1944 2238
6598.00	Europe Air traffic EUR A		USB
6600.00	UNID		LSB CB style (Italy) 1640
6603.00	UNID		LSB CB style (Italy) 2120
6604.00	Gander VOLMET, Canada	CZQX	USB 0654 0753 1827 1958 2121 2224
6604.00	New York VOLMET, USA	KZNY	USB 0047 0642 0744 0810 1906 2117 2245 2303
6605.00	UNID		LSB CB style (Italy) 1932
6610.00	UNID		LSB CB style (Fr) 1855
6617.00	CIS VOLMET channel		USB 0635 0739 0823 1516 1623 2136 2325
6622.00	N Atlantic Air traffic NAT F		USB
6622.00	Gander ATC, Canada	CZQX	USB 0711
6622.00	Shanwick ATC, UK/Eire	EGGX	USB 0643 0825 1400 1423 1616
6626.70	Egyptian Embassy traffic		SITOR Selcal XBVY 1937
6628.00	N Atlantic Air traffic NAT E		USB
6628.00	New York ATC, USA	KZNY	USB 0704 0822 (Springbok 201) 0727
6628.00	Santa Maria ATC, Azores	LPAZ	USB 0609 0654 0832 1334 2213
6630.00	UNID		LSB CB style (Ital) 0827 0937 2146
6631.00	Middle East Air traffic MID 1/3		USB
6634.00	Portishead (in-flight R/T service)		USB 0859 (with British Midland "Mike Oscar") 2212

kHz.	Station	Call	Mode / Heard/Times GMT
6636.00	UNID		LSB CB style (Span) 0819
6637.00	Houston (in-flight R/T service)		USB 0724
6637.00	St Lys (in-flight R/T service)		USB 0729 0754 0824 1924
6640.00	Honolulu (in-flight R/T service)		USB
6640.00	New York (in-flight R/T service)		USB 0728
6640.00	San Francisco (in-flight R/T service)		USB
6643.00	Berne (in-flight R/T service)		USB 0653 0808 0855 1743
6643.00	UNID		LSB CB style (Italy) 2318
6645.00	UNID		LSB CB style (Eng) 2119
6647.00	British Naval		USB 1617 "Foxtrot 94" & "Foxtrot 91" radio check 1454
6655.00	UNID		LSB CB style (France) 0908 1634 1739
6660.00	UNID		USB CB style (Fr) 1009 1857
6665.00	UNID		LSB CB style (Fr) 0828 1742
6668.00	UNID		USB CB style (France) 0803
6668.20	UNID		SITOR rig support vessels cargo lists (Gulf area) 1730
6670.00	UNID		LSB CB style (Norway/Germany) 0707 Eng 1050
6673.00	UNID		LSB CB style (Dutch) 0829 (Eng) 0934
6674.00	UNID		LSB CB style (Gary, in N Ireland) 2226
6675.00	UNID		LSB CB style (Eng) 1635
6675.50	UNID		LSB CB style (Eng) 1641
6676.00	Bangkok VOLMET, Thailand	VTBD	USB (Eng) 1612 1912 2214 2341
6676.00	Singapore VOLMET	WSJC	USB 0731 0901 1633 2121
6676.00	UNID		LSB (Scottish) 2157
6678.70	UNID		300Bd packet (FRA3KN/FD5COM) 1335 (FRA3GV/FD3GO/FR3BM) 2329
6679.00	Hong Kong VOLMET		USB 0651 2118
6679.00	Sydney VOLMET, Australia		USB 0754 2246
6681.00	UNID		300Bd packet (FRA2CP) 0907 (FD3GO/FRA3CP) 1425
6683.00	USAF Andrews AFB, USA		USB (to "200") 1953
6684.90	Spa Publications		

6685-6765
AERONAUTICAL MOBILE (MAINLY MILITARY) 3KHz channels

kHz.	Station	Call	Mode / Heard/Times GMT
6685.00	Moscow Air, Russia	RFNV	CW air meteo 0638 0810 0942 1344 1912 2111 2213
6685.00	Saudi Airlines company frequency		USB 1048 1716
6685.00	US Military		USB "Masterpiece" radio check 0936
6688.00	Portland Naval, UK		USB with "7UN" 0756
6690.00	UNID		LSB CB style (Ger) 1430
6693.00	Canadian Military		USB Search/Rescue channel
6693.00	CIS VOLMET channel		USB 0731 1638 1706 1919 2200 2319
6693.00	US Naval		USB "M9X" (going "green") 0626 "9JL" radio check 1459
6697.00	US Military		USB "2RE" 0657
6700.00	CIS VOLMET channel		USB 2147
6700.00	UNID		LSB CB style (Italy) 1837
6705.00	Canadian Military		USB
6705.00	UNID		LSB CB style (Fr) 0636
6708.00	Numbers Station		USB Ger (female voice) 1613
6712.00	French Military		USB Fr 0718 1710
6715.00	UNID		AM Asian lang religious programme 2319
6720.00	US Naval		USB "1FU" (to "XB") 0645 "4QJ"/"9HQ" 2210
6723.00	US Naval		USB "7IC" & "D5J" 2227
6725.00	UNID		LSB CB style (Fr) 0946
6730.00	CIS VOLMET channel		USB 1838 1947 2137 2210 2248
6736.00	Addis Ababa Air, Ethiopia	ETD3	50r 1955 2152 2247
6738.00	RAF, UK		USB "ARCHITECT" 0732 0810 2201 2300
6738.00	USAF Andrews AFB, USA		USB
6738.00	USAF Croughton, UK		USB
6738.00	USAF Incirlik, Turkey		USB 2337
6738.00	USAF Lajes, Azores		USB 2153 2239 2339
6738.00	USAF Thule, Greenland		USB wx 0845
6741.80	Tunisian Embassy traffic		SITOR 1948
6745.00	Numbers Station		AM "CIO2" (female voice) 0142 2150 2248 "VLB2" 1946
6750.00	PBS China		AM Chinese 2215
6750.00	USAF Croughton, UK		USB 0741 0814
6753.00	Canadian Military		USB wx 0641 0733 1838 2331 (reports H + 20 30 40)
6758.00	Numbers Station		AM Slav (female voice) 0710 0804 1010 1500 1859
6758.00	RAF Pitreavie, Scotland	MKL	CW wx 0709 0909 1401 1905 2205
6759.00	Prague, Czech Republic	OLX	CW ID 0900 1457
6761.00	USAF		USB 1746 2230 2328
6764.90	Spa Publications		Test

6765-7000
FIXED & LAND MOBILE

kHz.	Station	Call	Mode / Heard/Times GMT
6770.00	UNID		50r Arab (with passport details in French of Nigerian subjects) 1720
6779.00	German Military		USB "EA659" radio check 0643
6783.00	UNID		75n 5 let grps (long msg) 1900
6784.00	Numbers Station		AM Eng (female voice) 2122
6790.00	Ankara Met	YMA20	FAX wx maps 0647 1615
6790.00	R Moscow feeder		USB Slav feeder 2038
6792.00	INTERPOL	FSB	SITOR 0856 0901 1614 Selcal IPBM 1501 IPBK 1813
6798.00	French Military, Orleans	FDY	50r "Voyez le Brick...." 1337 1642
6798.50	Spanish Police		SITOR p/lang 0910
6807.00	Polish Embassy traffic		100POL-ARQ 5 fig grps 1904
6808.00	UNID	UCT	CW (clg RMEU) 2004
6810.00	UNID		CW "042/00" repeatedly 0731
6812.00	USAF Andrews AFB, USA		USB (VIP channel)
6817.00	USAF Andrews AFB, USA		USB phonepatch tfc 0841
6819.00	UNID		75n 5 let grps 1907
6821.00	USAF weather service		FAX wx maps 0911 0928 1338 1839
6825.00	French Military	FAV22	CW "QLH 3881/6825kHz" 0900 ID 1031
6830.00	Madrid Met, Spain	ECA7	FAX wx maps 2217
6835.00	Bracknell Met, UK	GFL22	50r 1816 1940 2041 2207 (1800-0600)
6840.00	Numbers Station		AM phonetics (female voice) 1909 2005 2234
6840.00	PBS China		AM Chinese 0947 2143 2222
6845.00	Numbers Station		AM Slav (male voice) 1839
6847.50	UNID		72ARQ/E/4 Idle 1034
6853.00	Numbers Station		USB "KR" (Ger female voice) & tones 0734 1404 2207
6859.50	French Military, Metz	FDC	CW 0813 1035
6867.20	UNID		SITOR Selcal QEMP 1429
6873.00	VOA feeder		LSB Eng 0646
6880.00	Moscow Met, Russia	RAN77	FAX wx maps 0713 0807 0922 1339 1430 1643 1921
6880.00	Numbers Station		USB Eng (female voice) 2124
6883.00	INTERPOL, Zurich	HEP	CW 1054
6887.30	UNID		50r RYs & QBF 0931
6890.00	French Military		200ARQ/M2/4 ch A p/lang msgs 1645
6890.00	R Bosnia-Herzegovina		AM Slav 1910
6905.00	INTERPOL	FSB	SITOR 0904 1432 1941 2126
6911.70	Egyptian Embassy traffic		SITOR 1813
6913.00	UNID		75n 5 let grps (long msg) 1842
6914.50	UNID		SITOR "BMBX" with mailbox msgs (Eng) 1502
6918.50	Madrid Met, Spain	ECA7	FAX wx maps 0735 0905 1019 1340 1405 1648 2205
6920.00	Kiev Met, Ukraine		50n 0732 0949 1014 1552 1907 2125
6925.30	US Embassy frequency (rptd Warrenton)	KKN50	CW 0734 0925 0932
6930.00	Numbers Station		AM Eng (female voice) 2206
6930.00	Spanish Naval	EBA	CW 0832 wx p/lang Span 0838 1706
6933.00	R China International		AM Slav 1724 1831 Span 2126 2138 2232
6934.00	CIS Naval	RIT	CW 1743 (to UHGU) 2200
6943.00	UNID		72ARQ/E/4 Idle 0903
6950.00	Kiev Met, Ukraine		FAX wx maps 0736 1015 1850 1943 2207
6950.00	Numbers Station		USB Eng (female voice) 2101
6950.00	R China International		AM Eng 2127 2152 Slav 1707 Ger 1912
6954.00	Polish Embassy traffic		100POL-ARQ p/lang 0827
6955.00	R China International		AM Eng 1913 Asian lang 1832
6959.00	Numbers Station		USB Eng (female voice) 2236
6960.00	UNID		LSB CB style (Fr) 1341
6963.00	French Military		72ARQ/E/4 p/lang 1021 1852
6963.50	UNID		USB Slav simplex R/T 1038
6964.00	Bandirma, Turkey	YMB20	CW wx sea fcsts (Eng) 0719 1900 1927 (also msrd 6966.0)
6966.00	French Military, Orleans	FDY	50r "Voyez le Brick.." 0905 1421
6972.00	Bucharest Press (ROMPRES)	YOG59	50r Fr 1650
6974.30	UNID		SITOR Selcal TVQX (probably UN traffic) 1845
6975.00	UNID		50n RYs & encrypted 2146
6976.00	UNID		72ARQ/E/4 Idle 0822 1915
6985.00	Polish Embassy traffic		100POL-ARQ 5 fig grps 0840 1432
6985.00	China Met		75r 2130
6985.00	UNID		USB CB style (Spain) 1022
6991.50	Spanish Police		SITOR p/lang 0644 Selcals TWBB & TWBM 1434
6992.00	RAF London	MKK	50r(VFT) QBF & RYls 0720 1040 (LSB ch 6995.0)
6992.30	British Military cadet tng net	MFI51	CW 1123
6994.80	UNID		50r 5 let grps 0736
6999.90	Spa Publications		

7000-7100
AMATEUR RADIO

| 7001.00 | UNID | | 81Bd spec code type 0907 |

kHz.	Station	Call	Mode / Heard/Times GMT
7030.00	UNID		AM Mid-East or Asian lang & music 2129
7034.00	Amateur packet radio	EA1ECY	300Bd packet net (to EA2DA) 1437
7034.20	Amateur packet radio	EA2CMM	300Bd packet net (to EA4EIU) 1652
7038.80	Single Letter Beacon	S	CW 1506 2211
7038.90	Single Letter Beacon	C	CW 0908 1834 1848 2044
7099.90	Spa Publications		

7100-7300
BROADCASTING & AMATEUR RADIO (USA)

kHz.	Station	Mode / Heard/Times GMT
7105.00	BBC	AM Fr 0613 Slav 1709
7105.00	REE Spain	AM Span 1910
7105.00	R Moscow	AM Eng 1845
7110.00	R Moscow	AM Eng 2312 2350
7115.00	R Moscow	AM Eng 2114
7115.00	R Svoboda	AM Slav 1515 1849 1915
7120.00	BBC	AM Slav 1800
7120.00	Deutsche Welle	AM Port 2209 Slav 2221
7120.00	R Netherland	AM Eng 1835
7125.00	BBC	AM Eng 2132
7125.00	IRRS Italy	AM Eng 0625 0816 1742 2341 (UN radio relay 0700 0739)
7125.00	R Conakry	AM Fr 2201 2224
7125.00	R Moscow	AM Eng 2252
7130.00	Deutsche Welle	AM Ger 2210
7130.00	R Netherland	AM Dutch 0712 1423
7135.00	R France International	AM Fr 1835 1916
7135.00	R Netherland	AM Dutch 0810
7140.00	R Moscow	AM Eng 2231 Fr 1846
7145.00	Algeria	AM Arab 2202
7145.00	Polish Radio Warsaw	AM Ger 1508 1516
7150.00	BBC	AM Eng 0626 0721
7150.00	R Moscow	AM Eng 2229 2239
7150.00	R Ukraine International	AM Eng 2105 2133 (2100-2200 0000-0100) Slav 2222
7155.00	R Tirana	AM Eng 1538
7165.00	R Moscow	AM Eng 0722 0830
7170.00	Deutsche Welle	AM Portuguese (German lang lessons) 2204
7170.00	R Australia	AM Eng 1600
7170.00	R China International	AM Eng 2201 2254
7170.00	R Moscow	AM Eng 1711 1912 2135
7170.00	VOA	AM Eng 0541 0627 0650 Slav 1956
7175.00	RTV Italiana	AM Ital 0626 0719
7180.00	BBC	AM Eng 2314
7180.00	R Moscow	AM Eng 1957 2134 2241 Fr 2310
7180.00	AWR	AM Eng 0744
7181.00	Intership working	USB (Scottish) 0713
7185.00	Deutsche Welle	AM Ger 1839 1925 2047
7185.00	Voice of Turkey	AM Eng 2223 2258 2315
7190.00	R Svoboda	AM Slav 0853 1055 1851
7195.00	R Canada International	AM Eng 2205 2224
7195.00	R Romania International	AM Eng 2140 2156 Ger 1841
7195.00	R Ukraine International	AM Eng 2204 2256
7200.00	VOA	AM Fr 2048
7205.00	R Moscow	AM Eng 1712 1913 2205 Fr 2257
7210.00	BBC	AM Fr 1135 Polish 1708
7215.00	VOA	AM Eng 1744
7220.00	R Budapest	AM Eng 2135 Ger 1854
7220.00	R Svoboda	AM Slav 0842 1410
7225.00	Deutsche Welle	AM Eng 1646 Urdu 1514
7225.00	R Romania International	AM Eng 0634 2115
7225.00	R Bulgaria	AM Eng 2355
7230.00	AWR	AM Eng 1049 Ger 0811 Multilingual ID 0658
7230.00	R Japan	AM Eng 0729
7230.00	R Moscow	AM Eng 2136
7235.00	RTV Italiana	AM Fr 1637 Ital 1720
7240.00	R Ukraine International	AM Eng 2206 2218 2245 Ger 1749 1801
7245.00	R Svoboda	AM Slav 1100
7250.00	R Canada International	AM Eng 0010
7250.00	R Vatican	AM Eng 0736 Latin mass 1510 Fr 0722
7255.00	Deutsche Welle	AM Eng 1606 Slav 1042
7255.00	R Nigeria	AM Eng 0631
7260.00	R Australia	AM Eng 1519 1633 1719 1816 1858 1901 1958
7260.00	R Canada International	AM Eng 2207
7265.00	SWF, Germany	AM Ger 0939 1102
7270.00	Polish Radio Warsaw	AM Ger 1640
7270.00	VOA	AM Slav 1959

kHz.	Station	Call	Mode / Heard/Times GMT
7275.00	Deutsche Welle		AM Ger 2225
7275.00	REE Spain		AM Span 1713 2051 2244
7280.00	R France International		AM Fr 0647
7280.00	R Moscow		AM Ger 1641 1817
7285.00	Polish Radio Warsaw		AM Eng 1654 1813 Ger 1520
7285.00	R Ukraine International		AM Eng 2159
7294.00	UNID		AM Ital 0701
7295.00	BBC		AM Eng 0737 Fr 0615
7295.00	R Moscow		AM Eng 2303
7295.00	R Svoboda		AM Slav 1411
7299.90	Spa Publications		

7300-8100
FIXED & LAND MOBILE

kHz.	Station	Call	Mode / Heard/Times GMT
7300.00	R Moscow		AM Eng 2229 2253
7310.00	R Moscow		AM Slav 2000
7311.00	French Military, Orleans	FDY	50r "Voyez le Brick...." 1103
7311.50	French Military, Metz	FDC	CW 0734 1337
7315.00	R Moscow		AM Slav 2052
7315.00	WHRI, USA		AM Eng 0652 0723 0832 0940 1104
7325.00	BBC		AM Eng 0741 0815 2054 2141 2208 2245
7325.00	VOA		AM Eng 0656
7330.00	R Moscow		AM Eng 1715
7332.00	UNID		CW 5 fig grps 2139
7335.00	Ottawa Time Station, Canada	CHU	USB 0616 0738 0743 0833
7335.00	R China International		AM Fr 2055 2137
7335.00	R Moscow		AM Eng 2235
7337.00	Numbers Station		USB Eng (female voice) 1842
7340.00	R Moscow		AM Slav 2213
7340.00	Voz del Cid		AM Span 0640 0658
7340.00	UNID		72ARQ/E/4 Idle 1027
7340.00	VOA		AM Fr 2155
7345.00	R Prague		AM Eng 0722 1722 2104 Ger 0932 Span 2055 Fr 2244
7345.00	R Slovakia International		AM Eng 1837 Fr 1931
7350.00	R China International		AM Fr 2056 2158
7355.00	WHRI, USA		AM Eng 0659 0744 0941
7360.00	R Moscow		AM Ger 1839 1907 1947
7370.00	R Moscow		AM Fr 1716 1840
7375.00	Radio for Peace International		USB Eng 0616 0641
7378.00	French Military	FDE2	CW 1044
7380.00	R Moscow		AM Eng 2209 2244
7385.00	TWR		AM Eng 0703 0735 0817 0834
7390.00	R Moscow		AM Ger 1841 1916
7400.00	R Moscow		AM Ger 1656 1842 Span 2248
7401.00	Tehran Press (IRNA)	9BC	50n Eng 1919 Arab 1846
7405.00	R China International		AM Ital 1843
7405.00	VOA		AM Eng 0636 1105
7412.00	All India Radio		AM Eng 1534 1745 1812 2209 2224
7415.00	VOA		AM Eng 2001 2036 2158
7420.00	R Moscow		AM Eng 1804
7425.00	WEWN, USA		AM Eng 0638 0740 0942
7428.50	Buenos Aires Press (TELAM)		50r Span 2249
7430.00	Voice of Greece		AM Greek 2150
7435.00	WWCR, USA		AM Eng 0006 0857
7440.00	R Yerevan		AM Eng 2246 2251
7450.00	Voice of Greece		AM Eng 1920
7451.50	French Military	RFFP	200ARQ/M2/4 msg to RFFVAY for flight departure to Sarajevo 1359
7453.00	Single Letter Beacon	R	CW 0008 1428 1535 1940 2216
7454.00	RAF London	MKK	50r (VFT) QBF & RYIs 1849 (LSB ch 7457.0)
7455.00	R Bulgaria		AM Eng 0011 2246 2305 Ger 1717 Fr 1805
7465.00	Kol Israel		AM Eng 1806 2003 2236 2255
7465.00	Monitor Radio International		AM Eng 0944 1046 1106
7470.00	R China International		AM Ital 1844 Slav 1941
7475.00	RTV Tunis		AM Arab 1850 1909 2152 2210 2244
7485.00	R Pakistan		AM Asian lang 1806
7489.00	RAF Akrotiri, Cyprus	MKD	50r(VFT) QBF & RYIs 1847 (LSB ch 7492.0)
7490.00	WJCR, USA		AM Eng 0725 0852 0945
7495.00	Tbilisi Met, Georgia		FAX wx maps 1820 1921 2217
7504.00	PBS China		AM Chinese 1732 2153 2240
7508.00	UNID	USG2	CW (clg UIL2) 2246
7508.50	Pretoria Met, RSA	ZRO2	FAX wx maps 0520
7510.00	Monitor Radio International		AM Eng 0946 2037 2252 Span 2306
7512.50	USAF weather service		75r 1849

kHz.	Station	Call	Mode / Heard/Times GMT
7520.00	Beijing Press (XINHUA)	BZP57	75r Eng 1847 1923 ID & RYs 1807
7520.00	Monitor Radio International		AM Eng 0718
7520.00	WEWN, USA		AM Ital 0653 2253
7521.50	French Military, Orleans	FDY	50r "Voyez le Brick.." 1652
7530.00	Boston CG, USA	NMF	FAX wx maps 2057 (1730-2215)
7532.00	INTERPOL	FSB	SITOR 1048 1446 1850
7533.00	British Naval	GYA	75r QBF & test call to MTT 1448
7535.00	Darwin Met, Australia	AXI33	FAX wx maps 1537 (1100-2300)
7541.00	UNID		75n 5 let grps 1851
7550.00	R Korea		AM Eng 0819 Ger 1944
7552.50	UNID		100ARQ/E3/8 Idle 1851
7570.00	Tashkent Met, Uzbekistan	RBX72	FAX wx maps 0140 0435 0735 1030
7572.50	French Military, Metz	FDC	CW 0815
7580.00	RAF Akrotiri, Cyprus	MKD	50r(VFT) QBF & RYls 1339 1721 (LSB ch 7583.0)
7582.00	US Naval, Diego Garcia	NKW	FAX wx maps 1658 1822 2211 2301
7584.00	Numbers Station		AM Ger (female voice) 1108
7586.00	UNID		96ARQ/E/4 Idle 1852 2212
7588.00	French Military	QO9Y	CW test call with "Voyez le Brick.." 1451
7592.00	Belgrade Press (TANJUG)	YZD6	50r Fr 1823
7594.50	USAF weather service Croughton, UK	EGWR	75n 1912 1924
7597.70	German Govt net		96ARQ/E/8 1451
7607.00	Swedish Embassy traffic		100SWED-ARQ p/lang 0817 1049 aircraft route plan 1453
7610.00	Cairo Press (MENA)	SUA231	75r Fr 1913
7611.70	Egyptian Embassy traffic		SITOR 1722 1808
7614.00	UNID		72ARQ/E/4 Idle 1415 1655 1825
7621.00	USAF weather service		75n 1855
7622.00	UNID		50n p/lang Slav (possibly Balkan area) 0730
7625.00	Jeddah Met, Saudi Arabia	HZN47	100n 1914 2218 2248 2302
7627.00	US Embassy frequency (rptd Athens)	KWS78	CW 0742 1540 1729 2226
7640.00	Minsk Met, Byelorussia	RST76	FAX wx maps 1109 1453 1947 2243
7642.20	UNID		200ARQ/M2/4 5 let grps 1724
7646.00	Hamburg (Quickborn) Met, Germany	DDH7	50r 0652 0947 1032 1110 1416 1458 1810 2219
7650.00	Beijing Press (XINHUA)	BZR67	75r Eng 1857 1939 ID & RYs 1810
7655.00	French Police		100ARQ/E3/8 1812
7658.00	Belgrade Press (TANJUG)	YZD	50r Eng 0654 1416 1454 1725 2220 ID & RYs 1700
7659.00	UNID		SITOR 5 let grps 0835
7660.00	R China International		AM Slav 1813 1948
7663.00	UNID		SITOR 5 let grps (long msg) 0955
7663.50	French Military, Orleans	FDY	50r "Voyez le Brick.." 1700
7670.00	Moscow Met, Russia	RCC76	FAX wx maps 1033 1111 1455 1814 2244
7678.30	Swiss Embassy traffic	HBD	SITOR p/lang 0957
7680.00	British Military	GXQ	50r (VFT) RYls 1051 1112 1515 1811 (LSB ch 7683.0)
7685.00	Moscow Met, Russia	RVM53	50r 1430 1545 1949 2221
7697.50	UNID		SITOR Selcal QEMP (probably Spanish) 1052 1410
7700.00	R China International		AM Fr 1812 1859
7701.60	Dutch Embassy traffic	PCW1	SITOR 5 let grps 1456
7706.00	UNID	8A5	CW (clg "SHWX") 1950
7710.00	RAF London	MKK	50r (VFT) QBF & RYls 0641 2304 (LSB 7713.0)
7724.00	US Embassy frequency (rptd London)	KRH50	CW 1433 1517 2245 2306
7750.00	Moscow Met, Russia	RAW78	FAX wx maps 1034 1113 1419 1546
7756.00	Cairo Press (MENA)	SUA34	75r Arab 1904 1952
7760.00	Archangel Met, Russia	RGH77	50n 1431 1517 1547 ID & RYs 1813
7762.00	Archangel Met, Russia	RGH77	FAX wx maps 1053 1701 2307
7766.00	Polish Embassy traffic		100POL-ARQ "Claris Nr 462" 1459
7776.50	Ostend, Belgium	OST33	SITOR Mode B tfc list 1810 (each hour + 10 mins)
7777.50	Italian Naval	IDR	CW 1802
7780.00	R China International		AM Slav 1531 1814
7800.00	R China International		AM Fr 1905 2222
7800.70	Egyptian Embassy traffic		SITOR 2256
7801.00	Tehran Press (IRNA)	9BC22	50r Eng 1551
7806.00	Belgrade Press (TANJUG)	YZD7	50r Eng 1727 1815 1906 ID & RYs 1701
7808.00	Serbian Embassy traffic	DFZG	75n p/lang Slav 0643 1420 1532 Eng 1501 1515
7822.10	UNID		200ARQ/M2/4 Idle 1910
7836.00	CIS Naval	RIW	CW (to RMEJ) 1533 (to RMLP) 1728
7842.40	Rabat Press (MAP)	CNM20/1X	50r Eng 1330 Fr 1035 1552 (1000-1130 1530-1700)
7845.70	Egyptian Embassy traffic		SITOR 1913
7852.50	Tirana Press (ATA)	ZAA	50r Eng 1915
7855.00	Moscow Met, Russia	ROK24	50r 1535 1825 2252
7863.00	China Met		75r 1827 1916
7863.50	Warsaw, Poland	SPW	SITOR 0920
7870.00	UNID		USB Scand (probably Icelandic Radio) 1919
7880.00	Hamburg (Quickborn) Met, Germany	DDK3	FAX wx maps 1433 1841 2223
7887.00	Beijing Press (XINHUA)	BZS27	75r Eng 1830 1842
7896.00	Austrian Embassy traffic	OEC	96SI-ARQ(5 char) p/lang 1056
7900.00	German Govt press info service		96FEC-A p/lang 1703 1731
7902.00	French Police		100ARQ/E3/8 1055 "RPT CRS MARSEILLE" 1002
7910.00	Almaty Met, Kazakhstan	RCW79	FAX wx maps 2246 2258

kHz.	Station	Call	Mode / Heard/Times GMT
7911.00	UNID		USB simplex R/T (Fr) 1845
7917.00	French Military, Metz	FDC	CW 1057
7924.70	Egyptian Embassy traffic		SITOR Selcal RCVB 2255
7935.00	PBS China		AM Chinese 2248
7946.00	UNID		96ARQ/E/4 Idle 1923
7954.00	Turkish Embassy traffic	TAD	144FEC 5 let grps 1833
7959.00	Tehran Press (IRNA)	9BC23	50r Eng 1537 1556 1919 1954 Arabic 1846
7960.00	RAF Akrotiri, Cyprus	MKD	50r (VFT) QBF & RYIs 1816 2255 (LSB 7963.0)
7964.20	Portuguese Military		SITOR msgs from Ponta Delgada, Azores 1927
7970.00	UNID		USB Slav feeder 2227 2257
7975.00	Warsaw Press		SITOR Mode B Polish 1818
7996.00	Belgrade Press (TANJUG)	YZD9	50r Eng 1704 1956
8005.00	R Moscow feeder		LSB & USB 0640 2159 2230
8011.70	Spanish Embassy traffic		SITOR Selcal QEMP 0705 0811
8012.00	Israeli Naval	4XZ	CW 1550 1746 1848 2146
8020.00	Pyongyang Press (KCNA)	HMF	50r Eng 1804
8030.00	Rome Press (ANSA)	IRF50	50n Eng 1100 1544
8031.00	UN traffic		SITOR msg to UNHCR Zagreb 0754
8031.00	UNID		72ARQ/E/4 p/lang Fr 2234
8040.00	Bracknell Met, UK	GFA	FAX wx maps 0706 0943 1617 1805
8040.00	R Moscow feeder		USB Slav 2205 2231
8045.00	CIS Naval	RCV	CW (to RVWVT) 0708
8049.00	Tehran Press (IRNA)	9BC	50r Eng 2147 Arab 1806 1825
8068.00	Czech Embassy traffic		75n p/lang Slav 0945
8071.30	Spanish Police		50n 1648
8080.00	US Naval	NAM	FAX wx maps 2235
8083.00	RAF London	MKK	50n (VFT) QBF & RYIs 1215 (LSB ch 8086.0)
8083.00	Tashkent Met, Uzbekistan	RIJ75	FAX wx maps 1545 1849 2028
8090.00	US Naval, Norfolk	NAM	CW 0710 0806 0918 2256
8099.90	Spa Publications		

8100-8195
FIXED

kHz.	Station	Call	Mode / Heard/Times GMT
8105.00	French Military, Versailles	RFFX	72ARQ/E/4 0643 1640 1850 2151
8107.00	Ships/Coast Stations simplex wkg		USB Scand 2237
8109.70	UNID		SITOR Eng (order for materials, poss UN tfc) 1520
8117.00	Taipei Met, Taiwan	BMB	CW 1525 1600 1619 2139 2200
8123.00	Brazzaville Air, Congo	TNL	96ARQ/M2/4 ch B 1809 2152 2239 ch A 1851
8128.00	Australian Naval	VHI	CW 1554
8128.00	UNID		72ARQ/E/4 Idle 1609
8130.00	French Military, Metz	FDC	CW 1652
8137.50	Ankara Press (AA)	TCY	50n Turkish 1537 1545
8140.00	Italian Naval	IGJ44	CW 0711 0757 0924 1001 1106 1424
8142.50	French Military, Orleans	FDY	50r "Voyez le Brick.." 0808
8145.00	Shannon Air, Eire	EIP	50n 1107
8146.60	Rome Met, Italy	IMB55	FAX wx maps 0713 1452 1620 2233
8148.00	Danish Naval	OVG8	CW 0946 1002 1127 1528 1810 2029
8149.00	Dutch Naval	PBB	75r 0809 1108 1547 1811
8155.00	RAF Akrotiri, Cyprus	MKD	50r (VFT) QBF & RYIs 2201 2241 (LSB 8158.0)
8164.90	Nairobi Air, Kenya	5YD	50n 0019 1548 1610 1852 2155 2257
8165.00	Numbers Station		USB Slav (male voice) 2215
8166.00	Turkish Embassy traffic	TAD	144FEC p/lang 1505 (after CW contact from 10056kHz)
8167.50	UNID		CW 5 let grps (not Eng morse) 0948
8170.00	Portishead (in-flight R/T service)		USB 2121
8179.00	Spanish Police		SITOR Selcal TWBB 1003
8188.00	Numbers Station		USB Ger (female voice) 0810
8192.00	Malaysian Naval	9MR	75r (RMMJ) RYs & SGs 0022 1556
8194.90	Spa Publications		

8195-8815
MARITIME MOBILE

kHz.	Station	Call	Mode / Heard/Times GMT
8195.00	Ships wkg ch 1 dup. 8719.0kHz		USB 0903 2125 (to UUI) 0740 (to 4XO) 2234
8198.00	Ships wkg ch 2 dup. 8722.0kHz		USB 0756 0814 1710 1752 "Discovery" (GLNE) 1724
8201.00	Ships wkg ch 3 dup. 8725.0kHz		USB 1853 "Siba Grescia" (3EMB9) 0849
8204.00	Ships wkg ch 4 dup. 8728.0kHz		USB (to 3AC) 0713 (to EHY) 0832 1453 2240
8207.00	Ships wkg ch 5 dup. 8731.0kHz		USB 0631 2132 (to UAT) 2127
8210.00	Ships wkg ch 6 dup. 8734.0kHz		USB 1425 1823 1943 2141
8211.70	Egyptian Embassy traffic		SITOR 1557 1612 1813 2130
8213.00	Ships wkg ch 7 dup. 8737.0kHz		USB (to UGC) 0738 0933 (to 5BA) 0747 1622
8216.00	Ships wkg ch 8 dup. 8740.0kHz		USB 1807 (to OXZ) 0715 2235 (to WOO) 2219
8219.00	Ships wkg ch 9 dup. 8743.0kHz		USB 0819 (to FFL) 0718 P3NA5 (to LFL) 0736

kHz.	Station	Call	Mode / Heard/Times GMT
8221.50	UNID		SITOR Oil rig rpts (Eng) 2244
8222.00	Ships wkg ch 10 dup. 8746.0kHz		USB 0656 1549 (to LZW) 0715 SQAZ (to SPO) 0804
8225.00	Ships wkg ch 11 dup. 8749.0kHz		USB (to TAN) 0630 "Argonaut" (KFDV to WOO) 2140
8228.00	Ships wkg ch 12 dup. 8752.0kHz		USB 0824 1824 2144 (to UDH) 0700 (to SPC) 1633
8228.00	UNID	VDE2	CW "de VDE2" repeatedly 1816
8231.00	Ships wkg ch 13 dup. 8755.0kHz		USB 0852 1908 2225 (to LFL) 2124 CNAG 0726
8234.00	Ships wkg ch 14 dup. 8758.0kHz		USB 0720 1854
8235.40	UK Coast Control		USB "GF" with radio check 0828
8237.00	Ships wkg ch 15 dup. 8761.0kHz		USB 1558 1702 1750 9HBA3 (to SVN) 0707
8240.00	Ships wkg ch 16 dup. 8764.0kHz		USB 0827 (to GKU) 0741 1454 1626
8243.00	Ships wkg ch 17 dup. 8767.0kHz		USB 1004 (to DAJ) 0649 1008 (to UAT) 1602
8246.00	Ships wkg ch 18 dup. 8770.0kHz		USB 0711 0823 1238 (to USO5) 0823
8249.00	Ships wkg ch 19 dup. 8773.0kHz		USB 0737 2158
8252.00	Ships wkg ch 20 dup. 8776.0kHz		USB 0647 0908 1825 2134
8255.00	Ships wkg ch 21 dup. 8779.0kHz		USB 0734 (to IAR) 1851
8258.00	Ships wkg ch 22 dup. 8782.0kHz		USB 0831 0842 2142 2235 "Volgobalt 239" (UIDC) 0644
8261.00	Ships wkg ch 23 dup. 8785.0kHz		USB 0650 0844 0923 1038 1540
8264.00	Ships wkg ch 24 dup. 8788.0kHz		USB (to SPC) 0713 1905 2154
8267.00	Ships wkg ch 25 dup. 8791.0kHz		USB 0812 1005 1538
8270.00	Ships wkg ch 26 dup. 8794.0kHz		USB 0849 0854 1623 2142 (to PCG) 1753
8273.00	Ships wkg ch 27 dup. 8797.0kHz		USB 0633 0759
8276.00	Ships wkg ch 28 dup. 8800.0kHz		USB 0744 0851 1540 (to PPO) 2218
8279.00	Ships wkg ch 29 dup. 8803.0kHz		USB (to OHG) 0724 0821 0841 1603
8282.00	Ships wkg ch 30 dup. 8806.0kHz		USB 0813 1549 1853 (to FFL) 0707 0949 7THK 1900
8285.00	Ships wkg ch 31 dup. 8809.0kHz		USB 0648 1817 TCTI 0745
8288.00	Ships wkg ch 32 dup. 8812.0kHz		USB 0858 1426 2202
8291.00	Ships/Coast stations simplex		USB (calling, distress & safety ch) 0751 0838
8294.00	Ships/Coast stations simplex		USB 0642 0709 1006 1109 1855 2205
8294.00	Archangel, Russia	UCE	USB 0738
8297.00	Ships/Coast stations simplex		USB 0648 0659 0758 1752 2233
8299.00	Intership working		USB 0716
8300.00	Intership working		USB 0648 0836
8300.00	UNID		75n RYs 0928
8303.00	UNID		75n 5 let grps 0649
8305.00	Intership working		USB 0758 1110
8307.00	Intership working		USB 1007 1921
8320.00	Gibraltar Naval	GYU	75n 2300
8320.00	Intership working		USB 0852 1111 1624
8331.50	London Naval	GYA	FAX wx maps 0951 1217 2032
8333.00	Intership working		USB 1614 2144
8339.00	Ships working		CW "Cielo di Amalfi" (IBJU) 0825
8340.00	Ships working		CW WHTU (to IAR) 1800 "Moulares" (TSLK) 2257
8341.00	Ships working		CW "Camelia" (4XLQ) 0807 "Shamss" (EPCB) 1541
8342.00	Ships working		CW "Segre" (EGBZ) 0750 "Novkong" (P3IU3) 0825
8342.50	Ships working		CW "AG 1358" (EVVM) 1925
8343.00	Ships working		CW "Jolly Arancione" (IBOR) 0815 "Buona Speranza" (IBSN) 2000
8343.50	Ships working		CW 0827 2206
8344.00	Ships working		CW "Nefterudovoz 6" 0905
8344.50	Ships working		CW "Sea Cross" (9HPS2) 1611
8345.00	Ships working		CW "Kathrin" (J8IO2) 1007 "Cape Breton" (P3UN2) 1632
8345.50	Ships working		CW "Przemysl" (SPZH) 1707
8346.00	Ships working		CW "Federal Danube" (P3OZ2) 0720 "Vered" (4XLU) 1908
8346.50	Ships working		CW "Tartu" (UYSL) 1403 "Rosina Topic" (ELAJ6) 2217
8347.00	Ships working		CW "Sir Charles Parsons" (GDXQ) 0728 "Jollity" (H3QB) 1004
8347.50	Ships working		CW 2236
8348.00	Ships working		CW "Lydia 2" (SVVM) 0757 "Superitas" (9HSE3) 1627
8348.50	Ships working		CW "Trident Mariner" (SZNU) 1905 "Seishin Maru" (JMOA) 2254
8349.00	Ships working		CW "Poong Emon" (6LRR) 2256 "Tirgu Ocna" (YQGO) 1902
8349.50	Ships working		CW "Syn Pulku" (SQDX) 1142
8350.00	Ships working		CW "Puma" (5BTZ) 0725 "Po" (ICJR) 1654 "Beeco Europe" (ELFO9) 1806
8350.50	Ships working		CW ESMD (to ESF) 1545
8351.00	Ships working		CW "Super Lady" (9HEI4) 0752 "Rio Amazonas" (HCRA) 0843
8351.50	Ships working		CW LYJI (to LYL) 2131
8352.00	Ships working		CW "Furia" (5MVE) 1009 "Georgiy Chicherin" (UYUY) 1916
8352.50	Ships working		CW "STM 8352" (LYHB to LYL) 2208
8353.00	Ships working		CW "Salonta" (YQHS) 0752
8353.50	Ships working		CW 0644
8354.00	Ships working		CW UDXS 1548
8354.50	Ships working		CW "Iasi" (YQAH) 0736
8355.00	Ships working		CW "Jemima-M" (C6MF6) 1543 "Avar" (TCVJ) 1851
8355.50	Ships working		CW 1855
8356.00	Ships working		CW "Baltiyskiy 110 " (UUPL) 0932 "Conquistador" (9HXB2) 2249
8356.50	Ships working		CW USZA 0653 9HGC3 (to URL) 1031

kHz.	Station	Call	Mode / Heard/Times GMT
8357.00	Ships working		CW "Corvus" (UOID) 0648
8357.50	Ships working		CW 1458
8358.00	Ships working		CW "Republica Del Ecuador" (HCRE) 2306
8358.50	Ships working		CW "Hilda" (3EIK5) 0712
8359.00	Ships working		CW 0845 1915
8359.50	Ships working		CW "Terutoku Maru" (JHTE) 1556 "Fierbinti" (YQHH) 2227
8360.00	Ships working		CW "Mare Glaciale" (IBBB) 1052 LAEE4 2126
8360.50	Ships working		CW "Suzdal" (UVEQ) 1740
8361.00	Ships working		CW "Sansovino" (ICYO) 0655 "Manthos" (SVFZ) 1002
8361.50	Ships working		CW "Iclios Glory" 1651 "Tobruk" (SQBP) 2213
8362.00	Ships working		CW "Dora Riparia" (IMBW) 1100
8362.50	Ships working		CW EVEN (to UIW) 0657 "Kota Jati" (9VLB) 1829
8363.00	Ships working		CW "MC Coral" (C6HP5) 0959
8363.50	Ships working		CW 2128
8364.00	Ships working		CW "Sealand Achiever" (WPKM) 0804 "Krasnoyarskiy" (ULKT) 0823
8364.50	Ships working		CW USLB (to URL) 2248
8365.00	Ships working		CW "Isola Turchese" (IBLN) 0847 "Bright Star" (9VVA) 1553
8365.50	Ships working		CW "Brisas 1" (3EXU5) 1922
8366.00	Ships calling ch 1		CW 9HCS3 0625 9HXB2 (to FFL) 1000
8366.50	Ships calling ch 2		CW URWY 0909 EMZT (to UON) 2124
8367.00	Ships calling ch 5		CW UPHD (to IAR) 0749 YQCN (to CNP) 0813
8367.50	Ships calling ch 6		CW C4DB (to CNP) 0909 6KWP 1740
8368.00	Ships calling ch 3		CW 3EWR4 (to TAH) 0839 ULRT (to TAH) 1033
8368.50	Ships calling ch 7		CW ELMP6 (to 9AR) 0835 "Mokhni" (URWE) 0943
8369.00	Ships calling ch 4		CW J8GC3 (to IAR) 2003 UZTE (to A9M) 2157
8369.50	Ships calling ch 8		CW 3EIK5 (to KFS) 0710 "Khudozhnik Gabashvili" (UKKE) 1912
8369.50	Ship working		170/50rc "Kherson" (UHRU) 1640
8370.00	Ships calling ch 9		CW SFTZ (to PCH) 0751
8370.00	Ship working		CW "Zelenoborsk" (UIRV) 0814
8370.50	Ships calling ch 10		CW "Mramorny" (UUXN) 0826
8370.50	Ships working		170/50nc "Priozersk" (ESUO) 1549
8371.00	Ships working		CW "Kompozitor Novikov" (UIDB) 0730 "Mikola Bazhan" (URUS) 0904
8371.50	Ships working		CW "Anatoly Lunacharskiy" (UKFK) 1855
8372.00	Ships working		CW "Lex Almendro" (YJZS8) 2240
8372.50	Ships working		CW "Odoyev" (LYGY) 1840
8373.00	Ships working		CW "Euterpe" (C4PU) 2135
8374.00	Ships working		CW "Sea Fox" (9HFR3) 0818 "Annitsa L" (SXBP) 2219
8374.50	Ships working		CW "Nikolay Kremlyanskiy" (UTYE) 1813
8375.00	Ships working		CW "Ladoga 11" (EMFG) 1025 UWLO (to UZP2) 1642
8375.50	Ships working		CW 0725
8376.00	Ships working		CW "Valaams" (YLMH) 1020 "Oakwell" (9HUU3) 1639
8376.50	Maritime Safety channel		SITOR Mode B 0838 1556
8377.00	Ships wkg ch 2 dup. 8417.0kHz		SITOR "Mekhanik Evgrafov" (EKMN) 1057 "CPC Helvetia" (V2EM) 1337
8377.50	Ships wkg ch 3 dup. 8417.5kHz		SITOR Selcal KYXQ (Odessa) 1835
8378.00	Ships wkg ch 4 dup. 8418.0kHz		SITOR "Agip Piemonte" (IBXT) 1218
8378.50	Ships wkg ch 5 dup. 8418.5kHz		SITOR "Norsk Barde" (LCZO3) 0901
8379.00	Ships wkg ch 6 dup. 8419.0kHz		SITOR Selcal KYVX (Moscow) 1831
8379.50	Ships wkg ch 7 dup. 8419.5kHz		SITOR "Wani Swan" (3FAJ2) 0919 "Cast Polarbear" (C6JX9) 1040
8380.00	Ships wkg ch 8 dup. 8420.0kHz		SITOR "Edouard L D" (FNFD) 0718 "Agip Piemonte" (IBXT) 0726
8380.50	Ships wkg ch 9 dup. 8420.5kHz		SITOR "Sandvik" (SXDK) 0734 "Kaliope" (3ECE6) 2252
8381.00	Ships wkg ch 10 dup. 8421.0kHz		SITOR "Merete Wonsild" (C6HR5) 0814 Selcal VFKQ (Lyngby) 0737
8381.00	Ship working		CW "Babor" (7TGQ) 0932
8381.50	Ships wkg ch 11 dup. 8421.5kHz		SITOR "Hassir' Mel" (7TCL) 1004 "Ramdane Abane" (7TGH) 1832
8382.00	Ships wkg ch 12 dup. 8422.0kHz		SITOR Selcal KYVS (Tallinn) 1231
8382.50	Ships wkg ch 13 dup. 8422.5kHz		SITOR "Komsomolets Azerbaydzhana" (UJXG) 1952
8383.00	Ships wkg ch 14 dup. 8423.0kHz		SITOR "Gulbene" (ESBV) 0658 "Burgas" (USQS) 0726
8383.50	Ships wkg ch 15 dup. 8423.5kHz		SITOR "Bytom" (SQJW) 0645
8384.00	Ships wkg ch 16 dup. 8424.0kHz		SITOR "Paraskevi 2" (SVKY) 1756 "Santos" (DGWH) 2308
8384.50	Ships wkg ch 17 dup. 8424.5kHz		SITOR "Rimba Meranti" (9MWS) 0938 "Norlandia" (PJGB) 1012
8385.00	Ships wkg ch 18 dup. 8425.0kHz		SITOR "Larbi Ben M'Hidi" (7THK) 1743 "Ruby" (C6HW5) 2215
8385.50	Ships wkg ch 19 dup. 8425.5kHz		SITOR "Marshal Zakharov" (UKED) 0850
8386.00	Ships wkg ch 20 dup. 8426.0kHz		SITOR "Agip Napoli" (IBMJ) 1224
8386.50	Ships wkg ch 21 dup. 8426.5kHz		SITOR "Serafin Topic" (ELBZ2) 1753 "Jag Pari" (VTBP) 1940
8387.00	Ships wkg ch 22 dup. 8427.0kHz		SITOR Selcal VFKQ (Lyngby) 0821
8387.50	Ships wkg ch 23 dup. 8427.5kHz		SITOR "Oldendorf" (ELIU5) 1009 "Powstaniec Slaski" (SPZL) 1250
8388.00	Ships wkg ch 24 dup. 8428.0kHz		SITOR "Mekhanik Artsev" (UNFW) 0910 "Leon" 1100
8388.50	Ships wkg ch 25 dup. 8428.5kHz		SITOR "Sasha Borodulin" (USCC) 2051 "Konstantin Korshunov" (UUHS) 1951
8389.00	Ships wkg ch 26 dup. 8429.0kHz		SITOR "Jose Antonio Nores" (EHLX) 2043

kHz.	Station	Call	Mode / Heard/Times GMT
8389.00	Ships working		CW "Ohanet" (7TQF) 1915
8389.50	Ships wkg ch 27 dup. 8429.5kHz		SITOR "Ville de Dakar" (6WAD) 0725
8390.00	Ships wkg ch 28 dup. 8430.0kHz		170/50nc "Kapitonas Reutov" (LYBM) 0837
8390.50	Ships wkg ch 29 dup. 8430.5kHz		170/50nc 0833
8391.00	Ships wkg ch 30 dup. 8431.0kHz		SITOR "Rauf Bey" (TCGS) 2227
8391.50	Ships wkg ch 31 dup. 8431.5kHz		SITOR "Dubulti" (YLBZ) 0945 "Slavyanka" (UGSH) 2241
8392.00	Ships wkg ch 32 dup. 8432.0kHz		SITOR "Taurupe" (YLBL) 0912 "Mehanikis Fjodorovs" (YLBJ) 0930
8392.50	Ships wkg ch 33 dup. 8432.5kHz		SITOR "Valentin Khutorskoy" (UIDK) 1902
8393.00	Ships wkg ch 34 dup. 8433.0kHz		170/50nc "Sventoji" (LYDD) 1015
8393.50	Ships wkg ch 35 dup. 8433.5kHz		RTTY
8394.00	Ships wkg ch 36 dup. 8434.0kHz		SITOR "Zvolen" (OLMD) 0942
8394.50	Ships wkg ch 37 dup. 8434.5kHz		RTTY
8395.00	Ship working		CW "Wave Crest" (3FHG) 1721 out of normal sub-band
8395.00	Ships wkg ch 38 dup. 8435.0kHz		SITOR 1844
8395.50	Ships wkg ch 39 dup. 8435.5kHz		SITOR "CMB Ensign" (C4VE) 0758 Selcal VMFV (Ostend) 1754
8396.00	Ships wkg ch 40 dup. 8436.0kHz		SITOR Selcal QSPV (Goeteborg) 0722
8396.50	Ships working (non paired)		170/50nc "Skulptor Konenkov" (UUXO) 1835
8397.00	Ships working (non paired)		SITOR "Nikolay Novikov" (UWPI) 0937 "Kapitan Glazachev" (UHCK) 0946
8397.50	Ships working (non paired)		170/50nc "Kaliningradneft" (UNXR) 1133 "Alatyrles" (UYST) 1831
8398.00	Ships working (non paired)		170/50nc "17 Syezd Profsoyazov" (UIHO) 1958
8398.50	Ships working (non paired)		SITOR "Safe Gothia" (SJVA) 0835
8399.00	Ships working (non paired)		170/50nc "Milgravis" (YLFR) 2010 "Professor Tovstykh" (UOJQ) 1926
8399.50	Ships working (non paired)		170/50nc "General Vladimir Zaimov" (UYCB) 1905 "Yarkiy Luch" (UTSS) 1052
8400.00	Ships working (non paired)		170/50nc "Dmitriy Shostakovich" (UMYN) 1725
8400.50	Hungarian Embassy traffic		125DUP-ARQ 0910
8400.50	Ships working (non paired)		170/50nc 0741
8401.00	Ships working (non paired)		170/50rc "Mikhail Vladimirskiy" (UFEK) 1944
8401.50	Ships working (non paired)		170/50nc "Sevan" (UVWU) 1825
8402.00	Ships working (non paired)		170/50nc 0844
8402.50	Ships working (non paired)		170/50nc "Kokand" (UUZQ) 2220 "Kurskaya Kosa" (UBCI) 2252
8403.00	Ships working (non paired)		170/50nc "Dusetos" (LYEO) 1551
8403.50	Ships working (non paired)		170/50nc UOZO (to UIW) 0648 "Engure" (UWFL) 0820
8404.00	Ships working (non paired)		170/50nc "Kompositor Musorgskiy" (UONY) 0944
8404.50	Ships working (non paired)		170/50nc "Ivorales" 0802
8405.00	Ships working (non paired)		170/50nc "Nikolay Morozov" (UNDX) 2150
8405.50	Ships working (non paired)		170/50nc "Geroi Monkady" (UTYN) 1907
8406.00	Ships working (non paired)		SITOR 1754
8406.50	Ships working (non paired)		170/50nc 0845 ESMY 0937
8407.00	Ships working (non paired)		170/50nc "Vladimir Mayakovskiy" (UNXG) 2230
8407.50	Ships working (non paired)		RTTY
8408.00	Ships working (non paired)		SITOR 1245 1514 & 170/50nc "Volga" (UDZS) 1915
8408.50	Ships working (non paired)		170/50nc UEMP 2254
8409.00	Ship working		CW "Soura" (UPOS to ROD9) 1408
8409.00	Ships working (non paired)		170/50nc "Bakaritsa" (UUBY) 1248
8409.50	Italian Naval	IDR8	CW 0754 1132
8410.00	Ships working (non paired)		170/50nc 1924
8410.00	Ship working		CW "Kingfisher" (P3GH4) 0624 RMMV (to RIT) 2223 "Arabat" (EOYW) 2232
8410.50	Ships working (non paired)		170/50nc "Aleksandrit" (USGH) 1017 "Korundovyy" (UQAP) 1647
8411.00	Ships working (non paired)		170/50nc "MB-0100" 0757
8411.00	Ship working		CW "Volgobalt 196" 1121
8411.50	Ships working (non paired)		170/50nc 2207
8412.00	Ships working (non paired)		170/50nc MB-0131 0950 "Izumrudnyy Bereg" (EKNB) 1016
8412.50	Ships working (non paired)		SITOR 2246 & 170/50nc "Leningradskaya Slava" (USWD) 1745
8413.00	Ships working (non paired)		SITOR "Grigoriy Mikheev" (URZC) 1022 "Slavyanka" (UGSH) 2255
8413.50	Ships working (non paired)		SITOR "Terral" (SQKW) 1828
8414.00	Ships working (non paired)		170/50nc "Vostok-2" (UHBE) 1432
8414.50	Maritime Safety channel		SITOR
8415.00	Ships digital selective calling		RTTY
8415.50	Ships digital selective calling		RTTY
8416.00	Ships digital selective calling		RTTY
8416.50	Maritime Safety channel		SITOR
8416.50	Boston CG, USA	NMF	SITOR Ice bulletins 0030 & 1218 wx 0140 & 1630
8417.00	Coast stations ch 2 dup. 8377.0kHz		RTTY
8417.00	Portishead, UK	GKE4	SITOR 0902 1737 1925 2255 Mode B tfc list 0700 wx 0935
8417.50	Coast stations ch 3 dup. 8377.5kHz		RTTY
8417.50	Odessa, Ukraine	UUI	SITOR 1748 1825 2245
8418.00	Coast stations ch 4 dup. 8378.0kHz		RTTY
8418.00	Argentine Radio	LSD836	SITOR 0714 0756 2209 2239

kHz.	Station	Call	Mode / Heard/Times GMT
8418.00	Novorossiysk, Russia	UFN	SITOR 2110 2338
8418.00	Rome, Italy	IAR	SITOR 0648 1335 1625 1858 1946 2247
8418.50	Coast stations ch 5 dup. 8378.5kHz		RTTY
8418.50	Rogaland, Norway	LGB2	SITOR 1124 1435 1855 Mode B 1600
8419.00	Coast stations ch 6 dup. 8379.0kHz		RTTY
8419.00	Helsinki, Finland	OFJ	SITOR Mode B news 1714
8419.00	Mobile, USA	WLO	SITOR 0720 0852 2255
8419.00	Moscow, Russia	UAT	SITOR 1839 1851 Mode B tfc list 2000
8419.00	Perth, Australia	VIP33	SITOR 1709 1739 1844 2258
8419.50	Coast stations ch 7 dup. 8379.5kHz		RTTY
8419.50	Goeteborg, Sweden	SAG	SITOR 0748 1757 1845
8419.50	Halifax, Canada	VCS	SITOR 2212
8419.50	Rio de Janeiro, Brazil	PPR	SITOR 0754 2138 2247
8419.50	Stettin, Poland	SPB	SITOR 0827 1129 1329 1833
8420.00	Coast stations ch 8 dup. 8380.0kHz		RTTY
8420.00	St Lys, France	FFT41	SITOR 1239 2147 Mode B tfc list 0903 1103
8420.50	Coast stations ch 9 dup. 8380.5kHz		RTTY
8420.50	Berne, Switzerland	HEC18	SITOR 0840 1248 1740 1904 2249 Mode B tfc list 0631
8420.50	Singapore	9VG78	SITOR 1756 wx 0030 1230
8421.00	Coast stations ch 10 dup. 8381.0kHz		RTTY
8421.00	Doha, Qatar	A7D	SITOR 1707 1742
8421.00	Lisbon, Portugal	CUL	SITOR
8421.00	Lyngby, Denmark	OXZ	SITOR 0755 1336 1708 2159 Mode B tfc list 1133 news 0831
8421.00	Mobile, USA	WLO	SITOR 0822 2300
8421.50	Coast stations ch 11 dup. 8381.5kHz		RTTY
8421.50	Hong Kong	VPS38	SITOR 1743 1841 1952
8421.50	Rijeka, Croatia	9AR	SITOR 0821 0854 2250
8421.50	Varna, Bulgaria	LZW4	SITOR 1452 1709 1948 2146 2240 Mode B tfc list 1708
8421.50	Yalta, Ukraine	UCO	SITOR 2214
8422.00	Coast stations ch 12 dup. 8382.0kHz		RTTY
8422.00	Boston CG, USA	NMF	SITOR 0954 2241
8422.00	Perth, Australia	VIP43	SITOR 1910
8422.00	Tallinn, Estonia	ESA	SITOR 0757 1124 1513 1703 1842 1949 2144
8422.50	Coast stations ch 13 dup. 8382.5kHz		RTTY
8422.50	Portishead, UK	GKP4	SITOR
8422.50	Mariupol, Ukraine	USU	SITOR 0804 0938 1126 1249 1743 1947 2248
8423.00	Coast stations ch 14 dup. 8383.0kHz		RTTY
8423.00	Athens, Greece	SVT4	SITOR 1852 2153 2204
8423.00	Novorossiysk, Russia	UFN	SITOR 0717 1724 1843 2147 2258
8423.00	Varna, Bulgaria	LZW	SITOR 1015 1740 1827 2150
8423.50	Coast stations ch 15 dup. 8383.5kHz		RTTY
8423.50	Mobile, USA	WLO	SITOR 2301
8423.50	Norddeich, Germany	DCL	SITOR 0827 1126 1242 1640 1843 2148
8423.50	Tallinn, Estonia	ESA	SITOR 0012
8424.00	Coast stations ch 16 dup. 8384.0kHz		RTTY
8424.00	Athens, Greece	SVU4	SITOR 1250 1626 1705
8424.00	Chatham, USA	WCC	SITOR 0757 2140 2205
8424.50	Coast stations ch 17 dup. 8384.5kHz		RTTY
8424.50	Scheveningen, Holland	PCH45	SITOR 1125 1350 1745 2217
8425.00	Coast stations ch 18 dup. 8385.0kHz		RTTY
8425.00	St Lys, France	FFT43	SITOR 0758 1554 1905 2259
8425.50	Coast stations ch 19 dup. 8385.5kHz		RTTY
8425.50	Berne, Switzerland	HEC28	SITOR 1134 1344 1746 1838 2232
8425.50	Portishead, UK	GKY4	SITOR
8425.50	Slidell, USA	WNU	SITOR 0828
8426.00	Coast stations ch 20 dup. 8386.0kHz		RTTY
8426.00	Genoa, Italy	ICB	SITOR 0649 1126 1601
8426.00	Portishead, UK	GKL4	SITOR
8426.50	Coast stations ch 21 dup. 8386.5kHz		RTTY
8426.50	Chatham, USA	WCC	SITOR 0758 0803 2141
8426.50	Singapore	9VG79	SITOR 1715 2216
8427.00	Coast stations ch 22 dup. 8387.0kHz		RTTY
8427.00	Lyngby, Denmark	OXZ	SITOR 0843 0938 1747 2154 2218
8427.50	Coast stations ch 23 dup. 8387.5kHz		RTTY
8427.50	Bahrain	A9M	SITOR 1627 1839 1906 2155 2302
8427.50	Gdynia, Poland	SPA41	SITOR 1234 1502 1642 Mode B tfc list 0850 1050
8428.00	Coast stations ch 24 dup. 8388.0kHz		RTTY
8428.00	Goeteborg, Sweden	SAG	SITOR 0756 0833 1849
8428.00	Chesapeake CG, USA	NMN	SITOR 0759
8428.50	Coast stations ch 25 dup. 8388.5kHz		RTTY
8428.50	Capetown, RSA	ZSC62	SITOR 2257
8428.50	Scheveningen, Holland	PCH46	SITOR 1351 1559 1842
8428.50	Vancouver, Canada	VAI	SITOR
8429.00	Coast stations ch 26 dup. 8389.0kHz		RTTY
8429.00	Berne, Switzerland	HEC38	SITOR 1711
8429.00	Madrid, Spain	EAD	SITOR 1706 1908 2150 2219 Mode B tfc list 0900
8429.00	Mobile, USA	WLO	SITOR 0825

kHz.	Station	Call	Mode / Heard/Times GMT
8429.50	Coast stations ch 27 dup. 8389.5kHz		RTTY
8429.50	Portishead, UK	GKQ4	SITOR
8429.50	Italian Naval	IDR4	CW 0802 0943 1145 1338 1741
8429.50	Murmansk, Russia	UMV	SITOR 1021 1251 1643
8430.00	Coast stations ch 28 dup. 8390.0kHz		RTTY
8430.00	Batumi, Georgia	UHK	SITOR 2136 2255
8430.00	Gdynia, Poland	SPA42	SITOR 2221
8430.50	Coast stations ch 29 dup. 8390.5kHz		RTTY
8430.50	Mobile, USA	WLO	SITOR 0650 0800 0832
8431.00	Coast stations ch 30 dup. 8391.0kHz		RTTY
8431.50	Coast stations ch 31 dup. 8391.5kHz		RTTY
8431.50	Dixon, USA	KMI	SITOR
8431.50	Moscow, Russia	UAT	SITOR 1708 1748 2151 2220 Mode B tfc list 2002
8432.00	Coast stations ch 32 dup. 8392.0kHz		RTTY
8432.00	Mobile, USA	WLO	SITOR 0728
8432.00	Riga, Latvia	UDH	SITOR 0852 1008 1709 1843 Mode B 1033 1133 1555 tfc list 1942
8432.50	Coast stations ch 33 dup. 8392.5kHz		RTTY
8432.50	Pennsuco, USA	WOM	SITOR
8432.50	Novorossiysk, Russia	UFN	SITOR 1910 2158 2241
8433.00	Coast stations ch 34 dup. 8393.0kHz		RTTY
8433.00	New York (Ocean Gate), USA	WOO	SITOR Mode B wx 0827 tfc list 2251
8433.50	Coast stations ch 35 dup. 8393.5kHz		RTTY
8433.50	UNID	PPQ	SITOR 0751 0846 2216 2317
8434.00	Coast stations ch 36 dup. 8394.0kHz		RTTY
8434.50	Coast stations ch 37 dup. 8394.5kHz		RTTY
8434.50	General Pacheco, Argentina	LPD	SITOR 0800 0848 2159 2211
8435.00	Coast stations ch 38 dup. 8395.0kHz		RTTY
8435.00	Guangzhou, China	XSQ	SITOR 1656 1713 1911 2059 2152 2213
8435.50	Coast stations ch 39 dup. 8395.5kHz		RTTY
8435.50	General Pacheco, Argentina	LPD	SITOR
8435.50	Ostend, Belgium	OST40	SITOR 1002 1238 1503 1600 1645
8436.00	Coast stations ch 40 dup. 8396.0kHz		RTTY
8436.50	Coast stations		RTTY
8436.50	Nakhodka, Russia	UKK3	SITOR 1542 1601 1710 1753
8436.50	St Petersburg, Russia	UGC	SITOR 2204
8437.00	Coast stations		RTTY
8437.00	Israeli Naval	4XZ	CW 1556 1657 1752 1844 wx 2215
8437.50	Coast stations		RTTY
8439.00	Dutch Naval	PBC	75r 0904 1128 1605
8439.00	Hamburg Press (HAB), Germany	DGH	CW Ger news summary 1720
8440.00	Halifax, Canada	VCS	CW 0639 0851 0902 1034 1325 1812 2153 tfc list 2106 wx 2208
8440.60	Moscow, Russia	UAT	CW 0758 1814 1920 tfc list 0900 1100 1300 1500 1900
8441.40	Aden	7OA	CW 1658 1723 1737 1808 1915
8441.40	Mombassa, Kenya	5ZF2	CW 1826
8442.30	Istanbul, Turkey	TCR	CW 0801 0907 2204 tfc list 0902
8444.50	Palo Alto, USA	KFS	CW 0647 0851 1711
8445.00	Banana, Zaire	9PA	CW 1940 2146
8445.00	Keelung, Taiwan	XSX	CW 1356 tfc list 1600 1900 2300 nav wng (Eng) 1828
8445.00	Muscat, Oman	A4M	CW 1357 1449
8445.00	Rijeka, Croatia	9AR	CW 1618 1717 tfc list 1600 1800
8445.50	Mobile, USA	WLO	CW 0014 0834 0943 2222 tfc list 1005
8446.00	Riga, Latvia	UQK	CW 2205 2232
8448.00	Bahrain	A9M	CW 1437 1529 1640 1748 1810 2142
8449.30	Bridgetown, Barbados	8PO	CW 2301 2317
8450.00	Benghazi, Libya	5AB	CW 0645 0748 0913 1531 1720 (also msrd 8451.0)
8450.00	Karlskrona, Sweden	SAA	CW (listens 8375.5) 0818 1743 2305
8450.00	UNID	RUF9	CW ID 1003
8450.50	Murmansk, Russia	ROD9	CW 1608 tfc list 0800 1000 1400 1600 1800 2300
8451.00	St Petersburg, Russia	UBF2	CW (to "4LT3") 1639 1902 2209 2223 tfc list 1404
8452.00	Townsville, Australia	VIT	CW
8453.00	French Naval, Paris	HWN	CW 0729 1129 1239 1900 2214
8454.00	Kaliningrad, Russia	UIW	170/50nc 1504 1522 1713 2222 nav wngs 1000 1630 1634
8454.70	Sabah, Malaysia	9WH	CW tfc list 2336
8455.00	Gelendzhik, Russia	UVA	CW (listens 8369.5) 1752 tfc list 1603 1700
8457.00	Boca, Argentina	LSA4	CW 0914 2213 2247
8457.00	Helsinki, Finland	OFJ	CW 0648 0906 1236 1302 1901 tfc list 2208
8459.00	Constanza, Romania	YQI4	CW 1240 1353 1715 tfc list 1700 1800 1900 2300
8460.00	Juncao, Brazil	PPJ	CW 0632 0738 0817 2156 2206 2318 (freq varies to 8459.7)
8460.00	Varna, Bulgaria	LZW4	CW 1531 1956 tfc list 1511 1902
8461.00	Capetown, RSA	ZSC42	CW wx 0930 1730
8461.00	Antofagasta, Chile	CBA	CW 2216 2226 2257
8466.00	Kaliningrad, Russia	UIW	CW 0739 0836 1435 1603 1847 2221 tfc list 0910
8466.00	Kaliningrad, Russia	UIW	170/50nc 1244 1353
8468.00	Ship working		CW "Atlantic Express" (3EFO4) 0702 out of normal sub-band
8469.00	Cape Verde	D4A6	CW 0731 0751 1539 1741 2134 2147

kHz.	Station	Call	Mode / Heard/Times GMT
8469.00	Lisbon, Portugal	CUL8	CW 2138 2205 2241
8471.00	Chesapeake CG, USA	NMN	CW 0740 0802 0904 1131 1242 2051 2141 2221 2304
8471.00	RSA Naval	ZRH	75r 1800 wx bulletin 1950
8471.50	Haiphong, Vietnam	XVG	CW 1857
8472.00	UNID	3SA	CW (clg BJCC) several times 1700
8473.00	Klaipeda, Lithuania	LYK	CW 1534 1810 tfc list 1501 1801
8473.00	Port Said, Egypt	SUP	CW 0726 1502 1659 1813 1841 tfc list 2011
8473.50	Doha, Qatar	A7D	CW 0752 1507 1549 1646 1753 1811 1958 2232 2305
8473.50	Mobile, USA	WLO3	CW 0741 0848 0900 2308
8474.00	Aqaba, Jordan	JYO	CW 0833 0917 1557 1648 1736 1813
8475.00	Murmansk, Russia	UMV	170/50rc 1508
8475.50	French Naval, Reunion	FUX	CW 1903 2150 2223
8476.00	Singapore	9VG56	CW 1536 1754 1816 2158 2337
8478.00	Australian Naval	VHP	CW 0732 0826 1848
8478.00	Ostend, Belgium	OST4	CW 0941 1139 1338 1647 2248 tfc list 1310 1710 2008
8478.00	Sydney, Australia	VIX4	CW 0944
8478.50	French Naval, Martinique	FUF	CW 0654 0803 2145 2245
8479.00	Choshi, Japan	JCU	CW 1718
8482.00	Gdynia, Poland	SPH41	CW 0905 1057 2309 tfc list 1210 1604 2010
8483.50	Norddeich, Germany	DAN	CW 0907 1253 1407 1746 1904 2225 2338
8484.50	Dammam, Saudi Arabia	HZG	CW 1533 1648 1700 1822 1923 2159
8485.00	Haifa, Israel	4XO	CW 1647 1816 2216 2325 (freq varies)
8486.00	Italian Naval	IDQ4	CW 0733 1549
8487.00	Darwin, Australia	VID	CW
8489.00	Havana, Cuba	CLS	CW 2249
8490.00	Lisbon, Portugal	CUL7	CW 1545 tfc list 0732
8490.00	Pakistan Naval	AQP	CW 1534 1849 1905 2226 2306 wx (Eng) 2216
8492.00	Rio de Janeiro, Brazil	PPR	CW 0530 0838 2217 2326 tfc list 2116
8493.00	UNID		100n RYs & encrypted 0942 1247 1609
8494.60	Single Letter Beacon	D	CW 1649 2152 2227
8494.90	Single Letter Beacon	S	CW 0905 1453 1645 2218
8495.00	Single Letter Beacon	C	CW 0817 0906 1305 1535 1818
8496.00	Havana, Cuba	CLA	CW 0730 0732 0838 1859 2145 tfc list 2227
8500.00	Baku, Azerbaijan	UON	CW 1903
8500.10	Indian Naval	VTH	50r RYs & SGs 2003 2045 2227 2305
8501.80	Shanghai, China	XSG	CW 1601
8502.00	Belem, Brazil	PPL	CW 0919 2148 2220 2255 nav wng 2242
8505.00	St Petersburg, Russia	UCW4	CW 1502 1611 (to "Ladoga 7" UKKC) 0624
8505.00	Turkish Naval	TBO	CW 0748 1520
8506.00	Riga, Latvia	UDH	CW 0728 1243 1438 1509 1800 2210 tfc list 1000 1100 1600 2200
8509.00	UNID		72ARQ/E/4 Idle 2134
8510.00	St Lys, France	FFS4	CW 0840 tfc list 1041
8510.00	Klaipeda Harbour, Lithuania	LYL	CW 0734 0805 1445 1522 1818
8511.00	Taichung, Taiwan	XSW2	CW 1510 1812 1927
8511.90	Norddeich, Germany	DAL	CW 0646 0809 0944 1245 1608 1819
8512.80	Australian Naval	VHI	CW 1650 2218 2229
8514.00	Mobile, USA	WLO	CW 0820 wx 0725 tfc list 0706
8514.00	Mobile, USA	WLO	SITOR (Jan to May) tfc list every hour + 35
8514.00	Guangzhou, China	XSQ	CW 1614 1735 1813 2145 tfc list 1730
8515.00	Tripoli, Libya	5AT	CW 0015 0705 1307 1416 1545 1622 1908 2055 2228 2310
8516.00	Portishead, UK	GKC	CW reserve frequency 1141
8520.00	Odessa, Ukraine	UUI	CW 1350 1814 2219
8520.00	Odessa, Ukraine	UUI	170/50rc 1542 1552 1623 1821
8520.00	Olinda, Brazil	PPO	CW 0652 0909 1824 2254 2312
8521.00	Perth, Australia	VIP	CW 0851 1702 1804 2248
8522.00	Valparaiso, Chile	CBV	CW 0655 0813
8522.50	St Lys, France	FFL4	CW 0945 1340 2237 2306 wx 0629 tfc list 2230
8523.40	Nagasaki, Japan	JOR	CW 0815
8525.00	Slidell, USA	WNU33	CW 0657 0707 2143 2210
8527.50	Rogaland, Norway	LFN	CW 2252 tfc list 2300
8528.50	Spanish Naval	EBA	CW nav wngs 1652 1752 1859
8528.50	Spanish Naval	EBA	75n 1100 nav wngs (Eng) 1005 1712
8530.00	Rome, Italy	IAR28	CW 0807 0828 tfc list 1200 2000 wx 0836 0916 2048
8530.00	Kiev, Ukraine	UTQ	CW 0739 0946 1250 1603
8532.00	Varna, Bulgaria	LZW42	CW 0943 1133 1541 tfc list 0700 0900 1300 1500 2100 2300
8534.00	Mobile, USA	WLO	CW 0820 0946 1127 2256
8534.00	Mobile, USA	WLO	SITOR Mode B wx 0736
8535.00	Tallinn, Estonia	ESF	CW 1244 tfc list 2200
8536.50	Athens, Greece	SVF4	CW 1546 1604 1926 2157 2307
8538.00	French Naval, Dakar	6WW	CW 0708 0741
8539.00	Hong Kong	VPS35	CW 1628 1656 1731 1753 tfc list 1904
8540.00	Mariupol, Ukraine	USU	CW 1828 1843 tfc list 1827
8540.00	Mariupol, Ukraine	USU	170/50nc 0830 1355 1718 1829 1909
8541.00	Klaipeda Harbour, Lithuania	LYL	CW 0713 0740 0859 1341 1547 1736 tfc list 0803
8541.00	Klaipeda Harbour, Lithuania	LYL	170/50nc 0819 (to "Kastitis") 0745 (to LYBF) 0835
8542.00	Jakarta, Indonesia	PKX	CW 1653 1735 1753

kHz.	Station	Call	Mode / Heard/Times GMT
8543.00	Hong Kong	VPS37	CW 2308
8545.90	Portishead, UK	GKA4	CW tfc list 0900 1100 1200 1300 1400 1900 2100 wx 0930 2130
8546.00	Batumi, Georgia	UHK	CW 2039 2246
8547.00	UNID	HVN7	CW (clg "L2OL") 1440
8548.00	Olinda, Brazil	PPO	CW 2144 tfc list 2214
8549.00	Archangel, Russia	UCE	SITOR 0836 (to EKHO) 0922 Mode B 1043 1102
8549.50	Brazilian Naval	PWZ33	CW nav wngs 0715
8550.00	Murmansk, Russia	UQA4	CW (to 4LS) 2141 2149 2222
8550.00	St Lys, France	FFT41	CW 1817 1840 wx 0850 1750 wx map (code) 0915 1831
8551.50	Portuguese Naval	CTP95	CW 0910 1134 1309 1749 2131 2226
8552.00	Moscow, Russia	UHF3	CW 1047
8552.00	Portishead, UK	GKK4	CW reserve frequency
8554.00	Pt Louis, Mauritius	3BM4	CW 1754 1912
8555.50	Kaliningrad, Russia	UIW	CW 0835 1924 2253
8556.00	Goeteborg, Sweden	SAG	SITOR 0833 0911 1135 1755
8557.00	Stettin, Poland	SPE41	CW 0710 0820 0948 1251 1343 2225 tfc list 1431 2231
8558.40	Palo Alto, USA	KFS	CW 0638 0713 0853 1537
8559.50	Portishead, UK	GKB4	CW 0918 1247 1605 1839 1917 2221
8562.00	Scheveningen, Holland	PCH40	CW 1105 1227 2147 2308
8564.00	Bourgas, Bulgaria	LZL4	CW 1616 1659 1907
8565.00	Luanda, Angola	D3E51	CW 1833 2159 2222 2254
8566.00	RSA Naval	ZSJ	CW 1925 2239
8568.00	French Naval, Djibouti	FUV	CW 1655 1745 1904 2149 2309
8568.60	Manzanillo, Mexico	XFM	CW 0717 0746 0853 0913 (also msrd 8569.2)
8569.00	CIS Naval	RIW	CW (with RMEU) 1536 1626
8569.00	Portishead, UK	GKD4	CW reserve frequency
8570.00	Provideniya, Russia	UPB	CW 1538 1620 tfc list 1404
8570.00	San Francisco, USA	NMC	CW 1439 1457 1547 1615 (joint call NMC/NRV)
8570.00	Slidell, USA	WNU43	CW 0742 0803 0945 1028 2241
8570.50	Magadan, Russia	RWHB	CW 0717 0800 1447
8571.00	Novorossiysk, Russia	UFN	CW 0713 1310 1512 1837 tfc list 1603 1904 2109 2200
8571.00	Novorossiysk, Russia	UFN	170/50nc 1442 (to "Marshal Zakharov" UKED) 1343
8571.00	Tokyo Naval, Japan	JNA	CW 0739 0748 0823 1135 1615 1818
8573.00	Havana, Cuba	CLA21	CW 0635 0719 0837 0950 1906 2140
8573.50	Bangkok, Thailand	HSA4	CW 1632 tfc list 1634
8574.00	Rogaland, Norway	LGB	CW 1045 1106 1246 1850 2136 tfc list 1103 1513
8574.80	Buenaventura, Colombia	HKC	CW 0626 0753 0854 2155 2239 (freq varies to 8575.5)
8575.00	St Petersburg, Russia	UGC	CW 1136 1938 wx 1600 (Russ) tfc list 0920 1836 1933
8575.00	St Petersburg, Russia	UGC	170/50nc 0831
8576.70	UNID		SITOR diving log reports 2204
8577.00	Seoul, S Korea	HLO	CW 0825 0858 1530 1747 1814
8578.00	Alexandria, Egypt	SUH3	CW 0936 1555 1659 1735 1820 2240 2302 tfc list 2113
8580.00	Archangel, Russia	RKLM	CW (to "4LY") 0527 0656 1203 tfc list 1500
8580.00	Murmansk, Russia	UQA4	CW 0018
8580.00	Sebastopol, Ukraine	URL	CW 1545 1752 1821 2152 2232
8580.00	Sebastopol, Ukraine	URL	170/50rc 2005
8580.40	Bulacan, Phillipines	DZO	CW 0857
8581.60	Portishead, UK	GKM4	CW reserve frequency
8582.00	Ningbo, China	XSN	CW 0804
8582.50	Seattle, USA	KLB	CW 0825 0838
8584.00	Hong Kong	VPS36	CW 1221
8585.00	Vladivostok, Russia	UFL	CW (with USFE for wx) 1802
8586.00	Chatham, USA	WCC	CW 0714 0827 1142 1625 2117 2223
8589.00	Panama	HPP	CW 0718 0858 2239 tfc list 2301
8591.50	Portishead, UK	GKG4	CW wkg freq to ships (to "Joy Venture) 1016
8593.00	Odessa, Ukraine	UUI	CW 0709 0801 1659 1812 2310 tfc list 1700 1900
8595.00	Vladivostok, Russia	UFL	CW 1629 nav wng 1527 1621
8595.50	Pinang, Malaysia	9MG	CW 0850
8598.00	Lyngby, Denmark	OXZ4	CW 0623 1107 1247 1908 2221
8600.00	CIS Naval	RIT	CW ID 1505
8600.00	St Petersburg, Russia	UGC	CW (to "4KB") 0700
8600.00	St Petersburg, Russia	UGC	170/50nc 0720 1402 nav wngs 0752 1514
8600.00	Tianjin, China	XSV	CW 0822 2151 tfc list 1502
8601.30	New Zealand Naval	ZLO	CW 0751 1553 1700 1906 2258
8602.00	Cerrito, Uruguay	CWA	CW 0019 0716 2113 2238
8604.00	Portishead, UK	GKH4	CW reserve frequency
8604.20	Bulacan, Philippines	DZJ	CW 1659 1701 1756 tfc list 2203 (freq varies slightly)
8604.30	RSA Naval	ZRH	CW 1701 1838 1909 2256
8606.00	Portishead, UK	GKI4	CW reserve frequency
8606.00	RSA Naval	ZRQ	CW 1702 2132 2237
8607.00	Mariupol, Ukraine	USU	170/50nc 1910 (to "Stepan Spondaryan") 1824
8609.50	Singapore	9VG73	CW 1540 1701 1743 1959 2224
8610.00	Archangel, Russia	UCE	CW 0717 0838 1426 1742 1832 2151 2258 tfc list 1801 2102
8610.00	Archangel, Russia	UCE	170/50nc (to "Pertominsk") 1830
8611.50	Istanbul, Turkey	TAH	CW 0720 1312 2254 tfc list 1703 1904 2103 2303
8614.00	Sebastopol, Ukraine	URL	CW 1840 2223 2250 tfc list 2104

kHz.	Station	Call	Mode / Heard/Times GMT
8616.50	Klaipeda Harbour, Lithuania	LYL	CW 1705 1944 2003 2236 tfc list 1700 2200
8618.00	Madrid, Spain	EDZ4	CW 1603
8618.00	San Francisco, USA	KPH	CW 0718 0902
8619.00	Hong Kong	VRN35	CW tfc list 1705 1905
8620.00	Mariupol, Ukraine	USU	CW 0816 1314 tfc list 1505 1800 1900
8622.00	Scheveningen, Holland	PCH41	CW 0807 0838 1248 1344 1445 2226 tfc list 0850 1250
8622.50	Nicosia, Cyprus	5BA	CW 0759 1544 2215 tfc list 1521 1955 (gives QSW as 8623.0)
8624.00	Guangzhou, China	XSQ	CW 1711 1827 1836 tfc list 1730 1830
8625.00	British Naval, Gibraltar	GYU	75n test tx 1053 2055
8625.00	French Military, Papeete	FUM	CW 1510
8630.00	Chatham, USA	WCC	CW 0833 0947 1138 1629 1842 1953 2225 tfc list 0653 2255
8632.00	Kaohsiung, Taiwan	XSW	CW 1227 2153 2239 wx (Eng) 1705
8634.00	Indian Naval	VTG6	CW 1824 2321 wx 1530
8634.00	Rio de Janeiro, Brazil	PPR	CW 2205 2322 tfc list 2304
8635.00	Kiev, Ukraine	UTQ	CW 1605 1849 1912
8636.00	Seoul, S Korea	HLW	CW 1532 1848
8638.00	Sydney Time Station, Australia	VNG	CW 0626
8638.50	Norddeich, Germany	DAM	CW 0721 0840 1112 1249 1945 2235 tfc list 0830 1130 1530
8639.50	Portuguese Naval	CTV8	CW 1915
8642.00	San Francisco, USA	KPH	CW
8643.50	Odessa, Ukraine	UUI	CW 1631 1846 2006 tfc list 1807
8643.50	Odessa, Ukraine	UUI	170/50nc 0923 1916
8644.00	CIS Naval	RMP	CW (clg UGJV) 2153
8646.00	French Military, Numea	FUJ	CW 0818 1632
8646.00	General Pacheco, Argentina	LPD86	CW 2142 2255
8646.00	Indian Naval	VTP6	CW 1831 2056 wx 1735
8649.50	Genoa, Italy	ICB	CW 0841 1129 1253 1400 1632 1706 1850
8650.00	Stettin, Poland	SPB43	SITOR (dup. 8404.5) 0753 0917 2231 Mode B tfc list 1601 1755
8650.00	Tallinn, Estonia	ESA	CW 1503 tfc list 0801 2203
8651.00	Dammam, Saudi Arabia	HZG	CW 1827 wx (Eng) 1830
8651.90	Ostend, Belgium	OST	CW 0701 1234 1345 1558 tfc list 1110
8652.50	Paramaribo, Surinam	PZN3	CW 2053
8653.60	Choshi, Japan	JCS	CW 1140 1446 1506 1633 1947
8656.00	Rome, Italy	IAR38	CW 0746 0929 1345 1709 1937 2051
8657.00	UNID		CW 2301 nav wngs (Slav lang) tfc list ("U" vessels) 1603 1803
8658.00	Karachi, Pakistan	ASK	CW 1754
8658.00	Mobile, USA	WLO2	CW 0705 0839 0948 2218 2300
8660.50	Kiev, Ukraine	UTQ7	CW 1931 2051 2142 2229
8661.00	Guangzhou, China	XSQ	CW 1447 1511 1549
8662.00	Istanbul, Turkey	TAH	CW 0814 1316 1605 1716 tfc list 0900 1100 1500 1700
8663.00	Novorossiysk, Russia	UFN	CW tfc list 1302
8665.00	Shanghai, China	XSG3	CW 1516 1707 1842 2242 tfc list 2030 2230
8670.00	Rome, Italy	IAR8	CW 0835 0927 1350 1543 1611 2009 wx (Eng) 1808
8672.50	Norddeich, Germany	DAF	CW 2319
8672.60	British Naval	MTO	75r 0816 0949 1114 1839 2059
8674.40	Madras, India	VWM	CW 1546
8677.50	St Petersburg, Russia	UGC	SITOR 0641 0811 0958 1551 (to UQRM) 2030 Mode B 1509 1708
8679.00	Trieste, Italy	IQX	CW 1111 1254 1346 1544 1711 1851 2010
8680.00	Tuckerton, USA	WSC	CW 1925 2143 tfc list 2318
8681.00	Athens, Greece	SVI4	CW 1351 1606 1645 1927 2233 wx (Eng) 0950 1527 2118
8682.00	Madrid, Spain	EAD3	CW 0846 1141 1317 1520 1821 tfc list 1809
8684.00	Luanda, Angola	D3E52	CW 2230 2234
8684.00	Portishead, UK	GKJ4	CW reserve frequency
8685.00	Rome (Medical Centre), Italy	IRM	CW 0740 0848 1120 1145 1529 1613
8686.00	Bangkok, Thailand	HSA2	CW 1635 tfc list 1628
8686.00	Belawan, Indonesia	PKB	CW 1515
8686.00	Casablanca, Morocco	CNP	CW 0817 1207 1318 1715 1819 1917 2111
8687.00	Athens, Greece	SVA4	CW 0857 1325 1534 1719 2227 tfc list 1420
8687.60	St Petersburg, Russia	UGC	CW 0628 0928 1248 1353 1717 1923 2006 tfc list 1502 1701 2302
8688.00	Singapore	9VG36	CW 1536 1713 1753 1834
8688.00	Slidell, USA	WNU53	CW 0706 0805 0859 0949 1150
8688.50	Capetown, RSA	ZSC6	CW 1740 1757 2235
8689.20	Dakar, Senegal	6VA5	CW 2134 2156 wx (French) 1000 2200
8690.00	Murmansk, Russia	UMV	CW tfc list 0800
8690.00	Suva, Fiji	3DP3	CW 0723 0750 0821
8691.00	Qingdao, China	XST	CW 0900 1517 1636 1836 2146 tfc list even hrs + 40
8692.50	Athens, Greece	SVD4	CW 0929 1354 1449 1720 1928 freq varies to 8693.0
8694.00	Curacao, Neth Antilles	PJC	CW 1852 2309 tfc list 0700
8694.10	Haifa, Israel	4XO	CW 0724 1545 1758 2013 2244 (freq varies slightly)
8695.00	Batumi, Georgia	UHK	CW 0836 1548 1821 tfc list 1505 2303
8698.00	Boufarik, Algeria	7TF6	CW 0813 1024 1121 1354 1607 1744 2122 2229 tfc list 1142
8698.00	Murmansk, Russia	UDK2	CW 1448 1834
8698.00	Murmansk, Russia	UDK2	170/50rc gtgs msgs 1549
8698.00	Pinang, Malaysia	9MG2	CW 1442 1637 1719 1840 tfc list 2010
8698.80	Bangkok, Thailand	HSA23	CW 1531 (harmonic of 4349.4)

kHz.	Station	Call	Mode / Heard/Times GMT
8700.00	Rijeka, Croatia	9AR3	CW 0827 1143 1345 1542 1800 2303 tfc list 1405 1811 2205
8701.00	Klaipeda, Lithuania	LYK	170/50nc 0752 0924 0950 nav wngs 0757 1525
8701.00	Klaipeda, Lithuania	LYK	CW 0810 1355 1820 nav wngs 1833 tfc list 1300 1500
8701.40	Barranquilla, Colombia	HKB	CW 0645
8703.00	Archangel, Russia	UCE	170/50nc 0725 0741 1107 1153 1533
8704.00	Athens, Greece	SVB4	CW 0917 1826 1926 2114 (also msrd on 8703.7)
8704.50	Novorossiysk, Russia	UNQ	CW 1721 1812 1817 tfc list 2102 2211
8705.00	Yalta, Ukraine	UCO	CW (to UUYX) 0822
8706.00	Nagasaki, Japan	JOS	CW 1450 1638 1747 1803 1847
8707.00	Coast/Ship stations simplex (ch 34)		USB 1519 2241
8710.00	Coast/Ship stations simplex (ch 35)		USB 0726 0805 0951 1451 1914
8713.00	Coast/Ship stations simplex (ch 36)		USB 1551 1854
8716.00	Coast/Ship stations simplex (ch 37)		USB 0708 0726 1721 2220
8716.00	UK Coast Control		USB 0720 0825 0920
8719.00	Coast stations ch 1 dup. 8195.0kHz		USB
8719.00	Goeteborg, Sweden	SAG	USB 1940
8719.00	Haifa, Israel	4XO	USB 0536 1807 1829
8719.00	Odessa, Ukraine	UUI	USB 0742
8722.00	Coast stations ch 2 dup. 8198.0kHz		USB
8722.00	Athens, Greece	SVN41	USB 0826 1915
8722.00	Boufarik, Algeria	7TA37	USB 0752 0901 0952 tfc list 0800 1000 1600 wx (Fr) 0800
8722.00	Cape Verde	D4A	USB ("Vicente Radio") 0904
8722.00	Lisbon, Portugal	CUL	USB 0815 0840
8722.00	Pennsuco, USA	WOM	USB 0804
8722.00	Portishead, UK	GKT42	USB 0825
8722.00	Sydney, Australia	VIS	USB 0538 0817 1711
8722.00	Taipei, Taiwan	BVA	USB tfc list 1500
8725.00	Coast stations ch 3 dup. 8201.0kHz		USB
8725.00	Berne, Switzerland	HEB48	USB 1942 2228
8725.00	Klaipeda Harbour, Lithuania	LYL	USB 1550
8725.00	Vladivostok, Russia	UFL	USB 0723
8728.00	Coast stations ch 4 dup. 8204.0kHz		USB
8728.00	Aqaba, Jordan	JYO	USB (with 3EJS6) 1513
8728.00	Monaco	3AC	USB 0721 1623
8728.00	Madrid, Spain	EHY	USB 0640 0701 0830 1115 1356 2148
8728.00	Singapore	9VG63	USB 1835
8731.00	Coast stations ch 5 dup. 8207.0kHz		USB
8731.00	Capetown, RSA	ZSC	USB
8731.00	Haifa, Israel	4XO	USB 1733 1928
8731.00	Moscow, Russia	UAT	USB 2128
8731.00	Pennsuco, USA	WOM	USB (with KFDV) 2130
8734.00	Coast stations ch 6 dup. 8210.0kHz		USB
8734.00	Athens, Greece	SVN42	USB 0859 1610 1830 2327
8734.00	Bahrain	A9M	USB 1801
8734.00	General Pacheco, Argentina	LPL	USB tfc list 2133
8734.00	Genoa, Italy	ICB	USB 1524
8734.00	Perth, Australia	VIP	USB
8737.00	Coast stations ch 7 dup. 8213.0kHz		USB
8737.00	Nicosia, Cyprus	5BA	USB 0727 0903 1638 2059 2216 2311
8737.00	St Petersburg, Russia	UGC	USB 0739 0934 1143 1356
8737.00	Vancouver, Canada	VAI	USB
8740.00	Coast stations ch 8 dup. 8216.0kHz		USB
8740.00	Athens, Greece	SVN43	USB 2230 2320
8740.00	Lyngby, Denmark	OXZ	USB 0714 0854 1520 2236
8743.00	Coast stations ch 9 dup. 8219.0kHz		USB
8743.00	Athens, Greece	SVN44	USB 1920
8743.00	Dixon, USA	KMI	USB
8743.00	Monaco	3AC	USB 2237 wx 0715 1830
8743.00	Rogaland, Norway	LFL5	USB 0746 1114 1552 1640 (with "Antares") 0818
8746.00	Coast stations ch 10 dup. 8222.0kHz		USB
8746.00	Istanbul, Turkey	TAN	USB 0805
8746.00	Madrid, Spain	EHY	USB 2154
8746.00	Pennsuco, USA	WOM	USB 2145
8746.00	Rijeka, Croatia	9AR	USB 0657 0809 1612 1653
8746.00	Stettin, Poland	SPO	USB 0657 1200 1347 1831 tfc list 1838
8746.00	Tokyo, Japan	JBO	USB
8746.00	Varna, Bulgaria	LZW	USB 0718
8749.00	Coast stations ch 11 dup. 8225.0kHz		USB
8749.00	General Pacheco, Argentina	LPL	USB
8749.00	Istanbul, Turkey	TAN	USB 1507 1737 2147 2224
8749.00	New York (Ocean Gate), USA	WOO	USB 0801 2141 tfc list & CW ID 0853
8749.00	Perth, Australia	VIP	USB (on request)
8749.00	Rogaland, Norway	LFL7	USB 0653 wx 2315
8752.00	Coast stations ch 12 dup. 8228.0kHz		USB
8752.00	Batumi, Georgia	UHK	USB 2105
8752.00	Gdynia, Poland	SPC41	USB 0728 1632
8752.00	Haifa, Israel	4XO	USB

kHz.	Station	Call	Mode / Heard/Times GMT
8752.00	Riga, Latvia	UDH	USB 0702 0726 0851
8755.00	Coast stations ch 13 dup. 8231.0kHz		USB
8755.00	Boufarik, Algeria	7TF	USB 1738 (to 9HID3) 1002
8755.00	Lisbon, Portugal	CUL	USB 0812 1047 2239
8755.00	Ostend, Belgium	OSU45	USB 0753 1607
8755.00	Rogaland, Norway	LFL8	USB 0730 1822 1931 2125
8758.00	Coast stations ch 14 dup. 8234.0kHz		USB
8758.00	Pennsuco, USA	WOM	USB
8758.00	Rome, Italy	IAR	USB 1722
8761.00	Coast stations ch 15 dup. 8237.0kHz		USB
8761.00	Athens, Greece	SVN46	USB
8761.00	Darwin, Australia	VID	USB (on request)
8761.00	Norddeich, Germany	DAK	USB
8761.00	Novorossiysk, Russia	UDN	USB 0802 1521 1703
8761.00	Ostend, Belgium	OSU41	USB 0635 0709 1900 tfc list 0902 1102 1702
8761.00	Perth, Australia	VIP	USB (on request)
8761.00	Singapore	9VG64	USB
8764.00	Coast stations ch 16 dup. 8240.0kHz		USB
8764.00	Barbados	8PO	USB
8764.00	Kaliningrad, Russia	UIW	USB 1946
8764.00	Madrid, Spain	EHY	USB 0007 2222 2308
8764.00	Portishead, UK	GKU46	USB 0711 0825 1627 1900 tfc list 2200
8764.00	Chesapeake CG, USA	NMN	USB (with P3UW3) 2312 wx 0535 2203 2222
8767.00	Coast stations ch 17 dup. 8243.0kHz		USB
8767.00	Moscow, Russia	UAT	USB 1603
8767.00	Norddeich, Germany	DAJ	USB 0734 0800 1401 1552 tfc list 0745 0845 1245 1745 2145 2245
8767.00	St Lys, France	FFL	USB 1451
8767.00	Townsville, Australia	VIT	USB
8770.00	Coast stations ch 18 dup. 8246.0kHz		USB
8770.00	Izmail, Ukraine	USO5	USB 0725 0750 0822
8770.00	Lyngby, Denmark	OXZ	USB
8770.00	Nicosia, Cyprus	5BA	USB 0721 1750
8773.00	Coast stations ch 19 dup. 8249.0kHz		USB
8773.00	Kaliningrad, Russia	UIW	USB 0747 0757
8773.00	Portishead, UK	GKU49	USB 1054 1612 2128
8773.00	Rome, Italy	IAR	USB 1329
8776.00	Coast stations ch 20 dup. 8252.0kHz		USB
8776.00	Athens, Greece	SVN48	USB 1826 2140 (with "Sirena" 9H4104) 2158 tfc list 2206
8776.00	Liepaja, Lithuania		USB 0706
8776.00	Norddeich, Germany	DAI	USB 2100
8776.00	Rome, Italy	IAR	USB 1451
8779.00	Coast stations ch 21 dup. 8255.0kHz		USB common calling ch
8779.00	Havana, Cuba	CLT	USB
8779.00	Moscow, Russia	UAT	USB 1457
8779.00	Rogaland, Norway	LGQ	USB 0916 1447 tfc list 0801 1801
8779.00	Rome, Italy	IAR	USB 0733 1051 1643 1840
8779.00	Singapore	9VG89	USB
8782.00	Coast stations ch 22 dup. 8258.0kHz		USB
8782.00	Berne, Switzerland	HEB18	USB 0718 0838 1119 1553 1705 1814 tfc list 0817
8782.00	Budapest, Hungary	HAR	USB
8782.00	Portishead, UK	GKV42	USB 0714 0748 2209
8782.00	Townsville, Australia	VIT	USB (on request)
8785.00	Coast stations ch 23 dup. 8261.0kHz		USB
8785.00	Athens, Greece	SVN49	USB 2200
8785.00	Genoa, Italy	ICB	USB 0735 2102
8785.00	Halifax, Canada	VCS	USB wx 0805
8785.00	Lyngby, Denmark	OXZ	USB
8785.00	Rogaland, Norway	LGQ	USB 0910
8788.00	Coast stations ch 24 dup. 8264.0kHz		USB
8788.00	Berne, Switzerland	HEB28	USB 1800
8788.00	Gdynia, Poland	SPC42	USB 0712 1903 2153 2223
8788.00	Mobile, USA	WLO	USB wx 0008
8788.00	Norddeich, Germany	DAP	USB
8788.00	Singapore	9VG65	USB
8791.00	Coast stations ch 25 dup. 8267.0kHz		USB
8791.00	Lyngby, Denmark	OXZ	USB
8791.00	Pennsuco, USA	WOM	USB 2234 2309
8791.00	Resolute Bay, Canada	VFR	USB
8791.00	St Lys, France	FFL	USB 0636 0739 0905 1402
8794.00	Coast stations ch 26 dup. 8270.0kHz		USB
8794.00	Inuvik, Canada	VFA	USB
8794.00	New York (Ocean Gate), USA	WOO	USB 0715
8794.00	Scheveningen, Holland	PCG41	USB 0754 0921 1145 1533 1613 1756 tfc list each odd hr + 05
8794.00	Portishead, UK	GKV46	USB
8794.00	Rome, Italy	IAR	USB 0834
8794.70	Single Letter Beacon	P	CW 1554

kHz.	Station	Call	Mode / Heard/Times GMT
8797.00	Coast stations ch 27 dup. 8273.0kHz		USB
8797.00	Bar, Montenegro	YUW	USB 0930 1358 1555
8797.00	Haifa, Israel	4XO	USB
8797.00	Lyngby, Denmark	OXZ	USB tfc list 0906
8800.00	Coast stations ch 28 dup. 8276.0kHz		USB
8800.00	Casablanca, Morocco	CNP	USB 1115
8800.00	Norddeich, Germany	DAH	USB 0752 0950
8800.00	Olinda, Brazil	PPO	USB 2219
8800.00	St Lys, France	FFL	USB 1422 2227
8800.00	Yalta, Ukraine	UCO	USB (with "Kapitan V Kulibin") 1908
8803.00	Coast stations ch 29 dup. 8279.0kHz		USB
8803.00	Helsinki, Finland	OHG	USB 0649 0736 0840 0922 1604 1725 (used by Russian vessels)
8803.00	Mobile, USA	WLO	USB 0753 tfc list 0700
8803.00	Sydney, Australia	VIS	USB with HQFQ4 0700
8806.00	Coast stations ch 30 dup. 8282.0kHz		USB
8806.00	Mobile, USA	WLO	USB 2127
8806.00	St Lys, France	FFL	USB 0710 0951 1404 1657 1835 1922 tfc list 1400
8809.00	Coast stations ch 31 dup. 8285.0kHz		USB
8809.00	Berne, Switzerland	HEB38	USB 1746
8809.00	Istanbul, Turkey	TAN	USB 0756 1608 1640 1819 2136
8809.00	Pennsuco, USA	WOM	USB 2253
8809.00	Portishead, UK	GKW41	USB
8809.00	Rome, Italy	IAR	USB 0652
8812.00	Coast stations ch 32 dup. 8288.0kHz		USB
8812.00	Istanbul, Turkey	TAN	USB 0654
8812.00	Malta	9HD	USB
8814.90	Spa Publications		

8815-8965
AERONAUTICAL MOBILE (MAINLY CIVIL) 3KHz channels

kHz.	Station	Call	Mode / Heard/Times GMT
8815.00	Intership working		USB Scottish 0917
8816.00	Russian air traffic	RXH	CW (wkg UGN) 1510
8816.00	Russian air traffic	UGN	CW (wkg RXH) 1512
8819.00	St John's (in-flight R/T service)		USB "Rainbow Radio" 2235
8819.00	CIS VOLMET channel		USB 1551 1644 1843 2144 2220
8825.00	N Atlantic Air traffic NAT A		USB
8825.00	Canaries ATC	GCCC	USB
8825.00	New York ATC, USA	KZNY	USB 2137 2208 2245 2314
8825.00	Piarco ATC, Trinidad	MKPP	USB 2310
8825.00	Sal ATC, Cape Verde	GVSC	USB
8825.00	Santa Maria ATC, Azores	LPAZ	USB 1118 1340 1402 1535 1729 1853 2232 2322
8825.00	UNID	VDE2	CW ID call 0700
8828.00	Auckland VOLMET, New Zealand	NZZA	USB 0651 0823
8828.00	Hong Kong VOLMET		USB 2115 2145
8828.00	Honolulu VOLMET, Hawaii		USB 0702
8831.00	N Atlantic Air traffic NAT F		USB
8831.00	Gander ATC, Canada	CZQX	USB 1202 1626 1717 1854
8831.00	Shanwick ATC, UK/Eire	EGGX	USB 1205 1339 1849
8837.00	El Al Company frequency		USB 0902 1751 1940 1949 2156
8843.00	Central East Pacific Air traffic		USB
8843.00	San Francisco ATC, USA	KSFO	USB
8846.00	Caribbean Air traffic CAR B		USB
8846.00	New York ATC, USA	KZNY	USB 2050 2146 2153 2210 2246 2315
8855.00	S America Air traffic SAM		USB
8855.00	Brasilia ATC, Brazil	SBBS	USB (with American 987) 0720
8855.00	Campo Grande ATC, Brazil	SBCD	USB 0807 2151
8855.00	Manaus ATC, Brazil	SBMU	USB 0717 0754
8855.00	Paramaribo ATC, Suriname	MEPM	USB 0633 2239
8855.00	Piarco ATC, Trinidad	MKPP	USB 2048 2224
8855.00	Porto Velho ATC, Brazil	SBPH	USB 2215
8855.00	Santa Cruz ATC, Bolivia	SLCZ	USB 2152
8860.00	UNID		AM Asian lang & music 1915
8861.00	Africa Air traffic AFI 1		USB
8861.00	Bamako ATC, Mali	GABS	USB 2137
8861.00	Canaries ATC	GCCC	USB 0042 0809 0824 1007 1611
8861.00	Dakar ATC, Senegal	GOOO	USB 0741 0812 0923 2222 2240
8861.00	Monrovia (Roberts) ATC, Liberia	GLRB	USB 2206
8861.00	S Atlantic Air traffic SAT 1		USB
8861.00	Recife ATC, Brazil	SBRE	USB 2135
8861.00	Sal ATC, Cape Verde	GVSC	USB (with Springbok 202) 0714
8864.00	N Atlantic Air traffic NAT B		USB
8864.00	Gander ATC, Canada	CZQX	USB 1350 1451 1557 1721 2148
8864.00	Reykjavik ATC, Iceland	BIRD	USB 1351

kHz.	Station	Call	Mode / Heard/Times GMT
8864.00	Shanwick ATC, UK/Eire	EGGX	USB 1247 1354
8867.00	S Pacific Air traffic SP		USB
8867.00	Auckland ATC, N Zealand	NZZA	USB 0717
8867.00	Sydney ATC, Australia	ASSY	USB 0648 0824
8867.00	Tahiti ATC	NTAA	USB
8873.00	Brazzaville ATC, Congo	FCCC	USB 1856 2301
8873.00	Garoua ATC, Cameroon	FKKR	USB 2101 2200
8879.00	Indian Ocean Air traffic INO 1		USB
8879.00	Beira ATC, Mozambique	FQBE	USB 1722
8879.00	Dar es Salaam ATC, Tanzania	HTDC	USB 2240
8879.00	Nairobi ATC, Kenya	HKNA	USB 1607 1839
8879.00	Mauritius ATC	FIMM	USB 1643 1758
8879.00	Seychelles ATC	FSSS	USB 1536
8879.00	Tananarive ATC, Madagascar	FMMM	USB 1629
8879.00	N Atlantic Air traffic NAT C		USB
8879.00	Gander ATC, Canada	CZQX	USB 1117 1248 1423 1536 1700 1855 1926 2245
8879.00	Reykjavik ATC, Iceland	BIRD	USB 1336 1642 1701
8879.00	Shanwick ATC, UK/Eire	EGGX	USB 1145 1323 1628 1725 1810
8888.00	CIS VOLMET channel		USB 0907 1403 1610 1730 1901 2147
8891.00	N Atlantic Air traffic NAT D		USB
8891.00	Bodo ATC, Norway	ENBO	USB 0643 1346 1531 1920
8891.00	Cambridge Bay ATC, Canada	CYCB	USB 2217
8891.00	Gander ATC, Canada	CZQX	USB 2312
8891.00	Reykjavik ATC, Iceland	BIRD	USB 0649 0716 1116 1258 1553 1726
8891.00	Shanwick ATC, UK/Eire	EGGX	USB 1054 1146 1553
8894.00	Africa Air traffic AFI 2		USB
8894.00	Algiers ATC, Algeria	DAAA	USB 0751 0826 0920 1731 1802 2151
8894.00	Niamey ATC, Niger	DRRR	USB 2331
8897.00	East Asia Air traffic EA 1		USB
8898.00	Indian Air Force		USB "K2" & "C5" with SITREP on search mission 1637
8900.00	Intership working		USB Scottish 1046
8903.00	Africa Air traffic AFI 4		USB
8903.00	Accra ATC, Ghana	DGAC	USB (with Springbok 201) 2227"Air Portugal 232" 2156
8903.00	Brazzaville ATC, Congo	FCCC	USB 1932 2230 2247 2320
8903.00	Dakar ATC, Senegal	GOOO	USB 1453
8903.00	Kano ATC, Nigeria	DNKN	USB 0040 2157 2218 2253 2315
8903.00	Kinshasa ATC, Zaire	FZZA	USB 2203 2225 2308
8903.00	Luanda ATC, Angola	FNAN	USB 1829 (with Springbok 234) 2225 (with Angola 658) 2226
8903.00	N'Djamena ATC, Chad	FTTT	USB 0044 2140 2234 2250 2257 2332
8903.00	Niamey ATC, Niger	DRRR	USB 2148 2246 2321
8906.00	India Air traffic		USB
8906.00	Bombay ATC, India	VABF	USB 1425 1600
8906.00	Delhi ATC, India	VIDF	USB 1555
8906.00	N Atlantic Air traffic NAT E		USB
8906.00	Gander ATC, Canada	CZQX	USB 0938 1336 1500 1646 1829
8906.00	New York ATC, USA	KZNY	USB 1322 1426 2238 (with Condor 601) 2231
8906.00	Santa Maria ATC, Azores	LPAZ	USB 1026 1118 1249 1348 1456 1742 2156 2228
8906.00	Shanwick ATC, UK/Eire	EGGX	USB 0752 1029 1319 1454 1551 1612 1742
8911.00	UNID		USB Asian lang simplex R/T 0908 2158 2241
8913.00	Kinshasa ATC, Zaire	FZAZ	USB 2244
8918.00	Mid East air traffic		USB
8918.00	Amman ATC, Jordan	OJAC	USB 2308
8918.00	Bahrain ATC	OBBB	USB 2143
8918.00	Damascus ATC, Syria	OSTT	USB
8918.00	Caribbean Air traffic CAR A		USB
8918.00	Havana ATC, Cuba	MUHA	USB 2143
8918.00	Jeddah ATC, Saudi Arabia	OEJD	USB
8918.00	New York ATC, USA	KZNY	USB
8918.00	Tehran ATC, Iran	OIIX	USB
8921.00	British Airways Company frequency		USB 0847 1130 1630 2207 2245
8924.00	El Al Company frequency		USB 0515 2126 2248
8924.00	KLM Company frequency		USB 0703 0751 0807 1749
8924.00	Polish Airline Company frequency		USB 2208
8924.00	West Indies Airline Company frequency		USB 0921
8925.00	UNID		USB CB style (Eng, West Indian accents) 2300
8927.00	Saudi Airline Company frequency		USB 1358 1753 2259
8930.00	Stockholm (in-flight R/T service)		USB 0637 0719 0739 0820 0909 1647 1837 2141 2245
8933.00	South African Airline Company frequency		USB 2207 2301
8936.00	Berne (in-flight R/T service)		USB 1542 2145 2238
8939.00	CIS VOLMET channel		USB 0654 0909 1118 1206 1554 1822 2121 2239
8942.00	E & S E Asia Air traffic EA 2 SEA 1		USB
8942.00	Hong Kong ATC	VHHK	USB 1702 2302
8942.00	Bangkok ATC, Thailand	VTBD	USB 1919 2132 2227
8942.00	Hochiminhville ATC, Vietnam	VVTS	USB 1342
8942.00	Manila ATC, Philippines	RPMM	USB 1426 1726 1817
8942.00	Singapore ATC	WSJC	USB 1609 1644 1838
8951.00	Middle East Air traffic MID 1/3		USB

kHz.	Station	Call	Mode / Heard/Times GMT
8951.00	Jeddah Air		USB 0732
8957.00	Shannon VOLMET, Eire	EINN	USB 0655 0924 1119 1207 1532 2241
8960.00	Portishead (in-flight R/T service)		USB 1051 1121 1527 1639 1903 2142 2208
8963.00	Nigerian Airways Company frequency		USB 1842 2129
8965.00	German Air Force	DHM91	USB aviation wx forecasts (in Eng) 0858
8964.90	Spa Publications		

AERONAUTICAL MOBILE (MAINLY MILITARY) 3KHz channels

kHz.	Station	Call	Mode / Heard/Times GMT
8967.00	USAF Andrews AFB		USB 2139
8967.00	USAF Hickham AFB, Hawaii		USB
8967.00	USAF Lajes, Azores		USB 0847 1010 2209 2236 2246
8967.00	USAF Thule, Greenland		USB 0709 0730 1839
8970.00	USAF		USB 1724 2154 (Rhein-Main Metro) 2017 2217
8972.00	Canadian Military		USB 2242
8972.00	US Naval		USB "H4A" 1600 "H709" 2210 "5YJ" 2303
8976.00	R Australian Air Force		USB 0706
8980.00	Italian Air Force		USB 2141
8984.00	Boston CG, USA	NMF	USB "COMSTA BOSTON" 2350
8984.00	Miami CG, USA	NOM	USB "COMSTA MIAMI" 2314 2321
8984.00	New Orleans CG, USA	NMG	USB "COMSTA NEW ORLEANS"
8984.00	New York CG, USA		USB (with search aircraft "1719" off Cape Cod) 2351
8984.00	Chesapeake CG, USA	NMN	USB "CAMSLANT CHESAPEAKE" (with "Rescue 1711") 2307
8988.00	RAF Pitreavie, Scotland	MKL	CW wx 0904 1208 1405 2206 2302
8989.00	Belgian Air Force		USB 0705
8989.00	USAF McClellan AFB		USB
8991.00	Italian Air Force		USB 0822
8992.00	Portuguese Military, Azores		USB 0858 1407 1534 1610 1858
8993.00	USAF Albrook AFB, Panama		USB
8993.00	USAF Andrews AFB		USB 0847 2157
8993.00	USAF Ascension Island		USB 0653
8993.00	USAF Incirlik, Turkey		USB 2210
8993.00	USAF MacDill AFB		USB 0934 2313
8997.00	Spanish Air Force		USB 0732
9003.00	Alia Jordan Airline Company frequency		USB 1905 1935 2019 2053 2210
9006.00	Canadian Military		USB 1859
9013.00	Prestwick Naval, UK		USB (clg) "X0F" 0816
9014.00	RAF		USB "U9V" radio check with "8WH" 1350
9017.00	USAF Andrews AFB		USB
9017.00	USAF MacDill AFB		USB
9022.00	R Tehran		AM Eng 0041 1942 Fr 0656 0721 1859 2240 Ger 1806 Span 2122
9023.00	USAF		USB 0849
9027.00	USAF		USB 0746 0816 0900 2046 2242 2316
9027.70	UNID		SITOR Oil Rig traffic (in Eng) 0658
9032.00	RAF Akrotiri, Cyprus		USB "CYPRUS FLIGHT WATCH" Akrotiri wx 2215
9032.00	RAF Ascension Island		USB
9032.00	RAF Falkland Isles		USB "VIPER"
9032.00	RAF Gibraltar		USB
9032.00	RAF, UK		USB "ARCHITECT" 0652 0758 0841 1452 wx 0700 1100 1400
9039.90	Spa Publications		

9040-9500
FIXED

kHz.	Station	Call	Mode / Heard/Times GMT
9041.00	Nairobi Met, Kenya	5YE	100r 2035
9045.00	Nairobi Met, Kenya	5YE	FAX wx maps 1812 2157
9046.00	Serbian Embassy traffic	DFZG	75n p/lang Slav 0658 Eng (TANJUG rpts) 0744
9050.00	US Naval, Italy	NSY	FAX wx maps 0924
9057.00	USAF		USB
9057.00	Serbian Embassy traffic	DFZG	75n p/lang Slav 1408 Eng 1541
9059.50	USAF weather service		75r 1404
9064.00	PBS China		AM Chinese 2304
9066.00	Polish Embassy traffic		100POL-ARQ 5 fig grps 1406
9070.00	Numbers Station		USB Slav (male voice) 1701
9080.00	PBS China		AM Chinese 1533 2200
9081.80	Swedish Embassy traffic		100SWED-ARQ (short) 0713
9082.00	CIS Naval	RMP	CW (listening 4194.0kHz) 0957
9087.50	Italian Embassy traffic		SITOR 0746 0842
9090.50	Italian Embassy traffic		SITOR 0909
9096.70	UNID		SITOR Selcal XECX 0700
9100.00	Rostov Met, Russia		FAX wx maps 1533
9103.00	Czech Embassy traffic		100n p/lang 1403

kHz.	Station	Call	Mode / Heard/Times GMT
9106.50	Italian Embassy traffic		SITOR p/lang 0844 0910 1345 Selcal VQMX 0720
9114.00	Budapest Press (MTI)	HGG31	50n Eng 1702 1731
9117.70	Dutch Embassy traffic	PCW1	SITOR 1308 2038 2159
9121.00	UNID		CW 5 fig grps 1808
9126.50	Italian Embassy traffic		SITOR 0845 1408 Selcal VXQX & msgs Budapest/ Bucharest 0734
9130.00	British Naval	MTO	75r test tape 2040
9130.00	Numbers Station		AM phonetics (female voice) 1544 1640
9133.00	Tirana Press (ATA)	ZAA6	50n Eng 0806 0820 0912 1123 ID & RYs 1054 (tx unstable)
9135.00	RAF Akrotiri, Cyprus	MKD	50r (VFT) QBF & RYls 1545 (LSB 9138.0)
9139.00	Polish Embassy traffic		100POL-ARQ p/lang (CLARIS No 452) 0914
9150.00	Tashkent Met, Uzbekistan	RCH73	FAX wx maps 1534 1703 1809 2041
9153.00	Polish Embassy traffic		75n 5 fig grps 0704
9154.00	Sal Air, Cape Verde	GVAC	50n 0721 2230 ID & RYs 0750
9162.00	Swiss Embassy traffic	HBD56	SITOR p/lang Fr (abt Bosnian wounded evacuation) 0821
9165.00	R Omdurman		AM Eng 1836 Arab 1535 Fr 1743
9167.50	Swiss Embassy traffic	HBD	SITOR 5 let grps 0736
9170.00	PBS China		AM Chinese 1546
9190.00	Moscow Met, Russia	RDZ75	50r 0825 0927 1352 1455 1556 1705
9198.00	Polish Embassy traffic		200POL-ARQ 5 fig grps 1347
9212.00	UNID		72ARQ/E/4 1121
9220.00	Novosibirsk Met, Russia	RTB26	FAX wx maps 1706 1811
9230.00	Khabarovsk Met, Russia	RXO70	FAX wx maps 1600
9251.00	Numbers Station		AM Eng (female voice) 1711 (& "Lincolnshire Poacher" jingle)
9259.00	UNID		72ARQ/E/8 Idle 0937
9268.00	UNID		75n Slav p/lang 0757
9275.00	Norwegian Embassy traffic		SITOR p/lang 0753
9278.00	Czech Embassy traffic		100n p/lang 0722 0828 (news summary) 0917
9280.00	WYFR, USA		AM Asian lang 1409 1557 2145 2201
9287.00	UNID		48ARQ/E3/4 Idle 2043
9306.00	UNID	SCY	CW (clg "1UH") 1123
9318.00	Grengel Met, Germany	DHJ51	100n 1056 1535
9318.00	US Naval, Iceland		FAX wx maps 0739 0822 2045 2124
9325.00	R Pyongyang		AM Eng 1527 1714 Span 2046
9333.50	Italian Embassy traffic		SITOR 0921
9340.00	Tashkent Met, Uzbekistan	RCH72	FAX wx maps 1459 1856 2202
9341.50	French Military, Orleans	FDY	50r RYs & "Voyez le Brick..." 0824
9345.00	R Pyongyang		AM Eng 2047 Span 1813
9349.50	French Military, Bordeaux	FDG	CW 0742
9350.00	UNID		AM Eng (US religious) 0831
9355.00	Monitor Radio International		AM Eng 1500 1806
9360.00	Copenhagen Met	OXT	FAX wx maps 1152
9365.00	R China International		AM Ital 2125
9370.00	WEWN, USA		AM Ger 2205
9373.00	US Naval, Spain	AOK	FAX wx map 0823 1445
9375.00	R for Peace International		AM Eng UN Radio programme 1059
9380.00	PBS China		AM Chinese 2207
9382.00	US Naval		FAX wx maps 0724 1349
9387.00	UNID		144FEC-A encrypted tfc ending "QSL ALL TKS 73" 1101
9387.50	French Military, Metz	FDC	CW 0921
9388.00	Kol Israel		AM Hebrew 1421 1655 2202
9395.00	Pyongyang Press (KCNA)	HMF84	50n Fr 1814 1859 2209
9395.00	Voice of Greece		AM Greek 1645
9400.00	Radiocentras Vilnius, Lithuania		CW test and request for rpts 1856
9400.00	FEBC Manila		AM Chinese 1100 1422
9410.00	BBC		AM Eng 0849 0924 1211 1356 1502 1714 2125 2208 (0300-2315)
9417.00	Beijing Press (XINHUA)	BXP59	75r Eng 1733 1853 1950 2034 ID 2141
9420.00	Swiss Radio International		AM Eng 1504
9425.00	Voice of Greece		AM Eng 0745 1356 Greek 1646 1900
9430.00	Taiwan Press (CNA)	3MA	CW & FAX
9430.00	Tirana Press (ATA)	ZAT	50n Eng 0832 1127 ID & RYs 0849 1102
9435.00	Kol Israel		AM Eng 2231 2239 (2230-2300) Span 2227
9440.00	R China International		AM Arab 1600
9445.00	Voice of Turkey		AM Eng 2210 Fr 2250
9445.00	Numbers Station		AM Ger (female voice) 1614
9450.00	R Yerevan		AM Eng 2148 Fr 2132
9455.00	TWR		AM Eng 1647
9455.00	Monitor Radio International		AM Eng 0644 0827 0912 0945
9463.00	Amman Press (PETRA)	JYF	50n Arab 0942
9465.00	Monitor Radio International		AM Eng 2203 2240 2251 (2200-2359)
9470.00	R Moscow		AM Slav 0946 Fr 1615 Portuguese 2136
9480.00	R Moscow		AM Eng 2212
9480.00	TWR		AM Eng 0655 0708 0850 0931
9485.00	R Prague		AM Span 2051
9490.00	R Moscow		AM Fr 1645 1902 2233
9491.00	Beijing Press (XINHUA)	BZR69	75r Eng 1847 1953 2037 2201

kHz.	Station	Call	Mode / Heard/Times GMT
9495.00	R France International		AM Fr 1825 2151
9495.00	Monitor Radio International		AM Eng 0650 1128 1214
9499.90	Spa Publications		

9500-9900
BROADCASTING

kHz.	Station	Call	Mode / Heard/Times GMT
9505.00	R Bratislava		AM Eng 1130
9505.00	R Prague		AM Eng 0625 0712 Span 1131
9505.00	R Ukraine International		AM Eng 2254
9510.00	R Australia		AM Eng 1603
9510.00	R Romania International		AM Eng 0631
9520.00	R Svoboda		AM Slav 1054 1135
9525.00	Polish Radio Warsaw		AM Eng 1231 1648 Ger 1132 1730
9530.00	R Moscow		AM Eng 1627
9535.00	R Swiss International		AM Eng 1103 1718 Fr 0735 0948 1735 Ger 1215 Ital 1818
9540.00	REE Spain		AM Eng 0013
9545.00	Deutsche Welle		AM Ger 0740 0946 1136 1219 1400 1526 1850 2244
9550.00	R Canada International		AM Eng 1630
9550.00	R Moscow		AM Eng 1630 1715 2236
9550.00	R Ukraine International		AM Eng (0000-0100)
9555.00	R Svoboda		AM Slav 0940
9560.00	R Amman		AM Eng 1711 Arab 2212
9560.00	R Australia		AM Eng 1618 1649 1748
9560.00	R Finland		AM Eng 0654 0748
9560.00	R Moscow		AM Eng 1712
9565.00	Deutsche Welle		AM Arab 0700
9565.00	R Svoboda		AM Slav 1541
9575.00	R Mediterranean International		AM Fr & Arab 1903
9580.00	R Bratislava		AM Eng (0200-0230)
9580.00	R Moscow		AM Eng 0812 1525 Fr 0741
9585.00	Deutsche Welle		AM Eng 1648
9585.00	VOA		AM Slav 2158
9590.00	BBC		AM Eng 2213
9590.00	R Denmark		AM Danish 1354
9590.00	VOA		AM Eng 1104 1138
9595.00	R Svoboda		AM Slav 1442
9600.00	BBC		AM Eng 0633 0713 0750 Ger 1158
9605.00	BBC		AM Eng (Eng lang lessons) 1755
9605.00	R Abu Dhabi		AM Eng 2201 2250 2345 (2200-2359) Arab 2141
9605.00	R Netherland		AM Eng 1836 1905
9605.00	R Prague		AM Eng 1800 2100 Ger 1722
9610.00	R Moscow		AM Eng 0534
9615.00	R Finland		AM Eng 2236
9620.00	R Moscow		AM Eng 2238 2307
9620.00	R Sweden		AM Scand 1140 Fr 1200
9620.00	R Yugoslavia		AM Eng 2058
9620.00	REE Spain		AM Span 1443 1542 1650 1817 1905 2142
9625.00	R Svoboda		AM Slav 0930 0942 1902
9635.00	R Portugal International		AM Portuguese 1906
9640.00	BBC		AM Eng 0701 0743
9640.00	R Moscow		AM Eng 2105
9640.00	R Ukraine International		AM Eng (0000-0100)
9645.00	R Australia		AM Eng 2202 2220
9645.00	R Sweden		AM Eng 1740
9645.00	R Vatican		AM Eng 0635 Ital 0714 Ger 1444 Fr 1607 Arab 1831
9650.00	Deutsche Welle		AM Ger 1654 2201 Slav 0948
9655.00	R Sweden		AM Eng 2117
9660.00	BBC		AM Eng 0715 1201 1311 1445
9665.00	Deutsche Welle		AM Eng 1907 Ger 1204
9680.00	R Portugal International		AM Portuguese 1446 1656
9685.00	R Moscow		AM Eng 1908 Fr 2310
9685.00	R Ukraine International		AM Eng 2146 (2100-2200 0000-0100)
9690.00	Deutsche Welle		AM Ger 0656
9690.00	R Romania International		AM Ger 1216 1635 1820
9700.00	R New Zealand		AM Eng 0818
9700.00	R Bulgaria		AM Eng 1754 2248 Fr 0745 1802
9700.00	VOA		AM Eng 1529 1651 1753 1814 1909 (1500-2200) Slav 2000
9705.00	R Svoboda		AM Slav 1716
9710.00	R Australia		AM Eng 1124
9710.00	R Vilnius		AM Eng 2147
9715.00	R Netherland		AM Eng 0753
9720.00	R Netherland		AM Eng 0747
9720.00	R Netherland		AM Eng 0950 Dutch 0653
9720.00	R Yugoslavia		AM Eng 2150

kHz.	Station	Call	Mode / Heard/Times GMT
9725.00	R Moscow		AM Eng 2236
9725.00	R Svoboda		AM Slav 1312
9730.00	Deutsche Welle		AM Ger 2208 2239 2308
9730.00	R Finland		AM Eng 1833 1837
9735.00	Deutsche Welle		AM Ger 0853 0939 1908
9735.00	R Nacional, Paraguay		AM Span 2248
9740.00	BBC		AM Eng 1106 1529 1612 1732 1821
9740.00	R Finland		AM Eng 2258
9745.00	HCJB, Ecuador		AM Eng 0758 0840 0854 (0730-1100)
9745.00	R Ukraine International		AM Eng 2220 2240
9750.00	BBC		AM Eng 0754 0947 1122 1205 1313 1447 1530 Ger 1657
9750.00	R Moscow		AM Eng 0535 0702 2200
9755.00	R Canada International		AM Eng 2210
9760.00	BBC		AM Eng 0841 0951 1128 1448 1530
9760.00	R Tirana		AM Eng 1540 2205
9760.00	VOA		AM Eng 1653 1700 1744 1855 1912 2001
9765.00	Deutsche Welle		AM Ger 2309
9765.00	R Moscow		AM Eng 0536 0623
9770.00	Deutsche Welle		AM Slav 1130
9770.00	R Abu Dhabi		AM Eng 2226 (readings from Holy Koran) 2214
9770.00	R Australia		AM Eng 1526 1546
9770.00	VOA		AM Eng 1834 2206
9785.00	KTWR, Guam		AM Eng 1108
9785.00	R Moscow		AM Fr 1654
9790.00	R France International		AM Fr 1824 1909 2002 2238 2313
9797.00	Bucharest Press (ROMPRES)	YOJ27	50r ID & RYs 0850 0856 Eng 0932 0940
9805.00	R France International		AM Eng 1236 Fr 0749 1123 1217
9810.00	R Swiss International		AM Eng 2212
9815.00	R Moscow		AM Eng 2207
9820.00	R Moscow		AM Eng 2004 2155
9830.00	R Croatia		AM Slav 2200
9830.00	R Amman		AM Arab 1914
9835.00	R Budapest		AM Eng 2109 (2100-2200)
9840.00	Monitor Radio International		AM Eng 0745 0857 0949
9860.00	R Moscow		AM Eng 1912
9860.00	R Netherland		AM Eng 1138
9860.00	R Ukraine International		AM Eng 2242
9870.00	R Austria International		AM Eng 1441 Ger 2213 2312
9875.00	REE Spain		AM Span 1206 1416 1548
9880.00	R Austria International		AM Eng 1534 Ger 1514
9880.00	R China International		AM Eng 2203
9880.00	R Moscow		AM Eng 1825 Fr 1638
9885.00	R Swiss International		AM Eng 0900 0920 1700 2005 2214 Fr 0933
9890.00	R Moscow		AM Eng 1515 1532 1715
9890.00	R Netherland		AM Eng 1552
9899.90	Spa Publications		

9900-9995
FIXED

kHz.	Station	Call	Mode / Heard/Times GMT
9900.00	R Cairo		AM Eng 2158 2215 Ger 1910
9905.00	R Vlaanderen International		AM Eng 0914 Ger 0953 Dutch 1206 1314
9910.00	All India Radio		AM Eng 1533 2216 2310
9915.00	BBC		AM Eng 1917 2202 2250 2315
9920.00	R China International		AM Eng 2100 Ger 1827 1837
9925.00	R Vlaanderen International		AM Eng 0647
9928.00	Almaty Met, Kazakhstan		FAX wx maps 0733
9941.50	Voz del Cid, Costa Rica		AM Span 2216
9945.00	R China International		AM Chinese 0954
9950.00	All India Radio		AM Eng 1838 2223
9970.00	French Military	FDC	CW 0801 1831
9985.00	WEWN, USA		AM Eng 1919
9994.00	Santa Maria Air, Azores	CSY	50n 0745 0854 0943 1534 2008 & msrd 9994.5kHz
9996.00	Moscow Time Station, Russia	RWM	CW 1218 1615 (CQ call 1710 2210)
10000.00	Fort Collins Time Station, USA	WWV	USB 0631 0900 2149
10000.00	Xian Time Station, China	BPM	CW ID 1500 1558
10004.00	Irkutsk Time Station, Russia	RID	CW 1756
10004.90	Spa Publications		

10005-10100
AERONAUTICAL MOBILE (MAINLY CIVIL) 3KHz channels

kHz.	Station	Call	Mode / Heard/Times GMT
10012.00	UNID		USB simplex R/T (with wx rpt in Spanish) 1808
10018.00	Africa & Mid East Air traffic AFI 3 MID 2		USB
10018.00	Bombay ATC, India	VABB	USB 1419 1637 1822 2100
10018.00	Colombo ATC, Sri Lanka	VCCC	USB
10018.00	Delhi ATC, India	VIDF	USB 2224
10018.00	Karachi ATC, Pakistan	OPKR	USB 1826 2102
10024.00	S America Air traffic SAM		USB
10024.00	Lima ATC, Peru	SPLI	USB 0633
10024.00	Santiago ATC, Chile	SCSC	USB
10027.00	Iberia Company frequency		USB 2244
10027.00	Prague Air, Czech Republic		USB 0746
10030.00	LTU Company frequency		USB 1900
10042.00	E Asia Air traffic EA 1		USB
10046.00	Israeli Naval	4XZ	CW 0905 1446 1559 1823 2150
10048.00	N Pacific Air traffic NP		USB
10048.00	Honolulu ATC	PHZH	USB 0736
10051.00	Gander VOLMET		USB 0625 0750 0951 1250 1556 1757 1822
10051.00	New York VOLMET		USB 2105 2134
10056.00	Turkish Embassy traffic	TAD	144FEC p/lang 1436 1500
10057.00	Brazzaville VOLMET	FCCC	USB 2108 2247
10066.00	S E Asia Air traffic SEA 1/3		USB
10066.00	Bombay ATC, India	VABB	USB 1511 2128
10066.00	Calcutta ATC, India	VECF	USB 1447 1543 1617 1730 1831 1907
10066.00	Colombo ATC, Sri Lanka	VCCC	USB 1526
10066.00	Dhaka ATC, Bangladesh	VGFR	USB 2150
10066.00	Kuala Lumpur ATC, Malaysia	WMFC	USB
10066.00	Madras ATC, India	VOMF	USB 1635
10066.00	Male ATC, Maldives	VRMM	USB 1625 1831
10066.00	Yangon ATC, Myanmar	VBRR	USB 1517 1731 1833 1909
10069.00	Berne (in-flight R/T service)		USB 0906 1626 2219
10072.00	Air India Company frequency		USB 1643 (with wx) 1621 1652
10072.00	British Airways Company frequency		USB 0936 1422 1521 1635 1641
10075.00	Houston (in-flight R/T service)		USB 1632
10078.00	Lufthansa Company frequency		USB 0811 1055 1121 1428 1738 2108
10084.00	Malta		USB (with Aeroflot 360) 1627
10090.00	CIS VOLMET channel		USB Eng 1613 1822
10096.00	N Central Asia Air traffic NCA 2		USB
10096.00	S America Air traffic		USB
10096.00	Caracas ATC, Venezuela	MVZM	USB 2239
10096.00	Piarco ATC, Trinidad	MKPP	USB
10096.00	Porto Velho ATC, Brazil	SBPV	USB 0753 2203
10099.90	Spa Publications		

10100-10150
AMATEUR & FIXED

kHz.	Station	Call	Mode / Heard/Times GMT
10103.70	French Embassy traffic		96ARQ/E/8 "DE PARIS 5870 0020910 CONTROLE DE VOIE" 0910
10108.00	UNID		200Bd spec code type 0949
10117.00	Beijing Met, China		FAX wx maps 1834 2159
10125.00	Numbers Station		AM "CIO2" (female voice) 1448
10130.00	Murmansk Met, Russia		FAX wx maps 0748 1545
10130.00	Tashkent Met, Uzbekistan		50n 0713
10132.70	Amateur Packet Radio	GB7PLY	300Bd packet net 1332
10138.60	Amateur Packet Radio	FF6RAC	300Bd packet (to F2XC) 2109 (G4JB/FF1SHI) 1751
10141.50	Amateur Packet Radio	FE6EQZ	300Bd packet net 0904
10144.00	Amateur Radio Beacon, Germany	DK0WCY	CW 0715 0912 (propagation rpt, in Eng) 0901 1157
10146.30	Amateur Packet Radio	UT4UX	300Bd packet net 1639
10147.20	Amateur Packet Radio	GB7GMX	300Bd packet net 1334
10148.00	UNID		80Bd spec code type 0950
10149.90	Spa Publications		

10150-11175
FIXED & MOBILE

kHz.	Station	Call	Mode / Heard/Times GMT
10150.00	Cairo Press (MENA)	SUA	75r Arab 0914 0933 1602 1753 1801 2033 2110
10151.80	Swedish Embassy traffic		100SWED/ARQ (long) 1549
10162.50	Baghdad Press (INA)	YIL70	50r Eng 1335 1516 (freq varies)
10165.00	Stockholm (in flight R/T service)		USB 1855
10165.00	UNID		100n Slav p/lang (probably Czech Embassy traffic) 1400
10166.00	Swedish Embassy traffic		100SWED-ARQ (mid) 0759
10170.00	Bangkok Met, Thailand	HSW63	85/50n 1824 1836
10186.00	Polish Embassy traffic		100POL-ARQ 1419

kHz.	Station	Call	Mode / Heard/Times GMT
10200.00	RAF London	MKK	50r (VFT) QBF & RYIs 0717 0915 1158 1920 (LSB 10203.0)
10215.00	Jeddah Met, Saudi Arabia	HZN48	100n 0718 1548 1758 1803 1831
10220.00	RAF Akrotiri, Cyprus	MKD	50r (VFT) QBF & RYIs 1636 1814 (LSB 10223.0)
10230.00	Moscow Met, Russia	RKA78	FAX wx maps 0800 1159 1605 1654 1832
10235.00	Taiwan Press (CNA)	3MA	50r Eng 1337
10250.00	Madrid Met, Spain		FAX wx maps 1640 1815
10255.00	US Embassy frequency (rptd Athens)	KWS78	CW 0801 1200 1837 2200
10260.00	PBS China		AM Chinese 2106 2114
10260.00	UNID		75n 5 let grps 1655
10280.00	RAF London	MKK	50r (VFT) QBF & RYIs 1201 (LSB 10283.0)
10295.00	INTERPOL	FSB	SITOR Selcal IPUC 1754
10298.70	Bangkok Met, Thailand	HSW	50n 1831
10304.00	UNID		USB Span simplex R/T 2107
10344.00	R Moscow feeder		USB Eng 1202 1807 2118
10380.00	Murmansk Met, Russia	RBW43	50n New Year gtngs (to "Rudnik Piramida") 0918
10390.00	INTERPOL	FSB	SITOR 0919 1812 2119 Selcal IPEC 0857
10400.20	French Military		200ARQ/M2/4 ch A 5 let grps 2120
10407.00	Dakar Air, Senegal	6VU	50 ID & RYs 0803
10408.00	Singapore Press (ANSA)	9VF63	50n Eng 1811 1819
10408.70	Beacon, Sveio, Norway	LN2A	SITOR & CW 1338 (ITU propagation tests, 1kW)
10412.00	UNID		75n 5 let grps 2201
10412.00	UNID		72ARQ/E/4 Idle 1645
10415.00	Polish Embassy traffic		75n 5 fig grps 0804
10417.00	Rabat Press (MAP)	CNM31/6X	50r Span 1938
10423.50	Ankara Met, Turkey	YMA20	50r 0910 0920 RYs 0805 1203
10425.00	Austrian Embassy traffic		96SI-ARQ(6 char) p/lang Ger 1339
10426.00	Numbers Station		USB "Lincolnshire Poacher" 2203
10495.00	RAF Akrotiri, Cyprus	MKD	50r (VFT) QBF & RYIs 0806 0921 1656 (LSB 10498.0)
10523.10	Pyongyang Press (KCNA)		50n Fr 1205
10536.00	Halifax Met, Canada	CFH	FAX wx maps 0911 1827 2109 2125
10536.00	Halifax Met, Canada	CFH	75r 1550 1756
10540.50	Santa Maria Air	CSY	50n 1206
10551.30	Bracknell Met, UK	GFL23	50r 0907 1340 1638 1836
10555.00	Darwin Met, Australia	AXI34	FAX wx maps 1757 2204 (schedule 0030) analysis 1430
10580.00	Pyongyang Press (KCNA)	HMF85	50r Eng 1452 1533 1541
10586.00	RAF Akrotiri, Cyprus	MKD	50r (VFT) QBF & RYIs 1922 (LSB 10589.0)
10599.90	Hanoi Press (VNA)	XVN37	50r Fr 1536 1652 Eng 1506 1535 1542
10610.00	Cairo Press (MENA)	SUA30	75r Eng 1537 1556 2115 Fr 1633 RYs 1654
10634.10	Rabat Press (MAP)	CNM37/9X	50r Fr 1613 1641 (1000-1130 1530-1700)
10638.60	French Military, Djibouti	RFQP	200ARQ/M2/4 Idle 1923
10654.00	RAF, UK	MKK	50r (VFT) QBF & RYIs 1643 (LSB ch 10657.0)
10654.20	Bangkok Air, Thailand	HSD	85/50n (VTBB) RYs 1614
10686.00	Tehran Met, Iran		50r 0940 1554 1616 1837
10690.00	R Moscow feeder		USB Slav 0910
10710.00	Moscow Met, Russia	RKA73	FAX wx maps 1849 2024 2249 2328
10720.00	Buenos Aires Met, Argentina	LRB72	FAX wx maps 2205
10723.00	Numbers Station		USB Eng (female voice) 1450
10757.50	Rabat Press (MAP)	CNM39/1X	50r Span 1946
10798.20	UNID		96ARQ/E3/8 Idle 0941
10805.00	Buenos Aires Press (NA)	LRO	75r Span 2118 2202 2227 2255 2324
10855.00	British Military	GXQ	50r (VFT) QBF & RYIs 1055 (LSB 10858.0)
10855.00	R Moscow feeder		USB Slav 0810 0912 1341 1839
10865.00	US Naval, Norfolk	NAM	FAX wx maps 2206
10871.70	Single Letter Beacon	D	CW 0811
10871.90	Single Letter Beacon	S	CW 1209 1520 1840
10872.00	Single Letter Beacon	C	CW 1342 1500 1618 1823
10873.80	UNID		100ARQ/E3/8 Idle 1841 1924
10888.00	CIS Naval	RIT	CW (to UAJN) 1807
10890.00	British Military	GXQ	50r (VFT) 0812 1210 1343 1645 (LSB 10893.0)
10893.50	Buenos Aires Press (TELAM)	LRB39	50r Span 2130 2313 2325
10896.80	Hungarian Embassy traffic		125DUP-ARQ(reverse polarity) msg from Zurich 1823
10945.00	Halifax Naval, Canada	CFH	CW 1211 1344 1827 2115
10960.70	French Military, Paris	RFFP	200ARQ/M2 Idle 1557
10970.00	Numbers Station		AM "VLB2" (female voice) 1345
10980.00	Moscow Met, Russia	RDD79	FAX wx maps 1521 1842
11000.00	PBS China		AM Chinese 2116
11002.00	Prague Telecom	OLX	CW 1058
11030.00	Canberra Met, Australia	AXM34	FAX wx maps 1522
11035.00	Barencburg, Spitzbergen	UKS	50rc Russ wx tfc 1544
11039.00	Hamburg (Quickborn) Met, Germany	DDH9	50r 1059 1212 1346 1830
11053.00	USAF Andrews AFB		USB
11063.00	Sofia Met, Bulgaria	LZU2	50n 1213 1348 1523
11080.00	Damascus Press (SANA)		50r Arab 1524 1600
11092.50	R St. Helena		USB one-day special tx 2000-2300
11095.00	RAF Akrotiri, Cyprus	MKD	50r (VFT) QBF & RYIs 0945 (LSB 11098.8)
11100.00	PBS China		AM Chinese 1332 1601
11111.00	UNID		USB Asian lang simplex R/T 2118

kHz.	Station	Call	Mode / Heard/Times GMT
11123.50	German Govt press info service	DFX	96FEC Ger news 1345 (also on 123.7kHz)
11125.00	Grengel Met, Germany	DHJ	100n 1334 1525 1602 1843
11133.00	Beijing Press (XINHUA)	BZG41	50r Fr 1810 1829
11142.00	US Embassy frequency (rptd London)	KRH50	CW 1157 1349 1603 1844
11145.00	Portuguese Naval, Madeira	RPTMB	75n QBF & RYs test run for RPFN 1158
11159.50	USAF weather service		75r 1811
11174.90	Spa Publications		

11175-11275
AERONAUTICAL MOBILE (MAINLY MILITARY)

kHz.	Station	Call	Mode / Heard/Times GMT
11176.00	USAF Albrook AFB, Panama		USB 2147 2227
11176.00	USAF Andrews AFB, USA		USB 1631 2318
11176.00	USAF Ascension Island		USB 0547 0715 2126 2210
11176.00	USAF Croughton, UK		USB 1336 1542 2115
11176.00	USAF Incirlik, Turkey		USB 0609 0754 0910 1738
11176.00	USAF Lajes, Azores		USB 1218
11176.00	USAF MacDill AFB, USA		USB 2149
11193.00	Moscow Air, Russia		USB 1536 1603 1830 2138
11200.00	RAF VOLMET		USB 0634 0940 1337 1723 1859 2107 2233
11201.00	US Coastguard stations		USB
11204.00	RAF, UK		USB "ARCHITECT" airfield states 1901
11212.00	RAF Pitreavie, Scotland	MKL	CW 0705 1605
11214.00	Canadian Military, Trenton		USB
11217.00	German Air Force		USB 0756 1830
11226.00	USAF Andrews AFB		USB (VIP channel)
11226.00	USAF Lajes, Azores		USB
11226.00	USAF MacDill AFB		USB
11228.00	US Military		USB "DN066/DN08" 1605
11233.00	Canadian Military		USB 1543
11234.00	RAF Ascension Island		USB "TURTLE"
11234.00	RAF Akrotiri, Cyprus		USB "CYPRUS FLIGHT WATCH" 0756 0948
11234.00	RAF Falkland Isles		USB "VIPER"
11234.00	RAF Gibraltar		USB "GIBRALTAR FLIGHT WATCH" (with "Z4S") 1146
11234.00	RAF, UK		USB "ARCHITECT" 1623
11239.00	USAF McClellan AFB		LSB 1753
11241.70	Egyptian Embassy traffic		SITOR 1501 1732
11243.00	USAF Incirlik, Turkey		USB 0630 1550 1820
11243.00	USAF Thule, Greenland		USB 1633
11246.00	Danish Air Force		USB 1523 1848
11246.00	USAF Andrews AFB		USB 0907
11246.00	USAF MacDill AFB		USB 1531
11255.00	US Naval (N Atlantic)		USB "F7T"/"0DF" 0811 "C0J"/"Z7F" 1846
11267.00	US Naval		USB "Y4H"/"2NX" 2140
11270.00	Numbers Station		AM Slav (male voice) 0827
11274.90	Spa Publications		

11275-11400
AERONAUTICAL MOBILE (MAINLY CIVIL) 3KHz channels

kHz.	Station	Call	Mode / Heard/Times GMT
11279.00	N Atlantic Air traffic NAT D		USB
11279.00	Cambridge Bay ATC, Canada	CYCB	USB 0632
11279.00	CIS VOLMET channel		USB 0910 0946 1113
11282.00	Central E Pacific Air traffic CEP 1/2		USB
11282.00	Honolulu ATC	PHZH	USB
11288.00	Saudi Airlines Company frequency		USB 1545 2108
11291.00	S Atlantic air traffic		USB
11291.00	Dakar ATC, Senegal	GOOO	USB 0757 2307
11297.00	CIS VOLMET channel		USB 0744 0941 1119 1339 1604
11300.00	Africa & Mid East Air traffic AFI 3 MID 2		USB
11300.00	Addis Ababa ATC, Ethiopia	HAAA	USB 1544 2145 2208
11300.00	Aden ATC	ODAA	USB 1738
11300.00	Benghazi ATC, Libya	HLLB	USB 1713
11300.00	Cairo ATC, Egypt	HECA	USB 1538 1847 2144
11300.00	Khartoum ATC, Sudan	HSSS	USB 1536 1812 2109 2142 2233
11300.00	Mahe ATC, Seychelles	FSSS	USB 1849
11300.00	Mogadishu ATC, Somalia	HCMM	USB 2253
11300.00	Nairobi ATC, Kenya	HKEA	USB 1606 2111 2141
11300.00	Sana ATC, Yemen	OYSN	USB 2236
11300.00	Tripoli ATC, Libya	HLLL	USB 0759 2145 2225 2323
11305.50	North Korean Embassy traffic		50n p/lang (Eng text of letter to Yassir Arafat) 1351
11306.00	Lima (in-flight R/T service)		USB (American 56) 2244
11306.00	Portishead (in-flight R/T service)		USB 0758 0948 1101

kHz.	Station	Call	Mode / Heard/Times GMT
11308.00	UNID		USB Slav simplex R/T 1103
11309.00	N Atlantic Air traffic NAT E		USB
11309.00	New York ATC, USA	KZNY	USB 1530 1825 1902
11309.00	Santa Maria ATC, Azores	LPAZ	USB 1355 1456 1739 1910
11318.00	CIS VOLMET channel		USB 0633 0706 1101 1237 1400
11330.00	New York ATC, USA	KZNY	USB 2135 2146 2234
11330.00	PBS China		AM Chinese 1606 2205
11336.00	N Atlantic Air traffic NAT C		USB
11336.00	Gander ATC, Canada	CZQX	USB 1357 1508 1531
11345.00	Stockholm (in-flight R/T service)		USB 0741 0942 1345 1618 1624
11346.70	Egyptian Embassy traffic		SITOR 1607
11351.00	St Lys (in-flight R/T service)		USB 1816 1831
11360.00	S America Air traffic SAM		USB
11363.00	Brittania Airways company frequency		USB 1649 2120 2144
11375.00	Middle East Air traffic MID 1/3		USB
11375.00	Numbers Station		USB Span (female voice) 0703
11384.00	Bulgarian Airlines Company frequency		USB 1455
11384.00	Central W Pacific Air traffic CWP 1/2		USB 1423
11387.00	Caribbean Air traffic CAR B		USB
11387.00	Singapore VOLMET	WSJC	USB 2311
11387.00	Sydney VOLMET	ASSY	USB 1031 1503 1901 2130
11390.00	Moscow Air, Russia		USB 0707
11393.00	Italian Embassy traffic		96ARQ/E/8 Idle 1605
11396.00	Caribbean Air traffic CAR A		USB
11396.00	New York ATC, USA	KZNY	USB 1607 2225
11396.00	Panama ATC	MPZL	USB 2228
11396.00	E & S E Asia Air traffic EA 2 SEA 1/3		USB
11396.00	Darwin ATC, Australia	ADDA	USB 1743
11396.00	Jakarta ATC, Indonesia	WIIZ	USB 1610 2122
11396.00	Perth ATC, Australia	APPH	USB 1547
11399.90	Spa Publications		

11400-11650
FIXED

kHz.	Station	Call	Mode / Heard/Times GMT
11402.00	R Iceland		USB Icelandic 1852
11405.00	UN traffic		SITOR p/lang Eng msg to UNHCR Zagreb 1458
11407.00	USAF Andrews AFB		USB (VIP channel)
11412.00	British Military	GXQ	50r (VFT) QBF & RYls 1834 (LSB ch 11415.0)
11423.50	Warsaw Press (PAP)		SITOR Mode B Polish 1814 1839
11430.00	Pyongyang Press (KCNA)	HMF55	50n Eng 1500 Fr 2207
11439.00	UNID		72ARQ/E/4 Idle 1150 1528
11445.00	R China International		AM Asian lang 1731 Span 1903
11450.00	Moscow Met, Russia	RDD77	50r 0728 0912 1347 1504
11453.00	Rome Met, Italy	IMB33	50n 0737 1103 1126 1402 1851 2114 2210
11455.50	US Embassy frequency (rptd Warrenton)	KKN50	CW 2116
11466.00	Santa Maria Air	CSY	50n 1400 1510 (also msrd 11469.0)
11467.00	Italian Embassy traffic		96ARQ/E/8 p/lang 0914
11476.00	Pyongyang Press (KCNA)	HMF52	FAX 0002
11476.00	Pyongyang Press (KCNA)	HMF52	50r Eng 1816 1841 1904 2212
11480.00	Italian Embassy traffic		96ARQ/E/8 5 let grps 0916 1501 1511
11485.00	US Naval, Spain	AOK	FAX wx maps 0944 0959 1547
11485.50	Abidjan Air, Ivory Coast	TUH	50n ID & RYs 2125
11500.00	R China International		AM Eng 2123 Slav 1701 Ger 1845
11507.50	Khartoum Air, Sudan	STK	50r 1752 2226
11515.00	R China International		AM Eng 1911 Ger 1832
11525.00	Moscow Met, Russia	RWZ77	FAX wx maps 0738 0945 1104 1905
11530.00	Wings of Hope, Lebanon		AM Eng 1349 2125
11536.00	Pyongyang Press (KCNA)	HMF49	50n Fr 1842 1906 ID & RYs 1745
11542.00	UNID		96ARQ/E3/8 Idle 0750
11545.00	Numbers Station		USB Eng (fem voice) 1512 1734 "Lincolnshire Poacher" 1505
11550.00	RTV Tunis		AM Arab 0729 0946 1401 1502
11550.00	Numbers Station		USB Eng (female voice) 1422
11560.00	R Cairo		AM Arab 1424
11565.00	Numbers Station		AM Eng 1732 & phonetics (female voice) 2138
11570.00	R Pakistan		AM Eng 1601 1625 1702
11572.00	UNID		CW "305" repeatedly 2133
11575.00	R China International		AM Eng 1614 1738
11580.00	Monitor Radio International		AM Eng 1645
11580.00	WEWN, USA		AM Eng 0723
11580.00	WYFR, USA		AM Eng 0533
11587.00	Kol Israel		AM Eng 1703 1912 2139 Fr 1935
11595.00	Voice of Greece		AM Greek 1434 1527 1848
11604.00	Belgrade Press (TANJUG)	YZJ2	50r Eng 0933 1153 (0400-1700)
11605.00	Kol Israel		AM Eng 1913 2140 (also msrd on 11603.0)

kHz.	Station	Call	Mode / Heard/Times GMT
11606.00	Beijing Press (XINHUA)		75r Eng 1439 1503 1856 1936
11610.00	PBS China		AM Chinese 0947 1435 2310
11620.00	All India Radio		AM Eng 1745 1849 1902 2112 2141 2224
11620.00	R Moscow		AM Eng 2110
11625.00	R Vatican		AM Latin mass 1844
11630.00	R Moscow		AM Ital 1850 Fr 1703 2136
11630.00	R Prague		AM Fr 1530
11638.00	Hamburg (Quickborn) Met, Germany	DDK8	50r 0855 0929 1105 1350 1639 1937
11640.00	UNID		AM Eng (religious) 1613
11645.00	Voice of Greece		AM Eng 0746
11649.90	Spa Publications		

11650-12050
BROADCASTING

kHz.	Station	Call	Mode / Heard/Times GMT
11650.00	KFBS, Saipan		AM Slav 0915
11655.00	R Netherland		AM Dutch 1640
11655.00	R Moscow		AM Asian lang 1559
11660.00	R Australia		AM Eng 1507 1554 1736 1903
11660.00	R France International		AM Fr 2313
11660.00	R Bulgaria		AM Span 2153
11668.50	Santa Maria Air, Azores	CSY	50n ID & RYs 0830
11670.00	R France International		AM Fr 0856 0948 1106 1300
11670.00	R Moscow		AM Fr 1855
11675.00	Kol Israel		AM Eng 1915 2142 Span 2113 2137
11680.00	BBC		AM Eng 0717 0917
11680.00	Beijing Press (XINHUA)	BZP51	75r Eng 1437 1512 1646
11680.00	R Australia		AM Eng 1848
11685.00	R Moscow		AM Eng 1916 2114
11690.00	R Moscow		AM Eng 0536 0839 1504
11695.00	R Australia		AM Eng 0949 1602 1706
11705.00	R France International		AM Eng 1605 1640
11705.00	R Moscow		AM Eng 0800 1001 1505 1615 1737
11705.00	R Ukraine International		AM Slav 1301
11705.00	VOA		AM Eng 1514 1520
11705.00	Monitor Radio International		AM Eng 0940
11710.00	R Abu Dhabi		AM Eng 2320
11710.00	R Moscow		AM Eng 0707
11715.00	All India Radio		AM Eng 2143
11715.00	R Korea		AM Eng 1031
11715.00	R Moscow		AM Eng 1352 1403 1857 1917
11715.00	VOA		AM Eng 1302
11720.00	R Moscow		AM Eng 2128
11720.00	R Bulgaria		AM Eng 1756 2156 2215 Fr 1900
11720.00	R Ukraine International		AM Eng (0000-0100)
11725.00	HCJB, Ecuador		AM Eng 0708 0731
11725.00	R Svoboda		AM Slav 0850 1642
11730.00	BBC		AM Arab 1900
11730.00	R Canada International		AM Eng 2322 Fr 2139
11730.00	R Moscow		AM Eng 2115 2158
11735.00	R Moscow		AM Eng 1804
11740.00	All India Radio		AM Eng 1536
11740.00	Deutsche Welle		AM Eng 1901 1928
11740.00	R Vatican		AM Fr 0718 Ital 1104
11745.00	R China International		AM Port 2201
11745.00	R Moscow		AM Eng 0801 1002
11750.00	BBC		AM Eng 1648 1734 2323
11750.00	Channel Africa (RSA)		AM Eng 1747
11750.00	R Moscow		AM Eng 2134
11755.00	R Finland		AM Eng 0749 1838 2131 Ger 0941
11760.00	BBC		AM Eng 0802
11760.00	R Moscow		AM Eng 2116 Fr 2212
11770.00	R Svoboda		AM Slav 1602
11770.00	WYFR, USA		AM Ital 0709
11780.00	BBC		AM Eng 0720
11780.00	R Austria International		AM Eng 1535 1553 1643 Ger 1505 1603
11785.00	Deutsche Welle		AM Eng 1646 1904 1929 2121
11790.00	REE Spain		AM Span 0851 2118
11795.00	Deutsche Welle		AM Ger 0710 0933 1506 2140
11795.00	R Dubai		AM Arab 1910
11800.00	R Moscow		AM Eng 2132
11800.00	R Portugal International		AM Eng (Sats & Suns) 0900
11805.00	R Moscow		AM Eng 0804 0950 1003
11805.00	VOA		AM Eng 0648
11810.00	R Romania International		AM Eng 1501

kHz.	Station	Call	Mode / Heard/Times GMT
11825.00	R Tirana		AM Eng 2131
11830.00	R Romania International		AM Eng 1735
11835.00	R Yugoslavia		AM Fr 1615
11835.00	HCJB, Ecuador		AM Eng 0711
11840.00	Polish Radio Warsaw		AM Eng 1507
11840.00	R Portugal International		AM Port 2141
11845.00	R France International		AM Fr 1132 1450 1531
11850.00	R Moscow		AM Fr 1355 1857
11855.00	R Australia		AM Eng 1452
11855.00	R Canada International		AM Eng 1356
11860.00	R Moscow		AM Eng 1656 Fr 0608 0725 Portuguese 2130
11865.00	Deutsche Welle		AM Ger 0833 0920
11870.00	R Moscow		AM Eng 1616 1631 2136
11870.00	VOA		AM Eng 1911
11875.00	R Canada International		AM Eng 2204
11880.00	R Moscow		AM Fr 1646 1705
11885.00	R Svoboda		AM Slav 1140
11895.00	R Netherland		AM Eng 0733 0935
11895.00	R Svoboda		AM Slav 1848
11910.00	R Australia		AM Eng 0805 0850
11910.00	R Budapest		AM Eng 2111
11915.00	VOA		AM Eng 1026 1105 Asian lang 0900
11920.00	R Yerevan		AM Eng (2245-2300)
11920.00	VOA		AM Eng 1912
11925.00	R Japan		AM Eng 2145
11925.00	V of the Mediterranean		AM Eng 1402 1458
11935.00	R Moscow		AM Eng 1533
11940.00	R Romania International		AM Eng 1353 1902 1918 Fr 1142 Ger 1651 1807
11945.00	R Moscow		AM Fr 1913
11945.00	R Yerevan		AM Eng (2245-2300)
11955.00	BBC		AM Eng 2123
11960.00	R Moscow		AM Eng 1710 1737
11960.00	R Yerevan		AM Eng (2245-2300)
11965.00	VOA		AM Eng 0539 0650
11980.00	R Moscow		AM Ger 1106 1534 1617 1712 1903 Fr 1554 2139
11985.00	R Moscow		AM Eng 1310
11990.00	R Prague		AM Eng 0734 1134
11990.00	R Kuwait		AM Arab 1509
11990.00	R Moscow		AM Portuguese 2141
11995.00	FEBC, Manila		AM Eng 1540
11995.00	VOA		AM Eng 1914
12000.00	R Moscow		AM Arab 1634
12005.00	RTV Tunis		AM Arab 1535 1616 2146
12010.00	R Moscow		AM Eng 0713 0902 0943 1043 Ger 1713 1739 1904 Portuguese 2142
12020.00	R Moscow		AM Eng 0903 0936 1100 Fr 1312 1400 1510 1908 Portuguese 2143
12030.00	R Moscow		AM Span 2139 Fr 2147
12035.00	REE Spain		AM Span 0912 1143 1536 1740 1909
12040.00	R Vilnius		AM Eng (2300-2359)
12049.90	Spa Publications		

12050-12230
FIXED

kHz.	Station	Call	Mode / Heard/Times GMT
12050.00	R Cairo		AM Arab 1714 2148
12050.00	R Vatican		AM ID & Asian lang 1316
12055.00	R Moscow		AM Eng 0911 1101 1910
12060.00	R Moscow		AM Fr 1653 1741 Span 1905 2154 2309
12065.00	R Moscow		AM Eng 1544
12065.00	UNID		AM Arab 1618
12070.00	R Moscow		AM Eng 0654 0854 0903 1024 1135 Fr 1742 2149
12080.00	VOA		AM Eng 0541 Fr 2150
12085.00	R Bulgaria		AM Eng 1549 1619
12085.00	R Damascus		AM Eng 2118 2151 Fr 1911
12095.00	BBC		AM Eng 0904 0937 1025 1144 1401 1512 1906 2152 (0300-2245)
12103.00	Swedish Embassy traffic		100SWED-ARQ(long) 5 let grps 1136
12110.00	Danish Naval	OVG	CW 0655 0921 1545 1603
12124.00	Bulgarian Embassy traffic	DOR	75n p/lang 0944
12135.00	US Naval, Norfolk	NAM	CW 0633 1908 2141
12140.00	French Naval	HWN	75r RYs & SGs 1235 1620 1714 1915
12148.00	RAF Akrotiri, Cyprus	MKD	50r (VFT) QBF & RYIs 0945 (LSB 12151.0)
12148.00	Warsaw Press (PAP)		SITOR Mode B news 1502 1908
12165.00	Moscow Met, Russia	RKB78	FAX wx maps 0657 0922 1550 1811

kHz.	Station	Call	Mode / Heard/Times GMT
12175.00	Pyongyang Press (KCNA)	HMF42	50r Eng 2142
12175.00	R Moscow feeder		USB Slav 1551 1601 1626
12186.00	Tripoli Press (JANA)		50r Fr 1520
12210.00	Czech Embassy traffic		100n p/lang 0924
12212.50	Belgrade Press (TANJUG)	YZO3	50r Eng 1154 1604 1622 Fr 1514
12216.00	Czech Embassy traffic		100n p/lang 0758
12220.00	UNID		50r 5 let grps (with 5 fig headings) 1628
12228.40	Beijing Press (XINHUA)	BZB62	75r Eng 1504 1515 1654
12229.90	Spa Publications		

12230-13200
MARITIME MOBILE

kHz.	Station	Call	Mode / Heard/Times GMT
12230.00	Ships wkg ch 1 dup. 13077.0kHz		USB (to UAT) 0757 1019 1509 1907 (to EHY) 0811 1513
12233.00	Ships wkg ch 2 dup. 13080.0kHz		USB 0810 (to HEB) 0722 (to GKT) 1916
12236.00	Ships wkg ch 3 dup. 13083.0kHz		USB 0847 SQNC (to CUL) 1524 CNTD (to CUL) 2144
12238.00	Numbers Station		USB Eng (female voice) 2105
12238.00	UNID		75n 5 let grps 1621
12239.00	Ships wkg ch 4 dup. 13086.0kHz		USB (to UGC) 0638 0717 1524
12242.00	Numbers Station		AM Eng (female voice) 1605
12242.00	Ships wkg ch 5 dup. 13089.0kHz		USB (to ICB) 0656 (to 9AR) 0727 (to UHK) 0821 & 0916
12245.00	Ships wkg ch 6 dup. 13092.0kHz		USB (to OHG) 0747 "Nordic Prince" (LAPJ3 to WOM) 2210
12248.00	Ships wkg ch 7 dup. 13095.0kHz		USB 0900 2145 (to OST) 0717 (to CUL) 1028 1317
12251.00	Ships wkg ch 8 dup. 13098.0kHz		USB SYWH (to 5BA) 0847 (to WOM) 2148
12254.00	Ships wkg ch 9 dup. 13101.0kHz		USB 1512 2110 (to WOM) 1112 1922
12255.00	Reflections Europe		AM Eng (Gospel Crusade Ministry) 1600
12257.00	Ships wkg ch 10 dup. 13104.0kHz		USB 0704 1546 1915 2150
12260.00	Ships wkg ch 11 dup. 13107.0kHz		USB (to ICB) 1615 LAQP4 (to LGQ) 1027 "Horizon" (to WOO) 2102
12262.40	Hungarian Embassy traffic		125DUP-ARQ 5 let grps 1506 1607 p/lang 0846
12263.00	Ships wkg ch 12 dup. 13110.0kHz		USB 0622 0850 (to DAN) 0640
12266.00	Ships wkg ch 13 dup. 13113.0kHz		USB 1210 "Mouna" (PGBG) 0724 UKYY (to PCG) 0931
12269.00	Ships wkg ch 14 dup. 13116.0kHz		USB 0733 0800 2153 (to OXZ) 2202
12272.00	Ships wkg ch 15 dup. 13119.0kHz		USB 0815 (to TFA) 0835 1707
12275.00	Ships wkg ch 16 dup. 13122.0kHz		USB 0907 (to SPC) 0803
12278.00	Ships wkg ch 17 dup. 13125.0kHz		USB 2109 (to LZW) 0910 V2CW (to LZW) 0806
12281.00	Ships wkg ch 18 dup. 13128.0kHz		USB 0636 1946 2139 (to TAN) 0631 1854
12282.00	UNID	8BY	CW 0947 1045 1148 1552 1948
12283.00	UNID	DEA47	CW 0639 0847 0938 1041 1102 (rptd German propagation test)
12284.00	Ships wkg ch 19 dup. 13131.0kHz		USB 1139 1505 1713
12287.00	Ships wkg ch 20 dup. 13134.0kHz		USB 0648 1738
12290.00	Ships wkg ch 21 dup. 13137.0kHz		USB 1213 (to IAR) 1619 (to LGQ) 1713 5BXF (to PCG) 1623
12292.00	UNID	CT4C	CW 0636
12293.00	Ships wkg ch 22 dup. 13140.0kHz		USB (to St Lys) 1722
12296.00	Ships wkg ch 23 dup. 13143.0kHz		USB 1643 1747 "Fantasy" (to WOO) 2320
12299.00	Ships wkg ch 24 dup. 13146.0kHz		USB 1801 "HMS Amazon" (GNID to GKV) 0755
12302.00	Ships wkg ch 25 dup. 13149.0kHz		USB 1947 2146
12305.00	Ships wkg ch 26 dup. 13152.0kHz		USB 1149 1514 1912 2155 (to FFL) 0612
12308.00	Ships wkg ch 27 dup. 13155.0kHz		USB 0626 0707 2151 (to SPO) 0707 ELCW9 (to HEB) 1852
12311.00	Ships wkg ch 28 dup. 13158.0kHz		USB 0705 0829 1055 1554 1930 (to UTQ) 0700
12314.00	Numbers Station		USB Ger (female voice) 0808 1147
12314.00	Ships wkg ch 29 dup. 13161.0kHz		USB 1641 1925 2140 (to UQK) 0650 (to FFL) 0930
12317.00	Ships wkg ch 30 dup. 13164.0kHz		USB 0715 0933 1214 1404 "Kanaris" (to HEB) 1625
12320.00	Novosibirsk, Russia		FAX wx maps 0654 0707 0840
12320.00	Ships wkg ch 31 dup. 13167.0kHz		USB 0946 1714 1856 (to SPC) 1759 2129
12323.00	Ships wkg ch 32 dup. 13170.0kHz		USB 0719 1002 1514 1633 1715 2108
12326.00	Ships wkg ch 33 dup. 13173.0kHz		USB 0729 0809 0858 1112 1506 1539
12329.00	Ships wkg ch 34 dup. 13176.0kHz		USB 2149 (to EHY) 1629 2155
12332.00	Ships wkg ch 35 dup. 13179.0kHz		USB 0837 0902
12335.00	Ships wkg ch 36 dup. 13182.0kHz		USB 0927 1507 IBJM (to IAR) 2131
12338.00	Ships wkg ch 37 dup. 13185.0kHz		USB 0809 1029 (to FFL) 1002
12341.00	Ships wkg ch 38 dup. 13188.0kHz		USB 0749 1058 1900 (to UAT) 1003
12344.00	Ships wkg ch 39 dup. 13191.0kHz		USB 1406 1516 1631 (to LZW) 0703
12347.00	Ships wkg ch 40 dup. 13194.0kHz		USB 0639 1101 2038
12350.00	Ships wkg ch 41 dup. 13197.0kHz		USB (to UUI) 0641 0811 1633
12353.00	Ship/Coast stations simplex		USB 0701 0822 1541 1919 2141
12356.00	Ship/Coast stations simplex		USB 0902 0948 1431 1601 2206
12359.00	Ship/Coast stations simplex		USB 0749 1046 1534
12362.00	Ship/Coast stations simplex		USB 0640 1136 2147
12365.00	Ship/Coast stations simplex		USB 0653 1003 1515 1634 SRQP 1906
12365.00	Darwin, Australia	VID	USB wx
12365.00	Melbourne, Australia	VIM	USB wx
12365.00	Perth, Australia	VIP	USB wx
12365.00	Sydney, Australia	VIS	USB wx
12365.00	Townsville, Australia	VIT	USB wx

kHz.	Station	Call	Mode / Heard/Times GMT
12368.00	Intership working		USB 0903
12370.00	Intership working		USB 1517 1918
12373.00	Intership working		USB 2050
12374.00	Intership working		USB 1141
12380.00	Intership working		USB 1600 1907 1920
12381.70	Egyptian Embassy traffic		SITOR Selcal YZZY 1151
12390.00	Intership working		USB 0819 1932
12392.00	Intership working		USB 2142
12405.00	Intership working		USB 1558
12420.00	Ships working		CW "Petrozavodsk" (EWZF) 1436
12421.00	Ships working		CW "Jupiteris" (LYAT) 1548
12422.00	Ships working		CW "Desyataya Pyatiletka" (UVKR) 0745 "Maximo Gomez" (CLDY) 1856
12422.50	Ships working		CW UYAY (to UIW) 1741
12423.00	Ships working		CW "Prometey" (UZFR) 0820 "Adonis" (3FUZ) 1512
12423.50	Ships working		CW LYEP (to LYL) 0649
12424.00	Ships working		CW "Flag Eva" (SZLW) 1516 "Export Freedom" (WCJS) 2114
12425.00	Ships working		CW "Baia De Arama" (YQNO) 0715 "Yantarnyy" (UYOV) 0802
12425.50	Ships working		CW 0905 "Mixteco" (3EIO3) 1600
12426.00	Ships working		CW "Negba" (4XLV) 0758 "Zim Anglia" (9HAG4) 1444
12426.50	Ships working		CW 1745
12427.00	Ships working		CW 1750
12428.00	Ships working		CW "Camocim" (PPXZ) 0824 "Pina Prima" (IBWR) 0832
12429.00	Ships working		CW "Baia de Noua" (YQRO) 1543
12430.00	Ships working		CW "Aspidoforos" (SVJC) 1853
12431.00	Ships working		CW "Yargora" (UYXN) 0944
12432.00	Ships working		CW "Ashbury" (C6IP4) 1045 IBEC (to GKB) 1056
12433.00	Ships working		CW "Olayne" 0804
12433.50	Ships working		CW "Barbosi" (YQTS) 1803
12434.00	Ships working		CW "Amy" 0903
12434.50	Ships working		CW "Norchem" (3FIY2) 0900
12435.00	Ships working		CW "Korean Trader" (5MQF) 0908
12435.50	Ships working		CW (to ESA) 1554
12436.00	Ships working		CW (to UUI) 0823
12437.00	Ships working		CW "Sunny Napier" (DZGY) 1610
12437.00	UNID		SITOR p/lang Eng drilling report (rig "HLS-2000") 2158
12438.00	Ships working		CW "Baronia" (HOFP) 1612
12438.50	Ships working		CW 1819
12439.00	Ships working		CW "Havjo" (LALA2) 1102
12439.50	Ships working		CW "Bizon" (UZTM) 1438
12440.00	Ships working		CW "Montgomery" (C6JR5) 1511
12441.00	Ships working		CW "Sunny Cedar" (D8FY) 1403 "Ohgishima Maru" (JQUV) 2058
12441.50	Ships working		CW "Kapitan Vasiliy Kulik" (UQZW) 2126
12442.00	Ships working		CW "Volgoneft 130" (UFDG) 0820 UDUO (to UIS) 0910
12442.50	Ships working		CW "Litkes Sala" (LYDV) 1008 LYIW (to LYL) 1453
12443.00	Ships working		CW "MSC Laura" (3EME6) 1105
12443.50	Ships working		CW EOHR (to RWHB) 0901
12444.00	Ships working		CW COGA (to CLA) 2144
12445.00	Ships working		CW "Verazzano" (IBUM) 0842 "Benwalid" (TCJV) 1823
12445.50	Ships working		CW CLDQ (to CLA) 2001
12446.00	Ships working		CW "Sormovskiy 14" (EULR) (to RSGV) 0726
12446.50	Ships working		CW 1606
12447.00	Ships working		CW UYCX 0828
12447.50	Ships working		CW UTNI (to UIW) 1910
12448.00	Ships working		CW 1012
12449.00	Ships working		CW "Havtroll" (LAEV4) 0700
12450.00	Ships working		CW "Militos" (ELBV) 1440 "Fantasy L" (SVUV) 1752
12451.00	Ships working		CW "Amur 2516" (USXX) 0836
12451.30	Ships working		CW "Premnitz" (Y5DR) 1128
12452.00	Ships working		CW "Silver An" (ELNK3) 1515 "Anangel Glory" (SWZX) 1639
12453.00	Ships working		CW "Maria M" (5BWP) 1455
12454.00	Ships working		CW "Shipka" (LZDV) 0914
12454.50	Ships working		CW "Nikolay Brovtsyev" (UHUZ) 2112
12455.00	Ships working		CW "Mee May" (C4WW) 1215 DVFO (to PPL) 1357
12456.00	Ships working		CW "Ocean Trader" (SQDO) 1617
12457.00	Ships working		CW "Capo Noli" (ICUH) 1903
12458.00	Ships working		CW "Annoula" (SVZD) 1635
12459.00	Ships working		CW 1921 UDST (to UDK2) 0917
12459.50	Ships working		CW 3ENF8 1744
12460.00	Ships working		CW "Safina E Arab" (AQVA) 1718
12461.00	Ships working		CW "Sunny Lady" (LAMC2) 0817 "Ionian Wind" (SZVY) 2132
12462.00	Intership working		CW "Pliska" (LZNC) 0937 "Seahappy" (5BRG) 1550
12463.00	Ships working		CW "Bright State" (ELNK2) 2305
12464.00	Ships working		CW "Inessa Armand" (UYUV) 1630 "Castillo Di Butron" (EFHF) 1840
12465.00	Ships working		CW "Rizcun Trader" (ZDBI2) 1025 "Pan Journey" (D7QZ) 1805

kHz.	Station	Call	Mode / Heard/Times GMT
12465.50	Ships working		CW "Pan Tide" (D8ZP) 2147
12466.00	Ships working		CW "Eleveit" (TCVT) 1513 "Yamak" (TCYT) 1656 TCHY 1819
12467.00	Ships working		CW 1555
12467.50	Ships working		CW "Estejnlis" 1818
12468.00	Ships working		CW "Lucky Field" 1446
12468.50	Ships working		CW 1629
12469.70	Egyptian Embassy traffic		SITOR Selcal TVVQ 0623
12470.00	Ships working		CW "Salvador 1" (3EMR9) 0902 "Manila Bay" (C6MA7) 2116
12471.00	Ships working		CW "Stenjohan" (J8BZ7) 1520
12472.00	Ships working		CW "No 6 Maya" (DZRE) 1638
12473.00	Ships working		CW "Cary" (9HAL3) 1403 "Vasiliy Kalashnikov" (UVGC) 1538
12474.00	Ships working		CW UPWU (to UUI) 1353
12474.50	Ships working		CW 1630
12475.00	Ships working		CW 1229
12476.00	Ships working		CW 9HTP3 1124 DPSM (to PPJ) 2106
12476.50	Ships working		CW UQEA (to UFJ) 1243
12477.00	Ships wkg ch 1 dup. 12579.5kHz		SITOR "Taganroga" (YLCM) 0804 "Kompozitor Chaykovskiy" (UKVG) 0926
12477.50	Ships wkg ch 2 dup. 12580.0kHz		SITOR "Treana" (P3IK2) 1011 "QE2" (GBTT) 1923
12478.00	Ships wkg ch 3 dup. 12580.5kHz		SITOR UJDQ 0934 "Inzhener Plavinskiy" (UBFX) 1650
12478.50	Ships wkg ch 4 dup. 12581.0kHz		SITOR
12479.00	Ships wkg ch 5 dup. 12581.5kHz		SITOR DQEB 1230 C6LM2 1826
12479.50	Ships wkg ch 6 dup. 12582.0kHz		SITOR "Christina 2" 0914 "Racise" 1758
12480.00	Ships wkg ch 7 dup. 12582.5kHz		SITOR "Gniezno 11" (SQJM) 0748 "Mekhanik Evgrafov" (EKMN) 1645
12480.50	Ships wkg ch 8 dup. 12583.0kHz		SITOR "Harry Pollit" (UKFM) 0922 Selcal KYVV (St Petersburg) 1830
12481.00	Ships wkg ch 9 dup. 12583.5kHz		SITOR "Kazakhstan" (ULSB) 1522
12481.50	Ships wkg ch 10 dup. 12584.0kHz		SITOR Selcal MFKV (Dammam) 1623
12482.00	Ships wkg ch 11 dup. 12584.5kHz		SITOR 1042
12482.50	Ships wkg ch 12 dup. 12585.0kHz		SITOR "B Semarak" (9MBD6) 1049 "Antonio Gramsi" (YLBQ) 1402
12483.00	Ships wkg ch 13 dup. 12585.5kHz		SITOR "Walther Herwig" (DBFP) 0840
12483.50	Ships wkg ch 14 dup. 12586.0kHz		SITOR 2236
12484.00	Ships wkg ch 15 dup. 12586.5kHz		SITOR "Multitank Ascania" (T2CC) 0831 "Litzen" (OEMV) 1835
12484.50	Ships wkg ch 16 dup. 12587.0kHz		SITOR "Zahari Stoianov" (LZKF) 0754 "Varna" (LZEF) 0930
12485.00	Ships wkg ch 17 dup. 12587.5kHz		SITOR 2125
12485.50	Ships wkg ch 18 dup. 12588.0kHz		SITOR "Xanadu" (9HAM3) 0810 "Ivanovo" (ULVC) 1145
12486.00	Ships wkg ch 19 dup. 12588.5kHz		SITOR 1335
12486.50	Ships wkg ch 20 dup. 12589.0kHz		SITOR "Polytraveller" (LHRM) 1259 "Bonita" (HCQO) 2114
12487.00	Ships wkg ch 21 dup. 12589.5kHz		SITOR "Clary" (9VVE) 1342 "Conti Hammonia" (ELGA7) 1943
12487.50	Ships wkg ch 22 dup. 12590.0kHz		SITOR "Smit Lloyd 110" (C6DF7) 1731 "Iran Motahari" (EQLK) 1734
12488.00	Ships wkg ch 23 dup. 12590.5kHz		RTTY
12488.50	Ships wkg ch 24 dup. 12591.0kHz		SITOR "Sea Victory" (ELXR) 1044 "Mekhanik Kraskovskiy" (UFHZ) 1313
12489.00	Ships wkg ch 25 dup. 12591.5kHz		SITOR 1105 1632
12489.50	Ships wkg ch 26 dup. 12592.0kHz		SITOR "Valdivia" (VRGW) 0940 "Jaguar" (OWWA2) 1450
12490.00	Ships wkg ch 27 dup. 12592.5kHz		SITOR wx msg 1838 Selcal XCKM (St Lys) 1539
12490.50	Ships wkg ch 28 dup. 12593.0kHz		SITOR ESBQ 1002 "Taeschorn" (5LGE) 1610
12491.00	Ships wkg ch 29 dup. 12593.5kHz		RTTY
12491.50	Ships wkg ch 30 dup. 12594.0kHz		SITOR "Valkla" (ESAN) 1655
12492.00	Ships wkg ch 31 dup. 12594.5kHz		SITOR "Moscenice" (J8EZ7) 1847
12492.50	Ships wkg ch 32 dup. 12595.0kHz		SITOR "Burak-M" (TCET) 0800
12493.00	Ships wkg ch 33 dup. 12595.5kHz		RTTY
12493.50	Ships wkg ch 34 dup. 12596.0kHz		SITOR 2258
12494.00	Ships wkg ch 35 dup. 12596.5kHz		SITOR "Bataafgracht" (PCZH) 1047 "Frio Africa" (3ERB5) 1702
12494.50	Ships wkg ch 36 dup. 12597.0kHz		SITOR "Cedynia" (SQDL) 1013 "Belchatow" (SQHE) 1927
12495.00	Ships wkg ch 37 dup. 12597.5kHz		SITOR "Grigoriy Nesterenko" UBWR) 0947
12495.50	Ships wkg ch 38 dup. 12598.0kHz		SITOR Selcal QSKV (Gdynia) 1012
12496.00	Ships wkg ch 39 dup. 12598.5kHz		SITOR 9HNF3 1113
12496.50	Ships wkg ch 40 dup. 12599.0kHz		RTTY
12497.00	Ships wkg ch 41 dup. 12599.5kHz		SITOR "Ivan Babushkin" (UUKB) 1619 ESBE 1800
12497.50	Ships wkg ch 42 dup. 12600.0kHz		SITOR "Weimar" (Y5KU) 1541 "Kapitan Danilkin" (UIAO) 1844
12498.00	Ships wkg ch 43 dup. 12600.5kHz		SITOR "Arkadiy Sverdlov" (UGWT) 1613 "Puppy-P" (9HWL2) 1714
12498.50	Ships wkg ch 44 dup. 12601.0kHz		SITOR "Vidal" (J8FN) 1905
12499.00	Ships wkg ch 45 dup. 12601.5kHz		SITOR "Cinchona" (3EBJ4) 1431 "Danica White" (OXMG2) 1708
12499.50	Ships wkg ch 46 dup. 12602.0kHz		SITOR Selcal KYXX (Novorossiysk) 2116
12500.00	Ships wkg ch 47 dup. 12602.5kHz		RTTY
12500.50	Ships wkg ch 48 dup. 12603.0kHz		SITOR "Ionic Reefer" (SYPI) 1542 "Balsa" (LAPN4) 1618
12501.00	Ships wkg ch 49 dup. 12603.5kHz		SITOR "Alandia Wave" (C6CN6) 1505 "Kalliopi T" (P3TC2) 1750
12501.50	Ships wkg ch 50 dup. 12604.0kHz		SITOR 1015 1918
12502.00	Ships wkg ch 51 dup. 12604.5kHz		SITOR "Velebit" (9HOJ3) 2149
12502.50	Ships wkg ch 52 dup. 12605.0kHz		SITOR "Leinebris" (JWNF) 0856
12503.00	Ships wkg ch 53 dup. 12605.5kHz		SITOR "Pargolovo" (URYH) 0825 "Pella" (J4FC) 1833

kHz.	Station	Call	Mode / Heard/Times GMT
12503.50	Ships wkg ch 54 dup. 12606.0kHz		SITOR "Aconcagua" (3FOQ3) 1918
12504.00	Ships wkg ch 55 dup. 12606.5kHz		170/50nc "Professor Multanovskiy" (UJFO) 0834
12504.50	Ships wkg ch 56 dup. 12607.0kHz		SITOR "Pavel Korchagin" (URQW) 1232 "Caribou" (J4UW) 1803
12505.00	Ships wkg ch 57 dup. 12607.5kHz		170/50nc "Kretinga" (LYAE) 1805
12505.50	Ships wkg ch 58 dup. 12608.0kHz		170/50nc 0730
12506.00	Ships wkg ch 59 dup. 12608.5kHz		170/50nc "Professor Vize" (UPUI) 0730 UJFO (to RNO) 1250
12506.50	Ships wkg ch 60 dup. 12609.0kHz		RTTY
12507.00	Ships wkg ch 61 dup. 12609.5kHz		SITOR "Sonia" (9HFB3) 2215
12507.50	Ships wkg ch 62 dup. 12610.0kHz		RTTY
12508.00	Ships wkg ch 63 dup. 12610.5kHz		RTTY
12508.50	Ships wkg ch 64 dup. 12611.0kHz		RTTY
12509.00	Ships wkg ch 65 dup. 12611.5kHz		RTTY
12509.50	Ships wkg ch 66 dup. 12612.0kHz		SITOR Selcal KQQV (Portishead) 1549
12510.00	Ships wkg ch 67 dup. 12612.5kHz		RTTY
12510.50	Ships wkg ch 68 dup. 12613.0kHz		RTTY
12511.00	Ships wkg ch 69 dup. 12613.5kHz		170/50nc 1242
12511.50	Ships wkg ch 70 dup. 12614.0kHz		RTTY
12512.00	Ships wkg ch 71 dup. 12614.5kHz		170/50nc "Pioner Moldavii" (UKDC) 0805
12512.50	Ships wkg ch 72 dup. 12615.0kHz		SITOR "Vera Khoruzhaya" (UEUG) 1008
12513.00	Ships wkg ch 73 dup. 12615.5kHz		RTTY
12513.50	Ships wkg ch 74 dup. 12616.0kHz		RTTY
12514.00	Ships wkg ch 75 dup. 12616.5kHz		170/50nc "Teodor Nette" (UGOK) 0931
12514.50	Ships wkg ch 76 dup. 12617.0kHz		RTTY
12515.00	Ships wkg ch 77 dup. 12617.5kHz		RTTY
12515.50	Ships wkg ch 78 dup. 12618.0kHz		RTTY
12516.00	Ships wkg ch 79 dup. 12618.5kHz		RTTY
12516.50	Ships wkg ch 80 dup. 12619.0kHz		RTTY
12517.00	Ships wkg ch 81 dup. 12619.5kHz		RTTY
12517.50	Ships wkg ch 82 dup. 12620.0kHz		RTTY
12518.00	Ships wkg ch 83 dup. 12620.5kHz		RTTY
12518.50	Ships wkg ch 84 dup. 12621.0kHz		SITOR 1544
12519.00	Ships wkg ch 85 dup. 12621.5kHz		RTTY
12519.50	Ships wkg ch 86 dup. 12622.0kHz		RTTY
12520.00	Maritime Safety channel		SITOR
12520.50	Ships wkg ch 88 dup. 12622.5kHz		RTTY
12521.00	Ships wkg ch 89 dup. 12623.0kHz		RTTY
12521.00	Indian Naval	VTP	50r RYs & SGs 1243
12521.50	Ships wkg ch 90 dup. 12623.5kHz		SITOR 1508
12522.00	Ships wkg ch 91 dup. 12624.0kHz		170/50nc "Neringa" (LYAW) 1709
12522.50	Ships wkg ch 92 dup. 12624.5kHz		RTTY
12523.00	Ships wkg ch 93 dup. 12625.0kHz		SITOR "Pioner Litvy" (USRS) 1216 "Pavel Shternbergs" (YLAP) 1816
12523.50	Ships wkg ch 94 dup. 12625.5kHz		SITOR "Isakogorka" (UUKC) 1831 Selcal KYVF (Archangel) 1826
12524.00	Ships wkg ch 95 dup. 12626.0kHz		RTTY
12524.50	Ships wkg ch 96 dup. 12626.5kHz		SITOR 1635
12525.00	Ships wkg ch 97 dup. 12627.0kHz		170/50rc "Kherson" (UHRU) 1652
12525.50	Ships wkg ch 98 dup. 12627.5kHz		SITOR "Satyamurti" (ATJW) 1512 "Lokamanya Tilak" (ATJY) 1622
12526.00	Ships wkg ch 99 dup. 12628.0kHz		RTTY
12526.50	Ships wkg ch 100 dup. 12628.5kHz		170/50nc "Proliv Viktoriya" (to URL) 1800
12527.00	Ships wkg ch 101 dup. 12629.0kHz		RTTY
12527.50	Ships wkg ch 102 dup. 12629.5kHz		RTTY
12528.00	Ships wkg ch 103 dup. 12630.0kHz		RTTY
12528.50	Ships wkg ch 104 dup. 12630.5kHz		RTTY
12529.00	Ships wkg ch 105 dup. 12631.0kHz		SITOR "Kremnica" (OLMC) 1521 Selcal MCYX (Prague) 1529
12529.50	Ships wkg ch 106 dup. 12631.5kHz		RTTY
12530.00	Ships wkg ch 107 dup. 12632.0kHz		SITOR 1600 1800
12530.50	Ships wkg ch 108 dup. 12632.5kHz		SITOR "Kostromales" (UEPA) 1128 Selcal KYVV (St Petersburg) 1841
12531.00	Ships wkg ch 109 dup. 12633.0kHz		RTTY
12531.50	Ships wkg ch 110 dup. 12633.5kHz		SITOR "Viktorio Kodovilja" (UKWY) 0815 "Mate Zalka" (YLAC) 0900
12532.00	Ships wkg ch 111 dup. 12634.0kHz		RTTY
12532.50	Ships wkg ch 112 dup. 12634.5kHz		RTTY
12533.00	Ships wkg ch 113 dup. 12635.0kHz		RTTY
12533.50	Ships wkg ch 114 dup. 12635.5kHz		RTTY
12534.00	Ships wkg ch 115 dup. 12636.0kHz		RTTY
12534.50	Ships wkg ch 116 dup. 12636.5kHz		170/50nc "Vasiliy Polenov" (USCW) 1810
12535.00	Ships wkg ch 117 dup. 12637.0kHz		170/50nc "Vadim Glazunov" (UUSJ) 1506 "Yulius Fuchik" (ENTD) 1144
12535.50	Ships wkg ch 118 dup. 12637.5kHz		SITOR "Yuta Bondarovskaya" (USBZ) 0816 "Posyet" (UGWB) 2331
12536.00	Ships wkg ch 119 dup. 12638.0kHz		RTTY
12536.50	Ships wkg ch 120 dup. 12638.5kHz		RTTY
12537.00	Ships wkg ch 121 dup. 12639.0kHz		RTTY

kHz.	Station	Call	Mode / Heard/Times GMT
12537.50	Ships wkg ch 122 dup. 12639.5kHz		SITOR "Crystal Prince" (LXPC) 1626 Selcal VMFV (Ostend) 1611
12538.00	Ships wkg ch 123 dup. 12640.0kHz		RTTY
12538.50	Ships wkg ch 124 dup. 12640.5kHz		RTTY
12539.00	Ships wkg ch 125 dup. 12641.0kHz		RTTY
12539.50	Ships wkg ch 126 dup. 12641.5kHz		RTTY
12540.00	Ships wkg ch 127 dup. 12642.0kHz		SITOR 1034
12540.50	Ships wkg ch 128 dup. 12642.5kHz		RTTY
12541.00	Ships wkg ch 129 dup. 12643.0kHz		RTTY
12541.00	Ship working		CW UIZN (to YLN2) 0626
12541.50	Ships wkg ch 130 dup. 12643.5kHz		RTTY
12542.00	Ships wkg ch 131 dup. 12644.0kHz		RTTY
12542.50	Ships wkg ch 132 dup. 12644.5kHz		RTTY
12543.00	Ships wkg ch 133 dup. 12645.0kHz		RTTY
12543.50	Ships wkg ch 134 dup. 12645.5kHz		SITOR "Matvey Muranov" (UULN) 0733 "General Gorbatov" (UMTM) 0919
12544.00	Ships wkg ch 135 dup. 12646.0kHz		170/50nc "Komsomolets Litvy" (UGNX) 1720
12544.50	Ships wkg ch 136 dup. 12646.5kHz		RTTY
12545.00	Ships wkg ch 137 dup. 12647.0kHz		RTTY & CW "Tama Caribbean" (H9JL) 2220
12545.50	Ships wkg ch 138 dup. 12647.5kHz		RTTY
12546.00	Ships wkg ch 139 dup. 12648.0kHz		RTTY
12546.50	Ships wkg ch 140 dup. 12648.5kHz		RTTY
12547.00	Ships wkg ch 141 dup. 12649.0kHz		RTTY
12547.50	Ships wkg ch 142 dup. 12649.5kHz		RTTY
12548.00	Ships wkg ch 143 dup. 12650.0kHz		RTTY
12548.50	Ships wkg ch 144 dup. 12650.5kHz		RTTY
12549.00	Ships wkg ch 145 dup. 12651.0kHz		170/50nc 2202
12549.50	Ships wkg ch 146 dup. 12651.5kHz		RTTY
12550.00	Ships calling ch 1		CW URET (to UUI) 0910 "Feng Yan" (BOWC) 1643
12550.50	Ships calling ch 2		CW 9HZO2 (to UUI) 0805 9HGO4 (to USU) 1621
12551.00	Ships calling ch 5		CW C6DA8 (to SUH) 0829 A6LW (to XSG) 1820
12551.50	Ships calling ch 6		CW UBST (to RKLM) 1353 "Andria" (SYNY) 1528
12552.00	Ships calling ch 3		CW 3EJG6 (to JCU) 0756 9HYK2 (to OST) 1047
12552.50	Ships calling ch 7		CW UFDG (to OFJ) 0817 YLEV (to UQK) 1637
12553.00	Ships calling ch 8		CW "Geolog Fersman" (UKKI) 0722
12553.50	Ships calling ch 4		CW 5BRJ (to SVB) 1922
12554.00	Ships calling ch 9		CW UYGO (to UAT) 1630
12554.50	Ships calling ch 10		CW EVPR 0906 UVDI 1407
12555.00	Ships wkg ch 147 dup. 12652.0kHz		170/50nc "Professor Zubov" (UMFW) 1739
12555.50	Ships wkg ch 148 dup. 12652.5kHz		RTTY
12556.00	Ships wkg ch 149 dup. 12653.0kHz		RTTY
12556.50	Ships wkg ch 150 dup. 12653.5kHz		170/50nc "Kompozitor Novikov" (UIDB) 1554
12557.00	Ships wkg ch 151 dup. 12654.0kHz		SITOR "Burak M" (TCET) 1144 "Mehmet Emin" (TCJM) 1240
12557.50	Ships wkg ch 152 dup. 12654.5kHz		RTTY
12558.00	Ships wkg ch 153 dup. 12655.0kHz		170/50nc "Akademik Mstislav Keldysh" (UFJI) 1809
12558.50	Ships wkg ch 154 dup. 12655.5kHz		RTTY
12559.00	Ships wkg ch 155 dup. 12656.0kHz		170/50nc "Geolog Fersman" (UKKI) 0823
12559.50	Ships wkg ch 156 dup. 12656.5kHz		RTTY
12560.00	Ships working (non paired)		170/50nc "Nikolay Tulpin" (UEWA) 1010 "Sergey Gritsevets" (UIXD) 1018
12560.50	Ships working (non paired)		170/50nc "Ukraina" 0845 "Akhtarskiy Liman" (URWR) 1833
12561.00	Ships working		CW "Wang Jiang" (BOUH) 0841 "Dzhafar Dzhabarly" (UMYV) 1205
12561.00	Ships working (non paired)		170/50nc "Ognyan Naydov" (UKAR) 1017
12561.00	UNID		SITOR Mode B news (in German) 1652 1658
12561.50	Ships working (non paired)		170/50nc "Novoukraina" (UHCF) 1739
12562.00	Ships working (non paired)		170/50rc "LI-8092" (LYEZ) 0807 UBHT (to UDK2) 1700
12562.50	Ships working (non paired)		170/50nc "More Sudruzhestva" (UYDV) 1701 "Ulan-Ude" (ESOB) 1840
12563.00	Ships working (non paired)		170/50nc "Pertominsk" (UWFN) 0854 "Pioner Litvy" (USRS) 1010
12563.00	Ships working		CW "Pavel Shternbergs" (YLAP) 1155 "Volgobalt 118" (EUCI) 1557
12563.50	Ships working (non paired)		SITOR "Vera" (PIFE) 0704 "Mekhanik Slauta" (UBLA) 0824
12564.00	Ships working (non paired)		170/50nc "Mikhail Isakovskiy" (UVGA) 0755
12564.50	Ships working (non paired)		170/50nc "Uragan" (UYZL) 1134 "Zefir" (UWNX) 2216
12565.00	Ships working (non paired)		170/50nc "Aleksander Mironenko" (UBAU) 0705 UVKW (to USO5) 1631
12565.50	Ships working (non paired)		170/50nc "Sarata" (UQGL) 1451 "Grigoriy Kozintsev" (UVQR) 1720
12566.00	Ships working (non paired)		170/50nc UWYL 1227
12566.50	Ships working (non paired)		170/50rc "Pyotr Tomasevich" (UIEU) 1540 "Novotcheboksarsk" (UGVJ) 2027
12567.00	Ships working (non paired)		170/50nc "Otto Grotevol" (EWJQ) 1544 "Ivan Aivazovskiy" (UHAJ) 1821
12567.50	Ships working (non paired)		170/50nc "Moldaya Gvardia" (UIWN) 0954 UVWB (to URL) 1700
12568.00	Ships working (non paired)		170/50nc "Ivan Zimakov" (UIAE) 1601 "Polessk" (UGMX) 2218

kHz.	Station	Call	Mode / Heard/Times GMT
12568.50	Ships working (non paired)		170/50nc "Kapitan Lukhmanov" (URFB) 1815
12569.00	Ships working (non paired)		170/50nc "Toyvo Antikaynen" (UWQZ) 1626 "Galdor" (UKFA) 1820
12569.50	Ships working (non paired)		170/50nc "Izmail" 0935 "Nataliya Kovshova" (UJZY) 1820
12570.00	Ships working (non paired)		170/50nc "Kildin" 0927 "Sevryba" (UKFY) 1623
12570.00	Ship working		CW "El Sharkia" (SUYN) 0812 "Energy" (P3TV3) 2112
12570.50	Ships working (non paired)		SITOR "Koscierzyna" (SQJX) 2117
12571.00	Ships working (non paired)		SITOR "Pioner Kazakhstana" (UJDG) 0802
12571.50	Ships working (non paired)		170/50nc "Lyudmila Pavlichenko" (UJEI) 1502
12572.00	Ships working (non paired)		170/50nc "Izumrudnyy Bereg" (EKNB) 1032
12572.50	Ships working (non paired)		SITOR SQRQ 1039
12573.00	Ships working (non paired)		170/50nc "MB-0003" 1656 LYEJ
12573.50	Ships working (non paired)		170/50nc "Mys Pavlovskiy" (UQTL) 1550 "Ikarion" 2304
12574.00	Ships working (non paired)		170/50nc "Professor Baranov" (UZDW) 1604
12574.50	Ships working (non paired)		170/50nc "Mys Pavlovskiy" (LYEJ) 1436
12575.00	Ships working (non paired)		170/50nc "Polyarnyy" 1335
12575.00	Ship working		CW "Chang Ting" (BOSA) 1356 (out of normal sub-band)
12575.50	Ships working (non paired)		RTTY
12576.00	Ships working (non paired)		170/50nc "MA-0067" 0840 "MA-1810" (to UDK2) 1459
12576.50	Ships working (non paired)		170/50nc "Ernst Thalmann" (EWJR) 1822
12577.00	Ship working		170/50nc "Khibinskie Gory" (UJOC) 1830 - out of normal sub-band
12577.00	Maritime Safety channel		RTTY
12577.50	Ships digital selective calling		RTTY
12578.00	Ships digital selective calling		RTTY
12578.50	Ships digital selective calling		RTTY
12579.00	Maritime Safety channel		SITOR
12579.00	Boston CG, USA	NMF	SITOR Mode B High Seas wx forecast 1635
12579.50	Coast stations ch 1 dup. 12477.0kHz		RTTY
12579.50	Riga, Latvia	UDH	SITOR 0756 1035 1612 1707 1818
12579.50	Singapore	9VG80	SITOR 1755 2121 wx 0030 1230 tfc list 1530
12580.00	Coast stations ch 2 dup. 12477.5kHz		RTTY
12580.00	Portishead, UK	GKE5	SITOR 0833 0952 1552 1625
12580.50	Coast stations ch 3 dup. 12478.0kHz		RTTY
12580.50	Gdynia, Poland	SPA61	SITOR
12580.50	Palo Alto, USA	KFS	SITOR 1548
12581.00	Coast stations ch 4 dup. 12478.5kHz		RTTY
12581.00	Argentine Radio	LSD836	SITOR 0810 1840 2124 2154 2224 Mode B tfc list 2130
12581.50	Coast stations ch 5 dup. 12479.0kHz		RTTY
12581.50	Mobile, USA	WLO	SITOR 1535 1704 1745
12581.50	Stettin, Poland	SPB61	SITOR 1152 2030
12582.00	Coast stations ch 6 dup. 12479.5kHz		RTTY
12582.00	Goeteborg, Sweden	SAG	SITOR 0845 1125 1626
12582.00	Perth, Australia	VIP34	SITOR 1550 1643 1707 1845 2121
12582.50	Coast stations ch 7 dup. 12480.0kHz		RTTY
12582.50	St Lys, France	FFT61	SITOR 0938 1037 1517 1658 2010 Mode B wx & nav wngs 1800
12583.00	Coast stations ch 8 dup. 12480.5kHz		RTTY
12583.00	Panama	HPP	SITOR 0658 2115 2248
12583.50	Coast stations ch 9 dup. 12481.0kHz		RTTY
12583.50	Odessa, Ukraine	UUI	SITOR 0938 1133 1553 1621 1645 1823 Mode B 0707 0849
12583.50	Valparaiso, Chile	CBV	SITOR 2123 2227 2300
12584.00	Coast stations ch 10 dup. 12481.5kHz		RTTY
12584.00	Lyngby, Denmark	OXZ	SITOR (on request)
12584.50	Coast stations ch 11 dup. 12482.0kHz		RTTY
12584.50	Mobile, USA	WLO	SITOR 1552 2133 2226
12584.50	Nakhodka, Russia	UKK3	SITOR 1556 1755
12584.50	UNID	UFC2	SITOR 0847
12585.00	Coast stations ch 12 dup. 12482.5kHz		RTTY
12585.00	Apra Harbour CG, Guam	NRV	SITOR 1828
12585.00	Perth, Australia	VIP44	SITOR
12585.00	Scheveningen, Holland	PCH55	SITOR 1518 1630 1838 2126
12585.50	Coast stations ch 13 dup. 12483.0kHz		RTTY
12585.50	Hong Kong	VPS63	SITOR 1348 1548 1736 1828
12586.00	Coast stations ch 14 dup. 12483.5kHz		RTTY
12586.50	Coast stations ch 15 dup. 12484.0kHz		RTTY
12586.50	Mobile, USA	WLO	SITOR 2134 Mode B 1800
12586.50	Norddeich, Germany	DCL	SITOR 0740 1134 1245 1438 1515
12587.00	Coast stations ch 16 dup. 12484.5kHz		RTTY
12587.00	Varna, Bulgaria	LZW5	SITOR 1245 1453 1738 1928 2128 Mode B tfc list 0845
12587.50	Coast stations ch 17 dup. 12485.0kHz		RTTY
12588.00	Coast stations ch 18 dup. 12485.5kHz		RTTY
12588.00	Berne, Switzerland	HEC13	SITOR 0732 0941 1323 1439 1554
12588.50	Coast stations ch 19 dup. 12486.0kHz		RTTY
12589.00	Coast stations ch 20 dup. 12486.5kHz		RTTY
12589.00	Rogaland, Norway	LGJ3	SITOR 1519 1646 1830 2129
12589.50	Coast stations ch 21 dup. 12487.0kHz		RTTY

kHz.	Station	Call	Mode / Heard/Times GMT
12589.50	Chatham, USA	WCC	SITOR 1140 1412 1601 2135
12589.50	St Lys, France	FFT62	SITOR 0817 0943 1739 2230
12590.00	Coast stations ch 22 dup. 12487.5kHz		RTTY
12590.00	Madrid, Spain	EAD	SITOR 0651 1129 1526 1623 2125
12590.00	Singapore	9VG94	SITOR 1648 1733 1831 2130
12590.50	Coast stations ch 23 dup. 12488.0kHz		RTTY
12591.00	Coast stations ch 24 dup. 12488.5kHz		RTTY
12591.00	Boston CG, USA	NMF	SITOR 1844 2212
12591.00	Doha, Qatar	A7D	SITOR 0708 0851
12591.00	Goeteborg, Sweden	SAG	SITOR 0918 1005 1558
12591.00	Hong Kong	VPS64	SITOR
12591.50	Coast stations ch 25 dup. 12489.0kHz		RTTY
12591.50	Mobile, USA	WLO	SITOR 1649 2136
12591.50	Portishead, UK	GKL5	SITOR
12591.50	Tallinn, Estonia	ESA	SITOR 1552 1601 1748 1941
12592.00	Coast stations ch 26 dup. 12489.5kHz		RTTY
12592.00	Lyngby, Denmark	OXZ	SITOR 1247 1650 2131 Mode B tfc list 0930
12592.50	Coast stations ch 27 dup. 12490.0kHz		RTTY
12592.50	Chesapeake CG, USA	NMN	SITOR 0940 1142 1905 2143
12593.00	Coast stations ch 28 dup. 12490.5kHz		RTTY
12593.00	Portishead, UK	GKP5	SITOR 1509 1740 2126
12593.00	Tallinn, Estonia	ESA	SITOR 1003 1555 1622 1827 2203 Mode B 1542 1600 1649
12593.50	Coast stations ch 29 dup. 12491.0kHz		RTTY
12593.50	Mobile, USA	WLO	SITOR 0659 1351 1553 1809 2208
12594.00	Coast stations ch 30 dup. 12491.5kHz		RTTY
12594.00	Italian Naval	IDR5	CW 0652 0932 1537
12594.00	Rio de Janeiro, Brazil	PPR	SITOR 0913 2138 2201
12594.50	Coast stations ch 31 dup. 12492.0kHz		RTTY
12594.50	Bahrain	A9M	SITOR 1337 1545 1653 1742 2200
12594.50	Tallinn, Estonia	ESA	SITOR 0833 0948 1054 1430 1507 1734
12595.00	Coast stations ch 32 dup. 12492.5kHz		RTTY
12595.00	Aqaba, Jordan	JYO	SITOR
12595.50	Coast stations ch 33 dup. 12493.0kHz		RTTY
12595.50	Helsinki, Finland	OFA	SITOR
12596.00	Coast stations ch 34 dup. 12493.5kHz		RTTY
12596.00	Mobile, USA	WLO	SITOR 1131 1651 2139
12596.50	Coast stations ch 35 dup. 12494.0kHz		RTTY
12596.50	Scheveningen, Holland	PCH56	SITOR 0856 1231 1606 1656
12597.00	Coast stations ch 36 dup. 12494.5kHz		RTTY
12597.00	Singapore	9VG95	SITOR 1655 1802
12597.00	Stettin, Poland	SPB62	SITOR 1102 1520 1743 2132 Mode B tfc list 0800 1600 1800
12597.50	Coast stations ch 37 dup. 12495.0kHz		RTTY
12597.50	Novorossiysk, Russia	UFN	SITOR 1517 1658 1726 1914
12598.00	Coast stations ch 38 dup. 12495.5kHz		RTTY
12598.00	Chatham, USA	WCC	SITOR 1143 1714 1744 1833 2012
12598.00	Gdynia, Poland	SPA62	SITOR 1041 1246 1511 1735 Mode B tfc list 1852
12598.50	Coast stations ch 39 dup. 12496.0kHz		RTTY
12598.50	Halifax, Canada	VCS	SITOR 1623
12599.00	Coast stations ch 40 dup. 12496.5kHz		RTTY
12599.00	Mobile, USA	WLO	SITOR 2140
12599.50	Coast stations ch 41 dup. 12497.0kHz		RTTY
12599.50	Moscow, Russia	UAT	SITOR 0858 1057 1540 1624 1745 2133 Mode B tfc list 1803
12600.00	Coast stations ch 42 dup. 12497.5kHz		RTTY
12600.00	San Francisco, USA	KPH	SITOR 1554 1811 2139 2210
12600.50	Coast stations ch 43 dup. 12498.0kHz		RTTY
12600.50	Berne, Switzerland	HEC23	SITOR 0819 1339 1440 1557
12601.00	Coast stations ch 44 dup. 12498.5kHz		RTTY
12601.00	Capetown, RSA	ZSC63	SITOR 1559 1754 1845 2105 Mode B tfc list 1820
12601.50	Coast stations ch 45 dup. 12499.0kHz		RTTY
12601.50	Lyngby, Denmark	OXZ	SITOR 1252 1700 1813 Mode B news 0850 tfc list 1130
12602.00	Coast stations ch 46 dup. 12499.5kHz		RTTY
12602.00	Novorossiysk, Russia	UFN	SITOR 2117 2140 2201
12602.50	Coast stations ch 47 dup. 12500.0kHz		RTTY
12602.50	Rome, Italy	IAR	SITOR 2232
12603.00	Coast stations ch 48 dup. 12500.5kHz		RTTY
12603.00	Portishead, UK	GKY5	SITOR 1042 1340 1658 2127
12603.00	Numbers Station		USB Eng (female voice) 1811
12603.50	Coast stations ch 49 dup. 12501.0kHz		RTTY
12603.50	Athens, Greece	SVS	SITOR 0859 0940 1441 1625 1950 Mode B tfc list 1620 1820
12603.50	Berne, Switzerland	HEC33	SITOR
12604.00	Coast stations ch 50 dup. 12501.5kHz		RTTY
12604.00	Goeteborg, Sweden	SAG	SITOR 2235
12604.50	Coast stations ch 51 dup. 12502.0kHz		RTTY
12604.50	Mobile, USA	WLO	SITOR 1758 2211
12604.50	Rijeka, Croatia	9AR	SITOR 0653 0736 2139
12605.00	Coast stations ch 52 dup. 12502.5kHz		RTTY
12605.00	Rogaland, Norway	LGJ4	SITOR 0852 0946 1624 1702 2142

kHz.	Station	Call	Mode / Heard/Times GMT
12605.50	Coast stations ch 53 dup. 12503.0kHz		RTTY
12605.50	St Lys, France	FFT64	SITOR 1044 1103 1601 2136
12606.00	Coast stations ch 54 dup. 12503.5kHz		RTTY
12606.00	Genoa, Italy	ICB	SITOR 0900 1540 1700 1746
12606.00	Mobile, USA	WLO	SITOR 0837 1043 1133 2137 2223
12606.50	Coast stations ch 55 dup. 12504.0kHz		RTTY
12607.00	Coast stations ch 56 dup. 12504.5kHz		RTTY
12607.00	Portishead, UK	GKQ5	SITOR 0733 0941 1747 2128
12607.50	Coast stations ch 57 dup. 12505.0kHz		RTTY
12607.50	Slidell, USA	WNU	SITOR 0808 1340 2141 2215
12608.00	Coast stations ch 58 dup. 12505.5kHz		RTTY
12608.50	Coast stations ch 59 dup. 12506.0kHz		RTTY
12609.00	Coast stations ch 60 dup. 12506.5kHz		RTTY
12609.50	Coast stations ch 61 dup. 12507.0kHz		RTTY
12609.50	Mobile, USA	WLO	SITOR 0838 1134 1341 1521 2143
12610.00	Coast stations ch 62 dup. 12507.5kHz		RTTY
12610.50	Coast stations ch 63 dup. 12508.0kHz		RTTY
12610.50	UNID	RUF9	CW (to "Baltiyskiy 15") 0813 (to "Sibirskij") 1505
12611.00	Coast stations ch 64 dup. 12508.5kHz		RTTY
12611.50	Coast stations ch 65 dup. 12509.0kHz		RTTY
12612.00	Coast stations ch 66 dup. 12509.5kHz		RTTY
12612.50	Coast stations ch 67 dup. 12510.0kHz		RTTY
12613.00	Coast stations ch 68 dup. 12510.5kHz		RTTY
12613.00	Guangzhou, China	XSQ	SITOR 1558 1701 2016 2137 wx (Eng) 1830 Mode B 1355
12613.50	Coast stations ch 69 dup. 12511.0kHz		RTTY
12614.00	Coast stations ch 70 dup. 12511.5kHz		RTTY
12614.50	Coast stations ch 71 dup. 12512.0kHz		RTTY
12615.00	Coast stations ch 72 dup. 12512.5kHz		RTTY
12615.00	Mariupol, Ukraine	USU	SITOR 0901 0930 1325 1518 1617 1750 Mode B nav wngs 1435
12615.50	Coast stations ch 73 dup. 12513.0kHz		RTTY
12616.00	Coast stations ch 74 dup. 12513.5kHz		RTTY
12616.50	Coast stations ch 75 dup. 12514.0kHz		RTTY
12617.00	Coast stations ch 76 dup. 12514.5kHz		RTTY
12617.50	Coast stations ch 77 dup. 12515.0kHz		RTTY
12618.00	Coast stations ch 78 dup. 12515.5kHz		RTTY
12618.50	Coast stations ch 79 dup. 12516.0kHz		RTTY
12619.00	Coast stations ch 80 dup. 12516.5kHz		RTTY
12619.50	Coast stations ch 81 dup. 12517.0kHz		RTTY
12620.00	Coast stations ch 82 dup. 12517.5kHz		RTTY
12620.50	Coast stations ch 83 dup. 12518.0kHz		RTTY
12621.00	Coast stations ch 84 dup. 12518.5kHz		RTTY
12621.50	Coast stations ch 85 dup. 12519.0kHz		RTTY
12622.00	Coast stations ch 86 dup. 12519.5kHz		RTTY
12622.50	Coast stations ch 88 dup. 12520.5kHz		RTTY
12623.00	Coast stations ch 89 dup. 12521.0kHz		RTTY
12623.50	Coast stations ch 90 dup. 12521.5kHz		RTTY
12623.50	Rogaland, Norway	LGJ	SITOR 0933 1233 1704
12624.00	Coast stations ch 91 dup. 12522.0kHz		RTTY
12624.50	Coast stations ch 92 dup. 12522.5kHz		RTTY
12625.00	Coast stations ch 93 dup. 12523.0kHz		RTTY
12625.50	Coast stations ch 94 dup. 12523.5kHz		RTTY
12625.50	Archangel, Russia	UCE	SITOR 1150 1357 1602 1624 1703 1749 Mode B tfc list 1205 1715
12626.00	Coast stations ch 95 dup. 12524.0kHz		RTTY
12626.50	Coast stations ch 96 dup. 12524.5kHz		RTTY
12626.50	Baku, Azerbaijan	UON	CW (to m/v "Fizuli" on 12561.0) 0640 (to ULCH) 0656
12627.00	Coast stations ch 97 dup. 12525.0kHz		RTTY
12627.50	Coast stations ch 98 dup. 12525.5kHz		RTTY
12627.50	Mariupol, Ukraine	USU	SITOR 1248 1514 1600 1623
12628.00	Coast stations ch 99 dup. 12526.0kHz		RTTY
12628.50	Coast stations ch 100 dup. 12526.5kHz		RTTY
12629.00	Coast stations ch 101 dup. 12527.0kHz		RTTY
12629.50	Coast stations ch 102 dup. 12527.5kHz		RTTY
12630.00	Coast stations ch 103 dup. 12528.0kHz		RTTY
12630.00	Dixon, USA	KMI	SITOR
12630.50	Coast stations ch 104 dup. 12528.5kHz		RTTY
12631.00	Coast stations ch 105 dup. 12529.0kHz		RTTY
12631.00	Pennsuco, USA	WOM	SITOR Mode B tfc list 0734 1135 1842
12631.50	Coast stations ch 106 dup. 12529.5kHz		RTTY
12632.00	Coast stations ch 107 dup. 12530.0kHz		RTTY
12632.00	New York (Ocean Gate), USA	WOO	SITOR 1137 Mode B wx 1628 tfc list 1004 1800 2020
12632.50	Coast stations ch 108 dup. 12530.5kHz		RTTY
12632.50	St Petersburg, Russia	UGC	SITOR 0634 1235 1521 1706 Mode B tfc list 1107
12633.00	Coast stations ch 109 dup. 12531.0kHz		RTTY
12633.50	Coast stations ch 110 dup. 12531.5kHz		RTTY
12634.00	Coast stations ch 111 dup. 12532.0kHz		RTTY

kHz.	Station	Call	Mode / Heard/Times GMT
12634.50	Coast stations ch 112 dup. 12532.5kHz		RTTY
12635.00	Coast stations ch 113 dup. 12533.0kHz		RTTY
12635.50	Coast stations ch 114 dup. 12533.5kHz		RTTY
12636.00	Coast stations ch 115 dup. 12534.0kHz		RTTY
12636.50	Coast stations ch 116 dup. 12534.5kHz		RTTY
12637.00	Coast stations ch 117 dup. 12535.0kHz		RTTY
12637.50	Coast stations ch 118 dup. 12535.5kHz		RTTY
12637.50	Murmansk, Russia	UMV	SITOR 0736 0903 1359 1524 1705 1807
12638.00	Coast stations ch 119 dup. 12536.0kHz		RTTY
12638.50	Coast stations ch 120 dup. 12536.5kHz		RTTY
12639.00	Coast stations ch 121 dup. 12537.0kHz		RTTY
12639.50	Coast stations ch 122 dup. 12537.5kHz		RTTY
12639.50	Ostend, Belgium	OST50	SITOR 1045 1542 1630 1707 1823 2122
12640.00	Coast stations ch 123 dup. 12538.0kHz		RTTY
12640.50	Coast stations ch 124 dup. 12538.5kHz		RTTY
12641.00	Coast stations ch 125 dup. 12539.0kHz		RTTY
12641.50	Coast stations ch 126 dup. 12539.5kHz		RTTY
12642.00	Coast stations ch 127 dup. 12540.0kHz		RTTY
12642.50	Coast stations ch 128 dup. 12540.5kHz		RTTY
12643.00	Coast stations ch 129 dup. 12541.0kHz		RTTY
12643.50	Coast stations ch 130 dup. 12541.5kHz		RTTY
12644.00	Coast stations ch 131 dup. 12542.0kHz		RTTY
12644.50	Coast stations ch 132 dup. 12542.5kHz		RTTY
12645.00	Coast stations ch 133 dup. 12543.0kHz		RTTY
12645.50	Coast stations ch 134 dup. 12543.5kHz		RTTY
12645.50	Mariupol, Ukraine	USU	SITOR 0734 1440 1525 1909 2021
12646.00	Coast stations ch 135 dup. 12544.0kHz		RTTY
12646.00	Istanbul, Turkey	TAH	SITOR 1416 (to TCAG) 1506
12646.50	Coast stations ch 136 dup. 12544.5kHz		RTTY
12647.00	Coast stations ch 137 dup. 12545.0kHz		RTTY
12647.00	General Pacheco, Argentina	LPD	SITOR 0654 0737 0853 1137 1856 2224
12647.50	Coast stations ch 138 dup. 12545.5kHz		RTTY
12648.00	Coast stations ch 139 dup. 12546.0kHz		RTTY
12648.00	General Pacheco, Argentina	LPD	SITOR
12648.50	Coast stations ch 140 dup. 12546.5kHz		RTTY
12649.00	Coast stations ch 141 dup. 12547.0kHz		RTTY
12649.50	Coast stations ch 142 dup. 12547.5kHz		RTTY
12649.50	Shanghai, China	XSG	SITOR 2217
12650.00	Coast stations ch 143 dup. 12548.0kHz		RTTY
12650.50	Coast stations ch 144 dup. 12548.5kHz		RTTY
12651.00	Coast stations ch 145 dup. 12549.0kHz		RTTY
12651.50	Coast stations ch 146 dup. 12549.5kHz		RTTY
12652.00	Coast stations ch 147 dup. 12555.0kHz		RTTY
12652.50	Coast stations ch 148 dup. 12555.5kHz		RTTY
12653.00	Coast stations ch 149 dup. 12556.0kHz		RTTY
12653.50	Coast stations ch 150 dup. 12556.5kHz		RTTY
12654.00	Coast stations ch 151 dup. 12557.0kHz		RTTY
12654.00	Istanbul, Turkey	TAH	SITOR 0909 1137 1250 1347 1603
12654.50	Coast stations ch 152 dup. 12557.5kHz		RTTY
12655.00	Coast stations ch 153 dup. 12558.0kHz		RTTY
12655.50	Coast stations ch 154 dup. 12558.5kHz		RTTY
12656.00	Coast stations ch 155 dup. 12559.0kHz		RTTY
12656.50	Coast stations digital selective calling		RTTY
12657.00	Coast stations digital selective calling		RTTY
12657.50	Coast stations digital selective calling		RTTY
12658.00	Coast stations digital selective calling		RTTY
12659.00	Varna, Bulgaria	LZW5	CW 1555 1604 tfc list 1513
12659.50	Singapore	9VG37	CW 0913 1405 1631 2141
12660.00	Banana, Zaire	9PA	CW tfc list 1959
12660.00	Basrah, Iraq	YIR	CW 0800 0856
12660.00	Mobile, USA	WLO	CW 0735 0859 0949 1837 2156 2225
12660.50	Novorossiysk, Russia	UNQ	CW 1410 1636 1711 1943 tfc list 1011 1811
12661.50	Murmansk, Russia	UMV	CW (listens for wx 12426.0) 1745
12661.50	Murmansk, Russia	UMV	170/50rc 0841 1425 1538 1809 (to "Arktika") 0928
12662.00	Boufarik, Algeria	7TF8	CW 0951 1046 1327 1601 2022 2210 tfc list 1743
12663.00	Valparaiso, Chile	CBV	CW 0831 0857 2157 2226
12664.50	French Naval, Tahiti	FUM	CW 1556 1655
12671.50	Riga, Latvia	UDH	CW 0800
12671.50	Riga, Latvia	UDH	170/50nc 1437 (with exchange rates) 1013 1945 (news) 1948
12673.50	Havana, Cuba	CLA33	CW 1215 1623 2124 2225
12673.50	Nagasaki, Japan	JOU	CW 0726 0832 0911 0943
12675.00	Karlskrona, Sweden	SAA	CW 0744 0841 1657 1719 tfc list 1301 1015
12675.50	Muscat, Oman	A4M	CW
12678.00	Pinang, Malaysia	9MG3	CW 1440 1505 1605 wx (Eng) 1752 2153 tfc list 1730 2130
12682.50	Ujungpandang, Indonesia	PKF	CW 1238
12687.00	Helsinki, Finland	OFJ32	CW 0952 1251 1548 1604 tfc list even hrs + 05
12688.50	Riga, Latvia	UQK	CW 0655 0727 0911 1328 1456 1550 1637 1851

kHz.	Station	Call	Mode / Heard/Times GMT
12688.50	Riga, Latvia	UQK	170/50nc 0914 1045 1709
12689.50	Juncao, Brazil	PPJ	CW 0833 1033 2023 2229 wx 0130 0730 1900 tfc list 2200
12690.00	Kaliningrad, Russia	UIW	CW 2132 (to UWNX for RTTY wkg) 2214
12690.00	Khomeyni, Iran	EQN	CW 1008
12691.00	French Naval, Reunion	FUX	CW 1442 1534 1631 1707 2058
12693.00	RSA Naval		75r news in Eng 1847 Afrikaans 2022
12694.20	Italian Naval	IGJ41	CW 1746 1805
12695.50	Palo Alto, USA	KFS	CW 0736 1559 1642 2025 2059 2159 wx 1134
12695.50	UNID	RWHB	CW (to UJDM) 0920 tfc list 1536
12695.80	Casablanca, Morocco	CNP	CW 1035 1047 tfc list 1030 1430
12697.00	Mariupol, Ukraine	USU	CW 0906 1110 1329 tfc list 0704 1820
12697.00	Mariupol, Ukraine	USU	170/50nc 0910 1018 nav wngs 1606
12698.00	Bahrain	A9M	CW (with ATUD) 1649 (with EPBZ) 1709 tfc list 0805 1700
12698.00	Capetown, RSA	ZSC9	CW 1739 1844 tfc list 1702
12699.00	Panama	HPP	CW 0944 2200 2226 tfc list 2302
12700.00	Archangel, Russia	UCE	170/50nc 0738 1139 nav wngs 0729
12700.00	Guangzhou, China	XSQ4	CW 1048 1251 1751 1835 2026 2227 tfc list 1230 1730 2130
12703.00	Klaipeda, Lithuania	LYK	CW 0954 (to LYCB) 0919 tfc list 1001
12704.50	Argentine Naval	LOR	100n ID & 5 let grps 2229
12704.50	Mobile, USA	WLO	CW 0656 0953 1129 1330 1809 2227
12707.00	Singapore	9VG34	CW 1445 1632 2027
12709.00	Bahrain	A9M	CW 0739 0914 1409 1534 1710 1911
12709.00	Bridgetown, Barbados	8PO	CW 1807 2130 tfc list 0140 1320 2100
12709.20	Salina Cruz, Mexico	XFQ	CW 2201
12710.00	Bombay, India	VWB	CW 1554 wx 0848 1548
12711.00	Guayaquil, Ecuador	HCG	CW 2113 2202
12711.00	Mariupol, Ukraine	USU	CW 1255 1455
12711.00	Mariupol, Ukraine	USU	170/50nc (to "Moskowskiy Komsomolets") 1726
12712.00	Seoul, S Korea	HLW3	CW 1140 1446 1557 2052
12714.00	Archangel, Russia	UCE	SITOR 0834 0915 1156 1605 1748 Mode B tfc list 1005 1904
12714.00	Portishead, UK	GKM5	CW reserve frequency
12715.00	Kiev, Ukraine	UTQ	CW 0918 1624 1830 1947 2047 tfc list 1004
12718.50	Chesapeake CG, USA	NMN	CW 0732 0921 1239 1410 1537 1857 2203
12719.80	New Zealand Naval	ZLO	CW 0725 0835 1049
12720.00	Athens, Greece	SVI5	CW 0945 1456 1629 1823 1929 2131
12721.00	Gdynia, Poland	SPH61	CW 0733 1500 1606 1809 tfc list 1200 1600
12723.00	Tallinn, Estonia	ESA	CW 1603 1925 tfc list 1833
12724.00	Capetown, RSA	ZSC43	CW 1538 1611 1721
12724.00	Singapore	9VG57	CW 1448 2147
12726.00	Halifax Naval, Canada	CFH	CW 1050 1639 1747 2135 wx 1400 1800 (also msrd 12724.0)
12727.00	Seoul, S Korea	HLJ	CW 1558 1617 2112
12727.50	Rogaland, Norway	LGJ	CW 0739 0836 0955 1253 tfc list hrly 0700-2000
12729.00	Vladivostok, Russia	UFL	CW 1731 wx 0916 nav wngs 1613
12729.00	Vladivostok, Russia	UFL	170/50r 0837
12729.00	Gelendzhik, Russia	UVA	CW 0703 0914 1018 1242 1449 1608 tfc list 1503 1601
12730.00	Murmansk, Russia	UMV	CW 1017 tfc list 0801 1601
12732.00	Mariupol, Ukraine	USU	CW 2204 tfc list 0800 1200 1300 1500 1600 2200
12733.50	Singapore	9VG20	CW tfc list 1257
12735.00	Sebastopol, Ukraine	URL	CW 0852 0956 1457 1538 1857 1937 2249 tfc list 1103 1803
12735.00	Sebastopol, Ukraine	URL	170/50rc 0807 (to "General Patrov") 1533
12736.60	Istanbul, Turkey	TAH	CW 0731 1240 tfc list 1100 1500 1600 1700 2200
12738.00	Rio de Janeiro, Brazil	PPR	CW 0837 0957 1458 1900 2230 tfc list 2304
12739.00	Moscow, Russia	UAT	CW (listens for wx on 12425.0kHz) 1555 1816
12739.00	Moscow, Russia	UAT	170/50nc 0847 1255 1614 (to UGSH) 1243 (to UIJR) 2057
12741.00	French Naval, Paris	HWN	75r RYs & SGs 0740 0958 1049 1811
12743.00	San Diego CG, USA	NOR	CW 0737
12745.50	Tokyo Press (KYODO)	JJC	FAX 0742 0852 1051 1735
12748.00	Rome (Medical Centre), Italy	IRM	CW 0959 1459 1538 1609
12750.00	Boston CG, USA	NIK	CW requests for ice sighting reports 1256
12750.00	Cerrito, Uruguay	CWA	CW 0642 0839 0925 1841 2114 2232
12750.00	Australian Naval	VHI	CW 0921 1526 1600 2206
12752.00	CIS Naval	RIW	CW 0921 1052
12753.50	Lyngby, Denmark	OXZ62	CW 0924 tfc list (cont) 1014
12755.00	Tallinn, Estonia	ESF	CW 0956 1053 1641
12760.00	Odessa, Ukraine	UUI	CW 1139 1801
12763.50	Norddeich, Germany	DAM	CW 0735 1658 1812 2233 tfc list 2030
12765.00	St Petersburg, Russia	UCW4	CW 0729 0839 0935 tfc list 1504
12772.50	Capetown, RSA	ZSC38	CW 1749 tfc list each even hour + 30 wx 1735
12780.00	Luanda, Angola	D3E61	CW 1901 2116 2236
12780.50	Rijeka, Croatia	9AR5	CW 0736 0840 1659 tfc list 1600 2200
12781.50	Malaysian Naval	9MB	CW 1259 1606 1856
12781.50	Ostend, Belgium	OST5	CW 1244 1450 1539 tfc list 1500
12784.50	Keelung, Taiwan	XSX	CW 0926 1228 tfc list 1900
12788.50	Portishead, UK	GKD5	CW (reserve frequency)
12790.00	Portishead, UK	GKG5	CW (working frequency to ships) 0842 1642 1723
12791.00	Turkish Naval	TBA	CW 1857
12791.50	Portishead, UK	GKH5	CW reserve frequency

kHz.	Station	Call	Mode / Heard/Times GMT
12792.00	Dammam, Saudi Arabia	HZG	CW 1613
12792.00	Havana, Cuba	CLA31	CW 2249 2349
12792.00	Turkish Naval	TBA	CW 2151
12793.00	Moscow Met Centre, Russia	RNO	CW (to UJFO) 1257
12795.00	Archangel, Russia	UCE	CW 0825 0916 1101 1245 1409 1627 tfc list 1501
12795.00	Archangel, Russia	UCE	170/50nc 1258 1540 "to "Pioner Moldavii" UKDC) 1618
12797.00	Brazilian Naval	PWZ33	CW nav wngs (in Eng) 2231 also rptd with 75Bd RTTY
12797.00	Murmansk, Russia	UDK2	CW 0844 0929 1428 1542 1726 (to "4LS") 1624
12797.00	Murmansk, Russia	UDK2	170/50nc 1430 1503 1608 1751
12799.50	Scheveningen, Holland	PCH51	CW 0742 0926 1547 1620 1700 2156 tfc lists even hrs + 50
12800.00	Bangkok, Thailand	HSA3	CW tfc list 0900
12801.00	Istanbul, Turkey	TAH	CW 0928 1246 1900 tfc list 0903 1503 1903 1703 2303
12803.00	Murmansk, Russia	UDK2	CW 0837 0854 0950 1000 1134 1442 1727
12803.00	Murmansk, Russia	UDK2	170/50nc 2144
12804.00	Constanza, Romania	YQI5	CW 0933 1415 tfc list 1003 1104 1904 2304
12806.00	US Naval, Diego Garcia	NKW	FAX wx maps 1543 1621 1739
12808.50	Indian Naval	VTG7	CW 1414 1647 2130 2158 2305 wx 0930 1530
12808.50	San Francisco, USA	KPH	CW 0844
12810.00	Moscow, Russia	UJE	CW 1003 1259
12811.30	Ras Tannurah, Saudi Arabia	HZY	CW 1544 tfc list 1001
12815.00	Klaipeda Harbour, Lithuania	LYL	CW 0750 1038 1136 1723 (giving QSX 12442.5/4207/480)
12815.00	Klaipeda Harbour, Lithuania	LYL	170/50nc 0808 1007 1050
12815.00	Portishead, UK	GKF5	CW reserve frequency
12817.50	Petrozavodsk, Russia	RSGV	CW 0658 0922 (to "Amur 2528") 0904
12818.00	Goeteborg, Sweden	SAG	SITOR 0931 1300 1627 1556 Mode B news 1705
12822.00	Portishead, UK	GKA5	CW wx 0930 1130 2130 tfc list 1100 1500 1600 1900 2000
12823.50	Portuguese Naval	CTP	CW 0752 0843 1611 1837
12824.00	British Naval, Gibraltar	GYU	75n 0852 1636
12826.50	British Naval, Gibraltar	GYU	75n 1052
12826.50	Choshi, Japan	JCS	CW 1017
12826.50	Slidell, USA	WNU34	CW 0804 2233 wx 1613
12829.30	Manzanillo, Mexico	XFM	CW 0818
12831.00	Mauritius	3BM5	CW 1725 1916 tfc list 1530
12832.50	Norddeich, Germany	DAF	CW
12833.00	Athens, Greece	SVF5	CW 0845 0934 1250 1623 tfc list 0810 1411 1608
12833.50	Novaliches, Philippines	DZP	CW 1454 1539 1625 2155 tfc list 1510
12835.00	UNID	URK9	CW Russian telegrams 1820
12835.40	Portishead, UK	GKB5	CW 0743 0810 1105 1558 1637 1817 2207
12840.30	Dutch Naval	PBC	75n 0717 1231
12843.00	Seoul, S Korea	HLO	CW 0753 1052 1144 1232 1308 1625
12844.50	Palo Alto, USA	KFS	CW 1456 1532 2100 tfc list 1728
12844.50	British Naval	GYA	FAX wx maps 0825 1648
12847.00	Chatham, USA	WCC	CW 0744 1106 1247 1615 1845 2208 tfc list 1050
12849.00	RSA Naval	ZSJ	CW 1743 2209
12853.10	Buenaventura, Colombia	HKC	CW (tx drifts very badly) 2132 2309
12853.50	Scheveningen, Holland	PCH52	CW 0846 1548 1818 2101 2234
12854.50	Kaliningrad, Russia	UIW	170/50nc 1649
12855.00	St Petersburg, Russia	UBF2	CW (to "4LT3") 0815 0827 1009 1107 1507 1628 tfc list 1405
12856.00	Shanghai, China	XSG	CW 0854 0936 1248 1602 1751 1838 tfc list 1230 1630 1830
12857.00	French Naval, Dakar	6VW	CW 0704 0849 1056 1550 1638 1743 1819
12858.00	Portishead, UK	GKI5	CW reserve frequency
12859.00	Athens, Greece	SVD5	CW 1111 1309 1616 1753 2146 2235
12860.90	Haifa, Israel	4XO	CW 0854 1617 1923 2100 tfc list even hrs + 25
12864.00	Kaohsiung, Taiwan	XSW	CW 0903 1234 1310 1549 1600 1746 2100
12865.00	Liepaja, Latvia	UPW2	CW 1123 1225 tfc list 1103 1803
12869.00	Slidell, USA	WNU54	CW 0741 0830 1618 1855 2147 2201
12870.00	Bulacan, Philippines	DZO	CW 1249
12870.00	Vladivostok, Russia	UKA	CW 0828 1659 1826
12871.50	Portishead, UK	GKJ5	CW reserve frequency
12871.50	Shanghai, China	XSG	CW 0935 1320 1533 1627
12874.00	Halifax, Canada	VCS	CW 0831 0900 1111 1203 1619 2101 wx 1543 2237
12875.00	French Naval, La Regine	FUG	CW (clg FAAW) 1844
12876.00	Vancouver, Canada	VAI	CW 2229
12877.50	Kaliningrad, Russia	UIW	CW 2102 2121 nav wngs 2125
12878.00	Choshi, Japan	JCU	CW 1124 1245
12879.50	Tuckerton, USA	WSC	CW 1246 1534 1628 2238 tfc list 1920 2220
12886.50	Mobile, USA	WLO	CW wx 1827
12887.50	Madrid, Spain	EAD44	CW 0937 1305 1524 1742 1845
12888.50	Bulacan, Philippines	DZK	CW 1322
12889.50	Honolulu CG, Hawaii	NMO	CW 0708
12889.50	Italian Naval	IDQ	CW 0706
12891.00	Novorossiysk, Russia	UFN	CW 0711 1112 1412 1529 1614 1835 tfc list 1840
12895.00	Klaipeda, Lithuania	LYK	CW 0911 1019 1505 tfc list 1602 1702 1802
12895.00	Klaipeda, Lithuania	LYK	170/50nc 0905 0928 1042 nav wngs 0800
12898.50	Norddeich, Germany	DAN	CW 1010 1639 1730 2149 2239
12901.50	St Petersburg, Russia	UGC	170/50nc 0709 0720 1429 1510
12903.00	Indian Naval	VTH	50r ID 1753

kHz.	Station	Call	Mode / Heard/Times GMT
12905.70	British Naval	GYA/MTO	75r 0834 1057
12906.00	Bulacan, Philippines	DZJ	CW 1247 1324 1630 1716 tfc list 1600
12907.50	Australian Naval	VHP	CW 0832 1012 1411 1515 1640 2240
12907.50	Sydney, Australia	VIX5	CW 0947
12910.00	Moscow, Russia	UAT	CW 1325 1513 tfc list 1301 1701 2301
12912.00	Batumi, Georgia	UHK	CW 1641
12912.60	St Lys, France	FFL6	CW 0744 1347 1530 1846 tfc list even hrs + 30 wx 1635
12916.50	Lyngby, Denmark	OXZ6	CW 1637 2104 2220 tfc list 1442 1539 2037
12916.50	Seoul, S Korea	HLF	CW 0938
12923.00	Seoul, S Korea	HLW2	CW 0802 0901 1514 1633 1748 2105
12925.50	Chatham, USA	WCC	CW 1542 1757 tfc list 2254 wx 1713
12925.50	St Petersburg, Russia	UGC	CW (to "4KB") 0746 0836 1044 1104 1523 1956 2157
12930.50	Aqaba, Jordan	JYO	CW 0711 0840 1532 1641 1758 1821
12932.50	Spanish Naval		100r encrypted 1634
12935.00	Seoul, S Korea	HLG	CW 1516 1800 2241 tfc list 1408 1608 2008
12940.00	Varna, Bulgaria	LZW52	CW 0712 1042 1624 2203 tfc list 1110 1310 2107
12942.00	Archangel, Russia	RKLM	CW 0822 0845 0941 1801
12942.00	Archangel, Russia	RKLM	170/50nc 0911
12943.10	Lisbon, Portugal	CUL	CW 1749 1831 1922 2009 2256
12947.00	Odessa, Ukraine	UUI	170/50rc 1511 1545 (to "Akademik Millionshchikov" UWFW) 1613
12947.00	Odessa, Ukraine	UUI	CW 0942 1902 2151 tfc list 1013
12950.00	Numbers Station		USB "MIW2" (female voice) 0816
12952.50	Perth, Australia	VIP	CW 0937 1706 1720
12954.00	Shanghai, China	XSG28	CW 1356 tfc list 1830 2230
12955.00	Vladivostok, Russia	UFL	CW 2011 tfc list 1312
12958.50	Olinda, Brazil	PPO	CW 0941 1016 1641 1749 nav wng (Eng) 2044 2100 tfc list 2140
12963.50	Jamestown, St Helena	ZHH	CW 1832
12965.00	Izmail, Ukraine	USO5	CW 0804 0813 0932 tfc list 1102 1603
12966.80	Doha, Qatar	A7D	CW 1328 1406 1520 1642 1756
12967.00	Moscow, Russia	UJE	CW 0913 (to UYKB) 1102
12969.00	Alexandria, Egypt	SUH	CW 1007 1120 1357 1604 (freq varies to 12971.2)
12969.00	Tianjin, China	XSV	CW 0847 1121 1354 1555 tfc list 1602
12970.00	Sebastopol, Ukraine	URL	CW 1800
12970.50	Jakarta, Indonesia	PKX	CW 1206 1355 1824
12973.00	Kaliningrad, Russia	UIW	CW 1237 1428 tfc list 1300 1700
12973.00	Kaliningrad, Russia	UIW	170/50nc 2120 2242
12975.00	Trieste, Italy	IQX	CW 0713 1029 1122 1436 1505 1556
12978.00	Genoa, Italy	ICB	CW 0835 1030 1413 1553 1605 1827 2109
12979.50	Sydney, Australia	VIS	CW
12979.60	Belem, Brazil	PPL	CW 0942 1043 1624 1839 2154
12984.00	Darwin, Australia	VNG	CW (Time Station) 0859 1239 1625 1641
12984.00	Israeli Naval	4XZ	CW 0805 1546 1643 1828 wx anal 1039 1550 2129
12988.50	General Pacheco, Argentina	LPD88	CW 1035 2107 tfc list 0913 2102
12992.00	Mobile, USA	WLO	CW 1023 1111 1523 2234
12992.00	Mobile, USA	WLO	SITOR Mode B tfc list (and for Lyngby) 0835 wx 0817
12993.00	Sebastopol, Ukraine	URL	CW 1414 1608 1730 1829 2117 2320
12993.00	Sebastopol, Ukraine	URL	170/50rc 2200
12996.00	Rome, Italy	IAR33	CW news (Ital) 2202
12997.50	Odessa, Ukraine	UUI	CW 1753 2108 tfc list 0700 1600 2200
12999.50	Portuguese Naval	CTU2	CW nav wng 0853 wx 1812 2044 wx analysis ("CANAL" code) 1800
13002.00	San Francisco, USA	KPH	CW 1617 2109
13006.50	Portishead, UK	GKK5	CW (reserve frequency)
13008.00	Nagasaki, Japan	JOR	CW 0730 0839 1044 1240 1547 1645 1748 1830
13010.00	Murmansk, Russia	UQA4	CW (to 4LS) 1315 1645 2212 tfc list 0835 1832
13011.00	Rome, Italy	IAR23	CW tfc list 0755 1215 1602 wx (Eng) 0831 2031 2204
13011.00	Slidell, USA	WNU44	CW 2118
13012.00	Pakistan Naval	AQP4	CW 1040 1433 1437
13014.00	Havana, Cuba	CLS	CW 1229 1434
13015.50	Rome, Italy	IAR3	CW 1241 1548 1646 1809 2151
13020.40	Hong Kong	VPS60	CW 0900 1333 1448 wx 0822
13022.00	Stettin, Poland	SPE63	CW 1607 1755 tfc list 1813 2228
13023.00	Luanda, Angola	D3E62	CW 1229 1549 1606 1735
13024.40	Karachi, Pakistan	ASK	CW 1230 1618 1809 tfc list 1801
13024.90	Mobile, USA	WLO	CW 1112 1533 2051 2118 2207
13027.50	Norddeich, Germany	DAL	CW
13029.00	Athens, Greece	SVB5	CW 1124 1626 1756 1833 2203
13030.00	St Petersburg, Russia	UGC	170/50nc 0902 0933
13030.00	St Petersburg, Russia	UGC	CW 1023 1126 1526 2119
13031.00	Hong Kong	VRN60	CW wx 1338 1348
13031.20	French Naval, Martinique	FUF	CW 0821 1040 1637 1834 2204
13033.50	Chatham, USA	WCC	CW 1125 1627 1757 tfc list 0853 2057
13034.70	Egyptian Embassy traffic		SITOR 0748
13040.00	Novorossiysk, Russia	UFN	CW 0900 1044 1114 1622 1711 1815 2204
13041.00	Odessa, Ukraine	UUI	CW 1550 1624 1758

kHz.	Station	Call	Mode / Heard/Times GMT
13041.50	Hochiminhville, Vietnam	XVS	CW 1222 tfc list 1113 1513
13042.50	French Military, Djibouti	FUV	CW 0736 1415 1538 1746 2238 2304
13042.50	Curacao, Neth. Antilles	PJC	CW 1105 1849 2120
13044.00	Hong Kong	VPS61	CW 1216 1242
13046.00	Paramaribo, Surinam	PZN4	CW
13050.00	Murmansk, Russia	UDK2	170/50rc 0921 1024 1812 1835
13050.00	Murmansk, Russia	UDK2	CW (to 4LS) 0822 0901 1025 1143 1748 2119
13051.00	Haifa, Israel	4XO	CW 1008 1531 1650 1812 tfc list 1628 1830 (freq varies)
13054.00	Kaliningrad. Russia	UIW	CW (to UOLF) 1440
13054.00	Kaliningrad, Russia	UIW	170/50nc 0824 1035 1351 nav wngs 1006
13055.00	Kiev, Ukraine	UTQ	CW 0715 1551
13059.00	Spanish Naval	EBA	CW nav wngs (Eng & Span) 1629 1835
13059.00	Spanish Naval	EBA	75n NAVAREA THREE nav wngs (Eng) 1006 1702
13060.00	UNID	UFJ	CW tfc list 0735 1030 (gives QSW as 6369/13060, QSX as 16622.5)
13060.50	Aden	7OA	CW 1417 1441
13062.00	Havana, Cuba	CLA32	CW 1223 1535 1651 1814 2122
13063.00	Nagasaki, Japan	JDB	CW 0724 0852 0906 1045 1115 1243
13065.00	Parnu, Estonia	ESP	CW 0938 tfc list 1201
13067.00	Ostend, Belgium	OST52	CW 0751 0826 1037 1630 2121 tfc list 1011
13069.50	Nagasaki, Japan	JOS	CW 0907 1800 tfc list odd hrs + 30
13070.00	Riga, Latvia	UDH	CW 1058 1252 1558 1631 1810 2123
13073.80	St Lys, France	FFT6	CW 1813 wx f/casts (Fr) 0856 1838
13076.50	Tokyo, Japan	JNA	CW 1252 1523 2122
13076.70	Dammam, Saudi Arabia	HZG	CW 1126 1404 1430 1557 1652
13077.00	Coast stations ch 1 dup. 12230.0kHz		USB
13077.00	Doha, Qatar	A7D	USB (with DTFI) 2125 (with LRBK) 2308
13077.00	Madrid, Spain	EHY	USB 0945 1538 tfc list 1804
13077.00	Moscow, Russia	UAT	USB 1019 1510 1611 1800
13077.00	Portishead, UK	GKT51	USB
13080.00	Coast stations ch 2 dup. 12233.0kHz		USB
13080.00	Athens, Greece	SVN51	USB time signals 1734
13080.00	Berne, Switzerland	HEB13	USB 0652 0723 1453
13080.00	Dammam, Saudi Arabia	HZG	USB
13080.00	Portishead, UK	GKT52	USB
13083.00	Coast stations ch 3 dup. 12236.0kHz		USB
13083.00	Dixon, USA	KMI	USB tfc list 0000 + 4 hrly
13083.00	Goeteborg, Sweden	SAG	USB tfc list 0800 1000 1600
13083.00	Lisbon, Portugal	CUL	USB 0852 1543 2143 (with SQNC) 1524 (with CNTD) 1623
13083.00	Monaco	3AC	USB 0751 1559
13083.00	New York (Ocean Gate), USA	WOO	USB 2145
13083.00	Sydney, Australia	VIS	USB 0747 0930
13083.00	Townsville, Australia	VIT	USB (on request)
13086.00	Coast stations ch 4 dup. 12239.0kHz		USB
13086.00	Haifa, Israel	4XO	USB
13086.00	Rogaland, Norway	LFL31	USB 1047 1745
13086.00	St Petersburg, Russia	UGC	USB 0659 1526
13089.00	Coast stations ch 5 dup. 12242.0kHz		USB
13089.00	Batumi, Georgia	UFA	USB 0822 0917
13089.00	General Pacheco, Argentina	LPL	USB 2121
13089.00	Genoa, Italy	ICB	USB 0657 1727
13089.00	Klaipeda, Lithuania	LYK	USB
13089.00	Norddeich, Germany	DAP	USB 2300
13089.00	Chesapeake, USA	NMN	USB wx 1146 1714 2204 2214
13089.00	Riga, Latvia	UDH	USB 1621
13092.00	Coast stations ch 6 dup. 12245.0kHz		USB
13092.00	Helsinki, Finland	OHG	USB 0748 0754
13092.00	Istanbul, Turkey	TAN	USB
13092.00	Pennsuco, USA	WOM	USB 2211 wx 1300 1500 1703
13092.00	Portishead, UK	GKT56	USB 1350
13092.00	Rome, Italy	IAR	USB 0838 0940
13095.00	Coast stations ch 7 dup. 12248.0kHz		USB
13095.00	Boufarik, Algeria	7TK41	USB wx 0800 tfc list 1605
13095.00	Haifa, Israel	4XO	USB 2105
13095.00	Lisbon, Portugal	CUL	USB 0806 0945 1027
13095.00	Murmansk, Russia	UMV	USB 1608
13095.00	Ostend, Belgium	OSU51	USB 0718 2124 tfc list 0802 1600
13095.00	Vancouver, Canada	VAI	USB
13098.00	Coast stations ch 8 dup. 12251.0kHz		USB
13098.00	Nicosia, Cyprus	5BA	USB 0738 1140 1454 1612
13098.00	Norddeich, Germany	DAK	USB 0821 0912
13098.00	Pennsuco, USA	WOM	USB 1324
13101.00	Coast stations ch 9 dup. 12254.0kHz		USB
13101.00	Bahrain	A9M	USB (with C6DB2) 1635
13101.00	Capetown, RSA	ZSC	USB 0706
13101.00	Pennsuco, USA	WOM	USB 1113
13101.00	Novorossiysk, Russia	UDN	USB 0814 1325

kHz.	Station	Call	Mode / Heard/Times GMT
13104.00	Coast stations ch 10 dup. 12257.0kHz		USB
13104.00	Berne, Switzerland	HEB43	USB 1856 (with YQKD) 0843
13104.00	Lyngby, Denmark	OXZ	USB
13104.00	Madrid, Spain	EHY	USB 1542 2125 tfc list 1801
13104.00	New York (Ocean Gate), USA	WOO	USB
13107.00	Coast stations ch 11 dup. 12260.0kHz		USB
13107.00	Genoa, Italy	ICB	USB 0912 1521
13107.00	New York (Ocean Gate), USA	WOO	USB 0637 (with "Horizon") 2100
13107.00	Rogaland, Norway	LFL34	USB 0947 1423
13110.00	Coast stations ch 12 dup. 12263.0kHz		USB
13110.00	Athens, Greece	SVN55	USB 0609 1406 1657 (with SZUJ) 1844
13110.00	Norddeich, Germany	DAH	USB 0642 1010
13113.00	Coast stations ch 13 dup. 12266.0kHz		USB
13113.00	Halifax, Canada	VCS	USB wx 0806 2206
13113.00	Scheveningen, Holland	PCG51	USB 0725 0922 1638 1818 2145 tfc list each odd hour + 05
13116.00	Coast stations ch 14 dup. 12269.0kHz		USB
13116.00	Inuvik, Canada	VFA	USB
13116.00	Lyngby, Denmark	OXZ	USB 0716 0811 2141 2203
13119.00	Coast stations ch 15 dup. 12272.0kHz		USB
13119.00	Haifa, Israel	4XO	USB 1010 1352 1443 2150
13119.00	Pennsuco, USA	WOM	USB 2229
13119.00	Reykjavik, Iceland	TFA	USB 0836 1707 tfc list 1005
13122.00	Coast stations ch 16 dup. 12275.0kHz		USB
13122.00	Gdynia, Poland	SPC61	USB 0901 0941 1501 1613 1804
13122.00	Singapore	9VG	USB 0908
13125.00	Coast stations ch 17 dup. 12278.0kHz		USB
13125.00	Kiev, Ukraine	UTQ	USB (with ULSB) 0752
13125.00	Rogaland, Norway	LFL37	USB 0754 1803
13125.00	Varna, Bulgaria	LZW	USB 0724 0750 0911 0918 1502 1639 1804
13128.00	Coast stations ch 18 dup. 12281.0kHz		USB
13128.00	Istanbul, Turkey	TAN	USB 0630 0956 1847
13128.00	Norddeich, Germany	DAI	USB
13128.00	Rome, Italy	IAR	USB 1524
13131.00	Coast stations ch 19 dup. 12284.0kHz		USB
13131.00	Lyngby, Denmark	OXZ	USB
13131.00	Singapore	9VG	USB 0725
13134.00	Coast stations ch 20 dup. 12287.0kHz		USB
13134.00	Aqaba, Jordan	JYO	USB
13134.00	Athens, Greece	SVN58	USB 1852
13137.00	Coast stations ch 21 dup. 12290.0kHz		USB common calling ch
13137.00	Capetown, RSA	ZSC	USB
13137.00	Havana, Cuba	CLT	USB
13137.00	Monaco	3AC	USB
13137.00	Rogaland, Norway	LGQ	USB 1835
13137.00	Ostend, Belgium	OSU56	USB
13137.00	Rio de Janeiro, Brazil	PPR	USB
13137.00	Rome, Italy	IAR	USB 0732 0953
13137.00	Scheveningen, Holland	PCG	USB 1624
13137.00	Singapore	9VG	USB
13140.00	Coast stations ch 22 dup. 12293.0kHz		USB
13140.00	Istanbul, Turkey	TAN	USB 1627
13140.00	Rogaland, Norway	LFL40	USB
13140.00	St Lys, France	FFL	USB 1432 1543
13143.00	Coast stations ch 23 dup. 12296.0kHz		USB
13143.00	Casablanca, Morocco	CNP	USB
13143.00	Lyngby, Denmark	OXZ	USB
13143.00	Mariupol, Ukraine	USU	USB 0816 0750 0900 1522 (clg "Aleksandr Pokalchuk" UPXX) 1723
13143.00	Pennsuco, USA	WOM	USB 2215
13146.00	Coast stations ch 24 dup. 12299.0kHz		USB
13146.00	Monaco	3AC12	USB (with UOVA) 0853 (with ODDV) 0856
13146.00	Norddeich, Germany	DAJ	USB 0807 0959 1627 1805 tfc list 1544
13146.00	Portishead, UK	GKV54	USB 1207 1550 1803 tfc list 0900
13149.00	Coast stations ch 25 dup. 12302.0kHz		USB
13149.00	Murmansk, Russia	UMV	USB 1050 1256 1528
13152.00	Coast stations ch 26 dup. 12305.0kHz		USB
13152.00	Lyngby, Denmark	OXZ	USB 0721
13152.00	Mobile, USA	WLO	USB
13152.00	Perth, Australia	VIP	USB
13152.00	St Lys, France	FFL	USB 0656 0741 1046 1114 1644
13155.00	Coast stations ch 27 dup. 12308.0kHz		USB
13155.00	Adelaide, Australia	VIA	USB (on request)
13155.00	Berne, Switzerland	HEB23	USB 0801 1205
13155.00	Darwin, Australia	VID	USB
13155.00	Helsinki, Finland	OHG2	USB 0650 (with EKUR) 0814
13155.00	Stettin, Poland	SPO62	USB 0747 0909 1028 1055 1241 (to C6DF6) 2219
13158.00	Coast stations ch 28 dup. 12311.0kHz		USB

kHz.	Station	Call	Mode / Heard/Times GMT
13158.00	Belem, Brazil	PPL	USB 2036 2139
13158.00	Kiev, Ukraine	UTQ	USB 0702 0745 1545
13158.00	New York (Ocean Gate), USA	WOO	USB 1224 1510 2126 (gives CW ID)
13158.00	Portishead, UK	GKV58	USB
13158.00	Rogaland, Norway	LFL44	USB 1056 1542 2125 wx 1226
13161.00	Coast stations ch 29 dup. 12314.0kHz		USB
13161.00	Brisbane, Australia	VIB	USB
13161.00	Darwin, Australia	VID	USB (on request)
13161.00	Dixon, USA	KMI	USB
13161.00	Doha, Qatar	A7D	USB (to 6NBH) 2211
13161.00	Perth, Australia	VIP	USB (on request)
13161.00	Riga, Latvia	UDH	USB 0651
13161.00	St Lys, France	FFL	USB 0754 0929
13164.00	Coast stations ch 30 dup. 12317.0kHz		USB
13164.00	Berne, Switzerland	HEB33	USB 0853 0910 1001 1156 1626
13164.00	Pennsuco, USA	WOM	USB (gives CW ID marker) 1000
13164.00	Portishead, UK	GKV50	USB
13167.00	Coast stations ch 31 dup. 12320.0kHz		USB
13167.00	Benghazi, Libya	5AB	USB
13167.00	Gdynia, Poland	SPC64	USB 1758
13167.00	Rogaland, Norway	LFL45	USB 1858
13167.00	St Lys, France	FFL	USB 1033 1807
13167.00	Sydney, Australia	VIS	USB (on request)
13167.00	Townsville, Australia	VIT	USB
13170.00	Coast stations ch 32 dup. 12323.0kHz		USB
13170.00	Athens, Greece	SVN59	USB 0658 0903 1353 1533 1848 tfc list 0805
13170.00	Portishead, UK	GKW52	USB
13170.00	US Coastguard stations		USB (common channel)
13173.00	Coast stations ch 33 dup. 12326.0kHz		USB
13173.00	Archangel, Russia	UCE	USB 0742 1113 1231
13173.00	Malta	9HD	USB
13176.00	Coast stations ch 34 dup. 12329.0kHz		USB
13176.00	Madrid, Spain	EHY	USB 1628 2153 tfc list 1804
13179.00	Coast stations ch 35 dup. 12332.0kHz		USB
13179.00	Riga, Latvia	UDH	USB 0743
13179.00	St Lys, France	FFL	USB 0713 0733
13182.00	Coast stations ch 36 dup. 12335.0kHz		USB
13182.00	Rome, Italy	IAR	USB 0648 0741 0928 1257 1846 2130
13185.00	Coast stations ch 37 dup. 12338.0kHz		USB
13185.00	Berne, Switzerland	HEB53	USB 0917 0944
13185.00	Haifa, Israel	4XO	USB
13185.00	St Lys, France	FFL	USB 1001
13188.00	Coast stations ch 38 dup. 12341.0kHz		USB
13188.00	Izmail, Ukraine	USO5	USB 1057
13188.00	Moscow, Russia	UAT	USB 0702 0723 1003
13191.00	Coast stations ch 39 dup. 12344.0kHz		USB
13191.00	Doha, Qatar	A7D	USB 2144
13191.00	Novorossiysk, Russia	UDN	USB 1843
13191.00	St Lys, France	FFL	USB 1604 1722
13191.00	Varna, Bulgaria	LZW	USB 0706 0710 1119
13194.00	Coast stations ch 40 dup. 12347.0kHz		USB (Portuguese 0903 1120 2137)
13197.00	Coast stations ch 41 dup. 12350.0kHz		USB
13197.00	Odessa, Ukraine	UUI	USB 0640 0755 0804 1634
13199.90	Spa Publications		

13200-13260
AERONAUTICAL MOBILE MAINLY MILITARY

kHz.	Station	Call	Mode / Heard/Times GMT
13201.00	USAF Anderson AFB, Guam		USB 0825
13201.00	USAF Croughton, UK		USB 1818
13201.00	USAF Elmendorf, Alaska		USB 0729
13201.00	USAF Hickham AFB, Hawaii		USB
13201.00	USAF McClellan AFB		USB 0543 0726 1624 1725 2215
13201.00	USAF Thule, Greenland		USB 1457 1814
13205.00	Berne (in-flight R/T service)	HEE	USB 1430
13207.00	R Australian Air Force		USB
13209.00	UNID		USB simplex R/T (Dutch) 2128
13210.00	USAF MacDill AFB		USB
13213.70	Egyptian Embassy traffic		SITOR 5 let grps 1657
13214.00	USAF Andrews AFB		USB 0908 2150
13214.00	USAF Croughton, UK		USB wx 1726
13214.00	USAF Incirlik, Turkey		USB 1030 1456
13214.00	USAF Lajes, Azores		USB 1017 1521
13217.00	USAF Andrews AFB		USB (VIP channel)
13220.00	Aeroflot Company frequency		USB 0816 1104

kHz.	Station	Call	Mode / Heard/Times GMT
13225.00	Alia Jordan Company frequency		USB 0818 1354 1621
13237.00	British Military	MQS	USB test call 0945 & CW MQS1 with MQS2 0947
13241.00	USAF		USB 0546 Skyking msg 2301
13244.00	USAF Lajes, Azores		USB 1625
13244.00	USAF MacDill AFB		USB 2119 2320
13245.50	Japanese Air Force		USB (Jap AF001 with Jap AF002 in Eng, then Japanese) 0850
13248.00	German Air Force		USB (in Eng) 0911 1725
13250.00	Swedish Air Force		USB (on Bosnian relief flight) 1501
13251.00	RNZAF		USB (Auckland & McMurdo Sound)
13252.00	Numbers Station		AM Slav (female voice) 1025
13257.00	Canadian Military, St John's		USB 2001
13259.90	Spa Publications		

13260-13360
AERONAUTICAL MOBILE (MAINLY CIVIL) 3KHz channels

kHz.	Station	Call	Mode / Heard/Times GMT
13261.00	Central E Pacific Air traffic CEP 1/2		USB
13264.00	Shannon VOLMET	EINN	USB 1049 1407 1644 1736 1833 2136
13267.00	Miami, USA	KJY74	USB (Hurricane hunters ch "GOLF") "42" at 39.29N 68.25W 2200
13270.00	Gander VOLMET		USB 0948 1026 1158 1452 1525 1746 2127
13270.00	New York VOLMET		USB 0733 0842 1031 1147 1408 1743 1834 2133 2217
13273.00	Africa Air traffic AFI 2		USB
13278.50	CIS VOLMET channel		USB (in English) 0824 1423
13282.00	Auckland VOLMET	NZZA	USB 0820
13282.00	Hong Kong VOLMET		USB 1516 1615 1821 1916 1922 2118
13282.00	Honolulu VOLMET	PHZH	USB 0731
13285.00	St John's (in-flight R/T service)		USB "Rainbow Radio" 1504 1744 1921
13285.00	UNID		USB Volmet (Eng) probably Far East 0756
13288.00	Europe Air traffic EUR A		USB
13288.00	Africa & Mid East Air traffic AFI 3 MID 2		USB
13291.00	N Atlantic Air traffic NAT B & D		USB
13291.00	Gander ATC, Canada	CZQX	USB 1345 1435 1505 1559
13291.00	New York ATC, USA	KZNY	USB 1639
13291.00	Shanwick ATC, UK/Eire	EGGX	USB 1346
13294.00	Africa & N Pacific Air traffic AFI 4 NP		USB
13294.00	Brazzaville ATC, Congo	FCCC	USB 1857
13297.00	Caribbean Air traffic CAR A		USB
13297.00	S America Air traffic SAM		USB
13300.00	Central W Pacific Air traffic CWP 1/2		USB
13300.00	Tokyo ATC, Japan	RJTG	USB
13303.00	N Central Asia Air traffic NCA 3		USB
13304.00	El Al Company frequency		USB 0654 0801 0821 0918 0949
13306.00	Indian Ocean Air traffic INO 1		USB
13306.00	N Atlantic Air traffic NAT A & C		USB
13306.00	Gander ATC, Canada	CZQX	USB 1506 1527 1833
13306.00	New York ATC, USA	KZNY	USB 1421 1458 1629 1745 1821
13306.00	Santa Maria ATC, Azores	LPAZ	USB 1244 1313 1355 1405
13306.00	Shanwick ATC, UK/Eire	EGGX	USB 1839
13309.00	E & S E Asia Air traffic EA 2 SEA 1		USB
13309.00	Bangkok ATC, Thailand	VTBB	USB 1447
13309.00	Hong Kong ATC	VHHK	USB 0925 1358 1449
13310.00	French Military, Paris	RFFA	72ARQ/E/4 2218
13315.00	S Atlantic Air traffic SAT 2		USB
13318.00	S E Asia Air traffic SEA 1/3		USB
13318.00	Hong Kong ATC	VHHK	USB 1823
13324.00	LTU Airline Company frequency		USB (Duesseldorf) 0852 1331 1823
13327.00	Iberia Company frequency		USB 0744 1026 2129
13327.00	Lufthansa Company frequency		USB Frankfurt 0950
13330.00	New York (in-flight R/T service)		USB 0746 0837 2128
13330.00	South African Airlines company frequency		USB 1559
13333.00	British Airways Company frequency		USB 0655 0835 2132 (with BA 11) 1617
13339.00	N Pacific Air traffic NP		USB
13339.00	Saudi Airline Company frequency		USB "Saudia 7668" clg Jeddah 1754
13342.00	Honolulu (in-flight R/T service)		USB
13342.00	Stockholm (in-flight R/T service)		USB 0632 0746 1048 1236 1509 (with Japan Air Force 002) 0854
13347.70	Egyptian Embassy traffic		SITOR 1354 1424 1637 1750
13348.00	San Francisco (in-flight R/T service)		USB 1901
13351.00	Ostend (in-flight R/T service)		USB 0732
13351.00	St Lys (in flight R/T service)		USB 1247 1435 1746
13356.00	Cuban Embassy Traffic	CLP	50n 5 fig grp msg (to African embassies) 2220
13357.00	Africa & S Atlantic Air traffic AFI 1 SAT 1		USB
13357.00	Dakar ATC, Senegal	GOOO	USB 1051

kHz.	Station	Call	Mode / Heard/Times GMT
13359.90	Spa Publications		

13360-13410
FIXED & RADIO ASTRONOMY

kHz.	Station	Call	Mode / Heard/Times GMT
13360.00	UNID		USB Russian wx info 0933
13366.00	Nairobi Air, Kenya	5YD	50n 1451 1646 1738 1831 2133 (freq varies)
13372.70	Nairobi Air, Kenya	5YD	50n 0639 1436 1808 2045 2057
13374.50	UNID		96ARQ/E/8 0920 1028
13375.00	Numbers Station		USB Eng (female voice) 1531 1630 "Lincolnshire Poacher" 1503
13375.50	UNID		96ARQ/E/8 Idle 0641
13380.00	Hungarian Embassy traffic		125DUP-ARQ 1601 5 let grps 1454
13395.30	Serbian Embassy traffic	DFZG	75n p/lang then encrypted 1108
13399.00	Serbian Embassy traffic	DFZG	75n RYs 1359 p/lang Slav 1409 1438 1446 1610 Eng 1505
13401.70	Egyptian Embassy traffic		SITOR 1506 Selcal TVXX 0949
13409.90	Spa Publications		

13410-13600
FIXED & MOBILE

kHz.	Station	Call	Mode / Heard/Times GMT
13413.00	Bulgarian Embassy traffic	DOR	75n p/lang 1031
13415.10	Dutch Embassy traffic	PCW1	SITOR 1642 2043 2100 2204
13420.00	UNID		75n 5 Let grps 1033
13421.00	Polish Embassy traffic		100POL-ARQ p/lang 0921
13423.00	Numbers Station		AM Eng (female voice) 1824
13425.00	Bulgarian Embassy traffic		75n msg to several embassies
13425.00	Italian Embassy traffic		USB 1052
13425.20	Italian Embassy traffic		SITOR 0826 1259
13430.00	R Moscow feeder		USB Slav 1836 2207
13440.00	Belgrade Press (TANJUG)	YZJ5	50r Eng 0858 0923 1054 1300 1358 1457 1531 (0400-1700)
13444.30	UNID		100ARQ/E3/8 Idle 1508
13459.00	UNID		USB Scandinavian lang simplex R/T 0924
13467.00	Polish Embassy traffic		100POL-ARQ 5 fig grps 1411
13470.00	Moscow Met, Russia	RKU71	FAX wx maps 0804 1055 1159 1400 1500 1648 1809
13479.50	UNID		200ARQ/M2/4 Idle 1056
13480.00	Numbers Station		USB Eng (male voice)
13481.70	Egyptian Embassy traffic		SITOR 0641 1440
13496.00	Danish Embassy traffic		SITOR p/lang 1058
13508.50	UNID		USB feeder (Eng, with Australian accents) 1417
13510.00	Halifax Met, Canada	CFH	75r 1035 1059 1155 1301 1644 1740 1837 2058
13510.00	Halifax Met, Canada	CFH	FAX wx maps 1412 1509 1616 1810 2134
13515.00	RAF Akrotiri, Cyprus	MKD	50r (VFT) QBF & RYIs 0808 0926 1053 1818 2044 (LSB 13518.0)
13520.00	INTERPOL	FSB	SITOR 1742 Selcal IPEC 1100
13522.00	Numbers Station		AM Slav (male voice) 2045
13524.00	Baghdad Press (INA)	YIO	50r Eng 1617
13526.00	Grengel Met, Germany	DHJ51	100n 0701 0927 1532
13530.00	Moscow Met, Russia	RVW53	50r 0642 0703 0809 0931 1302 1401
13533.00	Numbers Station		USB "EZI" (female voice) 1403
13538.50	Pretoria, RSA	ZRO3	FAX wx maps
13544.00	Polish Embassy traffic		100POL-ARQ 5 fig grps 1101
13544.00	UNID		CW 5 fig grps 0933
13546.00	UNID	Z4D	CW (clg "P6Z") 1511 (probably French)
13548.00	UNID		192FEC-A Fr p/lang 0842
13550.00	Auckland Met, N Zealand	ZKLF	CW wx p/lang 0840 0901 1811 2045
13550.00	Auckland Met, N Zealand	ZKLF	FAX wx maps 1502
13551.00	UNID	RBPP	50n (clg RBCY) RYs & Russian ATC msgs UWWBOH/UNIIOH 0930
13555.00	Numbers Station		USB Eng (female voice) 1202 1627
13560.00	Taipei Met, Taiwan	BMB	CW 1538 1839 2135
13561.00	Ankara Press (AA)		50r Eng 0939
13563.00	Taiwan Press (CNA)	3MA22	50r Eng 0828 1259 1404 1429
13566.00	RAF Akrotiri, Cyprus	MKD	50r (VFT) QBF & RYIs 0704 0934 1812 2129 2205 (LSB 13568.7)
13571.00	Swiss Embassy traffic	HBD	SITOR p/lang Ger 0736 0817 5 let grps 1620 1738
13571.10	Russian Amateur	UA1TAN	LSB clg "CQ Contest" (in Eng) 0832 (tx way off beam !!)
13574.00	French Embassy traffic	U3H	192FEC-A test call with RYs then 5 let grp msg to RFGW 1406
13580.00	Pyongyang Press (KCNA)	HMF36	50r Eng 2130
13582.00	UNID	DEA47	CW 0644 0705 0935 1054 1110 (rptd German propagation tests)
13590.00	R Pakistan		AM Eng 1628
13595.00	AWR		AM Asian lang (ID in Eng) 1500
13597.40	Rome Met, Italy	IMB56	FAX wx maps 0936 1435 2127

kHz.	Station	Call	Mode / Heard/Times GMT

13600-13800
INTERNATIONAL BROADCASTING

kHz.	Station	Call	Mode / Heard/Times GMT
13600.00	R Prague		AM Eng 0742 1505
13605.00	R Australia		AM Eng 0932 0942 1100 1125 Chinese 1300
13609.50	Tunis Press (TAP)	3VF40	50r Fr 1355 1524
13610.00	Deutsche Welle		AM Eng 0619 Fr 0700 Ger 2105 2131
13615.00	WEWN, USA		AM Eng 2135
13615.00	Monitor Radio International		AM Eng 0831 0846
13615.00	R Moscow		AM Eng 0832 1112
13620.00	R Kuwait		AM Eng 1804 1840 Arab 1746
13620.00	R Moscow		AM Eng 1058 Fr 1647
13625.00	R Moscow		AM Slav 1101 1301
13625.00	Monitor Radio International		AM Eng 1028 1055 1506
13635.00	R Swiss International		AM Eng 1104 1126 1502 Fr 1749 Ital 0701 1825 Ger 1600
13635.80	Single Letter Beacon	S	CW 1102 1507 2136
13636.00	Single Letter Beacon	D	CW 1600
13636.10	Single Letter Beacon	C	CW 1035 1439 2047 2133
13640.00	R Croatia		AM Eng 2110
13640.00	R France International		AM Eng 1201 1254
13650.00	R Canada International		AM Eng 2106 2117
13650.00	R Moscow		AM Eng 0752 0812 1021 1105 Fr 1814
13653.00	Cairo Press (MENA)	SUA	75r Fr 1006 2126
13655.00	R Vlaanderen International		AM Dutch 2207
13660.00	BBC		AM Slav 1100 Arab 1633 1826
13660.00	R Havana		AM Span 2132
13661.30	UNID		50n West African meteo rpts 0707
13670.00	R Canada International		AM Eng 2048 2107 2118 2210 Fr 2134
13670.00	R Bulgaria		AM Eng 1755 1815
13670.00	R Korea		AM Eng 0804
13675.00	R Dubai		AM Eng 1030 1611 1624
13680.00	Deutsche Welle		AM Eng 1624
13680.00	R Moscow		AM Eng 0807 1202 Fr 0934 1603 Portuguese 2212
13685.00	R Swiss International		AM Eng 1325 Ger 1007 Ital 0844
13690.00	Deutsche Welle		AM Eng 2108 2133 Ger 1333 1440 1648
13690.00	VOA		AM Eng 1812
13695.00	WYFR, USA		AM Eng 0725 1302
13700.00	R Netherland		AM Eng 1431 1534 1559 Dutch 0813 1816 2135 Fr 2049
13707.00	Almaty Met, Kazakhstan		FAX wx maps 1032
13710.00	R Moscow		AM Eng 1647
13710.00	VOA		AM Eng 1634 1754 1826 1900 2109 2136
13715.00	Slovak Radio		AM Slav 1304
13725.00	R Moscow		AM Eng 2111 2211
13730.00	R Austria International		AM Eng 0753 0834 1442 2144 Ger 0702 0944 1106 1441 1817
13745.00	BBC		AM Eng 0922 Slav 1629
13750.00	Kol Israel		AM Hebrew 1535 1650
13755.00	R Australia		AM Eng 1256 1303 1432 1455 1510 1543 1620 1748
13760.00	WHRI, USA		AM Eng 1755 2135 2213 (1700-2400)
13766.00	Taiwan Press (CNA)	3MA	CW & FAX
13770.00	R Netherland		AM Dutch 0618 1503
13770.00	Monitor Radio International		AM Eng 1107 1438 2050 2120 Ger 2136
13780.00	Pyongyang Press (KCNA)	HMF84	50n Eng 1531
13780.00	Deutsche Welle		AM Ger 0706 0835 1008 1203 1442 1536 2212
13785.00	R Pyongyang		AM Eng 1511 (1500-1550) Ger 2147
13790.00	Deutsche Welle		AM Eng 0619 0647 Ger 1445 Portuguese 2137
13799.90	Spa Publications		

13800-1400
FIXED & LAND MOBILE

kHz.	Station	Call	Mode / Heard/Times GMT
13803.00	Khabarovsk Met, Russia	RCR78	50r 1433
13804.50	UNID		SITOR Idle 0838
13815.00	US Embassy frequency (rptd London)	KRH50	CW 1127
13820.00	R Moscow feeder		USB Slav 1009 1108 1444 2148
13830.00	R Croatia		AM Slav 1512 1651 1800 1829
13835.00	R Iceland		USB Icelandic 1205 1257
13839.50	British Military	GXQ	50r(VFT) QBF & RYIs 2216 (LSB ch 13842.5)
13840.00	Monitor Radio International		AM Eng 2121
13845.00	WWCR, USA		AM Eng 1445 1606 1652 2138 2213
13855.00	Turkish Embassy traffic	TAD	144FEC-A p/lang Eng (abt Danish conference) 0838
13856.00	UNID		50n p/lang Eng (North Korean origin ??) 0735
13864.00	Turkish Embassy traffic	TAD	144FEC-A p/lang 0712 (Eng) 0649
13872.00	Polish Embassy traffic		100POL-ARQ 5 fig grps 0949 1620

kHz.	Station	Call	Mode / Heard/Times GMT
13875.50	Hungarian Embassy traffic		125DUP-ARQ 5 fig grps 0651 p/lang 1309
13877.00	UNID		CW 5 fig grps 1447
13880.00	RAF London	MKD	50n (VFT) QBF & RYIs 1506 (LSB ch 13883.0)
13882.50	Hamburg (Quickborn) Met, Germany		FAX wx maps 0932 1010
13895.00	Turkish Embassy traffic	TAD	144FEC p/lang Eng 1448
13896.50	UNID		96ARQ/E/8 Idle 0845 1041
13913.00	Turkish Embassy traffic	TAD	144FEC p/lang 1607
13920.00	Canberra Met, Australia	AXM35	FAX wx maps 0722 0833 1617 1718 1852 2120 2218
13926.00	RAF London	MKD	50n (VFT) QBF & RYIs 1507 (LSB ch 13929.0)
13933.00	Turkish Embassy traffic	TAD	144FEC p/lang 1447
13938.00	Bulgarian Embassy traffic	DOR	150n nx in Bulgarian 0848 (150Bd very rare)
13941.50	Tunisian Embassy traffic	NQ1	SITOR Mode B 5 let grps 1102 1449
13947.00	Tashkent Met, Uzbekistan		FAX wx maps 0736 0840 1129
13952.50	Canadian MARS		USB phonepatch tfc 1515
13966.30	International Red Cross traffic	HBC	SITOR msg N'Djamena/Geneva 0807
13996.50	Khartoum Air, Sudan	STK	50r 1615 1708 1722 1936 2122 2315
13999.90	Spa Publications		

14000-14350
AMATEUR RADIO

kHz.	Station	Call	Mode / Heard/Times GMT
14060.00	UNID		81Bd spec code type 1116
14089.70	Amateur Packet Radio	RK3P	300Bd (to DK0MWX) 0845 (to SM5BKI) 1522
14091.00	Amateur Packet Radio	UZ1AWT	300Bd 0951
14091.90	Amateur Packet Radio	I6KL	300Bd CQ call 1635
14092.00	Amateur Packet Radio	TA2EM	300Bd 1510
14093.10	Amateur Packet Radio	YU1DP	300Bd (to PA3FDT) 0810
14094.70	Amateur Packet Radio	UZ4FXT	300Bd (to RB4VWA) 1436
14097.10	Amateur Packet Radio	CT1XK	300Bd (to OH2BAR) 0953 (to EA3BBD) 1611
14098.00	Amateur Packet Radio	OH2BAR	300Bd (to HA3TK) 1511
14099.30	Amateur Packet Radio	EA8AOP	300Bd (to EA5HX) 1524
14099.50	Amateur Packet Radio	CT1REP	300Bd (to CU1AF) 1804
14100.00	Amateur Radio Beacon, Stanford, USA	W6WX/B	CW
14103.30	Amateur Packet Radio	SM2TEZ	300Bd (to EA3BBD) 1527 (to SM2IRZ) 1831
14104.80	Amateur Packet Radio	CU6NS	300Bd (to CT1JQ) 1832
14105.80	Amateur Packet Radio	EA8IY	300Bd (to EA4AUU) 0847
14107.50	Amateur Packet Radio	CU2ARA	300Bd (to EA5RQ) 1734
14109.40	Amateur Packet Radio	LA2K	300Bd (to LA9OCA) 1736
14111.00	Amateur Packet Radio	UT4UX	300Bd (to I5SGG) 0927
14113.00	Amateur Packet Radio	LZ2XA	300Bd (to IK7NXQ) 1132
14117.30	Amateur Packet Radio	UA3ZU	300Bd (to SM7TDC) 1119
14135.00	UNID		81Bd spec code type 0929
14141.00	UNID		81Bd spec code type 0850 0955
14160.00	UNID		40Bd spec code type 0930
14171.00	UNID		50Bd spec code type 0701
14240.00	R Rossiya (Russian Regional)		AM Slav/pop music 1526 1833 (harmonic of 7120kHz)
14286.00	UNID		81Bd spec code type 0812
14325.00	Emergency Net - Hurricanes		USB (monitored each season)
14349.90	Spa Publications		

14350-14990
FIXED & MOBILE

kHz.	Station	Call	Mode / Heard/Times GMT
14356.00	Bracknell Met, UK	GFL24	50r 0633 1505 1608 1739
14359.00	Polish Embassy traffic	SNN299	75n p/lang Polish 0713 ID & RYs 1607
14360.00	US Embassy frequency (rptd Athens)	KWS78	CW 1121 1744
14367.00	Beijing Met, China	BAF8	FAX wx maps 0936
14367.00	Beijing Press (XINHUA)	BZP54	75r Eng 0634 0737 0807 0854 1122
14374.00	USMARS	AGA1AH	300Bd packet net (with AFA7ML in Azores) 1746 (with CUW20) 1749
14376.00	Beijing Press (XINHUA)	BZT34	50r Russ 0816 (ID prints as NUB34)
14381.00	British Military	GXQ	50r (VFT) QBF & RYIs 1615 (LSB 14384.0)
14387.00	Bulgarian Embassy traffic	DOR	75n p/lang 0855 0937
14396.40	USAF Croughton, UK	EGWR	75n air meteo 1507
14405.00	RAF Akrotiri, Cyprus	MKD	50r (VFT) QBF & RYIs 0808 1748 1834 (LSB 14408.0)
14410.00	Portuguese Naval	RPTI	50r ID & RYs 0728
14410.00	R Moscow feeder		LSB + USB Eng 1656
14420.00	French Military, Dakar	RFTJ	72ARQ/E/4 1513 1612
14436.00	Bracknell Met, UK	GFA	FAX wx maps 1741
14445.00	RAF London	MKK	50r (VFT) QBF & RYIs 1540 1637 (LSB ch 14448.0)
14452.00	Pyongyang Press (KCNA)	HMF	50r Eng 0809
14452.50	MARS (Canadian Forces)		USB (VXV9/CIW301) 1658
14455.00	Jeddah Met, Saudi Arabia		50n 1512

kHz.	Station	Call	Mode / Heard/Times GMT
14460.00	R Moscow feeder		USB (World Service Eng) 0856
14461.50	MARS (Canadian Forces)		USB (in French) 1706
14467.30	Hamburg (Quickborn) Met, Germany	DDH8	50r ID & RYs 1517
14480.00	Slovak Embassy traffic		100n msg Bratislava to several embassies 0943
14482.00	UNID		48ARQ/E3/8 Idle 0807 0939 1707
14487.20	UNID		200ARQ/M2/4 0938
14497.50	Santa Maria Air, Azores	CSY	50n 0941 1451 1515 1639 1744 1750 (freq varies)
14508.00	Sal Air, Cape Verde	D4B	50n wx (GVAC) 1812
14518.00	Austrian Embassy traffic		96SI-ARQ(5 characters) p/lang 0821 1518
14524.00	Swedish Embassy traffic		100SWED-ARQ(long) 5 let grps 1520
14526.00	VOA feeder		USB & LSB Slav 1751 1814
14540.00	RAF London	MKK	50r(VFT) QBF & RYls 0811 (LSB ch 14543.0)
14546.50	Italian Embassy traffic		SITOR 5 let grps 0725 1104 p/lang 1414 Selcal VXQQ 1352
14556.00	CIS Naval	RIW	CW ID 1745
14560.00	Amman Press (PETRA)	JYF2	50r Eng 0812
14564.00	Nicosia, Cyprus	5BA	USB (dup. 16326.0) 0810 0831 1522 1610 1815
14573.00	Tripoli Press (JANA)		50r Arab 0945 1640 1745
14578.00	French Military, Beirut	RFFXL	72ARQ/E/4 1516 1821
14585.80	French Military		200ARQ/M2/4 1823
14598.00	UNID		200ARQ/M2/4 ch A long 5 let grp msg "RFFTD 21") 0833
14602.00	RAF Akrotiri, Cyprus	MKD	50r (VFT) QBF & RYls 1621 (LSB 14605.5)
14626.60	UNID		192ARQ/E3/8 Idle 0812 1825
14639.00	Polish Embassy traffic		100POL-ARQ 5 fig grps & p/lang 1036
14641.00	Spanish Naval	EBA	CW Span wx 1709
14642.00	UN traffic		SITOR 0946 1748
14645.00	Stockholm (in-flight R/T service)		USB 0645
14654.50	Warsaw, Poland	SPW	SITOR 1037 1247 1435 1749 2127 Mode B tfc list 0900
14656.00	Warsaw, Poland	SPW	USB 0813 0948 1453 1517 2215
14663.50	USMARS		USB 1039
14668.00	UNID		72ARQ/E/4 Idle 2129
14670.00	Canadian Time Station, Ottawa	CHU	USB (Eastern Standard Time each min) 1454 1544 1809
14670.00	French Military	RFFVAT	200ARQ/M2/4 ch A 5 let grps 1519
14674.00	Serbian Embassy traffic	DFZG	75n p/lang Eng press rpts 1526 1613 Slav 1455
14679.00	Polish Embassy traffic		100POL-ARQ 5 fig grps 1041
14685.00	Taiwan Press (CNA)	3MA	CW & FAX
14692.50	Tokyo Met, Japan	JMJ	FAX wx maps 0817
14699.00	Baghdad Press (INA)	YIX	50r Arab 0637 1456 1759
14750.00	Numbers Station		AM "MIW2" (female voice) 1520
14754.00	UNID		72ARQ/E/4 Idle 2132
14760.10	Rabat Press (MAP)	CNM61	50r Fr 1042
14764.00	Bahrain Press (GNA)		75r Eng 1521 1528 Arab 0638 0818
14776.80	Portuguese Naval	RPTI	75r QBF RYs & SGs 1522
14785.80	Indian Govt Press service	ATP65	50n Eng 1453 Fr 1530 (msrd also 14785.0 & 14784.5)
14808.00	British Military	GXQ	50r (VFT) QBF & RYls 1234 (LSB ch 14011.0)
14821.70	Egyptian Embassy traffic		SITOR 1045
14838.50	USMARS		USB "ZTI" (with "CYC" & "CUX") 2134
14880.00	Tokyo Met, Japan	JMG4	50r 0820 1803
14901.00	UNID		CW "CQ DE A4I QSX 01" 0823
14912.00	Serbian Embassy traffic	DFZG	75n p/lang Eng press reports 1615
14926.70	French Military		192ARQ/E3/8 p/lang (abt UN action in Bosnia) 1523
14931.50	Algiers Press (APS)		50n Span 1531
14936.50	USMARS (Navy)	NNNOCRW	SITOR msgs from USS "GUAM" 1532
14941.00	Turkish Embassy traffic	TAD	144FEC-A 5 let grps 1539
14950.00	R Moscow feeder		USB Slav 1753 1804
14956.00	Turkish Embassy traffic	TAD	144FEC p/lang 1049
14964.00	French Military, Bangui	RFFX	72ARQ/E/4 1542
14982.50	Tashkent Met, Uzbekistan	RBV76	FAX wx maps 1525 1545 1805
14989.00	Brazzaville Air, Congo	TNL77	96ARQ/M2/4 Ch B aireps & ship OBS 1755
14989.90	Spa Publications		

14990-15010
STANDARD FREQUENCY & TIME SIGNALS

kHz.	Station	Call	Mode / Heard/Times GMT
14991.70	Egyptian Embassy traffic		SITOR 1459
14996.00	Moscow Time Station	RWM	CW 1439 1544
15000.00	Fort Collins Time Station, USA	WWV	USB/CW 1747 2220
15000.00	Tokyo Time Station, Japan	JJY	USB/CW
15004.00	Irkutsk Time Station, Russia	RID	CW 1548
15009.90	Spa Publications		

15010-15100
AERONAUTICAL MOBILE (MAINLY MILITARY)

kHz.	Station	Call	Mode / Heard/Times GMT
15010.00	Voice of Vietnam		AM Eng 1605 1817 Fr 1314 1831 (freq varies to 15009.0)
15011.70	Egyptian Embassy traffic		SITOR 0944 1525
15015.00	USAF Albrook AFB, Panama		USB 2224
15015.00	USAF Ascension Island		USB 0912 1807
15015.00	USAF Croughton, UK		USB 1142 1622
15015.00	USAF Incirlik, Turkey		USB 0748 0902 1534 1652 1809
15015.00	USAF Lajes, Azores		USB 0945 1057 1611 1823 2224
15015.00	USAF MacDill AFB, USA		USB 1625 2204
15015.00	USAF McClellan AFB, USA		USB
15015.00	USAF Offut, USA		USB "Skyking" msg 2253
15016.70	Egyptian Embassy traffic		SITOR 1442
15020.00	All India Radio		AM Asian lang 1445
15030.00	Radio for Peace International		USB Eng 2203 2222
15035.00	Canadian Military, Edmonton		USB wx 1440 1532 1632 2223 2237
15041.70	Egyptian Embassy traffic		SITOR 1556
15046.00	Berne (in-flight R/T service)		USB 1832
15050.00	All India Radio		AM Eng 1016 1053 Arabic 1153
15060.00	R Riyadh, Saudi Arabia		AM Arab 0947 1350 1444
15070.00	BBC		AM Eng 0829 1030 1549 1848 1925 2205 2256
15075.00	All India Radio		AM Eng 1833
15080.00	VOA		AM Eng 0619
15084.00	R Tehran		AM Farsi 0653 1154 1533
15090.00	R Vatican		AM Eng 0642 0655 1551 1608
15095.00	R Damascus		AM Eng 2204 Arab 1650
15099.90	Spa Publications		

15100-15600
INTERNATIONAL BROADCASTING

kHz.	Station	Call	Mode / Heard/Times GMT
15100.00	R China International		AM Fr 1807 1843 2054
15105.00	Deutsche Welle		AM Eng 1600 Ger 0656 0911
15105.00	R Moscow		AM Eng 1413
15105.00	WHRI		AM Eng 1720
15110.00	REE Spain		AM Span 0903 1913 2223
15115.00	R Svoboda		AM Slav 1514 1545 1601
15125.00	AWR		AM Eng 1624
15125.00	R Moscow		AM Eng 0620 0732 1205 1316 1414
15130.00	R China International		AM Eng 1636
15135.00	BBC		AM Eng 0720
15135.00	Deutsche Welle		AM Eng 2103 Ger 1515 1710 1730
15140.00	All India Radio		AM Slav 1625
15140.00	R Veritas Asia		AM Eng ID 1553
15140.00	R Moscow		AM Eng 0617 0733 0904 1206
15145.00	Deutsche Welle		AM Eng 1505 1520 1626
15150.00	R Netherland		AM Eng 1542 1556
15150.00	R Moscow		AM Eng 0904
15160.00	VOA		AM Eng 1317
15170.00	R Australia		AM Eng 1043
15175.00	R Moscow		AM Eng 1031 1208 1602
15180.00	R Moscow		AM Eng 0627
15180.00	R Ukraine International		AM Eng (0000-0100)
15185.00	Deutsche Welle		AM Eng 0636
15185.00	VOA		AM Eng 2226
15190.00	R Moscow		AM Eng 0831 2205 2257 Ger 1032 1101
15195.00	R Ukraine International		AM Eng (0000-0100) Slav 0737 1825 2206
15205.00	VOA		AM Eng 1449 1543 1611 1721 1850
15210.00	R Moscow		AM Eng 0840 0954 1102 1156 Fr 1545
15210.00	R Vatican		AM Ital 1209
15215.00	R Svoboda		AM Slav 0659 0735 0859 1547
15220.00	BBC		AM Eng 1110
15220.00	R Golos Rossii		AM Russian 0959
15230.00	R Denmark (via Norway)		AM Danish 1653
15230.00	R Moscow		AM Eng 0841
15240.00	R Channel Africa, S Africa		AM Eng 1637 1644
15240.00	R Sweden		AM Eng 1450
15245.00	VOA		AM Eng 1637 Arab 1852
15255.00	VOA		AM Eng 1421 1543 1655
15260.00	BBC		AM Eng 1536 2208 2226
15260.00	R Tehran		AM Ger 1752 1826 Fr 1838
15260.00	R Canada International		AM Fr 1850
15265.00	R Moscow		AM Eng 1001 2305
15265.00	R Brazil		AM Ger 1931
15270.00	HCJB, Ecuador		AM Eng 0735
15275.00	Deutsche Welle		AM Ger 0912 1202 1517 1544 1811 2109
15280.00	BBC		AM Eng 2306

kHz.	Station	Call	Mode / Heard/Times GMT
15280.00	R Moscow		AM Eng 0643 0701 0735 0900 1103 1209
15290.00	R Moscow		AM Eng 1615 1723 1810 2110 2230
15290.00	R Svoboda		AM Slav 0632
15300.00	R France International		AM Fr 1638
15305.00	R Moscow		AM Eng 0710
15305.00	VOA		AM Eng 2210
15310.00	BBC		AM Eng 1109
15315.00	R Abu Dhabi		AM Eng 2228 2309
15315.00	R Canada International		AM Eng 1443
15315.00	R Netherland		AM Dutch 2111 2201
15320.00	R Australia		AM Eng 0702 2242 (2030-0800)
15320.00	R Dubai		AM Eng 1605 1623
15320.00	R Moscow		AM Eng 0737 0858 1543
15325.00	R Canada International		AM Eng 1445 1714 2112 Ukrainian 1856 Fr 1915
15330.00	R Finland		AM Eng 0903 0914
15335.00	RTV Morocco		AM Arab 1724 2240
15345.00	R Moscow		AM Eng 0832 0925 1034 1104 1446
15350.00	Deutsche Welle		AM Eng 2114
15355.00	WYFR, USA		AM Eng 1606 1916 Ger 1639 1715 Italian 1857
15360.00	Deutsche Welle		AM Eng 1652 2115
15380.00	R Moscow		AM Eng 0833 0904 1447
15395.00	VOA		AM Eng 1516 1607 1633
15400.00	BBC		AM Eng 1018 1728 1859 1932 2213 2311
15400.00	R Moscow		AM Eng 1105
15410.00	R Austria International		AM Eng 0739 Ger 0720
15410.00	VOA		AM Eng 1842 1900 (1600-2200)
15420.00	BBC		AM Eng 1654
15420.00	R Moscow		AM Eng 0620 0712
15435.00	R Moscow		AM Eng 0905
15440.00	R Finland		AM Eng 1831
15440.00	R Moscow		AM Eng 0825 1015 1112 1200
15445.00	VOA		AM Eng 1608 1717
15450.00	R Austria International		AM Eng 0834 1035 1053 Ger 1213
15455.00	R Moscow		AM Eng 1424 Span 2219
15465.00	R Moscow		AM Eng 0726 1107 1517 1544
15470.00	R Moscow		AM Eng 0906 1214
15475.00	Africa No 1, Gabon		AM Fr 1610 1843
15480.00	R Moscow		AM Eng 1526
15485.00	R Moscow		AM Eng 1918
15505.00	R Swiss International		AM Eng 1856
15525.00	R Moscow		AM Eng 0713 0820 1901 2312
15540.00	R Moscow		AM Eng 0927 1519 1545 Ger 1105
15544.00	Beijing Press (XINHUA)	BZS	75r Eng 0706 1216 ID & RYs 1426
15550.00	R Moscow		AM Eng 0916 1037 1108 1520
15555.00	R Pakistan		AM Eng 1620 (also msrd 15550.1 at 1730 1750)
15566.00	WYFR, USA		AM Eng 2116 2150
15566.50	Novosibirsk Met, Russia		50r 0708 0929
15575.00	BBC		AM Eng 0645 0710 1019 1106 1217 1428
15580.00	R Ukraine International		AM Eng (0000-0100)
15580.00	VOA		AM Eng 1902
15590.00	KTBN, USA		AM Eng 1718 1752
15590.00	R Moscow		AM Eng 0715 0727 0821
15599.90	Spa Publications		

15600-16360
FIXED

15610.00	KTWR, Guam		AM Eng 1542 1549
15617.00	Kol Israel		AM Fr 1043 Heb 1934 (freq varies 15614.3-15618.0)
15630.00	Voice of Greece		AM Eng 1531 (1530-1540) Greek 1719
15640.00	Kol Israel		AM Eng 1902
15650.00	Kol Israel		AM Eng 1905
15650.00	Voice of Greece		AM Eng 0747 1532 1848
15654.90	Rabat Press (MAP)	CNM29	50r Eng 1218 (1200-1400) Fr 1543 1615 1635 (1000-1130 1330-1700)
15665.00	Monitor Radio International		AM Eng 1429 1450 1526 1850 1904 2122 2222
15676.00	Hungarian Embassy traffic		125DUP-ARQ 5 let grps 1059 p/lang Eng 1217
15681.50	UNID		SITOR Selcal VQMY (probably Italian Embassy) 1056
15685.00	WWCR, USA		AM Eng 1522 1544 1611 1700 1906
15695.00	WEWN, USA		AM Eng 1907
15705.00	Belgrade Press (TANJUG)	YZJ6	50r Fr 1100
15708.00	UNID		192FEC-A 5 let grps 1431
15731.10	Khartoum Press (SUNA)		50r Arab 1433 1525 (ID prints as "XTNB")
15770.00	R Iceland		USB Icelandic 1244
15817.00	RAF Akrotiri, Cyprus	MKD	50r (VFT) QBF & RYls 2223 (LSB 15820.0)

kHz.	Station	Call	Mode / Heard/Times GMT
15826.00	UNID		75n 5 let grps 1636
15845.00	Cairo Press (MENA)	SUA289	75r Arab 0920 1108 1435 1526
15873.00	UNID		192FEC 5 let grps 0923
15878.00	Taiwan Press (CNA)	3MA	CW ID & FAX 1504
15935.20	Cairo Press (MENA)	SUA291	75r Eng 1105 Fr 0925 1825
15942.00	Czech Embassy traffic		100n 5 fig grps & diplomatic news bulletin 0928
15950.00	Moscow Met, Russia	RBI77	FAX wx maps 0721 1044 1436 1545 1638
15950.00	Tokyo Time Station, Japan	JJD2	CW 1221
15959.00	US Naval	NAM	FAX wx maps
15964.00	Portishead (in-flight R/T service)		USB 1508 1542 1708
15970.50	US Embassy frequency (rptd Warrenton)	KKN50	CW 1437 1526 1827
16013.80	German Govt, press info service	DGQ	96FEC-A Ger p/lang 0855
16025.00	Bulgarian Embassy traffic	DOR	75n RYs & 5 fig grps 0930
16025.00	Beijing Met, China	BAF	FAX wx maps 0622
16040.00	RAF London	MKK	50r (VFT) QBF & RYIs 0731 (LSB 16043.0)
16062.70	Egyptian Embassy traffic		SITOR 1107
16067.00	Rome Press (ANSA)	IRO30	50n Eng 1704 1829
16077.50	French Military, Orleans	FDY	50r "Voyez le brick.." 0724
16103.70	Norwegian Embassy traffic		SITOR 0734
16111.00	Swiss Embassy traffic	HBD	SITOR p/lang Ger 1444
16136.00	Beijing Press (XINHUA)	BZR	75r Eng 0725 1048 1108 1322
16148.10	RAF Akrotiri, Cyprus	MKD	50r (VFT) QBF & RYIs 1706 1910 (LSB 16151.0)
16171.70	Egyptian Embassy traffic		SITOR 0736 1109
16173.50	USMARS		SITOR "NAP"/"NHA" 1832
16180.00	US Naval, Norfolk	NAM	CW 1530 1642 1836 1907
16183.00	Nairobi Met, Kenya	5YE	100r 1853 1913 2000
16193.10	French Military, Djibouti	RFQP	200ARQ/M2/4 p/lang 0739
16213.00	Polish Embassy traffic		100POL-ARQ p/lang 0624
16264.00	Turkish Embassy traffic	TAD	144FEC p/lang 1110
16265.00	Singapore Press (ANSA)	9VF206	50r Eng 1840 1854
16270.00	Singapore Press (KYODO)	9VF207	FAX (Japanese text) 0758
16273.00	Portishead (in-flight R/T service)		USB 1724
16275.00	British Military	GXQ	50r (VFT) QBF & RYIs 1855 (LSB 16278.0)
16280.00	RAF Akrotiri, Cyprus	MKD	50r (VFT) QBF & RYIs 0727 (LSB 16283.0)
16291.00	UNID		72ARQ/E/4 Idle 0750 0933 1112
16295.00	Serbian Embassy traffic	DFZG	75n p/lang 0627
16302.00	Serbian Embassy traffic	DFZG	75n p/lang Slav 0934 1446
16304.00	Czech Embassy traffic		100n p/lang 0752
16312.50	UNID	C37A	100n (clg 6XM8) with QBF test 1448
16318.70	Egyptian Embassy traffic		SITOR 0753
16321.70	Egyptian Embassy traffic		SITOR 1049
16323.00	Danish Naval	OVG16	CW 2002
16324.70	French Military, Douala	RFTJ	192ARQ/E3/8 1856
16339.50	UNID		96ARQ/E/4 Idle 0729 "QRU 1 PSE GA" 1500 "PLS QRX" 1518
16339.50	UNID		100r RYs "CJL PSE QSY 70" 0801
16340.10	Auckland Met, N Zealand	ZKLF	CW p/lang wx 0925
16340.10	Auckland Met, N Zealand	ZKLF	FAX wx maps 1829
16346.70	Egyptian Embassy traffic		SITOR 0728
16354.00	Nicosia, Cyprus	5BA	USB (listens 16504.0) 0623 1050 1246
16355.00	Czech Embassy traffic		100n p/lang 0754
16359.90	Spa Publications		

16360-17410
MARITIME MOBILE

16360.00	Ships wkg ch 1 dup. 17242.0kHz		USB (to UDN) 0733 0753 1000 (to LPL) 2147
16363.00	Ships wkg ch 2 dup. 17245.0kHz		USB H3AT 1534 "HMS Broadsword" (GUUS) 2049
16366.00	Ships wkg ch 3 dup. 17248.0kHz		USB 1111 "Amarito" (P3DC5) 2126
16369.00	Ships wkg ch 4 dup. 17251.0kHz		USB 0726 1353 1508
16372.00	Indian Embassy traffic		50r 5 let grp msg Tehran/New Delhi 0912
16372.00	Ships wkg ch 5 dup. 17254.0kHz		USB (to URD) 1259 (to FFL) 1811
16375.00	Ships wkg ch 6 dup. 17257.0kHz		USB (to UAT) 0717 (to IAR) 1644
16378.00	Ships wkg ch 7 dup. 17260.0kHz		USB 1546 1857 A8WL (to SPC) 0729
16381.00	Ships wkg ch 8 dup. 17263.0kHz		USB C6KF2 1744
16384.00	Ships wkg ch 9 dup. 17266.0kHz		USB 2143 (to WOM) 2227
16384.00	UNID		50r Fr (about reunification of Korea) 1454
16387.00	Ships wkg ch 10 dup. 17269.0kHz		USB 1747
16390.00	Ships wkg ch 11 dup. 17272.0kHz		USB ZDAD9 0815
16393.00	Ships wkg ch 12 dup. 17275.0kHz		USB 0727 1114 1444
16396.00	Ships wkg ch 13 dup. 17278.0kHz		USB 1748
16399.00	Ships wkg ch 14 dup. 17281.0kHz		USB 1858
16402.00	Ships wkg ch 15 dup. 17284.0kHz		USB 0712 0933 2150
16405.00	Ships wkg ch 16 dup. 17287.0kHz		USB 1020 (to IAR) 0801 (to DAJ) 1631
16408.00	Ships wkg ch 17 dup. 17290.0kHz		USB 1533 (to 4XO) 0731
16411.00	Ships wkg ch 18 dup. 17293.0kHz		USB (to A9M) 1307 1504 (to TAN) 1503 (to GKU) 1846

kHz.	Station	Call	Mode / Heard/Times GMT
16414.00	Numbers Station		AM Ger (female voice) 0929
16414.00	Ships wkg ch 19 dup. 17296.0kHz		USB (to LGQ) 0702 1632
16417.00	Ships wkg ch 20 dup. 17299.0kHz		USB LAQA4 (in Black Sea to Rogaland LFN24) 0734
16420.00	Ships wkg ch 21 dup. 17302.0kHz		USB "Royal Viking Sun" (to LGQ) 1306
16423.00	Ships wkg ch 22 dup. 17305.0kHz		USB 1749 (to HEB) 1755
16426.00	Ships wkg ch 23 dup. 17308.0kHz		USB 1246 1314 (to UTQ) 1309
16429.00	Ships wkg ch 24 dup. 17311.0kHz		USB 0815 1723
16432.00	Ships wkg ch 25 dup. 17314.0kHz		USB 1537
16435.00	Ships wkg ch 26 dup. 17317.0kHz		USB 1238 SVHJ (to SVN) 0750
16438.00	Ships wkg ch 27 dup. 17320.0kHz		USB 0806 1722
16441.00	Ships wkg ch 28 dup. 17323.0kHz		USB 1015 1915 EDKN 1538
16444.00	Ships wkg ch 29 dup. 17326.0kHz		USB 0902 1220 1708 (to Boufarik) 1747
16447.00	Ships wkg ch 30 dup. 17329.0kHz		USB (to EHY) 1314 (to UFA) 2142
16450.00	Ships wkg ch 31 dup. 17332.0kHz		USB 2241
16451.00	Numbers Station		USB Eng (female voice) 0733
16453.00	Ships wkg ch 32 dup. 17335.0kHz		USB 1753
16453.50	Hungarian Embassy traffic		125DUP-ARQ(inv polarity) 5 let grps 0836 p/lang 1110
16456.00	Ships wkg ch 33 dup. 17338.0kHz		USB 0641 1222
16459.00	Ships wkg ch 34 dup. 17341.0kHz		USB 0615 1055 1520 2144
16462.00	Ships wkg ch 35 dup. 17344.0kHz		USB 0737 1340 1655
16465.00	Ships wkg ch 36 dup. 17347.0kHz		USB 1113 1537
16468.00	Ships wkg ch 37 dup. 17350.0kHz		USB 1710 1858
16471.00	Ships wkg ch 38 dup. 17353.0kHz		USB 0752 (to YUW) 1337 "Shura Buranchenko" (UPWW) 1436
16474.00	Ships wkg ch 39 dup. 17356.0kHz		USB 0917 1239 (to EHY) 1017
16477.00	Ships wkg ch 40 dup. 17359.0kHz		USB (to CBV) 2234 HO3882 (to GKW) 1222
16480.00	Ships wkg ch 41 dup. 17362.0kHz		USB 1354 1551
16483.00	Ships wkg ch 42 dup. 17365.0kHz		USB (to FFL) 0714
16486.00	Ships wkg ch 43 dup. 17368.0kHz		USB (to A7D) 1346
16489.00	Ships wkg ch 44 dup. 17371.0kHz		USB
16492.00	Ships wkg ch 45 dup. 17374.0kHz		USB 1116
16495.00	Ships wkg ch 46 dup. 17377.0kHz		USB 0734
16498.00	Ships wkg ch 47 dup. 17380.0kHz		USB 1745
16501.00	Ships wkg ch 48 dup. 17383.0kHz		USB 1018 1446
16504.00	Ships wkg ch 49 dup. 17386.0kHz		USB 1535 2118 SVTP (to 5BA) 1726
16507.00	Ships wkg ch 50 dup. 17389.0kHz		USB (to UDN) 1320
16510.00	Ships wkg ch 51 dup. 17392.0kHz		USB 0934 1543 1916
16513.00	Ships wkg ch 52 dup. 17395.0kHz		USB 0654 1558 1718
16516.00	Ships wkg ch 53 dup. 17398.0kHz		USB 0816 0911 2243
16519.00	Ships wkg ch 54 dup. 17401.0kHz		USB 0738 1409 (to UFB) 1518 1723
16522.00	Ships wkg ch 55 dup. 17404.0kHz		USB 1734
16525.00	Ships wkg ch 56 dup. 17407.0kHz		USB 2154
16528.00	Ships/Coast stations simplex		USB 1518 1711 2145
16531.00	Ships/Coast stations simplex		USB 0740 DQET (with Y5DR) 0819
16534.00	Ships/Coast stations simplex		USB 1555
16537.00	Ships/Coast stations simplex		USB 0816 2132 2244
16540.00	Ships/Coast stations simplex		USB 0735 0935 1439
16543.00	Ships/Coast stations simplex		USB 1117 1900
16546.00	Ships/Coast stations simplex		USB 1534 1721
16547.00	Intership working		USB 0756
16548.00	Intership working		USB 2146
16550.00	Intership working		USB 1712
16565.00	Intership working		USB 2121 2201
16570.00	Intership working		USB 1638 1917
16577.00	Intership working		USB 1934
16605.00	Intership working		USB 1113 2133
16610.00	Ships working		CW "Licorne Pacifique" (J8CV5) (out of normal sub-band) 1541
16615.00	Ships working		CW 1707
16619.00	Ships working		CW SQIM (to WCC) 1538
16619.50	Ships working		CW "Vera" (9HFX3) 1223
16620.00	Ships working		CW "Additya Kiran" (VTGC) 1142 "Sea Fighter" (9HCV2) 1337
16620.50	Ships working		CW "Kasan" (UROO) 1756 URMT 1914
16621.00	Ships working		CW "United Might" (9HQG3) 0841
16621.50	Ships working		CW 1734
16622.00	Ships working		CW "Brij" (C6DE6) 1404 "Star London" (C6IS8) 1757
16622.50	Ships working		CW "Filioara" (YQHL) 1228
16623.00	Ships working		CW "Bursa" (TCJX) 1758 "Geroi Adzhimuskaya" (EOXO) 1808
16623.50	Ships working		CW "Partnership Sea" (3FFO2) 0918 "Alka" 1440
16624.00	Ships working		CW "White Stone" (C6KI7) 1618 "Sea Song" 1802
16624.50	Ships working		CW "Rio Coari" (PPXY) 1445 "Ivory Bay" (3ELP8) 1624
16625.00	Ships working		CW "Vishva Madhuri" (ATGR) 0750 "Smyrni" (C4VB) 1551
16625.50	Ships working		CW "Marzario Francia" 1009 "No.7 Maya" (DZJS) 1753
16626.00	Ships working		CW "Diego Gomes" (ELOB6) 1615 "Livezeni" (YQDF) 1804
16627.00	Ships working		CW "Apjanjli" (VTFY) 0912 "Minerva" (5BVU) 1728
16627.50	Ships working		CW "Gavrila" 0931
16628.00	Ships working		CW "Superitas" (9HSE3) 0918 P3HQ3 1715
16628.50	Ships working		CW UNES (to UFN) 1040
16629.00	Ships working		CW "Searanger" (H2ZV) 1713

kHz.	Station	Call	Mode / Heard/Times GMT
16630.00	Ships working		CW "Lia" (SZJG) 1348
16631.00	Ships working		CW "Oocl Hope" (VRIC) 1223 "Samos" (SWLJ) 1640
16632.00	Ships working		CW "Kopalnia Piaseczno" (SQAM) 1343
16632.50	Ships working		CW "Gediz" (TCDL) 1624
16633.00	Ships working		CW "Faith Star" (P3DR2) 1638
16634.00	Ships working		CW "Amur 2508" (UEIO) 0851 "Arcadia 1" (3EBA9) 1557
16635.00	Ships working		CW ELBM2 (to VPS) 1133 "Ocean Breeze 1" (3EUV2) 1507
16636.00	Ships working		CW "Andreas P" (9HDY4) 0845
16637.00	Ships working		CW 0741
16637.50	Ships working		CW 1727
16638.00	Ships working		CW "MSC Alexandra" (3EHT8) 1227
16638.50	Ships working		CW 0046
16639.00	Ships working		CW "Valkalp" 1219 "Lavender" (LALZ2) 1934
16639.50	Ships working		CW 1618
16640.00	Ships working		CW "Garden Green" (5MKH) 1653
16641.00	Ships working		CW "Depa Giulia" (IBFQ) 1511
16641.50	Ships working		CW "Southern Princess" (DUCF) 0758 "Federal Fuji" (7LDY) 1020
16642.00	Ships working		CW 1709 3EGU6 (to JDB) 1023
16643.00	Ships working		CW 1619
16644.00	Ships working		CW "Akademik Shuleykin" (UBNZ) 0825
16645.00	Ships working		CW "El Cordero" (3ERB4) 1029
16646.00	Ships working		CW 1703
16647.00	Ships working		CW P3PN3 (to GKB) 1210
16648.00	Ships working		CW "Marianne 1" (LAYY2) 1855
16649.00	Ships working		CW "Dryso" (C6CS2) 1643
16649.50	Ships working		CW "Freccia dell Ovest" (ICAH) 1030
16650.00	Ships working		CW "Golden Fortune" (3FCU4) 1230
16651.00	Ships working		CW "Buena Fortuna" (J4FE) 1803
16651.50	Ships working		CW "Probo Baro" (LAZE2) 1248
16652.00	Ships working		CW 1226
16653.00	Ships working		CW "Lentz" (P3LL3) 2149
16654.00	Ships working		CW 1449 2143
16655.00	Ships working		CW "Sophie C" (SYLB) 1710
16656.00	Ships working		CW 1845
16656.50	Ships working		CW "Ursa Major" (IBFH) 0829
16657.00	Ships working		CW 0850
16658.00	Ships working		CW "Sea Progress" (9HBN3) 1255 "Sea Wish" (9HJQ4) 1753
16659.00	Ships working		CW "Havjo" (LALA2) 1253
16660.00	Ships working		CW 3EXC8 1259
16661.00	Ships working		CW 1558
16662.00	Ships working		CW "Double Glory" (VRUH6) 0752
16663.00	Ships working		CW "Violet Islands" (C4WU) 2146
16664.00	Ships working		CW 1256
16665.00	Ships working		CW "Haight" (C6IR8) 1748
16666.00	Ships working		CW "Flag Epos" (SVJS) 1557
16666.50	Ships working		CW 0852 1722
16667.00	Ships working		CW 1634
16667.50	Ships working		CW "Ustrica" 1753
16668.00	Ships working		CW (to CLS) 1557
16669.00	Ships working		CW 1539 1624
16670.00	Ships working		CW "Giorita" (P3TW3) 1805 "Docelotus" (PPVD) 2233
16671.00	Ships working		CW 1733
16671.50	Ships working		CW "Ostrov Litke" (ESSQ) 1746
16672.00	Ships working		CW "Maria Angelicoussi" (J4BK) 1550 "Khoms" (TCAW) 1715
16673.00	Ships working		CW "Havfalk" (LAKZ2) 0858
16673.50	Ships working		CW ESBT 1447
16674.00	Ships working		CW 1128 1902
16674.50	Ships working		CW 2005
16675.00	Ships working		CW 1257 1456
16676.00	Ships working		CW UFAA (to UQA4) 1541
16676.50	Ships working		CW (wx) 1756
16677.00	Ships working		CW "Flora C" (SYJR) 1723
16678.00	Ships working		CW "Alexandria" (SXCQ) 1645
16678.50	Ships working		CW "Star Magnate" (ZCKU) 1608
16679.00	Ships working		CW "Agrari" (P3GE4) 1444 "Hong Kong Glory" (SWDI) 1557
16680.00	Ships working		CW 1705 "Olivebank" (3ETQ5) 1155 "World Spear" (VPIB) 1628
16681.00	Ships working		CW "Olenegorsk" (UGXU) 1506
16682.00	Ships working		CW "Gulf Wave" (P3HY4) 1200
16683.00	Ships working		CW "Clipper Atlantic" (C4PA) 1541 "Pranas Zibertas" (UUCP) 1846
16683.50	Ships wkg ch 1 dup. 16807.0kHz		SITOR "Akademik Zavaritskiy" (UNUG) 1627 "Mulbera" (S6EP) 1803
16684.00	Ships wkg ch 2 dup. 16807.5kHz		SITOR "Almida Star" (ZDBR9) 1840
16684.50	Ships wkg ch 3 dup. 16808.0kHz		SITOR "Tadeusz Kosciuszko" (SQLB) 1213 Selcal QSKV (Gdynia) 1743

kHz.	Station	Call	Mode / Heard/Times GMT
16685.00	Ships wkg ch 4 dup. 16808.5kHz		SITOR 1338
16685.50	Ships wkg ch 5 dup. 16809.0kHz		SITOR "Kintampo" (5VKO) 2347 & 170/50nc UFJI 1746
16686.00	Ships wkg ch 6 dup. 16809.5kHz		SITOR SWHK 1428 & 170/50nc "Akademik Sergei Vavilov" (UKOS) 2214
16686.50	Ships wkg ch 7 dup. 16810.0kHz		RTTY
16687.00	Ships wkg ch 8 dup. 16810.5kHz		SITOR "Esram" (TCDI) 0900 "An Avel" (FNDC) 1845
16687.50	Ships wkg ch 9 dup. 16811.0kHz		SITOR 1221 2133
16688.00	Ships wkg ch 10 dup. 16811.5kHz		SITOR Selcal MCPV (Bahrain) 1901
16688.50	Ships wkg ch 11 dup. 16812.0kHz		SITOR "Burg" (Y5OY) 1503
16689.00	Ships wkg ch 12 dup. 16812.5kHz		170/50nc "Kapitan Reutov" (LYBM) 1335
16689.50	Ships wkg ch 13 dup. 16813.0kHz		SITOR "Kapitan Vodyenko" (ULUA) 1631 "Neftegorsk" (UWEE) 1845
16690.00	Ships wkg ch 14 dup. 16813.5kHz		SITOR "Hebe" (LJPF3) 1539 "Fullnes" (LAPD4) 1731
16690.50	Ships wkg ch 15 dup. 16814.0kHz		SITOR 1445
16691.00	Ships wkg ch 16 dup. 16814.5kHz		SITOR UYVP 1506
16691.50	Ships wkg ch 17 dup. 16815.0kHz		SITOR "Mimosa" (LAHM2) 1151 "Tiger River" (P3GR2) 1506
16692.00	Ships wkg ch 18 dup. 16815.5kHz		SITOR "Sangha" (C6JN4) 1718 "Maersk Despatcher" (OWFG2) 2008
16692.50	Ships wkg ch 19 dup. 16816.0kHz		SITOR "Iran Eghbal" (EQPQ) 1332
16693.00	Ships wkg ch 20 dup. 16816.5kHz		SITOR 1717 1802
16693.50	Ships wkg ch 21 dup. 16817.0kHz		SITOR "Acadia Forest" (D5DI) 1815
16694.00	Ships wkg ch 22 dup. 16817.5kHz		RTTY
16694.50	Ships wkg ch 23 dup. 16818.0kHz		SITOR "Anemone" 2245 Selcal XYFV (Athens) 1748
16695.00	Maritime Safety channel		SITOR
16695.50	Ships wkg ch 25 dup. 16818.5kHz		SITOR "Jablanica" (9HPP3) 1653 "Iran Jamal" (EQPS) 1734
16696.00	Ships wkg ch 26 dup. 16819.0kHz		SITOR Selcal QPVV (Rogaland) 1426
16696.50	Ships wkg ch 27 dup. 16819.5kHz		SITOR "Overseas Alice" (WOVL) 1731
16697.00	Ships wkg ch 28 dup. 16820.0kHz		SITOR "Agip Liguria" (IBPQ) 1335 "Aquitania" (ICGA) 1500
16697.50	Ships wkg ch 29 dup. 16820.5kHz		SITOR "Patchara Naree" (HPCW) 1721
16698.00	Ships wkg ch 30 dup. 16821.0kHz		SITOR "Barenbels" (SYMY) 1348
16698.50	Ships wkg ch 31 dup. 16821.5kHz		SITOR "Kate Maersk" (OZSV2) 1254 "Arktis Atlantic" (OVTK2) 1300
16699.00	Ships wkg ch 32 dup. 16822.0kHz		RTTY
16699.50	Ships wkg ch 33 dup. 16822.5kHz		SITOR Selcal QSPV (Goeteborg) 1037
16700.00	Ships wkg ch 34 dup. 16823.0kHz		SITOR "Cartagena De Columbia" (3EMG9) 1055
16700.50	Ships wkg ch 35 dup. 16823.5kHz		SITOR "Mekhanik Bardetskiy" (UVMH) 1116
16701.00	Ships wkg ch 36 dup. 16824.0kHz		SITOR "Elver" (P3GE5) 1235 "Dyvi Skagerak" (LAEL4) 1739
16701.50	Ships wkg ch 37 dup. 16824.5kHz		SITOR "Akademikis Vavilovs" (YLDB) 0910
16702.00	Ships wkg ch 38 dup. 16825.0kHz		SITOR "Rhine Forest" (ELFO3) 1600
16702.50	Ships wkg ch 39 dup. 16825.5kHz		170/50nc "Niko Nikoladze" (UVLF) 1546
16703.00	Ships wkg ch 40 dup. 16826.0kHz		SITOR "Khelermaa" 0751 "Gulbene" (UIIY) 1814 & 170/50nc 1902
16703.50	Ships wkg ch 41 dup. 16826.5kHz		SITOR "Tania" (9HYG3) 0742 "Ivan Korotyev" (UFSS) 1702
16704.00	Ships wkg ch 42 dup. 16827.0kHz		SITOR 9HLL3 1045 & 170/50rc "Akta" 1613
16704.50	Ships wkg ch 43 dup. 16827.5kHz		SITOR 1041 & 170/50nc (to UUI) 2137
16705.00	Ships wkg ch 44 dup. 16828.0kHz		SITOR "Coastal Eagle Point" (WHMK) 1820 "Sirius" (DJKL) 1829
16705.50	Ships wkg ch 45 dup. 16828.5kHz		SITOR Selcal QFMP (Norddeich) 1032
16706.00	Ships wkg ch 46 dup. 16829.0kHz		SITOR "Yuri Levitan" (UYPG) 1130
16706.50	Ships wkg ch 47 dup. 16829.5kHz		SITOR "Pushlakhta" 1339
16707.00	Ships wkg ch 48 dup. 16830.0kHz		SITOR "St Cacergue" (HBDJ) 1412
16707.50	Ships wkg ch 49 dup. 16830.5kHz		SITOR "Anangel Spirit" (SVUJ) 1443 "Anangel Faith" (SXRY) 2218
16708.00	Ships wkg ch 50 dup. 16831.0kHz		SITOR Selcal XVSV (Mobile) 1818
16708.50	Ships wkg ch 51 dup. 16831.5kHz		SITOR "Echo Pioneer" (LASV2) 1836
16709.00	Ships wkg ch 52 dup. 16832.0kHz		SITOR "Arild Viking" (LAIM) 1438
16709.50	Ships wkg ch 53 dup. 16832.5kHz		SITOR 1236
16710.00	Ships wkg ch 54 dup. 16833.0kHz		SITOR "Atlas Trader 4" (9HOV3) 1525 "Hennigsdorf" (Y5EH) 2352
16710.50	Ships wkg ch 55 dup. 16833.5kHz		RTTY
16711.00	Ships wkg ch 56 dup. 16834.0kHz		SITOR Selcal KPCV (Lisbon) 1756
16711.50	Ships wkg ch 57 dup. 16834.5kHz		SITOR "Mekhanik Yakovenko" (UEUQ) 1505
16712.00	Ships wkg ch 58 dup. 16835.0kHz		SITOR 1653
16712.50	Ships wkg ch 59 dup. 16835.5kHz		RTTY
16713.00	Ships wkg ch 60 dup. 16836.0kHz		SITOR "Ivans Polzunovs" (YLBG) 1229 "Rhine" (P3GT4) 1509
16713.50	Ships wkg ch 61 dup. 16836.5kHz		SITOR "Fredericksburg" (KNJN) 1517 "Tillie Lykes" (WMLH) 1626
16714.00	Ships wkg ch 62 dup. 16837.0kHz		RTTY
16714.50	Ships wkg ch 63 dup. 16837.5kHz		RTTY
16715.00	Ships wkg ch 64 dup. 16838.0kHz		SITOR 0715
16715.50	Ships wkg ch 65 dup. 16838.5kHz		SITOR "Baltik" (to 9AR) 1748
16716.00	Ships wkg ch 66 dup. 16839.0kHz		SITOR "Reefer Cape" (5BEZ) 0904
16716.50	Ships wkg ch 67 dup. 16839.5kHz		SITOR "Grigoriy Nesterenko" (UNWR) 1205 "Petr Schmit" (UERJ) 2025
16717.00	Ships wkg ch 68 dup. 16840.0kHz		SITOR "St Helena" (MMHE5) 1120
16717.50	Ships wkg ch 69 dup. 16840.5kHz		SITOR "Kery" (to UHK) 1433 "Vysokovsk" (URTK) 1553
16718.00	Ships wkg ch 70 dup. 16841.0kHz		170/50nc "Akademik Sergey Vavilov" (UKOS) 2225
16718.50	Ships wkg ch 71 dup. 16841.5kHz		RTTY

kHz.	Station	Call	Mode / Heard/Times GMT
16719.00	Ships wkg ch 72 dup. 16842.0kHz		RTTY
16719.50	Ships wkg ch 73 dup. 16842.5kHz		RTTY
16720.00	Ships wkg ch 74 dup. 16843.0kHz		170/50nc "Professor Zubov" (UMFW) 0920
16720.50	Ships wkg ch 75 dup. 16843.5kHz		RTTY
16721.00	Ships wkg ch 76 dup. 16844.0kHz		170/50nc 1422
16721.50	Ships wkg ch 77 dup. 16844.5kHz		RTTY
16722.00	Ships wkg ch 78 dup. 16845.0kHz		RTTY
16722.50	Ships wkg ch 79 dup. 16845.5kHz		RTTY
16723.00	Ships wkg ch 80 dup. 16846.0kHz		SITOR "Nadezhda Obukhova" (UKET) 0850 "Grigoriy Mikheev" (URZC) 1134
16723.50	Ships wkg ch 81 dup. 16846.5kHz		RTTY
16724.00	Ships wkg ch 82 dup. 16847.0kHz		170/50nc 0900
16724.50	Ships wkg ch 83 dup. 16847.5kHz		RTTY
16725.00	Ships wkg ch 84 dup. 16848.0kHz		RTTY
16725.50	Ships wkg ch 85 dup. 16848.5kHz		RTTY
16726.00	Ships wkg ch 86 dup. 16849.0kHz		RTTY
16726.50	Ships wkg ch 87 dup. 16849.5kHz		RTTY
16727.00	Ships wkg ch 88 dup. 16850.0kHz		RTTY
16727.50	Ships wkg ch 89 dup. 16850.5kHz		RTTY
16728.00	Ships wkg ch 90 dup. 16851.0kHz		RTTY
16728.00	CIS Naval	UMFE	CW (to RIW) 1447
16728.50	Ships wkg ch 91 dup. 16851.5kHz		RTTY
16729.00	Ships wkg ch 92 dup. 16852.0kHz		RTTY
16729.50	Ships wkg ch 93 dup. 16852.5kHz		RTTY
16730.00	Ships wkg ch 94 dup. 16853.0kHz		RTTY
16730.50	Ships wkg ch 95 dup. 16853.5kHz		RTTY
16731.00	Ships wkg ch 96 dup. 16854.0kHz		RTTY
16731.50	Ships wkg ch 97 dup. 16854.5kHz		170/50nc 1639 2124
16732.00	Ships wkg ch 98 dup. 16855.0kHz		RTTY
16732.50	Ships wkg ch 99 dup. 16855.5kHz		170/50nc 1733
16733.00	Ships wkg ch 100 dup. 16856.0kHz		170/50nc "Neringa" (LYMO) 0943
16733.50	Ships wkg ch 101 dup. 16856.5kHz		170/50rc "Khersones" (ENFI) 1517
16734.00	Ship working		170/50nc "Professor Zhubov" (UMFW) 0838 (out of normal sub-band)
16734.00	Ships calling ch 1		CW "Vulcan" (YQAV) 0903 "Oravita" (YQEH) 1107 YQNW 1702
16734.50	Ships calling ch 2		CW USGU (to UUI) 1114 UZZF (to UUI) 1222
16735.00	Ships calling ch 5		CW YQCN (to YQI) 1103 VRDP (to GKB) 1226
16735.50	Ships calling ch 6		CW SXMN (to SVB) 1158 C4VB (to GKB) 1541
16736.00	Ships calling ch 3		CW "Liza Chaykina" (UZYO) 0853 C4RF (to SVB) 1558
16736.50	Ships calling ch 7		CW "Yun Ling" (BOKN) 0935 "Balsa 31" (DUKD) 2156
16737.00	Ships calling ch 8		CW 9HPR3 (to 9AR) 1100 9HMM3 (to UVA) 1543
16737.50	Ships calling ch 9		CW EHJB (to EDZ6) 1625 URSP 1803 UFJI (to UNM2) 1805
16738.00	Ships calling ch 4		CW "Agios Aimilianos" (5BDK) 1110
16738.50	Ships calling ch 10		CW "El Cordero" (3ERB4) 1027
16739.00	Ships wkg ch 102 dup. 16857.0kHz		170/50nc 1257
16739.50	Ships wkg ch 103 dup. 16857.5kHz		SITOR "Akademik Millionshchikov" (UWFW) 1618 "Serov" (UOVC) 1619
16740.00	Ships wkg ch 104 dup. 16858.0kHz		170/50nc "Krasnokamsk" (UVXP) 2230
16740.50	Ships wkg ch 105 dup. 16858.5kHz		RTTY
16741.00	Ships wkg ch 106 dup. 16859.0kHz		RTTY
16741.50	Ships wkg ch 107 dup. 16859.5kHz		RTTY
16742.00	Ships wkg ch 108 dup. 16860.0kHz		RTTY
16742.50	Ships wkg ch 109 dup. 16860.5kHz		RTTY
16743.00	Ships wkg ch 110 dup. 16861.0kHz		RTTY
16743.50	Ships wkg ch 111 dup. 16861.5kHz		RTTY
16744.00	Ships wkg ch 112 dup. 16862.0kHz		RTTY
16744.50	Ships wkg ch 113 dup. 16862.5kHz		RTTY
16745.00	Ships wkg ch 114 dup. 16863.0kHz		RTTY
16745.50	Ships wkg ch 115 dup. 16863.5kHz		RTTY
16746.00	Ships wkg ch 116 dup. 16864.0kHz		RTTY
16746.50	Ships wkg ch 117 dup. 16864.5kHz		RTTY
16747.00	Ships wkg ch 118 dup. 16865.0kHz		RTTY
16747.50	Ships wkg ch 119 dup. 16865.5kHz		RTTY
16748.00	Ships wkg ch 120 dup. 16866.0kHz		RTTY
16748.50	Ships wkg ch 121 dup. 16866.5kHz		RTTY
16749.00	Ships wkg ch 122 dup. 16867.0kHz		RTTY
16749.50	Ships wkg ch 123 dup. 16867.5kHz		RTTY
16750.00	Ships wkg ch 124 dup. 16868.0kHz		RTTY
16750.50	Ships wkg ch 125 dup. 16868.5kHz		RTTY
16751.00	Ships wkg ch 126 dup. 16869.0kHz		RTTY
16751.50	Ships wkg ch 127 dup. 16869.5kHz		RTTY
16752.00	Ships wkg ch 128 dup. 16870.0kHz		RTTY
16752.50	Ships wkg ch 129 dup. 16870.5kHz		RTTY
16753.00	Ships wkg ch 130 dup. 16871.0kHz		RTTY
16753.50	Ships wkg ch 131 dup. 16871.5kHz		RTTY
16754.00	Ships wkg ch 132 dup. 16872.0kHz		RTTY
16754.50	Ships wkg ch 133 dup. 16872.5kHz		RTTY

kHz.	Station	Call	Mode / Heard/Times GMT
16755.00	Ships wkg ch 134 dup. 16873.0kHz		RTTY
16755.50	Ships wkg ch 135 dup. 16873.5kHz		RTTY
16756.00	Ships wkg ch 136 dup. 16874.0kHz		RTTY
16756.50	Ships wkg ch 137 dup. 16874.5kHz		RTTY
16757.00	Ships wkg ch 138 dup. 16875.0kHz		RTTY
16757.50	Ships wkg ch 139 dup. 16875.5kHz		RTTY
16758.00	Ships wkg ch 140 dup. 16876.0kHz		RTTY
16758.00	UNID		SITOR Mode B Press summary (Eng, about Philipino matters) 0834
16758.50	Ships wkg ch 141 dup. 16876.5kHz		RTTY
16759.00	Ships wkg ch 142 dup. 16877.0kHz		RTTY
16759.50	Ships wkg ch 143 dup. 16877.5kHz		RTTY
16760.00	Ships wkg ch 144 dup. 16878.0kHz		RTTY
16760.50	Ships wkg ch 145 dup. 16878.5kHz		RTTY
16761.00	Ships wkg ch 146 dup. 16879.0kHz		RTTY
16761.50	Ships wkg ch 147 dup. 16879.5kHz		RTTY
16762.00	Ships wkg ch 148 dup. 16880.0kHz		SITOR "An Xin Jiang" (BOAR) (to XSQ) 1552
16762.50	Ships wkg ch 149 dup. 16880.5kHz		RTTY
16763.00	Ships wkg ch 150 dup. 16881.0kHz		SITOR "Marine Pacer" (TCSX) 1438 Selcal MKCV (Istanbul) 1420
16763.50	Ships wkg ch 151 dup. 16881.5kHz		RTTY
16764.00	Ships wkg ch 152 dup. 16882.0kHz		RTTY
16764.50	Ships wkg ch 153 dup. 16882.5kHz		RTTY
16765.00	Ships wkg ch 154 dup. 16883.0kHz		SITOR LXCP 1514
16765.50	Ships wkg ch 155 dup. 16883.5kHz		RTTY
16766.00	Ships wkg ch 156 dup. 16884.0kHz		RTTY
16766.50	Ships wkg ch 157 dup. 16884.5kHz		170/50nc 1359
16767.00	Ships wkg ch 158 dup. 16885.0kHz		RTTY
16767.50	Ships wkg ch 159 dup. 16885.5kHz		RTTY
16768.00	Ships wkg ch 160 dup. 16886.0kHz		RTTY
16768.50	Ships wkg ch 161 dup. 16886.5kHz		170/50nc "Ivan Burmistsrov" (UUUT) 1835
16769.00	Ships wkg ch 162 dup. 16887.0kHz		RTTY
16769.50	Ships wkg ch 163 dup. 16887.5kHz		RTTY
16770.00	Ships wkg ch 164 dup. 16888.0kHz		RTTY
16770.00	Ship working		CW "Batna" (7THP to NMN) 1725 (out of normal sub-band)
16770.00	Bulgarian Naval		CW unknown station calling LZS36 (then QSY to 16773.0) 1350
16770.50	Ships wkg ch 165 dup. 16888.5kHz		RTTY
16771.00	Ships wkg ch 166 dup. 16889.0kHz		RTTY
16771.50	Ships wkg ch 167 dup. 16889.5kHz		RTTY
16772.00	Ships wkg ch 168 dup. 16890.0kHz		RTTY
16772.50	Ships wkg ch 169 dup. 16890.5kHz		RTTY
16773.00	Ships wkg ch 170 dup. 16891.0kHz		RTTY
16773.50	Ships wkg ch 171 dup. 16891.5kHz		RTTY
16774.00	Ships wkg ch 172 dup. 16892.0kHz		RTTY
16774.50	Ships wkg ch 173 dup. 16892.5kHz		RTTY
16775.00	Ships wkg ch 174 dup. 16893.0kHz		RTTY
16775.50	Ships wkg ch 175 dup. 16893.5kHz		RTTY
16776.00	Ships wkg ch 176 dup. 16894.0kHz		SITOR 1014 1634
16776.50	Ships wkg ch 177 dup. 16894.5kHz		RTTY
16777.00	Ships wkg ch 178 dup. 16895.0kHz		170/50nc 1040
16777.50	Ships wkg ch 179 dup. 16895.5kHz		RTTY
16778.00	Ships wkg ch 180 dup. 16896.0kHz		RTTY
16778.50	Ships wkg ch 181 dup. 16896.5kHz		RTTY
16779.00	Ships wkg ch 182 dup. 16897.0kHz		RTTY
16779.50	Ships wkg ch 183 dup. 16897.5kHz		RTTY
16780.00	Ships wkg ch 184 dup. 16898.0kHz		RTTY
16780.50	Ships wkg ch 185 dup. 16898.5kHz		RTTY
16781.00	Ships wkg ch 186 dup. 16899.0kHz		RTTY
16781.50	Ships wkg ch 187 dup. 16899.5kHz		SITOR 1741
16782.00	Ships wkg ch 188 dup. 16900.0kHz		SITOR 1027
16782.50	Ships wkg ch 189 dup. 16900.5kHz		RTTY
16783.00	Ships wkg ch 190 dup. 16901.0kHz		170/50nc "Novozybkov" (UWUA) 1125
16783.50	Ships wkg ch 191 dup. 16901.5kHz		RTTY
16784.00	Ships wkg ch 192 dup. 16902.0kHz		170/50nc 1613
16784.50	Ships wkg ch 193 dup. 16902.5kHz		RTTY
16785.00	Ships working (non paired)		170/50nc "Komsomolets Uzbekistana" (ULBI) 1020
16785.50	Ships working (non paired)		SITOR 1759 & 170/50nc "MB-0014" 2233
16786.00	Ships working (non paired)		SITOR Mode B "Havelland" (DQET) 0816 & 170/50nc ULIZ 0950
16786.50	Ships working (non paired)		170/50nc 1409
16787.00	Ships working (non paired)		170/50nc 0822 1819 2235
16787.50	Ships working (non paired)		170/50nc UEFN (to UIW) 0719
16788.00	Ships working (non paired)		170/50nc "More Sodruzhestva" (UYDN) 1550
16788.50	Ships working (non paired)		170/50nc "Sosnogorsk" (UOWG) 1133 "Khariton Greku" (EKXP) 1440
16789.00	Ships working (non paired)		170/50nc "Aleksandr Starostenko" (UNUZ) 1526
16789.50	Ships working (non paired)		170/50nc 1033

kHz.	Station	Call	Mode / Heard/Times GMT
16790.00	Ships working (non paired)		170/50nc 1733 1821
16790.50	Ships working (non paired)		SITOR "Maersk Faust" 1250 "Grigoriy Nesterenko" (UNWR) 1546
16791.00	Ships working (non paired)		170/50nc "Pioner Murmana" (UFPS) 1237 "Fyodor Gladkov" (UWMA) 1625
16791.50	Ships working (non paired)		170/50nc "Kapitan Radionov" (UWAP) 1742
16792.00	Ships working (non paired)		170/50nc "Kolskiy Zaliv" (UIAL) 1647
16792.50	Ships working (non paired)		170/50nc 1824
16793.00	Ships working (non paired)		170/100nc 1410
16793.50	Ships working (non paired)		170/50nc USJE (to URL) 1512
16794.00	Ships working (non paired)		SITOR "Professor Szafer" (SQJD) 1134 "Karlowicz" (SQLW) 1613
16794.50	Ships working (non paired)		SITOR Mode B news in Eng (abt Philippino matters) 1025 1615 1724
16795.00	Ships working (non paired)		170/50nc "Vidnoye" (UJEH) 1604
16795.50	Ships working (non paired)		170/50nc 1726 1811
16796.00	Ships working (non paired)		170/50nc "Motovskiy Zaliv" (UGTM) 1117
16796.50	Ships working (non paired)		170/50nc "MB 0019" (to Murmansk) 0926
16797.00	Ships working (non paired)		170/50nc "Valentin Zolotaryev" (UBPE) 1357 "Gazgan" (UNCH) 1725
16797.50	Ships working (non paired)		SITOR 1530
16798.00	Ships working (non paired)		170/50nc "MB-0015" (UHLW) 2228 "MA-0065" 2243
16798.50	Ships working (non paired)		170/50nc "Geroyevka" (UBJA) 1038
16799.00	Ships working (non paired)		170/50nc 0852
16799.50	Ships working (non paired)		170/50nc "General Chernyakovskiy" (UWUD) 1608
16800.00	Ships working (non paired)		170/50nc "MB 0389" 1919
16800.50	Ships working (non paired)		170/50nc UHUZ 2226
16801.00	Ships working (non paired)		SITOR "Vladimir Ilyich" (UQJX) 1656
16801.50	Ships working (non paired)		170/100nc "Timofey Gornov" (EMXD) 1628 & 1730
16802.00	Ships working (non paired)		170/50nc 1238 "Vasya Aleksayev" (UUHJ) 1035 "MA-0801" 1700
16802.50	Ships working (non paired)		170/50nc "Bereg Nadezhdy" (UFBH) 1251
16803.00	Ships working (non paired)		170/50nc "Bernard Koenen" (USMM) 1210 "Milgravis" (YLFR) 1541
16803.50	Ships working (non paired)		170/50nc "Lyudmila Pavlichenko" (UJEI) 1529
16804.00	Ships working (non paired)		170/50nc "MB-0133" (to Murmansk) 1253
16804.50	Maritime Safety channel		SITOR
16805.00	Ships digital selective calling		RTTY
16805.50	Ships digital selective calling		RTTY
16806.00	Ships digital selective calling		RTTY
16806.50	Maritime Safety channel		SITOR
16806.50	Boston CG, USA	NMF	SITOR wx bulletin 1631 nav wngs 1648
16806.50	Kodiak, USA	NOJ	SITOR 1547
16807.00	Coast stations ch 1 dup. 16683.5kHz		RTTY
16807.00	Singapore	9VG82	SITOR 1442 1503 wx 0030 1230 tfc list 1530 1730
16807.50	Coast stations ch 2 dup. 16684.0kHz		RTTY
16807.50	Portishead, UK	GKE6	SITOR 0750 1545 1848 2121
16808.00	Coast stations ch 3 dup. 16684.5kHz		RTTY
16808.00	Gdynia, Poland	SPA81	SITOR 1045 1412 1549 1652 1726 Mode B tfc list 0853 1453
16808.50	Coast stations ch 4 dup. 16685.0kHz		RTTY
16808.50	Argentine Radio	LSD836	SITOR 1516
16809.00	Coast stations ch 5 dup. 16685.5kHz		RTTY
16809.00	Goeteborg, Sweden	SAG	SITOR 1043
16809.00	Mobile, USA	WLO	SITOR 1504 1803
16809.00	Rogaland, Norway	LGX2	SITOR 1339 1754 2004
16809.50	Coast stations ch 6 dup. 16686.0kHz		RTTY
16809.50	Madrid, Spain	EAD	SITOR 1758 Mode B tfc list 1300 1500
16809.50	Stettin, Poland	SPB81	SITOR
16809.50	Perth, Australia	VIP35	SITOR 1036 1421 1505 1708
16810.00	Coast stations ch 7 dup. 16686.5kHz		RTTY
16810.50	Coast stations ch 8 dup. 16687.0kHz		RTTY
16810.50	St Lys, France	FFT81	SITOR 1034 1357 1534 Mode B wx 0802 tfc list 1502 1804
16811.00	Coast stations ch 9 dup. 16687.5kHz		RTTY
16811.00	Dammam, Saudi Arabia	HZG	SITOR
16811.00	Valparaiso, Chile	CBV	SITOR 0709 1049 1851 2123
16811.50	Coast stations ch 10 dup. 16688.0kHz		RTTY
16811.50	Bahrain	A9M	SITOR 0734 0838 0921 1139 1356 1550 1650 1905
16812.00	Coast stations ch 11 dup. 16688.5kHz		RTTY
16812.00	Mobile, USA	WLO	SITOR 1413 1523 1805 2214
16812.50	Coast stations ch 12 dup. 16689.0kHz		RTTY
16812.50	Apra Harbour CG, Guam	NRV	SITOR 1037 1107 1800 1829
16812.50	Boston CG, USA	NMF	SITOR 1553 2217
16812.50	Perth, Australia	VIP45	SITOR
16812.50	San Francisco CG, USA	NMC	SITOR 0830 1050
16813.00	Coast stations ch 13 dup. 16689.5kHz		RTTY
16813.00	Moscow, Russia	UAT	SITOR 0927 1252 1350 1450 1618 Mode B tfc list 1400 1800
16813.50	Coast stations ch 14 dup. 16690.0kHz		RTTY

kHz.	Station	Call	Mode / Heard/Times GMT
16813.50	Goeteborg, Sweden	SAG	SITOR 0837 1507
16814.00	Coast stations ch 15 dup. 16690.5kHz		RTTY
16814.00	Mobile, USA	WLO	SITOR 1205 1506 1759
16814.50	Coast stations ch 16 dup. 16691.0kHz		RTTY
16814.50	Berne, Switzerland	HEC17	SITOR 1405 2125 Mode B tfc list 1632
16815.00	Coast stations ch 17 dup. 16691.5kHz		RTTY
16815.00	Singapore	9VG83	SITOR 0950 1539 1653 1800
16815.50	Coast stations ch 18 dup. 16692.0kHz		RTTY
16815.50	Lyngby, Denmark	OXZ	SITOR 0710 1045 1801
16815.50	Pinang, Malaysia	9MG17	SITOR
16816.00	Coast stations ch 19 dup. 16692.5kHz		RTTY
16816.00	Aqaba, Jordan	JYO	SITOR
16816.00	Capetown, RSA	ZSC64	SITOR 1506 1542 1651 1733 1849
16816.50	Coast stations ch 20 dup. 16693.0kHz		RTTY
16816.50	San Francisco CG, USA	NMC	SITOR 1556
16817.00	Coast stations ch 21 dup. 16693.5kHz		RTTY
16817.00	Chatham, USA	WCC	SITOR 1143 1508 1730 Mode B 1646 tfc list 1840 (news, Suns) 1802
16817.50	Coast stations ch 22 dup. 16694.0kHz		RTTY
16818.00	Coast stations ch 23 dup. 16694.5kHz		RTTY
16818.00	Athens, Greece	SVT6	SITOR 0752 1358 1513 1825 2151 Mode B 2108
16818.00	Odessa, Ukraine	UUI	SITOR 0930 1241 1406
16818.50	Coast stations ch 25 dup. 16695.5kHz		RTTY
16818.50	Mobile, USA	WLO	SITOR 1206 1410
16818.50	Singapore	9VG	SITOR 1338 1444 1509 1616 1702 1908
16819.00	Coast stations ch 26 dup. 16696.0kHz		RTTY
16819.50	Coast stations ch 27 dup. 16696.5kHz		RTTY
16819.50	Chesapeake CG, USA	NMN	SITOR 1351 1507 1620 2230 Mode B 1904
16820.00	Coast stations ch 28 dup. 16697.0kHz		RTTY
16820.00	Rome, Italy	IAR	SITOR 0839 0928 1215 1254 2126
16820.50	Coast stations ch 29 dup. 16697.5kHz		RTTY
16820.50	Mobile, USA	WLO	SITOR 1412 1549 1703 2232
16820.50	Odessa, Ukraine	UUI	SITOR 1409
16821.00	Coast stations ch 30 dup. 16698.0kHz		RTTY
16821.00	Hong Kong	VPS82	SITOR 1036 1551
16821.00	St Lys, France	FFT83	SITOR 0742 1442
16821.50	Coast stations ch 31 dup. 16698.5kHz		RTTY
16821.50	Halifax, Canada	VCS	SITOR 1036
16821.50	Lyngby, Denmark	OXZ	SITOR 1253 1835 Mode B tfc list 1332
16822.00	Coast stations ch 32 dup. 16699.0kHz		RTTY
16822.00	Vancouver, Canada	VAI	SITOR
16822.50	Coast stations ch 33 dup. 16699.5kHz		RTTY
16822.50	Panama	HPP	SITOR
16822.50	Singapore	9VG97	SITOR 1101
16823.00	Coast stations ch 34 dup. 16700.0kHz		RTTY
16823.00	Genoa, Italy	ICB	SITOR 1109 1352 1615
16823.50	Coast stations ch 35 dup. 16700.5kHz		RTTY
16823.50	Odessa, Ukraine	UUI	SITOR 0757 0921 1411
16824.00	Coast stations ch 36 dup. 16701.0kHz		RTTY
16824.00	Portishead, UK	GKP6	SITOR 1011 1141 1317 1525 2019
16824.50	Coast stations ch 37 dup. 16701.5kHz		RTTY
16824.50	General Pacheco, Argentina	LPD	SITOR 0838 0945 2128 2208
16825.00	Coast stations ch 38 dup. 16702.0kHz		RTTY
16825.00	Chatham, USA	WCC	SITOR 0659 1047 1216 1420 1508 1732 1812
16825.00	Helsinki, Finland	OFA	SITOR
16825.50	Coast stations ch 39 dup. 16702.5kHz		RTTY
16825.50	General Pacheco, Argentina	LPD	SITOR
16826.00	Coast stations ch 40 dup. 16703.0kHz		RTTY
16826.00	Mobile, USA	WLO	SITOR 1542 1837 2229
16826.00	Tallinn, Estonia	ESA	SITOR 0746 0840 1421 Mode B 1112 1655 news & weather 1545-1615
16826.50	Coast stations ch 41 dup. 16703.5kHz		RTTY
16826.50	Scheveningen, Holland	PCH65	SITOR 0711 1412 1555 1921 2129 2222
16827.00	Coast stations ch 42 dup. 16704.0kHz		RTTY
16827.00	Portishead, UK	GKY6	SITOR 1038 1518 1612
16827.50	Coast stations ch 43 dup. 16704.5kHz		RTTY
16827.50	Berne, Switzerland	HEC37	SITOR 1424 1552 2228
16828.00	Coast stations ch 44 dup. 16705.0kHz		RTTY
16828.00	Mobile, USA	WLO	SITOR 1319 1353 1422 1500 1727 2130
16828.00	Novorossiysk, Russia	UFN	SITOR 1756 2110 Mode B (to UZIS) 1645
16828.50	Coast stations ch 45 dup. 16705.5kHz		RTTY
16828.50	Italian Naval	IDR6	CW 0822 2131
16829.00	Coast stations ch 46 dup. 16706.0kHz		RTTY
16829.00	Mariupol, Ukraine	USU	SITOR 0641 0751 0935 1146 1557 1730 1813 2020 Mode B 1438
16829.50	Coast stations ch 47 dup. 16706.5kHz		RTTY
16830.00	Coast stations ch 48 dup. 16707.0kHz		RTTY

kHz.	Station	Call	Mode / Heard/Times GMT
16830.00	Berne, Switzerland	HEC27	SITOR 1038 1217 1446 2208
16830.00	Odessa, Ukraine	UUI	SITOR 1526
16830.50	Coast stations ch 49 dup. 16707.5kHz		RTTY
16830.50	Athens, Greece	SVU6	SITOR 0735 0946 1617 1851 Mode B tfc list 1420 2020 2220
16831.00	Coast stations ch 50 dup. 16708.0kHz		RTTY
16831.00	Hong Kong	VPS83	SITOR 0916 1105
16831.00	Mobile, USA	WLO	SITOR 1413 1554 2227
16831.50	Coast stations ch 51 dup. 16708.5kHz		RTTY
16831.50	St Lys, France	FFT84	SITOR 0923 1455 1545 2131
16832.00	Coast stations ch 52 dup. 16709.0kHz		RTTY
16832.00	Rogaland, Norway	LGX3	SITOR 1402 1529 1622 1816
16832.50	Coast stations ch 53 dup. 16709.5kHz		RTTY
16833.00	Coast stations ch 54 dup. 16710.0kHz		RTTY
16833.00	Mobile, USA	WLO	SITOR 1546 1751 1922
16833.50	Coast stations ch 55 dup. 16710.5kHz		RTTY
16834.00	Coast stations ch 56 dup. 16711.0kHz		RTTY
16834.50	Coast stations ch 57 dup. 16711.5kHz		RTTY
16834.50	Goeteborg, Sweden	SAG	SITOR 0646 0813 0931 1150
16834.50	Slidell, USA	WNU	SITOR 1330 1456 1622 2226
16835.00	Coast stations ch 58 dup. 16712.0kHz		RTTY
16835.50	Coast stations ch 59 dup. 16712.5kHz		RTTY
16836.00	Coast stations ch 60 dup. 16713.0kHz		RTTY
16836.00	Norddeich, Germany	DCF	SITOR 1046 1322 1515 1733 1817 2210
16836.00	Vladivostok, Russia	UFL	SITOR 2141
16836.50	Coast stations ch 61 dup. 16713.5kHz		RTTY
16836.50	Boufarik, Algeria	7TK27	SITOR 1745
16836.50	Mobile, USA	WLO	SITOR 1143 1320 1657 2226 wx 1600
16837.00	Coast stations ch 62 dup. 16714.0kHz		RTTY
16837.50	Coast stations ch 63 dup. 16714.5kHz		RTTY
16838.00	Coast stations ch 64 dup. 16715.0kHz		RTTY
16838.00	Stettin, Poland	SPB81	SITOR 0754 0935 1404 1855
16838.50	Coast stations ch 65 dup. 16715.5kHz		RTTY
16838.50	Rijeka, Croatia	9AR	SITOR 1039 1457 1607 1818
16839.00	Coast stations ch 66 dup. 16716.0kHz		RTTY
16839.00	Gdynia, Poland	SPA82	SITOR 1117 1500 1704
16839.00	Scheveningen, Holland	PCH66	SITOR 1427 1544 2013 2211
16839.50	Coast stations ch 67 dup. 16716.5kHz		RTTY
16839.50	Genoa, Italy	ICB	SITOR 0950 1353 1619
16839.50	Novorossiysk, Russia	UFN	SITOR 0751 0946 1938 (to "Akademik Verestchagin" UUOA) 1610
16840.00	Coast stations ch 68 dup. 16717.0kHz		RTTY
16840.00	Portishead, UK	GKQ6	SITOR 0929 1403 1520 1614 2132 2223
16840.50	Coast stations ch 69 dup. 16717.5kHz		RTTY
16840.50	Batumi, Georgia	UHK	SITOR 1355
16841.00	Coast stations ch 70 dup. 16718.0kHz		RTTY
16841.50	Coast stations ch 71 dup. 16718.5kHz		RTTY
16842.00	Coast stations ch 72 dup. 16719.0kHz		RTTY
16842.50	Coast stations ch 73 dup. 16719.5kHz		RTTY
16843.00	Coast stations ch 74 dup. 16720.0kHz		RTTY
16843.50	Coast stations ch 75 dup. 16720.5kHz		RTTY
16844.00	Coast stations ch 76 dup. 16721.0kHz		RTTY
16844.50	Coast stations ch 77 dup. 16721.5kHz		RTTY
16845.00	Coast stations ch 78 dup. 16722.0kHz		RTTY
16845.50	Coast stations ch 79 dup. 16722.5kHz		RTTY
16846.00	Coast stations ch 80 dup. 16723.0kHz		RTTY
16846.00	St Petersburg, Russia	UGC	SITOR 0926 1153 1621 1808 1900 Mode B tfc list 1950
16846.50	Coast stations ch 81 dup. 16723.5kHz		RTTY
16847.00	Coast stations ch 82 dup. 16724.0kHz		RTTY
16847.50	Coast stations ch 83 dup. 16724.5kHz		RTTY
16848.00	Coast stations ch 84 dup. 16725.0kHz		RTTY
16848.50	Coast stations ch 85 dup. 16725.5kHz		RTTY
16849.00	Coast stations ch 86 dup. 16726.0kHz		RTTY
16849.00	Odessa, Ukraine	UUI	SITOR 1731
16849.50	Coast stations ch 87 dup. 16726.5kHz		RTTY
16850.00	Coast stations ch 88 dup. 16727.0kHz		RTTY
16850.50	Coast stations ch 89 dup. 16727.5kHz		RTTY
16851.00	Coast stations ch 90 dup. 16728.0kHz		RTTY
16851.50	Coast stations ch 91 dup. 16728.5kHz		RTTY
16851.50	Odessa, Ukraine	UUI	SITOR 1800
16852.00	Coast stations ch 92 dup. 16729.0kHz		RTTY
16852.50	Coast stations ch 93 dup. 16729.5kHz		RTTY
16853.00	Coast stations ch 94 dup. 16730.0kHz		RTTY
16853.50	Coast stations ch 95 dup. 16730.5kHz		RTTY
16854.00	Coast stations ch 96 dup. 16731.0kHz		RTTY
16854.50	Coast stations ch 97 dup. 16731.5kHz		RTTY
16855.00	Coast stations ch 98 dup. 16732.0kHz		RTTY
16855.50	Coast stations ch 99 dup. 16732.5kHz		RTTY

kHz.	Station	Call	Mode / Heard/Times GMT
16856.00	Coast stations ch 100 dup. 16733.0kHz		RTTY
16856.50	Coast stations ch 101 dup. 16733.5kHz		RTTY
16857.00	Coast stations ch 102 dup. 16739.0kHz		RTTY
16857.50	Coast stations ch 103 dup. 16739.5kHz		RTTY
16857.50	Odessa, Ukraine	UUI	SITOR 0926 1118 1500 1745 1822 (to "Kremenchug" UTYZ) 0926
16858.00	Coast stations ch 104 dup. 16740.0kHz		RTTY
16858.50	Coast stations ch 105 dup. 16740.5kHz		RTTY
16859.00	Coast stations ch 106 dup. 16741.0kHz		RTTY
16859.50	Coast stations ch 107 dup. 16741.5kHz		RTTY
16860.00	Coast stations ch 108 dup. 16742.0kHz		RTTY
16860.50	Coast stations ch 109 dup. 16742.5kHz		RTTY
16861.00	Coast stations ch 110 dup. 16743.0kHz		RTTY
16861.50	Coast stations ch 111 dup. 16743.5kHz		RTTY
16862.00	Coast stations ch 112 dup. 16744.0kHz		RTTY
16862.50	Coast stations ch 113 dup. 16744.5kHz		RTTY
16863.00	Coast stations ch 114 dup. 16745.0kHz		RTTY
16863.50	Coast stations ch 115 dup. 16745.5kHz		RTTY
16863.50	Odessa, Ukraine	UUI	SITOR 1802 (to "Azerbajdzhan" UFZX) 1409
16864.00	Coast stations ch 116 dup. 16746.0kHz		RTTY
16864.00	Riga, Latvia	UDH	SITOR 1700
16864.50	Coast stations ch 117 dup. 16746.5kHz		RTTY
16865.00	Coast stations ch 118 dup. 16747.0kHz		RTTY
16865.50	Coast stations ch 119 dup. 16747.5kHz		RTTY
16866.00	Coast stations ch 120 dup. 16748.0kHz		RTTY
16866.50	Coast stations ch 121 dup. 16748.5kHz		RTTY
16867.00	Coast stations ch 122 dup. 16749.0kHz		RTTY
16867.50	Coast stations ch 123 dup. 16749.5kHz		RTTY
16868.00	Coast stations ch 124 dup. 16750.0kHz		RTTY
16868.50	Coast stations ch 125 dup. 16750.5kHz		RTTY
16869.00	Coast stations ch 126 dup. 16751.0kHz		RTTY
16869.50	Coast stations ch 127 dup. 16751.5kHz		RTTY
16870.00	Coast stations ch 128 dup. 16752.0kHz		RTTY
16870.00	Dixon, USA	KMI	SITOR 2209
16870.50	Bulacan, Philippines	DZJ	CW 1242 1321 1546 1744 1912 (to 3EBA9) 1555
16870.50	Coast stations ch 129 dup. 16752.5kHz		RTTY
16871.00	Coast stations ch 130 dup. 16753.0kHz		RTTY
16871.50	Coast stations ch 131 dup. 16753.5kHz		RTTY
16872.00	Coast stations ch 132 dup. 16754.0kHz		RTTY
16872.50	Coast stations ch 133 dup. 16754.5kHz		RTTY
16873.00	Coast stations ch 134 dup. 16755.0kHz		RTTY
16873.50	Coast stations ch 135 dup. 16755.5kHz		RTTY
16874.00	Coast stations ch 136 dup. 16756.0kHz		RTTY
16874.50	Coast stations ch 137 dup. 16756.5kHz		RTTY
16875.00	Coast stations ch 138 dup. 16757.0kHz		RTTY
16875.50	Coast stations ch 139 dup. 16757.5kHz		RTTY
16876.00	Coast stations ch 140 dup. 16758.0kHz		RTTY
16876.50	Coast stations ch 141 dup. 16758.5kHz		RTTY
16877.00	Coast stations ch 142 dup. 16759.0kHz		RTTY
16877.50	Coast stations ch 143 dup. 16759.5kHz		RTTY
16878.00	Coast stations ch 144 dup. 16760.0kHz		RTTY
16878.50	Coast stations ch 145 dup. 16760.5kHz		RTTY
16879.00	Coast stations ch 146 dup. 16761.0kHz		RTTY
16879.50	Coast stations ch 147 dup. 16761.5kHz		RTTY
16880.00	Coast stations ch 148 dup. 16762.0kHz		RTTY
16880.00	Guangzhou, China	XSQ	SITOR 1100 1257 1547 1809 Mode B 0638
16880.50	Coast stations ch 149 dup. 16762.5kHz		RTTY
16881.00	Coast stations ch 150 dup. 16763.0kHz		RTTY
16881.00	Istanbul, Turkey	TAH	SITOR 1501
16881.50	Coast stations ch 151 dup. 16763.5kHz		RTTY
16882.00	Coast stations ch 152 dup. 16764.0kHz		RTTY
16882.50	Coast stations ch 153 dup. 16764.5kHz		RTTY
16883.00	Coast stations ch 154 dup. 16765.0kHz		RTTY
16883.00	Ostend, Belgium	OST60	SITOR 0753 0813 1041 1623 1734 2134
16883.50	Coast stations ch 155 dup. 16765.5kHz		RTTY
16884.00	Coast stations ch 156 dup. 16766.0kHz		RTTY
16884.50	Coast stations ch 157 dup. 16766.5kHz		RTTY
16885.00	Coast stations ch 158 dup. 16767.0kHz		RTTY
16885.50	Coast stations ch 159 dup. 16767.5kHz		RTTY
16886.00	Coast stations ch 160 dup. 16768.0kHz		RTTY
16886.50	Coast stations ch 161 dup. 16768.5kHz		RTTY
16887.00	Coast stations ch 162 dup. 16769.0kHz		RTTY
16887.50	Coast stations ch 163 dup. 16769.5kHz		RTTY
16888.00	Coast stations ch 164 dup. 16770.0kHz		RTTY
16888.50	Coast stations ch 165 dup. 16770.5kHz		RTTY
16889.00	Coast stations ch 166 dup. 16771.0kHz		RTTY
16889.50	Coast stations ch 167 dup. 16771.5kHz		RTTY

kHz.	Station	Call	Mode / Heard/Times GMT
16890.00	Coast stations ch 168 dup. 16772.0kHz		RTTY
16890.50	Coast stations ch 169 dup. 16772.5kHz		RTTY
16891.00	Coast stations ch 170 dup. 16773.0kHz		RTTY
16891.50	Coast stations ch 171 dup. 16773.5kHz		RTTY
16892.00	Coast stations ch 172 dup. 16774.0kHz		RTTY
16892.00	Shanghai, China	XSG	SITOR 1200
16892.50	Coast stations ch 173 dup. 16774.5kHz		RTTY
16893.00	Coast stations ch 174 dup. 16775.0kHz		RTTY
16893.50	Coast stations ch 175 dup. 16775.5kHz		RTTY
16894.00	Coast stations ch 176 dup. 16776.0kHz		RTTY
16894.50	Coast stations ch 177 dup. 16776.5kHz		RTTY
16895.00	Coast stations ch 178 dup. 16777.0kHz		RTTY
16895.50	Coast stations ch 179 dup. 16777.5kHz		RTTY
16896.00	Coast stations ch 180 dup. 16778.0kHz		RTTY
16896.50	Coast stations ch 181 dup. 16778.5kHz		RTTY
16897.00	Coast stations ch 182 dup. 16779.0kHz		170/50nc 2201
16897.50	Coast stations ch 183 dup. 16779.5kHz		RTTY
16898.00	Coast stations ch 184 dup. 16780.0kHz		RTTY
16898.00	Turkish Embassy traffic	TAD	144FEC 5 let grps 1356
16898.50	Coast stations ch 185 dup. 16780.5kHz		RTTY
16899.00	Coast stations ch 186 dup. 16781.0kHz		RTTY
16899.50	Coast stations ch 187 dup. 16781.5kHz		RTTY
16900.00	Coast stations ch 188 dup. 16782.0kHz		RTTY
16900.00	Goeteborg, Sweden	SAG	SITOR 2136
16900.50	Coast stations ch 189 dup. 16782.5kHz		RTTY
16901.00	Coast stations ch 190 dup. 16783.0kHz		RTTY
16901.50	Coast stations ch 191 dup. 16783.5kHz		RTTY
16902.00	Coast stations ch 192 dup. 16784.0kHz		RTTY
16902.50	Coast stations ch 193 dup. 16784.5kHz		RTTY
16903.00	Coast stations digital selective calling		RTTY
16903.50	Coast stations digital selective calling		RTTY
16904.00	Coast stations digital selective calling		RTTY
16904.90	French Naval, Djibouti	FUV	CW 0737 1041 1357 1457 1628 1852 2215 wx 1004
16906.00	Basrah, Iraq	YIR	CW 1548 1609
16909.70	Izmail, Ukraine	USO5	CW 1322 1512 tfc list 1102
16910.00	Seoul, S Korea	HLJ	CW 0617 0830 0910
16911.20	Tokyo, Japan	JNA	CW 0642 0713 0755 0818 0952 1149
16912.00	British Naval	GYA	FAX wx maps
16912.50	Alexandria, Egypt	SUH5	CW 0910 1042 1359 1516 tfc list 0710
16914.50	Stettin, Poland	SPB83	SITOR (paired 16787.5) 1741 1840 Mode B 2207 tfc list 1800
16914.50	US Naval	NWC	FAX wx maps 0906
16914.50	Valparaiso, Chile	CBV	CW 1853 2223 tfc list 2205
16915.00	French Naval, Reunion	FUX	CW 1341 1532
16916.50	Shanghai, China	XSG8	CW 0831 0911 tfc list 1519
16916.50	Tuckerton, USA	WSC	CW 1135 1405 1502 1603 1749 1805 tfc list 1422 1522 2222
16918.00	Juncao, Brazil	PPJ	CW 1612 1806 1853 2029 2133 2216
16918.30	British Naval	GYA/MTO	75r 1623 2209
16918.80	Portishead, UK	GKJ6	CW reserve frequency
16919.00	Australian Naval	VHP	CW 0901 1358 1622 2136 2223
16919.60	Sydney, Australia	VIX6	CW 0911
16921.00	Havana, Cuba	CLS	CW 1137 1530 1854
16922.00	Indian Naval	VTH	50n (RBSL) p/lang (Eng) 1243 1325
16922.00	Murmansk, Russia	UQA4	CW 0618 1115 1151 1215 1406 1606 (to ESGK) 1504
16922.00	Murmansk, Russia	UQA4	170/50rc (to UNCC) 1703
16923.80	Helsinki, Finland	OFJ7	CW 0832 1201 1807 2208 tfc list 0806 2213
16927.00	Kaliningrad, Russia	UIW	170/50nc 1508 1519 list & nav wng 1620
16928.40	Rogaland, Norway	LFX	CW (listens 16736.5) 0848 1407 1855
16930.00	Gelendzhik, Russia	UVA	CW 1326 1344 tfc list 1503
16930.50	Malaysian Naval	9MR	75r (RMMJ) RYs & SGs 1427 1551 1630 1915 wx (in Eng) 1802
16932.00	Boufarik, Algeria	7TF10	CW 0815 0913 1048 1808 tfc list 0730 1533
16933.20	Chatham, USA	WCC	CW 1400 1508 1627 2156 tfc list 1253 2058 wx 1640 1710
16933.20	Nagasaki, Japan	JOS	CW 0819 0849 0917
16935.00	Doha, Qatar	A7D	CW 0918 0954 1043
16938.00	Indian Naval	VTG8	CW 0849 1408 1421 wx 0930
16940.00	Kaohsiung, Taiwan	XSW	CW 0833 0919
16942.50	Rijeka, Croatia	9AR7	CW 0756 1632 1810 2148 tfc list 1005 1200 1400 1600 2000
16947.00	Odessa, Ukraine	UUI	CW 0748 1140 1811 2200
16947.40	Bridgetown, Barbados	8PO	CW 1633 1923 tfc list 1620 1900
16947.60	St Lys, France	FFT8	CW nav wngs 0957
16948.50	Halifax, Canada	VCS	CW 1509 1624 1842 2158 ice wng 1409 wx 1535
16949.00	Liepaja, Latvia	UPW2	CW 0914 0958 1225
16950.00	Malaysian Naval	9MB	CW 0834 0922 1428 1534 1628 1744 1916
16951.50	French Naval, Dakar	6VW	CW 0850 1221 1524 1857 2147 2224
16953.00	Dammam, Saudi Arabia	HZG	CW (to "Maknassy" TSLU) 1425
16954.40	Portishead, UK	GKC6	CW 1858
16955.00	Riga, Latvia	UDH	SITOR 0754 1200 1410 1605 1803 Mode B 1535 1945

kHz.	Station	Call	Mode / Heard/Times GMT
16956.00	Hochiminhville, Vietnam	XVS	CW 1557 tfc list 1550
16957.00	French Naval, Fort de France	FUF	CW 2204
16957.80	French Naval, Numea	FUJ	CW 0844 0914
16959.20	Lisbon, Portugal	CUL22	CW 1417
16960.00	Murmansk, Russia	UMV	CW 1407
16960.00	Ras Tannurah, Saudi Arabia	HZY	CW 1019 tfc list 1000
16961.00	Havana, Cuba	CLA40	CW 1142 1247 1404 1525 1821 2144
16961.50	French Naval, Martinique	FUF	CW 0702 1121 1521 1635 1745 2148 2223
16963.00	Kaliningrad, Russia	UIW	170/50nc RYs & "ANS 16672.5 PSE" 1804
16966.00	Athens, Greece	SVI6	CW 0835 0852 1117 1409 1522 2203
16966.50	Singapore	9VG58	CW 1636 tfc list each even hour + 30
16968.00	Belem, Brazil	PPL	CW 1119 1558 1800 wx (Eng) 2006 nav wngs (Eng) 2220
16969.00	Mobile, USA	WLO	CW 0620 1411 1526 1629 1926 2151
16970.00	St Petersburg, Russia	UGC	170/50nc 0914 1412 nav wngs 1510 (to "4KB" exchange rates 0704)
16971.00	Tokyo Press (KYODO)	JJC	FAX 0653 0836 0910 1637
16972.00	Chatham, USA	WCC	CW 1446 1523 1832 1905 2204 wx 1740 tfc list 0650 1257
16974.00	Stettin, Poland	SPE81	CW 1204 1510 1900 2129 2202 tfc list 1810
16974.60	Portishead, UK	GKD6	CW reserve frequency
16975.00	Archangel, Russia	RKLM	CW 1329
16975.00	Madras, India	VWM	CW 1020 1337 tfc list 0200 0400 0600 0800 1000 1200 1400
16976.00	Chesapeake CG, USA	NMN	CW 1119 1341 1447 1527 1747 1924 2140
16978.40	Mauritius	3BM6	CW 1120 1348 1530 1605 wx 1630
16980.00	Novorossiysk, Russia	UNQ	CW 0915 1334 1512 2206 tfc list 0911 1416 1811 1911
16980.00	Novorossiysk, Russia	UNQ	170/50nc 0820 1250 1324 1738
16980.40	Norddeich, Germany	DAM	CW 0759 0829 1054 1833 2150 tfc list 0730 1530 1730
16981.50	Athens, Greece	SVG6	CW 0716 0846 1249 1322 2211
16982.50	UNID	KOAT	CW (clg HKMR) 1432
16984.00	Rio de Janeiro, Brazil	PPR	CW 0837 0917 1538 1815 2152 2204 tfc list 1901 2102
16986.00	Portuguese Naval	CTP	CW 0847 1003 1144 1448 1638 1748
16987.00	Gibraltar Naval	GYU	75n 0707 1331 2200
16990.00	Seoul, S Korea	HLO	CW 0838 0854
16992.80	Moscow, Russia	UAT	CW tfc list 1502
16993.50	UNID		CW nav wngs (Slav) 1353
16994.00	Singapore	9VG22	CW (with ELQR9) 0951
16997.00	Riga, Latvia	UDH	CW 0839 0911 1057 1413 1639 1814 tfc list 1902
16997.60	Mobile, USA	WLO	CW 0648 1313 1350 1403 1748 1834 2222
16997.60	Mobile, USA	WLO	SITOR Mode B tfc list 1540 wx 1145 1245
16998.50	Choshi, Japan	JDC	CW 0646
17002.40	Shanghai, China	XSG29	CW 0657 0850 0927 tfc list 1231 1631
17004.00	Barranquilla, Colombia	HKB	CW 1146 1246 1822 1907 2213
17004.30	RSA Naval	ZRH	CW 1616
17005.00	Rome, Italy	IAR37	CW
17007.20	Scheveningen, Holland	PCH61	CW 0919 1412 1640 2207
17008.50	Istanbul, Turkey	TAH	CW 0800 0954 1206 1639 1836 tfc list 0900
17010.00	St Petersburg, Russia	UGC	CW 1743
17010.00	St Petersburg, Russia	UGC	170/50nc 1740
17010.50	Keelung, Taiwan	XSX	CW 0709 0851 0928
17013.50	Nicosia, Cyprus	5BA	CW 0706 0830 1123 1512 tfc list 1437 1612 1839 (freq varies)
17014.00	Feodosia, Ukraine	UTM	CW 0958
17016.00	Gdynia, Poland	SPH82	CW
17016.00	Single Letter Beacon	C	CW 0746 0801 0929 1510 1749 1816
17016.10	Single Letter Beacon	S	CW 1447 1640 1933 2215
17017.10	Ostend, Belgium	OST6	CW 0831 0955 1448 1525
17018.00	Spanish Naval	EBA	CW 0854 1826 nav wngs 1725 1817
17018.00	Spanish Naval	EBA	75r 1007
17020.00	Murmansk, Russia	UDK2	CW 1207 1426 1749 tfc list 0730
17020.00	Murmansk, Russia	UDK2	170/50nc 1000 1405 1425 (to EORK) 0920
17021.50	Istanbul, Turkey	TAH	CW 0710 0855 1836 tfc list 0900 1903
17022.50	Mobile, USA	WLO	CW 1641 1902 wx & nav wngs 1317 1922 2131 tfc list 2200
17022.50	Mobile, USA	WLO	SITOR Mode B tfc list 1541
17024.00	Goeteborg, Sweden	SAG	SITOR 1208 1758 1936 2216
17025.00	Providenya, Russia	UPB	CW (to USDY) 0807
17026.00	Palo Alto, USA	KFS	CW 0622 1543 1641 1835 2206 tfc list 1838
17027.00	St Lys, France	FFL8	CW 0810 1318 1509 tfc list 0846 1836 wx 1642
17029.00	Tokyo Met, Japan	JMC6	CW 0832
17036.00	Archangel, Russia	UCE	170/50nc 1043 nav wngs 0726
17037.00	Constanza, Romania	YQI6	CW 0956 1234 1428 1449 1500 tfc list 1002 1802
17038.00	Slidell, USA	WNU55	CW 1430 1542 1752 1909 2218 2233
17038.50	Sebastopol, Ukraine	URL	CW 0930 1555 1815
17040.00	US Naval	NSY	FAX wx maps 1510
17040.80	St Lys, France	FFS8	CW
17043.20	Choshi, Japan	JCU	CW 0712 0755 1008
17045.60	Buenaventura, Colombia	HKC	CW 2154 2247 2321
17045.60	General Pacheco, Argentina	LPD46	CW 1432 1514 1628 1816 1903 2153 2222 (to USXG) 2201
17045.60	Rijeka, Croatia	9AR8	CW
17048.00	Norddeich, Germany	DAF	CW 1414 1618

kHz.	Station	Call	Mode / Heard/Times GMT
17049.00	Odessa, Ukraine	UUI	CW 0832 1720
17049.00	Odessa, Ukraine	UUI	170/50nc (news) 1433 & 170/50rc 1434 1515 (to UPJG) 1527
17050.00	Israeli Naval	4XZ	CW 0657 1319 1407 1753 2141 wx 0905 1304 1633 2207
17053.00	Keelung, Taiwan	XSX	CW 0714 0907 0932 1215 (frequency varies to 17052.0)
17060.00	Haifa, Israel	4XO	CW 1346 1516 1636 1837 2209 tfc list 1627 1828
17062.00	Dammam, Saudi Arabia	HZG	CW
17063.00	Odessa, Ukraine	UUI	CW 1448 1755 tfc list 0700 0800 1400 1500 1600 1800
17064.00	Gdynia, Poland	SPH83	CW 1105
17064.80	Madrid, Spain	EDZ6	CW 0959 1436 1643 1818 1910 tfc list 0800
17066.00	Moscow, Russia	UAT	CW 1320 (to USNN) 1239 tfc list 1235
17066.00	Moscow, Russia	UAT	170/50nc (to "Slavyanka") 1251
17068.40	Lyngby, Denmark	OXZ8	CW 1637 tfc list 1448
17069.50	Tokyo Press (KYODO)	JJC	FAX 0744 0909 1058 1644 2220
17072.00	Portishead, UK	GKG6	CW (wkg freq to ships) 1112
17074.00	Rogaland, Norway	LGX	CW 1513 1942 2159 tfc list 1620 1820
17077.00	Tallinn, Estonia	ESA	CW tfc list 1000 1102 1834
17079.00	Seoul, S Korea	HLF	CW 0743 1600
17084.00	Australian Naval	VHI	CW 2149
17084.00	Trieste, Italy	IQX	CW 1514 1644 1821 1943
17085.00	Mariupol, Ukraine	USU	CW tfc list 1605
17088.80	San Francisco, USA	KPH	CW 0852 2019 2211
17091.00	Guangzhou, China	XSQ	CW 0742 0954 1337 1544 1645 2158 tfc list 1431 1532
17092.00	Portishead, UK	GKH6	CW wkg freq to ships 1548
17093.00	Nagasaki, Japan	JOR	CW 0840 0934 1017 1124 1207
17093.60	Pakistan Naval	AQP	CW 0741 0830 1105 1217
17094.80	Athens, Greece	SVA6	CW 0955 1622 1732 tfc list 1400 1800 2200
17096.00	Hong Kong	VPS80	CW 0835 0936 1108 2211 wx 2220
17098.40	Portishead, UK	GKA6	CW 1059 2137 wx 0948 2131 tfc list 0825 1314 1418 1507 1907 2201
17103.20	Shanghai, China	XSG	CW 0937 1100 1218 1521 1818 2221
17104.20	Scheveningen, Holland	PCH62	CW
17105.00	Rome (Medical Centre), Italy	IRM	CW 1000 1339 1444 1515 1822 1911
17107.00	Tallinn, Estonia	ESF	CW 0958 1734
17112.60	Choshi, Japan	JCS	CW 0739 2222
17113.00	Portishead, UK	GKB6	CW 0842 1102 1516 1742 1839 2155 2213
17114.00	Stettin, Poland	SPE41	CW 1947 (harmonic of 8557.0)
17115.00	St Petersburg, Russia	UGC	CW 0625 0959 1341 1408 1446 1638
17117.60	Slidell, USA	WNU45	CW 1518 1545 1645 2157 tfc list 2137
17122.40	Brazilian Naval	PWZ	CW 1925 2113 2138
17124.70	Egyptian Embassy traffic		SITOR 1742
17130.00	Seoul, S Korea	HLW	CW 0843 2224
17132.00	RSA Naval	ZSJ6	CW 1713
17134.00	Klaipeda, Lithuania	LYK	CW 1104 1608 tfc list 1002 1302 1802
17134.00	Klaipeda, Lithuania	LYK	170/50nc 0912 1413 1641 1823
17135.00	Kiev, Ukraine	UTQ	CW 0840 1210 1451 1646 1826
17136.80	Portishead, UK	GKM6	CW reserve frequency
17137.00	Batumi, Georgia	UHK	CW 1822 tfc list 1301 1501
17138.00	Klaipeda Harbour, Lithuania	LYL	CW 0804 0831 1008 1409 1547 1743 tfc list 0801
17138.00	Klaipeda Harbour, Lithuania	LYL	170/50nc 1753
17141.00	Novorossiysk, Russia	UFN	170/50nc 1337 1839
17141.00	Novorossiysk, Russia	UFN	CW 1105 1301 1408 2152 2211 tfc list 1004 1610 1836
17141.60	Mariupol, Ukraine	USU	CW 0719 1221
17141.60	Mariupol, Ukraine	USU	170/50nc (to UPJU) 1108 (to UPLJ) 1127
17143.60	Norddeich, Germany	DAN	CW 1256 1415 1447 1552 1906
17145.00	Varna, Bulgaria	LZW63	CW 0844 1029 1452 tfc list 1305 1505
17146.40	Haifa, Israel	4XO	CW 0938 1033 1556 1907 2224 tfc list 1626 1825 (& msrd 17146.0)
17146.40	Valparaiso, Chile	CBV	CW nav wngs (Eng) 2215 (also rptd with wx FAX)
17147.00	Sebastopol, Ukraine	URL	CW 0729 1240 1555 1604 1732 1816 tfc list 1502
17147.00	Sebastopol, Ukraine	URL	170/50rc 1411 2007
17147.20	Athens, Greece	SVJ6	CW
17151.20	Portishead, UK	GKI6	CW reserve frequency
17151.30	San Francisco CG, USA	NMC	FAX wx maps 1518 1534
17152.00	Kaliningrad, Russia	UIW	CW 0703 0846 (to "German Matern") 1345
17155.00	Odessa, Ukraine	UUI	CW tfc list 1806
17155.00	Odessa, Ukraine	UUI	170/50rc Ukrainian news 1821
17160.80	Rome, Italy	IAR27	CW 1349 tfc list 1626 wx (Eng) 0834
17161.30	Perth, Australia	VIP	CW 0719 0940 2150 tfc list 1050
17162.00	Olinda, Brazil	PPO	CW 1229 1449 1605 1840 2219 tfc list 1919
17163.00	Moscow Met Centre, Russia	RNO	50nc 0705
17164.80	Capetown, RSA	ZSC7	CW 1504 1537 1649 1746 1908
17165.60	Havana, Cuba	CLA41	CW 1422 2228
17166.50	Choshi, Japan	JCT	CW 2214
17167.50	Portishead, UK	GKK6	CW reserve frequency
17169.00	Bahrain	A9M	CW 0728 1225 1245 1642 tfc list 1105 1505
17170.00	Belem, Brazil	PPL	CW 0945 1545 1606 2205 nav wng 1931 wx 2028
17170.00	Numbers Station		USB "CIO1" Eng (female voice) 0756 1350

kHz.	Station	Call	Mode / Heard/Times GMT
17170.40	Casablanca, Morocco	CNP	CW
17170.50	Curacao, Neth. Antilles	PJC	CW 1545 1527 1608 tfc list 1550 1700
17172.40	Pinang, Malaysia	9MG11	CW 0851 1230 1453 1646 tfc list 1931 wx (Eng) 1400 2205
17173.50	Mobile, USA	WLO	CW 0706 1119 1257 1550 1625 2201 2210
17175.20	Aden	7OA	CW 0722 0752 tfc list 0702
17175.20	Bahrain	A9M	CW 0829 1053 1118 1528 1644 1709
17175.20	Vancouver, Canada	VAI	CW 2144 2230
17177.60	Norddeich, Germany	DAL	CW 1451 1551 1607 1746
17180.00	French Naval, Paris	HWN	CW 1343 1416 1826 1908
17181.00	Riga, Latvia	UDH	CW 0852 1115 1455
17181.00	Riga, Latvia	UDH	170/50nc 1956 (with currency exchange rates) 1945
17182.00	Genoa, Italy	ICB	CW 0836 1120 1610 2202
17184.80	Amboina, Indonesia	PKE	CW 1232 1248
17184.80	Dumai, Indonesia	PKP	CW 0909
17184.80	Madrid, Spain	EAD5	CW
17184.80	North Post, Trinidad	9YL	CW 1536 tfc list 1200 1530
17184.80	Palo Alto, USA	KFS	CW 1512 1553 1625 1843 2148 2230 tfc list 1735
17186.00	Odessa, Ukraine	UUI	CW with QSS/QSX for wx rpts 1750
17187.00	Ostend, Belgium	OST62	CW 0855 1249 1552 1828
17188.00	Athens, Greece	SVD6	CW 0727 1344 1454 1827 1941 2226
17189.60	Luanda, Angola	D3E71	CW 1346 1403 1452 1645 1738 1910
17190.50	Batumi, Georgia	UHK	170/50nc 1334
17190.50	Batumi, Georgia	UHK	CW 0744 1323 1824 1829
17190.50	Boca, Argentina	LSA6	CW 2000
17192.00	Hong Kong	VRN80	CW tfc list 1300
17194.40	Rio de Janeiro, Brazil	PPR	CW 0757 1452 1624 1751 1831 2203 tfc list 1900
17195.00	Moscow, Russia	UJE	CW (to UFHK) 1106
17197.50	Argentine Naval	LOR	100n 5 let grps 1923
17198.30	Dammam, Saudi Arabia	HZG	CW 0709 0843 1121 1324 1429 1553
17198.40	Athens, Greece	SVM6	CW 2035 2117
17198.90	Scheveningen, Holland	PCH60	CW 0726 1053 1547 1626 2156
17203.90	Lyngby, Denmark	OXZ82	CW 0710 1417 tfc list 1551
17206.00	Pinang, Malaysia	9MG	CW
17206.10	Rome, Italy	IAR	CW 1122 1453 1623 1911
17210.60	Capetown, RSA	ZSC39	CW
17213.90	Gdynia, Poland	SPH81	CW 1234 1406 1554 1832
17215.00	Nagasaki, Japan	JDB	CW 0725 0854 1142
17220.40	Genoa, Italy	ICB	CW
17220.50	Nagasaki, Japan	JOU	CW 0729 0837 0912
17220.50	San Francisco CG, US	NMC	CW 1555 2233
17221.40	Doha, Qatar	A7D	CW 1545
17222.40	Genoa, Italy	ICB	CW 1748
17227.50	New Zealand Naval	ZLO	CW 0838 0914
17230.00	Cerrito, Uruguay	CWA	CW 1253 1454 1517 2115 2222 wx 1408 tfc list 2001
17231.50	Kaliningrad, Russia	UIW	CW 0647 0711 1408 1649
17232.00	Panama	HPP	CW 1300 1348 1420 1455 1912 2147 2207 (freq varies)
17232.90	Singapore	9VG53	CW 1337 1555 tfc list 1259
17233.90	Archangel, Russia	UCE	CW 0714 0839 0928 1359 1739 tfc list 1301
17238.80	Tianjin, China	XSV	CW 0744 0841 2238 tfc list 1401
17239.70	Jakarta, Indonesia	PKX	CW 1306 1325 1350 1525 1552
17239.70	Stettin, Poland	SPB	SITOR 1647
17242.00	Coast stations ch 1 dup. 16360.0kHz		USB
17242.00	General Pacheco, Argentina	LPL	USB 1356 2148 2229
17242.00	Klaipeda, Lithuania	LYK	USB 1456
17242.00	Novorossiysk, Russia	UDN	USB 0650 0729 1001 1510 1650
17242.00	Pennsuco, USA	WOM	USB 1437 1522 wx 1305
17242.00	Rogaland, Norway	LFN2	USB
17245.00	Coast stations ch 2 dup. 16363.0kHz		USB
17245.00	Dammam, Saudi Arabia	HZG	USB
17245.00	Dixon, USA	KMI	USB
17245.00	Portishead, UK	GKT62	USB 1012 1705 1834 2216 (with GCRJ) 1550 (with GUUS) 2058
17245.00	Sydney, Australia	VIS	USB
17248.00	Coast stations ch 3 dup. 16366.0kHz		USB
17248.00	Nicosia, Cyprus	5BA62	USB 0825 1135 1419 1609 2127
17248.00	Rogaland, Norway	LFN3	USB
17248.00	Rome, Italy	IAR	USB 1949
17251.00	Coast stations ch 4 dup. 16369.0kHz		USB
17251.00	Halifax, Canada	VCS	USB wx wng 1612 tfc list 1737
17251.00	Perth, Australia	VIP	USB
17251.00	Rogaland, Norway	LFN4	USB 0918 1319 1805 (with ELNR7) 1617
17251.00	St Lys, France	FFL83	USB 1809
17254.00	Coast stations ch 5 dup. 16372.0kHz		USB
17254.00	Goeteborg, Sweden	SAG	USB
17254.00	Lyngby, Denmark	OXZ	USB
17254.00	New York (Ocean Gate), USA	WOO	USB 2151
17254.00	St Petersburg, Russia	UGC	USB 1258 1457 1517

kHz.	Station	Call	Mode / Heard/Times GMT
17254.00	St Lys, France	FFL86	USB
17257.00	Coast stations ch 6 dup. 16375.0kHz		USB
17257.00	Istanbul, Turkey	TAN	USB (on request)
17257.00	Moscow, Russia	UAT	USB 0718
17257.00	Portishead, UK	GKT66	USB
17257.00	Reykjavik, Iceland	TFA	USB
17257.00	Rome, Italy	IAR	USB 0935 1643 1916
17260.00	Coast stations ch 7 dup. 16378.0kHz		USB
17260.00	Athens, Greece	SVN61	USB 0715 1855
17260.00	Gdynia, Poland	SPC81	USB 0700
17260.00	Mobile, USA	WLO	USB
17260.00	Monaco	3AC16	USB 0705
17260.00	Rogaland, Norway	LFN6	USB 1758
17263.00	Coast stations ch 8 dup. 16381.0kHz		USB
17263.00	Capetown, RSA	ZSC28	USB 1754
17263.00	Genoa, Italy	ICB	USB
17263.00	Goeteborg, Sweden	SAG	USB tfc list 1600
17263.00	Vancouver, Canada	VAI	USB
17266.00	Coast stations ch 9 dup. 16384.0kHz		USB
17266.00	Athens, Greece	SVN62	USB 1328
17266.00	Dammam, Saudi Arabia	HZG	USB
17266.00	Pennsuco, USA	WOM	USB 2144 2227
17266.00	Haifa, Israel	4XO	USB
17269.00	Coast stations ch 10 dup. 16387.0kHz		USB
17269.00	Norddeich, Germany	DAP	USB 0802
17269.00	Pennsuco, USA	WOM	USB 2007
17269.00	Rogaland, Norway	LFN8	USB
17269.00	Sydney, Australia	VIS	USB (on request)
17272.00	Coast stations ch 11 dup. 16390.0kHz		USB
17272.00	Berne, Switzerland	HEB17	USB 1014 1238 1348 tfc list 2020
17272.00	Istanbul, Turkey	TAN	USB (on request)
17272.00	Pennsuco, USA	WOM	USB wx 2215
17272.00	Portishead, UK	GKU61	USB
17272.00	Rijeka, Croatia	9AR	USB 0920 1345 1648 (to C6LS6) 1415
17272.00	Rio de Janeiro, Brazil	PPR	USB
17275.00	Coast stations ch 12 dup. 16393.0kHz		USB
17275.00	Aqaba, Jordan	JYO	USB
17275.00	Monaco	3AC	USB 1113
17275.00	Murmansk, Russia	UDK	USB 1218 1648 1821
17275.00	Perth, Australia	VIP	USB (on request)
17275.00	Townsville, Australia	VIT	USB
17278.00	Coast stations ch 13 dup. 16396.0kHz		USB
17278.00	Rio de Janeiro, Brazil	PPR	USB 2155 2225
17278.00	Ostend, Belgium	OSU63	USB 1529 tfc list each odd hr
17278.00	Rogaland, Norway	LFN9	USB
17281.00	Coast stations ch 14 dup. 16399.0kHz		USB
17281.00	Genoa, Italy	ICB	USB 2101
17281.00	Goeteborg, Sweden	SAG	USB
17281.00	Guangzhou, China	XSQ	USB tfc list 1500
17281.00	Helsinki, Finland	OHG2	USB
17281.00	Lyngby, Denmark	OXZ	USB
17284.00	Coast stations ch 15 dup. 16402.0kHz		USB
17284.00	Berne, Switzerland	HEB27	USB 2049
17284.00	Lisbon, Portugal	CUL	USB 1016 1948
17284.00	Portishead, UK	GKU65	USB
17287.00	Coast stations ch 16 dup. 16405.0kHz		USB
17287.00	Norddeich, Germany	DAJ	USB 0756 0906 1842 tfc list 1345 1545 1745 1845 2245
17287.00	Pennsuco, USA	WOM	USB
17287.00	Rome, Italy	IAR	USB 0922
17290.00	Coast stations ch 17 dup. 16408.0kHz		USB
17290.00	Haifa, Israel	4XO	USB 0732 0829 1553 1611
17290.00	Lyngby, Denmark	OXZ	USB
17293.00	Coast stations ch 18 dup. 16411.0kHz		USB
17293.00	Bahrain	A9M	USB (with P3HI3) 1305 (with 3ESZ9) 1506
17293.00	Istanbul, Turkey	TAN	USB (on request) 1428 1510
17293.00	Lyngby, Denmark	OXZ	USB 1801
17293.00	Portishead, UK	GKU68	USB 1845
17296.00	Coast stations ch 19 dup. 16414.0kHz		USB
17296.00	Athens, Greece	SVO63	USB 1420
17296.00	Rogaland, Norway	LFN23	USB (with ICPT) 1359
17296.00	St Lys, France	FFL84	USB 1512 1918 (with SWBT) 1528
17299.00	Coast stations ch 20 dup. 16417.0kHz		USB
17299.00	New York (Ocean Gate), USA	WOO	USB
17299.00	Rogaland, Norway	LFN24	USB
17302.00	Coast stations ch 21 dup. 16420.0kHz		USB common calling ch
17302.00	Capetown, RSA	ZSC59	USB
17302.00	Dammam, Saudi Arabia	HZG	USB

kHz.	Station	Call	Mode / Heard/Times GMT
17302.00	Doha, Qatar	A7D	USB (with J8HY) 2011
17302.00	Havana, Cuba	CLT	USB
17302.00	Luanda, Angola	D3E	USB
17302.00	Monaco	3AC	USB
17302.00	Ostend, Belgium	OSU66	USB
17302.00	Rio de Janeiro, Brazil	PPR	USB
17302.00	Rogaland, Norway	LGQ	USB (with "Royal Viking Sun") 1307
17302.00	Rome, Italy	IAR	USB
17302.00	Scheveningen, Holland	PCG60	USB
17302.00	Singapore	9VG	USB
17305.00	Coast stations ch 22 dup. 16423.0kHz		USB
17305.00	Berne, Switzerland	HEB47	USB 1206
17305.00	Darwin, Australia	VID	USB
17305.00	Lyngby, Denmark	OXZ	USB
17305.00	St Lys, France	FFL	USB
17305.00	Sydney, Australia	VIS	USB (on request)
17308.00	Coast stations ch 23 dup. 16426.0kHz		USB
17308.00	Kiev, Ukraine	UTQ	USB 1310 1416
17308.00	Odessa, Ukraine	UUI	USB 0835
17308.00	Portishead, UK	GKV63	USB
17308.00	Scheveningen, Holland	PCG63	USB
17311.00	Coast stations ch 24 dup. 16429.0kHz		USB
17311.00	Dixon, USA	KMI	USB
17311.00	Norddeich, Germany	DAK	USB
17311.00	Riga, Latvia	UQK	USB 1533
17311.00	Rome, Italy	IAR	USB 1251 1936
17314.00	Coast stations ch 25 dup. 16432.0kHz		USB
17314.00	Athens, Greece	SVN63	USB 1622
17314.00	Ostend, Belgium	OSU61	USB
17314.00	Stettin, Poland	SPO81	USB 1832 tfc list 1438
17314.00	US Coastguard stations		USB (common channel)
17317.00	Coast stations ch 26 dup. 16435.0kHz		USB
17317.00	Athens, Greece	SVN64	USB 1210 (with SVHJ) 0750
17317.00	Doha, Qatar	A7D	USB 0707
17317.00	New York (Ocean Gate), USA	WOO	USB
17320.00	Coast stations ch 27 dup. 16438.0kHz		USB
17320.00	Athens, Greece	SVN65	USB
17320.00	Klaipeda Harbour, Lithuania	LYL	USB
17320.00	Ostend, Belgium	OSU62	USB
17320.00	Rijeka, Croatia	9AR	USB 0920 1531 1733
17320.00	Rogaland, Norway	LFN26	USB
17323.00	Coast stations ch 28 dup. 16441.0kHz		USB
17323.00	St Lys, France	FFL81	USB 1017 1532
17326.00	Coast stations ch 29 dup. 16444.0kHz		USB
17326.00	Athens, Greece	SVN66	USB 1340 1534 (with SYPI) 1800
17326.00	Boufarik, Algeria	7TF	USB 1747
17326.00	Rogaland, Norway	LFN27	USB
17329.00	Coast stations ch 30 dup. 16447.0kHz		USB
17329.00	Batumi, Georgia	UFA	USB 0912 2142
17329.00	Madrid, Spain	EHY	USB 0818 1315 1624
17329.00	Ostend, Belgium	OSU67	USB 1836
17332.00	Coast stations ch 31 dup. 16450.0kHz		USB
17332.00	Berne, Switzerland	HEB37	USB 1906
17332.00	Gdynia, Poland	SPC82	USB 1258 1710 1823
17332.00	New York (Ocean Gate), USA	WOO	USB 2154
17332.00	Varna, Bulgaria	LZW	USB
17335.00	Coast stations ch 32 dup. 16453.0kHz		USB
17335.00	Lisbon, Portugal	CUL	USB
17335.00	Nicosia, Cyprus	5BA64	USB 1805
17335.00	Portishead, UK	GKW62	USB
17338.00	Coast stations ch 33 dup. 16456.0kHz		USB
17338.00	Athens, Greece	SVO67	USB
17338.00	Belem, Brazil	PPL	USB (with PPLA) 1544
17338.00	Capetown, RSA	ZSC	USB
17338.00	Gdynia, Poland	SPC83	USB
17338.00	St Lys, France	FFL82	USB 1742
17341.00	Coast stations ch 34 dup. 16459.0kHz		USB
17341.00	Athens, Greece	SVN67	USB 0859 1350 1458
17341.00	Norddeich, Germany	DAI	USB
17344.00	Coast stations ch 35 dup. 16462.0kHz		USB
17344.00	Lyngby, Denmark	OXZ	USB 0701 1837 tfc list 1505
17347.00	Coast stations ch 36 dup. 16465.0kHz		USB
17347.00	Scheveningen, Holland	PCG61	USB 0909 1514 (with CNZE) 1012 tfc list each odd hour + 05
17350.00	Coast stations ch 37 dup. 16468.0kHz		USB
17350.00	Madrid, Spain	EHY	USB 0637 1018 1421 1548 2104
17350.00	Portishead, UK	GKW67	USB
17353.00	Coast stations ch 38 dup. 16471.0kHz		USB

kHz.	Station	Call	Mode / Heard/Times GMT
17353.00	Bar, Montenegro	YUW	USB 1352 1834
17353.00	Helsinki, Finland	OHG2	USB 0847 1415 1432
17353.00	Stettin, Poland	SPO82	USB
17356.00	Coast stations ch 39 dup. 16474.0kHz		USB
17356.00	Madrid, Spain	EHY	USB 1717 2018
17356.00	Norddeich, Germany	DAH	USB
17356.00	Scheveningen, Holland	PCG62	USB
17359.00	Coast stations ch 40 dup. 16477.0kHz		USB
17359.00	Athens, Greece	SVN68	USB 1556 (with SWDM) 1551
17359.00	Portishead, UK	GKW60	USB 1229
17359.00	Valparaiso, Chile	CBV	USB 2231
17362.00	Coast stations ch 41 dup. 16480.0kHz		USB
17362.00	Goeteborg, Sweden	SAG	USB 1557
17362.00	Mariupol, Ukraine	USU	USB 1553
17362.00	Mobile, USA	WLO	USB
17362.00	Singapore	9VG69	USB
17365.00	Coast stations ch 42 dup. 16483.0kHz		USB
17365.00	St Lys, France	FFL87	USB 0715
17368.00	Coast stations ch 43 dup. 16486.0kHz		USB
17368.00	Doha, Qatar	A7D	USB 1343 1505 2021
17368.00	St Lys, France	FFL88	USB
17371.00	Coast stations ch 44 dup. 16489.0kHz		USB
17374.00	Coast stations ch 45 dup. 16492.0kHz		USB
17377.00	Coast stations ch 46 dup. 16495.0kHz		USB
17377.00	Rome, Italy	IAR	USB 1324 1444 1533 1558 1750
17380.00	Coast stations ch 47 dup. 16498.0kHz		USB
17383.00	Coast stations ch 48 dup. 16501.0kHz		USB
17386.00	Coast stations ch 49 dup. 16504.0kHz		USB
17386.00	Nicosia, Cyprus	5BA	USB 0809 1254 1603
17387.00	All India Radio		AM Eng 1011
17389.00	Coast stations ch 50 dup. 16507.0kHz		USB
17389.00	Novorossiysk, Russia	UDN	USB 0832 0915 1321 1412
17392.00	Coast stations ch 51 dup. 16510.0kHz		USB
17395.00	Coast stations ch 52 dup. 16513.0kHz		USB
17395.00	Rijeka, Croatia	9AR	USB 1116
17395.00	Scheveningen, Holland	PCG64	USB
17398.00	Coast stations ch 53 dup. 16516.0kHz		USB
17398.00	Guangzhou, China	XSQ	USB
17401.00	Coast stations ch 54 dup. 16519.0kHz		USB
17401.00	Odessa, Ukraine	UUI	USB 0844 1410 1507 1614
17404.00	Coast stations ch 55 dup. 16522.0kHz		USB
17407.00	Coast stations ch 56 dup. 16525.0kHz		USB
17407.00	Berne, Switzerland	HEB57	USB 1515
17409.90	Spa Publications		

17410-17550
FIXED

17410.00	Numbers Station		USB phonetics (fem voice) 1304 1406 1433
17412.50	Italian Embassy traffic		SITOR Selcal VQMP 0849
17432.00	Serbian Embassy traffic	DFZG	75n p/lang Eng (TANJUG rpts) 1536 1612 1650 Slav 1445
17435.00	UNID		100r 5 let grps 1628
17442.00	Nairobi Met, Kenya	5YE	100r 1020 1529 1545
17443.10	Beijing Press (XINHUA)	BZG48	50r Fr 1141 1212 1329
17445.00	USAF weather service		75r 1517
17445.60	Nairobi Met, Kenya	5YE	FAX wx maps 1757 2215
17447.00	USAF weather service		75r 1416 1553
17448.00	Serbian Embassy traffic	DFZG	75n p/lang 1436
17456.70	Egyptian Embassy traffic		SITOR 1652
17459.00	Austrian Embassy traffic		96SI-ARQ(6 char) p/lang Ger 0818 0925 1136 5 let grps 1314
17462.00	UNID		75n 5 let grps 1533
17465.00	Hamburg, Germany	DGR46	CW Ger news 1653
17470.00	Beijing Press (XINHUA)	BZR	75r Eng 1142
17476.70	Egyptian Embassy traffic		SITOR 0838 0900 1347 5 let grps 0828
17485.00	R Moscow		AM Eng 0821
17490.00	HCJB, Ecuador		USB Eng 1233 1330 1420 1502 1518 2156 Ger 2105
17500.00	R Tunis		AM Arab 1407 1534
17510.00	WEWN, USA		AM Eng 1546 1600
17521.50	Bangkok Met, Thailand	HSW	50n 1536
17524.50	USAF wx service		75n 1538
17525.00	R Vatican		AM Eng 1348
17525.00	Voice of Greece		AM Eng 0946 1533 1844 Greek 0834
17526.50	UNID		96ARQ/E/8 Idle 0823
17527.00	Portuguese Naval	RPTI	75n QBF RYs & SGs 1504
17535.00	R Prague		AM Eng 0731

kHz.	Station	Call	Mode / Heard/Times GMT
17535.00	Slovak Radio		AM Eng 0836 0850
17535.00	Voice of Greece		AM Eng 1439 1446
17539.50	R Pakistan		AM Eng 1602
17545.00	Kol Israel		AM Hebrew 0734 1003
17549.90	Spa Publishing		

17550-17900
INTERNATIONAL BROADCASTING

kHz.	Station	Call	Mode / Heard/Times GMT
17550.90	French Military	RFTJ	192ARQ/E3/8 Idle 1213 5 let grps (RFTJC msg) 1540
17553.00	Tehran Met, Iran		50r 1305
17555.00	Monitor Radio International		AM Eng 1014 1703 2109 2217
17560.00	Deutsche Welle		AM Ger 1426 1526 1635
17560.00	R Moscow		AM Eng 0824 0842 1110 2202
17565.00	R Swiss International		AM Fr 0700 Ger 0730
17565.00	R Ukraine International		AM Slav 1408 1423
17570.00	R Moscow		AM Eng 0840 1231 2203
17575.00	Kol Israel		AM Eng 1422 2153
17580.00	R Moscow		AM Eng 1519
17580.00	R Netherland		AM Dutch 1409 1517
17590.00	Jeddah Met, Saudi Arabia	HZN49	100n 0829 1541 1632 2204 2232
17590.00	R Moscow		AM Eng 1331 1414
17595.00	R Moscow		AM Eng 0704 0837 1123 1420 Ger 1004
17600.00	R Moscow		AM Eng 0637 0830 1013
17605.00	R Netherland		AM Dutch 2110
17605.00	R Moscow		AM Eng 1234 Fr 1440 1537
17610.00	R Moscow		AM Eng 1014 1334 1430
17610.00	R Netherland		AM Eng 1548
17612.50	WYFR, USA		AM Eng 1847 2111 2157 2219
17620.00	R France International		AM Eng 1518 1556 1617 1704
17625.00	R Moscow		AM Fr 0843 1005 1303
17630.00	Africa No 1, Gabon		AM Fr 1533 1557
17635.00	R Moscow		AM Eng 0702 0732 0838
17640.00	BBC		AM Eng 0711 0800 1013 1125 1326 1424 1505
17640.00	VOA		AM Fr 1848 2133 (1830-2200)
17641.00	Numbers Station		USB Eng (female voice) 1604
17650.00	R France International		AM Fr 1522
17655.00	R Netherland		AM Eng 1752 1803
17660.00	R Moscow		AM Eng 0703 0801 1146
17665.00	R Moscow		AM Eng 0623 0801 1112
17670.00	R Australia		AM Eng 0802
17670.00	R Moscow		AM Eng 1147 Portuguese 2113
17675.00	R Moscow		AM Eng 0711 2206 2245
17680.00	R Moscow		AM Eng 0803 1131
17685.00	R Moscow		AM Eng 0736 0928
17695.00	R Australia		AM Eng 0735 0831 0849
17695.00	R France International		AM Eng 1433
17700.00	R Moscow		AM Eng 1148
17705.00	BBC		AM Eng 1327 1425 1506 1558
17710.00	R Moscow		AM Eng 1025
17715.00	R Australia		AM Eng 0848
17715.00	REE Spain		AM Span 1435
17720.00	R Romania International		AM Eng 0713 1328 1502
17725.00	R Moscow		AM Eng 1026 1235 1333
17725.00	R Ukraine International		AM Eng 2115 Slav 2207
17730.00	R Moscow		AM Eng 0639
17735.00	R Moscow		AM Eng 0704 0737 1149 1436
17735.00	VOA		AM Eng 2135 2208 2234
17750.00	R Australia		AM Eng 0848
17750.00	Voice of Free China		AM Eng 2201 2221 (2200-2300) Ger 2116
17755.00	R Moscow		AM Eng 0738 0902 1150
17760.00	R Havana		AM Eng 2120
17760.00	R Moscow		AM Eng 1027 1236 1306 1423 1437 1507 1811
17765.00	R Moscow		AM Eng 0739 0832 0904 1507
17770.00	R Moscow		AM Eng 0714 0738
17775.00	R Japan		AM Eng 0640 1702 1753
17775.00	R Moscow		AM Eng 0640 1307 1542
17780.00	R Bulgaria		AM Eng (1945-2030)
17780.00	R Moscow		AM Eng 0621 1028 1151 1237
17780.00	Monitor Radio International		AM Eng 0715
17785.00	VOA		AM Eng 1611
17790.00	BBC		AM Eng 0722
17790.00	HCJB, Ecuador		AM Eng 1637 1720 2156 Span 2200
17800.00	R Finland		AM Eng 0812
17800.00	VOA		AM Eng 1825 2122

kHz.	Station	Call	Mode / Heard/Times GMT
17805.00	R Moscow		AM Eng 1029
17805.00	R Romania International		AM Eng 0705
17805.00	R Svoboda		AM Slav 1424 1440
17810.00	Deutsche Welle		AM Eng 1621 Ger 2125
17815.00	R Moscow		AM Eng 1030 1132 1152 1242 Fr 1638 Afrikaans 1738
17820.00	R Canada International		AM Eng 1356 1704 2128 Fr 2131
17830.00	BBC		AM Eng 0726
17840.00	BBC		AM Eng 1426 1508 1606
17845.00	Deutsche Welle		AM Ger 0707 0850 1233
17845.00	REE Spain		AM Span 1527 1722
17850.00	All India Radio		AM Eng 0732
17855.00	R Moscow		AM Fr 1608
17860.00	BBC		AM Eng 1602
17860.00	Deutsche Welle		AM Ger 1849 2132 2217
17865.00	R Vatican		AM Eng 1548 (1545-1640)
17870.00	R Austria International		AM Eng 1031
17870.00	R Bulgaria		AM Portuguese 2139 Slav 2201
17875.00	R Moscow		AM Eng 1153 Fr 1425
17880.00	R Moscow		AM Eng 1300
17885.00	R Moscow		AM Fr 1609
17890.00	HCJB, Ecuador		AM Eng 1412 1530
17895.00	BBC		AM Russian 1301
17895.00	R Netherland		AM Dutch 2218
17895.00	VOA		AM Eng 1648
17899.90	Spa Publishing		

17900-17970
AERONAUTICAL MOBILE (MAINLY CIVIL) 3KHz channels

kHz.	Station	Call	Mode / Heard/Times GMT
17900.00	R Pakistan		AM Eng 0829
17901.00	Miami, USA	KJY74	USB (Hurricane flights)
17904.00	Pacific Air traffic CEP/CWP 1/2 NP SP		USB
17907.00	Caribbean Air traffic CAR A/B		USB
17907.00	E & S E Asia Air traffic EA 2 SEA 1/2		USB
17907.00	S America Air traffic SAM		USB
17910.00	St John's (in-flight R/T service)		USB "Rainbow Radio"
17916.00	Stockholm (in-flight R/T service)		USB 1426 1706
17922.00	British Airways Company frequency		USB 2205
17925.00	Honolulu (in-flight R/T service)		USB
17925.00	New York (in-flight R/T service)		USB
17925.00	San Francisco (in-flight R/T service)		USB
17937.00	Lima (in-flight R/T service)		USB
17940.00	Houston (in-flight R/T service)		USB 1546 2224
17940.00	Iberia Airlines Company frequency		USB
17940.00	R Baghdad		AM Arab 2220
17946.00	N Atlantic Air traffic NAT A/B/E		USB
17946.00	New York ATC, USA	KZNY	USB
17946.00	Shanwick ATC, UK/Eire	EGGX	USB
17946.00	N Pacific Air traffic NP		USB
17950.00	UNID		AM Arab 2202
17955.00	Africa/S Atlantic Air traffic AFI 1 SAT 1/2		USB
17955.00	Dakar ATC, Senegal	GOOO	USB
17955.00	Jo'Burg ATC, RSA	FAJS	USB
17958.00	N Central & E Asia Air traffic NCA 1/2/3 EA 1		USB
17961.00	Africa/Mid East/Indian Ocean Air traffic		USB
17961.00	Europe Air traffic EUR A		USB
17961.70	Egyptian Embassy traffic		SITOR 0851
17969.90	Spa Publishing		

17970-18030
AERONAUTICAL MOBILE (MAINLY MILITARY)

kHz.	Station	Call	Mode / Heard/Times GMT
17972.00	USAF		USB
17975.00	USAF Andrews AFB, USA		USB 1008
17975.00	USAF Croughton, UK		USB
17975.00	USAF McClellan AFB, USA		USB 1532
17975.00	USAF Thule AFB, Greenland		USB
17995.00	Canadian Military		USB
18002.00	USAF McClellan AFB		USB
18010.00	UNID		USB Fr simplex R/T 1034
18012.00	Canadian Military		USB
18018.00	RAF Akrotiri, Cyprus		USB "CYPRUS FLIGHT WATCH" wx 0820 1418
18018.00	RAF, UK		USB "ARCHITECT" airfield states 1830

kHz.	Station	Call	Mode / Heard/Times GMT
18019.00	USAF Ascension Island		USB
18023.00	Berne (in-flight R/T service)	HEE81	USB 1935
18027.00	Bulgarian Embassy traffic	DOR	75n p/lang 1605
18029.90	Spa Publishing		

18030-18068
FIXED

kHz.	Station	Call	Mode / Heard/Times GMT
18040.50	Ankara Press (AA)	TCY4	50r Eng 1035 Turkish 1155 1253
18041.50	Hungarian Embassy traffic		125DUP-ARQ(inv polarity) 5 let grps 1524
18050.00	Polish Embassy traffic		100POL-ARQ p/lang 0854
18055.00	Serbian Embassy traffic	DFZG	75n RYs 1428 p/lang Eng 1429 1526 1621 1707
18060.00	Darwin Met, Australia	AXI37	FAX wx maps (2300-1100)
18061.00	British Naval	MTO	75r ch marker test slip 1156 1245 1449 1527 1610
18064.00	Polish Embassy traffic		100POL-ARQ p/lang 0856
18067.90	Spa Publishing		

18068-18168
AMATEUR

kHz.	Station	Call	Mode / Heard/Times GMT
18068.00	Amateur Beacon	IK6BAK	CW "QTH Locator JN63KR" 1036 1529
18167.90	Spa Publishing		

18168-18780
FIXED

kHz.	Station	Call	Mode / Heard/Times GMT
18173.50	Khartoum Air, Sudan	STK	50r ID & RYs 2157
18190.00	INTERPOL	FSB	SITOR 5 let grps 1533
18195.00	R Moscow feeder		LSB & USB Slav 1157 1254 1431 1544
18200.70	Egyptian Embassy traffic		SITOR 1724
18205.00	Bulgarian Embassy traffic	DOR	75n p/lang 0859
18220.00	Tokyo Met, Japan	JMH5	FAX wx maps 0740 0822
18220.90	Rabat Press (MAP)	CNM76/X9	50r Eng 1333 (1200-1400) Fr (1000-1130 1530-1700)
18230.00	Bracknell Met, UK	GFL25	50r 1430 1534 1708
18238.70	Pretoria, RSA	ZRO4	FAX wx maps
18254.00	Cairo Met, Egypt	SUU	75r 0755 1610 1710
18255.00	Indian Govt Press Service		50n Eng 1433
18261.00	Bracknell Met, UK	GFA	FAX wx maps 0833 1432 (0600-1800)
18263.50	Hanoi Press (VNA)		50n Fr 0757
18265.00	Rabat Press (MAP)	CNM	50r sked 1526 Eng (1200-1400) Fr 1613 (1000-1130 1530-1700)
18275.00	VOA feeder		LSB Slav 1620
18280.50	Argentine Naval	LOR	100n ID & 5 let grps 2110
18319.00	Czech Embassy traffic		100n p/lang 0913
18320.00	Czech Embassy traffic	7A1	CW "next OMZ88" 1300
18351.00	US Embassy frequency (rptd Athens)	KWS78	CW 1301 1453 1546
18388.50	Tripoli Air, Libya	5AF	50r (HLLTYF) RYs & QJH 0800 1548
18410.10	British Military	GXQ	50r (VFT) QBF & RYIs 1714 (LSB 18413.1)
18416.70	Indonesian Embassy traffic		50n p/lang 1320 1442 1611
18441.00	Tokyo Met, Japan	JMJ5	FAX wx maps 0802
18445.50	Danish Embassy traffic		SITOR Selcal KFQU (Rabat) & p/lang 0858
18449.00	RAF London	MKK	50n (VFT) QBF & RYIs 1434 1715 (LSB ch 18452.0)
18456.00	RAF London	MKK	50r (VFT) QBF & RYIs 1523 (LSB 18459.0)
18480.00	Berne (in-flight R/T service)		USB Fr 0908
18486.00	US Naval		FAX wx maps
18496.10	Rabat Press (MAP)	CNM80/X11	50r Eng 1334 (1200-1400) Arab 0915 1547 (0900-1030 1530-1700)
18535.00	RAF Akrotiri, Cyprus	MKD	50r (VFT) QBF & RYIs 1435 1625 1716 (LSB 18538.0)
18561.00	Tehran Press (IRNA)	9BC31	50r Eng 1002 1113 Arab 1132 (& msrd 10560.0)
18567.00	UNID		100r 5 let grps (long msg) 0803
18648.50	Warsaw Press (PAP)		SITOR Polish 1436
18680.00	UNID		CW 5 fig grps (each twice) 1442
18688.00	Swedish Embassy traffic		100SWED-ARQ(long) 1438
18702.50	German Govt, press info service	DGS	96FEC p/lang Ger 1440 1528
18710.00	Moscow Met, Russia	RIZ59	FAX wx maps 0846 0933 1114 1217 1301
18755.80	INTERPOL, Tokyo	JPA	CW Eng 1000 & SITOR Selcal IPIY 0926
18779.90	Spa Publishing		

18780-18900
MARITIME MOBILE

kHz.	Station	Call	Mode / Heard/Times GMT
18780.00	Ships wkg ch 1 dup. 19755.0kHz		USB
18783.00	Ships wkg ch 2 dup. 19758.0kHz		USB
18786.00	Ships wkg ch 3 dup. 19761.0kHz		USB
18789.00	Ships wkg ch 4 dup. 19764.0kHz		USB
18792.00	Ships wkg ch 5 dup. 19767.0kHz		USB
18795.00	Ships wkg ch 6 dup. 19770.0kHz		USB
18798.00	Ships wkg ch 7 dup. 19773.0kHz		USB
18801.00	Ships wkg ch 8 dup. 19776.0kHz		USB
18804.00	Ships wkg ch 9 dup. 19779.0kHz		USB
18807.00	Ships wkg ch 10 dup. 19782.0kHz		USB
18810.00	Ships wkg ch 11 dup. 19785.0kHz		USB
18813.00	Ships wkg ch 12 dup. 19788.0kHz		USB
18816.00	Ships wkg ch 13 dup. 19791.0kHz		USB
18819.00	Ships wkg ch 14 dup. 19794.0kHz		USB
18822.00	Ships wkg ch 15 dup. 19797.0kHz		USB
18825.00	Ships/Coast stations simplex		USB
18828.00	Ships/Coast stations simplex		USB 0906 1220
18831.00	Ships/Coast stations simplex		USB 1716
18834.00	Ships/Coast stations simplex		USB
18837.00	Ships/Coast stations simplex		USB
18840.00	Ships/Coast stations simplex		USB 1750
18843.00	Ships/Coast stations simplex		USB
18864.00	Numbers Station		USB Eng (female voice) 1235
18870.00	R Moscow feeder		LSB + USB Slav 0807 1300 1550
18870.50	Ships wkg ch 1 dup. 19681.0kHz		RTTY
18871.00	Ships wkg ch 2 dup. 19681.5kHz		RTTY
18871.50	Ships wkg ch 3 dup. 19682.0kHz		RTTY
18872.00	Beijing Press (XINHUA)	BZR68	75r Eng 0833 1302
18872.00	Ships wkg ch 4 dup. 19682.5kHz		RTTY
18872.50	Ships wkg ch 5 dup. 19683.0kHz		RTTY
18873.00	Ships wkg ch 6 dup. 19683.5kHz		RTTY
18873.50	Ships wkg ch 7 dup. 19684.0kHz		RTTY
18874.00	Ships wkg ch 8 dup. 19684.5kHz		RTTY
18874.50	Ships wkg ch 9 dup. 19685.0kHz		RTTY
18875.00	Ships wkg ch 10 dup. 19685.5kHz		RTTY
18875.50	Ships wkg ch 11 dup. 19686.0kHz		RTTY
18876.00	Ships wkg ch 12 dup. 19686.5kHz		RTTY
18876.50	Ships wkg ch 13 dup. 19687.0kHz		RTTY
18877.00	Ships wkg ch 14 dup. 19687.5kHz		RTTY
18877.50	Ships wkg ch 15 dup. 19688.0kHz		RTTY
18878.00	Ships wkg ch 16 dup. 19688.5kHz		RTTY
18878.50	Ships wkg ch 17 dup. 19689.0kHz		RTTY
18879.00	Ships wkg ch 18 dup. 19689.5kHz		RTTY
18879.50	Ships wkg ch 19 dup. 19690.0kHz		RTTY
18880.00	Cuban Embassy traffic	CLP	75n msg Havana/Vietnam 0834
18880.00	Ships wkg ch 20 dup. 19690.5kHz		RTTY
18880.50	Ships wkg ch 21 dup. 19691.0kHz		RTTY
18881.00	Ships wkg ch 22 dup. 19691.5kHz		RTTY
18881.50	Ships wkg ch 23 dup. 19692.0kHz		RTTY
18882.00	Ships wkg ch 24 dup. 19692.5kHz		RTTY
18882.50	Ships wkg ch 25 dup. 19693.0kHz		RTTY
18882.50	Turkish Embassy traffic	TAD	144FEC p/lang 0647 0955 1052 1117 1520 5 let grps 0936 1423
18883.00	Ships wkg ch 26 dup. 19693.5kHz		RTTY
18883.50	Ships wkg ch 27 dup. 19694.0kHz		RTTY
18884.00	Ships wkg ch 28 dup. 19694.5kHz		RTTY
18884.50	Ships wkg ch 29 dup. 19695.0kHz		RTTY
18885.00	Ships wkg ch 30 dup. 19695.5kHz		RTTY
18885.50	Ships wkg ch 31 dup. 19696.0kHz		RTTY
18886.00	Ships wkg ch 32 dup. 19696.5kHz		RTTY
18886.50	Ships wkg ch 33 dup. 19697.0kHz		RTTY
18887.00	Ships wkg ch 34 dup. 19697.5kHz		RTTY
18887.50	Ships wkg ch 35 dup. 19698.0kHz		SITOR 1222
18888.00	Ships wkg ch 36 dup. 19698.5kHz		RTTY
18888.50	Ships wkg ch 37 dup. 19699.0kHz		RTTY
18889.00	Ships wkg ch 38 dup. 19699.5kHz		RTTY
18889.50	Ships wkg ch 39 dup. 19700.0kHz		RTTY
18890.00	Ships wkg ch 40 dup. 19700.5kHz		RTTY
18890.50	Ships wkg ch 41 dup. 19701.0kHz		RTTY
18891.00	Ships wkg ch 42 dup. 19701.5kHz		RTTY
18891.50	Ships wkg ch 43 dup. 19702.0kHz		RTTY
18892.00	Ships wkg ch 44 dup. 19702.5kHz		RTTY
18892.50	Ships wkg ch 45 dup. 19703.0kHz		RTTY
18893.00	Ships working (non paired)		CW/RTTY
18893.50	Ships working (non paired)		CW/RTTY
18894.00	Ships working (non paired)		CW/RTTY
18894.50	Ships working (non paired)		CW/RTTY

kHz.	Station	Call	Mode / Heard/Times GMT
18895.00	Ships working (non paired)		CW/RTTY
18895.50	Ships working (non paired)		CW/RTTY
18896.00	Ships working (non paired)		CW UWUY (to UNQ) 0915
18896.50	Ships working (non paired)		CW/RTTY SITOR (Fr) 1752
18897.00	Ships working (non paired)		CW/RTTY
18897.50	Ships working (non paired)		CW/RTTY
18898.00	Ships working (non paired)		CW/RTTY
18898.50	Ships digital selective calling		RTTY
18899.00	Ships digital selective calling		RTTY
18899.50	Ships digital selective calling		RTTY
18899.90	Spa Publishing		

18900-19680
FIXED

kHz.	Station	Call	Mode / Heard/Times GMT
18905.00	British Military	GXQ	50r (VFT) QBF & RYIs 1548 1559 (LSB 18908.0)
18940.00	China Met	BDF	FAX wx maps 0739 0910
18972.00	Serbian Embassy traffic	DFZG	75n p/lang Eng 1718
18993.50	Warsaw, Poland	SPW	SITOR (dup. 16785.0) 0921 1044 1304
18995.00	Warsaw, Poland	SPW	USB 1250
19013.50	Ostend, Belgium	OST63	SITOR Mode B 1236 1820 tfc list each hour + 20
19101.80	French Military, Martinique	RFLI	192ARQ/E3/8 1053 1301 1600 1719
19117.50	Indonesian Embassy traffic		SITOR p/lang 1413
19156.50	UNID		SITOR (French, poss ICRC) 0923
19160.00	Bulgarian Embassy traffic	DOR	75n p/lang 0836
19171.10	Rabat Press (MAP)	CNM85/X11	50r Eng 1302 1335 (1200-1400) Fr 1531 (100-1130 1530-1700)
19183.00	UNID		CW 5 fig grps 1415
19204.70	French Military, Martinique	RFLI	192/ARQ/E3/8 0809 1602 1722
19275.00	Khabarovsk Met, Russia	RXO74	FAX wx maps 0940 1258 1444
19286.70	Egyptian Embassy traffic		SITOR Selcal OOVS (Kuala Lumpur) 1055
19379.00	VOA feeder		LSB Eng 1547 Slav 1723
19385.30	UNID		200ARQ/M2/4 Idle 0812 0841
19386.70	French Military, Djibouti	RFQP	200ARQ/M2/4 Idle 1306
19400.00	Delhi Met, India	VVD69	120/50r 0721 0900 1057 (0040-1400)
19430.00	RAF Akrotiri, Cyprus	MKD	50n(VFT) QBF & RYIs 1100 (LSB ch 19433.0)
19443.00	UNID		96ARQ/E/8 Idle 0844
19461.00	Italian Embassy traffic		96ARQ/E/8 0841
19463.20	Khartoum Press (SUNA)		50n Eng 1725
19529.00	Tokyo Met, Japan	JMG	50r 0843 1303
19672.00	Polish Embassy traffic		75n p/lang 0837
19679.90	Spa Publishing		

19680-19800
MARITIME MOBILE

kHz.	Station	Call	Mode / Heard/Times GMT
19680.00	Taiwan Press (CNA)	3MA	CW ID & FAX 1505
19680.50	Maritime Safety channel		RTTY
19681.00	Coast stations ch 1 dup. 18870.5kHz		RTTY
19681.50	Coast stations ch 2 dup. 18871.0kHz		RTTY
19682.00	Coast stations ch 3 dup. 18871.5kHz		RTTY
19682.50	Coast stations ch 4 dup. 18872.0kHz		RTTY
19683.00	Coast stations ch 5 dup. 18872.5kHz		RTTY
19683.50	Coast stations ch 6 dup. 18873.0kHz		RTTY
19684.00	Coast stations ch 7 dup. 18873.5kHz		RTTY
19684.50	Coast stations ch 8 dup. 18874.0kHz		RTTY
19685.00	Coast stations ch 9 dup. 18874.5kHz		RTTY
19685.50	Coast stations ch 10 dup. 18875.0kHz		RTTY
19685.50	Mobile, USA	WLO	SITOR 1405 1549
19686.00	Coast stations ch 11 dup. 18875.5kHz		RTTY
19686.50	Coast stations ch 12 dup. 18876.0kHz		RTTY
19687.00	Coast stations ch 13 dup. 18876.5kHz		RTTY
19687.50	Coast stations ch 14 dup. 18877.0kHz		RTTY
19688.00	Coast stations ch 15 dup. 18877.5kHz		RTTY
19688.50	Coast stations ch 16 dup. 18878.0kHz		RTTY
19689.00	Coast stations ch 17 dup. 18878.5kHz		RTTY
19689.50	Coast stations ch 18 dup. 18879.0kHz		RTTY
19689.50	Dixon, USA	KMI	SITOR
19690.00	Coast stations ch 19 dup. 18879.5kHz		RTTY
19690.50	Coast stations ch 20 dup. 18880.0kHz		RTTY
19691.00	Coast stations ch 21 dup. 18880.5kHz		RTTY
19691.50	Coast stations ch 22 dup. 18881.0kHz		RTTY
19692.00	Coast stations ch 23 dup. 18881.5kHz		RTTY
19692.50	Coast stations ch 24 dup. 18882.0kHz		RTTY

kHz.	Station	Call	Mode / Heard/Times GMT
19693.00	Coast stations ch 25 dup. 18882.5kHz		RTTY
19693.00	St Petersburg, Russia	UGC	SITOR 0847 1406 1712
19693.50	Coast stations ch 26 dup. 18883.0kHz		RTTY
19694.00	Coast stations ch 27 dup. 18883.5kHz		RTTY
19694.50	Coast stations ch 28 dup. 18884.0kHz		RTTY
19695.00	Coast stations ch 29 dup. 18884.5kHz		RTTY
19695.50	Coast stations ch 30 dup. 18885.0kHz		RTTY
19696.00	Coast stations ch 31 dup. 18885.5kHz		RTTY
19696.50	Coast stations ch 32 dup. 18886.0kHz		RTTY
19697.00	Coast stations ch 33 dup. 18886.5kHz		RTTY
19697.50	Coast stations ch 34 dup. 18887.0kHz		RTTY
19698.00	Coast stations ch 35 dup. 18887.5kHz		RTTY
19698.00	Ostend, Belgium	OST	SITOR 0647 1550 1604
19698.50	Coast stations ch 36 dup. 18888.0kHz		RTTY
19699.00	Coast stations ch 37 dup. 18888.5kHz		RTTY
19699:00	General Pacheco, Argentina	LPD	SITOR
19699.50	Coast stations ch 38 dup. 18889.0kHz		RTTY
19700.00	Coast stations ch 39 dup. 18889.5kHz		RTTY
19700.00	General Pacheco, Argentina	LPD	SITOR
19700.50	Coast stations ch 40 dup. 18890.0kHz		RTTY
19701.00	Coast stations ch 41 dup. 18890.5kHz		RTTY
19701.50	Coast stations ch 42 dup. 18891.0kHz		RTTY
19702.00	Coast stations ch 43 dup. 18891.5kHz		RTTY
19702.50	Coast stations ch 44 dup. 18892.0kHz		RTTY
19703.00	Coast stations ch 45 dup. 18892.5kHz		RTTY
19703.50	Coast stations digital selective calling		RTTY
19704.00	Coast stations digital selective calling		RTTY
19704.50	Coast stations digital selective calling		RTTY
19707.00	Archangel, Russia	UCE	SITOR 0848 1042 1306 1551
19712.00	St Petersburg, Russia	UGC	170/50nc 1407 (to T/H "Novgorod") 1110
19715.00	Numbers Station		AM phonetics (female voice) 1309 "EZI" 1102
19718.00	Murmansk, Russia	UDK2	CW 1813
19718.00	Murmansk, Russia	UDK2	170/50nc 1811
19731.60	Dutch Embassy traffic	PCW1	SITOR 0849 1103
19734.50	St Petersburg, Russia	UGC	SITOR 1112 1726
19747.50	Dakar Met, Senegal	6VU	50n 0845 1044 1114 1309 1552 1605 1727 1753
19751.50	Dakar Met, Senegal	6VU	FAX 1607
19755.00	Coast stations ch 1 dup. 18780.0kHz		USB
19755.00	Portishead, UK	GKT18	USB
19756.80	Indonesian Embassy traffic		96SI-FEC p/lang Eng 1302 1537 5 let grps 1444
19758.00	Coast stations ch 2 dup. 18783.0kHz		USB
19761.00	Coast stations ch 3 dup. 18786.0kHz		USB
19761.00	Portishead, UK	GKU18	USB
19764.00	Coast stations ch 4 dup. 18789.0kHz		USB
19767.00	Coast stations ch 5 dup. 18792.0kHz		USB
19770.00	Coast stations ch 6 dup. 18795.0kHz		USB
19770.00	Rome, Italy	IAR	USB
19773.00	Coast stations ch 7 dup. 18798.0kHz		USB
19776.00	Coast stations ch 8 dup. 18801.0kHz		USB
19776.00	Haifa, Israel	4XO	USB
19779.00	Coast stations ch 9 dup. 18804.0kHz		USB
19779.00	Berne, Switzerland	HEB19	USB 1419
19782.00	Coast stations ch 10 dup. 18807.0kHz		USB
19785.00	Coast stations ch 11 dup. 18810.0kHz		USB
19788.00	Coast stations ch 12 dup. 18813.0kHz		USB
19788.00	Rijeka, Croatia	9AR	USB
19791.00	Coast stations ch 13 dup. 18816.0kHz		USB
19791.00	St Lys, France	FFL89	USB
19794.00	Coast stations ch 14 dup. 18819.0kHz		USB
19794.00	Rijeka, Croatia	9AR	USB
19797.00	Coast stations ch 15 dup. 18822.0kHz		USB
19799.90	Spa Publishing		

19800-19990
FIXED

kHz.	Station	Call	Mode / Heard/Times GMT
19802.00	Hungarian Embassy traffic		125DUP-ARQ(inv polarity) 1115
19808.00	Swedish Embassy traffic		100SWED-ARQ(short) p/lang 1045
19810.50	Hungarian Embassy traffic		125DUP-ARQ(inv polarity) 1116
19822.50	Tripoli Air, Libya	5AF	50r (HLLTYF) RYs 0850 1554
19860.00	British Naval	GYA	75r 0849 1105 1420
19865.00	Numbers Station		AM Slav 1421
19865.50	Belgrade Press (TANJUG)		50r Span 1510 1603
19877.00	Italian Embassy traffic		96ARQ/E/8 p/lang 1047
19980.00	Tehran Press (IRNA)	9BC33	50n Eng 1001 1512 1555

kHz.	Station	Call	Mode / Heard/Times GMT
19989.90	Spa Publishing		

19990-20010
STANDARD FREQUENCY/TIME SIGNALS + SPACE

19993.00	Satellite Rescue Frequency		USB
20000.00	Fort Collins Time Station, USA	WWV	USB/CW 0800
20009.90	Spa Publishing		

20010-21000
FIXED & LAND MOBILE

20011.70	Pakistan Embassy traffic		SITOR Selcal KMEU 1002 p/lang 1106
20015.00	US Naval, Norfolk	NAM	FAX wx maps (reserve frequency)
20020.00	German Embassy traffic		96ARQ/E/8 1241
20022.50	German Govt, press info service	DGU	96FEC Ger 1529 1556
20065.00	Portishead (in-flight R/T service)		USB 1152
20085.00	Rome Press (ANSA)	ISX20	50n Eng 0852 1049 1223 1510 Fr 0924 1125
20101.70	Egyptian Embassy traffic		SITOR Selcal KKVA 1318
20113.00	UNID		96ARQ/E3/8 p/lang French 0732
20124.70	Egyptian Embassy traffic		SITOR 0925
20132.00	Serbian Embassy traffic	DFZG	75n p/lang Eng 1511
20179.80	French Military	RFGW	100ARQ/E3/8 1051 1513
20186.00	NASA, USA		USB relay of Shuttle press conference 1637 1710
20204.00	Belgrade Press (TANJUG)	YZJ	50r Eng 1245 Fr 1216 ID & RYs 1055
20221.70	Egyptian Embassy traffic		SITOR Selcal KKXU 0636
20225.00	US Naval, Norfolk	NAM	CW 1408 1630 1652
20286.50	Warsaw, Poland	SPW	SITOR Mode B news 1448
20300.00	US Naval, Diego Garcia		FAX wx maps 1054 1513
20330.00	RAF Akrotiri, Cyprus	MKD	50r (VFT) QBF & RYIs 1452 (LSB 20333.0)
20338.00	French Military, La Regine	FUG	CW 1516
20359.00	Bulgarian Embassy traffic	DOR	75n RYs 0929 p/lang 1038
20365.00	Italian Embassy traffic		96ARQ/N/4 p/lang 1040
20372.00	Rome Press (ANSA)	IRS23	50n Fr 1409
20410.00	UNID		USB Italian simplex R/T 1058
20422.50	German Embassy traffic		96ARQ/E/8 1557
20426.00	Rabat Press (MAP)		50r Fr 1048
20434.00	Turkish Embassy traffic	TAD	144FEC-A 5 let grps 0945
20469.00	Canberra Met, Australia	AXM37	FAX wx maps 1130
20498.50	German Govt, press info service	DGU	96FEC Ger 0857
20568.00	US Embassy frequency (rptd London)	KRH50	CW 0931 1411
20584.00	UNID		SITOR p/lang (Ital) 1121 1250 (abt dam construction costs)
20590.20	Swiss Embassy traffic	HBD	SITOR 0932 1131
20616.50	Czech Embassy traffic		100n p/lang Slav 1007
20633.80	French Military, Reunion	RFVI	100ARQ/E3/8 ID & "Controle de Voie" 1425 Idle 1600
20639.30	Cuban Embassy traffic	CLP	75n 5 fig grps 1133
20670.00	UN traffic		SITOR p/lang Eng 0950
20674.70	Italian Embassy traffic		SITOR p/lang 1058
20700.00	Swedish Embassy traffic		100SWED-ARQ(long) (to Algiers) 1100
20734.00	United Nations traffic		SITOR 1444 1521 Selcal HCIA 1453
20750.00	Austrian Embassy traffic		96SI-ARQ(6 char) 0933
20805.30	French Military, Djibouti	RFQP	200ARQ/M2/4 ch B 1346 1446 Idle 1057
20813.70	French Military		48ARQ/E3/4 1249
20820.00	Cuban Embassy traffic	CLP1	CW (clg CLP12) 1603
20822.00	French Military, Bangui	RFTJ	72ARQ/E/4 1526
20832.00	Moscow Telecom		USB 1104
20845.20	UNID		200ARQ/M2/4 Idle 1527
20850.00	R Moscow feeder		USB Slav 1105 1447
20865.20	French Military, Paris	RFFH	200ARQ/M2/4 ch B p/lang msg to MIBRIGALEGET DJIBOUTI 1530
20870.00	Berne (in-flight R/T service)		USB 0935
20905.00	R Moscow feeder		USB Slav 1010
20933.50	Warsaw, Poland	SPW	SITOR Mode B 1341 1433 1455 tfc list 1354
20976.70	Pakistan Embassy traffic		SITOR Eng 1145 1348
20991.70	Single Letter Beacon	S	CW 1104
20992.00	Single Letter Beacon	C	CW 0839 1146 1250 1450
20994.00	USMARS (Army)		USB 1358 1532
20999.90	Spa Publishing		

21000-21450
AMATEUR RADIO

kHz.	Station	Call	Mode / Heard/Times GMT
21094.50	Amateur Packet Radio	TU2BB	300Bd packet net (F8BK) 1107 (F8BK/TROA) 1604
21098.00	Amateur Packet Radio	ON4ABB	300Bd packet net 1147
21101.30	Amateur Packet Radio	UA3VGZ	300Bd packet net (5B4TX/UA3VGZ) 1059
21108.70	Amateur Packet Radio	VE2TEN	300Bd packet net (EA8AML/EA7UH) 1541
21109.50	Amateur Packet Radio	VU2RSB	300Bd packet net (SV1IW) 1535
21111.10	Amateur Packet Radio	FF6KDS	300Bd packet net 1454
21112.80	Amateur Packet Radio	UA6LQ	300Bd packet net 0935
21121.20	Amateur Packet Radio	EL2ED	300Bd packet net 1828
21150.00	Reserved for Amateur Beacons		
21284.00	UNID		50Bd spec code type 1120 (rptd CIS Naval)
21449.90	Spa Publishing		

21450-21850
BROADCASTING

kHz.	Station	Mode / Heard/Times GMT
21450.00	R Moscow	AM Eng 0822 0926 0936 1035 1108
21455.00	HCJB, Ecuador	USB Eng 1326 1457 1516 1639 1830 1915 2130
21460.00	All India Radio	AM Eng 1036
21460.00	R Ukraine International	AM Slav 1106
21465.00	R Moscow	AM Eng 0831 1109 1457
21470.00	BBC	AM Eng 0640 0949 1011 1108 1245 1500 1538
21480.00	HCJB, Ecuador	AM Eng 1638 1740 2131 Ger 1832 2120
21480.00	R Moscow	AM Eng 0823 0928 1012
21480.00	R Netherland	AM Dutch 1329
21485.00	VOA	AM Eng 2121
21490.00	R Austria International	AM Eng 0832 1450
21490.00	VOA	AM Span 1731
21495.00	R Riyadh, Saudi Arabia	AM Arab 1141
21500.00	R Sweden	AM Swedish 1351
21500.00	WYFR, USA	AM Eng 1756 1833 Ital 2122
21505.00	R Riyadh, Saudi Arabia	AM Arab 1302 1541
21515.00	R Moscow	AM Eng 0907 1038 1109 Fr 1537
21515.00	R Netherland	AM Eng 1754 1833
21515.00	R Portugal International	AM Eng 1537 Portuguese 1502 1641
21520.00	R France International	AM Fr 1106 1143
21520.00	R Moscow	AM Asian lang 1449
21520.00	R Pakistan	AM Eng 0829 1110
21520.00	VOA	AM Kurdish 1230
21525.00	R Australia	AM Eng 0614 0641 0734 (0100-0900)
21525.00	WYFR, USA	AM Eng 1615 1653 2123 2148 Fr 1834
21530.00	R France International	AM Fr 0812 1156
21535.00	RTV Italiana	AM Ital 1331 1642
21540.00	Deutsche Welle	AM Ger 0642 0707 0833 1231 1303
21540.00	R Moscow	AM Eng 0908 1047 1144
21545.00	R Canada International	AM Slav 1456 1500
21545.00	R Moscow	AM Eng 0930
21550.00	R Finland	AM Eng 0810 1531
21550.00	R Moscow	AM Eng 1144
21555.00	REE Spain	AM Span 1344
21560.00	Deutsche Welle	AM Ger 0735 1304 1501 1606
21575.00	R Japan	AM Eng 0728
21580.00	R France International	AM Fr 1107 1332 1520 1709
21585.00	R Moscow	AM Eng 0912 0931
21585.00	VOA	AM Chinese (Eng lessons) 1145
21590.00	R Netherland	AM Eng 1730 1806 1838 (1730-2030)
21600.00	R Moscow	AM Eng 1048 1431
21605.00	R Dubai	AM Eng 1031 1337 1606
21610.00	R Moscow	AM Eng 0610 0825
21615.00	R Moscow	AM Eng 0730 0822 0932 1039
21615.00	WYFR, USA	AM Eng 1616 1645 1654 2124 Ital 1836
21620.00	R France International	AM Fr 1146 1458 1711
21630.00	R Moscow	AM Eng 1235 1424
21635.00	R France International	AM Fr 1418 1521
21640.00	Monitor Radio International	AM Eng 1713 (1600-2000)
21645.00	R France International	AM Eng 1200 Fr 1502 Span 1307
21655.00	R Moscow	AM Eng 0612
21655.00	R Portugal International	AM Port 1014 1334 1806
21660.00	BBC	AM Eng 0744 0814 1111 1244 1338 1501 1606
21665.00	R Canada International	AM Eng 1020 Fr 1015
21670.00	Monitor Radio International	AM Eng 1837
21680.00	Deutsche Welle	AM Eng 1609 Ger 1347
21685.00	R France International	AM Fr 1245 1522 1655 1732
21710.00	R Vatican	AM Span 1147
21715.00	BBC	AM Eng 0615 0820

kHz.	Station	Call	Mode / Heard/Times GMT
21720.00	R Moscow		AM Ger 1532 1544
21720.00	R Portugal International		AM Port 1152
21720.00	Voice of Free China		AM Eng 2202 (2200-2300)
21725.00	R Australia		AM Eng 1041
21725.00	R Moscow		AM Eng 0708
21735.00	US Naval, Hawaii	NPM	FAX wx maps
21740.00	R Moscow		AM Eng 1112 1236 1545 1733
21745.00	R Australia		AM Eng 1017
21745.00	R Netherland		AM Dutch 1330
21770.00	R Swiss International		AM Eng 1503
21785.00	R Moscow		AM Eng 0709 0821 1128 1206 1310 1400
21820.00	Deutsche Welle		AM Ger 1635
21820.00	R Moscow		AM Eng 0717
21820.00	R Swiss International		AM Eng 1115 1504 Fr 1552
21825.00	R Moscow		AM Eng 1148 Fr 0616
21837.00	US Naval, Pearl Harbour	NPM	FAX wx maps
21845.00	R Moscow		AM Eng 1051
21849.90	Spa Publishing		

21850-21870
FIXED

kHz.	Station	Call	Mode / Heard/Times GMT
21850.00	R Vatican		AM Portuguese 1116 Span 1204
21857.80	UNID		200ARQ/M2/4 Idle 1426
21859.00	Serbian Embassy traffic	DFZG	75n p/lang Eng 1541
21862.00	UNID		50n 5 fig grps 1504
21863.00	Swedish Embassy traffic		100SWED-ARQ(short) p/lang 1325
21869.00	Serbian Embassy traffic	DFZG	75n p/lang Eng press statements 1324
21869.90	Spa Publishing		

21870-21924
AERONAUTICAL (FIXED)

kHz.	Station	Call	Mode / Heard/Times GMT
21923.90	Spa Publishing		

21924-22000
AERONAUTICAL MOBILE (MAINLY CIVIL) 3KHz channels

kHz.	Station	Call	Mode / Heard/Times GMT
21925.00	N Pacific Air traffic NP		USB
21964.00	Honolulu (in-flight R/T service)		USB
21964.00	Houston (in-flight R/T service)		USB
21964.00	New York (in-flight R/T service)		USB
21964.00	San Francisco (in-flight R/T service)		USB
21967.00	Lufthansa Company frequency	DLH	USB
21970.00	Iberia Company frequency		USB
21985.00	Central W Pacific Air traffic CWP 1/2		USB
21988.00	Berne (in-flight R/T service)	HEE92	USB
21994.00	Saudi Airline Company frequency		USB
21999.90	Spa Publishing		

22000-22855
MARITIME MOBILE

kHz.	Station	Call	Mode / Heard/Times GMT
22000.00	Ships wkg ch 1 dup. 22696.0kHz		USB 0822 1432
22003.00	Ships wkg ch 2 dup. 22699.0kHz		USB 1335
22006.00	Ships wkg ch 3 dup. 22702.0kHz		USB 1506 1714
22009.00	Ships wkg ch 4 dup. 22705.0kHz		USB
22012.00	Ships wkg ch 5 dup. 22708.0kHz		USB 0932 1807
22015.00	Ships wkg ch 6 dup. 22711.0kHz		USB 0922 1336 1516 (to GKT) 1550
22018.00	Ships wkg ch 7 dup. 22714.0kHz		USB (to UAT) 0720 (to DAJ) 1551 1806
22021.00	Ships wkg ch 8 dup. 22717.0kHz		USB 0909 1026 1501
22024.00	Ships wkg ch 9 dup. 22720.0kHz		USB 0825 1205 1538
22027.00	Ships wkg ch 10 dup. 22723.0kHz		USB 1010 1322 1518 SZYK 1413
22030.00	Ships wkg ch 11 dup. 22726.0kHz		USB 1216 1324 1505
22033.00	Ships wkg ch 12 dup. 22729.0kHz		USB 1213 YJXK3 1336 5ROP 1555
22036.00	Ships wkg ch 13 dup. 22732.0kHz		USB 0935 1311
22039.00	Ships wkg ch 14 dup. 22735.0kHz		USB 1418
22042.00	Ships wkg ch 15 dup. 22738.0kHz		USB 0933 1325 1519
22045.00	Ships wkg ch 16 dup. 22741.0kHz		USB 1107 1503

kHz.	Station	Call	Mode / Heard/Times GMT
22048.00	Ships wkg ch 17 dup. 22744.0kHz		USB (to SVN) 1051 1105 1503
22051.00	Ships wkg ch 18 dup. 22747.0kHz		USB 1021
22054.00	Ships wkg ch 19 dup. 22750.0kHz		USB 1433 1505 1808
22057.00	Ships wkg ch 20 dup. 22753.0kHz		USB "Oakgarth" (GDWU) 1829
22060.00	Ships wkg ch 21 dup. 22756.0kHz		USB 1547
22063.00	Ships wkg ch 22 dup. 22759.0kHz		USB 1121
22066.00	Ships wkg ch 23 dup. 22762.0kHz		USB 1845
22069.00	Ships wkg ch 24 dup. 22765.0kHz		USB (to SVN) 0700 1329 1053
22072.00	Ships wkg ch 25 dup. 22768.0kHz		USB
22075.00	Ships wkg ch 26 dup. 22771.0kHz		USB 0716 1130
22078.00	Ships wkg ch 27 dup. 22774.0kHz		USB 1118
22081.00	Ships wkg ch 28 dup. 22777.0kHz		USB
22084.00	Ships wkg ch 29 dup. 22780.0kHz		USB 1526
22087.00	Ships wkg ch 30 dup. 22783.0kHz		USB 0711 0837
22090.00	Ships wkg ch 31 dup. 22786.0kHz		USB 1056 1654
22093.00	Ships wkg ch 32 dup. 22789.0kHz		USB 0824 1206 1349 1457
22096.00	Ships wkg ch 33 dup. 22792.0kHz		USB 1019 1217 1507
22099.00	Ships wkg ch 34 dup. 22795.0kHz		USB 1000
22102.00	Ships wkg ch 35 dup. 22798.0kHz		USB 0936 1517 1542
22105.00	Ships wkg ch 36 dup. 22801.0kHz		USB 1439 1844
22108.00	Ships wkg ch 37 dup. 22804.0kHz		USB 0701 1403 1505
22111.00	Ships wkg ch 38 dup. 22807.0kHz		USB 1129 1312
22114.00	Ships wkg ch 39 dup. 22810.0kHz		USB 1507
22117.00	Ships wkg ch 40 dup. 22813.0kHz		USB 1537
22120.00	Ships wkg ch 41 dup. 22816.0kHz		USB 1020 1106 1527
22123.00	Ships wkg ch 42 dup. 22819.0kHz		USB
22126.00	Ships wkg ch 43 dup. 22822.0kHz		USB 1124 1350 1506
22129.00	Ships wkg ch 44 dup. 22825.0kHz		USB 1345 1405
22132.00	Ships wkg ch 45 dup. 22828.0kHz		USB
22135.00	Ships wkg ch 46 dup. 22831.0kHz		USB C6MB2 1316
22138.00	Ships wkg ch 47 dup. 22834.0kHz		USB 0948
22141.00	Ships wkg ch 48 dup. 22837.0kHz		USB 0838
22144.00	Ships wkg ch 49 dup. 22840.0kHz		USB
22147.00	Ships wkg ch 50 dup. 22843.0kHz		USB 1549 1631
22150.00	Ships wkg ch 51 dup. 22846.0kHz		USB 1319 1414
22153.00	Ships wkg ch 52 dup. 22849.0kHz		USB 1421
22156.00	Ships wkg ch 53 dup. 22852.0kHz		USB 1057
22159.00	Ship/Coast simplex ch 1		USB 1427
22162.00	Ship/Coast simplex ch 2		USB 0718 1149
22165.00	Ship/Coast simplex ch 3		USB 1052 1113 1330
22168.00	Ship/Coast simplex ch 4		USB 1247
22171.00	Ship/Coast simplex ch 5		USB 1131
22174.00	Ship/Coast simplex ch 6		USB 1206
22177.00	Ship/Coast simplex ch 7		USB 0914 1336 1539
22187.00	Intership working		USB 1044
22190.00	Intership working		USB 1351 1515 1539
22195.00	Intership working		USB 1337
22203.00	Intership working		USB 1221
22204.00	Intership working		USB 1507
22235.00	Ship working		CW "Marian T" (SYID) 1612 out of normal sub-band
22240.00	Ships working		CW "Cumbrian Express" (3ELR7) 1736
22242.00	Ships working		CW 9HKX3 (to SVB) 0828 "Cape Wind" (C4JA) 1525
22242.50	Ships working		CW "Vasiliy Polenov" (USCW) 0953 "Toron" (UKYS) 1419
22243.00	Ships working		CW "Alexis" (9HLR3) 1554
22243.50	Ships working		CW UPEQ 1240 "Matrose Baltiki" (UUQY) 1513
22244.00	Ships working		CW "Riureni" (YQRC) 1016 "Navarino" (SWGV) 1549
22244.50	Ships working		CW "Uragan" (UYZL) 1508
22245.00	Ships working		CW "Akhtarskiy Liman" (URWR) 1415 "Borg" (LAGQ2) 1519
22245.50	Ships working		CW 1222 1759
22246.00	Ships working		CW "Mineral Dampier" (VRKT) 1450
22246.50	Ships working		CW ESYO 1505
22247.00	Ships working		CW "Serifos" (J8FN3) 1538
22247.50	Ships working		CW "Stamina" (P3II2) 1356
22248.00	Ships working		CW "Bicas" (PPXS) 1238 "Kamari" (P3OR3) 1634
22248.50	Ships working		CW 0839
22249.00	Ships working		CW 1321
22249.50	Ships working		CW 1352
22250.00	Ships working		CW "Independente" (PPRZ) 1211 "Global Makatcha" (ELNE4) 1738
22251.00	Ships working		CW "Derby North" (C4XH) 0935 "Belatrix" (PPSI) 1713
22251.50	Ships working		CW 1632
22252.00	Ships working		CW "Puhos" (C6CS7) 0833 "Yick Wing" (3FIR) 0948
22252.50	Ships working		CW "Karatsarovo" (UWKI) 0857
22253.00	Ships working		CW 1222
22253.50	Ships working		CW 1623
22254.00	Ships working		CW "Caledonian Express" (ELKW5) 1631
22254.50	Ships working		CW "Holberg" (LATX) 1729

kHz.	Station	Call	Mode / Heard/Times GMT
22255.00	Ships working		CW "Wave Crest" (3FHG) 1355
22256.00	Ships working		CW "Brilliant" (5BWT) 0813 "Semsvann" (DVGS) 1214
22257.00	Ships working		CW "Faurei" (YQES) 1109
22258.00	Ships working		CW "Lamda" (5LJY) 1022
22258.50	Ships working		CW 1627
22259.00	Ships working		CW 0840 "Pontiaki Doxa" (H2VI) 1350
22259.50	Ships working		CW "Kimlien" (XVER) 1046
22260.00	Ships working		CW 1430
22261.00	Ships working		CW LYGA 1021
22261.50	Ships working		CW 1424
22262.00	Ships working		CW "Paithoon" (HSAZ) 0734 ICMX (to IAR) 1108
22262.50	Ships working		CW "Korundovyy" (UQAP) 1803
22263.00	Ships working		CW "An Yue Jiang" (BOAS) 0820 "Golden Singapore" (3ELU5) 1508
22264.00	Ships working		CW "Kota Jati" (9VLB) 1013
22264.50	Ships working		CW "Perigey" (EVBC) 1140
22265.00	Ships working		CW 1240
22266.00	Ships working		CW 1024 "Vytina" (C6KS2) 1410
22267.00	Ships working		CW 0939
22268.00	Ships working		CW "Global Rio" (PPXN) 1754
22269.00	Ships working		CW 0915
22269.50	Ships working		CW 1807
22270.00	Ships working		CW "Herfah" (3EIH5) 1026 "Captain Bataman" (P3SC2) 1049
22270.50	Ships working		CW 1115
22271.00	Ships working		CW "Coop Express V" (DVAS) 0821
22271.50	Ships working		CW "Suren Spandaryan" (UULY) 0822
22272.00	Ships working		CW "Lupex" (J8DP7) 1332 "Lara S" (J4UR) 1600
22272.50	Ships working		CW "Olivia" (C4DS) 1801
22273.00	Ships working		CW "Aleksey Danchenko" (UIFB) 1600
22273.50	Ships working		CW ESCS 1107
22274.00	Ships working		CW 1432 1708
22275.00	Ships working		CW 0701 1349
22276.00	Ships working		CW "MA 0710" 1209
22277.00	Ships working		CW 3EPS9 (to GKB) 1534
22277.50	Ships working		CW "Barbara D" (3EUK5) 0726 UVKG (to URL) 1050
22278.00	Ships working		CW "Kibinskiy Gory" (UJOC) 1318 "Tuman 2" (UOMC) 1746
22278.50	Ships working		CW (to URL) 1414
22279.00	Ships working		CW "Delphic Flame" (C6JJ3) 0826 YJYF5 1242
22279.50	Ships calling ch 1		CW "Fuhmo Venture" (5MYT) 0900
22280.00	Ships calling ch 2		CW "Eygenia K" (SVIM) 1229 3EHK9 (to SVD) 1418
22280.50	Ships calling ch 3		CW "Ken Sun" (ELNW9) 0838 "Petro Linas" (9VIM) 0935
22281.00	Ships calling ch 4		CW YLFP 1507 "Jacui" (PPKQ) 1707
22281.50	Ships calling ch 5		CW SVIM (to SVB) 1332 "Balaban 1" (TCQR) 1445
22282.00	Ships calling ch 6		CW PGEV (to PCH) 0823 "Borg" (LAGQ2) 1515
22282.50	Ships calling ch 7		CW "Dryso" (C6CS2) 1057
22283.00	Ships calling ch 8		CW UIPS (to UFN) 1055 LRUP (to LSA) 1540
22283.50	Ships calling ch 9		CW "Skulptor Konenkov" (UUXO) 0856
22284.00	Ships calling ch 10		CW SYUI (to VIP) 1105 "Westgate" (P3SC2) 1538
22284.50	Ships wkg ch 1 dup. 22376.5kHz		SITOR "Pasewalk" (Y5LV) 1718 Selcal QFMP (Norddeich) 1342
22285.00	Ships wkg ch 2 dup. 22377.0kHz		SITOR "Nielstor" (C6JZ4) 1023 "Aristarkh Belopolskiy" (ENVK) 1515
22285.50	Ships wkg ch 3 dup. 22377.5kHz		SITOR (Cyrillic) 1832
22286.00	Ships wkg ch 4 dup. 22378.0kHz		SITOR "Hebe" (J8ER6) 1245
22286.50	Ships wkg ch 5 dup. 22378.5kHz		SITOR "Capitan Sandra Tapias" 1622
22287.00	Ships wkg ch 6 dup. 22379.0kHz		SITOR "Artur Grottger" (SQKK) 1745 Selcal QSKX (Stettin) 1546
22287.50	Ships wkg ch 7 dup. 22379.5kHz		SITOR "Talusia" (9HQV2) 1334 "Crown Frost" (3EHQ9) 1718
22288.00	Ships wkg ch 8 dup. 22380.0kHz		SITOR "Reefer Majesty" (P3TU2) 1605 "Bataafgracht" (PCZH) 1608
22288.50	Ships wkg ch 9 dup. 22380.5kHz		SITOR "Brisa" (9HTB3) 1510
22289.00	Ships wkg ch 10 dup. 22381.0kHz		SITOR Selcal MCQV (Singapore) 0704
22289.50	Ships wkg ch 11 dup. 22381.5kHz		SITOR Selcal KPVQ (Berne) 0846
22290.00	Ships wkg ch 12 dup. 22382.0kHz		RTTY
22290.50	Ships wkg ch 13 dup. 22382.5kHz		SITOR 1244
22291.00	Ships wkg ch 14 dup. 22383.0kHz		SITOR Selcal QYYV (Rome) 1125
22291.50	Ships wkg ch 15 dup. 22383.5kHz		SITOR 1624
22292.00	Ships wkg ch 16 dup. 22384.0kHz		RTTY
22292.50	Ships wkg ch 17 dup. 22384.5kHz		RTTY
22293.00	Ships wkg ch 18 dup. 22385.0kHz		SITOR "Talisman" (OWPG6) 1613
22293.50	Ships wkg ch 19 dup. 22385.5kHz		SITOR 1641
22294.00	Ships wkg ch 20 dup. 22386.0kHz		SITOR "Nikoloz Baratashvili" (UWHN) 1420
22294.50	Ships wkg ch 21 dup. 22386.5kHz		SITOR Selcal XVSQ (Chatham) 1235 1532
22295.00	Ships wkg ch 22 dup. 22387.0kHz		RTTY
22295.50	Ships wkg ch 23 dup. 22387.5kHz		SITOR "Fayrouz 2" (SVWP) 1132 Selcal XYFV (Athens) 1355
22296.00	Ships wkg ch 24 dup. 22388.0kHz		RTTY
22296.50	Ships wkg ch 25 dup. 22388.5kHz		RTTY
22297.00	Ships wkg ch 26 dup. 22389.0kHz		SITOR "Tolmiros" (SYSE) 0903 "Jag Palak" (VWYB) 1128

kHz.	Station	Call	Mode / Heard/Times GMT
22297.50	Ships wkg ch 27 dup. 22389.5kHz		SITOR Selcal XVSY (Portsmouth CG) 1806
22298.00	Ships wkg ch 28 dup. 22390.0kHz		RTTY Chesapeake
22298.50	Ships wkg ch 29 dup. 22390.5kHz		SITOR "Novoklav 2" (UOAP) 1212 "Baco-Liner 1" (DCDP) 1544
22299.00	Ships wkg ch 30 dup. 22391.0kHz		SITOR "Sierra Express" (DNCE) 1134
22299.50	Ships wkg ch 31 dup. 22391.5kHz		SITOR 1435
22300.00	Ships wkg ch 32 dup. 22392.0kHz		SITOR "Trans Argo" (C6JF9) 0757 "Swan Bay" (3EDF2) 0830
22300.50	Ships wkg ch 33 dup. 22392.5kHz		RTTY
22301.00	Ships wkg ch 34 dup. 22393.0kHz		SITOR "Ruth Lykes" (KOHB) 1530
22301.50	Ships wkg ch 35 dup. 22393.5kHz		RTTY
22302.00	Ships wkg ch 36 dup. 22394.0kHz		SITOR "Adele" (OZOV2) 1511
22302.50	Ships wkg ch 37 dup. 22394.5kHz		RTTY
22303.00	Ships wkg ch 38 dup. 22395.0kHz		SITOR "Leon Popov" (UFFT) 1336
22303.50	Ships wkg ch 39 dup. 22395.5kHz		RTTY
22304.00	Ships wkg ch 40 dup. 22396.0kHz		SITOR "Chemnitz" (Y5BR) 1429
22304.50	Ships wkg ch 41 dup. 22396.5kHz		RTTY
22305.00	Ships wkg ch 42 dup. 22397.0kHz		RTTY
22305.50	Ships wkg ch 43 dup. 22397.5kHz		SITOR "Krivbass" (UUBD) 1023 "Sidor Kovpak" (UHTX) 1211
22306.00	Ships wkg ch 44 dup. 22398.0kHz		SITOR "Almare IV" (IMCP) 1233
22306.50	Ships wkg ch 45 dup. 22398.5kHz		RTTY
22307.00	Ships wkg ch 46 dup. 22399.0kHz		RTTY
22307.50	Ships wkg ch 47 dup. 22399.5kHz		RTTY
22308.00	Ships wkg ch 48 dup. 22400.0kHz		RTTY
22308.50	Ships wkg ch 49 dup. 22400.5kHz		SITOR 1505
22309.00	Ships wkg ch 50 dup. 22401.0kHz		SITOR 1335
22309.50	Ships wkg ch 51 dup. 22401.5kHz		RTTY
22310.00	Ships wkg ch 52 dup. 22402.0kHz		SITOR "Viva" (LACU2) 0853 & 1620
22310.50	Ships wkg ch 53 dup. 22402.5kHz		RTTY
22311.00	Ships wkg ch 54 dup. 22403.0kHz		SITOR 1637 1855
22311.50	Ships wkg ch 55 dup. 22403.5kHz		SITOR "Imkenturm" (ELDI6) 1034
22312.00	Ships wkg ch 56 dup. 22404.0kHz		SITOR "Marshal Rokossovskiy" (UTZR) 1147 "Sapphire" (DUJW) 1807
22312.50	Ships wkg ch 57 dup. 22404.5kHz		SITOR "Riesa" (Y5EJ) 0943
22313.00	Ships wkg ch 58 dup. 22405.0kHz		SITOR 1856 Selcal KQQV (Portishead) 1518
22313.50	Ships wkg ch 59 dup. 22405.5kHz		SITOR "Azerbaydzhan" (UFZX) 1049 "Odessa" (EWBK) 1226
22314.00	Ships wkg ch 60 dup. 22406.0kHz		SITOR "Dmitriy Mendeleyev" (UILS) 1532
22314.50	Ships wkg ch 61 dup. 22406.5kHz		SITOR Selcal KPCV (Lisbon) 1253
22315.00	Ships wkg ch 62 dup. 22407.0kHz		SITOR "Belita Star" (C6JU8) 1547
22315.50	Ships wkg ch 63 dup. 22407.5kHz		SITOR "Kehra" (ESAE) 0851
22316.00	Ships wkg ch 64 dup. 22408.0kHz		SITOR Selcal MKKX (Capetown) 1555
22316.50	Ships wkg ch 65 dup. 22408.5kHz		SITOR 0957 1241
22317.00	Ships wkg ch 66 dup. 22409.0kHz		SITOR "General Bagration" (UJSH) 1617
22317.50	Ships wkg ch 67 dup. 22409.5kHz		RTTY
22318.00	Ships wkg ch 68 dup. 22410.0kHz		SITOR (Cyrillic) 0928
22318.50	Ships wkg ch 69 dup. 22410.5kHz		RTTY
22319.00	Ships wkg ch 70 dup. 22411.0kHz		SITOR Selcal MKCV (Istanbul) 1352
22319.50	Ships wkg ch 71 dup. 22411.5kHz		RTTY
22320.00	Ships wkg ch 72 dup. 22412.0kHz		SITOR 2116
22320.50	Ships wkg ch 73 dup. 22412.5kHz		SITOR "San Pedro" (DHHO) 1330
22321.00	Ships wkg ch 74 dup. 22413.0kHz		RTTY
22321.50	Ships wkg ch 75 dup. 22413.5kHz		RTTY
22322.00	Ships wkg ch 76 dup. 22414.0kHz		170/50nc 1548
22322.50	Ships wkg ch 77 dup. 22414.5kHz		RTTY
22323.00	Ships wkg ch 78 dup. 22415.0kHz		RTTY
22323.50	Ships wkg ch 79 dup. 22415.5kHz		RTTY
22324.00	Ships wkg ch 80 dup. 22416.0kHz		RTTY
22324.50	Ships wkg ch 81 dup. 22416.5kHz		RTTY
22325.00	Ships wkg ch 82 dup. 22417.0kHz		RTTY
22325.50	Ships wkg ch 83 dup. 22417.5kHz		RTTY
22326.00	Ships wkg ch 84 dup. 22418.0kHz		RTTY
22326.50	Ships wkg ch 85 dup. 22418.5kHz		RTTY
22327.00	Ships wkg ch 86 dup. 22419.0kHz		RTTY
22327.50	Ships wkg ch 87 dup. 22419.5kHz		RTTY
22328.00	Ships wkg ch 88 dup. 22420.0kHz		RTTY
22328.50	Ships wkg ch 89 dup. 22420.5kHz		RTTY
22329.00	Ships wkg ch 90 dup. 22421.0kHz		RTTY
22329.50	Ships wkg ch 91 dup. 22421.5kHz		RTTY
22330.50	Luanda, Angola	D3E81	CW 0947 1015 1245 1327 1506 1621 1737
22330.00	Ships wkg ch 92 dup. 22422.0kHz		RTTY
22330.50	Ships wkg ch 93 dup. 22422.5kHz		RTTY
22331.00	Ships wkg ch 94 dup. 22423.0kHz		RTTY
22331.50	Ships wkg ch 95 dup. 22423.5kHz		RTTY
22332.00	Ships wkg ch 96 dup. 22424.0kHz		RTTY
22332.50	Ships wkg ch 97 dup. 22424.5kHz		RTTY
22333.00	Ships wkg ch 98 dup. 22425.0kHz		RTTY
22333.50	Ships wkg ch 99 dup. 22425.5kHz		RTTY
22334.40	Ships wkg ch 100 dup. 22426.0kHz		RTTY
22334.50	Ships wkg ch 101 dup. 22426.5kHz		RTTY

kHz.	Station	Call	Mode / Heard/Times GMT
22335.00	Ships wkg ch 102 dup. 22427.0kHz		RTTY
22335.50	Ships wkg ch 103 dup. 22427.5kHz		RTTY
22336.00	Ships wkg ch 104 dup. 22428.0kHz		RTTY
22336.50	Ships wkg ch 105 dup. 22428.5kHz		RTTY
22337.00	Ships wkg ch 106 dup. 22429.0kHz		RTTY
22337.50	Ships wkg ch 107 dup. 22429.5kHz		RTTY
22338.00	Ships wkg ch 108 dup. 22430.0kHz		RTTY
22338.50	Ships wkg ch 109 dup. 22430.5kHz		RTTY
22339.00	Ships wkg ch 110 dup. 22431.0kHz		RTTY
22339.50	Ships wkg ch 111 dup. 22431.5kHz		RTTY
22340.00	Ships wkg ch 112 dup. 22432.0kHz		RTTY
22340.50	Ships wkg ch 113 dup. 22432.5kHz		SITOR "Georgiy Tovstonogov" (USWE) 1552
22341.00	Ships wkg ch 114 dup. 22433.0kHz		RTTY
22341.50	Ships wkg ch 115 dup. 22433.5kHz		RTTY
22342.00	Ships wkg ch 116 dup. 22434.0kHz		RTTY
22342.50	Ships wkg ch 117 dup. 22434.5kHz		RTTY
22343.00	Ships wkg ch 118 dup. 22435.0kHz		RTTY
22343.50	Ships wkg ch 119 dup. 22435.5kHz		RTTY
22344.00	Ships wkg ch 120 dup. 22436.0kHz		RTTY
22344.50	Ships wkg ch 121 dup. 22436.5kHz		RTTY
22345.00	Ships wkg ch 122 dup. 22437.0kHz		RTTY
22345.50	Ships wkg ch 123 dup. 22437.5kHz		RTTY
22346.00	Ships wkg ch 124 dup. 22438.0kHz		RTTY
22346.50	Ships wkg ch 125 dup. 22438.5kHz		RTTY
22347.00	Ships wkg ch 126 dup. 22439.0kHz		RTTY
22347.50	Ships wkg ch 127 dup. 22439.5kHz		RTTY
22348.00	Ships wkg ch 128 dup. 22440.0kHz		RTTY
22348.50	Ships wkg ch 129 dup. 22440.5kHz		RTTY
22349.00	Ships wkg ch 130 dup. 22441.0kHz		RTTY
22349.50	Ships wkg ch 131 dup. 22441.5kHz		RTTY
22350.00	Ships wkg ch 132 dup. 22442.0kHz		RTTY
22350.50	Ships wkg ch 133 dup. 22442.5kHz		SITOR 1613
22351.00	Ships wkg ch 134 dup. 22443.0kHz		SITOR 1336
22351.50	Ships wkg ch 135 dup. 22443.5kHz		RTTY
22352.00	Ships working (non-paired)		170/50nc "MB 0035" 1715
22352.50	Ships working (non paired)		170/50nc 0855
22353.00	Ships working (non paired)		170/50nc 1440 "Apogey" (EVBF) 1537
22353.50	Ships working (non paired)		170/50nc "Sokolinoye" 0707
22354.00	Ships working (non paired)		170/50nc 1626
22354.50	Ships working (non paired)		170/50nc "Argus" (ESRL) 1348 & 170/100nc ESCF 1425
22355.00	Ships working (non-paired)		170/50nc "Budapesht" (UOJD) 0844
22355.50	Ships working (non paired)		170/50nc "Chernomorskaya Slava" (USZW) 1504
22356.00	Ships working (non paired)		170/50nc 1104
22356.50	Ships working (non paired)		170/50nc "Hermann Matern" (URPK) 1143
22357.00	Ships working (non paired)		170/50nc "Otto Grotewohl" (EWJQ) 1358
22357.50	Ships working (non paired)		170/50nc 1108
22358.00	Ships working (non paired)		170/100nc "Fyodor Korobkov" (UQRS) 1614
22358.50	Ships working (non paired)		170/50nc "Kurs" (ESHY) 1513
22359.00	Ships working (non paired)		170/50nc (to URD) 1110
22359.50	Ships working (non paired)		170/50nc "Pioner Volkov" (UFKT) 1013
22360.00	Ships working (non paired)		170/50nc 1609
22360.50	Ships working (non paired)		RTTY
22361.00	Ships working (non paired)		170/50nc 1235 1454 1700
22361.50	Ships working (non paired)		170/50nc "Pyatigorsk" (UHXM) 1358 "Karatsaravo" (UNKI) 1521
22362.00	Ships working (non paired)		170/50nc "Wilhelm Pieck" (UWGP) 1436
22362.50	Ships working (non paired)		170/100nc "Ilmen" (ESIZ) 1231 & 50nc "MB 0002" 1604
22363.00	Ships working (non paired)		170/50nc "Konstantin Olshanskiy" (UJIP) 1535
22363.50	Ships working (non paired)		170/50nc UPBC (to UJY) 1123
22364.00	Ships working (non paired)		RTTY
22364.50	Ships working (non paired)		170/50nc 1112
22365.00	Ships working (non paired)		170/50nc 1129
22365.50	Ships working (non paired)		170/50nc "Musson" (URXW) 0804
22366.00	Ships working (non paired)		170/50nc "STM 8335" (LYGA) 1356
22366.50	Ships working (non paired)		170/50nc 1239
22367.00	Ships working (non paired)		170/50nc "MA-0052" 1216 "Stakhanovets" (ULJV) 1530 "MA-803" 1628
22367.50	Ships working (non paired)		RTTY
22368.00	Ships working (non paired)		RTTY
22368.50	Ships working (non paired)		170/50nc "Samara" (ESKX) 1152
22369.00	Ships working (non paired)		170/50nc "MB 0371" 1527
22369.50	Ships working (non paired)		170/50nc 1551
22370.00	Ships working (non paired)		170/50rc "Gigant" (URJQ) 1301
22370.50	Ships working (non paired)		RTTY
22371.00	Ships working (non paired)		170/50nc "Malaya Zemlya" (UWFH) 1033
22371.50	Ships working (non paired)		170/50nc "Rizhskiy Zaliv" (ESWE) 1615
22372.00	Ships working (non paired)		170/50nc UDWW 1257

kHz.	Station	Call	Mode / Heard/Times GMT
22372.50	Ships working (non paired)		170/50nc "Khasan" (UJZX) 0914 "Ivan Pribiylskiy" (UNOG) 1526
22373.00	Ships working (non paired)		SITOR "William Foster" (UIIE) 1132
22373.50	Ships working (non paired)		170/50nc "Mitridat" (ESJV) 1343
22374.00	Ships working (non paired)		170/50nc "MA 0055" 1605
22374.50	Ships working		170/50nc "Vasily Polenov" (USCW) 1354 "Veteran" 1630
22375.00	Ships (digital selective calling)		RTTY
22375.50	Ships (digital selective calling)		RTTY
22376.50	Coast stations ch 1 dup. 22284.5kHz		RTTY
22377.00	Coast stations ch 2 dup. 22285.0kHz		RTTY
22377.00	Portishead, UK	GKE7	SITOR 0710 1103 1328 1416 1609 Mode B 0908 1901
22377.50	Coast stations ch 3 dup. 22285.5kHz		RTTY
22377.50	Gdynia, Poland	SPA	SITOR 1236 1342
22378.00	Coast stations ch 4 dup. 22286.0kHz		RTTY
22378.00	St Lys, France	FFT91	SITOR 0735 1236 1540 2109 Mode B wx 0802 1002 1304
22378.50	Coast stations ch 5 dup. 22286.5kHz		RTTY
22379.00	Coast stations ch 6 dup. 22287.0kHz		RTTY
22379.00	Hong Kong	VPS97	SITOR 0618
22379.00	Perth, Australia	VIP36	SITOR 0636 0835 1034
22379.50	Coast stations ch 7 dup. 22287.5kHz		RTTY
22379.50	Goeteborg, Sweden	SAG	SITOR 0949 1219 1330 1411 1533
22380.00	Coast stations ch 8 dup. 22288.0kHz		RTTY
22380.00	Scheveningen, Holland	PCH75	SITOR 0916 1410 1542 1744
22380.50	Coast stations ch 9 dup. 22288.5kHz		RTTY
22380.50	Valparaiso, Chile	CBV	SITOR 1222 1850
22381.00	Coast stations ch 10 dup. 22289.0kHz		RTTY
22381.00	Mobile, USA	WLO	SITOR 1409 1536 1635
22381.00	Singapore	9VG	SITOR 0917 1057 Mode B 1330 wx 0030 1230 tfc list odd hours + 30
22381.50	Coast stations ch 11 dup. 22289.5kHz		RTTY
22381.50	Berne, Switzerland	HEC52	SITOR 0954 1052 1105 1432 1520 Mode B 1230
22382.00	Coast stations ch 12 dup. 22290.0kHz		RTTY
22382.00	Apra Harbour CG, Guam	NRV	SITOR 1022
22382.00	Boston CG, USA	NMF	SITOR (1100-2300)
22382.00	Perth, Australia	VIP46	SITOR
22382.00	San Francisco CG, USA	NMC	SITOR 1113
22382.50	Coast stations ch 13 dup. 22290.5kHz		RTTY
22382.50	San Francisco, USA	KPH	SITOR 1638
22383.00	Coast stations ch 14 dup. 22291.0kHz		RTTY
22383.00	Scheveningen, Holland	PCH76	SITOR 1106 1357 1412 1533
22383.50	Coast stations ch 15 dup. 22291.5kHz		RTTY
22383.50	Mobile, USA	WLO	SITOR 1347 1403
22384.00	Coast stations ch 16 dup. 22292.0kHz		RTTY
22384.50	Coast stations ch 17 dup. 22292.5kHz		RTTY
22385.00	Coast stations ch 18 dup. 22293.0kHz		RTTY
22385.00	Lyngby, Denmark	OXZ	SITOR 0919 1050 1231 1331 1433
22385.50	Coast stations ch 19 dup. 22293.5kHz		RTTY
22385.50	Slidell, USA	WNU	SITOR 1345
22386.00	Coast stations ch 20 dup. 22294.0kHz		RTTY
22386.00	Novorossiysk, Russia	UFN	SITOR 1058 1237 1358 (to "Sovietskaya Neft" UMTX) 1634
22386.50	Coast stations ch 21 dup. 22294.5kHz		RTTY
22386.50	Chatham, USA	WCC	SITOR 1328 1438 1512 tfc list 1238 1438 wx 1245 1345 1645 1700
22387.00	Coast stations ch 22 dup. 22295.0kHz		RTTY
22387.50	Coast stations ch 23 dup. 22295.5kHz		RTTY
22387.50	Athens, Greece	SVT7	SITOR 0854 1107 1437 1600 1952 Mode B 0938
22388.00	Coast stations ch 24 dup. 22296.0kHz		RTTY
22388.50	Coast stations ch 25 dup. 22296.5kHz		RTTY
22388.50	Kaliningrad, Russia	UIW	170/50nc 0924 1042 1256
22389.00	Coast stations ch 26 dup. 22297.0kHz		RTTY
22389.00	Singapore	9VG	SITOR 0956 1023 1122 1411 1606 (to J8HI4) 1640
22389.50	Coast stations ch 27 dup. 22297.5kHz		RTTY
22389.50	Chesapeake CG, USA	NMN	SITOR 1341 1401 1522 2114 2224
22390.00	Coast stations ch 28 dup. 22298.0kHz		RTTY
22390.50	Coast stations ch 29 dup. 22298.5kHz		RTTY
22390.50	St Lys, France	FFT92	SITOR 0848 0947 1531 1640 2108
22391.00	Coast stations ch 30 dup. 22299.0kHz		RTTY
22391.00	Norddeich, Germany	DCL	SITOR 0711 0951 1232 1423 1457 1606 1837
22391.50	Coast stations ch 31 dup. 22299.5kHz		RTTY
22391.50	Panama	HPP	SITOR 0840 1556 1656 1739
22391.50	Vancouver, Canada	VAI	SITOR
22392.00	Coast stations ch 32 dup. 22300.0kHz		RTTY
22392.00	Goeteborg, Sweden	SAG	SITOR 0921 1202 2113
22392.50	Coast stations ch 33 dup. 22300.5kHz		RTTY
22393.00	Coast stations ch 34 dup. 22301.0kHz		RTTY
22393.00	Portishead, UK	GKP7	SITOR 1129 1359 1601 1929
22393.50	Coast stations ch 35 dup. 22301.5kHz		RTTY

kHz.	Station	Call	Mode / Heard/Times GMT
22394.00	Coast stations ch 36 dup. 22302.0kHz		RTTY
22394.00	Lyngby, Denmark	OXZ	SITOR 0922 1238 1553 Mode B tfc list 1132 news (Danish) 1630
22394.50	Coast stations ch 37 dup. 22302.5kHz		RTTY
22394.50	General Pacheco, Argentina	LPD	SITOR 1405 1600 1622
22395.00	Coast stations ch 38 dup. 22303.0kHz		RTTY
22395.00	Helsinki, Finland	OFA	SITOR
22395.00	Mariupol, Ukraine	USU	SITOR 0957 1054 1341 1412 1536
22395.00	San Francisco, USA	KPH	SITOR
22395.50	Coast stations ch 39 dup. 22303.5kHz		RTTY
22395.50	General Pacheco, Argentina	LPD	SITOR
22396.00	Coast stations ch 40 dup. 22304.0kHz		RTTY
22396.50	Coast stations ch 41 dup. 22304.5kHz		RTTY
22397.00	Coast stations ch 42 dup. 22305.0kHz		RTTY
22397.50	Coast stations ch 43 dup. 22305.5kHz		RTTY
22397.50	Novorossiysk, Russia	UFN	SITOR 0638 0713 0849 (to UUBD) 1027
22398.00	Coast stations ch 44 dup. 22306.0kHz		RTTY
22398.50	Coast stations ch 45 dup. 22306.5kHz		RTTY
22399.00	Coast stations ch 46 dup. 22307.0kHz		RTTY
22399.00	Bahrain	A9M	SITOR 0620 0735 0855 1055 1545 1642 1741
22399.50	Coast stations ch 47 dup. 22307.5kHz		RTTY
22400.00	Coast stations ch 48 dup. 22308.0kHz		RTTY
22400.50	Coast stations ch 49 dup. 22308.5kHz		RTTY
22401.00	Coast stations ch 50 dup. 22309.0kHz		RTTY
22401.00	Berne, Switzerland	HEC62	SITOR 0654 0807 1116 1221 1330 1641
22401.50	Coast stations ch 51 dup. 22309.5kHz		RTTY
22402.00	Coast stations ch 52 dup. 22310.0kHz		RTTY
22402.00	Rogaland, Norway	LGG3	SITOR 0954 1019 1349 1453 1525 1930
22402.50	Coast stations ch 53 dup. 22310.5kHz		RTTY
22403.00	Coast stations ch 54 dup. 22311.0kHz		RTTY
22403.00	Mobile, USA	WLO	SITOR 1131 1331 1403 1541
22403.50	Coast stations ch 55 dup. 22311.5kHz		RTTY
22403.50	Berne, Switzerland	HEC72	SITOR 0714 1030 1600
22404.00	Coast stations ch 56 dup. 22312.0kHz		RTTY
22404.00	Mobile, USA	WLO	SITOR
22404.50	Coast stations ch 57 dup. 22312.5kHz		RTTY
22405.00	Coast stations ch 58 dup. 22313.0kHz		RTTY
22405.00	Halifax, Canada	VCS	SITOR
22405.00	Portishead, UK	GKY7	SITOR 1526
22405.50	Coast stations ch 59 dup. 22313.5kHz		RTTY
22405.50	Odessa, Ukraine	UUI	SITOR 1150 1234 1347 1400 1449
22406.00	Coast stations ch 60 dup. 22314.0kHz		RTTY
22406.00	Mobile, USA	WLO	SITOR 1406 1436 1601
22406.00	Moscow, Russia	UAT	SITOR 1048 1226 1333 1610
22406.50	Coast stations ch 61 dup. 22314.5kHz		RTTY
22406.50	Lisbon, Portugal	CUL	SITOR
22407.00	Coast stations ch 62 dup. 22315.0kHz		RTTY
22407.00	Mobile, USA	WLO	SITOR 1350 1600 1932
22407.50	Coast stations ch 63 dup. 22315.5kHz		RTTY
22407.50	Moscow, Russia	UAT	SITOR 1056 1414 1507 (to "Georgiy Tovstonogov" USWE) 1602
22408.00	Coast stations ch 64 dup. 22316.0kHz		RTTY
22408.00	Capetown, S Africa	ZSC65	SITOR 0734 1050 1505 1555
22408.50	Coast stations ch 65 dup. 22316.5kHz		RTTY
22409.00	Coast stations ch 66 dup. 22317.0kHz		RTTY
22409.00	Gdynia, Poland	SPA	SITOR
22409.00	Portishead, UK	GKQ7	SITOR 1031 1528 1620 1643
22409.50	Coast stations ch 67 dup. 22317.5kHz		RTTY
22410.00	Coast stations ch 68 dup. 22318.0kHz		RTTY
22410.50	Coast stations ch 69 dup. 22318.5kHz		RTTY
22411.00	Coast stations ch 70 dup. 22319.0kHz		RTTY
22411.50	Coast stations ch 71 dup. 22319.5kHz		RTTY
22412.00	Coast stations ch 72 dup. 22320.0kHz		RTTY
22412.00	Mobile, USA	WLO	SITOR 1907 2131
22412.50	Coast stations ch 73 dup. 22320.5kHz		RTTY
22413.00	Coast stations ch 74 dup. 22321.0kHz		RTTY
22413.50	Coast stations ch 75 dup. 22321.5kHz		RTTY
22414.00	Coast stations ch 76 dup. 22322.0kHz		RTTY
22414.50	Coast stations ch 77 dup. 22322.5kHz		RTTY
22415.00	Coast stations ch 78 dup. 22323.0kHz		RTTY
22415.50	Coast stations ch 79 dup. 22323.5kHz		RTTY
22416.00	Coast stations ch 80 dup. 22324.0kHz		RTTY
22416.50	Coast stations ch 81 dup. 22324.5kHz		RTTY
22417.00	Coast stations ch 82 dup. 22325.0kHz		RTTY
22417.50	Coast stations ch 83 dup. 22325.5kHz		RTTY
22418.00	Coast stations ch 84 dup. 22326.0kHz		RTTY
22418.00	Mobile, USA	WLO	SITOR 1337 1435 1527

kHz.	Station	Call	Mode / Heard/Times GMT
22418.50	Coast stations ch 85 dup. 22326.5kHz		RTTY
22419.00	Coast stations ch 86 dup. 22327.0kHz		RTTY
22419.50	Coast stations ch 87 dup. 22327.5kHz		RTTY
22420.00	Coast stations ch 88 dup. 22328.0kHz		RTTY
22420.00	Guangzhou, China	XSQ	SITOR 0857 0955 1123
22420.50	Coast stations ch 89 dup. 22328.5kHz		RTTY
22421.00	Coast stations ch 90 dup. 22329.0kHz		RTTY
22421.50	Coast stations ch 91 dup. 22329.5kHz		RTTY
22422.00	Coast stations ch 92 dup. 22330.0kHz		RTTY
22422.00	British Naval	MTO	75r 0716 1032 1613
22422.50	Coast stations ch 93 dup. 22330.5kHz		RTTY
22423.00	Coast stations ch 94 dup. 22331.0kHz		RTTY
22423.50	Coast stations ch 95 dup. 22331.5kHz		RTTY
22424.00	Coast stations ch 96 dup. 22332.0kHz		RTTY
22424.50	Coast stations ch 97 dup. 22332.5kHz		RTTY
22425.00	Coast stations ch 98 dup. 22333.0kHz		RTTY
22425.50	Coast stations ch 99 dup. 22333.5kHz		RTTY
22425.50	Pennsuco, USA	WOM	SITOR 1354 Mode B tfc list 1403 1602 wx 1653
22426.00	Coast stations ch 100 dup. 22334.0kHz		RTTY
22426.50	Coast stations ch 101 dup. 22334.5kHz		RTTY
22427.00	Coast stations ch 102 dup. 22335.0kHz		RTTY
22427.50	Coast stations ch 103 dup. 22335.5kHz		RTTY
22428.00	Coast stations ch 104 dup. 22336.0kHz		RTTY
22428.50	Coast stations ch 105 dup. 22336.5kHz		RTTY
22429.00	Coast stations ch 106 dup. 22337.0kHz		RTTY
22429.50	Coast stations ch 107 dup. 22337.5kHz		RTTY
22430.00	Coast stations ch 108 dup. 22338.8kHz		RTTY
22430.50	Coast stations ch 109 dup. 22338.5kHz		RTTY
22431.00	Coast stations ch 110 dup. 22339.0kHz		RTTY
22431.50	Coast stations ch 111 dup. 22339.5kHz		RTTY
22432.00	Coast stations ch 112 dup. 22340.0kHz		RTTY
22432.50	Coast stations ch 113 dup. 22340.5kHz		RTTY
22432.50	Moscow, Russia	UAT	SITOR 0956 1151 1229 1455 1618 Mode B 1204
22433.00	Coast stations ch 114 dup. 22341.0kHz		RTTY
22433.50	Coast stations ch 115 dup. 22341.5kHz		RTTY
22434.00	Coast stations ch 116 dup. 22342.0kHz		RTTY
22434.50	Coast stations ch 117 dup. 22342.5kHz		RTTY
22435.00	Coast stations ch 118 dup. 22343.0kHz		RTTY
22435.50	Coast stations ch 119 dup. 22343.5kHz		RTTY
22436.00	Coast stations ch 120 dup. 22344.0kHz		RTTY
22436.50	Coast stations ch 121 dup. 22344.5kHz		RTTY
22437.00	Coast stations ch 122 dup. 22345.0kHz		RTTY
22437.50	Coast stations ch 123 dup. 22345.5kHz		RTTY
22438.00	Coast stations ch 124 dup. 22346.0kHz		RTTY
22438.50	Coast stations ch 125 dup. 22346.5kHz		RTTY
22439.00	Coast stations ch 126 dup. 22347.0kHz		RTTY
22439.50	Coast stations ch 127 dup. 22347.5kHz		RTTY
22440.00	Coast stations ch 128 dup. 22348.0kHz		RTTY
22440.50	Coast stations ch 129 dup. 22348.5kHz		RTTY
22441.00	Coast stations ch 130 dup. 22349.0kHz		RTTY
22441.50	Coast stations ch 131 dup. 22349.5kHz		RTTY
22442.00	Coast stations ch 132 dup. 22350.0kHz		RTTY
22442.50	Coast stations ch 133 dup. 22350.5kHz		RTTY
22443.00	Coast stations ch 134 dup. 22351.0kHz		RTTY
22443.00	Ostend, Belgium	OST	SITOR 0717 0850 1109 1403 1655 1742
22443.50	Coast Stations ch 135 dup. 22351.5kHz		RTTY
22444.00	Coast stations (digital selective calling)		RTTY
22444.50	Coast stations (digital selective calling)		RTTY
22445.00	Coast stations (digital selective calling)		RTTY
22445.00	Murmansk, Russia	UMV	SITOR 1336
22446.00	Madrid, Spain	EAD6	CW 0935 1057 1405 1440 1514 1557 tfc list 1603 1802
22447.00	French Naval, Djibouti	FUV	CW 0958 1125 1228 1334 1538
22448.00	Constanza, Romania	YQI	CW 1027 1228 1403 tfc list 1300 1400 1500
22448.70	Portishead, UK	GKB7	CW 1030 1133 1510 1619 1743
22450.00	Olinda, Brazil	PPO	CW 1230 1432 1547 1656 1915 1935 tfc list 1333
22452.00	Guangzhou, China	XSQ7	CW 0711 0850 0958 1058 1203 tfc list 0830 0930 1030 1130
22454.00	Panama	HPP	CW 1418
22455.00	Capetown, RSA	ZSC40	CW 1433 1742 nav wngs 1703 wx 1733 tfc list 0636 1638
22455.00	Riga, Latvia	UDH	CW
22458.00	Slidell, USA	WNU46	CW 1404 1442 1529 1841
22458.10	Keelung, Taiwan	XSX	CW 0925 1110
22459.00	Lyngby, Denmark	OXZ93	CW 1031 1204 1457 1604 tfc list 1001 1501
22463.00	Choshi, Japan	JCU	CW 0641 1443
22464.00	Odessa, Ukraine	UUI	CW 1149 1233
22464.00	Odessa, Ukraine	UUI	170/50nc 1503
22465.00	Pinang, Malaysia	9MG12	CW 0926 1205 1338 1506 1646 tfc list 1604
22467.00	Portishead, UK	GKA7	CW wx anal 1130 tfc list 0800 0900 1100 1300 1600 1700 1800

kHz.	Station	Call	Mode / Heard/Times GMT
22471.50	Athens, Greece	SVD7	CW 0712 1000 1032 1335 1405 1548 1942
22473.00	Valparaiso, Chile	CBV	CW 1511 1541 1616 1744
22473.50	Rogaland, Norway	LFG	CW 0946 1235 1518 1626 1740 tfc list 1618
22474.00	Perth, Australia	VIP	CW 0831 0913 1043
22476.00	Norddeich, Germany	DAM	CW 1134 1206 1435 1512 1620
22477.50	San Francisco, USA	KPH	CW tfc list 1700
22479.00	Lisbon, Portugal	CUL24	CW 2146
22479.00	Singapore	9VG27	CW 1033 1533 1812
22485.00	St Petersburg, Russia	UBF2	CW 0714 1002 1130 1400 1550
22485.00	Sydney, Australia	VIX7	CW
22487.00	Mobile, USA	WLO	CW wx fcsts 1130 1518 1722 1945 2219 tfc list 1513
22487.00	Mobile, USA	WLO	SITOR Mode B 1452
22490.00	Archangel, Russia	UCE	SITOR 1034
22490.00	Archangel, Russia	UCE	170/50nc 1031 1139
22491.00	Haifa, Israel	4XO	CW 0718 0934 1101 1514 1745 tfc list 1625
22493.00	Moscow, Russia	UAT	170/50nc 1239
22494.00	Portishead, UK	GKK7	CW reserve frequency
22496.00	Juncao, Brazil	PPJ	CW 1035 1435 1546 1610 1917
22497.00	Murmansk, Russia	UQA4	CW (to "4LS") 0947 1003 1207 1402 1526 1701
22497.00	Murmansk, Russia	UQA4	170/50nc 1152 1535
22500.00	Athens, Greece	SVF7	CW 0914 1032 1114 1407 1605 1943
22501.00	Novorossiysk, Russia	UFN	170/50nc 1335 1504
22501.00	Novorossiysk, Russia	UFN	CW 0719 0811 0902 1004 1408 tfc list 1000 1200 1400 1600
22503.00	Portishead, UK	GKG7	CW (working frequency to ships) 0855 0917 1029 1611
22505.00	Stettin, Poland	SPB93	SITOR (dup. 22352.5) 0903 1006 1237 1530 1620 1739
22509.00	St Lys, France	FFL9	CW 0746 0813 1436 1552 1715 tfc list 1850 2040
22512.00	Moscow, Russia	UAT	CW 0905 0933 tfc list 0905 1336 1505
22516.00	Norddeich, Germany	DAN	CW 0716 0735 1059 1209 1447 1622
22518.00	Chatham, USA	WCC	CW 1337 1515 1621 wx 1300 1522 tfc list 1457 1658 1852
22520.00	Riga, Latvia	UQK	170/50nc 1552 1716
22520.00	Riga, Latvia	UQK	CW 0747 0832 0907 1008 1154 1517 tfc list 1000
22525.00	Rome (Medical Centre), Italy	IRM	CW 1057 1613 1843
22525.50	Portishead, UK	GKH7	CW (working frequency to ships) 1435
22527.00	Mariupol, Ukraine	USU	CW 0950
22527.00	Mariupol, Ukraine	USU	170/50nc 0717 0813 1034 1119
22527.00	Portishead, UK	GKM7	CW reserve frequency
22527.00	San Francisco CG, USA	NMC	FAX wx maps 1507 1744
22528.50	Portishead, UK	GKI7	CW reserve frequency
22530.00	Brazilian Naval	PWZ33	CW nav wngs (in Eng) 1350
22530.00	Sebastopol, Ukraine	URL	CW (listens 22274.5) 1059
22533.00	Madrid, Spain	EDZ7	CW 1659
22533.00	Ostend, Belgium	OST7	CW 1446 1501 1746
22533.00	RSA Naval	ZSJ	CW 0730 0908 1052 1441 1610
22536.00	Hong Kong	VPS22	CW 0822
22537.00	French Naval, Martinique	FUF	CW 1214 1250 1516 1636 1918
22539.00	Scheveningen, Holland	PCH71	CW 0909 1037 1555 1614
22541.00	Tokyo, Japan	JJC	FAX wx maps 0823 1253
22543.00	Boufarik, Algeria	7TF	CW 0718 0731 0858 1152
22545.00	Portishead, UK	GKJ7	CW reserve frequency
22548.00	Istanbul, Turkey	TAH	CW 0719 1155 1223 1508 tfc list 0901 1101 1301 1701
22550.50	British Naval	MTO	75r 1326 1408 1427
22555.00	Odessa, Ukraine	UUI	CW 0846 1208 1532
22556.30	Boca, Argentina	LSA7	CW 1624 1708 1753
22557.00	San Francisco, USA	KPH	CW 1622 1719
22560.00	Sebastopol, Ukraine	URL	CW 0656 0733 1133 1237 tfc list 1100
22560.00	Sebastopol, Ukraine	URL	170/50rc 0826
22563.50	Rijeka, Croatia	9AR	CW 1124 1344 1439 tfc list 1200
22565.00	Kaohsiung, Taiwan	XSW	CW 0718 1117
22575.50	Jakarta, Indonesia	PKX	CW 0700 0754 0828 0926 1510 1649 1734 1817
22575.50	Slidell, USA	WNU36	CW 1449 1520 tfc list 1405
22576.50	Tokyo, Japan	JNA	CW 0654 0749 0824
22578.50	Singapore	9VG59	CW 0810 1118 1338 1558 tfc list 1039
22581.50	Palo Alto, USA	KFS	CW 1600 1643 1720
22583.00	French Military, Reunion	FUX	CW 0820 1112
22583.00	Gelendzhik, Russia	UVA	CW 0725
22587.00	Mauritius	3BM7	CW 0928 wx 0831
22587.50	General Pacheco, Argentina	LPD91	CW 1035 1240 1440 1618 1756 1919 tfc list 1605
22588.70	Dammam, Saudi Arabia	HZG	CW 0904 1146
22589.50	Athens, Greece	SVA7	CW 0754 1038 1521 1757 1944 tfc list 1203 1603 1803
22591.50	Norddeich, Germany	DAF	CW 0638 1033 1523
22592.50	Bahrain	A9M	CW 0910 1002 1241 1341 1619 1748
22595.90	Athens, Greece	SVB7	CW 1138 1242 1535 1758 1914
22596.50	Novorossiysk, Russia	UFN	CW 0717 0939 1352 tfc list 1714
22602.50	Lyngby, Denmark	OXZ	CW 0843 1016
22603.00	Rio de Janeiro, Brazil	PPR	CW 0935 1039 1518 1610 1721 tfc list 1708 1907
22603.50	Kaliningrad, Russia	UIW	CW 0931 tfc list 0911
22607.30	Goeteborg, Sweden	SAG	SITOR 1147 1233 1540

kHz.	Station	Call	Mode / Heard/Times GMT
22609.80	Helsinki, Finland	OFJ	CW 1119 1243 1611 1759
22610.50	Havana, Cuba	CLA	CW 1551
22611.50	Seoul, Korea	HLF	CW 0850
22619.50	Halifax, Canada	VCS	CW 1430 1534 1644 ice wng 1334 1353
22623.50	Sebastopol, Ukraine	URL	CW tfc list 1803 (also hrd callsign as UKG9 at 0626)
22628.50	Indian Naval	VTG	CW 1006 1339 wx 1038
22630.50	Rome, Italy	IAR	CW 0834 1105 1524 1620 1736 1804
22634.00	Rome, Italy	IAR	CW 1552 tfc list 1200 1600
22635.50	Sebastopol, Ukraine	URL	CW 0724 0902 0951 1345 1607 1720
22635.50	Sebastopol, Ukraine	URL	170/50nc (listens 22372.0) 1007
22636.50	Klaipeda Harbour, Lithuania	LYL	CW 0823 0914 1039 1217 1336 1452 1745
22636.50	Klaipeda Harbour, Lithuania	LYL	170/50nc 1148 1735
22641.00	Mariupol, Ukraine	USU	CW 1107
22641.00	Mariupol, Ukraine	USU	170/50nc 1039
22645.50	Hamburg, Germany	DGW64	CW ID 0916 news 0923 0930
22646.50	Nagasaki, Japan	JOS	CW 0756 0855 0952 1031
22651.50	Kaliningrad, Russia	UIW	CW 1344 1624
22652.00	Murmansk, Russia	UDK2	170/50nc 1112
22655.00	Ostend, Belgium	OST	CW 1043 1247 1330 1441 1621
22659.00	Capetown, RSA	ZSC20	CW 0627 0714 0822 1407 1503
22659.50	Murmansk, Russia	UDK2	CW tfc list 1408
22659.50	Nagasaki, Japan	JOR	CW 0713 0757 0856 1027
22666.00	Gibraltar Naval	GYU	75n 1541
22666.20	Norddeich, Germany	DAL	CW 0836 1014 1715
22670.50	Rio de Janeiro, Brazil	PPR	CW 1008 1355 1541 1613 1648 1749 1921
22673.50	Klaipeda, Lithuania	LYK	CW 0914
22677.00	Murmansk, Russia	UMV	170/50nc 1520 (to "Nina Kukoverova" USFB) 1517
22679.00	Athens, Greece	SVG7	CW 0737 0823 1043 1522 1805 1946
22681.50	Kaliningrad, Russia	UIW	CW 0725 1225 1525
22682.00	Scheveningen, Holland	PCH70	CW 0725 1057 1337 1510 1806 1922
22684.00	Batumi, Georgia	UHK	170/50nc 1333
22684.50	Bahrain	A9M	CW 1614
22685.50	Kaliningrad, Russia	UIW	170/50nc 0836 0932 1219 1438 1607 1626 nav wngs 1623
22686.50	Mobile, USA	WLO	CW 1629 2233
22688.00	Mobile, USA	WLO	CW 1411 1534
22688.00	Mobile, USA	WLO	SITOR Mode B 1600 wx for Caribbean & N Atlantic 1449
22690.50	Nagasaki, Japan	JOU	CW 0711 0840 0858 1029
22691.50	Kaliningrad, Russia	UIW	CW (listens 22282.0) 0848 1136 1250 1605
22696.00	Coast stations ch 1 dup. 22000.0kHz		USB
22696.00	Madrid, Spain	EHY	USB 1239 1523 1608
22696.00	New York (Ocean Gate), USA	WOO	USB
22699.00	Coast stations ch 2 dup. 22003.0kHz		USB
22699.00	Rome, Italy	IAR	USB
22702.00	Coast stations ch 3 dup. 22006.0kHz		USB
22702.00	Goeteborg, Sweden	SAG	USB 0911
22702.00	Sydney, Australia	VIS	USB
22705.00	Coast stations ch 4 dup. 22009.0kHz		USB
22705.00	Capetown, RSA	ZSC29	USB
22705.00	General Pacheco, Argentina	LPL	USB 2142
22705.00	Haifa, Israel	4XO	USB 0858 1029
22705.00	Helsinki, Finland	OHG	USB 1356 1712
22705.00	St Lys, France	FFL	USB 1454
22708.00	Coast stations ch 5 dup. 22012.0kHz		USB
22708.00	New York (Ocean Gate), USA	WOO	USB
22708.00	Scheveningen, Holland	PCG71	USB 1442 tfc list each odd hour + 05
22711.00	Coast stations ch 6 dup. 22015.0kHz		USB
22711.00	Gdynia, Poland	SPC	USB 0911
22711.00	Portishead, UK	GKT76	USB 1334 1420 1724
22711.00	US Coastguard stations		USB (common channel)
22714.00	Coast stations ch 7 dup. 22018.0kHz		USB
22714.00	Haifa, Israel	4XO	USB
22714.00	Moscow, Russia	UAT	USB 1029 1353
22714.00	Norddeich, Germany	DAJ	USB 1152 1338
22717.00	Coast stations ch 8 dup. 22021.0kHz		USB
22717.00	Rogaland, Norway	LGN	USB 1546
22720.00	Coast stations ch 9 dup. 22024.0kHz		USB
22720.00	Athens, Greece	SVN71	USB 0827 1011 1055
22723.00	Coast stations ch 10 dup. 22027.0kHz		USB
22723.00	Athens, Greece	SVN72	USB 1453 1527
22723.00	New York (Ocean Gate), USA	WOO	USB
22726.00	Coast stations ch 11 dup. 22030.0kHz		USB
22726.00	Lyngby, Denmark	OXZ	USB
22729.00	Coast stations ch 12 dup. 22033.0kHz		USB
22729.00	Nicosia, Cyprus	5BA	USB 0925 1250 1341 1524
22729.00	Perth, Australia	VIP	USB
22729.00	Portishead, UK	GKU72	USB
22729.00	Singapore	9VG	USB

kHz.	Station	Call	Mode / Heard/Times GMT
22732.00	Coast stations ch 13 dup. 22036.0kHz		USB
22732.00	Halifax, Canada	VCS	USB wx 0205 0805 1605 2205
22732.00	Istanbul, Turkey	TAN	USB (on request)
22732.00	Lyngby, Denmark	OXZ	USB
22732.00	St Petersburg, Russia	UGC	USB 1744
22735.00	Coast stations ch 14 dup. 22039.0kHz		USB
22735.00	Berne, Switzerland	HEB52	USB 1615
22735.00	Istanbul, Turkey	TAN	USB (on request)
22735.00	Portishead, UK	GKU74	USB
22738.00	Coast stations ch 15 dup. 22042.0kHz		USB
22738.00	Athens, Greece		USB 0938 1326
22738.00	Pennsuco, USA	WOM	USB wx 1302
22738.00	Rogaland, Norway	LFN35	USB
22738.00	St Lys, France	FFL	USB
22741.00	Coast stations ch 16 dup. 22045.0kHz		USB
22741.00	Genoa, Italy	ICB	USB 1455
22741.00	Lyngby, Denmark	OXZ	USB
22741.00	Pennsuco, USA	WOM	USB 1719
22744.00	Coast stations ch 17 dup. 22048.0kHz		USB
22744.00	Athens, Greece	SVN73	USB 1042 1120 1549
22744.00	Haifa, Israel	4XO	USB
22744.00	Norddeich, Germany	DAP	USB
22747.00	Coast stations ch 18 dup. 22051.0kHz		USB
22747.00	Lyngby, Denmark	OXZ	USB
22747.00	Odessa, Ukraine	UUI	USB
22750.00	Coast stations ch 19 dup. 22054.0kHz		USB
22750.00	Athens, Greece	SVN74	USB 0901 1725 (with SVZW) 1525
22750.00	Monaco	3AC	USB
22753.00	Coast stations ch 20 dup. 22057.0kHz		USB
22753.00	Berne, Switzerland	HEB72	USB
22753.00	Portishead, UK	GKU70	USB 1828
22753.00	Vancouver, Canada	VAI	USB
22756.00	Coast stations ch 21 dup. 22060.0kHz		USB (common calling ch)
22756.00	Capetown, RSA		USB
22756.00	Monaco	3AC	USB 1307
22756.00	Ostend, Belgium	OSU76	USB
22756.00	Rio de Janeiro, Brazil	PPR	USB
22759.00	Coast stations ch 22 dup. 22063.0kHz		USB
22759.00	Pennsuco, USA	WOM	USB
22759.00	Lisbon, Portugal	CUL	USB 0900
22759.00	Norddeich, Germany	DAH	USB
22762.00	Coast stations ch 23 dup. 22066.0kHz		USB
22762.00	Istanbul, Turkey	TAN	USB (on request)
22762.00	Norddeich, Germany	DAI	USB
22762.00	Rome, Italy	IAR	USB
22762.00	Sydney, Australia	VIS	USB
22765.00	Coast stations ch 24 dup. 22069.0kHz		USB
22765.00	Athens, Greece	SVN75	USB 1328
22768.00	Coast stations ch 25 dup. 22072.0kHz		USB
22768.00	Monaco	3AC	USB 1034
22768.00	Ostend, Belgium	OSU71	USB
22771.00	Coast stations ch 26 dup. 22075.0kHz		USB
22771.00	St Lys, France	FFL	USB 0903 1256 1600
22774.00	Coast stations ch 27 dup. 22078.0kHz		USB
22774.00	Boufarik, Algeria	7TF51	USB
22774.00	Portishead, UK	GKV77	USB
22777.00	Coast stations ch 28 dup. 22081.0kHz		USB
22777.00	Lyngby, Denmark	OXZ	USB
22780.00	Coast stations ch 29 dup. 22084.0kHz		USB
22780.00	Madrid, Spain	EHY	USB 1252 1528 1554 1650
22780.00	Portishead, UK	GKV79	USB
22783.00	Coast stations ch 30 dup. 22087.0kHz		USB
22783.00	Goeteborg, Sweden	SAG	USB
22783.00	Istanbul, Turkey	TAN	USB (on request)
22786.00	Coast stations ch 31 dup. 22090.0kHz		USB
22786.00	Athens, Greece	SVN76	USB 1120 1321 (with SZPH) 1348
22786.00	St Lys, France	FFL	USB
22789.00	Coast stations ch 32 dup. 22093.0kHz		USB
22789.00	Berne, Switzerland	HEB62	USB 1459
22792.00	Coast stations ch 33 dup. 22096.0kHz		USB
22792.00	Athens, Greece		USB 1218 1527
22792.00	Rogaland, Norway	LFN	USB
22795.00	Coast stations ch 34 dup. 22099.0kHz		USB
22795.00	Mexico City, Mexico	XDA	USB
22795.00	Rogaland, Norway	LFN41	USB
22798.00	Coast stations ch 35 dup. 22102.0kHz		USB
22798.00	Athens, Greece	SVN77	USB 1609

kHz.	Station	Call	Mode / Heard/Times GMT
22798.00	Doha, Qatar	A7D	USB 0650
22798.00	St Lys, France	FFL	USB
22801.00	Coast stations ch 36 dup. 22105.0kHz		USB
22801.00	Dixon, USA	KMI	USB
22801.00	Lyngby, Denmark	OXZ	USB tfc list 0906
22801.00	New York (Ocean Gate), USA	WOO	USB
22804.00	Coast stations ch 37 dup. 22108.0kHz		USB
22804.00	Genoa, Italy	ICB	USB 1441
22804.00	Mobile, USA	WLO	USB
22804.00	Rome, Italy	IAR	USB 1751
22807.00	Coast stations ch 38 dup. 22111.0kHz		USB
22807.00	Boufarik, Algeria	7TF	USB 0926
22807.00	Norddeich, Germany	DAK	USB
22807.00	Rio de Janeiro, Brazil	PPR	USB 1424
22810.00	Coast stations ch 39 dup. 22114.0kHz		USB
22810.00	Ostend, Belgium	OSU72	USB
22813.00	Coast stations ch 40 dup. 22117.0kHz		USB
22813.00	Portishead, UK	GKX70	USB
22816.00	Coast stations ch 41 dup. 22120.0kHz		USB
22819.00	Coast stations ch 42 dup. 22123.0kHz		USB
22822.00	Coast stations ch 43 dup. 22126.0kHz		USB
22825.00	Coast stations ch 44 dup. 22129.0kHz		USB
22825.00	Rome, Italy	IAR	USB 1359 1502
22828.00	Coast stations ch 45 dup. 22132.0kHz		USB
22831.00	Coast stations ch 46 dup. 22135.0kHz		USB
22831.00	Berne, Switzerland	HEB82	USB 1317
22834.00	Coast stations ch 47 dup. 22138.0kHz		USB
22837.00	Coast stations ch 48 dup. 22141.0kHz		USB
22840.00	Coast stations ch 49 dup. 22144.0kHz		USB
22843.00	Coast stations ch 50 dup. 22147.0kHz		USB
22843.00	Rio de Janeiro, Brazil	PPR	USB 1312
22846.00	Coast stations ch 51 dup. 22150.0kHz		USB
22849.00	Coast stations ch 52 dup. 22153.0kHz		USB
22852.00	Coast stations ch 53 dup. 22156.0kHz		USB
22854.90	Spa Publishing		

22855-23600
FIXED

kHz.	Station	Call	Mode / Heard/Times GMT
22863.00	Cuban Embassy traffic	CLP	50n p/lang Spanish ("Circular 388") 1810
22870.00	UNID		FAX wx map of Indian Ocean 1440
22876.00	Italian Embassy traffic		96ARQ/E/8 (Tel Aviv/Rome) 5 let grps 1240
22888.00	Serbian Embassy traffic	DFZG	75n p/lang Eng 1444 Slav 1503
22892.50	Rome Press (ANSA)	IAR76	50n Eng 0740 0746 0750
22930.50	Swedish Embassy traffic		100SWED-ARQ(long) p/lang Eng (Lagos/Stockholm) 1131
22955.00	Rome Press (ANSA)	ISX22	50n ID 1044 Fr 1103 1610
22975.50	Cuban Embassy traffic	CLP	75n p/lang Spanish 1817
22984.00	USMARS		USB 1427
22990.00	UNID		LSB Eng (US) R/T duplex (probably Ascension Isle) 1257
22999.90	Spa Publishing		

23000-23200
FIXED & MOBILE

kHz.	Station	Call	Mode / Heard/Times GMT
23040.00	Stockholm (in-flight R/T service)		USB 1010 1528
23120.00	Italian Embassy traffic		96ARQ/E/8 1131
23142.00	Portishead (in-flight R/T service)		USB 1533
23153.00	Russian Embassy traffic	RCF	75n long RYs & ID 0637
23199.90	Spa Publishing		

23200-23350
AERONAUTICAL

kHz.	Station	Call	Mode / Heard/Times GMT
23210.00	Stockholm (in-flight R/T service)		USB (alt freq to 23040.0) 1151 1241
23220.00	RAF, UK		USB "ARCHITECT" wx & calling "3WE15" 1130
23285.00	Berne (in-flight R/T service)	HEE91	USB 1534
23287.00	US Naval		USB Atlantic/Caribbean net
23349.90	Spa Publishing		

kHz.	Station	Call	Mode / Heard/Times GMT

23350-24890
FIXED & LAND MOBILE

23370.00	Jeddah Met, Saudi Arabia	HZN50	100n 1430 1505
23420.00	Berne (in-flight R/T service)		USB 0930
23523.00	Tokyo Met, Japan	JMH	FAX wx maps 0807 1011 1523
23545.00	German Govt, press info service		96FEC p/lang Ger 0857
23561.50	Dutch Embassy traffic	PCW1	SITOR 1820
23642.00	US Embassy frequency (rptd Athens)	KWS78	CW 0856
23716.80	UNID		96ARQ/E3/8 Idle 1821
23972.00	Tokyo Met, Japan	JMG	50r 0811 0901 1015 1421 1435
24102.00	Serbian Embassy traffic	DFZG	75n p/lang Slav 1507
24302.00	USAF weather service		75n 1127 1509
24790.00	Rome Press (ANSA)	ISX24	50n Fr 1117
24889.90	Spa Publishing		

24890-24990
AMATEUR RADIO

24989.90	Spa Publishing		

24990-25010
STANDARD FREQUENCY/TIME SIGNALS & SPACE

25009.90	Spa Publishing		

25010-25070
FIXED & LAND MOBILE

25069.90	Spa Publishing		

25070-25210
MARITIME MOBILE

25070.00	Ships wkg ch 1 dup. 26145.0kHz		USB
25073.00	Ships wkg ch 2 dup. 26148.0kHz		USB
25076.00	Ships wkg ch 3 dup. 26151.0kHz		USB 1455
25079.00	Ships wkg ch 4 dup. 26154.0kHz		USB
25082.00	Ships wkg ch 5 dup. 26157.0kHz		USB
25085.00	Ships wkg ch 6 dup. 26160.0kHz		USB 1517
25088.00	Ships wkg ch 7 dup. 26163.0kHz		USB 1358
25091.00	Ships wkg ch 8 dup. 26166.0kHz		USB
25094.00	Ships wkg ch 9 dup. 26169.0kHz		USB
25097.00	Ships wkg ch 10 dup. 26172.0kHz		USB
25100.00	Ship/Coast simplex ch 1		USB 1515
25103.00	Ship/Coast simplex ch 2		USB
25106.00	Ship/Coast simplex ch 3		USB
25109.00	Ship/Coast simplex ch 4		USB
25112.00	Ship/Coast simplex ch 5		USB
25115.00	Ship/Coast simplex ch 6		USB 1133
25118.00	Ship/Coast simplex ch 7		USB
25161.50	Ships working		CW
25162.00	Ships working		CW "Novotroisk" (UOUO) 1030
25162.50	Ships working		CW
25163.00	Ships working		CW
25163.50	Ships working		CW
25164.00	Ships working		CW
25164.50	Ships working		CW
25165.00	Ships working		CW 0928
25165.50	Ships working		CW
25166.00	Ships working		CW "Balabin" (TCQR) 0911
25166.50	Ships working		CW
25167.00	Ships working		CW
25167.50	Ships working		CW
25168.00	Ships working		CW
25168.50	Ships working		CW
25169.00	Ships working		CW

kHz.	Station	Call	Mode / Heard/Times GMT
25169.50	Ships working		CW
25170.00	Ships working		CW
25170.50	Ships working		CW
25171.00	Ships working		CW 0838
25171.50	Ships calling		CW
25172.00	Ships calling		CW
25172.50	Ships calling		CW
25173.00	Ships wkg ch 1 dup. 26101.0kHz		RTTY
25173.50	Ships wkg ch 2 dup. 26101.5kHz		SITOR "Mercadian Queen 2" (OUZV2) 1304
25174.00	Ships wkg ch 3 dup. 26102.0kHz		RTTY
25174.50	Ships wkg ch 4 dup. 26102.5kHz		RTTY
25175.00	Ships wkg ch 5 dup. 26103.0kHz		RTTY
25175.50	Ships wkg ch 6 dup. 26103.5kHz		RTTY
25176.00	Ships wkg ch 7 dup. 26104.0kHz		RTTY
25176.50	Ships wkg ch 8 dup. 26104.5kHz		RTTY
25177.00	Ships wkg ch 9 dup. 26105.0kHz		RTTY
25177.50	Ships wkg ch 10 dup. 26105.5kHz		RTTY
25178.00	Ships wkg ch 11 dup. 26106.0kHz		RTTY
25178.50	Ships wkg ch 12 dup. 26106.5kHz		RTTY
25179.00	Ships wkg ch 13 dup. 26107.0kHz		RTTY
25179.50	Ships wkg ch 14 dup. 26107.5kHz		RTTY
25180.00	Ships wkg ch 15 dup. 26108.0kHz		RTTY
25180.50	Ships wkg ch 16 dup. 26108.5kHz		SITOR 1018
25181.00	Ships wkg ch 17 dup. 26109.0kHz		RTTY
25181.50	Ships wkg ch 18 dup. 26109.5kHz		RTTY
25182.00	Ships wkg ch 19 dup. 26110.0kHz		RTTY
25182.50	Ships wkg ch 20 dup. 26110.5kHz		RTTY
25183.00	Ships wkg ch 21 dup. 26111.0kHz		RTTY
25183.50	Ships wkg ch 22 dup. 26111.5kHz		RTTY
25184.00	Ships wkg ch 23 dup. 26112.0kHz		RTTY
25184.50	Ships wkg ch 24 dup. 26112.5kHz		RTTY
25185.00	Ships wkg ch 25 dup. 26113.0kHz		RTTY
25185.50	Ships wkg ch 26 dup. 26113.5kHz		RTTY
25186.00	Ships wkg ch 27 dup. 26114.0kHz		RTTY
25186.50	Ships wkg ch 28 dup. 26114.5kHz		RTTY
25187.00	Ships wkg ch 29 dup. 26115.0kHz		RTTY
25187.50	Ships wkg ch 30 dup. 26115.5kHz		RTTY
25188.00	Ships wkg ch 31 dup. 26116.0kHz		RTTY
25188.50	Ships wkg ch 32 dup. 26116.5kHz		RTTY
25189.00	Ships wkg ch 33 dup. 26117.0kHz		RTTY
25189.50	Ships wkg ch 34 dup. 26117.5kHz		RTTY
25190.00	Ships wkg ch 35 dup. 26118.0kHz		RTTY
25190.50	Ships wkg ch 36 dup. 26118.5kHz		RTTY
25191.00	Ships wkg ch 37 dup. 26119.0kHz		RTTY
25191.50	Ships wkg ch 38 dup. 26119.5kHz		RTTY
25192.00	Ships wkg ch 39 dup. 26120.0kHz		RTTY
25192.50	Ships wkg ch 40 dup. 26120.5kHz		RTTY
25193.00	Ships working (non paired)		CW/RTTY
25193.50	Ships working (non paired)		CW/RTTY
25194.00	Ships working (non paired)		CW/RTTY
25194.50	Ships working (non paired)		CW/RTTY 170/50nc 1433
25195.00	Ships working (non paired)		CW/RTTY
25195.50	Ships working (non paired)		CW/RTTY
25196.00	Ships working (non paired)		CW/RTTY
25196.50	Ships working (non paired)		CW/RTTY 170/50nc 1607
25197.00	Ships working (non paired)		CW/RTTY 170/50nc "Vasiliy Fomin" (UVOF) 1245
25197.50	Ships working (non paired)		CW/RTTY 170/50nc 1228
25198.00	Ships working (non paired)		CW/RTTY 170/50nc 1434
25198.50	Ships working (non paired)		CW/RTTY 170/50nc 0904
25199.00	Ships working (non paired)		CW/RTTY
25199.50	Ships working (non paired)		CW/RTTY
25200.00	Ships working (non paired)		CW/RTTY
25200.50	Ships working (non paired)		CW/RTTY
25201.00	Ships working (non paired)		CW/RTTY 170/50nc UBHU 1356
25201.50	Ships working (non paired)		CW/RTTY 170/50nc "Oltshan" (LYHN) 1351
25202.00	Ships working (non paired)		CW/RTTY
25202.50	Ships working (non paired)		CW/RTTY
25203.00	Ships working (non paired)		CW/RTTY 170/50nc "Karl Linne" (UJMO) 1451
25203.50	Ships working (non paired)		CW/RTTY
25204.00	Ships working (non paired)		CW/RTTY
25204.50	Ships working (non paired)		CW/RTTY 170/50nc "Vasiliy Grechishnikov" (LYEU) 1346
25205.00	Ships working (non paired)		CW/RTTY 170/50nc 1534
25205.50	Ships working (non paired)		CW/RTTY 170/50nc "Aleksey Tazayev" (LYEE) 1415
25206.00	Ships working (non paired)		CW/RTTY
25206.50	Ships working (non paired)		CW/RTTY 170/50nc "Promyslovik" (EWWE) 1343
25207.00	Ships working (non paired)		CW/RTTY
25207.50	Ships working (non paired)		CW/RTTY

kHz.	Station	Call	Mode / Heard/Times GMT
25208.00	Ships working (non paired)		CW/RTTY
25208.50	Ships digital selective calling		RTTY
25209.00	Ships digital selective calling		RTTY
25209.50	Ships digital selective calling		RTTY
25209.90	Spa Publishing		

25210-25550
FIXED & MOBILE

kHz.	Station	Call	Mode / Heard/Times GMT
25255.00	Murmansk, Russia	UDK2	170/50rc 1314
25262.00	Lyngby, Denmark	OXZ	CW 0834 0949 1041 tfc list 0950
25271.50	Rome Press (ANSA)	ISX25	50n Eng 0830 Fr 0931
25308.00	Rogaland, Norway	LGB	CW 1019 1535 1611
25531.00	Argentine Naval	LOL	75n 5 let grps 1459
25549.90	Spa Publishing		

25550-25670
RADIO ASTRONOMY

kHz.	Station	Call	Mode / Heard/Times GMT
25669.90	Spa Publishing		

25670-26100
BROADCASTING

kHz.	Station	Call	Mode / Heard/Times GMT
25690.00	R Abu Dhabi		AM Arab 0927
25730.00	UNID		AM Scan 1344
25820.00	R France International		AM Fr 1135 1345 1500
26010.00	UNID		USB CB style (Ger) 0933
26015.00	UNID		USB CB style (Spain) 1604
26040.00	UNID		USB CB style (USA) 1606
26064.70	UNID		USB CB style (Italy) 0935
26075.00	UNID		USB CB style (UK) 1608
26080.00	UNID		USB CB style (Italy, in Eng) 1137
26099.90	Spa Publishing		

26100-26175
MARITIME MOBILE

kHz.	Station	Call	Mode / Heard/Times GMT
26100.50	Maritime Safety channel		SITOR
26101.00	Coast stations ch 1 dup. 25173.0kHz		RTTY
26101.50	Coast stations ch 2 dup. 25173.5kHz		RTTY
26101.50	Lyngby, Denmark	OXZ	SITOR 0907 1237 1303
26102.00	Coast stations ch 3 dup. 25174.0kHz		RTTY
26102.50	Coast stations ch 4 dup. 25174.5kHz		RTTY
26103.00	Coast stations ch 5 dup. 25175.0kHz		RTTY
26103.50	Coast stations ch 6 dup. 25175.5kHz		RTTY
26104.00	Coast stations ch 7 dup. 25176.0kHz		RTTY
26104.50	Coast stations ch 8 dup. 25176.5kHz		RTTY
26105.00	Coast stations ch 9 dup. 25177.0kHz		RTTY
26105.50	Coast stations ch 10 dup. 25177.5kHz		RTTY
26105.50	Mobile, USA	WLO	SITOR 2233
26106.00	Coast stations ch 11 dup. 25178.0kHz		RTTY
26106.00	Odessa, Ukraine	UUI	SITOR 1252
26106.50	Coast stations ch 12 dup. 25178.5kHz		RTTY
26107.00	Coast stations ch 13 dup. 25179.0kHz		RTTY
26107.50	Coast stations ch 14 dup. 25179.5kHz		RTTY
26108.00	Coast stations ch 15 dup. 25180.0kHz		RTTY
26108.00	Mariupol, Ukraine	USU	SITOR 0721
26108.50	Coast stations ch 16 dup. 25180.5kHz		RTTY
26108.50	Moscow, Russia	UAT	SITOR 1027
26109.00	Coast stations ch 17 dup. 25181.0kHz		RTTY
26109.50	Coast stations ch 18 dup. 25181.5kHz		RTTY
26110.00	Coast stations ch 19 dup. 25182.0kHz		RTTY
26110.50	Coast stations ch 20 dup. 25182.5kHz		RTTY
26111.00	Coast stations ch 21 dup. 25183.0kHz		RTTY
26111.50	Coast stations ch 22 dup. 25183.5kHz		RTTY
26112.00	Coast stations ch 23 dup. 25184.0kHz		RTTY
26112.50	Coast stations ch 24 dup. 25184.5kHz		RTTY
26113.00	Coast stations ch 25 dup. 25185.0kHz		RTTY

kHz.	Station	Call	Mode / Heard/Times GMT
26113.60	Coast stations ch 26 dup. 25185.5kHz		RTTY
26114.00	Coast stations ch 27 dup. 25186.0kHz		RTTY
26114.00	Odessa, Ukraine	UUI	SITOR 1030
26114.50	Coast stations ch 28 dup. 25186.5kHz		RTTY
26114.50	Novorossiysk, Russia	UFN	SITOR 1032
26115.00	Coast stations ch 29 dup. 25187.0kHz		RTTY
26115.60	Coast stations ch 30 dup. 25187.5kHz		RTTY
26116.00	Coast stations ch 31 dup. 25188.0kHz		RTTY
26116.50	Coast stations ch 32 dup. 25188.5kHz		RTTY
26117.00	Coast stations ch 33 dup. 25189.0kHz		RTTY
26117.50	Coast stations ch 34 dup. 25189.5kHz		RTTY
26118.00	Coast stations ch 35 dup. 25190.0kHz		RTTY
26118.50	Coast stations ch 36 dup. 25190.5kHz		RTTY
26119.00	Coast stations ch 37 dup. 25191.0kHz		RTTY
26119.00	General Pacheco, Argentina	LPD	SITOR
26119.50	Coast stations ch 38 dup. 25191.5kHz		RTTY
26120.00	Coast stations ch 39 dup. 25192.0kHz		RTTY
26120.00	General Pacheco, Argentina	LPD	SITOR
26120.50	Coast stations ch 40 dup. 25192.5kHz		RTTY
26121.00	Coast stations digital selective calling		RTTY
26121.50	Coast stations digital selective calling		RTTY
26122.00	Coast stations digital selective calling		RTTY
26133.50	Kaliningrad, Russia	UIW	170/50nc 1504 (to "Nikolay Papivin") 1242
26140.00	UNID		USB CB style (Switzerland, in Eng) 0937
26145.00	Coast stations ch 1 dup. 25070.0kHz		USB
26145.00	Lyngby, Denmark	OXZ	USB
26148.00	Coast stations ch 2 dup. 25073.0kHz		USB
26148.00	Lyngby, Denmark	OXZ	USB
26148.00	Portishead, UK	GKU25	USB
26151.00	Coast stations ch 3 dup. 25076.0kHz		USB
26151.00	Berne, Switzerland	HEB25	USB
26154.00	Coast stations ch 4 dup. 25079.0kHz		USB
26157.00	Coast stations ch 5 dup. 25082.0kHz		USB
26157.00	Haifa, Israel	4XO	USB
26160.00	Coast stations ch 6 dup. 25085.0kHz		USB
26163.00	Coast stations ch 7 dup. 25088.0kHz		USB
26166.00	Coast stations ch 8 dup. 25091.0kHz		USB
26169.00	Coast stations ch 9 dup. 25094.0kHz		USB
26172.00	Coast stations ch 10 dup. 25097.0kHz		USB
26174.90	Spa Publishing		

26175-27500
FIXED & MOBILE

kHz.	Station	Call	Mode / Heard/Times GMT
26220.00	UNID		USB CB style (Spain, in Eng) 1812
26241.80	French Military	RFTJ	100ARQ/E3/8 1137
26280.00	UNID		USB CB style (Italy, in Eng) 1138
26285.00	UNID		USB CB style (Eng) 1346
26302.00	UNID		USB CB style (Fr) 1233
26305.00	UNID		USB CB style (Eng) 1502
26360.00	UNID		USB CB style (Italy, in Eng) 0941
26495.00	UNID		LSB CB style (Italy) 1848
26535.00	UNID		USB CB style 1141
26640.00	UNID		USB CB style (France) 1643
27499.90	Spa Publishing		

27500-27600
METEOROLOGICAL AIDES (SONDES)

LAND MOBILE (GOVERNMENT)

27599.90   Spa Publishing

27600-28000
METEOROLOGICAL AIDS (SONDES)

MOBILE

UK CB RADIO

kHz.	Station	Call	Mode / Heard/Times GMT
27601.25	UK CB channel 1		FM
27611.25	UK CB channel 2		FM
27621.25	UK CB channel 3		FM
27631.25	UK CB channel 4		FM
27641.25	UK CB channel 5		FM
27651.25	UK CB channel 6		FM
27661.25	UK CB channel 7		FM
27671.25	UK CB channel 8		FM
27681.25	UK CB channel 9		FM
27691.25	UK CB channel 10		FM
27701.25	UK CB channel 11		FM
27711.25	UK CB channel 12		FM
27721.25	UK CB channel 13		FM
27731.25	UK CB channel 14		FM
27741.25	UK CB channel 15		FM
27751.25	UK CB channel 16		FM
27761.25	UK CB channel 17		FM
27771.25	UK CB channel 18		FM
27781.25	UK CB channel 19 (CALLING)		FM
27791.25	UK CB channel 20		FM
27801.25	UK CB channel 21		FM
27811.25	UK CB channel 22		FM
27815.00	UNID		USB CB style (Italy) 1237
27821.25	UK CB channel 23		FM
27825.00	UNID		USB CB style (Spain) 1239
27831.25	UK CB channel 24		FM
27841.25	UK CB channel 25		FM
27851.25	UK CB channel 26		FM
27861.25	UK CB channel 27		FM
27871.25	UK CB channel 28		FM
27881.25	UK CB channel 29		FM
27891.25	UK CB channel 30		FM
27901.25	UK CB channel 31		FM
27911.25	UK CB channel 32		FM
27921.25	UK CB channel 33		FM
27931.25	UK CB channel 34		FM
27941.30	UK CB channel 35		FM
27951.25	UK CB channel 36		FM
27961.25	UK CB channel 37		FM
27971.25	UK CB channel 38		FM
27981.25	UK CB channel 39		FM
27991.25	UK CB channel 40		FM
27999.90	Spa Publishing		

28000-297000
AMATEUR RADIO

kHz.	Station	Call	Mode / Heard/Times GMT
28175.00	Beacon Ottawa	VE3TEN	CW 1642 1706
28180.00	Beacon Bordighera	IK1PCB	CW "IK1PCB/B JN33UT20 5ERP A1A MULTIOMNI 5/8 300MT" 0949
28185.00	Beacon S Africa	ZS6PW	CW 1500
28195.00	Beacon Bologna	IY4M	CW "IY4M ROBOT QRV QRV" 0748 1037
28202.50	Beacon, S Africa	ZS1J	CW 1502
28205.00	Beacon Mt. Predigtstuhl	DL0IGI	CW "DL0IGI" & 20 second tone 0950
28219.00	Beacon Cyprus	5B4CY	CW "5B4CY" 1912
28219.50	Beacon, Argentina	LU4XS	CW "LU4XS LAT 5459S LONG 6644W"
28222.00	Beacon Chicago, Il	W9UXO	CW "W9UXO/B" 1440 1556 1709
28234.00	Beacon Jupiter, Fla	KD4EC	CW "KD4EC/BCN JUPITER FLORIDA" 1442
28237.00	Beacon Oslo	LA5TEN	CW "LA5TEN QTH NR OSLO" 1710 1951
28239.00	Beacon	YO2X	CW "YO2X KN05OS QRP 2W/DIPOLES" 0957 1414
28250.00	Beacon Bulawayo	Z21ANB	CW "Z21ANB" 1403 1500 1543 1605 1628
28252.50	Beacon	OH2TEN	CW "OH2TEN" 1038
28257.50	Beacon Kissimee, Fl	WB4JHS	CW "WB4JHS/B KISSIMEE FL QSL BURO 5W" 1446
28258.00	Beacon	DK0TEN	CW "DK0TEN" & tone 0952
28269.50	Beacon St Petersburg, Fla	KF4MS	CW "KF4MS/BCN QSL SASE TO KF4MS PO BOX 21247 ST PETERSBURG FL33742"
28271.00	Beacon Forest View, Ill	ND9X	CW "ND9X/B FOREST VIEW, ILL. PSE QSL RST"
28278.00	Beacon	DF0AAB	CW "DF0AAB" & tone 1954
28290.00	Beacon Straengnaes, Sweden	SK5TEN	CW "SK5TEN/BEACON/QTH STRENGNAES/LOC JO89KK/PWR 75W/ANT VERT OMNI" 1041
28294.00	Beacon Deerpark, Ohio	WC8E	CW "WC8E/BCN" 1436 1540 1646
28296.00	Beacon Laurel, Maryland	W3VD	CW "W3VD/BCN JHU/APL 39.17N 76.9W" 1407 1545 1619
28297.00	Beacon Ft Lauderdale, Fla	WA4DJS	CW "WA4DJS/BCN FORT LAUDERDALE FLORIDA 30 WATTS ANTENNA 5/8 GROUNDPLANE" 1410
29600.00	FM calling channel		FM

Frequency	Station	Details
1637.00	UNID (pirate)	AM Dutch/Eng 1925 2146 2228 (freq varies)
2485.00	ABC Katherine, Australia	AM Eng 2037
3222.00	R Kara, Togo	AM Fr 2204
3255.00	BBC	AM Eng 2141 2148
3270.00	R Namibia	AM Eng 2225
3316.00	SLBS Freetown, Sierra Leone	AM Eng 2205 2212 2236
3320.00	R Orion, S Africa	AM 2208 classical music 2227
3326.00	R Nigeria	AM Eng 2109 2230 2246
3356.00	R Botswana	AM Eng 1812 2154
3366.00	GBC Radio, Ghana	AM Eng 0032 2146 2155 2214 2243
3905.00	All India Radio	AM Eng 1600
3910.00	Reflections Europe	AM Eng 2159 2229
3915.00	BBC	AM Eng 1601 2233
3944.50	Scottish Free Radio (pirate)	AM Eng 2200
3955.00	BBC	AM Eng 0621 0713 1755 2246 (0300-0730 1700-2315)
3960.00	R Svoboda	AM Slav 1933 2243
3965.00	R France International	AM Fr 0034 0638 0813 1934 2210 2313 (0001-0900 1700-2400)
3970.00	R Svoboda	AM Romanian 2158
3980.00	VOA	AM Eng 0435 0623 0637 1831 1917 Slav 2314
3985.00	R China International	AM Eng 2124 2200 Ital 2232
3985.00	R Swiss International	AM Eng 0613 Fr 0640 0813 1842 Ger 2024
3995.00	Deutsche Welle	AM Ger 2012 2208 2247 2316
4000.00	R Bafoussam, Cameroon	AM Fr 2011
4220.00	PBS China	AM 0035 2326
4460.00	PBS China	AM Chinese 2225
4485.00	R Petropavlovsk	AM Slav 1611 1738 1943 2321
4500.00	PBS China	AM Chinese 2202 2318 English lessons 2245 (freq varies)
4615.00	R Baghdad	AM Arab 2000 2312 (under jamming and varies frequency)
4735.00	PBS China	AM Chinese 1614 2340
4740.00	R Dushanbe	AM Slav 1610 1947 2329
4750.00	PBS China	AM 2305
4760.00	ELWA, Liberia	AM Eng 2201
4760.00	PBS China	AM 2248 2308 2359
4765.00	R Brazzaville	AM Fr 1904 1920 2152 2208
4770.00	R Nigeria	AM Eng 2004 2132 2154 2212 2250 (0530-2300)
4783.00	RTM Bamako, Mali	AM Fr 2234 2310
4790.50	R Kashmir	AM Asian lang 1755
4795.00	R Cameroon	AM Fr 2148 2204 2220
4795.00	R Moscow	AM Eng 2135 2249 2301 2310 Slav 1640
4800.00	PBS China	AM Chinese 0015 2311 2342
4800.00	R Lesotho	AM 2213
4805.00	R Nac Amazonas, Brazil	AM Portuguese 0003 2223 2326
4810.00	R Yerevan	AM Slav 1836 1921 2009 2251
4815.00	RTV Burkina Faso	AM Fr 2201
4820.00	R Moscow	AM Slav 1837 1903 2327
4825.00	R Ukraine International	AM Eng 2229 2252 Slav 0650 2214 Ger 0001
4830.00	R Botswana	AM Eng 2116 2318
4830.00	R Tachira, Venezuela	AM Span 2236 2306
4835.00	RTM Bamako, Mali	AM Fr 1929 2006 2250
4845.00	R Nouakchott, Mauretania	AM Fr 1924 Arab 2032 2215 2245 2312
4850.00	R Tashkent	AM Slav 1839 1905 2139 2234
4850.00	R Yaounde, Cameroon	AM Fr 2202 2234
4860.00	R Moscow	AM Eng 2133 2253 2314 Ger 2007 Slav 1906
4865.00	PBS China	AM Chinese 0017 2203 2342
4865.00	R Cinaruco, Colombia	AM Span 0534 0704 2327
4870.00	R Cotonou, Benin	AM Fr 1923 2226
4885.00	R Belem, Brazil	AM Port 2141 2216
4885.00	R Kenya	AM Swahili 1840
4890.00	RTV Senegal	AM Fr 2227
4895.00	R Manaus, Brazil	AM Portuguese 0004 2256
4904.50	R Chad	AM Fr 1841 1912 2222
4910.00	R Zambia	AM Eng 1834
4915.00	R Accra, Ghana	AM Eng 0741 0818 1925 2008 2207 2230 2259
4925.80	R Nacional, Equatorial Guinea	AM Span 2328
4930.00	R Moscow	AM Slav 1842 1950 2217
4935.00	R Kenya	AM Eng 1819 1926
4940.00	R Moscow	AM Eng 2330 Slav 1745 1843
4955.00	R Belem	AM Portuguese 2258
4957.50	R Baku	AM Slav 1844 1927 2012
4975.00	PBS China	AM Chinese 2213
4975.00	R Moscow	AM Eng 1617
4976.00	R Kampala	AM Eng 2025
4980.00	R Ecos del Torbes, Venezuela	AM Span 0005 2227 2259 2320
4985.00	R Brazil Central	AM Portuguese 0006 2204
4990.00	R Nigeria	AM Eng 1931 2112 2231 2300
5003.70	R Nacional, Equatorial Guinea	AM Span 2137 2146

5010.00	R Cameroon	AM Fr 2148
5010.00	SBC Radio One, Singapore	AM Eng 1450
5015.00	R Asgabat, Turkmenistan	AM Slav 2250
5020.00	R Niamey, Niger	AM Fr 2237
5021.00	PBS China	AM 2240 2315
5025.00	R Benin	AM Fr 2150
5026.00	R Kampala, Uganda	AM African lang 2038
5030.00	R Continente, Venezuela	AM Span 2141
5034.90	R Bangui	AM Fr 0836 1815 2151
5035.00	R Almaty, Kazakhstan	AM Eng 1935 Slav 1618 1834
5040.00	R Ala, Russia	AM Slav 1538 1841 2055 2230
5045.00	R Cultura do Para, Brazil	AM Port 2251
5047.00	R Lome, Togo	AM Fr 0002 1750 1915 2152 2213 2308
5050.00	R Tanzania	AM Eng 1810
5052.00	SBC Radio One, Singapore	AM 1619 2247
5055.00	R Guyane, Fr Guiana	AM Fr 0536 2154 2205
5075.00	R Bogota, Colombia	AM Span 0632 0647 0833 2236 2258 2309
5145.00	R China International	AM Slav 1518
5240.00	PBS China	AM 2242
5260.00	R Almaty, Kazakhstan	AM Eng 1938 Slav 1619 1844 1931
5275.00	WYFR, Taiwan	AM Chinese 1524
5290.00	R Krasnoyarsk, Russia	AM Slav 0838 2101 2241 2303
5440.00	PBS China	AM Chinese 0134 1630
5510.00	UNID	AM Fr 1639
5810.00	WWCR, USA	AM Eng 0738 0808
5825.00	WEWN, USA	AM Ger 2313 2320
5850.00	Monitor Radio International	AM Eng 0136 0700 0740
5875.00	BBC	AM Eng 1855 Slav 1651 1817 1903 2100
5880.00	R Australia	AM Eng 1917
5885.00	R Vatican	AM Eng 1950 Ital 2105 2202 2239 (freq varies to 5882.0kHz)
5890.00	R Australia	AM Eng 1707 1857
5895.00	R Croatia	AM Slav 2236
5900.00	Kol Israel	AM Hebrew 1858
5905.00	R Moscow	AM Eng 1554 2237
5910.00	R Vlaanderen International	AM Eng 0650 1806 1818 Dutch 0742 0843 Ger 1734
5915.00	R Almaty, Kazakhstan	AM Eng 2303
5915.00	R Slovakia International	AM Eng 1836 1859
5920.00	R Croatia	AM Slav 0855 2238
5920.00	R Moscow	AM Eng 2259 Ital 2140
5930.00	R Prague	AM Eng 1723 Fr 1953 Slav 1633 Span 1905 2301 2322
5935.00	R Riga	AM Eng 1820 1827
5935.00	WWCR, USA	AM Eng 0848
5940.00	R Moscow	AM Fr 2257
5945.00	R Austria International	AM Eng 1951 2137 Ger 1807 1848 2102 2203
5950.00	R Moscow	AM Eng 2155 2239
5950.00	Voice of Free China	AM Chinese 2300 2324
5955.00	R Netherland	AM Eng 0859 1319 1525 1558 Dutch 0743 0803 1653
5955.00	R Romania International	AM Eng 1945
5955.00	R Svoboda	AM Slav 2157 2208
5960.00	R Canada International	AM Eng 2218
5960.00	R Prague	AM Eng 2103 Slav 1920
5960.00	R Sarejevo	AM Slav 2325
5960.00	R Ukraine International	AM Eng 2241
5965.00	BBC	AM Eng 0138
5970.00	R Svoboda	AM Slav 1909 2200
5975.00	BBC	AM Eng 1634 2158 2241 2305
5975.00	R Japan	AM Eng 0728
5975.00	R Moscow	AM Eng 2201
5980.00	Radioropa Info	AM Ger 0717 1037 1122 1322 2210 2225
5985.00	R Moscow	AM Eng 2323
5985.00	R Svoboda	AM Slav 1346 1910
5985.00	R Ukraine International	AM Eng 2242
5990.00	RTV Italiana	AM Eng 2205 Ital 1631 Ger 1821
5995.00	Polish Radio Warsaw	AM Eng 1829 1849
5995.00	R Australia	AM Eng 0900
5995.00	R Canada International	AM Eng 2109 2150 2222 Slav 1635 Fr 1952 2104
5995.00	VOA	AM Eng 0612 0646
6000.00	R Moscow	AM Eng 1632 Span 2326
6000.00	R Sweden	AM Slav 1503
6005.00	RIAS, Berlin	AM Ger 0823 1347 1620 1735 1920 2204
6005.00	RTV Italiana	AM Ital 2245
6010.00	Deutsche Welle	AM Slav 1600
6010.00	R Moscow	AM Eng 2139 Ger 1943
6020.00	R Netherland	AM Dutch 0900 2110 2205
6020.00	R Ukraine International	AM Eng 2238
6030.00	BBC	AM Arab (Eng lang lesson) 1924
6030.00	SDR, Germany	AM Ger 0725 0806 1049 1404

6035.00	VOA	AM Eng 0636 2249
6040.00	Deutsche Welle	AM Span 2327
6040.00	R France International	AM Fr 2210
6040.00	VOA	AM Eng 0641 1654 1731 1809 1923 2000 2127 Span 2307
6045.00	R Moscow	AM Slav 1658
6050.00	R Japan	AM Eng 0702 0744 0807 2306 2330
6055.00	R Moscow	AM Eng 2240
6055.00	R Prague	AM Eng 0615 1039 1601 2103 2114 2208 Ger 0955 Fr 1635
6055.00	R Ukraine International	AM Eng 2217
6060.00	R Denmark	AM Danish 2331
6060.00	R Japan	AM Eng 2309
6060.00	RTV Italiana	AM Ital 0805
6060.00	VOA	AM Eng 0637 Slav 0616 1700 1833
6065.00	R Sweden	AM Eng 1732 1840 2115 Ger 1830 Swed 0825
6070.00	R Svoboda	AM Slav 1810
6070.00	VOA	AM Eng 2224 2243
6075.00	Deutsche Welle	AM Ger 0703 1050 1123 1348 1623 2226 2325
6080.00	R Australia	AM Eng 1652 1811 1820
6085.00	Bayerische Rundfunk	AM Ger 1904 2116
6090.00	R Ukraine International	AM Eng 2104 2142 (2100-2200 0000-0100) Ger 2310
6090.00	RTL	AM Fr 0721 0800 0858 1602
6100.00	Deutsche Welle	AM Ger 2213 2327
6100.00	R Yugoslavia	AM Eng 1948 Fr 1700 2131 2147
6105.00	R Romania International	AM Eng 1946
6105.00	R Svoboda	AM Slav 0752 1349
6110.00	BBC	AM Eng 0644
6110.00	R Budapest	AM Eng 1906 2210 2250
6115.00	Deutsche Welle	AM Ger 1124 1405 1624 1811 2311
6120.00	R Finland	AM Eng 0646 0745 1834 1957 2142 Ger 1930 Russ 2000
6125.00	BBC	AM Eng 1249 1601 1705 Ger 1654 1812 1910
6125.00	REE Spain	AM Eng 2132 Span 0007 2333
6130.00	Deutsche Welle	AM Slav 1407
6130.00	R Moscow	AM Eng 2144 Ger 1745
6130.00	R Portugal International	AM Port 2200
6135.00	Polish Radio Warsaw	AM Eng 1350 Ger 1603 1816
6140.00	Deutsche Welle	AM Ger 0809 0900 1052 Span 1702
6140.00	VOA	AM Eng 0618 1638 Slav 2000
6145.00	R Moscow	AM Fr 1657 Ger 1713
6155.00	R Austria International	AM Eng 0850 1250 1440 1832 Ger 1002 1125 1819 Span 1351
6160.00	BBC	AM Eng 2314
6165.00	R Netherland	AM Eng 2338
6165.00	R Swiss International	AM Eng 1004 Ger 0723 1703 Fr 0950 Ital 1638
6175.00	R France International	AM Eng 1555 1645 Fr 1041 1126 1700 2001
6180.00	BBC	AM Eng 1704 1749 1835 1921
6180.00	VOA	AM Eng 1640
6183.10	R Nacional Amazonas	AM Port 2215 2302
6190.00	R Bremen	AM Ger 0951 1923
6195.00	BBC	AM Eng 0639 1721 1820 2002 2201 2251 2329
6205.00	HCJB, Ecuador	AM Eng 0643 0738 0801 0825 1738
6210.00	R Bulgaria	AM Slav 1414 1803 Ital 2331
6220.00	European Christian Radio	AM Eng ID & Romanian 1700
6221.50	UNID (pirate)	AM Eng 0850 1053 1352 1641
6226.10	R DLR-106 (Pirate)	AM Eng 1008 2201
6229.00	UNID (pirate)	AM Eng 0811 0856 1127
6230.00	R Cairo	AM Arab 1627
6230.00	TWR	AM Ger 0830 Ital 1009
6235.00	R Bulgaria	AM Eng 1845 1857 Fr 1807 Ger 1709
6238.80	R Merlin International (Pirate)	AM Eng 1011
6245.00	R Vatican	AM Eng 0637 Ital 1642 Fr 1013 1710 Ger 1924
6250.30	R Nacional, Equatorial Guinea	AM Span 2117 2200
6260.00	PBS China	AM Chinese 2258
6268.00	UNID (pirate)	AM Eng (Irish accent) 1056
6280.00	King of Hope, Lebanon	AM Eng 0125 1853 2151
6295.00	UNID (pirate)	AM Eng 1014 1130 1047
6300.00	WYFR, USA	AM Chinese (Taiwan relay) 2228
6305.40	Voz del Cid	AM Span 0547 0640 0707 0800
6400.00	Pirate Radio (UNID)	AM Eng 1240 1757
6400.00	R Pyongyang	AM Asian lang 2215
6480.00	R Korea	AM Eng 2219 Slav 2016 Asian lang 1819
6540.00	R Pyongyang	AM Asian lang 1824 1936 2019
6549.50	R Beirut	AM Arab 1713 1813 1941 2118 (freq varies to 6550)
6560.00	R Baghdad	AM 1622 1740 1946
6576.00	R Pyongyang	AM Eng 2046 Span 1814 Ger 1931 1942 Fr 1615 2119
6750.00	PBS China	AM Chinese 2215
6840.00	PBS China	AM Chinese 0947 2143 2222
6890.00	R Bosnia-Herzegovina	AM Slav 1910
6933.00	R China International	AM Slav 1724 1831 Span 2126 2138 2232

6950.00	R China International	AM Eng 2127 2152 Slav 1707 Ger 1912
6955.00	R China International	AM Eng 1913 Asian lang 1832
7105.00	BBC	AM Fr 0613 Slav 1709
7105.00	R Moscow	AM Eng 1845
7105.00	REE Spain	AM Span 1910
7110.00	R Moscow	AM Eng 2312 2350
7115.00	R Moscow	AM Eng 2114
7115.00	R Svoboda	AM Slav 1515 1849 1915
7120.00	BBC	AM Slav 1800
7120.00	Deutsche Welle	AM Port 2209 Slav 2221
7120.00	R Netherland	AM Eng 1835
7125.00	BBC	AM Eng 2132
7125.00	IRRS Italy	AM Eng 0625 0816 1742 2341 (UN radio relay 0700 0739)
7125.00	R Conakry	AM Fr 2201 2224
7125.00	R Moscow	AM Eng 2252
7130.00	Deutsche Welle	AM Ger 2210
7130.00	R Netherland	AM Dutch 0712 1423
7135.00	R France International	AM Fr 1835 1916
7135.00	R Netherland	AM Dutch 0810
7140.00	R Moscow	AM Eng 2231 Fr 1846
7145.00	Algeria	AM Arab 2202
7145.00	Polish Radio Warsaw	AM Ger 1508 1516
7150.00	BBC	AM Eng 0626 0721
7150.00	R Moscow	AM Eng 2229 2239
7150.00	R Ukraine International	AM Eng 2105 2133 (2100-2200 0000-0100) Slav 2222
7155.00	R Tirana	AM Eng 1538
7165.00	R Moscow	AM Eng 0722 0830
7170.00	Deutsche Welle	AM Portuguese (German lang lessons) 2204
7170.00	R Australia	AM Eng 1600
7170.00	R China International	AM Eng 2201 2254
7170.00	R Moscow	AM Eng 1711 1912 2135
7170.00	VOA	AM Eng 0541 0627 0650 Slav 1956
7175.00	RTV Italiana	AM Ital 0626 0719
7180.00	AWR	AM Eng 0744
7180.00	BBC	AM Eng 2314
7180.00	R Moscow	AM Eng 1957 2134 2241 Fr 2310
7185.00	Deutsche Welle	AM Ger 1839 1925 2047
7185.00	Voice of Turkey	AM Eng 2223 2258 2315
7190.00	R Svoboda	AM Slav 0853 1055 1851
7195.00	R Canada International	AM Eng 2205 2224
7195.00	R Romania International	AM Eng 2140 2156 Ger 1841
7195.00	R Ukraine International	AM Eng 2204 2256
7200.00	VOA	AM Fr 2048
7205.00	R Moscow	AM Eng 1712 1913 2205 Fr 2257
7210.00	BBC	AM Fr 1135 Polish 1708
7215.00	VOA	AM Eng 1744
7220.00	R Budapest	AM Eng 2135 Ger 1854
7220.00	R Svoboda	AM Slav 0842 1410
7225.00	Deutsche Welle	AM Eng 1646 Urdu 1514
7225.00	R Bulgaria	AM Eng 2355
7225.00	R Romania International	AM Eng 0634 2115
7230.00	AWR	AM Eng 1049 Ger 0811 Multilingual ID 0658
7230.00	R Japan	AM Eng 0729
7230.00	R Moscow	AM Eng 2136
7235.00	RTV Italiana	AM Fr 1637 Ital 1720
7240.00	R Ukraine International	AM Eng 2206 2218 2245 Ger 1749 1801
7245.00	R Svoboda	AM Slav 1100
7250.00	R Canada International	AM Eng 0010
7250.00	R Vatican	AM Eng 0736 Latin mass 1510 Fr 0722
7255.00	Deutsche Welle	AM Eng 1606 Slav 1042
7255.00	R Nigeria	AM Eng 0631
7260.00	R Australia	AM Eng 1519 1633 1719 1816 1858 1901 1958
7260.00	R Canada International	AM Eng 2207
7265.00	SWF, Germany	AM Ger 0939 1102
7270.00	Polish Radio Warsaw	AM Ger 1640
7270.00	VOA	AM Slav 1959
7275.00	Deutsche Welle	AM Ger 2225
7275.00	REE Spain	AM Span 1713 2051 2244
7280.00	R France International	AM Fr 0647
7280.00	R Moscow	AM Ger 1641 1817
7285.00	Polish Radio Warsaw	AM Eng 1654 1813 Ger 1520
7285.00	R Ukraine International	AM Eng 2159
7295.00	BBC	AM Eng 0737 Fr 0615
7295.00	R Moscow	AM Eng 2303
7295.00	R Svoboda	AM Slav 1411
7300.00	R Moscow	AM Eng 2229 2253
7310.00	R Moscow	AM Slav 2000

7315.00	R Moscow	AM Slav 2052
7315.00	WHRI, USA	AM Eng 0652 0723 0832 0940 1104
7325.00	BBC	AM Eng 0741 0815 2054 2141 2208 2245
7325.00	VOA	AM Eng 0656
7330.00	R Moscow	AM Eng 1715
7335.00	R China International	AM Fr 2055 2137
7335.00	R Moscow	AM Eng 2235
7340.00	R Moscow	AM Slav 2213
7340.00	VOA	AM Fr 2155
7340.00	Voz del Cid	AM Span 0640 0658
7345.00	R Prague	AM Eng 0722 1722 2104 Ger 0932 Span 2055 Fr 2244
7345.00	R Slovakia International	AM Eng 1837 Fr 1931
7350.00	R China International	AM Fr 2056 2158
7355.00	WHRI, USA	AM Eng 0659 0744 0941
7360.00	R Moscow	AM Ger 1839 1907 1947
7370.00	R Moscow	AM Fr 1716 1840
7375.00	Radio for Peace International	USB Eng 0616 0641
7380.00	R Moscow	AM Eng 2209 2244
7385.00	TWR	AM Eng 0703 0735 0817 0834
7390.00	R Moscow	AM Ger 1841 1916
7400.00	R Moscow	AM Ger 1656 1842 Span 2248
7405.00	R China International	AM Ital 1843
7405.00	VOA	AM Eng 0636 1105
7412.00	All India Radio	AM Eng 1534 1745 1812 2209 2224
7415.00	VOA	AM Eng 2001 2036 2158
7420.00	R Moscow	AM Eng 1804
7425.00	WEWN, USA	AM Eng 0638 0740 0942
7430.00	Voice of Greece	AM Greek 2150
7435.00	WWCR, USA	AM Eng 0006 0857
7440.00	R Yerevan	AM Eng 2246 2251
7450.00	Voice of Greece	AM Eng 1920
7455.00	R Bulgaria	AM Eng 0011 2246 2305 Ger 1717 Fr 1805
7465.00	Kol Israel	AM Eng 1806 2003 2236 2255
7465.00	Monitor Radio International	AM Eng 0944 1046 1106
7470.00	R China International	AM Ital 1844 Slav 1941
7475.00	RTV Tunis	AM Arab 1850 1909 2152 2210 2244
7485.00	R Pakistan	AM Asian lang 1806
7490.00	WJCR, USA	AM Eng 0725 0852 0945
7504.00	PBS China	AM Chinese 1732 2153 2240
7510.00	Monitor Radio International	AM Eng 0946 2037 2252 Span 2306
7520.00	Monitor Radio International	AM Eng 0718
7520.00	WEWN, USA	AM Ital 0653 2253
7550.00	R Korea	AM Eng 0819 Ger 1944
7660.00	R China International	AM Slav 1813 1948
7700.00	R China International	AM Fr 1812 1859
7780.00	R China International	AM Slav 1531 1814
7800.00	R China International	AM Fr 1905 2222
7935.00	PBS China	AM Chinese 2248
9022.00	R Tehran	AM Eng 0041 1942 Fr 0656 0721 1859 2240 Ger 1806 Span 2122
9064.00	PBS China	AM Chinese 2304
9080.00	PBS China	AM Chinese 1533 2200
9165.00	R Omdurman	AM Eng 1836 Arab 1535 Fr 1743
9170.00	PBS China	AM Chinese 1546
9280.00	WYFR, USA	AM Asian lang 1409 1557 2145 2201
9325.00	R Pyongyang	AM Eng 1527 1714 Span 2046
9345.00	R Pyongyang	AM Eng 2047 Span 1813
9355.00	Monitor Radio International	AM Eng 1500 1806
9365.00	R China International	AM Ital 2125
9370.00	WEWN, USA	AM Ger 2205
9375.00	R for Peace International	AM Eng UN Radio programme 1059
9380.00	PBS China	AM Chinese 2207
9388.00	Kol Israel	AM Hebrew 1421 1655 2202
9395.00	Voice of Greece	AM Greek 1645
9400.00	FEBC Manila	AM Chinese 1100 1422
9410.00	BBC	AM Eng 0849 0924 1211 1356 1502 1714 2125 2208 (0300-2315)
9420.00	Swiss Radio International	AM Eng 1504
9425.00	Voice of Greece	AM Eng 0745 1356 Greek 1646 1900
9435.00	Kol Israel	AM Eng 2231 2239 (2230-2300) Span 2227
9440.00	R China International	AM Arab 1600
9445.00	Voice of Turkey	AM Eng 2210 Fr 2250
9450.00	R Yerevan	AM Eng 2148 Fr 2132
9455.00	Monitor Radio International	AM Eng 0644 0827 0912 0945
9455.00	TWR	AM Eng 1647
9465.00	Monitor Radio International	AM Eng 2203 2240 2251 (2200-2359)
9470.00	R Moscow	AM Slav 0946 Fr 1615 Portuguese 2136

9480.00	R Moscow	AM Eng 2212
9480.00	TWR	AM Eng 0655 0708 0850 0931
9485.00	R Prague	AM Span 2051
9490.00	R Moscow	AM Fr 1645 1902 2233
9495.00	Monitor Radio International	AM Eng 0650 1128 1214
9495.00	R France International	AM Fr 1825 2151
9505.00	R Bratislava	AM Eng 1130
9505.00	R Prague	AM Eng 0625 0712 Span 1131
9505.00	R Ukraine International	AM Eng 2254
9510.00	R Australia	AM Eng 1603
9510.00	R Romania International	AM Eng 0631
9520.00	R Svoboda	AM Slav 1054 1135
9525.00	Polish Radio Warsaw	AM Eng 1231 1648 Ger 1132 1730
9530.00	R Moscow	AM Eng 1627
9535.00	R Swiss International	AM Eng 1103 1718 Fr 0735 0948 1735 Ger 1215 Ital 1818
9540.00	REE Spain	AM Eng 0013
9545.00	Deutsche Welle	AM Ger 0740 0946 1136 1219 1400 1526 1850 2244
9550.00	R Canada International	AM Eng 1630
9550.00	R Moscow	AM Eng 1630 1715 2236
9550.00	R Ukraine International	AM Eng (0000-0100)
9555.00	R Svoboda	AM Slav 0940
9560.00	R Amman	AM Eng 1711 Arab 2212
9560.00	R Australia	AM Eng 1618 1649 1748
9560.00	R Finland	AM Eng 0654 0748
9560.00	R Moscow	AM Eng 1712
9565.00	Deutsche Welle	AM Arab 0700
9565.00	R Svoboda	AM Slav 1541
9575.00	R Mediterranean International	AM Fr & Arab 1903
9580.00	R Bratislava	AM Eng (0200-0230)
9580.00	R Moscow	AM Eng 0812 1525 Fr 0741
9585.00	Deutsche Welle	AM Eng 1648
9585.00	VOA	AM Slav 2158
9590.00	BBC	AM Eng 2213
9590.00	R Denmark	AM Danish 1354
9590.00	VOA	AM Eng 1104 1138
9595.00	R Svoboda	AM Slav 1442
9600.00	BBC	AM Eng 0633 0713 0750 Ger 1158
9605.00	BBC	AM Eng (Eng lang lessons) 1755
9605.00	R Abu Dhabi	AM Eng 2201 2250 2345 (2200-2359) Arab 2141
9605.00	R Netherland	AM Eng 1836 1905
9605.00	R Prague	AM Eng 1800 2100 Ger 1722
9610.00	R Moscow	AM Eng 0534
9615.00	R Finland	AM Eng 2236
9620.00	R Moscow	AM Eng 2238 2307
9620.00	R Sweden	AM Scand 1140 Fr 1200
9620.00	R Yugoslavia	AM Eng 2058
9620.00	REE Spain	AM Span 1443 1542 1650 1817 1905 2142
9625.00	R Svoboda	AM Slav 0930 0942 1902
9635.00	R Portugal International	AM Portuguese 1906
9640.00	BBC	AM Eng 0701 0743
9640.00	R Moscow	AM Eng 2105
9640.00	R Ukraine International	AM Eng (0000-0100)
9645.00	R Australia	AM Eng 2202 2220
9645.00	R Sweden	AM Eng 1740
9645.00	R Vatican	AM Eng 0635 Ital 0714 Ger 1444 Fr 1607 Arab 1831
9650.00	Deutsche Welle	AM Ger 1654 2201 Slav 0948
9655.00	R Sweden	AM Eng 2117
9660.00	BBC	AM Eng 0715 1201 1311 1445
9665.00	Deutsche Welle	AM Eng 1907 Ger 1204
9680.00	R Portugal International	AM Portuguese 1446 1656
9685.00	R Moscow	AM Eng 1908 Fr 2310
9685.00	R Ukraine International	AM Eng 2146 (2100-2200 0000-0100)
9690.00	Deutsche Welle	AM Ger 0656
9690.00	R Romania International	AM Ger 1216 1635 1820
9700.00	R Bulgaria	AM Eng 1754 2248 Fr 0745 1802
9700.00	R New Zealand	AM Eng 0818
9700.00	VOA	AM Eng 1529 1651 1753 1814 1909 (1500-2200) Slav 2000
9705.00	R Svoboda	AM Slav 1716
9710.00	R Australia	AM Eng 1124
9710.00	R Vilnius	AM Eng 2147
9715.00	R Netherland	AM Eng 0753
9720.00	R Netherland	AM Eng 0747
9720.00	R Netherland	AM Eng 0950 Dutch 0653
9720.00	R Yugoslavia	AM Eng 2150
9725.00	R Moscow	AM Eng 2236
9725.00	R Svoboda	AM Slav 1312
9730.00	Deutsche Welle	AM Ger 2208 2239 2308

9730.00	R Finland	AM Eng 1833 1837
9735.00	Deutsche Welle	AM Ger 0853 0939 1908
9735.00	R Nacional, Paraguay	AM Span 2248
9740.00	BBC	AM Eng 1106 1529 1612 1732 1821
9740.00	R Finland	AM Eng 2258
9745.00	HCJB, Ecuador	AM Eng 0758 0840 0854 (0730-1100)
9745.00	R Ukraine International	AM Eng 2220 2240
9750.00	BBC	AM Eng 0754 0947 1122 1205 1313 1447 1530 Ger 1657
9750.00	R Moscow	AM Eng 0535 0702 2200
9755.00	R Canada International	AM Eng 2210
9760.00	BBC	AM Eng 0841 0951 1128 1448 1530
9760.00	R Tirana	AM Eng 1540 2205
9760.00	VOA	AM Eng 1653 1700 1744 1855 1912 2001
9765.00	Deutsche Welle	AM Ger 2309
9765.00	R Moscow	AM Eng 0536 0623
9770.00	Deutsche Welle	AM Slav 1130
9770.00	R Abu Dhabi	AM Eng 2226 (readings from Holy Koran) 2214
9770.00	R Australia	AM Eng 1526 1546
9770.00	VOA	AM Eng 1834 2206
9785.00	KTWR, Guam	AM Eng 1108
9785.00	R Moscow	AM Fr 1654
9790.00	R France International	AM Fr 1824 1909 2002 2238 2313
9805.00	R France International	AM Eng 1236 Fr 0749 1123 1217
9810.00	R Swiss International	AM Eng 2212
9815.00	R Moscow	AM Eng 2207
9820.00	R Moscow	AM Eng 2004 2155
9830.00	R Amman	AM Arab 1914
9830.00	R Croatia	AM Slav 2200
9835.00	R Budapest	AM Eng 2109 (2100-2200)
9840.00	Monitor Radio International	AM Eng 0745 0857 0949
9860.00	R Moscow	AM Eng 1912
9860.00	R Netherland	AM Eng 1138
9860.00	R Ukraine International	AM Eng 2242
9870.00	R Austria International	AM Eng 1441 Ger 2213 2312
9875.00	REE Spain	AM Span 1206 1416 1548
9880.00	R Austria International	AM Eng 1534 Ger 1514
9880.00	R China International	AM Eng 2203
9880.00	R Moscow	AM Eng 1825 Fr 1638
9885.00	R Swiss International	AM Eng 0900 0920 1700 2005 2214 Fr 0933
9890.00	R Moscow	AM Eng 1515 1532 1715
9890.00	R Netherland	AM Eng 1552
9900.00	R Cairo	AM Eng 2158 2215 Ger 1910
9905.00	R Vlaanderen International	AM Eng 0914 Ger 0953 Dutch 1206 1314
9910.00	All India Radio	AM Eng 1533 2216 2310
9915.00	BBC	AM Eng 1917 2202 2250 2315
9920.00	R China International	AM Eng 2100 Ger 1827 1837
9925.00	R Vlaanderen International	AM Eng 0647
9941.50	Voz del Cid, Costa Rica	AM Span 2216
9945.00	R China International	AM Chinese 0954
9950.00	All India Radio	AM Eng 1838 2223
9985.00	WEWN, USA	AM Eng 1919
10260.00	PBS China	AM Chinese 2106 2114
11000.00	PBS China	AM Chinese 2116
11100.00	PBS China	AM Chinese 1332 1601
11330.00	PBS China	AM Chinese 1606 2205
11402.00	R Iceland	USB Icelandic 1852
11445.00	R China International	AM Asian lang 1731 Span 1903
11500.00	R China International	AM Eng 2123 Slav 1701 Ger 1845
11515.00	R China International	AM Eng 1911 Ger 1832
11530.00	Wings of Hope, Lebanon	AM Eng 1349 2125
11550.00	RTV Tunis	AM Arab 0729 0946 1401 1502
11560.00	R Cairo	AM Arab 1424
11570.00	R Pakistan	AM Eng 1601 1625 1702
11575.00	R China International	AM Eng 1614 1738
11580.00	Monitor Radio International	AM Eng 1645
11580.00	WEWN, USA	AM Eng 0723
11580.00	WYFR, USA	AM Eng 0533
11587.00	Kol Israel	AM Eng 1703 1912 2139 Fr 1935
11595.00	Voice of Greece	AM Greek 1434 1527 1848
11605.00	Kol Israel	AM Eng 1913 2140 (also msrd on 11603.0)
11610.00	PBS China	AM Chinese 0947 1435 2310
11620.00	All India Radio	AM Eng 1745 1849 1902 2112 2141 2224
11620.00	R Moscow	AM Eng 2110
11625.00	R Vatican	AM Latin mass 1844
11630.00	R Moscow	AM Ital 1850 Fr 1703 2136
11630.00	R Prague	AM Fr 1530
11645.00	Voice of Greece	AM Eng 0746

11650.00	KFBS, Saipan	AM Slav 0915
11655.00	R Moscow	AM Asian lang 1559
11655.00	R Netherland	AM Dutch 1640
11660.00	R Australia	AM Eng 1507 1554 1736 1903
11660.00	R Bulgaria	AM Span 2153
11660.00	R France International	AM Fr 2313
11670.00	R France International	AM Fr 0856 0948 1106 1300
11670.00	R Moscow	AM Fr 1855
11675.00	Kol Israel	AM Eng 1915 2142 Span 2113 2137
11680.00	BBC	AM Eng 0717 0917
11680.00	R Australia	AM Eng 1848
11685.00	R Moscow	AM Eng 1916 2114
11690.00	R Moscow	AM Eng 0536 0839 1504
11695.00	R Australia	AM Eng 0949 1602 1706
11705.00	Monitor Radio International	AM Eng 0940
11705.00	R France International	AM Eng 1605 1640
11705.00	R Moscow	AM Eng 0800 1001 1505 1615 1737
11705.00	R Ukraine International	AM Slav 1301
11705.00	VOA	AM Eng 1514 1520
11710.00	R Abu Dhabi	AM Eng 2320
11710.00	R Moscow	AM Eng 0707
11715.00	All India Radio	AM Eng 2143
11715.00	R Korea	AM Eng 1031
11715.00	R Moscow	AM Eng 1352 1403 1857 1917
11715.00	VOA	AM Eng 1302
11720.00	R Bulgaria	AM Eng 1756 2156 2215 Fr 1900
11720.00	R Moscow	AM Eng 2128
11720.00	R Ukraine International	AM Eng (0000-0100)
11725.00	HCJB, Ecuador	AM Eng 0708 0731
11725.00	R Svoboda	AM Slav 0850 1642
11730.00	BBC	AM Arab 1900
11730.00	R Canada International	AM Eng 2322 Fr 2139
11730.00	R Moscow	AM Eng 2115 2158
11735.00	R Moscow	AM Eng 1804
11740.00	All India Radio	AM Eng 1536
11740.00	Deutsche Welle	AM Eng 1901 1928
11740.00	R Vatican	AM Fr 0718 Ital 1104
11745.00	R China International	AM Port 2201
11745.00	R Moscow	AM Eng 0801 1002
11750.00	BBC	AM Eng 1648 1734 2323
11750.00	Channel Africa (RSA)	AM Eng 1747
11750.00	R Moscow	AM Eng 2134
11755.00	R Finland	AM Eng 0749 1838 2131 Ger 0941
11760.00	BBC	AM Eng 0802
11760.00	R Moscow	AM Eng 2116 Fr 2212
11770.00	R Svoboda	AM Slav 1602
11770.00	WYFR, USA	AM Ital 0709
11780.00	BBC	AM Eng 0720
11780.00	R Austria International	AM Eng 1535 1553 1643 Ger 1505 1603
11785.00	Deutsche Welle	AM Eng 1646 1904 1929 2121
11790.00	REE Spain	AM Span 0851 2118
11795.00	Deutsche Welle	AM Ger 0710 0933 1506 2140
11795.00	R Dubai	AM Arab 1910
11800.00	R Moscow	AM Eng 2132
11800.00	R Portugal International	AM Eng (Sats & Suns) 0900
11805.00	R Moscow	AM Eng 0804 0950 1003
11805.00	VOA	AM Eng 0648
11810.00	R Romania International	AM Eng 1501
11825.00	R Tirana	AM Eng 2131
11830.00	R Romania International	AM Eng 1735
11835.00	HCJB, Ecuador	AM Eng 0711
11835.00	R Yugoslavia	AM Fr 1615
11840.00	Polish Radio Warsaw	AM Eng 1507
11840.00	R Portugal International	AM Port 2141
11845.00	R France International	AM Fr 1132 1450 1531
11850.00	R Moscow	AM Fr 1355 1857
11855.00	R Australia	AM Eng 1452
11855.00	R Canada International	AM Eng 1356
11860.00	R Moscow	AM Eng 1656 Fr 0608 0725 Portuguese 2130
11865.00	Deutsche Welle	AM Ger 0833 0920
11870.00	R Moscow	AM Eng 1616 1631 2136
11870.00	VOA	AM Eng 1911
11875.00	R Canada International	AM Eng 2204
11880.00	R Moscow	AM Fr 1646 1705
11885.00	R Svoboda	AM Slav 1140
11895.00	R Netherland	AM Eng 0733 0935
11895.00	R Svoboda	AM Slav 1848

11910.00	R Australia	AM Eng 0805 0850
11910.00	R Budapest	AM Eng 2111
11915.00	VOA	AM Eng 1026 1105 Asian lang 0900
11920.00	R Yerevan	AM Eng (2245-2300)
11920.00	VOA	AM Eng 1912
11925.00	R Japan	AM Eng 2145
11925.00	V of the Mediterranean	AM Eng 1402 1458
11935.00	R Moscow	AM Eng 1533
11940.00	R Romania International	AM Eng 1353 1902 1918 Fr 1142 Ger 1651 1807
11945.00	R Moscow	AM Fr 1913
11945.00	R Yerevan	AM Eng (2245-2300)
11955.00	BBC	AM Eng 2123
11960.00	R Moscow	AM Eng 1710 1737
11960.00	R Yerevan	AM Eng (2245-2300)
11965.00	VOA	AM Eng 0539 0650
11980.00	R Moscow	AM Ger 1106 1534 1617 1712 1903 Fr 1554 2139
11985.00	R Moscow	AM Eng 1310
11990.00	R Kuwait	AM Arab 1509
11990.00	R Moscow	AM Portuguese 2141
11990.00	R Prague	AM Eng 0734 1134
11995.00	FEBC, Manila	AM Eng 1540
11995.00	VOA	AM Eng 1914
12000.00	R Moscow	AM Arab 1634
12005.00	RTV Tunis	AM Arab 1535 1616 2146
12010.00	R Moscow	AM Eng 0713 0902 0943 1043 Ger 1713 1739 1904 Portuguese 2142
12020.00	R Moscow	AM Eng 0903 0936 1100 Fr 1312 1400 1510 1908 Portuguese 2143
12030.00	R Moscow	AM Span 2139 Fr 2147
12035.00	REE Spain	AM Span 0912 1143 1536 1740 1909
12040.00	R Vilnius	AM Eng (2300-2359)
12050.00	R Cairo	AM Arab 1714 2148
12050.00	R Vatican	AM ID & Asian lang 1316
12055.00	R Moscow	AM Eng 0911 1101 1910
12060.00	R Moscow	AM Fr 1653 1741 Span 1905 2154 2309
12065.00	R Moscow	AM Eng 1544
12070.00	R Moscow	AM Eng 0654 0854 0903 1024 1135 Fr 1742 2149
12080.00	VOA	AM Eng 0541 Fr 2150
12085.00	R Bulgaria	AM Eng 1549 1619
12085.00	R Damascus	AM Eng 2118 2151 Fr 1911
12095.00	BBC	AM Eng 0904 0937 1025 1144 1401 1512 1906 2152 (0300-2245)
12255.00	Reflections Europe	AM Eng (Gospel Crusade Ministry) 1600
13590.00	R Pakistan	AM Eng 1628
13595.00	AWR	AM Asian lang (ID in Eng) 1500
13600.00	R Prague	AM Eng 0742 1505
13605.00	R Australia	AM Eng 0932 0942 1100 1125 Chinese 1300
13610.00	Deutsche Welle	AM Eng 0619 Fr 0700 Ger 2105 2131
13615.00	Monitor Radio International	AM Eng 0831 0846
13615.00	R Moscow	AM Eng 0832 1112
13615.00	WEWN, USA	AM Eng 2135
13620.00	R Kuwait	AM Eng 1804 1840 Arab 1746
13620.00	R Moscow	AM Eng 1058 Fr 1647
13625.00	Monitor Radio International	AM Eng 1028 1055 1506
13625.00	R Moscow	AM Slav 1101 1301
13635.00	R Swiss International	AM Eng 1104 1126 1502 Fr 1749 Ital 0701 1825 Ger 1600
13640.00	R Croatia	AM Eng 2110
13640.00	R France International	AM Eng 1201 1254
13650.00	R Canada International	AM Eng 2106 2117
13650.00	R Moscow	AM Eng 0752 0812 1021 1105 Fr 1814
13655.00	R Vlaanderen International	AM Dutch 2207
13660.00	BBC	AM Slav 1100 Arab 1633 1826
13660.00	R Havana	AM Span 2132
13670.00	R Bulgaria	AM Eng 1755 1815
13670.00	R Canada International	AM Eng 2048 2107 2118 2210 Fr 2134
13670.00	R Korea	AM Eng 0804
13675.00	R Dubai	AM Eng 1030 1611 1624
13680.00	Deutsche Welle	AM Eng 1624
13680.00	R Moscow	AM Eng 0807 1202 Fr 0934 1603 Portuguese 2212
13685.00	R Swiss International	AM Eng 1325 Ger 1007 Ital 0844
13690.00	Deutsche Welle	AM Eng 2108 2133 Ger 1333 1440 1648
13690.00	VOA	AM Eng 1812
13695.00	WYFR, USA	AM Eng 0725 1302
13700.00	R Netherland	AM Eng 1431 1534 1559 Dutch 0813 1816 2135 Fr 2049
13710.00	R Moscow	AM Eng 1647
13710.00	VOA	AM Eng 1634 1754 1826 1900 2109 2136
13715.00	Slovak Radio	AM Slav 1304

13725.00	R Moscow	AM Eng 2111 2211
13730.00	R Austria International	AM Eng 0753 0834 1442 2144 Ger 0702 0944 1106 1441 1817
13745.00	BBC	AM Eng 0922 Slav 1629
13750.00	Kol Israel	AM Hebrew 1535 1650
13755.00	R Australia	AM Eng 1256 1303 1432 1455 1510 1543 1620 1748
13760.00	WHRI, USA	AM Eng 1755 2135 2213 (1700-2400)
13770.00	Monitor Radio International	AM Eng 1107 1438 2050 2120 Ger 2136
13770.00	R Netherland	AM Dutch 0618 1503
13780.00	Deutsche Welle	AM Ger 0706 0835 1008 1203 1442 1536 2212
13785.00	R Pyongyang	AM Eng 1511 (1500-1550) Ger 2147
13790.00	Deutsche Welle	AM Eng 0619 0647 Ger 1445 Portuguese 2137
13830.00	R Croatia	AM Slav 1512 1651 1800 1829
13835.00	R Iceland	USB Icelandic 1205 1257
13840.00	Monitor Radio International	AM Eng 2121
13845.00	WWCR, USA	AM Eng 1445 1606 1652 2138 2213
14240.00	R Rossiya (Russian Regional)	AM Slav/pop music 1526 1833 (harmonic of 7120kHz)
15010.00	Voice of Vietnam	AM Eng 1605 1817 Fr 1314 1831 (freq varies to 15009.0)
15020.00	All India Radio	AM Asian lang 1445
15030.00	Radio for Peace International	USB Eng 2203 2222
15050.00	All India Radio	AM Eng 1016 1053 Arabic 1153
15060.00	R Riyadh, Saudi Arabia	AM Arab 0947 1350 1444
15070.00	BBC	AM Eng 0829 1030 1549 1848 1925 2205 2256
15075.00	All India Radio	AM Eng 1833
15080.00	VOA	AM Eng 0619
15084.00	R Tehran	AM Farsi 0653 1154 1533
15090.00	R Vatican	AM Eng 0642 0655 1551 1608
15095.00	R Damascus	AM Eng 2204 Arab 1650
15100.00	R China International	AM Fr 1807 1843 2054
15105.00	Deutsche Welle	AM Eng 1600 Ger 0656 0911
15105.00	R Moscow	AM Eng 1413
15105.00	WHRI	AM Eng 1720
15110.00	REE Spain	AM Span 0903 1913 2223
15115.00	R Svoboda	AM Slav 1514 1545 1601
15125.00	AWR	AM Eng 1624
15125.00	R Moscow	AM Eng 0620 0732 1205 1316 1414
15130.00	R China International	AM Eng 1636
15135.00	BBC	AM Eng 0720
15135.00	Deutsche Welle	AM Eng 2103 Ger 1515 1710 1730
15140.00	All India Radio	AM Slav 1625
15140.00	R Moscow	AM Eng 0617 0733 0904 1206
15140.00	R Veritas Asia	AM Eng ID 1553
15145.00	Deutsche Welle	AM Eng 1505 1520 1626
15150.00	R Moscow	AM Eng 0904
15150.00	R Netherland	AM Eng 1542 1556
15160.00	VOA	AM Eng 1317
15170.00	R Australia	AM Eng 1043
15175.00	R Moscow	AM Eng 1031 1208 1602
15180.00	R Moscow	AM Eng 0627
15180.00	R Ukraine International	AM Eng (0000-0100)
15185.00	Deutsche Welle	AM Eng 0636
15185.00	VOA	AM Eng 2226
15190.00	R Moscow	AM Eng 0831 2205 2257 Ger 1032 1101
15195.00	R Ukraine International	AM Eng (0000-0100) Slav 0737 1825 2206
15205.00	VOA	AM Eng 1449 1543 1611 1721 1850
15210.00	R Moscow	AM Eng 0840 0954 1102 1156 Fr 1545
15210.00	R Vatican	AM Ital 1209
15215.00	R Svoboda	AM Slav 0659 0735 0859 1547
15220.00	BBC	AM Eng 1110
15220.00	R Golos Rossii	AM Russian 0959
15230.00	R Denmark (via Norway)	AM Danish 1653
15230.00	R Moscow	AM Eng 0841
15240.00	R Channel Africa, S Africa	AM Eng 1637 1644
15240.00	R Sweden	AM Eng 1450
15245.00	VOA	AM Eng 1637 Arab 1852
15255.00	VOA	AM Eng 1421 1543 1655
15260.00	BBC	AM Eng 1536 2208 2226
15260.00	R Canada International	AM Fr 1850
15260.00	R Tehran	AM Ger 1752 1826 Fr 1838
15265.00	R Brazil	AM Ger 1931
15265.00	R Moscow	AM Eng 1001 2305
15270.00	HCJB, Ecuador	AM Eng 0735
15275.00	Deutsche Welle	AM Ger 0912 1202 1517 1544 1811 2109
15280.00	BBC	AM Eng 2306
15280.00	R Moscow	AM Eng 0643 0701 0735 0900 1103 1209
15290.00	R Moscow	AM Eng 1615 1723 1810 2110 2230
15290.00	R Svoboda	AM Slav 0632
15300.00	R France International	AM Fr 1638

15305.00	R Moscow	AM Eng 0710
15305.00	VOA	AM Eng 2210
15310.00	BBC	AM Eng 1109
15315.00	R Abu Dhabi	AM Eng 2228 2309
15315.00	R Canada International	AM Eng 1443
15315.00	R Netherland	AM Dutch 2111 2201
15320.00	R Australia	AM Eng 0702 2242 (2030-0800)
15320.00	R Dubai	AM Eng 1605 1623
15320.00	R Moscow	AM Eng 0737 0858 1543
15325.00	R Canada International	AM Eng 1445 1714 2112 Ukrainian 1856 Fr 1915
15330.00	R Finland	AM Eng 0903 0914
15335.00	RTV Morocco	AM Arab 1724 2240
15345.00	R Moscow	AM Eng 0832 0925 1034 1104 1446
15350.00	Deutsche Welle	AM Eng 2114
15355.00	WYFR, USA	AM Eng 1606 1916 Ger 1639 1715 Italian 1857
15360.00	Deutsche Welle	AM Eng 1652 2115
15380.00	R Moscow	AM Eng 0833 0904 1447
15395.00	VOA	AM Eng 1516 1607 1633
15400.00	BBC	AM Eng 1018 1728 1859 1932 2213 2311
15400.00	R Moscow	AM Eng 1105
15410.00	R Austria International	AM Eng 0739 Ger 0720
15410.00	VOA	AM Eng 1842 1900 (1600-2200)
15420.00	BBC	AM Eng 1654
15420.00	R Moscow	AM Eng 0620 0712
15435.00	R Moscow	AM Eng 0905
15440.00	R Finland	AM Eng 1831
15440.00	R Moscow	AM Eng 0825 1015 1112 1200
15445.00	VOA	AM Eng 1608 1717
15450.00	R Austria International	AM Eng 0834 1035 1053 Ger 1213
15455.00	R Moscow	AM Eng 1424 Span 2219
15465.00	R Moscow	AM Eng 0726 1107 1517 1544
15470.00	R Moscow	AM Eng 0906 1214
15475.00	Africa No 1, Gabon	AM Fr 1610 1843
15480.00	R Moscow	AM Eng 1526
15485.00	R Moscow	AM Eng 1918
15505.00	R Swiss International	AM Eng 1856
15525.00	R Moscow	AM Eng 0713 0820 1901 2312
15540.00	R Moscow	AM Eng 0927 1519 1545 Ger 1105
15550.00	R Moscow	AM Eng 0916 1037 1108 1520
15555.00	R Pakistan	AM Eng 1620 (also msrd 15550.1 at 1730 1750)
15566.00	WYFR, USA	AM Eng 2116 2150
15575.00	BBC	AM Eng 0645 0710 1019 1106 1217 1428
15580.00	R Ukraine International	AM Eng (0000-0100)
15580.00	VOA	AM Eng 1902
15590.00	KTBN, USA	AM Eng 1718 1752
15590.00	R Moscow	AM Eng 0715 0727 0821
15610.00	KTWR, Guam	AM Eng 1542 1549
15617.00	Kol Israel	AM Fr 1043 Heb 1934 (freq varies 15614.3-15618.0)
15630.00	Voice of Greece	AM Eng 1531 (1530-1540) Greek 1719
15640.00	Kol Israel	AM Eng 1902
15650.00	Kol Israel	AM Eng 1905
15650.00	Voice of Greece	AM Eng 0747 1532 1848
15665.00	Monitor Radio International	AM Eng 1429 1450 1526 1850 1904 2122 2222
15685.00	WWCR, USA	AM Eng 1522 1544 1611 1700 1906
15695.00	WEWN, USA	AM Eng 1907
15770.00	R Iceland	USB Icelandic 1244
17387.00	All India Radio	AM Eng 1011
17485.00	R Moscow	AM Eng 0821
17490.00	HCJB, Ecuador	USB Eng 1233 1330 1420 1502 1518 2156 Ger 2105
17500.00	R Tunis	AM Arab 1407 1534
17510.00	WEWN, USA	AM Eng 1546 1600
17525.00	R Vatican	AM Eng 1348
17525.00	Voice of Greece	AM Eng 0946 1533 1844 Greek 0834
17535.00	R Prague	AM Eng 0731
17535.00	Slovak Radio	AM Eng 0836 0850
17535.00	Voice of Greece	AM Eng 1439 1446
17539.50	R Pakistan	AM Eng 1602
17545.00	Kol Israel	AM Hebrew 0734 1003
17555.00	Monitor Radio International	AM Eng 1014 1703 2109 2217
17560.00	Deutsche Welle	AM Ger 1426 1526 1635
17560.00	R Moscow	AM Eng 0824 0842 1110 2202
17565.00	R Swiss International	AM Fr 0700 Ger 0730
17565.00	R Ukraine International	AM Slav 1408 1423
17570.00	R Moscow	AM Eng 0840 1231 2203
17575.00	Kol Israel	AM Eng 1422 2153
17580.00	R Moscow	AM Eng 1519
17580.00	R Netherland	AM Dutch 1409 1517

17590.00	R Moscow	AM Eng 1331 1414
17595.00	R Moscow	AM Eng 0704 0837 1123 1420 Ger 1004
17600.00	R Moscow	AM Eng 0637 0830 1013
17605.00	R Moscow	AM Eng 1234 Fr 1440 1537
17605.00	R Netherland	AM Dutch 2110
17610.00	R Moscow	AM Eng 1014 1334 1430
17610.00	R Netherland	AM Eng 1548
17612.50	WYFR, USA	AM Eng 1847 2111 2157 2219
17620.00	R France International	AM Eng 1518 1556 1617 1704
17625.00	R Moscow	AM Fr 0843 1005 1303
17630.00	Africa No 1, Gabon	AM Fr 1533 1557
17635.00	R Moscow	AM Eng 0702 0732 0838
17640.00	BBC	AM Eng 0711 0800 1013 1125 1326 1424 1505
17640.00	VOA	AM Fr 1848 2133 (1830-2200)
17650.00	R France International	AM Fr 1522
17655.00	R Netherland	AM Eng 1752 1803
17660.00	R Moscow	AM Eng 0703 0801 1146
17665.00	R Moscow	AM Eng 0623 0801 1112
17670.00	R Australia	AM Eng 0802
17670.00	R Moscow	AM Eng 1147 Portuguese 2113
17675.00	R Moscow	AM Eng 0711 2206 2245
17680.00	R Moscow	AM Eng 0803 1131
17685.00	R Moscow	AM Eng 0736 0928
17695.00	R Australia	AM Eng 0735 0831 0849
17695.00	R France International	AM Eng 1433
17700.00	R Moscow	AM Eng 1148
17705.00	BBC	AM Eng 1327 1425 1506 1558
17710.00	R Moscow	AM Eng 1025
17715.00	R Australia	AM Eng 0848
17715.00	REE Spain	AM Span 1435
17720.00	R Romania International	AM Eng 0713 1328 1502
17725.00	R Moscow	AM Eng 1026 1235 1333
17725.00	R Ukraine International	AM Eng 2115 Slav 2207
17730.00	R Moscow	AM Eng 0639
17735.00	R Moscow	AM Eng 0704 0737 1149 1436
17735.00	VOA	AM Eng 2135 2208 2234
17750.00	R Australia	AM Eng 0848
17750.00	Voice of Free China	AM Eng 2201 2221 (2200-2300) Ger 2116
17755.00	R Moscow	AM Eng 0738 0902 1150
17760.00	R Havana	AM Eng 2120
17760.00	R Moscow	AM Eng 1027 1236 1306 1423 1437 1507 1811
17765.00	R Moscow	AM Eng 0739 0832 0904 1507
17770.00	R Moscow	AM Eng 0714 0738
17775.00	R Japan	AM Eng 0640 1702 1753
17775.00	R Moscow	AM Eng 0640 1307 1542
17780.00	Monitor Radio International	AM Eng 0715
17780.00	R Bulgaria	AM Eng (1945-2030)
17780.00	R Moscow	AM Eng 0621 1028 1151 1237
17785.00	VOA	AM Eng 1611
17790.00	BBC	AM Eng 0722
17790.00	HCJB, Ecuador	AM Eng 1637 1720 2156 Span 2200
17800.00	R Finland	AM Eng 0812
17800.00	VOA	AM Eng 1825 2122
17805.00	R Moscow	AM Eng 1029
17805.00	R Romania International	AM Eng 0705
17805.00	R Svoboda	AM Slav 1424 1440
17810.00	Deutsche Welle	AM Eng 1621 Ger 2125
17815.00	R Moscow	AM Eng 1030 1132 1152 1242 Fr 1638 Afrikaans 1738
17820.00	R Canada International	AM Eng 1356 1704 2128 Fr 2131
17830.00	BBC	AM Eng 0726
17840.00	BBC	AM Eng 1426 1508 1606
17845.00	Deutsche Welle	AM Ger 0707 0850 1233
17845.00	REE Spain	AM Span 1527 1722
17850.00	All India Radio	AM Eng 0732
17855.00	R Moscow	AM Fr 1608
17860.00	BBC	AM Eng 1602
17860.00	Deutsche Welle	AM Ger 1849 2132 2217
17865.00	R Vatican	AM Eng 1548 (1545-1640)
17870.00	R Austria International	AM Eng 1031
17870.00	R Bulgaria	AM Portuguese 2139 Slav 2201
17875.00	R Moscow	AM Eng 1153 Fr 1425
17880.00	R Moscow	AM Eng 1300
17885.00	R Moscow	AM Fr 1609
17890.00	HCJB, Ecuador	AM Eng 1412 1530
17895.00	BBC	AM Russian 1301
17895.00	R Netherland	AM Dutch 2218
17895.00	VOA	AM Eng 1648

17900.00	R Pakistan	AM Eng 0829
17940.00	R Baghdad	AM Arab 2220
21450.00	R Moscow	AM Eng 0822 0926 0936 1035 1108
21455.00	HCJB, Ecuador	USB Eng 1326 1457 1516 1639 1830 1915 2130
21460.00	All India Radio	AM Eng 1036
21460.00	R Ukraine International	AM Slav 1106
21465.00	R Moscow	AM Eng 0831 1109 1457
21470.00	BBC	AM Eng 0640 0949 1011 1108 1245 1500 1538
21480.00	HCJB, Ecuador	AM Eng 1638 1740 2131 Ger 1832 2120
21480.00	R Moscow	AM Eng 0823 0928 1012
21480.00	R Netherland	AM Dutch 1329
21485.00	VOA	AM Eng 2121
21490.00	R Austria International	AM Eng 0832 1450
21490.00	VOA	AM Span 1731
21495.00	R Riyadh, Saudi Arabia	AM Arab 1141
21500.00	R Sweden	AM Swedish 1351
21500.00	WYFR, USA	AM Eng 1756 1833 Ital 2122
21505.00	R Riyadh, Saudi Arabia	AM Arab 1302 1541
21515.00	R Moscow	AM Eng 0907 1038 1109 Fr 1537
21515.00	R Netherland	AM Eng 1754 1833
21515.00	R Portugal International	AM Eng 1537 Portuguese 1502 1641
21520.00	R France International	AM Fr 1106 1143
21520.00	R Moscow	AM Asian lang 1449
21520.00	R Pakistan	AM Eng 0829 1110
21520.00	VOA	AM Kurdish 1230
21525.00	R Australia	AM Eng 0614 0641 0734 (0100-0900)
21525.00	WYFR, USA	AM Eng 1615 1653 2123 2148 Fr 1834
21530.00	R France International	AM Fr 0812 1156
21535.00	RTV Italiana	AM Ital 1331 1642
21540.00	Deutsche Welle	AM Ger 0642 0707 0833 1231 1303
21540.00	R Moscow	AM Eng 0908 1047 1144
21545.00	R Canada International	AM Slav 1456 1500
21545.00	R Moscow	AM Eng 0930
21550.00	R Finland	AM Eng 0810 1531
21550.00	R Moscow	AM Eng 1144
21555.00	REE Spain	AM Span 1344
21560.00	Deutsche Welle	AM Ger 0735 1304 1501 1606
21575.00	R Japan	AM Eng 0728
21580.00	R France International	AM Fr 1107 1332 1520 1709
21585.00	R Moscow	AM Eng 0912 0931
21585.00	VOA	AM Chinese (Eng lessons) 1145
21590.00	R Netherland	AM Eng 1730 1806 1838 (1730-2030)
21600.00	R Moscow	AM Eng 1048 1431
21605.00	R Dubai	AM Eng 1031 1337 1606
21610.00	R Moscow	AM Eng 0610 0825
21615.00	R Moscow	AM Eng 0730 0822 0932 1039
21615.00	WYFR, USA	AM Eng 1616 1645 1654 2124 Ital 1836
21620.00	R France International	AM Fr 1146 1458 1711
21630.00	R Moscow	AM Eng 1235 1424
21635.00	R France International	AM Fr 1418 1521
21640.00	Monitor Radio International	AM Eng 1713 (1600-2000)
21645.00	R France International	AM Eng 1200 Fr 1502 Span 1307
21655.00	R Moscow	AM Eng 0612
21655.00	R Portugal International	AM Port 1014 1334 1806
21660.00	BBC	AM Eng 0744 0814 1111 1244 1338 1501 1606
21665.00	R Canada International	AM Eng 1020 Fr 1015
21670.00	Monitor Radio International	AM Eng 1837
21680.00	Deutsche Welle	AM Eng 1609 Ger 1347
21685.00	R France International	AM Fr 1245 1522 1655 1732
21710.00	R Vatican	AM Span 1147
21715.00	BBC	AM Eng 0615 0820
21720.00	R Moscow	AM Ger 1532 1544
21720.00	R Portugal International	AM Port 1152
21720.00	Voice of Free China	AM Eng 2202 (2200-2300)
21725.00	R Australia	AM Eng 1041
21725.00	R Moscow	AM Eng 0708
21740.00	R Moscow	AM Eng 1112 1236 1545 1733
21745.00	R Australia	AM Eng 1017
21745.00	R Netherland	AM Dutch 1330
21770.00	R Swiss International	AM Eng 1503
21785.00	R Moscow	AM Eng 0709 0821 1128 1206 1310 1400
21820.00	Deutsche Welle	AM Ger 1635
21820.00	R Moscow	AM Eng 0717
21820.00	R Swiss International	AM Eng 1115 1504 Fr 1552
21825.00	R Moscow	AM Eng 1148 Fr 0616
21845.00	R Moscow	AM Eng 1051
21850.00	R Vatican	AM Portuguese 1116 Span 1204

25690.00	R Abu Dhabi	AM Arab 0927
25730.00	UNID	AM Scan 1344
25820.00	R France International	AM Fr 1135 1345 1500

ABC Katherine, Australia	2485	AM Eng 2037
All India Radio	3905	AM Eng 1600
All India Radio	7412	AM Eng 1534 1745 1812 2209 2224
All India Radio	9910	AM Eng 1533 2216 2310
All India Radio	9950	AM Eng 1838 2223
All India Radio	11620	AM Eng 1745 1849 1902 2112 2141 2224
All India Radio	11715	AM Eng 2143
All India Radio	11740	AM Eng 1536
All India Radio	15050	AM Eng 1016 1053 Arabic 1153
All India Radio	15075	AM Eng 1833
All India Radio	17387	AM Eng 1011
All India Radio	17850	AM Eng 0732
All India Radio	21460	AM Eng 1036
AWR	7180	AM Eng 0744
AWR	7230	AM Eng 1049 Ger 0811 Multilingual ID 0658
AWR	13595	AM Asian lang (ID in Eng) 1500
AWR	15125	AM Eng 1624
Channel Africa (RSA)	11750	AM Eng 1747
Deutsche Welle	7225	AM Eng 1646 Urdu 1514
Deutsche Welle	7255	AM Eng 1606 Slav 1042
Deutsche Welle	9585	AM Eng 1648
Deutsche Welle	9665	AM Eng 1907 Ger 1204
Deutsche Welle	11740	AM Eng 1901 1928
Deutsche Welle	11785	AM Eng 1646 1904 1929 2121
Deutsche Welle	13610	AM Eng 0619 Fr 0700 Ger 2105 2131
Deutsche Welle	13680	AM Eng 1624
Deutsche Welle	13690	AM Eng 2108 2133 Ger 1333 1440 1648
Deutsche Welle	13790	AM Eng 0619 0647 Ger 1445 Portuguese 2137
Deutsche Welle	15105	AM Eng 1600 Ger 0656 0911
Deutsche Welle	15135	AM Eng 2103 Ger 1515 1710 1730
Deutsche Welle	15145	AM Eng 1505 1520 1626
Deutsche Welle	15185	AM Eng 0636
Deutsche Welle	15350	AM Eng 2114
Deutsche Welle	15360	AM Eng 1652 2115
Deutsche Welle	17810	AM Eng 1621 Ger 2125
Deutsche Welle	21680	AM Eng 1609 Ger 1347
ELWA, Liberia	4760	AM Eng 2201
European Christian Radio	6220	AM Eng ID & Romanian 1700
FEBC, Manila	11995	AM Eng 1540
GBC Radio, Ghana	3366	AM Eng 0032 2146 2155 2214 2243
HCJB, Ecuador	6205	AM Eng 0643 0738 0801 0825 1738
HCJB, Ecuador	9745	AM Eng 0758 0840 0854 (0730-1100)
HCJB, Ecuador	11725	AM Eng 0708 0731
HCJB, Ecuador	11835	AM Eng 0711
HCJB, Ecuador	15270	AM Eng 0735
HCJB, Ecuador	17490	USB Eng 1233 1330 1420 1502 1518 2156 Ger 2105
HCJB, Ecuador	17790	AM Eng 1637 1720 2156 Span 2200
HCJB, Ecuador	17890	AM Eng 1412 1530
HCJB, Ecuador	21455	USB Eng 1326 1457 1516 1639 1830 1915 2130
HCJB, Ecuador	21480	AM Eng 1638 1740 2131 Ger 1832 2120
IRRS Italy	7125	AM Eng 0625 0816 1742 2341 (UN radio relay 0700 0739)
King of Hope, Lebanon	6280	AM Eng 0125 1853 2151
Kol Israel	7465	AM Eng 1806 2003 2236 2255
Kol Israel	9435	AM Eng 2231 2239 (2230-2300) Span 2227
Kol Israel	11587	AM Eng 1703 1912 2139 Fr 1935
Kol Israel	11605	AM Eng 1913 2140 (also msrd on 11603.0)
Kol Israel	11675	AM Eng 1915 2142 Span 2113 2137
Kol Israel	15640	AM Eng 1902
Kol Israel	15650	AM Eng 1905
Kol Israel	17575	AM Eng 1422 2153
KTBN, USA	15590	AM Eng 1718 1752
KTWR, Guam	9785	AM Eng 1108
KTWR, Guam	15610	AM Eng 1542 1549
Monitor Radio International	5850	AM Eng 0136 0700 0740
Monitor Radio International	7465	AM Eng 0944 1046 1106
Monitor Radio International	7510	AM Eng 0946 2037 2252 Span 2306
Monitor Radio International	7520	AM Eng 0718
Monitor Radio International	9355	AM Eng 1500 1806
Monitor Radio International	9455	AM Eng 0644 0827 0912 0945
Monitor Radio International	9465	AM Eng 2203 2240 2251 (2200-2359)
Monitor Radio International	9495	AM Eng 0650 1128 1214
Monitor Radio International	9840	AM Eng 0745 0857 0949
Monitor Radio International	11580	AM Eng 1645
Monitor Radio International	11705	AM Eng 0940
Monitor Radio International	13615	AM Eng 0831 0846
Monitor Radio International	13625	AM Eng 1028 1055 1506
Monitor Radio International	13770	AM Eng 1107 1438 2050 2120 Ger 2136
Monitor Radio International	13840	AM Eng 2121
Monitor Radio International	15665	AM Eng 1429 1450 1526 1850 1904 2122 2222
Monitor Radio International	17555	AM Eng 1014 1703 2109 2217
Monitor Radio International	17780	AM Eng 0715
Monitor Radio International	21640	AM Eng 1713 (1600-2000)
Monitor Radio International	21670	AM Eng 1837
PBS China	4500	AM Chinese 2202 2318 English lessons 2245 (freq varies)
Pirate Radio (UNID)	6400	AM Eng 1240 1757
Polish Radio Warsaw	5995	AM Eng 1829 1849
Polish Radio Warsaw	6135	AM Eng 1350 Ger 1603 1816
Polish Radio Warsaw	7285	AM Eng 1654 1813 Ger 1520
Polish Radio Warsaw	9525	AM Eng 1231 1648 Ger 1132 1730
Polish Radio Warsaw	11840	AM Eng 1507
R Abu Dhabi	9605	AM Eng 2201 2250 2345 (2200-2359) Arab 2141
R Abu Dhabi	9770	AM Eng 2226 (readings from Holy Koran) 2214
R Abu Dhabi	11710	AM Eng 2320
R Abu Dhabi	15315	AM Eng 2228 2309
R Accra, Ghana	4915	AM Eng 0741 0818 1925 2008 2207 2230 2259
R Almaty, Kazakhstan	5035	AM Eng 1935 Slav 1618 1834

R Almaty, Kazakhstan	5260	AM Eng 1938 Slav 1619 1844 1931
R Almaty, Kazakhstan	5915	AM Eng 2303
R Amman	9560	AM Eng 1711 Arab 2212
R Australia	5880	AM Eng 1917
R Australia	5890	AM Eng 1707 1857
R Australia	5995	AM Eng 0900
R Australia	6080	AM Eng 1652 1811 1820
R Australia	7170	AM Eng 1600
R Australia	7260	AM Eng 1519 1633 1719 1816 1858 1901 1958
R Australia	9510	AM Eng 1603
R Australia	9560	AM Eng 1618 1649 1748
R Australia	9645	AM Eng 2202 2220
R Australia	9710	AM Eng 1124
R Australia	9770	AM Eng 1526 1546
R Australia	11660	AM Eng 1507 1554 1736 1903
R Australia	11680	AM Eng 1848
R Australia	11695	AM Eng 0949 1602 1706
R Australia	11855	AM Eng 1452
R Australia	11910	AM Eng 0805 0850
R Australia	13605	AM Eng 0932 0942 1100 1125 Chinese 1300
R Australia	13755	AM Eng 1256 1303 1432 1455 1510 1543 1620 1748
R Australia	15170	AM Eng 1043
R Australia	15320	AM Eng 0702 2242 (2030-0800)
R Australia	17670	AM Eng 0802
R Australia	17695	AM Eng 0735 0831 0849
R Australia	17715	AM Eng 0848
R Australia	17750	AM Eng 0848
R Australia	21525	AM Eng 0614 0641 0734 (0100-0900)
R Australia	21725	AM Eng 1041
R Australia	21745	AM Eng 1017
R Austria International	5945	AM Eng 1951 2137 Ger 1807 1848 2102 2203
R Austria International	6155	AM Eng 0850 1250 1440 1832 Ger 1002 1125 1819 Span 1351
R Austria International	9870	AM Eng 1441 Ger 2213 2312
R Austria International	9880	AM Eng 1534 Ger 1514
R Austria International	11780	AM Eng 1535 1553 1643 Ger 1505 1603
R Austria International	13730	AM Eng 0753 0834 1442 2144 Ger 0702 0944 1106 1441 1817
R Austria International	15410	AM Eng 0739 Ger 0720
R Austria International	15450	AM Eng 0834 1035 1053 Ger 1213
R Austria International	17870	AM Eng 1031
R Austria International	21490	AM Eng 0832 1450
R Botswana	3356	AM Eng 1812 2154
R Botswana	4830	AM Eng 2116 2318
R Bratislava	9505	AM Eng 1130
R Bratislava	9580	AM (0200-0230)
R Budapest	6110	AM Eng 1906 2210 2250
R Budapest	7220	AM Eng 2135 Ger 1854
R Budapest	9835	AM Eng 2109 (2100-2200)
R Budapest	11910	AM Eng 2111
R Bulgaria	6235	AM Eng 1845 1857 Fr 1807 Ger 1709
R Bulgaria	7225	AM Eng 2355
R Bulgaria	7455	AM Eng 0011 2246 2305 Ger 1717 Fr 1805
R Bulgaria	9700	AM Eng 1754 2248 Fr 0745 1802
R Bulgaria	11720	AM Eng 1756 2156 2215 Fr 1900
R Bulgaria	12085	AM Eng 1549 1619
R Bulgaria	13670	AM Eng 1755 1815
R Bulgaria	17780	AM Eng (1945-2030)
R Cairo	9900	AM Eng 2158 2215 Ger 1910
R Canada International	5960	AM Eng 2218
R Canada International	5995	AM Eng 2109 2150 2222 Slav 1635 Fr 1952 2104
R Canada International	7195	AM Eng 2205 2224
R Canada International	7250	AM Eng 0010
R Canada International	7260	AM Eng 2207
R Canada International	9550	AM Eng 1630
R Canada International	9755	AM Eng 2210
R Canada International	11730	AM Eng 2322 Fr 2139
R Canada International	11855	AM Eng 1356
R Canada International	11875	AM Eng 2204
R Canada International	13650	AM Eng 2106 2117
R Canada International	13670	AM Eng 2048 2107 2118 2210 Fr 2134
R Canada International	15315	AM Eng 1443
R Canada International	15325	AM Eng 1445 1714 2112 Ukrainian 1856 Fr 1915
R Canada International	17820	AM Eng 1356 1704 2128 Fr 2131
R Canada International	21665	AM Eng 1020 Fr 1015
R Channel Africa, S Africa	15240	AM Eng 1637 1644
R China International	3985	AM Eng 2124 2200 Ital 2232
R China International	6950	AM Eng 2127 2152 Slav 1707 Ger 1912
R China International	6955	AM Eng 1913 Asian lang 1832
R China International	7170	AM Eng 2201 2254
R China International	9880	AM Eng 2203
R China International	9920	AM Eng 2100 Ger 1827 1837
R China International	11500	AM Eng 2123 Slav 1701 Ger 1845
R China International	11515	AM Eng 1911 Ger 1832
R China International	11575	AM Eng 1614 1738
R China International	15130	AM Eng 1636
R Croatia	13640	AM Eng 2110
R Damascus	12085	AM Eng 2118 2151 Fr 1911
R Damascus	15095	AM Eng 2204 Arab 1650
R DLR-106 (Pirate)	6226	AM Eng 1008 2201
R Dubai	13675	AM Eng 1030 1611 1624
R Dubai	15320	AM Eng 1605 1623
R Dubai	21605	AM Eng 1031 1337 1606
R Finland	6120	AM Eng 0646 0745 1834 1957 2142 Ger 1930 Russ 2000
R Finland	9560	AM Eng 0654 0748
R Finland	9615	AM Eng 2236
R Finland	9730	AM Eng 1833 1837

R Finland	9740	AM Eng 2258
R Finland	11755	AM Eng 0749 1838 2131 Ger 0941
R Finland	15330	AM Eng 0903 0914
R Finland	15440	AM Eng 1831
R Finland	17800	AM Eng 0812
R Finland	21550	AM Eng 0810 1531
R for Peace International	9375	AM Eng UN Radio programme 1059
R France International	6175	AM Eng 1555 1645 Fr 1041 1126 1700 2001
R France International	9805	AM Eng 1236 Fr 0749 1123 1217
R France International	11705	AM Eng 1605 1640
R France International	13640	AM Eng 1201 1254
R France International	17620	AM Eng 1518 1556 1617 1704
R France International	17695	AM Eng 1433
R France International	21645	AM Eng 1200 Fr 1502 Span 1307
R Havana	17760	AM Eng 2120
R Japan	5975	AM Eng 0728
R Japan	6050	AM Eng 0702 0744 0807 2306 2330
R Japan	6060	AM Eng 2309
R Japan	7230	AM Eng 0729
R Japan	11925	AM Eng 2145
R Japan	17775	AM Eng 0640 1702 1753
R Japan	21575	AM Eng 0728
R Kampala	4976	AM Eng 2025
R Kenya	4935	AM Eng 1819 1926
R Korea	6480	AM Eng 2219 Slav 2016 Asian lang 1819
R Korea	7550	AM Eng 0819 Ger 1944
R Korea	11715	AM Eng 1031
R Korea	13670	AM Eng 0804
R Kuwait	13620	AM Eng 1804 1840 Arab 1746
R Merlin International (Pirate)	6239	AM Eng 1011
R Moscow	4795	AM Eng 2135 2249 2301 2310 Slav 1640
R Moscow	4860	AM Eng 2133 2253 2314 Ger 2007 Slav 1906
R Moscow	4940	AM Eng 2330 Slav 1745 1843
R Moscow	4975	AM Eng 1617
R Moscow	5905	AM Eng 1554 2237
R Moscow	5920	AM Eng 2259 Ital 2140
R Moscow	5950	AM Eng 2155 2239
R Moscow	5975	AM Eng 2201
R Moscow	5985	AM Eng 2323
R Moscow	6000	AM Eng 1632 Span 2326
R Moscow	6010	AM Eng 2139 Ger 1943
R Moscow	6055	AM Eng 2240
R Moscow	6130	AM Eng 2144 Ger 1745
R Moscow	7105	AM Eng 1845
R Moscow	7110	AM Eng 2312 2350
R Moscow	7115	AM Eng 2114
R Moscow	7125	AM Eng 2252
R Moscow	7140	AM Eng 2231 Fr 1846
R Moscow	7150	AM Eng 2229 2239
R Moscow	7165	AM Eng 0722 0830
R Moscow	7170	AM Eng 1711 1912 2135
R Moscow	7180	AM Eng 1957 2134 2241 Fr 2310
R Moscow	7205	AM Eng 1712 1913 2205 Fr 2257
R Moscow	7230	AM Eng 2136
R Moscow	7295	AM Eng 2303
R Moscow	7300	AM Eng 2229 2253
R Moscow	7330	AM Eng 1715
R Moscow	7335	AM Eng 2235
R Moscow	7380	AM Eng 2209 2244
R Moscow	7420	AM Eng 1804
R Moscow	9480	AM Eng 2212
R Moscow	9530	AM Eng 1627
R Moscow	9550	AM Eng 1630 1715 2236
R Moscow	9560	AM Eng 1712
R Moscow	9580	AM Eng 0812 1525 Fr 0741
R Moscow	9610	AM Eng 0534
R Moscow	9620	AM Eng 2238 2307
R Moscow	9640	AM Eng 2105
R Moscow	9685	AM Eng 1908 Fr 2310
R Moscow	9725	AM Eng 2236
R Moscow	9750	AM Eng 0535 0702 2200
R Moscow	9765	AM Eng 0536 0623
R Moscow	9815	AM Eng 2207
R Moscow	9820	AM Eng 2004 2155
R Moscow	9860	AM Eng 1912
R Moscow	9880	AM Eng 1825 Fr 1638
R Moscow	9890	AM Eng 1515 1532 1715
R Moscow	11620	AM Eng 2110
R Moscow	11685	AM Eng 1916 2114
R Moscow	11690	AM Eng 0536 0839 1504
R Moscow	11705	AM Eng 0800 1001 1505 1615 1737
R Moscow	11710	AM Eng 0707
R Moscow	11715	AM Eng 1352 1403 1857 1917
R Moscow	11720	AM Eng 2128
R Moscow	11730	AM Eng 2115 2158
R Moscow	11735	AM Eng 1804
R Moscow	11745	AM Eng 0801 1002
R Moscow	11750	AM Eng 2134
R Moscow	11760	AM Eng 2116 Fr 2212
R Moscow	11800	AM Eng 2132
R Moscow	11805	AM Eng 0804 0950 1003
R Moscow	11860	AM Eng 1656 Fr 0608 0725 Portuguese 2130
R Moscow	11870	AM Eng 1616 1631 2136
R Moscow	11935	AM Eng 1533
R Moscow	11960	AM Eng 1710 1737

R Moscow	11985	AM Eng 1310
R Moscow	12010	AM Eng 0713 0902 0943 1043 Ger 1713 1739 1904 Portuguese
R Moscow	12020	AM Eng 0903 0936 1100 Fr 1312 1400 1510 1908 Portuguese
R Moscow	12055	AM Eng 0911 1101 1910
R Moscow	12065	AM Eng 1544
R Moscow	12070	AM Eng 0654 0854 0903 1024 1135 Fr 1742 2149
R Moscow	13615	AM Eng 0832 1112
R Moscow	13620	AM Eng 1058 Fr 1647
R Moscow	13650	AM Eng 0752 0812 1021 1105 Fr 1814
R Moscow	13680	AM Eng 0807 1202 Fr 0934 1603 Portuguese 2212
R Moscow	13710	AM Eng 1647
R Moscow	13725	AM Eng 2111 2211
R Moscow	15105	AM Eng 1413
R Moscow	15125	AM Eng 0620 0732 1205 1316 1414
R Moscow	15140	AM Eng 0617 0733 0904 1206
R Moscow	15150	AM Eng 0904
R Moscow	15175	AM Eng 1031 1208 1602
R Moscow	15180	AM Eng 0627
R Moscow	15190	AM Eng 0831 2205 2257 Ger 1032 1101
R Moscow	15210	AM Eng 0840 0954 1102 1156 Fr 1545
R Moscow	15230	AM Eng 0841
R Moscow	15265	AM Eng 1001 2305
R Moscow	15280	AM Eng 0643 0701 0735 0900 1103 1209
R Moscow	15290	AM Eng 1615 1723 1810 2110 2230
R Moscow	15305	AM Eng 0710
R Moscow	15320	AM Eng 0737 0858 1543
R Moscow	15345	AM Eng 0832 0925 1034 1104 1446
R Moscow	15380	AM Eng 0833 0904 1447
R Moscow	15400	AM Eng 1105
R Moscow	15420	AM Eng 0620 0712
R Moscow	15435	AM Eng 0905
R Moscow	15440	AM Eng 0825 1015 1112 1200
R Moscow	15455	AM Eng 1424 Span 2219
R Moscow	15465	AM Eng 0726 1107 1517 1544
R Moscow	15470	AM Eng 0906 1214
R Moscow	15480	AM Eng 1526
R Moscow	15485	AM Eng 1918
R Moscow	15525	AM Eng 0713 0820 1901 2312
R Moscow	15540	AM Eng 0927 1519 1545 Ger 1105
R Moscow	15550	AM Eng 0916 1037 1108 1520
R Moscow	15590	AM Eng 0715 0727 0821
R Moscow	17485	AM Eng 0821
R Moscow	17560	AM Eng 0824 0842 1110 2202
R Moscow	17570	AM Eng 0840 1231 2203
R Moscow	17580	AM Eng 1519
R Moscow	17590	AM Eng 1331 1414
R Moscow	17595	AM Eng 0704 0837 1123 1420 Ger 1004
R Moscow	17600	AM Eng 0637 0830 1013
R Moscow	17605	AM Eng 1234 Fr 1440 1537
R Moscow	17610	AM Eng 1014 1334 1430
R Moscow	17635	AM Eng 0702 0732 0838
R Moscow	17660	AM Eng 0703 0801 1146
R Moscow	17665	AM Eng 0623 0801 1112
R Moscow	17670	AM Eng 1147 Portuguese 2113
R Moscow	17675	AM Eng 0711 2206 2245
R Moscow	17680	AM Eng 0803 1131
R Moscow	17685	AM Eng 0736 0928
R Moscow	17700	AM Eng 1148
R Moscow	17710	AM Eng 1025
R Moscow	17725	AM Eng 1026 1235 1333
R Moscow	17730	AM Eng 0639
R Moscow	17735	AM Eng 0704 0737 1149 1436
R Moscow	17755	AM Eng 0738 0902 1150
R Moscow	17760	AM Eng 1027 1236 1306 1423 1437 1507 1811
R Moscow	17765	AM Eng 0739 0832 0904 1507
R Moscow	17770	AM Eng 0714 0738
R Moscow	17775	AM Eng 0640 1307 1542
R Moscow	17780	AM Eng 0621 1028 1151 1237
R Moscow	17805	AM Eng 1029
R Moscow	17815	AM Eng 1030 1132 1152 1242 Fr 1638 Afrikaans 1738
R Moscow	17875	AM Eng 1153 Fr 1425
R Moscow	17880	AM Eng 1300
R Moscow	21450	AM Eng 0822 0926 0936 1035 1108
R Moscow	21465	AM Eng 0831 1109 1457
R Moscow	21480	AM Eng 0823 0928 1012
R Moscow	21515	AM Eng 0907 1038 1109 Fr 1537
R Moscow	21540	AM Eng 0908 1047 1144
R Moscow	21545	AM Eng 0930
R Moscow	21550	AM Eng 1144
R Moscow	21585	AM Eng 0912 0931
R Moscow	21600	AM Eng 1048 1431
R Moscow	21610	AM Eng 0610 0825
R Moscow	21615	AM Eng 0730 0822 0932 1039
R Moscow	21630	AM Eng 1235 1424
R Moscow	21655	AM Eng 0612
R Moscow	21725	AM Eng 0708
R Moscow	21740	AM Eng 1112 1236 1545 1733
R Moscow	21785	AM Eng 0709 0821 1128 1206 1310 1400
R Moscow	21820	AM Eng 0717
R Moscow	21825	AM Eng 1148 Fr 0616
R Moscow	21845	AM Eng 1051
R Namibia	3270	AM Eng 2225
R Netherland	5955	AM Eng 0859 1319 1525 1558 Dutch 0743 0803 1653
R Netherland	6165	AM Eng 2338
R Netherland	7120	AM Eng 1835
R Netherland	9605	AM Eng 1836 1905

R Netherland	9715	AM Eng 0753
R Netherland	9720	AM Eng 0747
R Netherland	9720	AM Eng 0950 Dutch 0653
R Netherland	9860	AM Eng 1138
R Netherland	9890	AM Eng 1552
R Netherland	11895	AM Eng 0733 0935
R Netherland	13700	AM Eng 1431 1534 1559 Dutch 0813 1816 2135 Fr 2049
R Netherland	15150	AM Eng 1542 1556
R Netherland	17610	AM Eng 1548
R Netherland	17655	AM Eng 1752 1803
R Netherland	21515	AM Eng 1754 1833
R Netherland	21590	AM Eng 1730 1806 1838 (1730-2030)
R New Zealand	9700	AM Eng 0818
R Nigeria	3326	AM Eng 2109 2230 2246
R Nigeria	4770	AM Eng 2004 2132 2154 2212 2250 (0530-2300)
R Nigeria	4990	AM Eng 1931 2112 2231 2300
R Nigeria	7255	AM Eng 0631
R Omdurman	9165	AM Eng 1836 Arab 1535 Fr 1743
R Pakistan	11570	AM Eng 1601 1625 1702
R Pakistan	13590	AM Eng 1628
R Pakistan	15555	AM Eng 1620 (also msrd 15550.1 at 1730 1750)
R Pakistan	17540	AM Eng 1602
R Pakistan	17900	AM Eng 0829
R Pakistan	21520	AM Eng 0829 1110
R Portugal International	11800	AM Eng (Sats & Suns) 0900
R Portugal International	21515	AM Eng 1537 Portuguese 1502 1641
R Prague	5930	AM Eng 1723 Fr 1953 Slav 1633 Span 1905 2301 2322
R Prague	5960	AM Eng 2103 Slav 1920
R Prague	6055	AM Eng 0615 1039 1601 2103 2114 2208 Ger 0955 Fr 1635
R Prague	7345	AM Eng 0722 1722 2104 Ger 0932 Span 2055 Fr 2244
R Prague	9505	AM Eng 0625 0712 Span 1131
R Prague	9605	AM Eng 1800 2100 Ger 1722
R Prague	11990	AM Eng 0734 1134
R Prague	13600	AM Eng 0742 1505
R Prague	17535	AM Eng 0731
R Pyongyang	6576	AM Eng 2046 Span 1814 Ger 1931 1942 Fr 1615 2119
R Pyongyang	9325	AM Eng 1527 1714 Span 2046
R Pyongyang	9345	AM Eng 2047 Span 1813
R Pyongyang	13785	AM Eng 1511 (1500-1550) Ger 2147
R Riga	5935	AM Eng 1820 1827
R Romania International	5955	AM Eng 1945
R Romania International	6105	AM Eng 1946
R Romania International	7195	AM Eng 2140 2156 Ger 1841
R Romania International	7225	AM Eng 0634 2115
R Romania International	9510	AM Eng 0631
R Romania International	11810	AM Eng 1501
R Romania International	11830	AM Eng 1735
R Romania International	11940	AM Eng 1353 1902 1918 Fr 1142 Ger 1651 1807
R Romania International	17720	AM Eng 0713 1328 1502
R Romania International	17805	AM Eng 0705
R Slovakia International	5915	AM Eng 1836 1859
R Slovakia International	7345	AM Eng 1837 Fr 1931
R Sweden	6065	AM Eng 1732 1840 2115 Ger 1830 Swed 0825
R Sweden	9645	AM Eng 1740
R Sweden	9655	AM Eng 2117
R Sweden	15240	AM Eng 1450
R Swiss International	3985	AM Eng 0613 Fr 0640 0813 1842 Ger 2024
R Swiss International	6165	AM Eng 1004 Ger 0723 1703 Fr 0950 Ital 1638
R Swiss International	9535	AM Eng 1103 1718 Fr 0735 0948 1735 Ger 1215 Ital 1818
R Swiss International	9810	AM Eng 2212
R Swiss International	9885	AM Eng 0900 0920 1700 2005 2214 Fr 0933
R Swiss International	13635	AM Eng 1104 1126 1502 Fr 1749 Ital 0701 1825 Ger 1600
R Swiss International	13685	AM Eng 1325 Ger 1007 Ital 0844
R Swiss International	15505	AM Eng 1856
R Swiss International	21770	AM Eng 1503
R Swiss International	21820	AM Eng 1115 1504 Fr 1552
R Tanzania	5050	AM Eng 1810
R Tehran	9022	AM Eng 0041 1942 Fr 0656 0721 1859 2240 Ger 1806 Span
R Tirana	7155	AM Eng 1538
R Tirana	9760	AM Eng 1540 2205
R Tirana	11825	AM Eng 2131
R Ukraine International	4825	AM Eng 2229 2252 Slav 0650 2214 Ger 0001
R Ukraine International	5960	AM Eng 2241
R Ukraine International	5985	AM Eng 2242
R Ukraine International	6020	AM Eng 2238
R Ukraine International	6055	AM Eng 2217
R Ukraine International	6090	AM Eng 2104 2142 (2100-2200 0000-0100) Ger 2310
R Ukraine International	7150	AM Eng 2105 2133 (2100-2200 0000-0100) Slav 2222
R Ukraine International	7195	AM Eng 2204 2256
R Ukraine International	7240	AM Eng 2206 2218 2245 Ger 1749 1801
R Ukraine International	7285	AM Eng 2159
R Ukraine International	9505	AM Eng 2254
R Ukraine International	9550	AM Eng (0000-0100)
R Ukraine International	9640	AM Eng (0000-0100)
R Ukraine International	9685	AM Eng 2146 (2100-2200 0000-0100)
R Ukraine International	9745	AM Eng 2220 2240
R Ukraine International	9860	AM Eng 2242
R Ukraine International	11720	AM Eng (0000-0100)
R Ukraine International	15180	AM Eng (0000-0100)
R Ukraine International	15195	AM Eng (0000-0100) Slav 0737 1825 2206
R Ukraine International	15580	AM Eng (0000-0100)
R Ukraine International	17725	AM Eng 2115 Slav 2207
R Vatican	5885	AM Eng 1950 Ital 2105 2202 2239 (freq varies to
R Vatican	6245	AM Eng 0637 Ital 1642 Fr 1013 1710 Ger 1924
R Vatican	7250	AM Eng 0736 Latin mass 1510 Fr 0722

R Vatican	9645	AM Eng 0635 Ital 0714 Ger 1444 Fr 1607 Arab 1831
R Vatican	15090	AM Eng 0642 0655 1551 1608
R Vatican	17525	AM Eng 1348
R Vatican	17865	AM Eng 1548 (1545-1640)
R Veritas Asia	15140	AM Eng ID 1553
R Vilnius	9710	AM Eng 2147
R Vilnius	12040	AM Eng (2300-2359)
R Vlaanderen International	5910	AM Eng 0650 1806 1818 Dutch 0742 0843 Ger 1734
R Vlaanderen International	9905	AM Eng 0914 Ger 0953 Dutch 1206 1314
R Vlaanderen International	9925	AM Eng 0647
R Yerevan	7440	AM Eng 2246 2251
R Yerevan	9450	AM Eng 2148 Fr 2132
R Yerevan	11920	AM Eng (2245-2300)
R Yerevan	11945	AM Eng (2245-2300)
R Yerevan	11960	AM Eng (2245-2300)
R Yugoslavia	6100	AM Eng 1948 Fr 1700 2131 2147
R Yugoslavia	6200	AM Eng 2058
R Yugoslavia	9720	AM Eng 2150
R Zambia	4910	AM Eng 1834
Radio for Peace International	7375	USB Eng 0616 0641
Radio for Peace International	15030	USB Eng 2203 2222
REE Spain	6125	AM Eng 2132 Span 0007 2333
REE Spain	9540	AM Eng 0013
Reflections Europe	12255	AM Eng (Gospel Crusade Ministry) 1600
Reflections Europe	3910	AM Eng 2159 2229
RTV Italiana	5990	AM Eng 2205 Ital 1631 Ger 1821
SBC Radio One, Singapore	5010	AM Eng 1450
Scottish Free Radio (pirate)	3945	AM Eng 2200
SLBS Freetown, Sierra Leone	3316	AM Eng 2205 2212 2236
Slovak Radio	17535	AM Eng 0836 0850
Swiss Radio International	9420	AM Eng 1504
TWR	7385	AM Eng 0703 0735 0817 0834
TWR	9455	AM Eng 1647
TWR	9480	AM Eng 0655 0708 0850 0931
UNID (pirate)	1637	AM Dutch/Eng 1925 2146 2228 (freq varies)
UNID (pirate)	6222	AM Eng 0850 1053 1352 1641
UNID (pirate)	6229	AM Eng 0811 0856 1127
UNID (pirate)	6268	AM Eng (Irish accent) 1056
UNID (pirate)	6295	AM Eng 1014 1130 1047
V of the Mediterranean	11925	AM Eng 1402 1458
VOA	3980	AM Eng 0435 0623 0637 1831 1917 Slav 2314
VOA	5995	AM Eng 0612 0646
VOA	6035	AM Eng 0636 2249
VOA	6040	AM Eng 0641 1654 1731 1809 1923 2000 2127 Span 2307
VOA	6060	AM Eng 0637 Slav 0616 1700 1833
VOA	6070	AM Eng 2224 2243
VOA	6140	AM Eng 0618 1638 Slav 2000
VOA	6180	AM Eng 1640
VOA	7170	AM Eng 0541 0627 0650 Slav 1956
VOA	7215	AM Eng 1744
VOA	7325	AM Eng 0656
VOA	7405	AM Eng 0636 1105
VOA	7415	AM Eng 2001 2036 2158
VOA	9590	AM Eng 1104 1138
VOA	9700	AM Eng 1529 1651 1753 1814 1909 (1500-2200) Slav 2000
VOA	9760	AM Eng 1653 1700 1744 1855 1912 2001
VOA	9770	AM Eng 1834 2206
VOA	11705	AM Eng 1514 1520
VOA	11715	AM Eng 1302
VOA	11805	AM Eng 0648
VOA	11870	AM Eng 1911
VOA	11915	AM Eng 1026 1105 Asian lang 0900
VOA	11920	AM Eng 1912
VOA	11965	AM Eng 0539 0650
VOA	11995	AM Eng 1914
VOA	12080	AM Eng 0541 Fr 2150
VOA	13690	AM Eng 1812
VOA	13710	AM Eng 1634 1754 1826 1900 2109 2136
VOA	15080	AM Eng 0619
VOA	15160	AM Eng 1317
VOA	15185	AM Eng 2226
VOA	15205	AM Eng 1449 1543 1611 1721 1850
VOA	15245	AM Eng 1637 Arab 1852
VOA	15255	AM Eng 1421 1543 1655
VOA	15305	AM Eng 2210
VOA	15395	AM Eng 1516 1607 1633
VOA	15410	AM Eng 1842 1900 (1600-2200)
VOA	15445	AM Eng 1608 1717
VOA	15580	AM Eng 1902
VOA	17735	AM Eng 2135 2208 2234
VOA	17785	AM Eng 1611
VOA	17800	AM Eng 1825 2122
VOA	17895	AM Eng 1648
VOA	21485	AM Eng 2121
VOA	21585	AM Chinese (Eng lessons) 1145
Voice of Free China	17750	AM Eng 2201 2221 (2200-2300) Ger 2116
Voice of Free China	21720	AM Eng 2202 (2200-2300)
Voice of Greece	7450	AM Eng 1920
Voice of Greece	9425	AM Eng 0745 1356 Greek 1646 1900
Voice of Greece	11645	AM Eng 0746
Voice of Greece	15630	AM Eng 1531 (1530-1540) Greek 1719
Voice of Greece	15650	AM Eng 0747 1532 1848
Voice of Greece	17525	AM Eng 0946 1533 1844 Greek 0834
Voice of Greece	17535	AM Eng 1439 1446
Voice of Turkey	7185	AM Eng 2223 2258 2315

Voice of Turkey	9445	AM Eng 2210 Fr 2250
Voice of Vietnam	15010	AM Eng 1605 1817 Fr 1314 1831 (freq varies to 15009.0)
WEWN, USA	7425	AM Eng 0638 0740 0942
WEWN, USA	9985	AM Eng 1919
WEWN, USA	11580	AM Eng 0723
WEWN, USA	13615	AM Eng 2135
WEWN, USA	15695	AM Eng 1907
WEWN, USA	17510	AM Eng 1546 1600
WHRI	15105	AM Eng 1720
WHRI, USA	7315	AM Eng 0652 0723 0832 0940 1104
WHRI, USA	7355	AM Eng 0659 0744 0941
WHRI, USA	13760	AM Eng 1755 2135 2213 (1700-2400)
Wings of Hope, Lebanon	11530	AM Eng 1349 2125
WJCR, USA	7490	AM Eng 0725 0852 0945
WWCR, USA	5810	AM Eng 0738 0808
WWCR, USA	5935	AM Eng 0848
WWCR, USA	7435	AM Eng 0006 0857
WWCR, USA	13845	AM Eng 1445 1606 1652 2138 2213
WWCR, USA	15685	AM Eng 1522 1544 1611 1700 1906
WYFR, USA	11580	AM Eng 0533
WYFR, USA	13695	AM Eng 0725 1302
WYFR, USA	15355	AM Eng 1606 1916 Ger 1639 1715 Italian 1857
WYFR, USA	15566	AM Eng 2116 2150
WYFR, USA	17613	AM Eng 1847 2111 2157 2219
WYFR, USA	21500	AM Eng 1756 1833 Ital 2122
WYFR, USA	21525	AM Eng 1615 1653 2123 2148 Fr 1834
WYFR, USA	21615	AM Eng 1616 1645 1654 2124 Ital 1836

5055.00	Amman Press (PETRA)	JYF	50n Eng 1714 Arab 1654
5112.00	Belgrade Press (TANJUG)	4OC3	75r Slav 0830 1716 1849
5220.00	Cairo Press (MENA)	SUA	75r Arab 1822 1842 1919 1930
5240.00	Belgrade Press (TANJUG)	4OC2	50r Eng 1643 1823 1901 2059 2150 2252 2302
5275.00	Cairo Press (MENA)		75r Eng 1839 1857 Fr 1734 1825 1922
5867.00	Baghdad Press (INA)	YIL	50r Arab 1720 1902
6418.50	Hamburg Press	DGF41	SITOR Mode B Ger news 1954 2009
6972.00	Bucharest Press (ROMPRES)	YOG59	50r Fr 1650
7401.00	Tehran Press (IRNA)	9BC	50n Eng 1919 Arab 1846
7428.50	Buenos Aires Press (TELAM)		50r Span 2249
7520.00	Beijing Press (XINHUA)	BZP57	75r Eng 1847 1923 ID & RYs 1807
7592.00	Belgrade Press (TANJUG)	YZD6	50r Fr 1823
7610.00	Cairo Press (MENA)	SUA231	75r Fr 1913
7650.00	Beijing Press (XINHUA)	BZR67	75r Eng 1857 1939 ID & RYs 1810
7658.00	Belgrade Press (TANJUG)	YZD	50r Eng 0654 1416 1454 1725 2220 ID & RYs 1700
7756.00	Cairo Press (MENA)	SUA34	75r Arab 1904 1952
7801.00	Tehran Press (IRNA)	9BC22	50r Eng 1551
7806.00	Belgrade Press (TANJUG)	YZD7	50r Eng 1727 1815 1906 ID & RYs 1701
7842.40	Rabat Press (MAP)	CNM20/1	50r Eng 1330 Fr 1035 1552 (1000-1130 1530-1700)
7852.50	Tirana Press (ATA)	ZAA	50r Eng 1915
7887.00	Beijing Press (XINHUA)	BZS27	75r Eng 1830 1842
7959.00	Tehran Press (IRNA)	9BC23	50r Eng 1537 1556 1919 1954 Arabic 1846
7975.00	Warsaw Press		SITOR Mode B Polish 1818
7996.00	Belgrade Press (TANJUG)	YZD9	50r Eng 1704 1956
8020.00	Pyongyang Press (KCNA)	HMF	50r Eng 1804
8030.00	Rome Press (ANSA)	IRF50	50n Eng 1100 1544
8049.00	Tehran Press (IRNA)	9BC	50r Eng 2147 Arab 1806 1825
8137.50	Ankara Press (AA)	TCY	50n Turkish 1537 1545
8439.00	Hamburg Press (HAB), Germany	DGH	CW Ger news summary 1720
9114.00	Budapest Press (MTI)	HGG31	50n Eng 1702 1731
9133.00	Tirana Press (ATA)	ZAA6	50n Eng 0806 0820 0912 1123 ID & RYs 1054 (tx unstable)
9395.00	Pyongyang Press (KCNA)	HMF84	50n Fr 1814 1859 2209
9417.00	Beijing Press (XINHUA)	BXP59	75r Eng 1733 1853 1950 2034 ID 2141
9430.00	Taiwan Press (CNA)	3MA	CW & FAX
9430.00	Tirana Press (ATA)	ZAT	50n Eng 0832 1127 ID & RYs 0849 1102
9463.00	Amman Press (PETRA)	JYF	50n Arab 0942
9491.00	Beijing Press (XINHUA)	BZR69	75r Eng 1847 1953 2037 2201
9797.00	Bucharest Press (ROMPRES)	YOJ27	50r ID & RYs 0850 0856 Eng 0932 0940
10150.00	Cairo Press (MENA)	SUA	75r Arab 0914 0933 1602 1753 1801 2033 2110
10162.50	Baghdad Press (INA)	YIL70	50r Eng 1335 1516 (freq varies)
10235.00	Taiwan Press (CNA)	3MA	50r Eng 1337
10408.00	Singapore Press (ANSA)	9VF63	50n Eng 1811 1819
10417.00	Rabat Press (MAP)	CNM31/6	50r Span 1938
10523.10	Pyongyang Press (KCNA)		50n Fr 1205
10580.00	Pyongyang Press (KCNA)	HMF85	50r Eng 1452 1533 1541
10599.90	Hanoi Press (VNA)	XVN37	50r Fr 1536 1652 Eng 1506 1535 1542
10610.00	Cairo Press (MENA)	SUA30	75r Eng 1537 1556 2115 Fr 1633 RYs 1654
10634.10	Rabat Press (MAP)	CNM37/9	50r Fr 1613 1641 (1000-1130 1530-1700)
10757.50	Rabat Press (MAP)	CNM39/1	50r Span 1946
10805.00	Buenos Aires Press (NA)	LRO	75r Span 2118 2202 2227 2255 2324
10893.50	Buenos Aires Press (TELAM)	LRB39	50r Span 2130 2313 2325
11080.00	Damascus Press (SANA)		50r Arab 1524 1600
11133.00	Beijing Press (XINHUA)	BZG41	50r Fr 1810 1829
11423.50	Warsaw Press (PAP)		SITOR Mode B Polish 1814 1839
11430.00	Pyongyang Press (KCNA)	HMF55	50n Eng 1500 Fr 2207
11476.00	Pyongyang Press (KCNA)	HMF52	50r Eng 1816 1841 1904 2212
11476.00	Pyongyang Press (KCNA)	HMF52	FAX 0002
11536.00	Pyongyang Press (KCNA)	HMF49	50n Fr 1842 1906 ID & RYs 1745
11604.00	Belgrade Press (TANJUG)	YZJ2	50r Eng 0933 1153 (0400-1700)
11606.00	Beijing Press (XINHUA)		75r Eng 1439 1503 1856 1936
11680.00	Beijing Press (XINHUA)	BZP51	75r Eng 1437 1512 1646
12148.00	Warsaw Press (PAP)		SITOR Mode B news 1502 1908
12175.00	Pyongyang Press (KCNA)	HMF42	50r Eng 2142
12186.00	Tripoli Press (JANA)		50r Fr 1520
12212.50	Belgrade Press (TANJUG)	YZO3	50r Eng 1154 1604 1622 Fr 1514
12228.40	Beijing Press (XINHUA)	BZB62	75r Eng 1504 1515 1654
12745.50	Tokyo Press (KYODO)	JJC	FAX 0742 0852 1051 1735
13440.00	Belgrade Press (TANJUG)	YZJ5	50r Eng 0858 0923 1054 1300 1358 1457 1531 (0400-1700)
13524.00	Baghdad Press (INA)	YIO	50r Eng 1617
13561.00	Ankara Press (AA)		50r Eng 0939
13563.00	Taiwan Press (CNA)	3MA22	50r Eng 0828 1259 1404 1429
13580.00	Pyongyang Press (KCNA)	HMF36	50r Eng 2130
13609.50	Tunis Press (TAP)	3VF40	50r Fr 1355 1524
13653.00	Cairo Press (MENA)	SUA	75r Fr 1006 2126
13766.00	Taiwan Press (CNA)	3MA	CW & FAX
13780.00	Pyongyang Press (KCNA)	HMF84	50n Eng 1531
14367.00	Beijing Press (XINHUA)	BZP54	75r Eng 0634 0737 0807 0854 1122

14376.00	Beijing Press (XINHUA)	
14452.00	Pyongyang Press (KCNA)	
14560.00	Amman Press (PETRA)	
14573.00	Tripoli Press (JANA)	
14685.00	Taiwan Press (CNA)	
14699.00	Baghdad Press (INA)	
14760.10	Rabat Press (MAP)	
14764.00	Bahrain Press (GNA)	
14785.80	Indian Govt Press service	
14931.50	Algiers Press (APS)	
15544.00	Beijing Press (XINHUA)	
15654.90	Rabat Press (MAP)	
1330-1700)		
15705.00	Belgrade Press (TANJUG)	
15731.10	Khartoum Press (SUNA)	
15845.00	Cairo Press (MENA)	
15878.00	Taiwan Press (CNA)	
15935.20	Cairo Press (MENA)	
16067.00	Rome Press (ANSA)	
16136.00	Beijing Press (XINHUA)	
16265.00	Singapore Press (ANSA)	
16270.00	Singapore Press (KYODO)	
16971.00	Tokyo Press (KYODO)	
17069.50	Tokyo Press (KYODO)	
17443.10	Beijing Press (XINHUA)	
17465.00	Hamburg, Germany	
17470.00	Beijing Press (XINHUA)	
18040.50	Ankara Press (AA)	
18220.90	Rabat Press (MAP)	
18255.00	Indian Govt Press Service	
18263.50	Hanoi Press (VNA)	
18265.00	Rabat Press (MAP)	
1530-1700)		
18496.10	Rabat Press (MAP)	
1530-1700)		
18561.00	Tehran Press (IRNA)	
18648.50	Warsaw Press (PAP)	
18872.00	Beijing Press (XINHUA)	
19171.10	Rabat Press (MAP)	
1530-1700)		
19463.20	Khartoum Press (SUNA)	
19680.00	Taiwan Press (CNA)	
19865.50	Belgrade Press (TANJUG)	
19980.00	Tehran Press (IRNA)	
20085.00	Rome Press (ANSA)	
20204.00	Belgrade Press (TANJUG)	
20372.00	Rome Press (ANSA)	
20426.00	Rabat Press (MAP)	
22645.50	Hamburg, Germany	
22892.50	Rome Press (ANSA)	
22955.00	Rome Press (ANSA)	
24790.00	Rome Press (ANSA)	

BZT34	50r Russ 0816 (ID prints as NUB34)
HMF	50r Eng 0809
JYF2	50r Eng 0812
	50r Arab 0945 1640 1745
3MA	CW & FAX
YIX	50r Arab 0637 1456 1759
CNM61	50r Fr 1042
	75r Eng 1521 1528 Arab 0638 0818
ATP65	50n Eng 1453 Fr 1530 (msrd also 14785.0 & 14784.5)
	50n Span 1531
BZS	75r Eng 0706 1216 ID & RYs 1426
CNM29	50r Eng 1218 (1200-1400) Fr 1543 1615 1635 (1000-1130
YZJ6	50r Fr 1100
	50r Arab 1433 1525 (ID prints as "XTNB")
SUA289	75r Arab 0920 1108 1435 1526
3MA	CW ID & FAX 1504
SUA291	75r Eng 1105 Fr 0925 1825
IRO30	50n Eng 1704 1829
BZR	75r Eng 0725 1048 1108 1322
9VF206	50r Eng 1840 1854
9VF207	FAX (Japanese text) 0758
JJC	FAX 0653 0836 0910 1637
JJC	FAX 0744 0909 1058 1644 2220
BZG48	50r Fr 1141 1212 1329
DGR46	CW Ger news 1653
BZR	75r Eng 1142
TCY4	50r Eng 1035 Turkish 1155 1253
CNM76/X	50r Eng 1333 (1200-1400) Fr (1000-1130 1530-1700)
	50n Eng 1433
	50n Fr 0757
CNM	50r sked 1526 Eng (1200-1400) Fr 1613 (1000-1130
CNM80/X	50r Eng 1334 (1200-1400) Arab 0915 1547 (0900-1030
9BC31	50r Eng 1002 1113 Arab 1132 (& msrd 10560.0)
	SITOR Polish 1436
BZR68	75r Eng 0833 1302
CNM85/X	50r Eng 1302 1335 (1200-1400) Fr 1531 (100-1130
	50n Eng 1725
3MA	CW ID & FAX 1505
	50r Span 1510 1603
9BC33	50n Eng 1001 1512 1555
ISX20	50n Eng 0852 1049 1223 1510 Fr 0924 1125
YZJ	50r Eng 1245 Fr 1216 ID & RYs 1055
IRS23	50n Fr 1409
	50r Fr 1048
DGW64	CW ID 0916 news 0923 0930
IAR76	50n Eng 0740 0746 0750
ISX22	50n ID 1044 Fr 1103 1610
ISX24	50n Fr 1117

BMBX	UNID
BMOC	Swiss Embassy traffic
BMRK	Swiss Embassy traffic
BMUQ	Swiss Embassy traffic
BQQQ	UNID
BYQI	UNID
CVVA	Irish Naval
CVVO	Irish Naval
CVVX	Irish Naval
DOPX	Pakistan Embassy traffic
ELSA	UNID
HBCG	International Red Cross
HBVX	International Red Cross
HCIA	United Nations traffic
IPBC	Interpol
IPBQ	Interpol
IPBV	Interpol
IPEC	Interpol
IPUS	Interpol
IPUX	Interpol
IPUY	Interpol
IPXX	Interpol
KCKC	Mariupol Coast Radio
KCPX	Odessa Coast Radio
KFKI	UNID
KFPR	Danish Embassy traffic
KFPT	UNID
KFPX	Rijeka Coast Radio
KFQU	Danish Embassy traffic
KKVA	Egyptian Embassy traffic
KKVD	Egyptian Embassy traffic
KKXU	Egyptian Embassy traffic
KMEU	Pakistan Embassy traffic
KPCV	Lisbon Coast Radio
KPVP	Swiss Embassy traffic
KPVQ	Berne Coast Radio
KQKM	Hebrides Coast Radio (or KQQV Portishead)
KQQV	Portishead Coast Radio
KQXX	Cullercoats Coast Radio (or KQQV Portishead)
KYUF	UNID (possibly Swiss)
KYVF	Archangel Coast Radio
KYVM	Riga Coast Radio
KYVQ	Batumi Coast Radio
KYVS	Tallinn Coast Radio
KYVV	St Petersburg Coast Radio
KYVY	Murmansk Coast Radio
KYVX	Moscow (UAT) Coast Radio
KYXM	Vladivostok Coast Radio
KYXX	Novorossiysk Coast Radio
MCKX	Hong Kong Coast Radio
MCPV	Hamala Coast Radio
MCQV	Singapore Coast Radio
MCSV	Doha Coast Radio
MFKV	Dammam Coast Radio
MFKX	Dammam Coast Radio
MKCV	Istanbul Coast Radio
MKKV	Durban Coast Radio
MKKX	Capetown Coast Radio
MREK	UNID (possibly Australian)
MRZK	Egyptian Embassy traffic
MVXV	Wellington Coast Radio
OFIP	UNID
OKUK	UNID
OOVK	Egyptian Embassy traffic
OOVS	Egyptian Embassy traffic
PKKB	Pakistan Embassy traffic
PKMV	UNID (possibly Spanish)
QBMX	UNID
QCVB	Swedish Embassy traffic
QCVZ	Swedish Embassy traffic
QEMP	UNID
QFMP	Norddeich Coast Radio
QKCV	Choshi Coast Radio
QKVP	Nigerian Embassy traffic
QPPV	Rogaland Coast Radio
QQTP	Egyptian Embassy traffic
QQVV	Jakarta Coast Radio
QSKK	Warsaw Coast Radio
QSKV	Gdynia Coast Radio
QSKX	Stettin Coast Radio
QSPV	Goeteborg Coast Radio
QVYM	Genoa Coast Radio
QVYV	Rome Coast Radio
QYYV	Scheveningen Coast Radio
QYYX	Scheveningen Coast Radio
RCVB	Egyptian Embassy traffic
RQAS	UNID
RXTF	UNID
SEEW	Swiss Embassy traffic
SEQU	UNID
STKH	UNID
TPEF	Swedish Embassy traffic
TPEX	Swedish Embassy traffic
TPOV	Swedish Embassy traffic
TQMV	UNID
TSQF	UNID

TSVF	UNID
TVKY	Egyptian Embassy traffic
TVQX	UNID
TVVQ	UN traffic
TVVX	Spanish Police
TWBB	Spanish Police
TWBL	Spanish Police
TWBM	Spanish Police
TWBT	Spanish Police
TWEL	Spanish Police
TWEN	Spanish Police
TWJC	Spanish Police
TWLA	Spanish Police
TWLB	Spanish Police
TWLV	Spanish Police
TWNA	UNID
TWNC	Spanish Police
TWNN	Spanish Police
TWNO	Spanish Police
TWNP	Spanish Police
TWNS	UNID
TXXX	Spanish Police
TYMG	UNID
TYVM	Italian Embassy traffic
UAYX	Pakistan Embassy traffic
VFKQ	Lyngby Coast Radio
VFKK	Lyngby Coast Radio
VFMY	Lyngby Coast Radio
VFXV	Varna Coast Radio
VKKX	Perth Coast Radio
VKPV	UNID
VMFV	Ostend Coast Radio
VOCA	UNID
VPFV	Halifax Coast Radio
VQFV	UNID
VQKM	Italian Embassy traffic
VQKS	Italian Embassy traffic
VQMC	UNID
VQMP	Italian Embassy traffic
VQMX	Italian Embassy traffic
VQMY	UNID
VQPK	UNID
VQYC	Italian Embassy traffic
VQYM	Italian Embassy traffic
VQXC	Italian Embassy traffic
VXQK	UNID
VXQQ	Italian Embassy traffic
VXQS	Italian Embassy traffic
VXQV	Italian Embassy traffic
VXQX	Italian Embassy traffic
VXXM	Italian Embassy traffic
VXXP	UNID (probably Italian Embassy traffic)
VXXQ	Italian Embassy traffic
XBVP	Egyptian Embassy traffic
XBVQ	Egyptian Embassy traffic
XBVY	Egyptian Embassy traffic
XBXF	Egyptian Embassy traffic
XCKM	St Lys Coast Radio
XCVP	Helsinki Coast Radio
XKTG	UNID
XQKU	Italian Embassy traffic
XSFC	Irish Naval
XSFM	Irish Naval
XVSM	Palo Alto Coast Radio
XVSP	Boston Coast Radio
XVSQ	Chatham Coast Radio
XVSV	Mobile Coast Radio
XVSX	San Francisco Coast Radio
XVSY	Portsmouth Coast Radio
XVYF	Madrid Coast Radio
XXVS	Slidell Coast Radio
XYFV	Athens Coast Radio

W9GR DSP Audio Filter - - transforms your SSB & CW reception

Digital Signal Processor

Here's a filter that will transform your listening. Based on digital techniques, this filter makes radical improvements to reception, not only on CW but on SSB, and that's a very big plus point for the majority of operators. But to call it a filter is perhaps over simplifying the way in which it works. So lets examine more closely what this filter has to offer and how it achieves its excellent performance.

If we want to improve SSB reception the standard technique has been to narrow the IF pass-band by purchasing a narrower filter, using IF shift or purchasing a traditional audio filter. All these methods reduce or modify the bandwidth, but unfortunately they also affect the intelligibility of the signal by chopping some of the wanted audio signal. To an extent this works but very quickly a point is reached whereby so much of the audio signal is missing, the speech cannot be copied. Enter the DSP filter which takes a completely new approach.

The filter uses the LMS algorithm which works on correlation or repetitiveness. The filter samples the audio signal at regular intervals (fractions of a second). Signals which are correlated from one sample to the next are regarded as being speech and passed to the audio output. Noise, static, and similar forms of interference which do not correlate and are of a random nature are classed as unwanted and rejected by the filter. This method of operation is termed adaptive because the characteristics of the filter change from one instant to the next. The net result of this filtering is to drastically reduce QRN from line noise, ignition noise, and other pulse interference.

For CW operation it uses more traditional techniques of narrow band-pass filtering with bandwidths of 200Hz, 100Hz and 30Hz. These are centred on 800Hz but there is an optional position giving 100Hz bandwidth centred on 400Hz for those who like a lower pitched note. The last feature is the auto notch filter which can lock onto not one, but many heterodynes to completely rid the copy of heterodyning, even swishing carriers. That's the theory, but does it work?

£299.95

"Makes SSB sound like a good S9 FM signal"

We checked a sample out from the first production run and boy what a difference! Would you believe that some SSB signals sounded like the local repeater? There was a dramatic reduction in background noise of all kinds and the SSB signal became much clearer without any perceptible difference in audio quality. The fatigue level fell to the extent that most signals were armchair copy with the filter switched in. Signals that were difficult to copy in the QRN became "S5" and those that had a background noise became almost silent. In fact you get four separate SSB positions to cater for differing forms of interference. This filter is a must for any serious DX worker or those that want to ragchew on 40m and 80m without the fatigue that goes with all the background noise.

On CW the filter performed just as spectacularly with an almost silent background and true single signal reception. The bandwidths gave more than enough choice for differing preferences and there was no sign of ringing that sometimes accompanies the lower cost filters. In fact this is a CW man's dream filter. And on SSB the notch filter completely eliminated heterodynes. They just weren't there any more! Even sweeping through an AM signal on SSB produced silence apart from the sidebands.

There are also filter positions for HF Packet, RTTY and SSTV which will make copy and operating much better with cleaner backgrounds and much easier signal acquisition.

Connection is simple, just take the audio output from the receiver into the unit and the output into speaker or headphones. A 12 Volt supply at 250mA max, completes the requirements. And there's plenty of audio, more than enough in fact. Setting up is just as easy. Advance the receiver audio gain to the point at which the LED bar graph is occasionally fully lit on speech peaks and then use the filter audio gain for adjusting reception levels. The filter can be switched in and out of circuit with a simple push switch. And that's all there is to it. Make no mistake, this filter performs like nothing else you have ever heard! Clearly it will have a great application in commercial circles as well where long term signal monitoring is required. In all cases it will greatly aid copy and reduce operator fatigue.

Modes:

CW .... 100Hz centred 400Hz
CW .... 200Hz centred 800Hz
CW .... 100Hz centred 800Hz
CW .... 30Hz centred 800Hz
SSB .... Noise & Notch
SSB .... Noise optimised
SSB .... Optimised notch
SSB .... Low signal notch
HF Packet .... 1550 - 1850Hz
RTTY .... 2075 - 2345Hz
SSTV .... 1150 - 2350Hz

General

Notch Rejection .... >40dB
Bandstop .... >40dB
Ripple .... >0.3dB
Power required .... 12V @ 250mA
Audio Out .... 2 Watts 8 Ohms
Audio sockets .... 2 x 3.5mm
Headphone .... 1/4 inch jack
DC Connector .... coaxial
Size .... 1.5" x 5.5" x 6.4"

Available from All Good Dealers

Have you got a copy of our VHF - UHF Frequency Guide?

It continues where this publication ends, covering the range 26MHz to 12GHz. Just like this guide, you'll find the band headings with details of the services occupying each segment. Then you'll find individual listings with full duplex information. If you own a scanner or are thinking of buying one, we recommend you purchase a copy of this fascinating publication. Its full of information you won't find elsewhere.

Available at your local ham radio store - accept no substitute!

/	With figures either side used to indicate RTTY width/speed
AGC	Automatic gain Control
AM	Amplitude Modulation
AMTOR	Amateur Teletype Over Radio
ARQ	Automatic Request for Repeat
ATC	Air Traffic Control Centre
BFO	Beat Frequency Oscillator
CW	Carrier Wave (Morse Code)
DUPLEX	Transmission and Reception on different frequencies
FAX	Facsimile
FM	Frequency Modulation
FREQ.	Frequency. (All entries in kHz unless otherwise stated).
GMT	Greenwich Mean Time
HF	High Frequency
kHz	KiloHertz
LSB	Lower Sideband (Phone)
Meteo	Meteorological
MHz	MegaHertz
n	Normal (RTTY polarity).
nav	Navigation
PACKET	System for sending computer data over radio
r	Reverse (RTTY polarity).
RF	Radio Frequency
RTTY	Radio Teletype
SELCAL	Selective Calling
SIMPLEX	Transmission and Reception on same frequency
SITOR	Simplex Teletype Over Radio
SSB	Single Sideband (Collective term for LSB/USB) Phone.
Tfc	Traffic
Times	GMT unless otherwise stated
UNID	Unidentified Stations
USB	Upper Sideband (Phone). Favoured for most utility stations.
UTILITY	Non-Broadcast stations.
USB	Non-Broadcast stations.
VHF	Very High Frequency
VOLMET	Aeronautical weather service
wkg	Working
wngs	Warnings
wx	Weather

NOTE: "Spa Publishing" entries are used as copy protection.